The Beatles and Sixties Britain

Though the Beatles are nowadays considered national treasures, this book shows how and why they inspired phobia as well as mania in 1960s Britain. As symbols of modernity in the early sixties, they functioned as a stress test for British institutions and identities, at once displaying the possibilities and establishing the limits of change. Later in the decade, they developed forms of living, loving, thinking, looking, creating, worshipping and campaigning which became subjects of intense controversy. The ambivalent attitudes contemporaries displayed towards the Beatles are not captured in hackneyed ideas of the 'swinging sixties', the 'permissive society' and the all-conquering 'Fab Four'. Drawing upon a wealth of contemporary sources, *The Beatles and Sixties Britain* offers a new understanding of the band as existing in creative tension with postwar British society: their disruptive presence inciting a wholesale re-examination of social, political and cultural norms.

MARCUS COLLINS is Senior Lecturer in Cultural History at Loughborough University and an elected member of the Council of the Royal Historical Society. A specialist on popular culture and social change in Britain since 1945, he is author of *Modern Love: An Intimate History of Men and Women in Twentieth-century Britain* (2003), editor of *The Permissive Society and Its Enemies: Sixties British Culture* (2007) and co-author of *Why Study History?* (2020).

The Beatles and Sixties Britain

MARCUS COLLINS

CAMBRIDGE
UNIVERSITY PRESS

CAMBRIDGE
UNIVERSITY PRESS

University Printing House, Cambridge CB2 8BS, United Kingdom

One Liberty Plaza, 20th Floor, New York, NY 10006, USA

477 Williamstown Road, Port Melbourne, VIC 3207, Australia

314–321, 3rd Floor, Plot 3, Splendor Forum, Jasola District Centre,
New Delhi – 110025, India

79 Anson Road, #06–04/06, Singapore 079906

Cambridge University Press is part of the University of Cambridge.

It furthers the University's mission by disseminating knowledge in the pursuit of
education, learning, and research at the highest international levels of excellence.

www.cambridge.org
Information on this title: www.cambridge.org/9781108477246
DOI: 10.1017/9781108769426

First published 2020

Printed in the United Kingdom by TJ International Ltd. Padstow Cornwall

A catalogue record for this publication is available from the British Library.

Library of Congress Cataloging-in-Publication Data
Names: Collins, Marcus, 1971– author.
Title: The Beatles and sixties Britain / Marcus Collins.
Description: New York : Cambridge University Press, 2020. | Includes bibliographical
references and index.
Identifiers: LCCN 2019031214 (print) | LCCN 2019031215 (ebook) | ISBN 9781108477246
(hardback) | ISBN 9781108769426 (epub)
Subjects: LCSH: Beatles. | Popular music – Social aspects – Great Britain – History – 20th
century. | Popular music – Great Britain – 1961–1970 – History and criticism. | Nineteen
sixties.
Classification: LCC ML421.B4 C63 2020 (print) | LCC ML421.B4 (ebook) | DDC
782.42166092/2–dc23
LC record available at https://lccn.loc.gov/2019031214
LC ebook record available at https://lccn.loc.gov/2019031215

ISBN 978-1-108-47724-6 Hardback

Contents

Figures

Tables

Preface: Imagining the Beatles

"GAD, SMITHERS, WHAT NEXT?"

Figure P.1 Phobes – *Daily Mirror* cartoonist Stanley Franklin anticipates the Beatles' appearance at the Royal Variety Performance, October 1963. Photo by *Daily Mirror/* Franklin/Mirrorpix/Mirrorpix via Getty Images

Four heads appeared on the front page of the *Daily Mail* in February 1964.[1] The sketches lacked mouths and ears, but on each a few thin, dark lines emanated from a crown and ended in a rough fringe. 'You can't get away from', stated the caption, the unfinished sentence at once assuming and reinforcing the iconic status of a band whose hair alone ensured instant recognition. The Beatles were their own logo. They were advertisements for themselves.

This book seeks to understand what the Beatles meant to people in 1960s Britain. It argues that they were iconic, divisive, atypical and prefigurative:

themes introduced and illustrated in the preface using contemporary cartoons. Their depiction as icons in the 1964 *Daily Mail* cartoon contrasted starkly with their first appearance in a Fleet Street cartoon twelve months previously, when theirs had been one of a barrage of British records raining down on the Kremlin in a display of soft power.[2] They received minor billing in February 1963 compared to Susan Maughan, Helen Shapiro, Cliff Richard, Adam Faith, Marty Wilde and the Tornados, as befitted a band whose second single ('Please Please Me') was competing for the number one spot with Frank Ifield's 'The Wayward Wind' (1963). Over the following year, they would achieve what commentators agreed to be an unprecedented level of celebrity.

The Beatles' iconic power, which seems self-evident in retrospect, struck contemporaries as being so fascinating and peculiar that it formed the principal subject of cartoons about them. Their appeal is represented in the cartoons as pervasive, extending from Smithfield Market to Rishikesh and encompassing everyone from Francis Chichester to Richard Nixon.[3] So omnipresent are the Beatles that you could not escape them if you were stranded on a desert island, entered a monastery or journeyed to other planets.[4] It is cause for comment if an entire day passes 'without a story about some shaggy-'air doing something or other!'[5]

In these cartoons, the Beatles' influence is as intensive as it is pervasive. Small children pray to them and teenagers fantasise about possessing them.[6] Owning a Beatle is the ultimate memento, so that two girls kidnap one and another puts one on her list for Santa Claus.[7] If a whole Beatle is not available, a piece of one would do, leading to a bidding war for Ringo Starr's tonsils.[8] These scenarios did not seem far-fetched at a time when *Honey* magazine photographed a fan's room featuring Beatles wallpaper, a Beatles ottoman, a Beatles blanket, a Beatles mirror, a Beatles rug, a Beatles record cabinet, a Beatles lilo, a Beatles tablecloth, a Beatles mug, a Beatles plate, a Beatles tele-set, a Beatles tea towel, a Beatles Christmas card, Beatles talcum powder, Beatles wall plaques, Beatles stickers and Beatles handbags.[9]

Fame pays. Cartoonists presented the Beatles as richer than royalty and as the only thing standing between Britain and bankruptcy.[10] They are so valuable that their body parts are auctioned at Sotheby's and 'Beatle-meat' is the most expensive joint a housewife can imagine.[11] Their convoy to the 1965 Shea Stadium concert consists of one armoured car to transport the band and another to carry their fee.[12] Their return to Britain a fortnight later empties Whitehall of every Treasury official, so eager is the government to claim its share of tour proceeds.[13]

What made these cartoons satirical rather than surreal was that they often exaggerated or simply replicated real events. The cartoonist who imagined the American president greeting the British prime minister in 1964 with witticisms about the Beatles was vindicated two days later, when Lyndon Johnson complimented Alec Douglas-Home on his 'advance guard'.[14] A cartoon showing the Beatles arriving at Buckingham Palace to receive their MBEs in 1965 is clearly based on a famous photograph of a police line buckling under the crush of fans.[15] The band actually arrived at Shea Stadium in an armoured car, sat cross-legged at the feet of an Indian guru and were asked to record 'O Come All Ye Faithful – Yeah! Yeah! Yeah!' by a Methodist minister, much as cartoonists depicted. John Lennon and Yoko Ono's later escapades hardly needed embellishment. The nude album cover, rude lithographs, Bed-Ins, Bag-Ins and donation of hair to the Black Power movement were if anything toned down by cartoonists when compared to the reality.[16]

The band's iconic status rested on more than their popularity, talent, wealth and fame. It existed because, as their press officer put it, 'The Beatles are not a pop group, they are an abstraction, a repository for many things.'[17] For cartoonists, they functioned as ready-made symbols of modernity and controversy. They are associated with new technology such as ham radio, computers and space rockets;[18] with the latest outfits and hairdos; with the current state of the 'Special Relationship' and the Cold War; and with all manner of social trends, including secularisation and embourgeoisement, multiculturalism and the 'brain drain', student protest and the 'generation gap'.[19] Cartoonists also pondered whether the Beatles' influence would shape Britain for decades to come. Would the Cavern Club become a coal cellar or a tourist attraction?[20] Would retired baby boomers in lapelless jackets and winkle-pickers drone on about the Beatles?[21] Would the Beatles mean anything to generations to come?[22]

The divisive effect of the Beatles is the second theme of the cartoons and the book. Inserting the Beatles into almost any situation, real or imagined, invited viewers to consider what a Beatlified Britain would look like, and what would need to change to make such a scenario conceivable. Cartoonists re-fashioned traditional symbols of nationhood to assess Britain's capacity for reinvention. Thatched cottages gain moptops, as do Highland cattle, the guy for Bonfire Night and the statue of Eros in Piccadilly Square.[23] Sartorial traditions perish as barristers wear Beatle-style wigs in court, public schools clothe their boys in Beatle-style 'with-it college gear' and stockbrokers trading shares in Northern Songs dress for the part.[24] A monocled officer in the Coldstream Guards can only wonder

'Gad ... what next?' upon receiving news that the Beatles are to appear in the Royal Variety Performance (see Fig. P.1). His question is answered as he speaks, as his troops march past in bearskins newly styled to resemble moptops.[25]

Cartoonists used motifs of inversion to explore the Beatles' effect on taken-for-granted institutions and identities. In the images they created, gender inversion occurs when female fans inflict violence on any male who stands in the way of their obsession. In one cartoon, young girls wielding slingshots and hammers lay siege to Buckingham Palace in response to an unflattering remark about the Beatles allegedly made by the Duke of Edinburgh. They debag a policeman, remove the helmet from his colleague and knock a soldier senseless.[26] Another cartoon shows a girl throttling a policeman and a third has a female lynch mob descending upon two boys who have offended their idols.[27] While girls transgress conventional feminine behaviour, men falter in their traditional masculine roles as providers and protectors. Henpecked husbands meekly agree to their newborn sons being named after the Beatles and are hectored to earn incomes as sizeable as Starr's.[28] Cowardice is displayed by a guard who deserts his post when the Beatles visit Buckingham Palace and policemen who flee upon news of their imminent arrival.[29] A police officer returns from a shift with his uniform torn, brained by a Beatles placard.[30]

Class inversion is symbolised by oiks chanting 'yeah, yeah, yeah?' when mocking the pre-eminence of Eton, and by Brian Epstein's NEMS vying with Oxbridge as a top destination for school-leavers.[31] A posh woman boasts that her husband is 'the first Knight Commander ever to get Ringo Starr's autograph' and a decorated officer shows off a medal containing a lock of Starr's hair.[32] It is the Beatles, not the royals, whom one fan expects to appear on the balcony of Buckingham Palace.[33] The Beatles try to purchase the place in a cartoon from 1963, and Lord Starr does so in one that appeared a decade or so later.[34]

Cultural hierarchies are toppled by the staging of a Beatles ballet, the prospect of operagoers behaving like Beatlemaniacs and the band rivalling William Shakespeare as the prime symbol of British creative genius.[35] Religious traditions crumble as church bells chime Beatles' melodies, monks translate Beatlisms into Latin, vicars sermonise about Lennon's apostasy and priests follow McCartney's example by discovering God through LSD.[36] The Beatles' global popularity mollifies patriots shaken by decolonisation and relative economic decline. As Malta gains independence, Britain loses yachting's America's Cup and BOAC considers removing the Union flag from its livery, an updated flag featuring the four Beatles is the one national symbol left flying at full mast.[37] A year after he had vetoed British membership of the Common Market, President de Gaulle feels threatened by the Beatles' visit to Paris.[38] Eighteen months after former US Secretary of State Dean Acheson stated that 'Great Britain has lost an empire and has not yet found a role', the 'British invasion' crowns the entire North American continent with a moptop.[39]

If scenes of inversion consider the possibilities of change, those depicting opposition to the Beatles draw attention to the obstacles. In public, the greatest resistance to the Beatles comes from mature men accustomed to running the country. In one image, an old duffer in a tuxedo is the only audience member who refuses to join Lennon and Ono in stripping off at the Royal Albert Hall.[40] Royal officials object to Starr's presence at court.[41] When the Beatles receive MBEs, one blimpish type in full uniform earns a medal for his bravery at the Battle of Buckingham Palace, a second shows off the medal he has been awarded in recognition for repudiating his own gong, and a third fumes over the Beatle wig that he was sent in exchange.[42] In 1969, a group of highly decorated retired military men in a gentlemen's club toast their decision to 'send our Beatle LPs back' in protest against Lennon returning his MBE.[43] When two youths spot a bowler-hatted, pinstripe-besuited, brolly-wielding gent skipping down the road in 1966, they surmise that he has either won the pools or heard confirmation that the Beatles had broken up.[44]

The Beatles also provoke resentment from two archetypal figures, the postman and the policeman, who are of lower status but of equal importance to the social order. Cartoons depict them as casualties of Beatlemania. Tons of fan mail clog up the sorting offices and make mailbags impossible to carry, threatening to bring an essential service to a standstill.[45] Policemen are charged with defending social order against hordes of Beatlemaniacs running riot through concert venues and streets. Order cannot be maintained when fans besiege the police at the Royal Variety Performance and corner a bald officer under the misapprehension that he is Starr in disguise.[46]

The middle-aged father serves as the usual foil to the young female Beatlemaniac in cartoons. Only the occasional image depicts a son as the fan or a mother as the disapproving parent.[47] In almost all family scenes, a trendy daughter is pitted against a trad dad determined to spoil her fun. Fathers refuse to sport moptops, complain about visiting Liverpool, grimace at news of McCartney's recovery from gastric flu and forbid their children from displaying Starr's tonsils in the family home.[48] One father shelters behind his paper and pipe while his daughter plays Beatles records, while another still refuses to talk to his daughter months after they were awarded MBEs.[49] The only enthusiastic father cuts a ludicrous figure playing a guitar. Looking on bemused is his daughter, whose mother explains that 'He's just found out what the Beatles earn!'[50]

The third theme is the Beatles' atypicality. This is signified by their distinctive appearance in the cartoons, which makes them as similar to one another as they are different from everyone else. In their first years of fame, they remain their inimitable selves whatever the circumstances. Whether being scalped by an oblivious Native American, harassed by gendarmes in Paris, placed before a firing squad in Manila, turned away at the gates of Buckingham Palace, forced to view the FA Cup Final on stilts, exiled to the South Seas or fired off into space, their environment changes while they stay the same.[51]

Cartoonists envisaged the Beatles as becoming increasingly divergent and distant from British society in the late sixties and early seventies. During Beatlemania, they are typically depicted as inciting bizarre behaviour in others, whether fan or foe. The Beatles' eccentricity is largely confined to their hairstyles. This changed from 1967 onwards, when their weird lives, art, looks, sayings and doings regularly became the target of ridicule. A later chapter will discuss what these cartoons depict: the identification of the Beatles with some of the least popular elements of late sixties society. They are associated with illegal immigrants, barefooted hippies, drug pushers, pornographers and Japanese performance artists.[52] Their eccentricity is indicated by their appearance in loincloths and turbans,[53] Pepper gear[54] and birthday suits.[55] They are so out of touch at the beginning of the seventies that they have not heard of 'inflation, unemployment, [or] food prices' and are unknown to a new generation of children.[56]

Parents who had previously been wrong-footed by the Beatles now impart wisdom to daughters who had mistaken Lennon for 'a stable, middle-class family man' and sons who are unable to accept that the Beatles have split up.[57] Even Harold Wilson sometimes appears favourably in comparison with them, being less of a 'champion bore' than Lennon and a safer bet as prime minister than Starr.[58] Most jarring are the later cartoons which portray the Beatles as elitist. Once viewed as Everymen, they are now pitted against working-class archetypes. Alf Garnett is rejected as a disciple of the Maharishi, dustmen chuck a bag containing Lennon and Ono into a compactor and a lavatory attendant keeps his facilities drug-free after hearing of Lennon's misbehaviour in Buckingham Palace.[59]

The Beatles' atypicality is also emphasised in cartoons on the theme of role reversal. In the early years, it is scarcely conceivable to envisage the Beatles as anything other than themselves. The most outlandish fantasy is that of a bald Beatle.[60] Cartoonists instead made mischief by bestowing authority figures with moptops to show their incapacity of being modern and popular. Politicians provided the ideal targets. Before Harold Macmillan suddenly resigned as prime minister in October 1963, cartoonists depict the Tory leadership forming a beat combo to court popularity.[61] In the search for his replacement, they alight on Quintin Hogg as 'the best Pop Minister' among the candidates, thanks to his demagoguery and occasionally unkempt hair.[62] Cartoonists had fun underscoring the contrast between the Beatles and the new prime minister Alec Douglas-Home, a skeletal and balding sixty-year-old aristocrat, by decking him out in Beatle gear and depicting his new Cabinet in similar attire under the banner of 'Modernisation'.[63] Still more debasing are the scenes which depict Tories comporting themselves like Beatlemaniacs. In one cartoon, a crowd of mini-skirted Alec Douglas-Homes at a Beatles concert scream 'We love you, yeah, yeah, yeah' at a nuclear weapon.[64] Another shows Home and Rab Butler joining the ranks of autograph hunters outside the stage door, hoping that the Beatles will sign up to become Tory candidates.[65]

The Tories cannot match the Beatles' appeal. They are billed as 'The Unpopular group' and appear desperate when promising the electorate 'anything that you want' in the manner of 'From Me to You' (1963).[66] Home's rendition of 'She Loves You' (1963) in front of President Johnson is no match for the Beatles' own US performances, which leave him in the shade.[67] After winning the Greater London Council elections in April 1964, it is Labour leader Harold Wilson who sings 'They love me, yeah, yeah, yeah', kitted out with drainpipe trousers, Chelsea boots, pipe and electric guitar.[68]

Once he becomes prime minister later that year, Harold Wilson proves to be as pathetically dependent on the Beatles as his predecessor. He beseeches a hospitalised Starr in December 1964 to 'tour the world to save the balance of payments situation!'[69] The poor reception accorded to the *Magical Mystery Tour* television special in December 1967 causes Wilson to reflect that the Beatles' failure would be more damaging to the British economy than the devaluation of sterling implemented the previous month.[70] His shameless populism naturally draws him to emulate the Beatles. In 1965, he is depicted joining senior Cabinet members in growing his hair, then deciding to appoint the Beatles in their stead after awarding the band MBEs.[71] By the late sixties, he is shown cravenly adopting their every fad, from flower power and transcendental meditation[72] to Bed-Ins and Bagism.[73] Wilson makes no more plausible a hippie than Starr makes a prime minister or Lennon an Archbishop of Canterbury when imagined as such in other cartoons.[74] The impossibility of squares becoming the Beatles or the Beatles becoming squares symbolises the divergence perceived by cartoonists between the young and old, the radical and the staid and the political and cultural worlds in 1960s Britain.

The fourth theme of the book, that the Beatles were prefigurative, is demonstrated by the familiarity to us of the events depicted in the cartoons and the unfamiliarity of their underlying assumptions. As the art historian Ernst Gombrich observed, cartoons draw upon a 'common stock of knowledge ... immediately accessible to anyone'.[75] In the Beatles' case, the cartoons show how large that stock had to be. At the minimum, cartoonists assumed that their audience knew the names of the band members plus those of their wives, girlfriends and children. In fact, the cartoon opening this chapter shows that the names were often considered superfluous.[76] The Beatles were expected to be readily identifiable by sight, and to be distinguishable from one another, throughout their myriad changes of appearance.[77]

Identifying the Beatles was only the first step towards understanding the jokes. A strong working knowledge was assumed of their songs,[78] tribute songs to them and their position in the charts.[79] Three cartoons appeared on the day in January 1964 that the Dave Clark Five dethroned the Beatles at number one, each imagining the Beatles' oblivion.[80] The viewer had to be aware of the band's whereabouts when they were abroad, including their first visit to the United States in 1964, their North American tours later that year, in 1965 and 1966,[81] their ill-starred trip to the Philippines[82] and their pilgrimage to India.[83] Events assumed to be common knowledge included the demise of the Cavern Club,[84] rumours of the band's break-up in 1966,[85] the opening and closing of the Apple Boutique[86] and the bad reviews of the *Magical Mystery Tour* TV special.[87]

Such was their fame that cartoonists took for granted the British public's familiarity with Starr's medical condition,[88] Harrison's sitar lessons, McCartney's facial hair, and the paint job on Lennon's Rolls Royce.[89] Viewers were expected to keep up to date with Lennon's controversial remarks about religion,[90] his claim to have smoked pot in Buckingham Palace[91] and the many and varied Happenings he staged with Ono.[92] The Beatles' weddings were assumed to be a matter of general knowledge,[93] as were the births of Starr's two sons.[94]

'Mummy, darling, what were the Beatles?' a young boy asks his incredulous mother in a 1971 cartoon by Osbert Lancaster.[95] It appeared days after McCartney had filed suit to dissolve the band, and looked ahead to a time when the band would be forgotten and cartoons about them rendered meaningless. This was the cartoon's natural fate, Gombrich observed, its wit inextricably intertwined with 'recondite allusions to long-forgotten issues and events'.[96] In the Beatles' case, however, that future has not yet arrived. We still remember them and something of their times. The volume of information which contemporaries needed to know in order to make sense of cartoons about the Beatles is remarkable enough. But what is truly extraordinary is that much of the same Beatle lore is recalled half a century later. The opening and closing ceremonies of the 2012 London Olympics placed the Beatles at the core of British national identity and assumed that the global audience would be familiar with their greatest hits.[97]

But the more we lionise the Beatles today, the harder it is for us to understand the controversy they caused in sixties Britain. '[O]ld cartoons are often so difficult to appreciate', Gombrich argued, because '[t]he analogies used, once topical and illuminating, so often have faded.'[98] In contemporary cartoons about the Beatles, those analogies were based on a series of attitudes and assumptions that from today's perspective are unfamiliar and unfathomable.

If you think it ludicrous that men's hair falls below their collars and women's skirts reach above their knees, that couples cohabit or that parents name their sons Zak, then you would experience little culture shock being transported back to sixties Britain.[99] The music, fashions and gossip which so captivated contemporary admirers of the Beatles provided an alternative form of entertainment for their critics, who were invited by cartoonists to have a laugh at the expense of the band and their fans. Mockery provided a means of engaging with the 'swinging sixties' without embracing its values, acknowledging the spectacle while upholding existing norms.

Conversely, the cartoons may leave you cold if you fail to see anything odd in the notion that pop stars are highly paid and much feted, that they marry, take drugs, express political and religious opinions and try their hand at other arts. Much of what seemed absurd to the cartoonists seems unexceptionable now. For popular culture to generate national pride, newspaper headlines, international earnings and collaborations with high art has lost much of its novelty, controversy and comedic potential.

If you are not amused or alarmed by such ideas, then the Beatles are part of the reason why. They are prefigurative because their viewpoints seem closer to our own than do those of their satirists. The transformation of values over the intervening half century has many causes, but the cartoons provide a comic-book account of how the Beatles catalysed debate about the social, political and cultural underpinnings of mid-twentieth-century Britain and consideration of the alternatives. To understand the Beatles in their time, we need to examine why their thoughts and actions were often considered so funny peculiar in 1960s Britain. To understand their legacy, we should consider why we struggle to laugh at these cartoons today.

Introduction

Figure I.1 Oddballs – Presenting their new look to the public in Hyde Park, May 1967.
Photo by Marvin Lichtner/The LIFE Images Collection via Getty Images/Getty Images

This book reassesses the Beatles, the sixties and the relationship between the two. In the preface, we saw cartoonists' profound ambivalence to the band and what they appeared to represent. The next chapter analyses opinion polls to measure broader public attitudes to the 'permissive society'. Polling provides the context necessary to understand the social, cultural and political debates about the Beatles explored in Chapters 2 to 5. Chapter 2 examines how the Beatles and Beatlemania were interpreted as social phenomena up to 1965. Chapter 3 considers how the band became semi-detached from the society in which they lived and worked in the second half of the decade. The questions of whether the Beatles were artists and their impact on cultural hierarchies are the subjects of Chapter 4. Chapter 5 deals with their political significance to Westminster politicians and the revolutionary left. The Conclusion compares the book's findings with narratives of the Beatles generated at the time of their break-up, in major popular accounts and in oral testimony recorded at the turn of the millennium. But first, this introduction will outline the book's scope and methods and explain how they offer a different approach to a familiar subject.

Half a century of debate on the role of the Beatles in 1960s Britain has produced three main models.[1] The first is that of the Beatles as trailblazers of change. The second presents the Beatles as exemplars, riding on the bandwagon of social transformation. The third is of the Beatles as outliers, pursuing their own path while largely divorced from wider society. The catalytic effect of the Beatles is envisaged in the first model as having revolutionised popular music, redefined celebrity, collapsed distinctions between popular and high culture and exerted a major influence over how their contemporaries looked, thought and lived. To their champions, they were emancipators; to their critics, destroyers of established norms. The second model presents the 1960s as an equally significant turning point but attributes less agency to the Beatles. They are not held to have created the 'permissive society' so much as have been notable participants in and proponents of it. The third model forms part of a wider scepticism about the significance of the 1960s and the concomitant emergence of permissiveness. It questions whether the changes associated with the decade actually happened; whether they occurred earlier or later than is commonly thought, or for reasons unrelated to figures such as the Beatles; and whether ordinary people were aware of, affected by or favourable towards such developments.

It is hard to find an academic historian who subscribes to the first model of the groundbreaking effect of the Beatles, although the political scientist Samuel Beer once portrayed them in true Romantic fashion as 'the "unacknowledged legislators" of Britain's populist revolt'.[2] Not only does the model smack of an antiquated Great Man view of history, it also assumes that the sixties were a transformational historical moment. This heroic view of the Beatles is intertwined with a series of Whiggish notions about the 1960s that historians have sought to nuance or refute. Many of them are no more convinced of the existence of the 'swinging sixties', 'permissive society', 'sexual revolution', 'global village', 'birth of the teenager' and 'Summer of Love' than they are of the 'Age of Aquarius'.[3] The notion of the sixties as a distinctive and cohesive period is itself widely disputed.[4]

The second model of the Beatles as representatives of the sixties enjoys more academic support. It moderates claims of the Beatles' agency by portraying them as embodying social trends rather than engineering them. It is compatible with several different conceptions of the sixties, from 'cultural revolution' at one pole to near stasis at the other. The main proponent of the 'cultural revolution' model, Arthur Marwick, argued that the Beatles *were* the sixties' inasmuch as they represented and promoted its quintessential qualities.[5] Conversely, Oded Heilbronner and Dominic Sandbrook argue that the Beatles were symptomatic of the lack of change in 1960s Britain. According to Heilbronner, the Beatles stood for an 'anti-revolutionary, consensual and conservative' form of Englishness.[6] Sandbrook cites the early Beatles as evidence that the sixties were 'a stage in a long evolution' of modern British history rather than 'a dramatic turning point'.[7]

Sandbrook switches to the third model of the Beatles as outliers in his account of their later career. Having depicted them as unthreatening in the early 1960s, he sees them as hypocritical, unpopular and out of touch in the late 1960s and early 1970s. David Fowler agrees that the Beatles were 'detached ... from youth culture by the late 1960s' and goes so far as to question '[w]hether the Beatles had a major influence on British youth culture' at any point.[8]

This book reconceives the relationship between the Beatles and sixties Britain as one of creative tension. The Beatles' own creativity does not need belabouring. The case for their musical inventiveness has been most powerfully made by the composer and broadcaster Howard Goodall. He quickly dispenses with claims that the Beatles were a generic rock 'n' roll outfit at the beginning of their career or the passive beneficiaries of George Martin's studio experimentation later on.[9] More startling is his contention that 'the Beatles rescued western music' through reclaiming harmonic and melodic systems discarded by twentieth-century classical composers.[10] When their mastery of melody is added to their groundbreaking recording techniques, eclectic instrumentation, audacious modulation and fusion of Eastern and Western musics, Goodall concludes that the Beatles were instrumental in creating a 'new musical mainstream':

There are very, very few composers in history whose work changed all the music that followed it. Beethoven was one, Wagner was another and I believe that posterity will add to their select ranks the Beatles, whose musical revolution and thrilling songs will rightly be regarded as one of the crowning glories of twentieth-century music.[11]

Contemporaries saw the Beatles' recordings as just one facet of their innovation. 'Everything about them is – first', maintained the *NME*'s Norrie Drummond in 1967: 'their music, their clothes, their ideas'.[12] There were few limits to their creative ambition. Having revolutionised popular music and become 'famous and loaded' in the process, they sought to parlay their creativity into pioneering new forms of living, loving, dressing, worshipping, working, selling, lobbying, thinking, performing and maturing.[13] This versatility was itself a form of creativity as they made a name for themselves not merely as musicians but as songwriters, actors, comics, authors, celebrities, artists, socialites, activists, businessmen, heartthrobs, missionaries, criminals, patrons and (whether they liked it or not) role models and oracles.

How the Beatles fared in these ventures will be the subject of the sequel to this book. This volume focuses not on the Beatles' actions but their contemporaries' reactions. The Beatles' creativity engendered creativity in others. Most obviously, they inspired the creation of countless bands. The music critic Henry Pleasants prefigured Goodall when crediting the Beatles in 1969 for creating a 'new mainstream'. He noted that 'thousands of groups have been founded in their image, all called the This, the That and the Other Thing, and all of them sounding more or less like the Beatles'.[14] The Beatles' impact beyond youth culture was manifested during Beatlemania in the '[m]illions of words' of newspaper copy which assessed their 'social significance'.[15]

This iconic status – one of the four themes previewed in the preface – may appear to be the Beatles' most obvious and least interesting characteristic. They are so iconic, indeed, that the *Cambridge Dictionary* illustrates the correct usage of the word with the sentence 'John Lennon gained iconic status following his death.'[16] But it is worth considering how this happened. The Beatles' exceptional talent, charisma and originality did not guarantee success – they might never have got the chance to record a note or make a broadcast. Success in pop music did not inevitably lead to fame or even name recognition beyond the young singles-buying public. And fame once attained need not have made its beneficiaries central to key debates about the current state and future trajectory of society. It was the Beatles' fulfilment of all these criteria that made them fit the dictionary definition of iconic figures 'considered to represent particular opinions or a particular time'.[17]

As David R. Shumway has argued in an American context, the type of rock stardom enjoyed by the Beatles came to be 'defined by the embodiment of cultural controversies'.[18] The controversy surrounding the Beatles in sixties Britain explains why their creativity generated tension and returns us to the preface's other three themes: namely, their divisive, atypical and prefigurative character. The divisive effect of the Beatles on contemporaries has been obscured by their subsequent veneration as national treasures and symbols of the sixties. Opposition to the Beatles is represented in conventional narratives of their career as a rearguard effort by forces of reaction.[19] It is difficult to empathise with those who inveighed against moptops and Beatlemaniacs and who swore that the Beatles' music would be rapidly and deservedly forgotten. But empathy is precisely what is necessary to understand the Beatles' world. In sixties Britain, many intelligent and educated observers could not envisage the Beatles' music as having any merit or lasting appeal. Others perceived the Beatles as grammar-school failures, half-formed Marxists, a substandard soul outfit or agents of moral degeneration. This book attempts to show that the Beatles' critics were not simply curmudgeons, killjoys and contrarians, but people who had reason to believe that their cardinal values were threatened by the band and what it represented.

By atypical, I mean that the Beatles' social attitudes placed them at odds with those of most of their contemporaries (see Fig 1.1). This is not to say that they were party-line permissives. On the contrary, the sequel to this book will argue that their behaviours and beliefs were characterised by ambivalence, contradiction and vacillation. Their open-mindedness towards a whole array of issues nonetheless positioned them far outside the mainstream of public opinion. Polls show that these putative spokesmen for their generation, region and class did not represent the attitudes of the young, the North-West, CDEs – or any sizeable segment of the population.

Furthermore, the evolution of the Beatles' attitudes over the course of the 1960s far outpaced that occurring in wider society. British social attitudes were different at the end of the 1960s than at the beginning, but they did not develop in a uniformly permissive manner and did not change anything like as fast as the Beatles had hoped. The Beatles responded by attempting to bridge the gap between themselves and the general population through campaigns of public enlightenment. Somewhat unwilling targets of social, cultural and political commentary in the first half of the 1960s, they instigated such debates in the late 1960s to effect societal change. Celebrity granted them a hearing but not acceptance. Their activism often simply highlighted their idiosyncrasy and associated them with some of the period's most unpopular and eccentric causes. The more the Beatles intervened in public affairs, the more alienated they became.

The Beatles were not prefigurative in the sense that later generations adopted their behaviours and beliefs wholesale. Most people in subsequent decades were scarcely more likely to take LSD, visit an ashram, flirt with communism, campaign for gay rights or women's liberation or seduce their best friend's spouse than they were to become pop stars. Yet these and other acts of the Beatles lost much of their shock value over time as they became incorporated into a nostalgic vision of the 1960s. Retrospective accounts of the decade as a time of experimentation and emancipation reveal more tolerance of the Beatles and less tolerance of the intolerance they once faced.[20]

The Beatles' cultural stature showed little sign of diminishing in the early twenty-first century. As Alina Kwiatkowska elegantly demonstrated through web searches, they overtook Shakespeare as the standard source for literary quotations and allusions. She discovered in 2010 that there were almost twice as many exact and fuzzy Google hits for 'All you need is love' than for seven famous Shakespearean quotations put together ('To be or not to be: that is the question'; 'All the world's a stage'; 'Something is rotten in the state of Denmark'; 'The green-eyed monster'; 'If music be the food of love, play on'; 'My kingdom for a horse!'; 'The lady doth protest too much'). There were ten times as many hits for 'We all live in a yellow submarine' as for 'My kingdom for a horse!' and for 'I read the news today, oh boy' as for 'The lady doth protest too much.'[21] References appeared in every kind of online text, from adverts to scientific papers, and often took the form of puns that demonstrated the adaptable and ever-evolving character of Beatles lyrics. Such wordplay exhibited the author's wit and taste and established bonds with equally savvy readers.

Opinion polls display the appeal of the sixties to subsequent generations. In 1985, 47 per cent of those questioned by Gallup considered that 'the British people "never had it so good"' as they did in the 1960s, even though the phrase was coined by Harold Macmillan during and about the previous decade. All age groups decidedly preferred the sixties to any other decade.[22] Sixties nostalgia showed little sign of waning when YouGov asked respondents in 2016 to name the decade in which 'Britain was at its greatest'. Although half declined to answer, the 1960s was over twice as popular a choice as its nearest rival, the 1980s, and as popular as the 1940s, 1950s and 1970s combined. Only 1 per cent of people thought Britain to be in its prime in 2016, the year of the Brexit referendum.[23]

Polls also show how Britain since the 1960s has become a more diverse nation, accustomed to (if not necessarily approving of) a multiplicity of lifestyles, cultures and tastes.[24] Consider the answers given in British Social Attitudes (BSA) surveys conducted around the turn of the millennium.[25] By this point, many more British people had personal experience of the permissive lifestyles modelled by the Beatles in the 1960s. A quarter said they had taken cannabis; a quarter's parents had divorced.[26] Almost half had discovered their 'own way connecting with God without churches or religious services', much like the Beatles in their meditative phase, and four fifths accepted the pluralistic notion that many religions shared 'basic truths'.[27] The kind of behaviour which earned John Lennon and Yoko Ono moral opprobrium in the 1960s mattered less at the end of the century. Although 28 per cent of people still disapproved of couples who decided to have children out of wedlock, half thought the matter had 'nothing to do with morals'.[28] One in fourteen disputed that 'divorce can be a positive first step towards a new life' and one in seven disapproved of cohabitation.[29] The same proportion said they would 'mind a lot' if a close relative married someone of Asian descent.[30] Only 6 per cent picked cannabis and 16 per cent picked LSD from a list of drugs 'most harmful to frequent users', whereas a third named tobacco and alcohol.[31] For almost every answer, permissive attitudes were strongest among the young and weakest among the old. This cohort effect indicated that Britain was likely to become more permissive as conservatives born in the early twentieth century came to the end of their lives, as later BSA surveys confirmed.

Time and Place

The core chapters of the book, which examine the social, cultural and political impact of the Beatles, cover the period 1963 to 1975. They begin when the Beatles attained national attention following the chart success of

'Please Please Me' (1963) and the outbreak of what was soon dubbed Beatlemania. Their formative years in Liverpool and Hamburg and their first record release fall outside the ambit of the book because they did not generate much printed discussion beyond the pages of *Mersey Beat*.[32] The significance of their first years of fame has been obscured by their later creative achievements, which relegated their earlier recordings to the unfavoured half of the 'pop'/'rock' split. The Beatles' subsequent embarrassment over their moptop phase added to the denigration and trivialisation of the Beatlemania era. Yet the extraordinary effect of their sudden rise to fame should not be understated. 'Peak Beatles' as measured in column inches and parliamentary speeches occurred in 1964, by which point most principal lines of argument about the band were well established. The purpose of incorporating material up to 1975, five years after their public break-up, is not to consider the Beatles' solo careers in the early seventies. It is to allow the book to consider the first retrospectives of the Beatles' career before punk and the murder of Lennon transformed debates about the band.[33] This Introduction and the conclusion have a wider brief, surveying more than half a century of interpretations of the Beatles and the 1960s.

As for place, this book concerns British attitudes to a British band who travelled widely but lived and recorded music almost entirely in Britain during the 1960s. Their Liverpudlian origins, German sojourns and global success often overshadow the national context in which they operated. For all the diversity and division within sixties Britain, the Beatles and their compatriots interpreted each other by drawing upon a medley of assumptions, experiences and cultural references peculiar to themselves. The sources examined here are essentially those produced for a national audience or polls based on a national sample, rather than for or about the United Kingdom's constituent nations, regions and localities. Domestic commentary on the Beatles was far from insular, ranging as it did across issues of Americanisation, Eastern religion, Western civilisation and Britain's post-imperial identity. Furthermore, the book's definition of a British primary source is expansive enough to include British commentators living overseas (e.g. the poet W. H. Auden and the New Age writer Alan Watts) and non-British commentators resident in Britain (e.g. the intellectuals Germaine Greer and George Steiner). However, it does not attempt to explore 'the intersection of global vectors across one local terrain' in the manner of Timothy Scott Brown's illuminating *West Germany and the Global Sixties* (2013).[34]

Primary Sources

The primacy given to contemporaneous sources stems from the book's aim to explore attitudes towards the Beatles during and immediately after their recording career. The band and the decade have generated powerful myths and countermyths over the past half-century. These narratives are at once an object lesson in the contested nature of the past and a substantial impediment to understanding how the band and the decade were conceived at the time. In theory, any contemporary British discussions of the Beatles and their work fall within the book's remit. Direct encounters with the Beatles occurred when attending their concerts, interviewing them or meeting them at social functions. More common were mediated encounters such as listening to their records, watching their films or reading about their sayings and doings. Contemporaries also encountered the Beatles through each other's commentary. They were the subject of thousands of newspaper articles and broadcasts. Politicians made speeches about them, academics wrote treatises on them and they were represented in novels, plays, ballets, films, paintings, sculptures and cartoons.

The volume of material on the Beatles is undeniably daunting, but in practice it is reduced by the requirement that sources were created at the time and have survived since. The primary sources available to the researcher testify to the elitist bias of the recording and preservation of past voices. As a rule of thumb, the more likely you were to appreciate the Beatles in the 1960s, the less likely it is that your opinions were documented at the time and have survived to this day. Young, working-class female fans were more prominent as consumers than producers of media, although the book draws heavily upon the girls' magazines and fan-club publications which published their views. The predominance of older, richer, educated males in the press, the arts, broadcasting, literature and scholarship – and consequently in the sources for this book – is a distortion of societal opinion but an accurate reflection of cultural authority. Their often reactionary perspectives provide an alternative narrative of the sixties in which the Beatles appear as undereducated, overpaid, talentless, clueless, unexceptional, objectionable, pretentious and preposterous figures whose comic hairstyles constituted their only cultural contribution of note.

Between these poles of mania and phobia exists a diverse and complex array of discourses about the Beatles and the sixties which digitisation has rendered accessible as never before. These include daily and Sunday papers (*The Telegraph, The Express, The Mirror, The Mail, The Times, The Sunday*

Times, The Guardian, The Observer and the non-digitised *Herald* and *Sun*).[35] Periodicals are used extensively, whether musical (*Melody Maker, New Musical Express, Record Mirror, Disc and Music Echo, Rave*), political (*Spectator, Economist, New Statesman, Tribune*), literary (*Times Literary Supplement*), social (*New Society*), countercultural (*Oz, International Times, Gandalf's Garden, Frendz, 7 Days*) or general interest (*Listener, Punch*).[36] Radio and television broadcasts and recordings of interviews and press conferences have been obtained thanks to the painstaking work of collectors and bootleggers. Physical archives have been used more sparingly. These include the BBC Written Archives Centre, the British Library Sound Archive and the Special Collections and Archives of Liverpool John Moores University.

Each chapter supplements these sources with more specialised ones. The cartoons examined in the preface mostly come from the British Cartoon Archive. In Chapter 1, top-line statistics from opinion polls are culled from digests issued by polling companies, while the cross-tabulations use raw data deposited in the UK Data Archive, the German-based GESIS Data Archive for the Social Sciences and the United States-based Inter-University Consortium for Political and Social Research. Chapters 2 and 3 on society make especial use of religious publications (*Church Times, Catholic Herald, Blackfriars*) and magazines targeted primarily or exclusively at teenage girls (*Beatles Book, Fabulous 208, Honey, Petticoat, Jackie, Girl*).[37] Academic journals and specialist arts and music publications feature prominently in Chapter 4, which focuses on culture.[38] Chapter 5, on politics, uses materials ranging from parliamentary debates recorded in Hansard through cyclostyled anarchist pamphlets to the digitised archives of the Communist Party of Great Britain.

Because it is concerned with representations of the Beatles, the book seldom features the Beatles' own creative output, interviews and writing. When they are quoted, for example when discussing their fall from grace in the second half of the 1960s, it is to explain how others reacted to them. This situation will be remedied by a companion volume, *The Beatles' World*, which will view the same issues from the opposite perspective by assessing how the Beatles themselves understood the society, culture and politics of 1960s Britain. *The Beatles' World* will argue that although they were the most celebrated figures of the 'permissive society', the Beatles exhibited uncertainty over most of its cardinal values. They both embraced and renounced materialism, secularism, drugs, self-disclosure, casual sex, revolutionary politics and artistic experimentation.[39]

Secondary Sources

The historian Gerd-Rainer Horn expressed incredulity in 2007 that 'no satisfactory study of the socio-political dimension of British rock music has been published to date' and, for the sixties, limited progress has been made since.[40] The work that has come closest to remedying the situation, Keith Gildart's *Images of England through Popular Music: Class, Youth and Rock 'n' Roll, 1955–1976* (2013), notes how popular music and youth culture remains 'stubbornly resistant to the focus of academic historians'.[41] His assertion that postwar British historians have belittled, marginalised or ignored the significance of popular music for working-class youth could be applied equally to their treatment of the Beatles.

There exists no book-length study of the Beatles by an academic British historian. Most of the standard surveys of postwar British history feel obliged to namecheck the band, but they struggle to relate it to their wider narratives and are often misinformed. The principal scholarly work on the Beatles' relationship to sixties Britain therefore consists of a modest number of chapters and articles. Gildart uses the Beatles' formative years in Liverpool as a case study of 'the connections between class, race, ethnicity, locality, popular music and youth culture'.[42] The chapter devoted to the Beatles in David Simonelli's *Working Class Heroes: Rock Music and British Society in the 1960s and 1970s* (2013) considers some of the same issues of class, youth and place from a national perspective as opposed to Gildart's local one.[43]

Simonelli and Gildart are primarily interested in the Beatles as popular musicians. *The Beatles and Sixties Britain* is closer in its ambitions to chapters by David Fowler, Dominic Sandbrook and Arthur Marwick, which situate the band within wider debates about continuity and change in 1960s Britain.[44] Its differences from Fowler and Sandbrook's accounts are explored below, but it accepts certain of their reservations about Marwick's approach. Marwick made his name as a historian of social change in the twentieth century, so it was appropriate that his last major work, *The Sixties* (1998), presented a similarly transformational narrative of that decade as his earlier work on 'total war'.[45] The analysis of opinion polls in *The Beatles and Sixties Britain* suggests the need to qualify his claim that 'the sixties was a time of liberation for majorities in all Western countries'.[46] Although most people became more prosperous and gained greater civil rights during the decade, they expressed doubts about the accompanying social and cultural changes. By the same token, Marwick's portrayal of the Beatles as 'the heroes of the age' seems overdrawn when we consider the sustained and substantial opposition towards them and what they represented in 1960s Britain.[47]

Notwithstanding its different conclusions, *The Beatles and Sixties Britain* shares with the work of Marwick, Fowler and Sandbrook a focus on the historical relationship between the band and British society. It bears fewer family resemblances to academic works on the Beatles which differ in their focus, methods, discipline or some combination of the three. Most scholarship on the Beatles is primarily concerned with their lives and art, whether as a band or as individuals.[48] There are three scholarly studies of Harrison,[49] still more of Lennon[50] and a major two-volume biography of George Martin.[51] The biographical approach also shapes the most significant popular works on the Beatles.[52] In contrast, this book adopts the reverse perspective of examining contemporary attitudes towards the band.

Work on the Beatles takes place within a thriving field of interdisciplinary research on canonical popular musicians of the 'long 1960s'. There are studies of American musicians including Bob Dylan, the Beach Boys, Janis Joplin, the Doors and the Grateful Dead[53] as well as their British counterparts the Rolling Stones,[54] the Kinks,[55] The Who,[56] David Bowie,[57] Dusty Springfield,[58] Led Zeppelin[59] and Pink Floyd.[60] Other scholars have studied genres of music instead of individual musicians. For Britain, there are notable studies of light music,[61] jazz,[62] folk,[63] blues,[64] rock 'n' roll and beat music,[65] Mod,[66] soul,[67] psychedelia,[68] prog,[69] glam,[70] disco,[71] punk,[72] post-punk,[73] indie[74] and metal.[75] A third approach is that of studying themes in popular music such as performance,[76] ethnicity and national identity,[77] class,[78] gender,[79] women[80] and men.[81]

At the outer limits of this book's reach are works on the 1960s or popular culture which concern neither Britain nor the Beatles. Many of the issues explored in this book have been studied more extensively in the United States than in Britain. Historical research on sixties culture and radicalism started early in the United States and has developed impressively since.[82] Some of the attention paid to the decade in the United States can be attributed to the ongoing 'culture wars'.[83] But this is not to gainsay the sophistication of the field, including debates on the origins[84] and aftermath of 'the sixties'.[85] Besides studies specifically about the Beatles' reception, the most relevant works on postwar America concern intellectuals' attitudes to popular culture,[86] pop audiences,[87] ethnicity and the development of the 'pop'/'rock' divide,[88] rock stardom,[89] rock criticism,[90] the counterculture[91] and countercultural music.[92] The widest context for this study is provided by transnational work on the 1960s. Though 1968 still forms the focus for such research,[93] there is increasing interest in the international dimensions of the counterculture and cultural experimentation.[94] Exploring the Beatles' impact on Britain provides a missing piece in the broader puzzle of the 'global sixties'.[95]

Methodology

The book's methodology is best expressed as a series of aspirations and distinctions: that is, what it endeavours to do and how this differs from alternative methods. Its four guiding principles are to be historical, broad, empirical and dispassionate. Let me clarify what I mean by each of these terms by comparing the book's approach to those of other works on the Beatles and the sixties.

First and foremost, this is a historical study of a subject largely studied by non-historians. The scarcity of historical work on the Beatles contrasts starkly with the scholarly interest in them displayed in other fields of scholarship, including literary criticism,[96] cultural studies,[97] geography,[98] philosophy,[99] sociology,[100] communications[101] and psychology.[102] *The Beatles and Sixties Britain* draws upon and benefits from research in these disciplines while addressing fundamentally different questions. For example, much formal musicological analysis of the Beatles does not dwell upon the Beatles' historical context, whereas this book touches upon the Beatles' music only insofar as it affected their perceived social, political and cultural significance.[103] Popular musicology therefore appears here less as a form of analysis to be applied than as a discipline whose origins were intertwined with interpretations of the Beatles in the 1960s. Chapter 4 accordingly excavates the prehistory of critical musicology and popular music studies. It shows that contemporary claims about the Beatles' artistry were made largely by writers with no formal musical training, whose comparisons between the Beatles and classical composers (positive and negative) were correspondingly superficial. Early attempts to evaluate the Beatles' canonical status rested instead on lyrical analysis and evaluations of the cultural capital of the Beatles and their supporters.

The Beatles and Sixties Britain is historical in the sense that it is funda-mentally concerned with the contemporary impact of the Beatles and not their legacy or lasting significance. Those interested in the band members' lives after the Beatles, the marketing of their music and image, the retelling of their narrative and the treatment of Lennon's death are referred to the fine work of writers such as Peter Doggett, Holly Tessler and Erin Weber.[104] The book is historicist as well as historical: that is, it seeks to understand the attitudes and actions of sixties figures in their own terms and within the context of their time and place. The book's historicism dovetails with its empiricism and dispassion in its ambition to identify and represent past perspectives in all their variety. It also situates the work on one side of 'the essential divide between history and criticism' identified by Elijah Wald:

> what made something timely is usually very different from what makes it timeless ... The critic's job is to assign value and importance on an artistic level, which necessarily is a judgement about how the work stands up in the present. The historian's is to sort out and explain what happened in the past, which means attempting to understand the tastes and environment of an earlier time.[105]

The book's broadness stems from its examination of the Beatles' cultural, political and social meaning in sixties Britain. This distinguishes it from works which deal with more discrete topics such as the Beatles' image,[106] artistry,[107] masculinity[108] or religion[109] and their relationship to Romanticism,[110] communications technology,[111] the music industry[112] or the Rolling Stones.[113] Its use of a variety of sources from over a dozen years differentiates it from works which cover shorter periods[114] or which focus on a single source such as an album[115] or film.[116]

The book's wide-ranging subject matter accounts for its eclectic research methods, which range from exegesis to regression analysis. It also means that the work is informed by and contributes to many fields of postwar British history. This is primarily a cultural history both in the sense of being about popular culture and in its concern with discourse and representation. It shares Shumway's ambition 'not to get at the truth of the individual life but the meaning of the star for the culture'.[117] But the chapter titles indicate that the book has social and political dimensions in addition to cultural ones and subsections of these chapters attest to the Beatles' encroachment on sixties debates about gender, sexuality, ethnicity, nation, region, generation, class, religion, education, consumerism and personal appearance. If the book does not examine every finger placed by each Beatle in every pie, it is not for lack of effort.

The multiplicity of contemporary perspectives it presents on the Beatles adds to the book's scope. In contrast to more specialised studies, which examine a single discourse or set of actors, it adopts what the literary critic Mikhail Bakhtin once described as a 'polyphonic' method which gives expression to a 'plurality of independent and unmerged voices and consciousnesses'.[118] One drawback to this approach is that, like the Russian novels examined by Bakhtin, the number of people given voice in this book runs into the hundreds. Another is that similarities between speakers can be lost among a babel of speakers. This book cannot circumvent the first issue, but seeks to address the second by grouping together like-minded thinkers and counterpoising their arguments to different and competing discourses.

Empiricism simply means seeking in the substantive chapters to ground every argument in evidence: primary sources when possible or else secondary sources based on primary sources.[119] Alternative methods exist. At the beginning of the century, a major university press issued a monograph about the Beatles which contained less than one reference per page. At that time, Charles Hamm struggled to name any examples of 'empirical work produced in popular music studies'.[120] This is no longer the case, but many chapters and articles on the band continue to be published which contain little primary research. Moreover, much significant scholarship on the Beatles employs theoretical models. Freudian, Lacanian, Gramscian, Weberian, post-structuralist and McLuhanite approaches have all been deployed to understand the band.[121]

I do not share the disdain of writers such as Dominic Sandbrook for 'the opaque theoretical discussions, invented abstract nouns and ... obscure Continental theorists' that in his view blight academic cultural criticism.[122] Remarks of this nature contribute to empiricism's sorry reputation as a byword for intellectual philistinism and political conservatism. Good old-fashioned common sense contains a welter of unexamined assumptions, and any historian deals with abstractions such as class which are ineluctably freighted with theory. However, this book illustrates how inductive and empirical research proceeds on different lines from that underpinned by a theoretical framework.

Empiricism stands or falls on the reliability of primary sources. Sparing use is therefore made here of memoirs written with the benefit of hindsight.[123] The oral history examined in the Conclusion is primarily included to understand the 1990s, when the interviews were conducted, rather than the 1960s, which were their ostensible subject. Quotations have been traced back to their original source wherever possible. The pitfalls of doing otherwise can be seen in the factual errors which bedevil surveys of postwar Britain based on secondary sources. Paul Addison writes of the Beatles receiving OBEs (not MBEs) and of William Mann (not Tony Palmer) as declaring them to be the greatest songwriters since Schubert.[124]

Sir Brian Harrison misdates and misquotes Lennon's pronouncement that the Beatles were 'more popular than Jesus' and Lord Morgan lists his sole source on the group as being '*The Beatles' Progress*, by Michael Brown (1974)'.[125] The title, author and date of this work are all incorrect.

From an empirical standpoint, as much care needs to be taken in the selection and interpretation of sources as in establishing their veracity. For example, you could find quotations to 'prove' that John Lennon was a capitalist, communist, anarchist, liberal, libertarian, socialist, environmentalist and (if used in combination) a hypocrite. Empirical rigour in this book is sought through selecting the least worst forms of evidence. Opinion polls with all their flaws furnish otherwise unobtainable measures of public opinion, especially when collected in bulk, analysed systematically, used judiciously and interpreted alongside qualitative sources. Equally, there is no way of telling whether the letters published by the *Beatles Book* were (as its editor claimed) 'truly representative of the thousands we received for each issue'.[126] They nonetheless provide a unique insight into fandom because they span almost the entirety of the Beatles' recording career, express a range of opinions and (thanks to Mike Kirkup's detective work) are known to contain the real words of actual fans.[127]

The findings of this book are based on such a process of accumulating, selecting, evaluating and interpreting evidence. Except here and in the Conclusion, I have subordinated my authorial voice to a curated assembly of past testimony and support every claim with a citation, usually accompanied by a quotation. This ventriloquising technique does not suggest that the sources speak for themselves or provide definitive proof. On the contrary, one advantage of empirical research is its falsifiability. Arguments resting on cited sources can be disproved or challenged by uncovering better sources or providing more plausible readings of existing ones.

Claims of dispassion, like those of empiricism, understandably raise suspicions of hidden agendas. After all, anyone possessing ears and eyes is unlikely to be indifferent to the Beatles, and this author is no exception. While I rate the Beatles' music and admire many of their accomplishments, this is not why I have written this book and is still less of a reason for anyone to read it. In this respect, it differs from a large body of writing in which authors explore how the band has shaped their lives. The first generation of American rock critics wrote movingly about the transformative effect of hearing the Beatles for the first time on themselves and their generation.[128] Dissatisfaction with 'gushing hero worship' inspired Ian

MacDonald to produce 'a detached, posterity-anticipating tally of what the Beatles did' in his peerless *Revolution in the Head* (1994).[129] He succeeded spectacularly in most respects but, as discussed further in the Conclusion, he was anything but detached on account of his spirituality, countercultural ethos and generational identification with the band. Although unafraid to question some of the band members' actions and to pan celebrated songs, he readily accepted one interviewer's characterisation of his book as an 'act of love'.[130]

Autobiographical accounts written by a later generation of Beatles fans were no less unstinting in their adulation. Devin McKinney self-identifies as a 'Beatle-besotted second-generation fan-fanatic' and Rob Sheffield describes how 'being born on the same planet as the Beatles is one of the ten best things that's ever happened to me'.[131] While their predecessors celebrated their experience of growing up alongside the Beatles, McKinney and Sheffield reflect on having been 'destined by fate to miss out on the 60s'.[132] The titles of their books, *Magic Circles: The Beatles in Dream and History* and *Dreaming the Beatles: The Love Story of One Band and the Whole World*, indicate how they intertwine biography with extreme subjectivity. *The Beatles and Sixties Britain* adopts the reverse approach. It is concerned with the past, not the present: with them, not me. It seeks to overcome the very 'psychological biases, intellectual limitations, aesthetic prejudices, and personal experiences' which McKinney decides are his true subjects of investigation.[133]

Whereas McKinney sets out to 'creat[e] my own myth from the facts and fancies of the time', other writers pursue the opposite objective of challenging myths surrounding the Beatles and the sixties, often for political purposes.[134] David Fowler and Dominic Sandbrook question the band's significance as part of their broader revisionist critique of the 1960s as a major turning point in modern British history. In *Youth Culture in Modern Britain, c.1920–1970* (2008), Fowler aims to scotch two 'powerful myths of the period': 'that British youth culture of the 1960s suddenly became "classless" due to the impact of pop music' and 'that the Beatles created a cohesive youth culture'.[135] The proponents of these myths are, however, hard to identify. No one is cited as crediting the Beatles for uniting youth culture and the one historian named as arguing for pop's classlessness (Arthur Marwick) categorically rejected the notion.[136]

Turning to the other myth, Fowler presents three reasons for it being 'highly unlikely' that 'the Beatles did shape youth culture during the 1960s': their greater popularity among young girls than Mods or students; their cross-generational appeal as 'family entertainment'; and their aloofness after they stopped touring.[137] Each does not withstand critical scrutiny. To claim that 'the Mods were a more important cultural phenomenon than the Beatles because they generated the first geographically mobile, national youth movement' privileges scooters over the power of mass communications to create imagined communities.[138] His assessment that the Beatles and other bands had 'quite modest fan bases' is based on the size of their official fan clubs and exhibits a similarly narrow conception of the nature of youth participation in the 1960s.[139] Still more troubling is Fowler's characterisation of the Beatles' audience as 'passive teenage (mainly female) fans'.[140] As Barbara Ehrenreich, Elizabeth Hess and Gloria Jacobs have argued, Beatlemaniacs were anything but passive, and to characterise them as such harks back to the androcentric form of subcultural studies undertaken in the 1970s.[141] Fowler's argument that student revolutionaries 'especially despised the Beatles' music' is based on two letters by one man, John Hoyland, who was no longer a student and who confessedly 'loved and admired' Lennon.[142] More broadly, Fowler does not take account of the Beatles' evolution in the second half of the 1960s. If their patronage of the counterculture and their experiments with avant-garde music, agitprop and psychoactive drugs did not place them at 'the cutting edge of youth culture', it is hard to imagine who else would qualify.[143]

A more sophisticated exercise in revisionism comes from Dominic Sandbrook, whose work, while heavily reliant on standard biographies of the band, is novel inasmuch as he uses the Beatles in support of his continuity thesis that the 1960s were 'a stage in a long evolution [of Britain] stretching back into the forgotten past'.[144] Four claims underpin his attempt to square the Beatles with his depiction of the 1960s as a conservative era in Britain. The first is that the Beatles were less popular than middle-of-the-road fare such as Cliff Richard and soundtrack albums such as *The Sound of Music*.[145] Sandbrook's second claim is that the Beatles' 'old-fashioned simplicity' largely accounted for their popularity in the early years.[146] Third, he maintains that 'the more the Beatles departed from their conservative image of 1963, the more people disliked them'.[147] And fourth, he seeks to undermine their exceptionalism by querying 'enduring myths associated with the rise of the Beatles'.[148] Musically, he questions both the uniqueness of the Merseybeat scene and the unique popularity of the Beatles within it. Socially, Sandbrook characterises the Beatles as 'lower middle class rather than working class' in order to diminish their threat to class hierarchy and to ridicule Lennon's credentials as a 'Working Class Hero'.[149] And politically, he concludes that the Beatles and other sixties luminaries were '[f]ar from being revolutionary pioneers' because they purchased expensive properties and hobnobbed with the rich.[150]

An analysis of each of these claims reveals Sandbrook's portrayal of the Beatles to be intelligent and thought-provoking but ultimately misconceived. His first claim about the greater popularity of Cliff Richard and *The Sound of Music* is misleading. Richard achieved more hits than the Beatles in the 1960s simply because he released twice as many singles. In fact, such was the Beatles' dominance of the singles charts that they released 18 of the top 60 (and 4 of the top 5) best-selling singles of the decade.[151] Sandbrook's further contention that soundtrack albums for musicals were the 'most popular group of the sixties' is not corroborated by chart placings and sales figures.[152] The Beatles topped the album charts for more weeks in the 1960s than all the original soundtrack albums combined. Sales figures compiled in 1992 showed that the Beatles produced seven of the UK's ten best-selling albums recorded in the 1960s, and that by this point *Sgt. Pepper* had sold more copies than *The Sound of Music*.[153]

Sandbrook's second claim that the Beatles were conservative at the beginning of their career is not borne out by this book, which shows how they were depicted from the outset as a comprehensive alternative to societal norms. There is more substance to the idea that the Beatles courted unpopularity in the late 1960s, but (contrary to Sandbrook's account) this did not translate into falling sales. What is remarkable about the Beatles is not their decline but their continuous supremacy in both singles and albums charts from 1963 to 1970, despite audacious changes of image, genre and target audience. His dismissal of the Beatles' political radicalism on account of their wealth does not take into account their post-materialism or explain why they became more politicised as they became richer.[154] To denigrate Lennon and Ono's Bed-Ins as 'gigantic exercises in self-indulgence' is insufficient.[155] The Bed-Ins operated on a number of levels: as political demonstrations, performance art, press conferences, publicity stunts, marital bonding and consciousness-raising.[156] Their actions did not bring about world peace, but it was not 'obviously nonsense' for them to campaign for it.[157]

The myth-busting of Sandbrook creates myths of its own. Mark Lewisohn has demonstrated that Liverpool hosted a singular musical scene in the late fifties and early sixties, and the Beatles occupied an unrivalled place in it.[158] The Shadows, Acker Bilk and Lonnie Donegan did not pave the way for the Beatles in the United States.[159] The band exhibited no 'dependence on music-hall traditions', which they drew upon at a time when they were throwing every other musical genre into the mix,

including folk, Indian classical music and *musique concrète*.[160] Sandbrook
asserts that '[o]nly Richard Starkey ... had a genuine claim to working-
class origins' because he alone 'grew up in anything resembling genuine
poverty'.[161] It is simplistic to label Harrison, McCartney and Lennon as
'lower middle class'; they were respectively the sons of a bus driver turned
trade unionist, an unsuccessful cotton salesman and a district nurse, and
a merchant seaman and a waitress.[162] He proceeds to characterise
'Working Class Hero' (1970) as 'pure self-mythologising' on the part of
Lennon, whose messy childhood he considers 'settled and loving'.[163] He
misreads the song as a first-person account of Lennon's heroism, even
though it is non-autobiographical and argues that a 'Working Class Hero'
is a contradiction in terms. Sandbrook's portrait of Lennon replaces
a plaster saint with an equally simplistic caricature of vanity and
hypocrisy.[164]

Sandbrook's work exemplifies the politicisation of writing on the
Beatles, in which they appear as proxies in the ongoing culture wars
over the 1960s.[165] He espouses conservatism in its core sense of opposing
rapid change. His narrative of the 1960s accordingly steers an uneasy
path between disclaiming any wish to 'return to the years when gay men
lived in fear of the law, or when landladies put up "No Coloureds" signs'
and chastising the 'permissive liberalism' which remedied such injustices
for its disrespect towards 'the disciplines of the past'.[166] His affection for
the Beatles' music sits awkwardly with his moral disapproval of what
they represented. Thus Paul Johnson is extolled as one of 'few brave
souls [who] dared to question the cult of youth' for his 1964 diatribe
against 'The Menace of Beatlism'. Sandbrook applauds Johnson's icono-
clasm while accepting his invective against Beatlemaniacs for their inferior education, intelligence, class, taste, appearance and behaviour was 'a
bit harsh'.[167]

Sandbrook's right-wing critique of the Beatles and the 1960s is relatively
benign when compared with that of his colleagues at the *Mail*, A. N. Wilson
and Peter Hitchens. Wilson considers the Beatles as 'con artists' of lesser
cultural significance than the modernist composer John McCabe.[168]
Hitchens self-parodically describes the Beatles as 'a popular musical combination' and analyses the sexual abandon caused by their falsetto singing
and 'loud and relentless drumbeat'.[169] But whereas Wilson maintains that
'any history could afford to overlook the Beatles', Hitchens sees them as
prime movers in the destruction of 'one of the happiest, fairest and kindest
societies which has ever existed'.[170] The band legitimised drug-taking,
Lennon did the same for atheism in 'Imagine' (1971) and he, Mick Jagger

and Elvis Presley together destroyed 'British sexual reserve'.[171] In Hitchens' overwrought account, the moral degeneration instigated by the Beatles culminated in New Labour. Tony Blair's identification with the Beatles and 'the rock and roll generation' signalled the victory of 'cultural revolution' over the 'Conservative imagination' and its defence of 'patriotism, faith, morality and literature'.[172]

The politicisation of the Beatles is not confined to the right. A centre-left critique has been provided by the distinguished political historian and Labour peer Kenneth O. Morgan, whose account of the Beatles is consistent only in its condescension. Morgan argues that 'the culture represented by the Beatles or Carnaby Street posed no questions' in one sentence, then contradicts himself in the next when referring to the controversy caused by 'John Lennon's observations on drugs and Jesus Christ'.[173] His characterisation of youth protest as 'perhaps anarchic, certainly apolitical' is likewise contradictory, as is his statement that 'the permissive era had no political implications at all' despite acknowledging the relaxation of censorship and the 'legislation on sexual issues'.[174] Also puzzling is his comment that 'the permissive pop artists of the sixties were in many cases self-indulgent nihilists with no message for society in general. It could hardly be otherwise since all you needed was love.'[175] 'All You Need Is Love' (1967) was more idealistic than nihilistic in tone, and the Beatles sought to spread its message to the extent that the words were inscribed on sandwich boards in multiple languages for worldwide broadcast.

Far-left analyses of the Beatles adopt a still more critical tone. Two articles by Oded Heilbronner tell us more about the author's politics than those of his subjects. His contention that the Beatles 'epitomised the anti-revolutionary character of British society' uncritically recapitulates Marxist arguments of the period and is based on a series of questionable contrasts.[176] He opposes Englishness to radicalism, the Beatles to the Rolling Stones, nativist pastoralism to Continental modernism, 'conservative-popular "Beatles culture"' to '68ers and *The Beatles* double album (1968) to 'the spirit of the time'.[177] Because the Beatles fail to accord with Heilbronner's conception of true revolutionaries, they are variously disparaged as being 'part and parcel of the British establishment', 'guardians of British order and restraint' and curiously unwilling 'to play the role that was assigned to them by the fighters on the barricades or the Manson Gang'.[178] Sandbrook's claims about the popularity of Cliff Richard and Hollywood musicals are based on a book chapter by the Trotskyist cultural critic Dave Harker.[179] Sandbrook's demolition of 'Working Class

Hero' similarly echoes one published by Harker in his pioneering critique of the political economy of popular music, *One for the Money* (1980).[180] This unlikely alliance between Marxist and Tory populist stems from their shared distaste for sixties permissiveness: Harker seeing it as a diversion from class struggle, Sandbrook as the faddish concern of a 'metropolitan elite'.[181]

For all their doctrinal differences, each of these authors writes about the Beatles as an ideological enterprise. Sandbrook's championing of the 'reticent, dutiful and quietly conservative' majority sidelined in the sixties is deployed in his *Daily Mail* columns to warn their latter-day successors against change for change's sake.[182] Hitchens and Wilson use the rise of the Beatles as an index of moral and artistic decline. Morgan, Heilbronner and Harker present them as exemplars of political inaction or misadventure according to their own socialist convictions. Such partisanship and polemicism runs contrary to the empiricist and historicist approach of this book which, insofar as it is possible, checks its politics at the door.

1 | The Other Sixties: An Anti-Permissive Permissive Society?

Figure 1.1 Pollsters – Anne Geldart conducts a door-to-door survey, March 1966.
Photo by Reg Burkett/Express/Getty Images

In July 1970, three months after the Beatles publicly broke up, a group of researchers surveyed public attitudes on the future of the nation. The six hundred or so 16–44-year-olds they interviewed had a generally optimistic and adaptable outlook. Over the past fifteen years, 85 per cent of them had experienced 'a great deal' or 'quite a lot' of social change. Two thirds of the group saw these changes as positive, versus a fifth who thought things had got worse. It was hard for them to envisage the next fifteen years being as frenetic and dramatic. Ten times as many people anticipated the pace of change would slow down than predicted that it would speed up in the 1970s and early 1980s. Whatever the velocity, respondents nonetheless believed they were heading in the right direction by a ratio of 5:1.[1]

Then came questions asking people to predict the likelihood of scenarios in the science-fiction world of 1985, ranging from robotic cleaners to every family possessing a telephone and a car. This being 1970, a large proportion of these questions concerned permissiveness.[2] The term was defined in the questionnaire as 'greater freedom from old customs and outdated moral codes, sexual freedom, decline of marriage as an institution, less [sic] restrictions on private conduct, [and] liberalisation of drug laws', but in its broadest sense encompassed other issues of interest including the rights of women, ethnic minorities and the young.[3]

Table 1.1 shows that in all but one case, most of those questioned predicted a more permissive future. By 1985, a majority expected further advances in the sexual revolution, greater freedom of expression, more secularisation and cohabitation, higher rates of drug addiction, an increase in teenage independence and gender equality in education, employment and the home. The sole exception was that respondents split down the middle over whether they expected immigrants to continue experiencing discrimination at work.

The respondents therefore predicted the inexorable growth of permissiveness, but for the most part hoped that they would be proven wrong. While broadly in favour of equal opportunities for women and (to a lesser extent) immigrants, they were overwhelmingly opposed to the decline of marriage, religion and parental power. Fewer people were for than against 'Freedom in attitudes to sexual behaviour by men and women'. The same went for the abolition of censorship, although greater freedom of expression was supported by a plurality of the sample.[4]

This chapter, which examines polls such as this one, is not about the Beatles or reactions to them but the social context in which they can be understood. The Beatles were the most celebrated figures of the 'permissive society'. Their iconic standing rested not simply on their music, but on their capacity to encapsulate the loosening of strictures that was perceived

Table 1.1 Predictions in 1970 of the likelihood and desirability of changes over the next fifteen years

Q: All the statements are about what might happen over the next 15 years . . . please say how much you agree or disagree with each one. Do you think that if this happened it would be a good thing or a bad thing on the whole, and how good or bad?	Agree (or *greater)	Disagree (or *less)	Good (or *better)	Bad (or *worse)
Women will be entirely equal with men in the education they get, the jobs they do, and the pay they get for similar jobs	76.3	16.2	70.5	19.8
Immigrants will be accepted as entirely equal with British people in all kinds of jobs	43.7	46.9	50	36.7
Boys and girls of 15 will be much less under the control of their parents than at present	80.2	13	12.8	80.4
Only half as many people as now will claim to have any religious faith	70.8	18.4	12.1	63.8
Men and women will take equal shares in housework and in looking after children	54.6	38.2	n/a	n/a
Many couples won't bother to get married	72.9	21.7	14	72.7
There will be more drug addiction than there is now	73.9	18.8	n/a	n/a
All forms of censorship will be abolished	51.2	37.4	35.2	47.3
Freedom in attitudes to sexual behaviour by men and women	71.5*	10.1*	32.4*	45.1*
The amount of freedom as to what can be shown or written about in the cinema, on TV and in news- papers, magazines and books	82.4*	5.6*	45.2*	35*

Source: Social Science Research Council (SSRC) Survey Unit, Future in Britain Survey, July 1970 (N=586 adults aged 16–44)

to be under way in the 1960s. During their career, their champions placed them alongside William Blake and Dr Spock as 'Priests and Prophets of Permissiveness', while their detractors yoked them to Harold Wilson as progenitors of a 'progressive and permissive orthodoxy'.[5] The Beatles' reputation as 'filters of Sixties liberation' has endured in the half-century since they split up and has been advanced by Paul McCartney as their primary non-musical accomplishment.[6] 'I think we gave some sort of freedom to the world', he reflected: 'I think we set free a lot of people who were blinkered.'[7]

The idea that the Beatles were the dynamos of the 'swinging sixties' rests on three debatable propositions concerning the Beatles' attitudes, those of wider society and the effect of one on the other. The degree to which the Beatles were permissive in thought and deed deserves a book of its own.

The question of how the Beatles exerted influence on social attitudes is dealt with in the remainder of this one. Although it is extremely difficult to establish causation in the field of ideas, especially on a society-wide scale, the chapters on society, culture and politics show that the Beatles at a minimum stimulated debates across an array of issues associated with permissiveness. This leaves the vexed issue of when (if ever) Britain became a 'permissive society'.

What is telling about the 1970 Future in Britain poll is that its results cannot be easily explained by the principal approaches to this issue. The respondents' conviction that they were living in a time of major upheaval contradicts Dominic Sandbrook's assertion that 'Britain in 1970 was still fundamentally the same country it had been twenty, thirty or a hundred years before'.[8] The same sense of rapid change appeared in a National Opinion Polls (NOP) survey conducted earlier that year. Twice as many people thought that attitudes to marriage had 'changed a lot' during the previous decade than those who discerned little change. Four fifths of the same sample agreed that 'people's attitudes to sex had changed a lot', but only a third of people thought such changes to be a 'good thing'.[9] Such misgivings, like those expressed in the Future in Britain poll, cast doubt on Arthur Marwick's rival vision of 'a "revolution", or "transformation" in material conditions, lifestyles, family relationships, and personal freedoms for the vast majority of ordinary people' or Jeffrey Weeks' conception of a 'democratisation of everyday life'.[10] While democratic in the sense of establishing basic human rights to live, love and behave as one pleased, the 'social, cultural and moral revolutions' described by Weeks were not democratic in the sense of commanding majority support. Such 'revolutions from below' were conducted by minorities in the face of widespread disapproval.[11]

Polls such as these furnish new answers to two long-standing puzzles concerning sixties Britain. To begin with, recognition that contemporaries' awareness of change co-existed with a preference for continuity erodes the false dichotomies underpinning current debates over the existence or absence of permissiveness, a cultural revolution or 'the sixties' itself. The first half of this chapter introduces the concept of an 'anti-permissive permissive society' to account for the ambivalence of public attitudes displayed in polling data. Most people perceived a permissive society as coming into being from the 1960s onwards, but they disapproved of most of its manifestations and legislative reforms.[12] The second half of the chapter drills down into the raw data of opinion polls to compare attitudes towards different issues across demographic groups. The variations seen across age, gender, class, religion, region, nation, education and marital status reveal a complexity not captured in standard models of sixties Britain and provide clarity about which elements of British society were more permissive than others.

Methods

As Mark Jarvis argues, the 'emotive and politicised' term 'permissiveness' is nonetheless a concept which 'can hardly be avoided ... [i]n any study dealing with material on social issues in this period'.[13] The term here is defined broadly, encompassing not only issues concerning private life and civil liberties, including abortion, the age of majority, birth control, censorship, capital punishment, corporal punishment, divorce, drugs, gambling, homosexuality, illegitimacy, prostitution, religion and suicide, all of which were subject to legislation, policymaking and public debate in this period. The chapter also considers attitudes towards women, ethnic minorities and the young, because these concerned matters of equality closely related to the anti-discriminatory intent of permissive reforms.

National polls conducted by the major polling and surveying organisations up to 1975 have been mined for their coverage of the twenty-three topics listed in Table 1.2. In most cases, only top-line statistics are available. These polls form the basis of the first half of the chapter, which uses descriptive statistics to survey society as a whole. The second half of the chapter uses cross-tabulation and regression analysis on the minority of

Table 1.2 Topics related to permissiveness covered in opinion polls, 1963–1975

abortion	homosexuality
authority	illegitimacy
capital punishment	permissiveness
censorship	race and immigration
cohabitation	religion and secularisation
contraception	sexual revolution
corporal punishment	sixties culture
the counterculture	student radicalism
criminal justice	upbringing of children
divorce	women's rights
drugs	youth
gambling	

polls which provide the requisite granular data to show how attitudes towards permissiveness varied across subpopulations of British society.

The type of polling data used in this chapter has been studied for decades by social scientists,[14] who have constructed sophisticated historical models in the process.[15] But their work has made little impression on twentieth-century British historians, who have gravitated instead towards the mixed-methods approach of Mass-Observation.[16] The 'cultural turn' has led historians away from the quantitative and social scientific approaches that accompany polling analysis, even though polls provide otherwise unavailable insights into the issues of mentality and belief that most fascinate cultural historians. In the absence of quantification, large claims about permissiveness sometimes rest on anecdotes. 'Sixties values seem to have gained more support from the young and the middle-class living in the southeast than elsewhere', concludes Brian Harrison. The only evidence he offers is that Mary Whitehouse came from the West Midlands and that the notoriously misanthropic Philip Larkin wrote from Hull that he had been 'little in touch … w[ith] the world since 1945'.[17] Even when polling and survey data are mentioned in studies of permissiveness, they tend to be used unsystematically. Thus Michael Schofield's findings that most teenagers were virgins in 1962–3 is often cited to disprove the existence of the 'swinging sixties', with much less mention made of the 'tremendous change in attitude, especially among the women' he discovered when he tracked down some of the same respondents in 1971.[18] Many historians also use Geoffrey Gorer's findings uncritically, despite his 1950 survey being based on an unrepresentative sample and his 1969 survey being compromised by methodological and interpretative flaws.[19]

Existing literature on opinion polling about social issues in twentieth-century Britain can be divided into two main strands. One focuses on the practices of polling organisations, their claims to provide a scientific analysis of public opinion and how parties and NGOs deployed their findings in political debate.[20] The other concerns the quantitative analysis of religious beliefs and practices undertaken by Clive Field, Ben Clements and Callum Brown.[21] Beyond those on religion, there are few studies of social change in postwar Britain centred on opinion polls.[22]

Historians' limited use of polling data helps to explain why the question of when (if ever) Britain became a 'permissive society' remains fundamentally unresolved due to problems with sourcing, sampling and conceptualisation. Those who identify a 'cultural revolution' largely base their arguments on canonical cultural artefacts of the period such as songs, films, writings and fashions.[23] Revisionists either point to a series of other cultural artefacts that provide a more conservative view of the sixties or else contrast a minority permissive 'culture' with a broader 'society' displaying stronger continuities with the earlier twentieth century.[24] The quandaries faced by cultural historians in establishing the representativeness of such sources and in finding testimony from subordinate groups can be understood from a quantitative standpoint as ones of sampling. Again, polling throws historians a lifeline. 'History from below' is aided by stratified sampling, which ensures that different social groups are adequately represented and records attitudinal differences between them. Without use of polling data, it is more difficult to access the past perspectives of women, manual workers, the young and other groups underrepresented in conventional historical records. Conceptually, the debate has suffered from a conflation of the separate issues of behaviours, perceptions and preferences. Polls provide limited evidence on behaviours, but they allow us to distinguish between what people thought was happening (perceptions) and what they wished to happen (preferences). This distinction between preferences and perceptions underpin the concept of an 'anti-permissive permissive society'.

The usual qualifications apply concerning the interpretation of polling statistics.[25] They measure attitudes rather than behaviours, and reported attitudes at that, which were collated by strangers with clipboards (see Fig. 1.1). Respondents were asked to choose between a predetermined set of answers which were open to interpretation, may not have corresponded with their unprompted opinions and did not capture their motivations for choosing one answer over another. The data used in this chapter are fragmentary, episodic and culled from a miscellany of sources and a variety of organisations. No breakdown by social group is possible for most surviving polls; no polls covered Northern Ireland; and pollsters did not sample or identify respondents by ethnicity until the 1980s. Polls require interpretation, like any other source. At the same time, historians studying the past century should appreciate how uniquely privileged we are to have access to sources which sample the attitudes of the entire population and its constituent elements.

The Other Sixties

Social and moral issues were not uppermost in the minds of many people in mid-twentieth-century Britain. That, together with respondents' reluctance to choose one of the specified options, accounts for the high number of 'don't knows' on several key questions relating to permissiveness. At least a fifth of people did not express an opinion on whether the Wolfenden Committee's recommendations on homosexuality should become law in 1958,[26] whether *Lady Chatterley's Lover* should be published in 1960,[27] whether pregnant women who had taken drugs such as thalidomide should be granted abortions in 1962,[28] whether divorce laws were fit for purpose in 1965,[29] whether pirate radio should be banned in 1966,[30] whether there should be a clampdown on drug-taking in 1967[31] or whether to side with student demonstrators or university administrations in 1968.[32] A substantial number were also hazy about the law governing personal behaviour. Large minorities believed that all abortions had been outlawed before 1967 and that all were allowed afterwards.[33] A 1967 poll discovered no difference between attitudes towards censorship laws on books and those on plays, even though plays remained subject to much stricter regulation.[34] And almost a third of people were unaware or unsure whether sex between men had been decriminalised in 1970, three years after the Sexual Offences Act had been signed into law.[35]

The fabled sixties may indeed have left a minority largely indifferent, unaffected, even oblivious. Yet almost everyone was aware of the great 'moral panics' of the age.[36] Well over 90 per cent of people had heard about the Notting Hill riots in 1958,[37] the clashes between mods and rockers in 1964[38] and Enoch Powell's 'Rivers of Blood' speech in 1968.[39] The percentage of 'don't knows' did not exceed single figures for hot-button issues such as immigration and race relations and almost no one was short of an opinion about pornography, sex education, premarital intercourse, the gravity of the drug problem and the best methods for disciplining adolescents.

Of the manifold social changes explored by pollsters, women's emancipation was one of the very few positive developments perceived by the generality of people in mid-twentieth-century Britain. Misgivings about sexual mores increased from 1959 to 1969, by which point over twice as many people considered that attitudes were worsening rather than improving.[40] There was unrelieved pessimism about race relations.[41] Those convinced that 'the feeling between white . . . and coloured people' was deteriorating outnumbered those seeing signs of improvement in every Gallup and NOP poll up to 1973. An unprecedented bout of optimism recorded by NOP in 1974 and 1975 gave way to despair following the 1976 Notting Hill riots.

Public opinion was gloomy about the state of religion, the polling evidence on which has been expertly explored by Ben Clements and

Clive Field.[42] Their analysis provides a more nuanced picture than the model of sudden secularisation advocated by Callum Brown, and is more in accord with the generally conservative sentiments highlighted in this chapter. A wide-ranging poll on religion commissioned by ITV in 1963 – a year which Brown pinpoints as the beginning of the end for 'Christian Britain' – indicates that almost everyone professed to be Christian.[43] Atheists were a tiny and unpopular minority.[44] At the same time, people consistently indicated widespread concern over secularisation. Three fifths (63 per cent) of the ITV sample thought that religion was 'losing its influence on British life', and proved their point by expressing less confidence in traditional Christian doctrine than those polled in 1957.[45]

The ITV poll recorded a sharp rise in those viewing religion as 'largely old-fashioned and out-of-date'.[46] Yet support waned during the sixties and early seventies for measures such as compulsory religious instruction which were intended to preserve Britain as a Christian nation, and respondents appeared to regard secularisation as inevitable but regrettable. The large minority who identified a worsening attitude to religion at the end of the 1950s had grown into a clear majority a decade later.[47] Such concerns extended to the moral condition of Britain in general, as measured by responses to Gallup's question 'Are you satisfied or dissatisfied with the honesty and standards of behaviour of people in this country?' Around 40 per cent expressed themselves satisfied in the first half of the 1960s, but the figure had plummeted to below a quarter by the end of the decade and hovered just above 20 per cent during the 1970s.

It is not possible to be precise about how much of this perceived moral decline was attributed to permissiveness. What is evident from a 1969 Opinion Research Centre (ORC) poll (see Table 1.3) is the disquiet created by the 'permissive society'. Permissive legislation topped the list of most objectionable sixties changes, closely followed by non-white immigration and student protest. Together these three phenomena were chosen by three quarters of people as their least favourite things about the sixties, compared with just 6 per cent who named them as particularly positive developments.[48] The same poll found that 77 per cent of people believed that 'There is too much publicity given to sex', slightly more than the number agreeing that 'There are too many coloured immigrants in the country now' (73 per cent) or 'Murderers ought to be hanged' (71 per cent).[49] Other polls indicated opposition to the moral relativism and social pluralism associated with permissiveness. The proposition that 'A group which tolerates too many differences of opinion among its members cannot exist for long' was

Table 1.3 Perceptions in 1969 of the best and worst changes during the 1960s

Here are some of the changes which have taken place in the 1960s	Which one are you most pleased with?	Which one do you most object to?
Easier laws for homosexuality, divorce, abortion, etc.	5	26
Immigration of coloured people	–	23
Student unrest	1	23
Higher family allowances	7	9
Rising standard of living	18	7
Schools going comprehensive	9	6
Having TV throughout Britain	6	1
Better old age pensions	51	–
None of these	3	5

Source: Opinion Research Centre for *New Society*, November 1969 (N=1071)[50]

accordingly backed by a ratio of almost 2:1 in a poll of 15–40-year-olds conducted during 1967's 'Summer of Love'.[51] Many aspects of permissiveness were perceived to be linked to the increase in crime that scared and scarred Britain in the second half of the twentieth century.[52] Perhaps Gallup stacked the deck in 1973 when asking those polled to explain the crime wave primarily in terms of anti-authoritarianism, media irresponsibility, drugs use and ethnic conflict. But many respondents were willing to play along by blaming such attitudinal changes for the spike in crime and violence.[53]

This sense of moral malaise provided the context in which British people responded to the postwar laws, policies and appointments listed in Table 1.4. The first thing to note is that – contrary to its reputation as a liberalising era – the three decades after the Second World War spawned a mixture of permissive and anti-permissive initiatives. This is not to gainsay the permissive reforms which expanded freedom of expression and transformed the civil rights of women, the young, gay men, ethnic minorities, convicted criminals and others hitherto ill-treated by the law. In fact, these achievements appear more significant and hard-won when considered alongside the array of illiberal measures introduced during the same period. All of the immigration acts were restrictive save for the first one, the British Nationality Act of 1948, which was by no means intended to usher in mass non-white migration.[54] Politicians also sought to outlaw a series of new threats thought to be undermining the moral fabric of the nation. They targeted horror comics and prostitutes openly soliciting for custom in the

Table 1.4 Permissive and anti-permissive laws, policies and appointments in postwar Britain

1948	British Nationality Act
1948	Criminal Justice Act
1955	*Children and Young Persons (Harmful Publications) Act*
<u>1958</u>	<u>John Trevelyan appointed Secretary of the British Board of Film Censors</u>
1959	Obscene Publications Act
1959	Legitimacy Act
1959	*Street Offences Act*
1960	Betting and Gaming Act
<u>1960</u>	<u>Hugh Carleton Greene appointed Director-General of BBC</u>
1961	Suicide Act
<u>1961</u>	<u>Michael Ramsey appointed Archbishop of Canterbury</u>
1962	*Commonwealth Immigrants Act*
<u>1962</u>	<u>Birching banned for prisoners</u>
1965	Race Relations Act
1965	Murder (Abolition of Death Penalty) Act
1967	*Marine Broadcasting (Offences) Act*
1967	Sexual Offences Act (England and Wales)
1967	National Health Service (Family Planning) Act
1967	Abortion Act
1968	*Commonwealth Immigrants Act*
1968	Race Relations Act
1968	Theatres Act
1968	*Gaming Act*
1969	Divorce Reform Act
1969	Family Law Reform Act
1969	Representation of the People Act
1970	Equal Pay Act
1971	*Misuse of Drugs Act*
1971	*Immigration Act*
1975	Sex Discrimination Act
1975	Employment Protection Act

Key:
Legislation with broadly permissive intentions
Legislation with broadly anti-permissive intentions
<u>Ministerial decisions and appointments to government-linked institutions</u>

1950s, pirate radio and casinos in the 1960s and recreational drug use in the 1970s.

What did the public make of these initiatives taken on their behalf? Polling does not provide answers in every instance. Contemporary reaction to the 1948 British Nationality Act, the 1959 Obscene Publications Act, the 1959 Legitimacy Act, the 1968 Theatres Act and the maternity-leave provisions of the 1975 Employment Protection Act apparently went unrecorded. In other cases, polls indicate surprisingly high levels of support for some of the earliest liberalising reforms. The postwar Attlee government heeded the desires of the 44 per cent of respondents who had wanted to outlaw flogging of criminals shortly before the war.[55] The majority (58 per cent) in favour of legalising off-course betting in 1949 likewise had their wish granted by the Betting and Gaming Act in 1960.[56] Half of those polled backed the legalisation of attempted suicide in 1958, three years before the law was changed to this effect.[57]

The 1960s deserve some of their reputation as a 'permissive moment' inasmuch as support grew during the decade for equal pay for women, the state provision of birth control, the relaxation of divorce and abortion laws and the decriminalisation of sex between men in private.[58] Increasing support did not necessarily mean majority support. For example, the percentage of respondents in favour of liberalising divorce never matched the combined total of those in favour of tougher laws or retaining the status quo.[59] The Divorce Reform Act enjoyed a honeymoon period in the period between its passage in 1969 and its implementation in 1971. The new laws were endorsed in 1970 by two thirds of people (66 per cent), of whom half cited the fact that 'unhappy marriage causes misery' as the major reason for their support. The same respondents were nonetheless opposed to couples refusing to marry in the first place by a margin of two to one (47 to 25 per cent).[60] The concurrent rise of cohabitation and divorce in the 1970s weakened any further appetite for divorce reform. In 1975, those against making divorces easier outnumbered those in favour by 48 to 35 per cent.[61]

Other permissive causes failed to win strong public approval during the 'long 1960s'. The abolition of capital punishment never attracted the backing of more than a quarter of the population from 1945 until the suspension of the death penalty in 1965.[62] A majority was opposed to lowering the age of majority to eighteen in 1969, albeit by a smaller margin than in 1954.[63] There was more support for parents slapping and teachers caning children in 1967 than had been the case in 1949.[64] Two thirds of people disapproved of sex before marriage, according to polls conducted in 1963 and 1964.[65] The same issue returned in a different guise in debates over whether unmarried women should be prescribed the contraceptive pill.[66] Only 37 per cent of people questioned in 1968 envisaged any circumstances in which it was acceptable for the unmarried to use birth control.[67] Two years later, respondents divided equally over whether or not to bestow moral approval on single women on the pill.[68]

There were indications of an anti-permissive backlash regarding some issues in the 1960s. The reintroduction of hanging predictably topped the wish list of respondents asked by NOP in 1969 to choose one law to put on the statute books. But corporal punishment vied with capital punishment in the public's affections. 'Bring back hanging' was picked by 26 per cent and 'Stricter punishment/bring back the birch' by another 25 per cent, with no other option attracting more than 5 per cent support.[69] A majority of people in 1961 and 1962 supported the restoration of flogging and birching as civilian judicial punishments.[70] Half considered the obscenity laws to be insufficiently severe in 1964, just five years after their revision.[71] Over half backed Mary Whitehouse's campaign against smut on television in 1965 and almost as many did so in 1967.[72] And half adjudged the custodial sentences imposed upon the editors of *Oz* in 1971 to be fair or lenient.[73] Lennon and Ono's benefit record 'God Save Us' (1971) fell largely on deaf ears.

The public was far from implacable in its opposition to discrimination. Those polled in 1968 about the Race Relations Bill were evenly split over the general principle of whether or not it should be illegal 'to discriminate against people because of their colour'. In the same poll, a plurality was opposed to specific provisions in the Bill outlawing discrimination when hiring workers and selling houses.[74] The Sex Discrimination Act 1975 obtained majority backing, but a third were opposed.[75] A broader measure of discriminatory attitudes was provided by a Gallup question asking respondents whether they would vote for a well-qualified parliamentary candidate different from themselves. Respondents were appreciably more tolerant of atheists and Jews in 1965 than in 1959. But the numbers willing to vote for a woman or a Catholic had barely altered over the same period and prejudices were hardening against non-whites.[76]

In contrast to the very mixed response accorded to permissive legislation, all but one of the anti-permissive measures introduced in this period enjoyed overwhelming support. Seventy-one per cent were in favour of the proposal to ban imported horror comics in 1954, with only 6 per cent against.[77] The public supported the Wolfenden Committee's proposals to remove prostitution from public view, except that half of them took exception to the committee's tolerance of call girls operating behind closed doors.[78] Home Secretary James Callaghan's refusal to reduce the penalties against cannabis users was in line with the views of 88 per cent of those polled in 1967.[79] Massive majorities endorsed every new curb on non-white immigration. Proponents of the 1962 Commonwealth Immigrants Act outnumbered opponents by a ratio of 6:1.[80] Although 90 per cent of respondents supported the immigration controls contained in the 1968 Commonwealth Immigrants Act, 63 per cent of them wished they went further still.[81] The harsher 1971 Immigration Act accordingly earned the approval of 59 per cent of respondents and disapproval of 17 per cent.[82] The only unpopular anti-permissive law enacted during this period was the outlawing of pirate radio, but the numbers tightened once the ban came into effect in 1967.[83]

Drug-taking provoked a moral panic in the late 1960s and early 1970s that was out of proportion to any personal exposure to the subject.[84] Ninety-seven per cent of people told Gallup in 1967 that neither they nor anyone else in their household knew anyone who had taken illegal drugs.[85] Yet the issue never ranked lower than third in importance in Gallup's polling on 'very serious social problems' from 1965 onwards, well above pornography, immigration or rape. Gallup polls conducted in 1967 and 1973 showed that the public drew few distinctions between how 'hard' and 'soft' drugs should be treated under the law. Fewer than 10 per cent of people in both polls were more prepared to decriminalise the use, possession or selling of cannabis than that of heroin.[86] The rationale for public opposition to soft drug use became apparent in an NOP poll conducted in 1972. It showed that two thirds of people considered cannabis more harmful than tobacco (67 per cent) and alcohol (66 per cent) and that four fifths (82 per cent) saw it as a gateway drug.[87] This was the lens through which ordinary people viewed the Beatles' drug use, as described in Chapter 3.

Disaggregating Sixties Society

So far, this chapter has taken British society as a single entity in order to establish broad trends in attitudes towards a variety of issues over the long 1960s. It now examines how these attitudes varied along lines of class, gender, age, nation, region, religion, education, voting intention and marital and parental status: first, by cross-tabulating the answers to questions concerning each of twenty-three topics related to permissiveness; then by conducting binary logistic regression analysis on one data-rich poll.

The data amenable to cross-tabulation are extensive but inconclusive, limited as they are to analysis using descriptive statistics. Answers to a total of 256 questions derived from a basket of 40 polls carried out between 1963 and 1975 were assigned to 23 topics related to permissiveness. A net permissive or anti-permissive score was then calculated for all social groups answering that question (see Table 1.5). For example, in 1965

Table 1.5 Sample questions by topic to assess permissiveness and anti-permissiveness within social categories

Topic	No. of questions	Sample question
abortion	15	Do you think that abortion should be legal in all cases, legal in some cases, or illegal in all cases? (net none minus all or some): Mar. 1965
authority	3	How do you feel about people showing less respect for authority? (net too far minus not far enough): Oct. 1974
capital punishment	1	Would you like to see the death penalty kept or abolished? (net kept minus abolished): Nov. 1964
censorship	32	Do you agree or disagree with the view that pornography is too easily available in Britain today? (net agree minus disagree): Sep. 1972
cohabitation	2	Cohabitation (lowest percentage approving): Jan. 1970
contraception	4	Birth control should be provided free for all who ask for it (net disapprove minus approve): Apr. 1975
corporal punishment	1	Corporal punishment should be reintroduced (percentage agreeing it would help to reduce crime): Jan. 1970
counterculture	3	Hippies (lowest percentage approving): Jan. 1970
criminal justice	12	What is your view about taking tougher measures to prevent crime? (net should minus should not): Oct. 1974
divorce	4	Would you say the divorce laws are …? (percentage answering completely/fairly satisfactory): Oct. 1965
drugs	10	Reduction in penalties for marijuana possession (net disapprove minus approve): Jan. 1969
gambling	3	Do you think that gambling is wrong in principle? (net yes minus no): Jan. 1963
homosexuality	4	Homosexual acts between consenting adults (21 years and over) in private should be regarded as criminal (net agree minus disagree): Oct. 1965
illegitimacy	3	It is morally wrong to have an illegitimate child (net agree minus disagree): Jan. 1970
morality	4	What are the most important changes in the past 15 years that you think have been changes for the worse? (percentage answering permissive society): Jul. 1970
race relations and immigration	39	Do you agree or disagree that there should be a drastic reduction on further immigration? (net agree minus disagree): Apr. 1968
religion and secularisation	12	If your present neighbours moved out, are there any of these you would not like to have as a neighbour? (percentage answering atheist): Dec. 1963–Jan. 1964
sexual revolution	37	Men and women should have sexual relations only for the purpose of having children (percentage agree): Dec. 1963–Jan. 1964
sixties culture	6	Miniskirts (lowest percentage approving): Sep. 1972

Table 1.5 (*cont.*)

Topic	No. of questions	Sample question
student radicalism	9	Do you think students are or are not justified in holding demonstrations on political subjects like the war in Vietnam? (net not justified minus justified): May 1968
upbringing of children	11	There isn't the discipline in school that there used to be (percentage agree): Jan. 1970
women's rights	33	How do you feel about the attempts to ensure equality for women? (net too far minus not far enough): Oct. 1974
youth	8	Do you think that people should be able to get married without their parents' consent at the age of 18 or not? (net no minus yes): Dec. 1965

NOP asked the question 'Do you think that abortion should be legal in all cases, legal in some cases, or illegal in all cases?'[88] A net anti-permissive score subtracted those answering 'legal in all cases' or 'legal in some cases' from those answering 'illegal in all cases'. In this instance, NOP provided answers broken down by class, age, gender, marital status, religion and region or nation, but did not publish any information showing how the answers varied according to how respondents intended to vote, whether they had dependent children, the age they left school, the type of area they lived in or (if female) whether they worked outside the home.

The quotidian detail provided by these cross-tabulations is both its strength and its weakness. It allows us to compare attitudes *within* polls: to see, for example, what the married and unmarried thought about an array of subjects over a dozen years. Direct comparisons *between* polls are stymied by the slightly different categories used from one poll to another. Take the example of categorisation by nation and region. The most common practice was to provide figures for Wales, Scotland and seven English regions (North, North-East, Midlands, London, East, South, South-West). But there were many variations: treating the English South or North as single categories, merging London with the South-East or Wales with the West or South-West, hiving off Yorkshire, omitting Scotland and so on. This means that, of the seventy-one polls containing information on nation and region, only twenty-eight use the same nine categories and as such are directly comparable.

The purpose of identifying directly comparable polls is to see which groups were the most and least permissive using uniform classifications.

Comparing like with like is a more robust method, admittedly at the cost of excluding polls employing irregular forms of categorisation. The results of this winnowing process are displayed in Tables 1.6 and 1.7. These tables show which group within a given social category gave the largest number of permissiveness and anti-permissive answers on each topic. To return to the example of abortion, the question asked by NOP in the 1965 poll is one of eight questions from five polls which provide some uniform cross-tabulations. Seven of these eight questions furnish data showing how attitudes to abortion varied between those intending to vote Conservative, Labour or Liberal. Conservatives were more opposed to abortion (and therefore more anti-permissive) than either Labour or Liberals in four of their seven answers. Liberals were more in favour of abortion on the same number of answers, so are listed as the most permissive group of voters. Likely Labour voters fell somewhere in the middle, providing the most permissive answer to one question and the most anti-permissive answer to three questions. The tables display which group within a given social category gave the largest number of permissive and anti-permissive answers. A blank cell indicates where no single group gave more anti-permissive or permissive answers than any of the others; dashes indicate where no data exist for that social category.

This method has its limitations, but nonetheless provides a useful indication of where support for and opposition to permissiveness was at its strongest within British society. The patterns which emerge are summarised in Table 1.8. It distils the data contained in Tables 1.6 and 1.7 to show which group was the most permissive or anti-permissive in the greatest number of topics. According to these polls, anti-permissive attitudes were more likely to be found among Conservatives, semi-skilled and unskilled manual workers, the elderly, women (especially housewives), the married and those without dependent children. There are more gaps in the data for the other categories (religion, education, region, nation and type of area), but the available evidence suggests that the less educated and those living in urban areas or north-east England tended to be less permissive. No religious denomination was clearly more anti-permissive than others, but the irreligious held conspicuously more permissive attitudes on most issues.

Men, women in paid work, the unmarried and those with dependent children were more permissive than their counterparts in the binary categories to which they belonged. The most permissive groups in terms of age, education and class were the opposites of the anti-permissive groups, being the youngest, the most educated and professionals or managers. Data on the most permissive region or nation are limited and the

Table 1.6 The most permissive groups by topic within social categories

	Voting intention	Class	Age	Gender	Employment (women only)	Marital status	Dependent children	Religion	Region/nation	Age completed education	Type of area
abortion	Liberal	AB	–	Male	Housewife	Married	Kids	Atheist/agnostic	Scotland	–	–
authority	Labour	DE	16 to 24	Male	–	Unmarried	Kids	Atheist/agnostic	London	15	–
capital punishment	Liberal	AB	–	Male	–	Unmarried	Kids	–	London	19 or over	–
censorship	Liberal	C2	16 to 24	Male	Paid work	Unmarried	Kids	Atheist/agnostic	–	19 or over	Rural
cohabitation	Liberal	AB	–	Male	Paid work	Unmarried	–	–	–	–	Rural
contraception	Liberal	AB	16 to 24	Male	–	–	Kids	Atheist/agnostic	Midlands	16	–
corporal punishment	Liberal	–	–	Female	–	–	–	–	–	–	–
counterculture	Liberal	–	–	Male	–	–	–	–	–	–	–
criminal justice	Liberal	AB	16 to 24	Male	Paid work	–	Kids	–	South	19 or over	–
divorce	–	–	–	Female	Housewife	Married	Kids	–	–	–	–
drugs	Liberal	–	16 to 24	Male	–	Unmarried	–	–	–	–	–
gambling	Liberal	–	–	Male	–	–	–	–	–	–	–
homosexuality	Liberal	–	–	Female	Paid work	Married	Kids	–	–	–	–
illegitimacy	Liberal	–	–	Male	–	–	–	–	–	–	–
morality	Conservative	–	16 to 24	Male	Paid work	Unmarried	Kids	Catholic	South-west	15	Rural
race rels/ immig.	Liberal	AB	16 to 24	Male	Paid work	Unmarried	Kids	–	–	19 or over	Rural
religion	Labour	–	16 to 24	Male	–	Unmarried	Kids	Atheist/agnostic	–	15	Conurbation
sexual revolution	Labour	–	16 to 24	Male	Paid work	–	–	–	South	17 to 18	Rural
sixties culture	–	–	–	–	–	–	–	–	–	–	–
student radicalism	Liberal	AB	16 to 24	Male	Housewife	Married	No kids	Atheist/agnostic	–	19 or over	–
upbringing	Labour	–	16 to 24	Male	Paid work	Unmarried	Kids	Catholic	–	15	Rural
women's rights	Liberal	C1	16 to 24	Female	Housewife	Married	No kids	Other	Wales	19 or over	Urban
youth	Labour	–	–	Male	–	–	Kids	–	North	–	–

Source: Basket of polls and surveys conducted by BBC, British Election Study, Eurobarometer, Gallup, NOP, SSRC Survey Unit, 1963–1975 (N=40)

Table 1.7 The most anti-permissive groups by topic within social categories

	Voting intention	Class	Age	Gender	Employment (women only)	Marital status	Dependent children	Religion	Region/nation	Age completed education	Type of area
abortion	Conservative	DE	65 plus	Female	Paid work	Unmarried	No kids	Catholic	East	–	–
authority	Conservative	AB	45 to 54	Female	–	Married	No kids	Other	North-east	17 to 18	–
capital punishment	Conservative	DE	65 plus	Female	–	Married	No kids	–	South	14 or under	–
censorship	Labour	AB	–	Female	Housewife	Married	No kids	Other	Wales	14 or under	Urban
cohabitation		Never employed	–	Female	Housewife	Married	–	–	–	14 or under	Urban
contraception	Conservative	–	65 plus	Female	–	–	No kids	Catholic	Scotland	14 or under	–
corporal punishment	Conservative	–	–	Male	–	–	–	–	–	–	–
counterculture	Conservative	–	–	Female	–	–	–	–	–	–	–
criminal justice	Conservative	–	65 plus	Female	Housewife	–	No kids	–	–	14 or under	–
divorce		–	–	Male	Paid work	Unmarried	No kids	–	–	–	–
drugs	Conservative	C2	–	Female	–	Married	–	–	–	–	–
gambling	Conservative	–	–	Female	–	–	–	–	–	–	–
homosexuality		–	–	Male	Housewife	Unmarried	No kids	–	–	14 or under	–
illegitimacy	Conservative	–	–	Female	–	–	–	–	–	–	–
morality	Labour	AB	55 to 64	Female	Housewife	Married	No kids	Presbyterian	North-east	19 or over	Conurbation
race rels/ immig.	Conservative	DE	65 plus	Female	Housewife	Married	No kids			14 or under	Urban
religion	Conservative	C2	65 plus	Female	–	Married	No kids		–	17 to 18	Urban
sexual revolution	Conservative		65 plus	Female	Housewife		–		North-east	14 or under	Urban
sixties culture		–	–		–	–	–	–	–	–	–
student radicalism	Conservative	DE	65 plus	Female	Paid work	Unmarried	Kids	Presbyterian		14 or under	–
upbringing	Conservative		65 plus	Female	Housewife	Married	No kids	Other Non-con	North-east	19 or over	–
women's rights	Labour		65 plus	Male	Paid work	Unmarried	Kids	Anglican		14 or under	Rural
youth	Conservative		65 plus	Female	–		No kids	–	Scotland	–	–

Source: Basket of polls and surveys conducted by BBC, British Election Study, Eurobarometer, Gallup, NOP, SSRC Survey Unit, 1963–1975 (N=40)

Table 1.8 Typical characteristics of permissive and anti-permissive respondents in opinion polls

	Permissive	Anti-Permissive
Voting intention	Liberal	Conservative
Class	AB	DE
Age	16 to 24	65 plus
Gender	Male	Female
Employment (women only)	Paid work	Housewife
Marital status	Unmarried	Married
Parental status	Dependent children	No dependent children
Religion	Atheist or agnostic	[N/A – inconclusive results]
Region or nation	London/South	North-east
Age completed education	19 or over	14 or under
Type of area	Rural	Urban

results variable, with London and the South being marginally ahead. Possibly the most surprising finding is that rural areas were more permissive than urban areas or conurbations for three quarters of the topics for which data exist. This, like the corresponding anti-permissiveness found in urban areas, merits further investigation. Although the ethnicity of respondents was not sampled or recorded in national polls during this period, a local 1971 study found that whites and (mostly Afro-Caribbean) non-whites in Brent discerned no ethnic difference in permissiveness among the young. In contrast, three quarters of Indian and Pakistani immigrants in Bradford believed that 'young white people are more permissive than young coloured people' and cited this as a major reason to keep their teenage children apart from whites.[89]

Table 1.8 therefore provides composite portraits – an identikit of sorts – of the typical permissive and anti-permissive groups in sixties and early seventies Britain. It is important to acknowledge the fragmentary and sometimes ambiguous nature of the data, the inexactitude of the methodology, the variation within groups and the arguably unpermissive character of the activity of creating stereotypes. That said, these composite portraits apply well to attitudes towards all but two of the 23 topics related to permissiveness. The fit is at its most precise for the counterculture, criminal justice, gambling, illegitimacy, race relations and immigration. Where a more permissive or anti-permissive group is identified for these topics, it corresponds to every one of the groups listed in the table. There is a single variation from the composite portraits in attitudes to capital punishment, cohabitation and drugs, and two or three for the topics of secularisation, contraception and the sexual revolution.

The composite portraits are less reliable in predicting attitudes to some other topics. Though housewives and the married were generally less permissive than women in paid work and the unmarried, these two groups tended to be more in favour of abortion and less opposed to student radicalism. Men were more opposed to homosexuality and more in favour of corporal punishment, although otherwise more permissive than women on almost every issue. The most liberal views on authority came from the DE classes, Labour supporters and those who had left school at 15: groups which did not usually typify permissive attitudes. These topics, in common with morality, youth and the upbringing of children, shared at least half of the typical characteristics of respondents listed in Table 1.8. Two topics – divorce and women's rights – were outliers in that the most permissive and anti-answers were largely given by groups not predicted by the composite portraits. There was greater enthusiasm for the liberalisation of the divorce laws among the married, women and housewives, who tended to be anti-permissive on other topics. The same groups were more in favour of women's rights, as were the ordinarily less permissive urban dwellers and those without dependent children. More predictable was the greater support for women's rights among Liberal voters, the most educated and those under 25.[90]

Greater precision in identifying variations among social groups becomes possible by using binary logistic regression analysis. Only one poll lends itself to this method in that its raw data are available and it included a range of questions about permissiveness. This is the British Election Study Cross-Section Survey, which was conducted from October 1974 to January 1975, at the tail-end of the period under consideration. It boasted an unusually large sample of 2,365 respondents (493 of which had missing cases and were excluded from the regression analysis). Table 1.9 summarises the responses to nine questions from the survey. The first seven questions asked whether certain permissive phenomena had gone too far (coded as 1) as against either having not gone far enough or being 'about right' (coded as 0). The last two questions asked whether respondents thought it important for the government to pursue anti-permissive policies (coded as 1) or were either indifferent or opposed to these policies (coded as 0). Odds ratios under 1, which are shaded in the table, indicate that the correspondingly shaded group listed at the top of the column was less permissive on that question; odds ratios over 1 indicate the opposite.

Table 1.9 Binary logistic regression analyses of selected questions from British Election Study, 1974–1975

	Voting intention		Class		Age		Gender		Marital status		Dependent children		Religion		Age completed education		Region/ nation	
	Tory	Non-Tory	ABC1	C2DE	<45	45+	Male	Female	Unmarried	Married	No Kids	Kids	Irreligious	Religious	Left <16	Left 16+	Sc, Wls, N	Mids, S
How do you feel (^What is your view) about . . .?																		
the attempts to ensure equality for women?	0.73*		1.23		1.20		1.25		0.73*		1.01		1.25		0.58*		1.13	
moves to go easier on people who break the law?	0.90		0.91		1.27*		0.79*		1.16		0.90		1.05		1.01		0.77*	
the right to show nudity and sex in films and magazines?	0.75*		0.86		4.05*		3.13*		0.93		0.76*		1.67*		0.77		0.73*	
people showing less respect for authority?	0.55*		0.83		1.45*		1.45*		1.70*		0.91		1.75*		1.03		0.57*	
recent attempts to ensure equality for coloured people?	0.64*		1.01		1.16		0.95		0.76*		0.74*		0.81		0.68*		1.01	
the change to modern methods in teaching children at school?	0.57*		0.68*		1.96*		1.38*		0.83		0.82*		0.93		1.86*		1.12	
the availability of abortion on the National Health Service?	0.74*		1.01		2.29*		1.57*		0.81		0.90		1.36*		0.64*		0.80*	
sending coloured immigrants back to their own country?^	0.67*		1.38*		1.22		1.33*		0.95		0.90		0.94		0.53*		1.14	
taking tougher measures to prevent crime?^	0.33*		1.12		2.03*		1.29		1.16		0.76		1.42		0.71		0.86	

Source: British Election Study Cross-Section Survey, Oct 1974 to Jan 1975 (N=2365)

Note: Results given as odds ratios (Exp(B)); *p <.05 or lower

The results are generally in line with those from other polls. For example, Conservative voters were less permissive than voters for other parties on every question. The difference between Tories and non-Tories was statistically significant in all but one case, and was especially marked on questions concerning criminal justice, modern teaching methods and authority. Age, gender, level of education and religiosity also had a strong relationship to social attitudes, with anti-permissiveness more likely to be found among older, female, less educated and more religious respondents. All of the statistically significant differences between regions and nations indicated less permissive attitudes in Wales, Scotland and Northern England, but these accounted for a minority of answers. Although those without dependent children were less permissive on all but one question, most of the odds ratios were narrow and not statistically significant. This poll differs from the cross-tabulations in providing weak evidence for class or marital status being consistently associated with attitudes towards permissiveness.

Conclusion

In 1966, the American literary critic Steven Marcus coined the term 'The Other Victorians' to describe the sexual fantasies and deviance lurking beneath the veneer of nineteenth-century British society. Marcus' Freudian model held that the strait-laced 'official culture' of sexuality created its Other in the form of licence, obscenity and sado-masochism. 'For every warning against masturbation issued by the official voice of culture', he wrote, 'another work of pornography was published.'[91] A sixties liberal, Marcus regarded Victorian sexual attitudes, whether prudish or perverted, as Other – '"foreign", distinct, exotic' – from those of his own time. The 'important, momentous, and enduring' sexual revolution under way in the 1960s would create a society less prone to repression or obsession.[92]

If the 'Other Victorians' represented immodest behaviour hidden by propriety, then the 'other sixties' uncovered in this chapter was the very opposite. The evidence from opinion polls indicates that the 'official culture' of the 1960s – the permissiveness endorsed by Marcus – contended with its Other in the form of conservative reaction. The concept of an 'anti-permissive permissive society' is not intended to blur the boundaries between expression and repression in the manner of Michel Foucault, whose analysis of permissiveness I have critiqued elsewhere.[93] Nor does acknowledging the power of this anti-permissive 'other sixties' negate the significance of permissiveness. In some respects, sixties Britain was an unusually tolerant place by contemporary standards. For example, Gallup asked British and American respondents in 1969 'Would you find pictures of nudes in magazines objectionable?' Seventy-one per cent of British people said no; 73 per cent of Americans said yes.[94] On most issues, however, reformers and minorities encountered an uphill struggle in the face of prevailing headwinds.

Where did the Beatles fit into this anti-permissive permissive society? First and foremost as avatars of permissiveness: hence NOP's inclusion of a question gauging approval of 'John and Yoko' in its *Report on Attitudes towards Crime, Violence and Permissiveness in Society* undertaken in January 1970. Just 13 per cent of people approved of the couple versus 75 per cent against. The negative response shows the Beatles' second role, especially towards the end of their recording career, as a warning against permissiveness taken to extremes.[95]

Popular newspapers of the period delighted to point out the Beatles' poor showing in polls which asked young people whom they most admired. 'Who'd have expected THIS teenage top ten?' asked the *Daily Mail* in November 1967 upon discovering that under 1 per cent of an NOP sample listed a Beatle as their main role model.[96] The full results were not provided and the small print suggested that only 'Mother', the Queen and Francis Chichester had gained any appreciable support, but the lowly showing of the Beatles and Mick Jagger provided the best copy. In June 1971 it was the *Daily Express'* turn to crow that 'There wasn't a Rolling Stone or Beatle in sight' when 16–29-year-olds were asked to name the public figure they most admired. Winston Churchill came top with 9 per cent of mentions, while the highest-ranked entertainer was the broadcaster, philanthropist and (it later transpired) child molester Jimmy Savile.[97]

The newspapers expressed surprise that the 'pop-singers and student militants' who were 'regarded as spokesmen for their entire generation' were not more highly esteemed by their own kind.[98] But the sheer atypicality of the Beatles becomes evident when considering not merely their views on permissiveness, which were much more libertarian than the norm, but also their deviation from the demographic categories used by pollsters to survey sixties Britain. The Beatles' political views could not be captured in a question about party affiliation and their later religious beliefs were beyond categorisation. They educated themselves in the late 1960s with the aid of hallucinogens and ashrams. The standard occupational classifications also proved wanting. While their wealth appeared to put

them top of any socioeconomic tree, the Beatles were issued with H2 visas
for their first American tour in recognition that their skills surpassed those
of trainees but did not exhibit the 'distinguished merit and ability' necessary for H1 status.[99] The Beatles were singularly unrepresentative representatives of sixties Britain. The next two chapters explore this paradox and
its consequences.

Figure 2.1 Fans – Awaiting the Beatles' arrival at the Liverpool premiere of
A Hard Day's Night, July 1964. Photo by Staff/Mirrorpix/Getty Images

> It sets girls screaming and gives policemen nightmares.
> It impels boys to cultivate mushroom style hair.
> It makes older folk go 'yeah, yeah, yeah', thinking they are young
> again.
> It has now even taken hold of the Royal Family . . .[1]

'It', needless to say, was Beatlemania, the transformative effect of which captivated the press in 1963–5. Newspapers ran dozens of stories about staid institutions falling under their sway. Troops petitioned the Beatles to 'Come and sing to us'.[2] Royals traded jokes with the band.[3] Schools issued boys with guitars and girls with 'Beatle-style uniforms'.[4] Symphony orchestras and military bands played their tunes and ballet companies danced to them.[5] Stockbrokers traded shares in their songs, barristers clashed over their cultural value, Cambridge dons discussed them at high table, clergymen pondered their significance, a duke had one down for a weekend and party leaders vied with each other to associate themselves with the band.[6] They could be heard in chapel, Sunday School and the Women's Institute and even seen in 'Squaresville', otherwise known as Cheltenham Spa.[7]

The press highlighted clashes between the Beatles' followers and their adversaries. Male apprentices at a Birkenhead engineering firm threatened to fast in protest against hair inspections and the suspension of a colleague for his hairstyle, and several reports emerged of female factory workers striking against restrictions on their Beatlemania.[8] Two hundred millworkers in Accrington who had been singing along to 'She Loves You' (1963) staged a sit-down strike when management turned off the piped music.[9] A reprimand issued to Ivy Lewis for wearing a Beatle wig resulted in a two-day walkout by 500 of her colleagues at a packaging factory in Neath. 'If you can't have a bit of fun it's not worth living', said Lewis in a phrase which captured how these disputes appeared to pit jobsworths against rebels, regulation against freedom.[10]

Such hyperbole was partly down to hype. Publicists blended biblical allusions ('they have come amongst us') with claims that 'the magic of the Beatles' transcended barriers of age, class and nationality.[11] There was also an undeniable element of whimsy in media reports of orthodoxies being upended and the whole nation being Beatlified in carnivalesque fashion. The saturation coverage of the band in turn prompted a backlash by 'Beatlephobes' (a term coined in January 1964) seeking to cut the band, their fans and their apologists down to size.[12]

Yet just as the Beatles themselves were not ephemeral and inconsequential, nor were the reactions to them. The publicised examples of institutions succumbing to the Beatles were not chosen by accident. They collectively represented the most venerable and fundamental elements of British society: the church and the factory, the gentlemen's club and the WI, the school and the university, the bandstand and the concert hall, the military and the monarchy, Westminster and the City, the law courts, the spa town and the stately home. The Beatles principally functioned in these accounts as symbols of modernity who tested each institution's capacity for change.[13] Scrutiny of institutions broadened out into questions of identity. Attitudes towards class and religion, gender and generation, region and nation, morality and sexuality were articulated and debated in reaction to the Beatles. Their transformative powers, whether actual or potential, led contemporaries to contemplate the possibility and desirability of social, cultural and political upheaval in 1960s Britain.

The Beatles did not transform social attitudes in sixties Britain. As Chapter 1 has argued, most people were much less permissive and much more averse to change than were the band. The Beatles nonetheless had a significant impact on discussions of social issues, both directly through their art, activism and interviews and indirectly by generating discourses about them and what they represented. This chapter analyses the contested nature of the band and their fans within discourses of class, nation, generation, gender and sexuality in the period from 1963 to 1965. Chapter 3 then considers how the evolution of the Beatles after 1965 placed them in greater conflict with British society, which increased their engagement with social issues while reducing their impact.

Generation, Gender and Sexuality

Initial reactions to the Beatles, much like the band itself, bore the imprint of deep-rooted British social and intellectual traditions. Generational analyses of the Beatles and their fans (see Fig. 2.1) were a case in point, drawing as they did on hoary debates about the 'youth question' which oscillated between conceptions of 'youth-as-fun' and 'youth-as-trouble'.[14] Commentators of the period generally conceived of adolescence as a perilous stage characterised by the need for excessive energy to be channelled into constructive outlets.[15] In the case of boys, delinquency was most likely to manifest itself through crime and violence; in girls, through disobedience and premature sexual activity. Overlaid on these essentialist models of childhood development was the notion that there was something unique about baby boomers. A 1964 *New Society* editorial reasoned that 'what is happening at the moment is surely more than simply the young enjoying themselves and rebelling as the young always have done'.[16] Postwar discourses on adolescent subcultures, fashion, education, crime, sexuality and consumerism doubled as meditations on the present and future state of British society.

Commentators agreed that the Beatles and Beatlemaniacs were important portents of generational change, but divided sharply over their meaning.[17] Optimists extolled the Beatles as representative of their generation's superior education, drive and creativity. The band's *joie de vivre* enthralled the president of the Mothers' Union, who credited them for banishing 'drabness' from teenage dress and dance, and journalist Maureen Cleave, who concluded that 'Everybody loves them because they look so happy.'[18] The *Daily Mail's* Vincent Mulchrone held them up as paragons of youth: 'shatteringly honest, incredibly modest, immediately friendly . . . refreshing . . . fun . . . kind'.[19]

Mulchrone defended Beatlemaniacs for expressing the same 'sheer outrageous joy of being young' as their idols.[20] Others shared his tolerant view of adolescent exuberance. When the *Daily Telegraph* asked its readers whether their screaming was 'a safety valve or symptomatic of youth's declining morals', most replied that the young needed '[s]ome form of energetic self-expression'.[21] The proliferation of beat combos had the tangible benefit of 'siphon[ing] off a great deal of surplus juvenile energy into socially innocuous channels', according to Liverpool University sociologist John B. Mays.[22]

Progressive educators considered how to channel the young's interest in the band into socially useful pursuits. In November 1963, the *Mirror* reported that a headmaster had allowed girls to design a lapelless jacket 'right in the Beatles' groove' as part of their new school uniform.[23] The next day, the same paper carried a photograph of boys at another school playing guitars behind their desks. 'We will not try to stop the boys playing pop music', commented their headmaster, who had acceded to their repeated requests for guitar tuition.[24] The noted principal of Kingsway further education college, Fred Flower, saw a learning opportunity in a pupil describing a Beatles' concert as 'Just fab'. Rather than berating the boy for his vagueness, the teacher should recognise that there were 'occasions when imprecise speech can not only be tolerated but is in fact appropriate' as a means of establishing social bonds.[25]

The Beatles' supporters saw hostility to youth culture as misplaced and ill-advised. The generation gap had become a gulf as a result of 'adult resentment', stated the Cavern Club's disc jockey Bob Wooler.[26] A Cavern regular, 16-year-old Tony Mizen, thought that the older generation 'hate our guts' and insulted the Beatles out of sexual jealousy and spite.[27] Psychoanalyst D. W. Winnicott agreed that 'envy of the teenager' accounted for adult criticism of the Beatles, and the chair of the National Council of Civil Liberties warned that 'The brazen contempt of some middle-aged people for the youth of the Beatle era has nearly driven the young to violent extremes.'[28] A divorce case made public an extreme example of generational struggles over the Beatles. In 1967 Mr Minter assaulted his stepson for defying an order to cut his hair and his step-daughter for objecting to his description of the Beatles as 'drips with long hair'. The judge granted Mrs Minter a divorce on grounds of cruelty, ruling that the boy's hair was not so extreme as to merit a beating and that it was 'fair and reasonable' for the girl to condemn her stepfather as 'square' for his views on the Beatles.[29]

The opposite approach was advanced by paternalists who did not trust children to act in their own best interests. Boys who preferred to listen to pop records over character-building activities such as exercising or collect-ing stamps did not know what was good for them.[30] 'I am sick of kids of your age listening to the Beatles instead of playing tennis, instead of playing cricket, instead of doing SOMETHING', Australian broadcaster Russell Braddon told an audience of sixth-formers in London. Fandom showed that Britain had become a 'spectator country' unable to win international sporting competitions.[31] Equally malign was the sirenic power exercised by the Beatles over 'suggestible . . . volatile and rudderless' teenage girls.[32] The Beatles' detractors portrayed the young as irrational by nature, their 'unformed adolescent minds' incapable of resisting the insidious designs of the music industry.[33] It was absurd to speak of their free will when psychologists found that beat music exercised the same hypnotic effect as a 'rapidly flickering light'.[34] Marketing was propaganda by another name, devised with the express intent of 'depriving young people of the chance to develop taste and discrimination'.[35] Beatlemaniacs were bamboozled into purchasing 'what they have been taught to buy', confusing their conformity for an assertion of agency.[36]

According to this logic, it was incumbent on adults to set an example to the young by withholding approval from the Beatles. All adults able to 'think for [them]selves and be true to [their] own feelings' would have a low estimation of the band and concede that '"it" is not worth being "with"'.[37] Those exhibiting enthusiasm forfeited all 'pride and dignity'.[38] '[I]t is pathetic to see those middle-aged fingers clicking', wrote Robert Pitman, who could not find any legitimate reason to praise the Beatles' 'extraordinarily unpleasant noise'.[39] Whereas Pitman upbraided adult fans for their faddishness and pretension, the *Mail*'s Marshall Pugh made the graver charge that they were undermining generational authority:

How much genuine contempt of society is instilled in young people when their elders and betters themselves adopt idols like the Beatles ... ape their dances, their haircuts and their clothes ...?[40]

It was patronising to pretend that adolescents were the equals of adults. Noël Coward likened the Beatles to little boys who should be 'seen but not heard' and Auberon Waugh thought no Beatlemaniac had yet 'evolve[d] into an ordinary human being'.[41]

Discussions of generation were highly gendered. Concerns over the Beatles' influence on boys were limited to petty if regrettable imitative behaviour such as growing hair.[42] Stories of schoolboys being punished for infringements were a regular occurrence in the mid-sixties. Reports came in of all types of schools imposing moptop bans: secondary moderns, grammar schools and public schools, from Cornwall to Scotland. The most draconian schools sheared their pupils *en masse*, as when between fifteen and twenty schoolboys were handed over to an army barber at Harraby Secondary School in Carlisle.[43] In other cases, boys with moptops were barred from sporting competitions, denied school prizes and threatened with suspension.[44] The *Express* reported that a school in Croydon had extended the embargo to Beatle-type attire and that a pupil at another school was suspended for wearing a 'Beatle suit'.[45] Some boys found ways to resist while remaining in school. A Warwickshire teenager threatened with expulsion for his unkempt hair returned to school with a smart Beatle-style cut, and four Sussex schoolboys forced to cut their hair submitted a protest to the local education department signed by 500 of their schoolmates.[46] But one London grammar schoolboy quit school when given the choice between losing his hair or the opportunity to sit GCE examinations. 'I would rather leave than change my hair style', he stated: 'I shall begin to look for work next week.'[47]

Accusations of effeminacy were occasionally levelled at long-haired boys. A 14-year-old boy in Dalkeith was ordered to sit in a girls' class, two brothers in Cornwall had their hair tied up with yellow ribbon and an 18-year-old apprentice baker in Perth was ordered to cover his head with the regulation turban issued to female colleagues.[48] A secondary modern teacher in London also raised the spectre of homosexuality when reporting how 'two of my most promising boys, both of whom sported

Beatle mops, had taken to walking about hand in hand'.[49] Yet there was surprisingly little attempt to portray the Beatles as effeminate, and the only suggestions that they were gay came in sarcastic fashion from the Beatles themselves.[50] The clampdown on boys' hairstyles was accordingly justified as upholding discipline rather than masculinity. 'Overlong hair can be treated as a symbol of successful rebellion against authority', stated the headmaster of Uppingham public school after imposing a ban on moptops. Parental reactions ranged from indignation ('Geoffrey's hair is tidy') to collaboration (one mother attempted to cut her sons' hair in their sleep). Adults as a whole agreed that 'schools should require boys to keep their hair cut short' by a margin of 5:1 according to a 1965 Gallup poll.[51]

A different concern was that starstruck boys might abandon their studies and jobs in pursuit of pop success. In August 1963, a 14-year-old boy from Folkestone made headlines for running away from home in the hope of securing a record contract on the strength of a fake Scouse accent and an electric guitar.[52] By early 1964, the National Association of Youth Clubs warned that beat groups were accruing debts and crashing vans while on tour, and Liverpool's principal youth employment officer despaired that 'Boys have thrown up good jobs and apprenticeships in the hope of becoming as famous as the Beatles.'[53] Later that year his organisation related that employers' habit of associating 'certain deficiencies in personality in a youth with a Beatle hairstyle' was proving a bar to employment.[54]

These skirmishes mattered to their participants and piqued the curiosity of the national press, but attracted much less attention than the antics of female Beatlemaniacs. They were also offset by a counter-narrative that the Beatles alleviated the graver problem of male juvenile delinquency. The value of beat music as an alternative to criminality in Liverpool featured strongly in a *Daily Express* article published in October 1963. A policewoman stated that the Cavern Club 'keeps the kids off the streets' and a Cavern employee characterised the music scene as being 'better than knocking down old ladies with bicycle chains'.[55] Some corroboration came in February 1964 when *New Society* published Colin Fletcher's autobiographical account of how beat music had displaced violence in the affections of Merseyside gang members such as himself in the late 1950s.[56] While bands provided gangs with a new source of identity and pride, clubs provided young Liverpudlians more generally with 'a music, a number of dances and a "place of their own"' in which they could develop a less aggressive adolescent subculture.[57]

Fletcher's article could hardly have been better timed. It appeared the same week that a senior police officer in Liverpool credited beat groups for his city's declining juvenile crime rate, a magistrate's clerk instructed a teenage bicycle thief to follow the Beatles' 'good example', cabinet minister Bill Deedes portrayed them as paragons of youthful enterprise and the Duke of Edinburgh applauded them for encouraging 'singing and dancing' instead of 'fighting and stealing' among youngsters.[58] The clashes between mods and rockers in seaside resorts later that year were seldom blamed on the Beatles, much to the relief of Brian Epstein.[59] On the contrary, suggestions for preventing future disturbances included the creation of a 'Beatles Anti-Vandalism Club, with badges' and a talent show for beat groups.[60] 'The Beatles have already proved that if young people can strum instruments, they won't become delinquents', stated Rediffusion television's head of variety when announcing the competition: 'If we can encourage more people to do this sort of thing, instead of doing a Clacton, then we'll be happy.'[61]

Epstein claimed in his ghost-written autobiography that 'the Beatles have never been associated with actual rioting, vandalism, or damage or any sort', but this was to overlook the other, female side of the youth question.[62] Elsewhere he acknowledged that Beatlemaniacs 'would kill the Beatles if they got their hands on them'.[63] Newspapers published daily accounts of rioting, fainting and screaming at concerts during the height of Beatlemania. The *Express'* account of an engagement in December 1963 was calculated to alarm:

A screaming blonde almost fell into the orchestra pit during a Beatles show at Southend last night. . . . then a near riot broke out. The fire curtain was dropped, and the performance stopped five minutes before time. Police moved in from the sides of the theatre. The screaming ended when the manager put on a record of the national anthem.[64]

The concert had been halted when some girls rushed the stage after the fan's fall and a dozen others 'fell to their knees in the centre aisle and started beating their head and fists on the carpet'. The second performance of the day was comparatively uneventful, after a bomb alert proved to be a hoax and just five girls fainted during the show.[65]

The press ran stories of girls led astray by Beatlemania. Searches were launched for a 13-year-old from Boston and two 16-year-olds from Cleveland who flew unaccompanied to Britain in search of their idols.[66] There was also the case of the 12-year-old from Sunderland who tried to post herself to the Beatles' fan club in a tea chest marked 'Presents of the

Beatles'. The chest was three-foot square, had no air holes and was stocked with a single toffee by way of provisions. She felt woozy after ten minutes and caused the box to wobble, which alerted porters to her predicament. 'I hadn't thought about fresh air or food', she explained: 'All I wanted to do was see the Beatles. I don't know what I would have done if I had really got there. I suppose I would have fainted.'[67]

Schools' problems with girls centred not on hair but on fandom. Fifteen pupils were carpeted for a rum-fuelled celebration of John Lennon's birthday on the tennis courts of Wrexham's Grove Park Grammar School for Girls.[68] An enterprising truancy officer and headmistress ambushed miscreants who had sagged off school to catch a sight of the Beatles arriving at Taunton station during the filming of *A Hard Day's Night*; they bundled the worst offenders into a car.[69] When grammar-school boys in nearby Minehead taunted female fans with a banner declaring 'The Empire is crumbling', the girls reportedly tore it up.[70] One school in Essex halted a concert by schoolboys when their Beatles impersonations caused 300 schoolgirls to 'riot'.[71] 'I don't like the Beatles. I've never seen anything like the mob hysteria they spark off', their headmistress exclaimed.[72]

The headmistress' censorious attitude was not uncommon. A music therapist wrote to the *Daily Telegraph* that

Subjecting immature young people, especially girls, to long strong doses of crude, coarse, often over-syncopated combinations of sound vibrations can, and obviously does, lead to loss of self-control and low-toned moral behaviour. The side- and after-effects can be seen in the next day's boredom, sullenness and, too often, anti-social behaviour.[73]

A *Telegraph* editorial the next day expressed alarm at how an all-consuming Beatlemania colonised 'otherwise empty ... heads and hearts'.[74] Some prominent male writers criticised Beatlemaniacs for failing to conform to their ideals of physical beauty. Anthony Burgess described them as 'pudgy, spotty', 'slack-mouthed, sallow, and empty-eyed' and lacking 'anything approaching comeliness', while Paul Johnson despaired at their 'chain-store makeup ... broken stiletto heels ... sagging mouths and glazed eyes'.[75] A brazen anti-feminism appeared in portrayals of female fans as a 'monstrous regiment' or the 'weaker sex'.[76]

Such attitudes invited accusations of sheer reaction. 'Why not turn the clock back completely and burn them as witches?' asked journalist Charles Hamblett in response to a facetious suggestion that girls should be caged during the Beatles' visit to Blackburn.[77] Epstein detected a double standard in criticisms of girls who shrieked at their idols when grown men did much the same at football matches. He also disputed the notion that Beatlemaniacs lacked self-control when recalling how one fan turned her screams on and off at will. 'That's not hysteria', he reasoned: 'That's self-expression.'[78]

Defenders of Beatlemania advanced a quasi-feminist argument that fandom empowered girls. When journalist Merrick Winn visited Liverpool in 1963, Merseybeat musicians told him that they cultivated an androgynous appearance because 'Girls like boys to look pretty.'[79] The blurred gender roles did not stop there, with Winn reporting that boys were now the wallflowers at dances and sang songs once considered too feminine.[80] Peter Laurie's *The Teenage Revolution* (1965) claimed that girls were the 'real dynamo' powering youth autonomy and gender equality.[81] He cited the objectification of male heart-throbs and the higher rates of female premarital intercourse as evidence that adolescent girls had discovered sexual agency and that 'traditional distinctions between men and women are melting away'.[82] Laurie and Winn echoed Margaret Mead's *Coming of Age in Samoa* (1928) when arguing that 'in all societies differences in the characters of the sexes are socially and not biologically imposed'.[83] Alun Owen's screenplay for *A Hard Day's Night* (1964) accordingly depicted the Beatles as flirting with androgyny by sitting under hairdryers, applying face powder, reading women's magazines, assuming girls' names and escaping from sexual predators. When Paul's grandfather scolds them for being a 'bunch of sissies', the Beatles tease him for being envious.[84]

In retrospect, however, the early Beatles posed a limited challenge to the taken-for-granted chauvinism of the time. Women were peripheral in *A Hard Day's Night*, their lines minimal and their roles limited to those of adoring fan, cougar, flirt, plumed dancer, beautician, secretary, battleaxe and a lady too dainty to step in a puddle. Ostensibly sympathetic accounts of Beatlemaniacs thought nothing of likening concerts to 'the conquest . . . of a village of virgins' or defending fans' appearance on the impolitic grounds that even 'an ugly girl can now look attractive' thanks to advances in make-up technology.[85] This was an era in which men were thought to 'attack' and 'conquer' women in courtship and obtain their 'physical surrender' during intercourse.[86] Even more jarringly, it was one in which a celebrated feminist, Edith Summerskill, considered Beatlemania an expression of 'women's primary instincts' to mother the Beatles.[87]

Beatlemania raised the awkward issue of adolescent female sexuality.[88] It was difficult to avoid the subject altogether, considering the goings-on at concerts and the eye candy on offer in girls' magazines. *Jackie* was launched

'for go-ahead teens' at the height of Beatlemania in January 1964. The cover
of one of its earliest issues captured the obsessional quality of its coverage:

Beatles the Beatles
the Beatles
the Beatles
Beatles
the Beatles
the Beatles
Beatles
Their fanpopstic success story in pictures inside!
You'll love it!
Yeah! Yeah! Yeah![89]

Fans were supplied with plentiful pin-ups, Beatlefacts, Beatles-themed
cartoon serials and, from May 1964, a dedicated Beatle Page each week.
Girl, which targeted younger readers, devoted its first centrefold to the
Beatles in July 1963, accompanied by an astrological forecast which ventured that 'The year ahead for the Beatles is good, but not necessarily
excellent.'[90] Even the otherwise wholesome *Beatles Book* printed a letter
in 1963 from a fan who warned that she'd 'never be able to go into my room
un-attended' if the magazine published photographs of the Beatles in their
underwear.[91]

However, childhood sexuality was as difficult to discuss then as now.
Monica Furlong noted how one broadcaster had alluded to Beatlemania's
sexual origins in a 'slightly embarrassed' fashion, then rapidly changed the
subject 'obviously feeling he had gone too far'.[92] Her suggestion of turning
over the matter to scientists was the usual way to broach the topic, but the
results were confused and confusing. For example, clinical psychologist
Frederick Casson found 'nothing to suggest sex' in the Beatles yet diagnosed their fans as suffering from a 'pent-up eroticism' which, when
released, was 'almost impossible to bring ... under control until its pres-
sure has spent itself'.[93] Adult male experts struggled to fathom the desires
of adolescent girls. So removed were they from their subjects that they
sought explanations for girls' behaviour in abnormal psychology and the
anthropology of ritual behaviour. The resulting models were condescend-
ing and uncomprehending. The biologist Julian Huxley labelled
Beatlemania 'ludicrously orgiastic' and the sexologist Alex Comfort characterised it as a 'discharge of unacceptable impulses'.[94]

Critics rejected suggestions that Beatlemania was a necessary if somewhat
unseemly stage in girls' normal sexual development on two grounds. The

first was that girls were being artificially and prematurely aroused by mass culture. Malcolm Muggeridge feared that Britain would imitate the commodification of sexuality befouling the United States, where 'tiny tots who ought to be reading about Peter Rabbit and the Seven Dwarfs wear padded bras, paint their faces, and howl like randy hyenas at the Beatles'.[95] His warnings were in vain, if fellow journalist David Griffiths was to be believed. The manner in which televised pop shows 'leer[ed] brazenly at writhing limbs in the audience' and the innuendo of A Hard Day's Night (1964) convinced Griffiths that the Beatles had legitimised 'blatant pop-eroticism'.[96]

A second concern was that Beatlemania arrested girls' sexual development at the juvenile stage of self-abuse. The 'mass masturbation orgy' witnessed by Noël Coward at a Beatles concert left him 'truly horrified and shocked'.[97] Cambridge don David Holbrook experienced the same revulsion when attending a primary school glove-puppet show featuring 'phallophoric' effigies of the Beatles:

As the taped Beatle music rose to a pitch, the [children's] jiggling became an almost indecent enactment of sexual rhythm, while the cries, sighs and shouts became those of people possessed by sexual ecstasy approaching orgasm. It became painfully clear that the Beatles are a masturbation fantasy, such as a girl presumably has during the onanistic act . . .[98]

Holbrook recounted this event in a letter to the *New Statesman* in 1964. In the same letter, he appealed to readers to provide him with children's accounts of fandom in order to test his hypothesis that the masturbation incited by pop music created a 'closed circuit' which prevented children from attaining maturity.[99] Three teachers replied. One testified that he caught schoolboys in the act of 'moving their pelvises rhythmically in time with each other' while listening to the Beatles on the radio.[100] The other two furnished Holbrook with exactly what he had requested: a bundle of their pupils' writings about the Beatles.

Holbrook's findings, which he published thirty years later, unsurprisingly indicated that some girls were sexually aroused by the Beatles. One girl described how 'you clinth [sic] yourself' when they appeared on television and another related how the band 'makes my body fill all funney [sic]'.[101] More remarkable was Holbrook's conviction that all the children's comments were not merely sexual but represented 'a kind of deep regression to ... the time of total dependence on the mother'.[102] Holbrook deployed the full array of Freudian techniques to make his case. He explained a 10-year-old's desire to sit on McCartney's lap as a projection of McCartney 'becom[ing] her baby': hence her attraction to his 'babies [*sic*] face' and 'appealing eyes'.[103] An 11-year-old's account of learning to masturbate to the Beatles ('he has a glorious voice it is so soft it makes you want to wriggle all over the plaice [*sic*]') was interpreted as a 'regression to infantile states' rather than a prelude to adult sexuality.[104] A 16-year-old betrayed 'her denial of inner problems' by disagreeing that the Beatles were masturbation material.[105] Holbrook saw the manner in which Beatlemaniacs screamed, cried and wet themselves as further evidence of their return to infanthood.[106] He claimed that the Beatles' 'jiggling ... hair-flopping ... [and] guitar-strumming' produced sensations akin to dand-ling and sucking, that the crowd provided maniacs with 'a symbolic womb' and that their experience of being 'sent' turned them into a 'mass polyglot baby'.[107]

Such conclusions did not impress everyone. The music critic Deryck Cooke charged Holbrook with failing to supply evidence that the Beatles incited masturbation and with displaying a 'puritanical disgust' at bodily movements common to all dancing.[108] The same behaviours which Holbrook interpreted as displays of infantile sexuality were cast as exam-ples of girls 'subconsciously preparing for motherhood' by a psychologist interviewed in the *News of the World*. Whereas Holbrook conjectured that Beatlemaniacs screamed like infants and identified themselves with the jelly babies that they hurled at their idols, the psychologist interpreted their screams as a 'rehearsal' for labour and the jelly babies as symbolising their future offspring.[109] This psychologist's insistence on the 'innocent and harmless' motivations of female fans was echoed by another set of (adult male) commentators who saw 'nothing nasty' about Beatlemania, by which they meant it was 'not sexual'.[110] They favourably contrasted the Beatles' performances with the suggestiveness of Elvis Presley's act and surmised that girls were drawn to the Beatles' 'innocence', viewing them as brothers rather than lovers.[111]

Class, Nation and Religion

In 1969, Richard Mabey observed that 'The pop music scene has become an arena in which the old lodestar divisions of class, age, sex, status and geography have been challenged and uprooted.'[112] What was a truism at the end of the decade was a matter of incredulity at its beginning, when the Beatles refreshed parts of social discourse that other musicians did not reach. Diverse interpretations of classlessness were employed to explain the Beatles' impact on Britain's social hierarchy.[113] Epstein advanced the idea that 'they don't seem to come from any particular class background' to explain their transcendent appeal.[114] A more common argument portrayed them as 'unimpressed by old-fashioned class barriers'.[115] The Beatles delighted Vincent Mulchrone by telling him that the train scene in *A Hard Day's Night* where they clash with a bowler-hatted curmudgeon was based on a real encounter. His impression that they gave 'no thought for the importance of the person they are speaking to' was precisely the message intended by the film's director, Richard Lester.[116] 'The Beatles sent the class thing sky high: they laughed it out of existence and, I think, introduced a tone of equality more successfully than any other single factor', he recalled.[117]

A differing right-wing interpretation of classlessness acclaimed the Beatles as models of upward social mobility. Cabinet minister Bill Deedes chose them to symbolise his dynamic and meritocratic vision of Britain, which was to mirror youth culture in being 'free of divisions of class or creed'.[118] Jonathan Aitken fleshed out this argument in *The Young Meteors* (1967), in which he claimed that 'a completely new class has been formed, running parallel to the existing system'. It consisted of those like the Beatles whose sheer talent allowed them to scale the social ladder without assuming 'the conventions of dress and manners of the upper-class world'.[119] Another journalist from a storied Tory family, Robin Douglas-Home, disputed that aristocrats were the 'privileged class' when imagining the following scenario:

If a 14th Earl with a grouse moor [Alec Douglas-Home] and George Harrison with Patti[e] Boyd walked together into a restaurant and there was only one table left, who would be given the table?[120]

The likely preference given to a Beatle and his wife over his uncle, a former prime minister, convinced him that 'It is the golden youth that is the "upper" class today.'[121]

Characterisations of the Beatles' fans also revealed the contested nature of classlessness. The Beatles' publicists touted the band's universal popularity. Epstein's contention that 'anybody can get on their wavelength' was echoed by NEMS press officer Tony Barrow, who noted how fans came from 'every walk of life'.[122] Sympathetic journalists joined in drawing attention to the 'almost completely classless' composition of the Cavern audience and the Beatles' popularity among 'the champagne and diamond set', public-school pupils, jodhpur-clad girls from Cheltenham, 'a certain countess' and habitués of cocktail parties in Kensington.[123] 'I daresay there is hardly a deb who wouldn't give up her heirlooms for Ringo', mused Marjorie Proops.[124] Some writers depicted fans as sharing their heroes' indifference to social stratification. To Derwent May, Merseybeat was the property of 'young working people who have begun to forget the idea of class, and to blend with the classless, cosmopolitan crowd'.[125] Others claimed that fans were undergoing the same process of *embourgeoisement* as the Beatles themselves. One girl's comment that 'They fought their way to the top and they took us with them' was presented by Alan Brien as evidence that 'Britain is no longer that Neapolitan ice with the classes frozen layer upon layer it was until the Fifties – with each snobbish sub-group cut off from its neighbours above and below by accent, money, education and dress.'[126]

For all their differences, these models of classlessness envisaged social hierarchies as undergoing profound and rapid change in Britain's postwar 'affluent society'.[127] Opposition to the Beatles was accordingly portrayed as a rearguard defence of the old class system from reactionaries from every station in life. Representing the unreconstructed working class were the shipyard workers unable after a day's riveting to take the 'deafening noise' of beat groups at their branch of the Royal Antediluvian Order of Buffaloes.[128] The 'stern world of trade unionism' received similarly negative coverage when carpenters and electricians downed tools and held up the filming of *A Hard Day's Night* until members of the Film Artistes' Association were looked after and child extras paid union rates.[129]

Fleet Street newspapers portrayed snobs who slighted the Beatles as lacking the very manners they claimed to uphold. The press named and shamed social clubs which rejected or ejected them. The Carlisle Golf Club received unwelcome coverage when expelling 'the vocal-instrumental group, the Four Beatles' for wearing leather jackets in February 1963, as did Mayfair's exclusive Annabel's nightclub when turning away Harrison for turning up in a polo neck.[130] '[W]e do have a rule that members and guests must wear ties', explained its owner, Lady Annabel Birley. 'If we decided to break it just because a Beatle wanted to come in with a polo-necked sweater, we might as well not have the rule in the first place', she argued, indicating the strict terms on which aristocrats would mix with the nouveau riche.[131] Newspapers goaded Lord Russell of Liverpool to condemn the 'damn silly' idea of the Beatles becoming members of London's Liver Club on the grounds that 'We're very careful who we have in.'[132] And they had a field day reporting the reception at the British Embassy in Washington, DC in 1964, where boorish attendees helped themselves to clumps of Ringo's hair.[133] Epstein's castigation of 'guests [who] believe themselves to be important or very significant young Englishmen with marvellous educations' contributed to an anti-gentlemanly discourse prevalent since the mid-1950s.[134]

The old boys' club of high finance was also tarnished by its disdain of the Beatles. The creation of a limited company to handle the Beatles' affairs in 1963 was greeted as a curious intrusion into 'our world of bowlers and brollies' and the *Daily Mail* had fun dressing up the band as City gents in 1964.[135] Its question – 'How would the Stock Exchange react to this?' – lost its whimsy when Northern Songs applied to be listed on the Stock Exchange the following year.[136] The floatation attracted 'unprecedented and almost universal criticism', since the Stock Exchange Council normally required ten years of profit records and assets more tangible than three songwriters' imaginations.[137] Having failed to prevent the share issue, City opinion-formers 'panned it to a man'.[138] Yet, as was so often the case in the first half of the 1960s, the Beatles successfully infiltrated a hallowed British institution. The offer was heavily over-subscribed and shares opened above their original selling price, prompting one cartoonist to imagine a stockbroker adding Chelsea boots, a polka-dot shirt and a Pierre Cardin suit to his traditional umbrella, briefcase and bowler hat.[139]

The monarchy's acceptance of the Beatles brought much more favourable coverage.[140] Encounters between Beatles and royals made for grand spectacles. Besides being the two most famous sets of British celebrities, they also personified two faces of sixties Britain: progress and tradition, North and South, accomplishment and entitlement. The *Mirror* accordingly presented the Beatles' appearance at the Royal Variety Performance in November 1963 as a triumph of social mobility and confirmation of their universal appeal. The warm reception accorded to Lennon's suggestion that well-heeled guests 'rattle your jewellery' in appreciation was presented as a transformational moment:

They had broken down the show's traditional 'stuffed-shirt' barrier.
From then on the usually sedate audience made it quite clear that they had
   been bitten by the Beatle bug. And that they were ENJOYING it. . . .
Princess Margaret, in a red and gold brocade gown, was snapping her
   fingers in time with the music.
Tony Armstrong-Jones, seated beside her, was smiling broadly.
The Queen Mother smiled happily – and clapped with the rest of 'em.
Last night EVERYBODY loved the Beatles – Yeah, Yeah, Yeah.[141]

The Beatles' publicists played along by representing the Royal Premiere of *A Hard Day's Night* as 'the ultimate' accolade, but acceptance was not hard to achieve from a monarchy eager to display its modernising zeal through cordial relations with the band.[142] Reported conversations showed the royals seeking common ground. Prince Philip offered to swap books with Lennon and telegraphed an apology to Epstein when quoted (accurately or otherwise) as saying that 'The Beatles are on the wane.'[143] Princess Margaret traded jokes with McCartney and the Beatles recounted how the Queen had acted 'just like a mum to us' at the investiture ceremony for the MBE.[144] The press concocted further affinities between the Beatles and the royals by depicting the Queen's children as proto-Beatles. The 'Beatle-style' hair of a windswept Charles made the front page of the *Daily Mail* in 1964 and the *Daily Telegraph* published a photo of Anne in a Lennon-esque cap in 1966.[145]

This more magnanimous admittance of the Beatles into elite circles carried a powerful symbolic charge, but risked exposing the rituals, traditions and privileges of that elite to the Beatles' ridicule. Lennon's quip about jewellery at the Royal Variety Performance in 1963 was calculated to raise a laugh at the same time as exposing class division, undermining elite authority and alleviating his discomfort over appearing at such an Establishment occasion.[146] If press reports were to be believed, his bandmates got in on the act when dining at Brasenose College, Oxford the following year. Legend had it that Harrison turned down smoked salmon in favour of a jam butty, McCartney drank milk brought to him on a silver platter and Starr quizzed his hosts about the prevalence of 'sex cases' in the college.[147] Accounts of the Beatles' discomfort at wearing formal attire indicated the limits of their willingness to cleave to tradition. Lennon and McCartney did not fit into the dinner suits they were required to don when receiving songwriting awards from Duke of Edinburgh in 1964, and a besuited Harrison complained that 'We would be much happier in jeans and T-shirts' at the premier of *Help!*[148]

The same choice between resistance and appeasement faced commentators who wished to sustain class hierarchies. Diehard opposition came from the leader columns of the *Daily Telegraph*, which sought to stem the tide of Beatlemania 'throb[bing] up from the slums', and from Paul Johnson in the *New Statesman*, who claimed that Beatlemaniacs represented the lumpen and 'least fortunate of their generation'.[149] Whereas Johnson skewered Tories for acclaiming the Beatles, the *Sunday Telegraph*'s Peregrine Worsthorne blamed Labour for creating a 'topsy-turvy' situation in which politicians derived authority from hobnobbing with the Beatles instead of wealth and rank.[150] The Beatles represented, in historian Max Beloff's dystopian vision, a society in which 'dustmen look down on dukes', and educationalist Bryan Wilson feared that fandom would destroy the 'class values' taught by decent families and schools.[151] Wilson viewed pop stars' success as undeserved and a poor example to others because '[t]heir social mobility has not depended on training, intellect, civilized values or liberal education (nor, be it noted, on competitive examination)'.[152] A hit parade which 'offers success in spite of educational failure' made a mockery of meritocracy in its truest sense.[153]

Such impolitic defences of the status quo provoked much the same sort of criticism as that directed towards snobs who barred entry to the Beatles or abused them as guests. Johnson was pilloried for expressing unacceptable views for the deputy editor of a left-of-centre publication. Accusations of 'rampant class snobbery' and 'upper-middle-class arrogance' dogged him for years to come.[154] Noël Coward's snooty barbs against the Beatles also threatened to harm his reputation more than theirs. He appeared uncharacteristically humourless when deploring Lennon's quip at the Royal Variety Performance as 'the height of bad taste', and peevish when complaining that the Beatles refused to meet a detractor such as himself.[155]

The recasting of national identity began as the internal matter of accepting that the pace was being set culturally outside London.[156] The Beatles built on the success over the previous decade of plays, novels and films set in the provinces, and the brief ascendancy of 'Merseybeat' led commentators to display an ethnographic interest in Scouse customs. Intrepid reporters ventured northwards to discover the secret of Liverpool's success, while those viewing events from Fleet Street marvelled at its 'typical meaty northern lack of inhibition' and unique ethnic mix.[157] From a metropolitan perspective, Liverpool was a 'polyglot city' bursting with 'Irish, Welsh and coloured influences' and music displaying 'a touch of the Negro' or, to put it less kindly, a 'compost heap' from which blossomed four 'exotic flowers'.[158] Liverpool's Otherness was exploited by the Beatles' publicity machine, as when their Crosby-born press officer Tony Barrow claimed that the Beatles 'epitomis[ed] Northern Man – his naturalness, directness, the "truthfulness" behind those hard and nobby faces'.[159]

The Beatles became national as well as regional symbols.[160] To Charles Hamblett, they undercut British reticence with 'the outspoken frankness of the true Liverpuddlian [sic]' and broke with the nation's moral and martial traditions.[161] He identified them with a contemporary worldview 'totally free from cant or prejudice'.[162] Their admiration of West Germany and the United States was of a piece with 'knocking the stuffing – and the stuffiness – out of the neo-Victorians'.[163] The Beatles represented an escape from Britain's mundane present as well as its moribund past. Peter Laurie interpreted Beatlemania as a release from adolescents' allotted role of 'squeezing into a narrow niche of this tight little isle', and psychologist Michael Karoly paired Beatlemania with Bondmania as offering temporary respite from 'the dullness of everyday life' in a post-Churchillian age.[164]

The Beatles' Britishness seemed especially significant within the world of popular entertainment. In his *Encounter* article 'Young England, Half English' (1957), Colin MacInnes lamented that the Americanisation of British popular music since the Great War had produced generations of 'English boys and girls [who] identified themselves, imaginatively, with a completely alien world'.[165] His faint hope that Tommy Steele would become 'the first English pop artist to sing English songs' went largely unrealised until the Beatles rekindled the prospect of a re-anglicisation of popular culture.[166] The Canadian writer Mordecai Richler wryly observed that British commentators would have disdained the Beatles 'as yet another example of bad taste Americana' had they originated in the United States. As it was, they were applauded for creating an inimitably British sound.[167] Tony Barrow parried the notion that they had a 'trans-Atlantic style' by claiming that 'their only real influence has been from the unique brand of Rhythm and Blues folk music which abounds on Merseyside'.[168] In December 1963, *Times* music critic William Mann credited Lennon and McCartney for composing songs which were 'distinctly indigenous in character' and an *Observer* feature published the previous month claimed that fans in their twenties were 'for the Beatles because they represent "a break with America"'.[169] Hopes rose that high art would develop an 'indigenous contemporary style' when a Beatles score was used in the *Mods and Rockers* ballet, staged in 1963.[170] '[A]t last Britain has the chance of evolving its own jazz-dance rather than copying the American pattern', declared dance critic Clive Barnes.[171]

The Beatles' international fame provided an opportunity to rebrand Britain abroad. George Him had created some of the most celebrated images for Home Front publicity drives, the 1946 Britain Can Make It campaign and the Festival of Britain in 1951. In 1966, he invoked the symbol of tournament mascot World Cup Willie when enjoining designers to 'Give the British lion a Beatle haircut and transform the foreigners' image of Britain'.[172] The Beatles represented near-perfect brand ambassadors for Him's vision of Britain as a 'really young country' divested of the 'paraphernalia of processions and castles'.[173] Charles de Hoghton, who worked for the progressive think tank Political and Economic Planning, commended the Beatles for helping to rectify 'the foreign vision of Britain as a country entirely populated by middle-aged conservatives of all sorts – e.g. stockbrokers, wildcat strikers, Beefeaters and Pembrokeshire coracle fisherman'.[174]

Press coverage of treatment of the Beatles overseas testified to the band's capacity to represent a modern and democratic model of Britishness. Articles regularly portrayed suppression of the Beatles and all their works as a way of illustrating Britain's comparative freedoms. As it happened, such clampdowns constituted a fairly accurate index of authoritarianism. Their records were banned in Cuba from 1964 to 1966 and in South Africa from 1966 to 1971.[175] A 1964 ban on the Beatles performing in Israel involved the cultural committee, the Education Ministry, the High Court of Justice and the Knesset.[176] President Sukarno of Indonesia pronounced 'the Beatles and Beatlism' to be a type of 'mental disease' in 1965.[177] The French Interior Ministry targeted foreign visitors with Beatle-style haircuts in 1966 and the Burmese, Egyptian and Greek dictatorships all launched campaigns against long hair in 1967.[178] The press also reported the Eastern Bloc's long-running struggle to contain the ideological threat of the Beatles and the West's attempt to exacerbate it, as when Radio Free Europe began to broadcast their records across the Iron Curtain in March 1964.[179]

Signs of the Beatles' ability to recast Britain's image abroad came from European listeners to the BBC, who placed them above the Queen and Winston Churchill as the British figures they would most like to meet, and from tourist trap Madame Tussaud's, which reported them to be its main draw.[180] They featured in American magazines in refutation of declinist models of Britain as hidebound and hierarchical. American *Vogue* presented George Harrison and Pattie Boyd as the very personification of the 'Youthquake'. 'They're young. They're doing things. They're in the Quant spirit', it declared in 1965.[181] A year later, *Time* magazine's portrait of 'Swinging London' attributed to the whole metropolis the qualities of classlessness, originality, informality, vitality and anti-Victorianism customarily associated with the Beatles.[182]

The admiration expressed by *Vogue*, *Time* and other American commentators towards British culture was not entirely reciprocated. Some of their British counterparts claimed the Beatles for the nation and portrayed America as a spent cultural force.[183] The first mention of the Beatles in the *Daily Mirror* was in a January 1963 piece which heralded British domination of the top ten.[184] The following year, the *Daily Mail* judged American entertainment to be 'middle-aged' and 'square'.[185] In 1966, the *Daily Mirror* responded to *Time* magazine's celebration of 'swinging London' by stating that 'in the world of mass culture Britain still has nothing to learn from its captive audience across the Atlantic'.[186]

However, none of these upbeat interpretations of the Beatles' effect on national identity went unchallenged. Metropolitan commentary about Liverpool was generally patronising and often insulting. Malcolm Muggeridge's comparison of the Beatles to the Beverly Hillbillies said much, as did the incomprehensibility of the Scouse dialect to certain Southerners. Cabinet minister Ted Heath doubted whether the Beatles spoke the Queen's English and Prince Philip displayed characteristic tact when telling Lennon and Starr that he 'almost had to have a list to translate the words' when docking at Liverpool during the war.[187] Just such a glossary of Scouse argot was compiled by the Association of Child Care Officers 'to get through to the swinging adolescent currently addicted to the Beatles and other Liverpool noises'.[188]

Although some writers celebrated the 'Negro origins' of Merseybeat, others denounced it as a reversion to primitivism.[189] Such accounts displayed the residual influence of imperialism, social Darwinism and G. Stanley Hall's recapitulation theory, which understood maturation in evolutionary terms. The sociologist Bryan Wilson maintained that 'Intrinsically, the youth culture's values are more animal'.[190] Psychologist Frederick Casson and psychiatrists Erwin Stengel and William Sargent drew upon anthropology when comparing Beatlemania to 'the frenzied dancing and shouting of voodoo worshippers', an 'epidemic hysteria in Nigeria' and the 'brainwashing, conversion and mass hysteria' induced by witch doctors in Kenya.[191] For 'tribal nonsense' to be taking place in Britain was potentially embarrassing at a time of rapid decolonisation and development in the 'third world'.[192] A vicar addressing the first national convention of Mary Whitehouse's National Viewers' and Listeners' Association placed the behaviour of the Beatles and the Animals beneath that of 'savages' encountered in the Congo.[193] In the same vein, the Daily Express ran a letter which recounted a colonial commoner saying that 'We in Jamaica used to carry on like [the Beatles] ... years ago until the British came to the island and taught us how to become civilised.'[194] The accompanying cartoon depicted a white imperial official receiving a guitar from a black man in exchange for his bowler hat.[195]

Traditionalists did not feel obliged to embrace the Beatles simply because they were 'British rubbish' instead of the foreign variety.[196] They disputed that national identity was in any need of updating and blamed the band for 'hav[ing] done so much to present a picture of Britain in the sixties as a long-haired frenetic sex-mad swinging people'.[197] Alan Pegler justified his plans to transport the 100-ton Flying Scotsman across the Atlantic as a means of 'correct[ing] the unfortunate impression created by the Beatles over there'.[198] Travelling in the opposite direction was the actress and self-confessed 'old-fashioned . . . snob' Hermione Gingold, to whom the Beatles represented the antithesis of gentlemanliness and high diction.[199]

The early Beatles seemed as far removed from organised religion as could be imagined: a situation played for laughs by Peter Sellers' rendition of 'Help!' (1965) in the manner of a sermonising vicar. At the same time, the adulation accorded to the Beatles lent itself to religious metaphors and many commentators, sympathetic and otherwise, likened Beatlemania to a cult.[200] They observed how girls queued for hours for 'a glimpse of their gods', showered them with '[v]otive offerings' on stage and were found 'kneeling, as if in prayer, in the aisles'.[201] Psychologists and psychiatrists explained the fans' hero worship as a developmental stage and equated mania to primitive religions practised by 'voodoo worshippers', snake-handlers and 'the religious hill-billy'.[202]

Puritanical clergymen condemned Beatlemania for its idolatry. The verdict of the Rector of Prestwich that '[i]f you do not worship God, you probably worship the Beatles' was echoed by the eminent Methodist minister Donald Soper, who pronounced the Beatles to be one of sundry 'rootless substitutes for that full life which flourish precisely because we have no overriding spiritual beliefs'.[203] But decrying modern society for its abject materialism did not solve the problem of declining congregations and waning moral influence. The mainstream churches in the 1960s feared for their survival which, as Callum Brown has argued, depended on turning young women in particular into regular churchgoers.[204] Moderate clerics therefore counselled against '[u]nnecessary and superior criticism' of the Beatles.[205] Their appeal 'has to be understood and lived with', maintained the Archbishop of Canterbury.[206]

Modernisers hoped that a church which accepted Beatlemania would in turn be accepted by Beatlemaniacs. To the Oxford theologian Canon Ian T. Ramsey, the fact that a fan's 'Beatle-language was virtually theological language' did not signify the opposition between popular culture and religion, but that fandom contained a germ of faith:

If, and in so far as some girl gave as her reason for behaving as she did towards the Beatles, the fact that they seemed overwhelming and so much bigger than herself, and even introduced the word 'heaven' into the discussion, it could be that for her the Beatles might be one stage in the progress towards a cosmic disclosure.[207]

Ramsey argued that the Church would only succeed in channelling this latent religiosity by conversing with the young in their own language and by seeking the divine in the contemporary world.[208]

Canon Ramsey's aspiration to 'make our theology meaningful' by updating its symbolism and language for the Beatles generation was shared by other liberal clergymen.[209] One outcome was the rise of the 'trendy vicar'. 'You've got to be up to date', stated the Bishop of Guildford, who mentioned the Beatles and the Animals in a sermon and posed for photographs strumming a guitar.[210] The Bishop of Liverpool and Dean of Liverpool Cathedral responded to young people's complaints that church music was 'terribly slow, heavy, and dull' by endorsing special services featuring pop.[211] Congregational minister Rev. Robert Bailey swapped organ music for Beatles records, preached about their songs and sported a moptop on the grounds that 'it helps to break down barriers' between himself and the young.[212] The founder of the St. Mary-of-the-Angels Song School in Beaconsfield, Fr Desmond Morse-Boycott, was too advanced in years to grow his hair or strap on a guitar, but urged the Archbishop of Canterbury to recruit young priests from ordinary backgrounds who could tell teenagers that 'I was a Beatle-maniac, too'.[213]

One of the most widely publicised, criticised and satirised of these clergymen was Methodist minister Ronald Gibbins, who made headlines in November 1963 with his plans to 'sell it [religion] through the Beatles'.[214] Gibbins' observation that churches had more trouble than the Beatles in attracting the young was unexceptional and unexceptionable. What attracted attention was his alleged comment that the Beatles could save religion or found a religion of their own, and his invitation to the Beatles to discuss 'sex, drinking and gambling' with his young congregants.[215]

The Beatles did not visit Gibbins in Basildon. Nor did they fulfil his request to record a rocking carol for his Christmas service, but this did not save him from the ridicule of cartoonists and columnists.[216] The *Daily Mail's* Anne Scott-James judged that 'If a parson cannot win a congregation with dignity, he might as well give up.'[217] The other modernisers likewise met with mirth and disdain. The most eminent of them, Canon Ramsey, was the subject of critical editorials in the *Times*, *Church Times* and *Daily Telegraph*. They accused him of having 'h[e]ld up to ridicule the liberalising movement now so powerful in all churches' through a 'desperate anxiety to be modern at all costs'.[218] The *Spectator's* Henry Fairlie thought it 'idolatrous' to equate Beatlemania with faith and accused the Modern Churchmen's Union conference at which Ramsey had spoken of having altered Anglicanism beyond all recognition.[219] From this perspective, the attempt to incorporate the Beatles within religious practice threatened to destroy the church it was meant to save.

Conclusion

The award of MBEs to the Beatles in 1965 marked the culmination of their first years of fame and brought together virtually every discourse about their impact on British society. The ambiguity surrounding what 'services of a conspicuous character' had been rendered by the Beatles placed no limits on debate. 'We don't have to say, and we don't always say', was the response of one official in the prime minister's office.[220] Another Downing Street source advanced the cultural case that 'the Beatles are leaders in their particular art', while Harold Wilson later recalled recommending the awards to recognise their social value in having 'got the kids off the streets'.[221] The band members and most contemporaries thought that it was for 'services to exports', with their contribution adjudged to be primarily economic. Others cynically concluded that the awards had nothing to do with the Beatles' accomplishments and everything to do with Wilson's election prospects.

Such confusion gave new legs to existing controversies over the Beatles' impact on concepts of nation, generation, class and gender in sixties Britain. To the music papers, the awards represented official recognition of the Beatles' refashioning of national and generational identity. They had 'rejuvenated the whole country' according to *Melody Maker*, while the *New Musical Express* (NME) saluted them for raising Britain's international standing:

Their efforts to keep the Union Jack fluttering proudly have been far more successful than a regiment of diplomats and statesmen. We may be regarded as a second-class power in politics, but at any rate we now lead the world in pop music![222]

The *NME* reasoned that the Beatles had accepted the awards on behalf of the young. It viewed the gesture as lessening the generation gap and remedying the adverse publicity generally given to teenagers.[223] In gendered terms, the awards contradicted Lennon's assumption that 'you had to drive tanks and win wars to win the MBE' and, with it, the supreme value accorded to masculine valour.[224] The spectacle of female fans laying siege to the gates of Buckingham Palace at the Beatles' investiture ceremony further disrupted class and gender norms. Joseph Lee's cartoon of the occasion combined all these themes into a single image. The pitting of female Beatlemaniacs against male police officers defending the palace was paired to those of outsiders against insiders, youth against maturity, meritocracy against heredity, crowds against cliques, emotion against reason, innovation against tradition, fashion against uniformity, nudity against propriety, pleasure against duty, smiles against grimaces, spontaneity against ritual, chaos against order and change against stolidity.[225]

The mailbags of the *Mirror*, *Mail* and 10 Downing Street suggested that public opinion was finely balanced for and against the Beatles' awards.[226] Commentators were similarly polarised, with opponents taking on proponents point by point. Class-inflected arguments against the Beatles receiving MBEs centred on the relationship between prestige and wealth. In 1964, the *Daily Mail*'s City editor had cuttingly informed Starr that 'If they knight you lot it will be for services to exports, not to music.'[227] When the MBEs were announced, *Mirror* columnist Donald Zec likewise dismissed the Beatles' cultural contribution while also questioning whether their commercial success deserved official recognition. To him, the Beatles' social standing should not be measured 'merely in terms of the dollars their records have earned'.[228] But even if honours were to be granted to those in trade, Lennon suspected that the music business remained beyond the pale. '[E]veryone would have applauded' an exporter of manufactured goods who was given a gong, he charged, so 'why should they knock us?'[229]

Critics made two objections to the notion that the awards symbolised Britain's embrace of meritocracy. The first was that the Beatles lacked merit. They appeared 'talentless' to Noël Coward and 'ephemeral rubbish' to Bernard Levin, for whom such nonsense was symptomatic of Britain's postwar malaise. '[O]ur age is not declining because it likes the Beatles; it likes the Beatles because it is declining', he observed.[230] The second objection was that elevating the Beatles undermined the ruling classes. Diehard conservative Peregrine Worsthorne argued that until recently, people of all stations had accepted 'the basic hierarchy as reasonable and right and permanent'. Now, however, a reverse snobbery was at work according to which 'the traditional trappings of authority – titles, cultivation, superior education, breeding, background, property – instead of continuing to excite respect and awe, tend ... to provoke ribaldry and ridicule'.[231] Coward admonished the Queen for agreeing to the awards.[232] From the left, George Melly agreed that the Establishment was discrediting itself in its doomed quest to be 'with it', oblivious to the Beatles' 'cold distaste' towards its overtures.[233]

Whereas Harrison was tickled to think himself the youngest ever recipient of an MBE, others were appalled. An editorial in the *Catholic Herald* summed up the generational case against granting the Beatles MBEs. It argued that the young did not deserve positions of authority, did not desire them, were 'not developed enough socially' to occupy them and were not in fact being granted them by such symbolic acts.[234] Quoodle in the *Spectator* contrasted the 'honourable men' returning their awards with the juvenile reaction of the Beatles to the news, relating how they declared 'Harold was a good lad' and pondered wearing the medals as ties.[235]

The men praised by Quoodle expressed their difference from the Beatles in terms of generation, national identity, gender and class. The generation gap dividing them from the Beatles was a matter not simply of age but the fact that almost all had been honoured for their service in the Second World War. They included two RAF squadron leaders, officers in the Royal Artillery and Anti-Aircraft Command, a sea captain torpedoed twice and an airman who escaped from German prison camps both times he was shot down behind enemy lines. That a large proportion of these decorated servicemen came from Canada and Australia was a reminder of Britain's imperial past, and their belief that the awards made Britain 'fall deeper into international ridicule and contempt' spoke to its inglorious present.[236] The martial masculinity represented by these veterans met its opposite in the Beatles, whose imagined enlistment seemed so absurd a prospect that it had featured in a hit satirical song, the Barron Knights' 'Call Up the Groups' (1964). These men had cause to fear that the Beatles represented a new kind of non-military hero. 'For the next war do not count on me – use the Beatles or the Beatniks', remarked Dr Gaeten Jarry, a former Surgeon Lieutenant-Commander in the Royal Canadian Navy.[237] Less creditable was the snobbery manifested by his compatriot Hector Dupuis in depicting the Beatles as 'undesirables' and 'sorry fellows' with whom he had no desire to be associated. RAF veteran Paul Pearson likewise felt the honours system had been 'debased and cheapened' by recognising the Beatles and another lower-class Northern entertainer, actress Ena Sharples.[238]

Although their protests may appear churlish in retrospect, these veterans raised valid questions about whether the Beatles' public service could be equated with their own. C. V. Hearn, a policeman who had hunted brigands and deserters in Southern Italy during the Second World War, said that 'I was told my award was for bravery, but there is nothing brave in yelping at a howling mob of teenagers while you have £1 million in the bank.'[239] His comment captured the disorientation and indignation felt by many of his generation. It was to no avail. The Irish Guards' rendition of 'Can't Buy Me Love' (1964) outside Buckingham Palace a few days after the announcement marked the Changing of the Guard.[240]

The Beatles had their own doubts about their suitability for state honours, as Lennon's close friend Pete Shotton observed:

John went along to the Buckingham Palace investiture as cheerfully as he had played the Royal Variety Show two years earlier ... he felt a certain flush of triumph, befitting the naughty boy who had got away with sneaking into a place he most assuredly didn't belong. That, in a nutshell, was John's general attitude towards his embrace by the Establishment and the bourgeoisie – until it started to dawn on him that perhaps *they* had got the better of him, rather than the other way around.[241]

Was the award a compliment or an embarrassment, a blessing or a burden, the reward or price of fame? Lennon eventually concluded that he had 'sold [his] soul' when accepting the MBE. He exorcised the memory by returning his medal and inventing a story about smoking cannabis in the Buckingham Palace toilets at the investiture ceremony.[242] The other Beatles did not join Lennon in returning their MBEs; McCartney continued to express pride in the 'great honour' bestowed upon him.[243] As with playing Shea Stadium and meeting Elvis Presley earlier that year, being presented to the Queen represented another superlative achievement to add to the list. In this respect, 1965 was the year when, as Mark Lewisohn notes, the Beatles 'consolidated all the successes and excesses of 1964 by virtually repeating everything already achieved'.[244] It was also a year of significant firsts and lasts. It was the last year that they released two new LPs, acted in a feature film, performed in panto, toured Britain and spent virtually all the time with each other. Not coincidentally, it was the last year when Epstein was fully in control of them, and of himself.[245]

New elements which appeared in the Beatles' lives and work in 1965 foreshadowed things to come. It was the first year in which some of them took LSD, were exposed to Indian music, recorded with strings and discussed their songwriting in any depth. It was also the first time that they gave much thought to their lyrics. Lennon responded to Maureen Cleave's observation that his songs were monosyllabic by including the words 'self-assured', 'insecure', 'appreciate' and 'independence' in Help! (1965).[246] Lyrical self-awareness was married to musical sophistication in

McCartney's 'Yesterday' (1965) and several tracks on December's *Rubber Soul*.[247] The Beatles' new direction meant that 1965 was possibly the last year when a prime minister or monarch could afford to award them MBEs. The backlash against Lennon's comments on Christianity would have rendered him too controversial for the honour in 1966, and their association with drugs would have blackballed the rest of the band a year after that.

As the Beatles evolved, so in its own way did sixties British society. London in 1965 hosted its first major Happening (the International Poetry Incarnation at the Royal Albert Hall) and received its first tributes from American tastemakers as being 'the most swinging city in the world'.[248] More ominously, London was singled out by a governmental report as the one British city in which 'addiction to dangerous drugs does . . . seem to be a serious problem'.[249] These phenomena were as yet embryonic. The term 'permissive society' was not in common parlance and 'counterculture' had yet to be coined. There were 753 known addicts of dangerous drugs in the entire United Kingdom, most of whom were supplied by six doctors.[250] In 1965, Northern Ireland was at peace, women's liberation had yet to coalesce into a movement and the liberalisation of the laws concerning abortion, male homosexuality and divorce lay in the future. Chapter 3 considers how the next five years reshaped British society, the Beatles and their perceptions of each other.

Figure 3.1 Butchers – Dismembering the moptop image, March 1966. Photo by Michael Ochs Archives/Getty Images

In the second half of the 1960s, Paul McCartney toyed with releasing an album of avant-garde experiments under the title *Paul McCartney Goes Too Far.*[1] These unissued *divertissements* were of a piece with the experimentation which characterised virtually every aspect of the later Beatles' lives and work. But how far was too far? This chapter examines public reactions to the Beatles' mounting transgressions of social norms. It argues that, although their popularity as a band remained undiminished, they became increasingly alienated and alienating figures within British society in four respects. First, they made little attempt to attain universal popularity (see Fig. 3.1). Second, their fabled transformational abilities often failed them. Third, they associated themselves with strikingly unpopular causes. Fourth, they were no longer indulged by the popular press. The chapter concludes by exploring how sex and drugs became polarising issues and prime examples of how the Beatles in the late sixties had gone too far.

Detachment

In many respects, the Beatles possessed similar qualities in the late 1960s as before. They remained the most popular of popular musicians, notwithstanding press scrutiny of each setback and misstep for evidence that their star had waned. The 'more popular than Jesus' controversy made no appreciable dent in the success of that summer's album *Revolver* and its spin-off single 'Eleanor Rigby'/'Yellow Submarine' (both 1966). The failure of 'Penny Lane'/'Strawberry Fields Forever' to reach number one was soon followed by the crowning achievement of *Sgt. Pepper* (both 1967). The poor reception accorded later that year to the *Magical Mystery Tour* television special inspired Bernard Levin to recycle portions of a column first published in 1965 in which he confidently predicted the Beatles' inevitable descent into 'total obscurity'.[2] Yet his doom-mongering was once again confounded by the Beatles' swift return to popularity with 'Lady Madonna' (1968), though that did not stop him from re-reissuing his prophecy in 1970.[3]

The Beatles retained some of their most prominent supporters in the second half of the sixties and acquired new ones such as Wilfrid Mellers, Tony Palmer and Hunter Davies, who provocatively declared them to be 'The best-known four people in the world today'.[4] They also continued to provide girls' magazines with dishy photographs, even though they now faced more competition as dreamboats than during the days of Beatlemania. In 1967, *Jackie* featured them only once on its cover and included pictures of the bespectacled Lennon inside the magazine mainly for comic effect, as when observing his resemblance to the Edwardian murderer Dr Crippen.[5] But *Petticoat* still honoured them as 'the world's best-known quartet' and the Beatles had been restored to *Jackie*'s favours by 1969, when it featured pin-ups of each Beatle.[6] McCartney was assumed to be its readers' favourite. A teaser of him inside a cupid's heart enticed readers to 'open up and ogle' the full spread inside a 1969 issue, and the magazine welcomed any 'excuse to print a picture of Paul' the following year.[7]

Their enduring fame and chart success, when combined with their evolving style, led to expanded claims about the Beatles as epochal figures in the late 1960s. Whereas Beatlemania had prompted a number of commentators to proclaim 1963 'The Year of the Beatles',[8] end-of-decade retrospectives regularly identified the entire 1960s with the band.[9] Hunter Davies credited them for helping people like himself to gain acceptance and, together with Mary Quant, for having 'made Britain known for something when otherwise we'd have been known for nothing'.[10] Lennon was the sole British representative in ITV's *Man of the Decade* series in December 1969 and the Beatles appeared prominently in a BBC retrospective of the sixties later that month.[11] All of the instant histories of the sixties published at the turn of the decade saw them as representing the zeitgeist, whether these had been written by friend or foe.[12]

The Beatles' challenge to orthodox notions of class, generation, gender, sexuality, nation and religion persisted, even escalated. Their disruption of class hierarchies was such that Kenneth Allsop discussed them in a 1967 symposium on the subject.[13] The Beatles featured regularly in late-sixties accounts of working-class dynamism[14] and middle-class reaction, as when Tony Palmer blamed 'cultural snobbery and bourgeois prejudice' for cavilling at their genius.[15] The case for the Beatles' growing generational influence was made by Tony Barrow. In 1968, he admitted that he had not grasped the Beatles' 'full social significance' when serving as their publicist during the Epstein era.[16] Having previously explained their importance in terms of behaving like 'fans rather than stars', he now credited them with having introduced the 'world's rising generation' to an 'entirely new way of life'.[17] It was an assertion which, however overblown, was echoed by two Reith lecturers. The psychiatrist G. M. Carstairs marvelled in 1972 at the 'astonishing impact' wrought by the Beatles since he delivered his Reith Lectures ten years earlier.[18] His claim that the Beatles 'imparted a new confidence to a generation of young people who suddenly felt free to give expression to their exuberant nonconformity' was expressed in more general terms by the social anthropologist Edmund Leach.[19] In his 1967 Reith Lectures, Leach portrayed the teenagers of 'Britain's pop generation' as in being opposition to 'the whole principle of a predetermined social order'.[20]

The Beatles increasingly defied norms of gender and sexuality in the late sixties and early seventies. Their hair fell below their shoulders, their faces sprouted moustaches and beards and their clothing became more androgynous and flamboyant.[21] In the early sixties, it had been uncertain whether their followers could stomach the prospect of a married Beatle. In the late sixties, fans had to accustom themselves to Lennon's desertion of his wife and son, adultery and divorce. Lennon publicly supported second-wave feminism and gay rights; the Gay Liberation Front returned the compliment by naming their magazine *Come Together*.[22] His disclosure to *Rolling Stone* in 1970 of Epstein's homosexuality and the Beatles' use of prostitutes dispelled any remaining traces of their once-wholesome image.[23]

The Beatles' eccentric appearance made it all the more remarkable that they were chosen to represent the nation to the rest of the planet in 1967's *Our World* satellite broadcast. Though they had long served in an ambassadorial role for Britain, they represented an unsettling ethnic proposition in the late sixties. They were Southern Northerners, cosmopolitan Englishmen, whites flirting with Eastern spirituality and Black Power, who by 1969 had joined their fortunes with a manager from Newark and wives from Tokyo and Westchester County. Much of this ethnic complexity was on display in their broadcast performance of 'All You Need Is Love' (1967), with its caftans, multilingual sandwich boards and snippets of quintessentially English, French, German and American tunes. Within Britain, such spectacles led Michael Wood to identify a 'new nationalism' centred on 'the swingingness of English art'[24] Overseas, Julian Critchley envisaged 'millions of foreigners [for whom] Britain is associated not with parliamentary democracy, nor with technology, nor even with banking, but with the Beatles'.[25]

The band's religious impact grew in the second half of the sixties as they oscillated between atheism and westernised variants of Hinduism. During Beatlemania, clerics had debated whether the Beatles' success offered lessons about modernising the image of Christian worship. Youth outreach initiatives in the late 1960s continued to reference the Beatles, as when St Paul's Cathedral staged a pop event in 1968 which featured McCartney's protégée Mary Hopkin, his brother Mike McGear and P. P. Arnold singing Beatles tunes as well as go-go dancers and a catwalk show in front of the

Duke of Wellington's funeral carriage.[26] But in the late 1960s, the Beatles additionally featured in debates over prayer and doctrine. The Archbishop of Canterbury welcomed their adoption of Transcendental Meditation for dispelling the notion that 'mysticism is something queer and abnormal'. He commended their 'searching for spiritual truth', even though it was leading them away from Christianity.[27] Several contributors to the *Church Times* took Anglicanism to task for failing to satisfy the 'spiritual hunger' displayed by the Beatles and others of their generation, resulting in the rise of New Age religion.[28] Anglican campaigners for peace and social justice found common cause with Lennon and Ono, who joined fasters protesting against global poverty at Rochester Cathedral, and against the Biafran War at London's St Martin-in-the-Fields.[29]

The Beatles took pride in achieving popularity and influence in the late sixties on their own terms, quite unlike the days of Beatlemania. Starr looked back on their career in the winter of 1968–9:

> when we first started we were the nice clean moptops and every mother's son. And everyone loved us . . . You can't live all your life by what they want, you know, we can't go on forever as four clean moptops playing 'She Loves You'.[30]

Starr and his bandmates used 'moptop' as a multipurpose metaphor for all that was wrong with the Beatles' early popularity. They came to disavow acclamation that was as broad as it was shallow. To appeal to 'everyone', the Beatles could afford to offend no one, at substantial cost to their integrity. Moptops had to do 'what they [the general public] want', which in Lennon's recollection involved 'cop-out' and 'compromise'.[31] Moptops were there to perform, both in the sense of staging 'a moptop show' in concert and in acting in accordance with a 'moptop image' bearing little relationship to their authentic selves.[32]

The qualities Starr associated with being a moptop indicate what he and his bandmates considered constraining and inauthentic. One was uniformity. Moptops came in a set of four, the individuality of each disguised by matching clothes and hair. Another was puerility. Starr chafed at being considered 'every mother's son' for the same reasons that McCartney objected to the patronising treatment of moptops as 'jovial' and 'idiotic'.[33] Rejecting this role was to Lennon an essential part of 'grow[ing] up'.[34] Musical development necessitated personal growth. Just as Starr disliked the idea of playing 'She Loves You' for eternity, McCartney feared that being typecast as 'four silly little puppets' would prevent them from becoming known as 'four people who made music that stands up to being remembered'.[35]

By pitting authenticity against popularity and musicianship against entertainment, the Beatles participated in separating 'rock' from 'pop' in a process discussed in Chapter 4.[36] They exhibited the same role conflict detected by James T. Coffman among contemporaneous West Coast musicians who sought to reconcile the expectations of fans, other musicians and the music industry.[37] Their towering popularity produced commensurately stronger pressures, but also the wealth and self-belief to change direction. Lennon stated that there would be 'No more tours, no more moptops' because it was pointless to seek 'More fame ... More money'.[38] They had 'compromised' in order to succeed, only to realise that being 'famous and rich' left them unfulfilled. And so they 'gave up being moptops'.[39]

The 'nice clean' image repudiated by Starr had been central to their initial appeal.[40] Epstein's marketing strategy had emphasised the Beatles' sheer niceness as much as their talent, portraying them as 'quite magnificent human beings, utterly honest, often irritating but splendid citizens shining in a fairly ordinary, not very pleasing world'.[41] Authenticity was a favourite theme of the authorised fan magazine *Beatles Book*. 'SUCCESS DOES NOT CHANGE THEM', it insisted, citing as proof their 'typically Northern' directness and partiality for steak and chips.[42] The magazine maintained that the Beatles hated miming on television shows and foreswore the dance routines and 'mechanical grins' purveyed by other acts.[43] Even their publicity events were presented as spontaneous occasions owing to Epstein's insistence that they 'answer questions [and] pose for pictures' without his direction.[44]

Many journalists testified to the Beatles' decency in their first years of fame. Peter Laurie detected 'gentleness [and] lovableness' and the *NME* considered them to be 'the same happy-go-lucky crowd, as modest as ever' before and after stardom.[45] The rougher elements of their character were often excused by their upbringing and youth or else interpreted in the best possible light: mockery as wit, conceit as candour, stroppiness as a refreshing lack of reserve. The Beatles were deemed so likeable that 'few mothers ... wouldn't welcome a Beatle into the family' and any detractor risked being labelled a 'real sour square'.[46] But Beatlephobes were in any case more likely to target the fans, apologists and the music industry rather than the Beatles themselves during Beatlemania. The same *Telegraph* editorial which laid into vacuous teens and 'with-it' intellectuals had to concede that the Beatles themselves were 'clean and friendly' and 'very hard to dislike'.[47]

This sanitised portrait of the Beatles suited most parties in the early sixties. It provided the press with access and copy, the fans with idols, the music industry with an unbeatable brand and the Beatles with approbation and protection from scandal. Dominic Sandbrook shrewdly observes that the press 'could probably have destroyed the Beatles' career almost before it had begun' if it had investigated incidents like Lennon's assault on his old friend Bob Wooler in 1963.[48] Instead, the main coverage of the event consisted of an exculpatory *Mirror* article entitled 'Beatle in Brawl Says "Sorry I Socked You"'. A contrite Lennon explained that he 'didn't realise what [he] was doing' after having one drink too many.[49]

Such whitewashing and backscratching could not continue indefinitely. Independent-minded journalists such as Peter Evans drew attention to how 'very much out of step with their scrubbed image' the Beatles had become by 1965. Evans enjoined 'these four little-boy men' to live up to public expectations by exhibiting responsibility and modesty.[50] But the Beatles reached the opposite conclusion. It was their image rather than their behaviour that had to change. In the second half of the 1960s, they set out to dismantle the idealised 'moptop' version of them existing in 'other people's minds'.[51] Telling indications came in a series of interviews conducted by Maureen Cleave during the spring of 1966, in which Lennon's notorious remark about Christianity was just one of several provocative statements. Epstein remained 'polite and restrained' with Cleave, and Starr came across as the avuncular family man.[52] But McCartney condemned working-class people who did not share his passion for the high arts and described the United States in incendiary fashion as 'a lousy country where anyone who is black is made to seem a dirty n****r'.[53] Lennon's pet hates included 'soft' and 'ugly' people, Labour, the Conservatives and the British and Roman empires.[54] Harrison declared his opposition to all wars and authority figures, 'religious or secular', with special criticism meted out to war heroes, the Pope and the prime minister.[55] It was a moot point whether the Beatles felt impelled to speak out, aimed to stoke controversy or simply did not consider the consequences of sharing their latest opinions with the public.

This confrontational stance did not come as a complete surprise given their earlier reputation for plain speaking. Some of their defenders went so far as to identify their 'persistent rudeness and aggressiveness' as the defining characteristic of their career.[56] Yet many of their later sayings and doings verged on self-sabotage. Harrison laid waste to their 'goody-goody' image by drawing attention to how 'parts of us are lousy and rotten'.[57] As if to prove the point, McCartney agreed with a journalist's characterisation of him as 'pleasantly insincere', yet seemed too honest for his own good when stating in the same interview that 'starvation in India doesn't worry me one bit'. He added that he did not 'really feel' for the Vietnamese people and that sympathy was wasted on the disabled.[58] This was not a good look for a band which had fronted an Oxfam campaign against famine a few years previously.[59]

The Beatles' self-sabotage was more than rhetorical. It involved foreswearing most of the activities which had brought them unprecedented success up to 1966. Their retirement from live performances save for the unannounced rooftop concert meant no foreign trips as a band, next to no collective press conferences, fewer photo opportunities and the shrinking of Beatlemania to a gaggle of Apple Scruffs.[60] The long-promised sequel to the films *A Hard Day's Night* and *Help!* never quite materialised. *Magical Mystery Tour* (1967) did not receive a theatrical release in Britain, *Yellow Submarine* (1968) was a film about, not by, the Beatles and *Let It Be* (1970) was hardly popcorn fodder. Their broadcast appearances became more selective well before Epstein died. They even treated their official fan magazine with a neglect which, in the case of Harrison, bordered on contempt.[61] They starved it of exclusive photos, cancelled plans for a concert after readers had won tickets and ruined the magazine's exclusive preview of *Get Back* by shelving the album the following month.[62]

They were not short of new promotional strategies, but their abandonment of most existing ones made them more dependent than ever upon record releases to generate money and publicity. This helped to explain why the inability of 'Penny Lane'/'Strawberry Fields Forever' (1967) to top the charts led to intense speculation about their future prospects. The *Record Mirror*'s Jeremy Walsh was unsurprised that Engelbert Humperdinck's 'Release Me' (1967) had outsold a double A-side that was by turns pretentious and parochial, from a band guilty of a 'lack of attention to their fans'.[63] When *Melody Maker* found that two-fifths of a sampling of 100 fans preferred the Monkees to the Beatles in March 1967, it attributed the result to the Beatles' 'no-appearances policy'.[64] True to the Beatles' growing disdain of blanket acclaim, Lennon told *Melody Maker* at the launch of *Sgt. Pepper* that he was happy for the Monkees to replace them in the affections of the young and undiscerning: 'I don't want to be a moptop. For those who want moptops, the Monkees are right up there, man. ... Let 'em dig their cuddly moptops till they change their minds.'[65]

Sgt. Pepper gave the lie to claims that the Beatles were a spent force: commercially, aesthetically or iconically. But it did so by exorcising the ghosts of Beatlemania. The album reinvented the group as Sgt. Pepper's Lonely Hearts Club Band, replaced a live audience with a canned one and

featured a cover which juxtaposed the new-look Beatles in all their psychedelic finery with waxworks representing their smaller, greyer, undiffer-
entiated and fabricated earlier selves. Lennon told *Disc and Music Echo*
how pleased they were to stop performing and no longer 'be screamed at'.[66]
Prioritising the creation of music over its consumption allowed him to
'answer to myself, man, nobody else'.[67] His subordination of audience
desires to artistic imperatives confirmed Alan Walsh's article about 'The
Danger Facing Pop' published the previous week. Walsh observed that the
Beatles' decision to 'devote their talents exclusively to the recording studios' meant that they had given up all the other 'trappings' of stardom
including tours, television appearances, feature films, interviews and interactions with fans.[68] Walsh worried that the Beatles' seclusion would render
them 'unworldly' and their music 'too hip' for a general audience. But he
acknowledged that the Beatles hoped what he feared. Their new 'freedom
to devote their talents exclusively to the recording studios' had been long
desired and hard earned.[69]

Transformation

It was intrinsic to the mystique of the early Beatles that they changed
virtually everything that they encountered with ease and insouciance.
They had triumphed in pantomime, cinema and literature and emerged
from encounters with royals, academics, politicians, City traders,
Continentals and Americans with their reputations enhanced. Without
any effort on their part, they had kept the prime minister's plane waiting on
the tarmac, had flown to Australia without a passport and, once there, had
been greeted by hosts behaving as if 'freed from captivity'.[70] Their good
example had 'helped reduce the number of juvenile delinquents' according
to the Master of the Rolls and had liberated British pop music from the
'shackles of Americanism' according to the Canon of Coventry
Cathedral.[71] They had helped to feed the hungry and reduce tooth decay
simply by lending their name to campaigns by Oxfam and the General
Dental Council. Their music and hair caused a sit-down strike at a mill, a
walk-out at a cardboard box factory and a threatened hunger strike at an
engineering works. Their healing powers were reputedly demonstrated in a
London hospital, where their images 'worked wonders' by calming children receiving injections.[72] The deaf artist Alfred Thomson exhibited a
painting of them after the 'big Beatle beat' became his first experience of
music through a new hearing aid.[73] If bringing comfort to the sick and

music to the deaf was not miraculous enough, they had defied expectations, precedent and gravity by remaining the top pop act years after their bubble was supposed to burst.

Since this was what they had achieved almost without trying, what could they accomplish if they put their minds to it? Their capacity to perform good works set imaginations racing. They could 'put their talent to Christian account' by joining the ranks of the Salvation Army or electing to 'plug the Ten Commandments, instead of pop songs'.[74] Gracie Fields wanted them to set a sartorial example.[75] The Lord Provost of Edinburgh asked them to donate £100,000 to the Festival.[76] The medical officers assembled at the Royal Society of Health congress in 1964 considered how a few choice words from the Beatles would cut teenage smoking at a stroke.[77]

Though often unwitting, even unwilling objects of such discussions during the years of Beatlemania, the Beatles later sought to use their fame to effect social change. As McCartney put it in 1968,

being suddenly rich and famous, and in a position to do something, we've got a choice of doing what either most people do, which is just making more and more money, and getting more and more rich and famous . . . or trying to DO something which will help.[78]

This philosophy shaped the Beatles' later songwriting. 'The Word', released in December 1965, announced their proselytising ambitions and contained their fundamental message for society: of the power of love to create community and to invest existence with meaning. Its instruction to an unspecified 'you' to change their lives in order to 'be like me' reappeared in songs such as 'Think for Yourself' (1965), 'Rain' (1966), 'A Day in the Life' (1967), 'The Inner Light' (1968), 'Come Together' and 'The End' (both 1969). The related theme of inclusivity appeared in 'With a Little Help from My Friends' (1967) and 'Dear Prudence' (1968). Parables including 'Nowhere Man' (1965), 'Eleanor Rigby' (1966), 'She's Leaving Home' (1967) and 'The Continuing Story of Bungalow Bill' (1968) illustrated the sorry condition of humanity excluded from community. 'Sgt. Pepper's Lonely Hearts Club Band' and 'Magical Mystery Tour' (both 1967) invited listeners to participate in an imagined act of togetherness. Lennon playfully revived the same theme when launching his first solo single in 1969:

The ad . . . said, 'YOU are the Plastic Ono Band.' So we are the Plastic Ono Band, and the audience is the Plastic Ono Band. There is no Plastic Ono Band . . . And that's the Plastic Ono Band. You're in it. Everybody's in it.[79]

The Beatles' musical missionising was accompanied by the promotion and sponsorship of a series of side projects and campaigns, most of which were associated with London's counterculture.[80] The Beatles had strong countercultural credentials. They provided the underground with its soundtrack, represented its most high-profile spokespeople, embraced its mysticism and bankrolled its activities. To McCartney, '[p]utting money into the counterculture was doing things about changing the world, politically'; to the counterculture, it was what kept them solvent.[81] '[I]f *IT* wanted anything, they could have it', was Apple's policy according to Derek Taylor.[82] The underground newspaper *IT* accordingly benefited from advertising revenue from Apple, circulation-boosting interviews with McCartney and Harrison, a loan to cover printing costs and a handout from McCartney to pay the wage bill.[83] Lennon was the most regular claimant on Apple funds. He favoured *IT*'s edgier rival, *Oz*, recording a charity single for them in 1971 and being responsible, with Ono, for placing the majority of Apple adverts in the magazine. McCartney personally subsidised the Indica gallery and bookshop and BIT, a phone service providing information on the counterculture. Harrison donated to the drug charity Release and the Beatles collectively sponsored the Soma advertisement calling for the decriminalisation of cannabis use.[84]

Apple was the Beatles' most concerted attempt to embed themselves into the London counterculture.[85] It presented itself in *Oz* as 'an "underground" company above ground' which existed to 'help, collaborate with, and extend all existing [underground] organizations as well as start many new ones', and in many respects fulfilled its mandate.[86] Taylor recalled that anyone who 'came in off the street with an idea and they looked right and felt right' could expect a handout from Apple headquarters. Apple Boutique clothed the counterculture, Apple Films produced avant-garde fare and Apple Theatre staged plays which, in true countercultural fashion, pursued a 'way to bewilderment'.[87]

The Beatles expressed their goals in vaultingly ambitious terms. Promoting Transcendental Meditation 'could turn on millions of people'.[88] Pulling off the *Magical Mystery Tour* film without any directorial experience would demonstrate that 'you don't need knowledge in this world to do anything'.[89] Bag-Ins would produce 'total communication', Bed-Ins would 'indoctrinat[e] them [people] to think about peace' and Lennon and Ono's collaborations would show that 'everything is art'.[90] Apple would become 'a complete business organisation on the lines of ICI', except that it would serve 'the general good' and foster a progressive 'social and cultural environment'.[91] 'The possibilities for Apple are unlimited', claimed the *Beatles Book*:

The Beatles see this as a vast concept, a massive environment, capable of making and selling all kinds of assorted goods and services. There is no reason why we should not be buying Apple electric shavers or Apple detergents before the year is out.[92]

The outcome was far from what the Beatles anticipated, but neither was it one of unrelieved disenchantment. Their music remained supremely popular and, for some, was inspirational. Several of their songs became anthems: sometimes intentionally, as in the case of Lennon's 'Come Together' and 'Give Peace a Chance' (both 1969), and sometimes with a little creative adaptation. Student protestors chorused 'We all live in a Red LSE', striking car workers serenaded Harold Wilson with the refrain 'We all live on bread and margarine' and hostages on a hijacked plane taunted their Arab captors by singing 'We all live in a blue and white machine.'[93] The televised singalongs of 'All You Need Is Love' in 1967 and 'Hey Jude' in 1968 unforgettably evoked their vision of an ideal community, and the 1969 rooftop concert portrayed the Beatles as dissidents taking on the law and its middle-aged and middle-class allies.[94]

The content and distribution of the Beatles' later music nonetheless had exclusive aspects as well as inclusive ones. Songs like 'Rain' (1966) trod a fine line between exhortation and condescension, which they crossed in the hectoring lyrics of 'And Your Bird Can Sing' (1966), 'Within You Without You' (1967) and 'Revolution' (1968). The humanity of 'Ob-La-Di, Ob-La-Da' was undercut by the misanthropy of 'Piggies' (both 1968). The uplift of 'Let It Be' (1970) conflicted with the aloofness of 'The Fool on the Hill' (1967). Filmed performances were no substitute for touring and were designed to control direct contact with the band's fans. For the television recordings, 'All You Need Is Love' and 'Hey Jude' were played in studios in front of invited audiences, while the rooftop concert was witnessed live only by their inner circle, local office workers and sundry passers-by. The primacy accorded to albums led them to sequester themselves in the studio and resulted in more irregular releases of more expensive records. An album was a major purchase for younger fans, even prohibitively so when *The Beatles* double LP (1968) was priced at £2 13s and the *Let It Be* box set (1970) was a penny under £3.

Their track record outside music was still more problematic. In June 1968, Alan Walsh had excitedly reported that Apple represented 'an ambitious and far-reaching attempt to create a British cultural revolution'.[95] Six months later, he returned to interview Taylor about what had gone wrong:

We certainly haven't brought about a revolution in the music business, we've failed in that. But all the other revolutions this year failed, too ... We started off with grandiose ideas but it's difficult to be grandiose in a glum society like the one which we have here.[96]

Apple was a reputational disaster as well as an organisational one for the Beatles, as the counterculture bit the hand that fed it. Going into business made the Beatles seem 'absolutely bound to the Establishment and accountants', claimed disc jockey John Peel.[97] One of Apple Electronics' proposed products, a device to prevent home taping, represented the unacceptable face of capitalism to student journalist Daniel Wiles.[98] *Oz* columnist Germaine Greer denounced the whole organisation as a venal part of 'The Establishment'.[99] Its editor Richard Neville suggested that the Beatles' philanthropy was insufficient when Harrison declined to participate in a benefit concert for the Vietnam Solidarity Campaign.[100] Such jibes forced McCartney to take out a full-page advertisement in *Oz* stating Apple's benign intentions.[101]

The films *Magical Mystery Tour* (1967) and *Let It Be* (1970) failed in their ambitions to be transformative spectacles. Harrison had commented before the screening of *Magical Mystery Tour* that 'We want everyone who watches to be able to freak out, but we don't want to frighten them.'[102] Viewers surveyed by the BBC did not freak out so much as lash out in a manner less unsettled than disgusted. Three-quarters of them

could hardly find a good word to say for the programme, considering it stupid, pretentious rubbish which was, no doubt, intended to be very clever and 'way out' but which was, they thought, a complete jumble with neither shape nor meaning, and certainly no entertainment value whatsoever.[103]

McCartney's boast about 'how easy it is to get involved in everything' in film-making came back to bite him.[104] 'Why on earth should anyone be surprised if they made a rotten film?' asked the *Sunday Times*' television critic Maurice Wiggin: 'What possible qualifications have they shown as film makers?'[105]

Let It Be captured in excruciating close-up the foundering of another transformational project.[106] Its premise was to show the creation of music from its sketchy origins to the finished article, starting in rehearsal rooms and ending in a spectacular concert. McCartney floated any number of suggestions for staging a concert like no other. They could halt flights at an airport, gatecrash the Houses of Parliament, wow their fan club or play in Harrison's house, an orphanage or a hospital ward where lame children would rise from their beds. What about flying to Biafra, 'rescu[ing] all the people' and playing some numbers on the runway?[107] But in order to create a game-changing spectacle, he first had to change his bandmates' minds. 'I'm here because I want to do a show. But I don't really feel an awful lot of support', he said, as if hoping to be corrected.[108] The transformation captured by the resulting film *Let It Be* (1970) was that of a band disintegrating.

Lennon and Ono's participatory rhetoric belied the alienation more commonly evoked by their avant-garde creations. Letters to the *Beatles Book* suggested that 'Revolution 9' (1968) was regarded as a 'monstrosity' by some fans and left others simply nonplussed.[109] 'I am unable to say very much in favour of it because I fail to see what it is trying to put over', confessed Elaine Danson: 'Maybe if someone could enlighten me I'd be able to understand and therefore appreciate it far more.'[110] The *Beatles Book* counterbalanced explicatory articles about Lennon and Ono's conceptual art with fan testimony accusing the couple of 'trying to make excuses for the fact that they don't know how to create really important works of art, paintings or sculptures'.[111] Lennon's response oscillated between pleas for open-mindedness and haughty claims that it would take many decades before his and Ono's art would be understood and admired.[112]

His partnership with Ono tried the patience of his most stalwart supporters. Adrian Henri's later assessment that 'artistically they were a disaster for each other' was expressed at the time by Tony Palmer.[113] Palmer's close working relationship with Lennon did not prevent him from penning a scathing review of *Grapefruit* (1964; reissued in 1970) which ended 'I wish and hope Miss Ono will go far. Soon.'[114] Some critics understandably wondered if the couple's art was a put-on. *The Spectator*'s art critic Evan Anthony considered Lennon 'a jokester' and George Barker hoped for Ono's sake that *Grapefruit* was 'a rather elaborate practical joke'.[115] When Hornsey art students sarcastically donated a rusty bike 'inadvertently left out' of Lennon's debut solo exhibition, he unrepentantly put it on display.[116]

The Bed-Ins proved counterproductive. In 1971 Lennon claimed that media coverage made them 'one of the great happenings of this century'. At the time, however, he admitted that he could not provide any 'concrete example' of their effects save for 'a few good cartoons ... and a few good reactions from readers' letters'.[117] Ono later conceded that the reactions were largely damning, with conservatives 'trying to ignore or suppress' the event and liberals pronouncing it 'too naïve'.[118] While they expected no better from political elites, criticism from 'our camp' and doubts over whether 'people had got the point' plunged Lennon and Ono into deep depression.[119] That an exercise in complete transparency provoked incredulity and befuddlement was an irony not lost on journalists. Alan Walsh puzzled at 'Lennon's apparent inability to communicate to ordinary people'. To deliver homilies from a king-sized bed in a five-star hotel was as 'ridiculous' as it was 'insulting' to the majority of people who lacked the time and money to do the same.[120] Donald Zec noted that there were likewise 'No takers' for Lennon's Bag-In and 'No planters' for his acorns for peace.[121]

Estrangement

To many observers, there was something perverse about the most popular and famous band of the era associating themselves with some of the most unpopular causes and fringe groupings in sixties Britain.[122] But what appeared paradoxical from the outside seemed logical to the Beatles and their inner circle. The Beatles' elevated position arguably granted them a wider perspective and the capacity to rise above public scorn. As Derek Taylor put it,

The Beatles have the capacity of very attractive children for really getting away with it. They've said, 'we are more popular than Jesus', tried LSD and admitted it, signed the Legalise Marijuana petition and two of them have been heavily fined for smoking it, and followed the Maharishi. They've survived all that and still people smile when they see them.[123]

Taylor had a point, but the Beatles sought to accomplish much more from their missionising than mere survival and did not emerge unscathed.

Some of the Beatles' controversial statements and esoteric causes received a surprisingly sympathetic hearing. Lennon's contention that the Beatles were 'more popular than Jesus now' produced little reaction in Britain until it was picked up in the United States.[124] British commentators had already debated the religious overtones of Beatlemania and the comparative appeal of Christianity at length during 1963 and 1964. These and related discussions indicated general acceptance that Britain was a secularising society, allowing for differences over whether secularisation could or should be resisted. The British reaction to the delayed American reaction to Lennon's remarks did not dwell on whether he should apologise. On the contrary, film director Bryan Forbes thought it absurd that Lennon was 'denounced from the pulpit for daring to utter one of the more obvious truths of this decade'.[125] Others saved their outrage for the 'fantastically unreasoned reaction' of the protestors.[126] Cartoons firmly associated the backlash with the Ku Klux Klan and depicted Beatles' records being immolated by the Statue of Liberty's torch.[127] *Melody Maker* concluded that those burning records in the States and banning them in South Africa proved Lennon's point that some Christians were a bit thick.[128]

Only one commentator, the *Sunday Times*' Maurice Wiggin, envisaged a moral majority repudiating Lennon's 'arrogant nihilism' and ushering in a new 'age of order'.[129] The remainder agreed with Lennon's ranking of Jesus below the Beatles in the British hit parade, even when (like the Catholic *Ready! Steady! Go!* presenter Cathy McGowan) they did not share Lennon's atheism.[130] The clergymen who weighed in on the matter generally blamed the populace for preferring entertainment over 'ideals and principles'.[131] A Derbyshire vicar argued that Jesus' teachings were 'far too demanding' for most people and the Bishop of Reading recalled that Barabbas had won an earlier popularity contest.[132] But the bishop was rebuked in the letter pages of the *Sunday Telegraph* for absolving himself and his fellow clerics from blame for the 'half-empty churches throughout the land'.[133] The controversy provided another opportunity for commentators to ride their usual hobby horses in the ongoing secularisation debate.

The Beatles' dalliance with the Maharishi Mahesh Yogi prompted a mixture of incredulity and curiosity, including some unexpectedly fair-minded coverage in the popular press.[134] A special investigation conducted by the *Express* in September 1967 empathised with the Beatles' quest to find meaning in life and concluded that Transcendental Meditation 'is a genuine belief . . . does appear to have had good effects, and . . . deserves to be considered'.[135] The *Express* followed up with an on-site report from Rishikesh which dispelled rumours about the Maharishi's wealth.[136] In the *Mirror*, Donald Zec and Don Short weighed their own scepticism against the sincerity of the Maharishi and the Beatles as well as the possibility that 'A new era is about to dawn.'[137]

In hindsight, Harrison had been gravitating towards Eastern religion since 1965, as had Lennon since 1966.[138] Yet to contemporaries, the whole band appeared to have converted overnight. This sudden and unanticipated turn of events, when coupled to the unfamiliarity of non-Christian religion in 1960s Britain, scrambled the usual dividing lines between supporters and critics of the Beatles. The normally supportive David

Frost and John Mortimer suggested to Lennon and Harrison on a chat show that Transcendental Meditation sanctioned selfish individualism.[139] Whereas Mortimer attacked the Maharishi from an atheist viewpoint, McCartney's close friend Barry Miles contrasted the Maharishi's huckster-ism with genuine Tibetan wisdom.[140]

Conversely, some of the Beatles' most prominent critics considered meditation to be the wrong answer to the right question. Peregrine Worsthorne attended the Maharishi's first meeting with the Beatles at the London Hilton and came away declaring it at once 'comic' and 'historic'. He was not taken in by the Maharishi's 'mystical mumbo jumbo', but was hopeful that the seeds of faith, having taken root in the Beatles, would be sown across millions of their followers.[141] Another conservative Christian, Christopher Booker, dismissed Transcendental Meditation as one of the 'blatantly dubious' paths to instant enlightenment. He nonetheless saw its popularity as heralding 'the most remarkable shift in Western conscious-ness for several hundred years': a repudiation of 'our collectivist, techno-logical, materialist, rational culture' in favour of a renewed 'sense of the sacred'.[142] Most striking was the change of heart displayed by the liberal Christian journalist Monica Furlong. In 1964, she had led a populist revolt against the 'four monumental bores' and the acclaim accorded to them.[143] But in 1973, she saw them as spearheading a religious revival of the same potential magnitude as the Reformation. She applauded the 'golden good-ness and wisdom' displayed in their lyrics.[144] The 'genuine mystical vision' of Harrison's *All Things Must Pass* (1970) earned her highest praise for reintroducing into popular music spiritual and humanitarian themes that had gone unheard for centuries. The 'discovery of inner riches' in the title track and the quest for 'wholeness' in 'My Sweet Lord' contended with the sombre warnings against hypocrisy and alienation contained in 'Beware of Darkness' and 'Isn't It a Pity'.[145]

The Beatles' association with the Maharishi and the Krishna Consciousness movement, Harrison's obsession with Indian music and Lennon's infatuation with Ono prompted discussions of 'the East' in ethnic terms.[146] Three main schools of thought emerged. The first welcomed multiculturalism. Nigel Gosling defended Lennon's nude studies of his wife for the unabashed, 'Oriental' way in which they displayed sexual subjects 'veiled in the West for centuries'.[147] Desmond Shawe-Taylor placed the Beatles' musical fusions alongside those of Peter Maxwell Davies, Benjamin Britten, Carl Orff, John Cage and Olivier Messiaen.[148] John Grigg greeted the 'Indian sound' of 'Norwegian Wood' (1965) as part of a 'cross-fertilisation' which prevented Western culture from being 'too self-sufficient', while Wilfrid Mellers saw 'the magical aspects of Beatle music' as revitalising the Western tradition.[149]

But the working-class schoolchildren who told Mellers that they disliked the 'Chinky' sound of *Revolver* (1966) revealed less cosmopolitanism outside the literati.[150] Lennon discovered the same thing when he released 360 helium balloons in 1968, each with a label attached asking the recipient to write back. He was shocked by the virulent racism of the respondents who thought it treasonous to fraternise with a Japanese woman so soon after the Second World War.[151] The Maharishi brought out the worst British stereotypes of Indians as wily, gnomic, avaricious, superstitious and unkempt. *Private Eye* dubbed him Veririshi Lotsa Moni Yogi Bear and Malcolm Muggeridge concluded that he was a 'delectable old Hindu con man' after the two of them debated the virtues of asceticism.[152] Shadow Home Secretary Quintin Hogg branded Lennon a race traitor for his discipleship. '[Y]ou have chosen to turn your backs [on] the literature, the art, the religion, the philosophy, the science, the genius of the dynamic West, of our own spiritual heritage', he thundered, in favour of an alien creed which 'can offer mankind nothing but the immemorial poverty of the East [and] its acceptance of human suffering'.[153]

A more generous approach was to attribute the Beatles' orientalism to ignorance. Only one commentator who sought to put the Beatles right about India was himself Indian. That said, Farrukh Dhondy's uncomplimentary portrait of the Maharishi differed little from most British analyses.[154] George Harrison was the Beatle whose profile grew most from the band's association with Indian religion during their hippie period and who found it hardest to live down thereafter. 'Curry powder' was the metaphor used by music critics George Melly, Nik Cohn and Charles Shaar Murray to describe his efforts on the sitar.[155] Melly found his ongoing devotion to Eastern mysticism 'rather pretentious and absurd' and Tony Palmer likened his homilies to those found in the *Reader's Digest*.[156]

Other phenomena associated with the Beatles faced more or less uniform hostility. The waning of public demonstrations of Beatlemania from 1966 onwards led commentators to assume that the Beatles had lost their young female fan base, even though their buoyant record sales suggested otherwise. The concurrent emergence of the counterculture was assumed to have provided the Beatles with their new core audience. A 1967 *Daily Express* feature on the new phenomenon of the underground identified the Beatles as its chief financial backer and propagandist for drugs, and a *Mirror* article provided Lennon and Ono as their ready-made answer to the question 'What is a hippie?'[157] An overlapping body of student radicals was also associated with the Beatles, despite Lennon's occasionally fractious dealings with them.[158] Academics presented the Beatles' popularity on campus as evidence of various changes within higher education, including the influx of working-class students, the adoption by middle-class students of working-class culture and the radicalisation of students for whom Beatles tunes served as 'marching songs'.[159]

If Beatlemaniacs had engendered controversy, hippies and student radicals encountered almost universal condemnation. A 1969 *New Society* poll placed student unrest equal second in a list of undesirable changes during the 1960s and, for every person who told NOP in 1970 that they approved of hippies, ten more disapproved of them.[160] Counterculturalists, student revolutionaries and the Beatles in the late 1960s stood accused of an immaturity unexcused by youth alone. To columnist Anne Scott-James, childishness was of a piece with the selfishness displayed by drug users and by meditators such as the Beatles, whose quest for self-realisation was 'a way of opting out of responsibility' for others in society.[161] A *Mirror* editorial slammed McCartney for being 'one of the oldest teenagers on record' when he admitted taking LSD.[162] Literary critic Michael Wood discerned in Lennon's writings a form of arrested development shared by other sixties rebels:

The Beatles have by-passed adulthood, and this links them with the revolutionary students who are asking why they should grow up when growing up means napalm, treachery, compromise and Porton Down. For years we have sold maturity as a virtue, we have preached the careful ethic of the status quo. But the Beatles are nearly 30 and wildly successful on anyone's terms. If they haven't grown up yet, why should they now?[163]

Newspaper commentators used Epstein's drug overdose to damn the 'Summer of Love'. To the *Daily Express*' Alix Palmer, 'The Epstein Era' had begun with a 'great desire among the young to see something constructive happen to Britain' and ended with hippies fruitlessly seeking in 'Flower Power, freakouts, love-ins [and] transcendental meditation' something to fill their moral void.[164] The *Daily Mail*'s Godfrey Winn included hippies, the Beatles and the 'Dorian Gray'-like Epstein among 'The Rootless Ones'. Their indiscipline and egocentrism were more than self-destructive, he warned. If left to fester, flower power 'could end in the decline and fall of Britain, and all that our country has stood for in the past'.[165]

The Beatles' influence on students concerned traditionalists who looked to universities to reproduce cultural authority. John Sparrow at Oxford tied the Beatles' repudiation of Western civilisation with the appearance in quadrangles of 'sloppy, shaggy' wastrels.[166] To Rudolf Klein, it was Lennon's denigration of Beethoven that epitomised students' revolt against 'every established value and every traditional hero-figure'.[167] Peter Simple denounced a Cambridge student for elevating the Beatles to the same level as Beethoven. '[I]f the cult of Pop had taken hold only of the minds of the immature, the stupid and the uneducated, other people could afford to laugh', he argued. But for a student at an ancient university to embrace cultural relativism was a harbinger of 'cultural collapse'.[168]

Peace need not have been an unpopular cause for the Beatles to champion. There was perpetual fear of nuclear conflagration and sufficient public opposition to prevent British involvement in the Vietnam War.[169] It was also the one political cause of the Beatles which seemed to resonate with fans. 'Dear Humanity', wrote Clyndwr Chambers from Ramsgate:

Love is the key word and it seems that the only two people who are just human in this world today are Big Uncle John und Auntie Yoko. And if more people listened to them instead of mocking them all the time, we wouldn't have all this unhappiness, I'm sure of it.[170]

However, the Beatles' pacifism extended beyond Vietnam and nuclear disarmament to encompass all wars. Harrison and Lennon (but not McCartney) broke ranks over the two world wars in which many of their fellow citizens had fought.[171] In 1966, Harrison criticised the British public's nostalgia for 'their Churchills and their Montys' and their pride in having 'killed a few more Huns here or there'.[172] Lennon followed suit by appearing in *How I Won the War* (1967). Its assault on the memory of the Second World War seemed 'distressing' to film critic Dilys Powell and 'smug' to a correspondent to the *Daily Mail*, who pointedly asked 'Who enjoys war, Mr Lennon?'[173] In 1969, Lennon unrepentantly devised a skit for *Oh! Calcutta!* (1969) in which a group of masturbators climax at the mention of Winston Churchill. That same year, he attempted to change his middle name by deed poll from Winston to Ono and claimed that Britain had spawned leaders just as murderous as Hitler. He held Britain and Germany jointly responsible for instigating the Second World War and committing atrocities during it.[174] Such crass comments meant that his 1969 protest against the Vietnam and Biafra wars was unlikely to be taken seriously, even had he not added the flagging sales of 'Cold Turkey' (1969) to his reasons for returning the MBE. As it was, he invited reprimands not just from the usual sources but from his own relatives, who 'keep writing saying, alright, so you want peace, but you're not growing up yet'.[175]

Another line of attack on the Beatles' outspoken pacifism came from the increasingly militant counterculture. If 'All You Need Is Love' was an apt sentiment during the Summer of Love, it seemed hackneyed by the turn of the decade, when underground papers were asking for clemency for Charles Manson and the Angry Brigade.[176] John Hoyland accused Lennon in 1968 of ignoring the need to '[r]uthlessly destroy' existing structures and build anew.[177] Undeterred by Lennon's barb that he was 'on a destruction kick', Hoyland took on 'The End's' (1969) 'reactionary supposition' that love was a form of karma.[178] According to this logic, 'if your family is being burnt alive by napalm, it's your own fault for not loving people enough. Or, alternatively, if you do love them enough you won't mind these things happening to you'.[179] A pacifism so passive left oppression unchecked.

The Beatles' supporters offered several justifications of the Beatles' confrontational stances. The mildest defence was that they were entitled to speak their minds, as when Lennon sounded off about religion in 1966. 'Lennon has the right to propound whatever views he honestly holds on absolutely any subject', stated *Melody Maker*'s editorial on the controversy, while David Frost insisted that toleration of dissent was a hallmark of a 'civilised society'.[180] This 'live and let live' defence drew upon long-standing discourses of Britain as a land of liberty and tolerance.[181] At their most patronising, commentators placed the Beatles within another venerable national tradition: that of the harmless eccentric. Virginia Ironside's defence of the 'Poor Beatles' as 'fallible' individuals was echoed by confirmed reactionary Robert Pitman, who allowed that 'even their wrong turnings are all their own'.[182] Such expressions of sympathy did not commit commentators to support the Beatles' actions. The *Mirror*'s Don Short argued that Lennon and Ono should not be treated as 'freaks', even when it was hard to 'digest or accept' their baffling sayings and doings.[183]

A stronger claim was that the Beatles deserved a hearing as representatives of their generation. Desmond Morris nominated Lennon as 'Man of the Decade' on the grounds that he personified the ongoing 'rebellion of youth in the sixties'.[184] Tony Palmer portrayed them as generational 'spokesmen' and proffered 'Dig a Pony' (1970) of all songs as having captured 'the mood of young people at the beginning of the seventies'.[185] Attributing a leadership role to the Beatles cast them as neither eccentric nor typical, but pioneering. 'Thank God for individualists breaking new ground, seeking, searching, questioning', wrote the editor of *Honey*, Audrey Slaughter.[186] The Beatles' spiritual mentors imagined the Beatles' sway over youth in much the same terms as had Ronald Gibbins in the early 1960s. The Maharishi Mahesh Yogi saw them as 'lead[ing] … the young' and A. C. Bhaktivedanta Swami Prabhupāda informed Harrison, Lennon and Ono that 'if something is accepted by the leading persons, the ordinary persons follow'.[187]

Such elitist sentiments were captured in Peter Finch's poem in hippie magazine *Gandalf's Garden*, which contrasted the ignorant to the enlightened:

the Beatles preach meditation
thru the wires and waves of mass media,
smiling guru's [sic],
perhaps the people will listen
and perhaps they won't.
They've ignored their previous chances thru the years, thru the decades, thru the
     centuries.
And they're still not quite ready … yet.[188]

Finch's pious hope that the populace would become 'illuminated' was not shared by the Beatles' staunchest defenders, who portrayed ordinary people as 'sheep-like', 'mindless' and 'revolting'.[189] The most extreme reaction came from Apple press officer Derek Taylor, who responded to the 'persecution' of Lennon and Ono with the novel public relations strategy of waging 'war with the Outside World'.[190] Taylor argued that Lennon was not a 'common man' and therefore unaccountable to any 'Normal Human'.[191] Suspending all 'critical reasoning', he criticised anyone who criticised Lennon.[192] His Manichean world view distinguished between 'naughty and nice people': the 'daft' and the Elect, 'grownups' and youth, the 'glum' and the fun, the selfish materialism exhibited by 'most people … for most of history' and the Beatles' 'mode of goodness'.[193]

The *Beatles Book* advanced all three defences of the Beatles as individuals, representatives and leaders in order to rationalise their increasingly trying behaviour. Its editor Sean O'Mahony kept to himself his misgivings about 'their "hairy" period', drug use and refusal to tour while doing his best to placate the readership.[194] The titles of three articles from 1967 – 'Why Did They Grow Moustaches?', 'Recording: Why It Takes So Long Now' and 'Is *Sgt. Pepper* Too Advanced for the Average Pop Fan to Appreciate?' – suggested fans were in a mutinous state.[195] The magazine parried fans' objections to facial hair and hippie garb by stating that 'each Beatle wears what he wants to wear and changes from day to day'.[196] Their slower pace of recording was put down to their perfectionism and their experimentation was not 'gimmicky' but an adventurous desire 'to do different things every time'.[197]

The *Beatles Book* aligned the Beatles to their generation in its article by Steve Turner about how fans such as himself had 'changed and grown up' alongside the band.[198] A 1968 editorial preferred to depict the Beatles as thought leaders when explaining why they 'always meet a lot of opposition when they put forward their revolutionary new ideas'.[199] Lennon's adventures with Ono presented the magazine with its trickiest PR task. 'Maybe there are things we don't understand', conceded a valedictory 1969 article, but that was testament to Lennon's originality and boldness. The article concluded that 'what being a real fan is all about' was not a matter of appreciating Lennon's every action, or the idiosyncrasies of the other band members.[200] True fans distinguished themselves from fair-weather ones by 'bear[ing] up in face of the laughter, the sneering'.[201] However, fans who wrote into the *Beatles Book* displayed more condescension than stoicism. 'Thank you so much for ... knocking sense into such an IGNORAMIC shower!' wrote Lennon Maniac No. 136649 after her hero was barracked by his fellow guests and a 'half-witted audience' on *The Eamonn Andrews Show* in 1969.[202]

Reaction

The Beatles enjoyed increasingly tetchy relations with the popular press in the late 1960s. To some extent, newspapers simply engaged in the same process of demythologisation undertaken by the Beatles themselves. A band which declared that 'we are pricks sometimes' could not reasonably complain when journalists seconded the motion.[203] Nor could the Beatles expect universal acceptance for their increasingly unconventional lives and art. Although Lennon justifiably detected racism and sexism in press coverage of Ono, a white English male conceptual artist given to screaming and exhibitionism who campaigned for Black Power and on behalf of convicted murderers would also attract widespread criticism, as he was to discover.[204]

The *Mail*'s later coverage of the Beatles pointed to another motive besides disillusionment and prejudice: the popular press's habit of knocking down what it had once built up. Whether or not following editorial orders, four *Mail* columnists who had been supportive during Beatlemania turned on the Beatles in the late 1960s. Anne Scott-James, who had declared the band to be 'clever and likeable' in 1963, chided McCartney for being 'fatuous' and callous in 1967 when claiming that Indians were 'laughing and smiling' as they starved.[205] Vincent Mulchrone found it hard to reconcile the 'pandered, primped, preening, pony-tailed' Lennon of 1969 with the 'quiet, composed, relaxed' foursome he had encountered in

1963.[206] The 'characteristic modesty' he had praised in 1965 had been eclipsed by 'arrogant presumption'.[207] Godfrey Winn (inaccurately) claimed to be the first national journalist to have praised the Beatles and had been friendly with George Martin in the early days. But in 1967 he took Epstein's death to be a judgement on the counterculture's aimlessness, contempt for 'ordinary decent behaviour' and refusal to 'assume any of the responsibilities of adult citizenship'.[208] Lennon's Amsterdam Bed-In and Harrison's conviction on drug charges in 1969 made him lament that 'wealth ... fame and ... adulation' had turned 'four charming, unspoilt young men' into objects of 'disillusionment and dislike'.[209] Virginia Ironside ran yearly obituaries from 1967 onwards for the Beatles she had known at the start of their fame. *Sgt. Pepper* prompted her to address the question of 'What's happening to the Beatles?' by juxtaposing an early photograph taken when they were 'everybody's next-door neighbour' with one showing the 'shrouded weirdies' of today.[210] In August 1968, she wrote of her disappointment over how each Beatle had turned out. Starr had degenerated into a 'Family Entertainer' and Harrison was to be found 'sitting cross-legged and writing pretentious songs'. Lennon no longer resembled the 'cynical, down-to-earth' character she had once adored, leaving only McCartney as a relatively 'untarnished' figure, albeit one who was incapable of singlehandedly arresting the decline.[211] In October 1969, images from what turned out to be their final photo shoot led her to surmise that 'The Beatles are Dead'.[212]

Whereas the Beatles had once been disparaged *de haut en bas*, their psychedelic phase provoked press critics to attack them from a populist angle as conceited and out of touch. In the *Sunday Express*, Hogg attributed their insensitivity to 'the needs and aspirations and suffering of ordinary men and women' to wealth, egotism, drugs and meditation.[213] Evidence of elitism was provided by *The Sun* in the Gypsy-influenced paint job of Lennon's Rolls Royce, which it interpreted as 'a public raspberry being blown loudly and continuously by the young and famous owner of a lot of money'.[214]

Jaundiced reporting about the Beatles in the popular press in the late 1960s was offset in part by their increasing coverage in broadsheets and other august publications. As Chapter 4 will explore in further detail, features and reviews concerning the Beatles became mainstays of the arts pages, while the *Sunday Times*' decision to publish extracts of Hunter Davies' *The Beatles: The Authorised Biography* (1968) was something of a media sensation. However, heavyweight critics were often highly critical of the band and Davies' biography provoked a backlash against its subjects, author and serialiser. The *Sunday Times*' advance publicity characterised the biography as a warts-and-all account which would 'make the Beatles more enemies than friends'.[215] Its predictions were borne out by reviews of the book which, as Jonathan Gould notes, 'found it hard to reconcile their admiration for the Beatles' music with the unflattering portraits of their personalities that emerged' in Davies' interviews.[216] This did not prevent criticism of Davies as being a fanboy writing 'press agents' handouts' and of the *Sunday Times* for 'cheapen[ing]' itself by publishing celebrity fluff.[217] When the *Observer* attempted to scoop the *Sunday Times* by running excerpts from Julius Fast's unofficial biography, eminent journalist Francis Williams was left incredulous:

> Who would have thought to see the day when the two heavies would be slugging it out for the shillings of the well-heeled intelligentsia with life stories of the Beatles as their principal weapons?[218]

The band's fall from grace is captured in press coverage from August 1968. At this point, there had been no single since 'Lady Madonna' in March and no long-player since the *Magical Mystery Tour* double EP the previous December. The poor reception of the *Magical Mystery Tour* television special had been followed by their trip to Rishikesh, the Lennons' separation, the release of the *Yellow Submarine* film and the closure of the Apple Boutique. The headlines provoked during this comparative lull in activity – 'Why Does Nobody Love The Beatles?', 'Nothing Left to Scream About', 'One Boob Too Many', 'Is It All Up for the Turds?' – seemed out of proportion to events.[219] Their single 'Hey Jude'/'Revolution', released on 30 August, sold in the region of a million copies in Britain, defying predictions that it would shift under a third that number.[220]

The growing disenchantment with the Beatles in the late 1960s was acknowledged by all sides. Their fan magazine characterised them as 'reviled, put down, hated' for their experimentation.[221] Sympathetic journalists like Alan Walsh and Ray Connolly held 'Fleet Street' in general and 'middle-aged pundits and columnists' in particular responsible for inciting Beatlephobia.[222] Unsympathetic ones charged that the Beatles had no one but themselves to blame that their 'love affair with the British public should be ending fast, in disillusionment and dislike'.[223] Some of the most poignant reactions came from fans writing to the *Beatles Book*. 'Dear Beatles, I feel very sorry for you at the moment!' exclaimed Joanna Thomson in Edinburgh a year later in response to 'all the destructive Press articles and rumours floating around at the moment'.[224] The first letters addressing criticism of this kind concerned McCartney's admission of LSD use.[225] Thereafter they mainly defended Lennon[226] and his activities with Ono.[227]

By 1969, the attacks appeared unrelenting. '[Q]uit knocking, knockers', pleaded 'A loyal Beatles fan', who perceived the forces of 'Press, TV, and most of the older generation (over 30s)' ranged against his favourites.[228]

This 'big cloud of anti-Beatle matter' fostered a siege mentality within the Beatles.[229] Starr blamed media bias. 'They only print the crap', he complained in 1967: 'They don't print the nice things.'[230] Harrison and Lennon's persecution complexes made them envisage the entire nation to be against them. 'It's only Britain that doesn't seem to like the Beatles', stated Harrison in March 1969; 'Britain appreciates us least', agreed Lennon a month later.[231]

The public relations strategies adopted by McCartney and Lennon in the late sixties were profoundly counterproductive. McCartney had hitherto been the most approachable Beatle, so his sudden reticence and stays in the Scottish Highlands stoked rumours that 'Paul Is Dead'.[232] As McCartney withdrew from Apple's day-to-day affairs and decamped to the Mull of Kintyre, Lennon and Ono often gave several interviews a day and embarked on a series of attention-seeking ventures in the name of consciousness-raising and transparency.[233]

The common ground between McCartney's reclusiveness and Lennon's exhibitionism was their refusal to continue the Epstein-era 'grinnings at nothings'.[234] Each asserted the right to say and do as they pleased even at the cost of disappointing their supporters and consequently faced similar charges of egotism and elitism. McCartney incurred further reputational damage when resurfacing in April 1970. The 'self-interview' he released to promote his solo album made him appear responsible for breaking up the Beatles. The following month the underground paper *Frendz* cited his refusal to give interviews, participate in Apple or work with Lennon as evidence that '[e]verything has been perfectly arranged to cut him off finally and completely from the people, his public'.[235] Lennon's many exhibitions, demonstrations and provocations in league with Ono were equally off-putting and left him overexposed and under attack. The *Mirror* accused him of turning Japanese, pronounced him 'Clown of the Year' and publicised a 'work-in' conducted by factory workers in Orpington as a riposte to his and Ono's 'lie-in'.[236] Whereas papers had once emphasised the affinity between the Beatles and working people by running stories about Beatle-inspired industrial action, they now contrasted the industriousness of the many with the indolence and self-indulgence of the few. It was a curious situation in which the poster boys of sixties Britain now found themselves.

Sex and Drugs

Figure 3.2 Deviants – John Lennon and Yoko Ono leave court after being charged with possession of marijuana, October 1968. Photo by Bettmann/Getty Images

The previous chapter examined how reactions to the Beatles receiving MBEs encapsulated their social impact during the era of Beatlemania. Their subsequent transgressions meant that much the same role was performed in the late sixties by the issues of sex and drugs. Public discussion of such matters had evolved rapidly since the beginning of their recording career. In 1963, when Beatlemania took on national proportions, *Melody Maker* elicited diverse opinions from musicians in response to the question 'Should a pop singer discuss teenage sex problems in public?'[237] It raised the problem of 'Sex in Songs' shortly afterwards in response to the faint innuendo of Mitch Murray compositions such as 'How Do You Do It?' (1963), a song the Beatles had turned down for being too twee.[238] Their anodyne earlier lyrics gave prudes little to complain about, though one or two detected double entendres in 'From Me to You' (1963) and 'A Hard Day's Night' (1964).[239]

Epstein apparently instructed the Beatles not to discuss their 'love lives [and] ... sexual preferences' and journalists had the tact not to ask.[240] As editor of *Disc* and *Melody Maker*, Ray Coleman 'used discretion when secrets were either unimportant to the public or impolitic to reveal for the sake of the Beatles or their families'.[241] The Beatles' affairs and one-night stands were accordingly unknown even to their wives and girlfriends in the early sixties, and the public remained oblivious to the baseless paternity suits dogging McCartney in Liverpool and Hamburg.[242] Epstein's homosexuality also remained unreported during his lifetime and for some years afterwards in Britain, long after it had been openly discussed in the American press.[243]

Sexual discussions of the early 1960s were therefore more likely to focus on Beatlemaniacs than on the Beatles themselves. Some of their detractors noted that fandom reached fever pitch when 'the performers start whirling their bodies about in very peculiar manners'.[244] But most writers initially gave the Beatles the benefit of the doubt and distinguished between the 'freshness and innocence' of the band and the unseemly lust of their fans.[245] Editorials in the *Daily Express* and *Daily Mirror* explicitly contrasted the Beatles to the sexual 'laxity' of the Swedes and entertainers who 'rely on off-colour jokes about homos'.[246] Although the *Observer* reported in 1963 that older fans credited the Beatles for being 'crude but direct about sex instead of sly and sentimental', they were soon outstripped in this regard by the trouser-splitting antics of P. J. Proby and the serial provocations of the Rolling Stones.[247] The Stones were duly credited by *Melody Maker* in 1965 for spearheading a permissive 'Avant Garde' of musicians who 'short-circuit conventional behaviour, wear far-out clothes and clamour for freedom of expression'.[248] The Beatles went unmentioned.

The sexual behaviour of pop stars off-stage (the worst of which has subsequently been exposed by investigations of historic child abuse) began to be discussed openly in the second half of the 1960s. Early hints came in a *Melody Maker* article published in 1965, which contended that girls 'know perfectly well that they aren't going to play *Monopoly*' when accompanying pop stars back to their hotel rooms.[249] The article nonetheless rejected as a 'sickening prejudice' any notion that musicians were 'morally more lax and abandoned' than other young people. Baby boomers were having more premarital sex than their parents' generation, and pop stars simply had more chance to sow their wild oats.[250] *Melody Maker* took the same line when countering the depiction of musicians as 'sex-happy gorillas' in such *romans à clef* as Thom Keyes' *All Night Stand* (1966) and Jenny Fabian and Johnny Byrne's *Groupie* (1969).[251]

Lennon took the lead in associating the Beatles with sexual permissiveness, especially in his extra-curricular activities. His books offered an early insight into his id, and critics noted that *A Spaniard in the Works* (1965) was ruder than *In His Own Write* (1964). His lyrics became explicit later, with 'I Am the Walrus' (1967) becoming the first Beatles song to be censored on sexual grounds.[252] The themes of nudity and obscenity featured strongly in Ono's art and were amplified by Lennon as soon as they became a couple. His penis granted an interview to *IT*, starred in the film *Self Portrait* (1969) and appeared with Ono in a full-frontal photo on the cover of *Unfinished Music I: Two Virgins* (1968).[253]

By contemporary reckoning, John Lennon's infidelity was immoral and his brazen desertion of Cynthia Lennon for Yoko Ono deserving of censure.[254] Lennon and Ono were publicly shamed in their first appearances as a couple in spring 1968, first by being refused permission as adulterers to plant acorns in consecrated ground, then when facing press catcalls of 'Where's your wife?' at the first night of the National Theatre's adaptation of *In His Own Write* (1968).[255] Their reputation plummeted still further that autumn. In the space of a month they were charged with possession of drugs (see Fig. 3.2), cited as guilty party and co-respondent in the Lennons' divorce proceedings and pilloried for the nude cover of *Two Virgins*. The double album *The Beatles* (1968) was released a day after Ono miscarried their illegitimate child.[256] Not one to shun controversy, Lennon's contributions to the album included songs referring to masturbation and nudity as well as a photograph and sketch of himself and Ono undressed.

If Lennon's infidelity seemed unseemly, news of the Beatles' drug habits was scandalous. They had used recreational drugs since their Hamburg days, but were long shielded from exposure by the naïveté of many journalists and the discretion of their inner circle. By the second half of the sixties, the Beatles found it increasingly difficult to keep their drug-taking to themselves because of the changing drug scene, mounting public awareness and their own outspokenness. In the fifties and early sixties, concerns about drug-taking within popular music had focused on jazz. Exposés of amphetamine use brought young club-goers under scrutiny in 1963–4, but left the Beatles untouched. '[A]udience response is their only stimulant drug', Epstein declared in his 1964 autobiography.[257] The music papers initially dismissed rumours of drug use among popular musicians as exaggerated and preju-diced, much the same line they took towards allegations of sexual misconduct.[258] In 1966, however, Donovan was filmed, and subsequently convicted for, using marijuana and Pete Townshend stated that 'everyone takes' hashish.[259] That August, *Melody Maker* coined the term 'Drug Rock' to describe the growing number of records which featured druggy lyrics, psychedelic artwork and musical evocations of trips.[260]

Politicians, the police and the mainstream press became increasingly aware of and alarmed by drug use by pop musicians and their associates in the counterculture. The missionising efforts of the World Psychedelic Centre led in quick succession to a raid, sensationalist stories about 'The Drug That Is Menacing Young Lives' and the outlawing of LSD in 1966.[261] In January and February 1967, a *News of the World* series on 'Pop Stars and Drugs' exposed LSD use among musicians, including an inaccurate charge against Mick Jagger. Jagger's attempt to silence all discussion of his drug use by suing the *News of the World* for libel backfired spectacularly when the paper instigated a bust. The ensuing trial of Jagger, his bandmate Keith Richards and the gallery owner Robert Fraser indelibly associated pop music and drugs.[262]

Meanwhile, the Beatles were dropping increasingly heavy hints about their own drug habits. 'Tomorrow Never Knows' (1966) was by no means the first time they had smuggled drug references into their songs, but lyrics which paraphrased the infamous Timothy Leary invited public scrutiny.[263] Whereas Kenneth Tynan congratulated the band on creating 'the best musical evocation of LSD I've ever heard', the conservative columnist Robert Pitman condemned the song for the same reason and a Birmingham doctor blamed it and other songs for a dramatic surge in acid consumption.[264] The Beatles' spokesman saw 'no reason to suspect' any connection with drugs in 'Tomorrow Never Knows', and the band affected innocence when the BBC banned 'A Day in the Life' the following year.[265]

Because most people knew little about drugs, and because even the band's cannabis smoking had been hitherto undisclosed, McCartney's sudden revelation of his LSD use in June 1967 was all the more shocking.[266] Only the month before, the *Beatles Book* had awarded a free subscription to a fan who had expressed pride that the Beatles had not got 'mixed up in this drugs business' and had singled out McCartney for being 'too sensible' to dabble. The Beatles' sponsorship of a *Times* advertisement calling for the decriminalisation of cannabis in July and Epstein's fatal overdose from prescription medication in August cemented the Beatles' notoriety as drug users second only to the Stones.

One defence of the Beatles' record on sex and drugs was to distinguish between their lives and art. *Melody Maker*'s Alan Walsh was exasperated by some of their activities, but he respected their privacy. Reminding his readers that the Beatles were 'really only a musical group and not the conscience of the nation', he counselled them to 'turn on the music. And forget the rest.'[267] The *Beatles Book* sometimes developed this line of argument into the libertarian case that an individual's personal life was his or her own affair. The Beatles had insisted that the magazine respect their privacy from the outset, and the only major airing of their personal relationships prior to the Lennons' separation came in a series of stage-managed visits to each of the Beatles' homes in 1967.[268] It attempted to hold the line in 1968 despite receiving a 'tremendous flood of letters' about McCartney's split from Jane Asher and Lennon's desertion of his wife.[269] The letters published that year argued that Lennon's 'private life should be kept exactly that'.[270] But Lennon and Ono's erasure of the distinction between public and private in their Bed-Ins, Bag-Ins and performance art tested this policy to destruction. The magazine published an open letter in March 1969 from three Geordie girls who asked 'Just how much are faithful Beatle fans expected to take?'[271] The publisher and editor Sean O'Mahony reached his own breaking point later that year over drugs. Having long waited in vain for the Beatles to realise how 'utterly stupid' they had been, he took it upon himself to denounce 'the pro-drug brigade' and close the magazine.[272]

Another argument advanced by the Beatles' defenders was to present them as performing a public service by pioneering alternative forms of thought, morality and community. *Melody Maker* placed them at the very 'vanguard of the drive towards liberation of the human spirit' and poet Adrian Mitchell thanked them for encouraging 'the average Englishman ... to explore what his body is for'.[273] Lennon's lewdness was accepted, if not exactly approved, by two of the major liberalisers of the age, Sir Hugh

Carleton Greene, Director-General of the BBC, and Sir John Trevelyan, Secretary of the British Board of Film Censors. 'I Am the Walrus' was not banned outright by the BBC, as Lennon later claimed.[274] In fact, some accounts maintain that it was Greene's refusal to excise it from the *Magical Mystery Tour* television special which contributed to his removal as Director-General.[275] His decision went against the recommendation of the incoming Chairman of the BBC, Lord Hill, who had been alerted to the song's reference to knickers by the moral crusader Mary Whitehouse. Greene won the battle by threatening to defy a direct order, but lost the war when pressured to announce his resignation the following year.[276] Trevelyan signalled his sympathy by defending the 'preposterous naked-ness' of the *Two Virgins* cover in 1968 and Lennon's right to exhibit explicit lithographs in 1970.[277] His outrage at police impounding Lennon's nude studies of Ono was unexpectedly echoed in the opinion columns of the *Daily Mail* and *Daily Express*. Bernard Levin put his loathing of the Beatles to one side when defending Lennon's right to artistic self-expression and Barbara Griggs expressed 'shock and dismay' not at Lennon's artworks but at their seizure by the police.[278]

Griggs' defence of Lennon was based on more than legal grounds. She viewed his nude studies of his wife as displaying a 'sensitivity and charm' sadly missing from most sexually explicit fare. 'Has our permissive society really reached the point at which anything goes except tender, conjugal love?' she wondered.[279] The art critic Nigel Gosling was less impressed by Lennon's artistic technique, but nonetheless welcomed how he treated sexuality with 'smiling relaxation'.[280] Drama critic Irving Wardle drew the same distinction between worthwhile ideas and inept execution in his review of *Oh! Calcutta!* The show was 'ill-written, juvenile and attention-seeking'. Yet it was important inasmuch as it used sensuality 'to bring people together by means of the last surviving natural link in urban culture'.[281]

The Beatles' drug-taking was also justified in terms of a new morality. McCartney and Harrison attested that LSD had led them to God and Epstein credited it with making him less angry and more self-aware. The 'new mood' created by psychedelic drugs among sixties youth led him to predict a future of 'gentleness, love and a desire for peace'.[282] Epstein's comments first appeared in a *Queen* feature about 'The Love Generation' which envisaged the drugs debate as part of a 'generation war' between 'the Establishment, determined to play the heavy father' on one side and 'the kids' and their leaders in the pop world on the other.[283] From Tony Palmer's perspective, the criminal charges and moral censure directed at

Lennon in 1968 were a case in point. His subjection to 'all that organised morality can throw at him' was part of society's determination to punish the Beatles. However evil they were made out to be, the Beatles were 'heroes' to him.[284]

Derek Taylor pled benefit of clergy in defence of Lennon and Ono's adultery, nudity and drug use in November 1968. Conventional morality did not apply to artists like them and 'anyone seeking to apply to John the values of Acacia Avenue is likely to become unstuccoed'.[285] Yet, according to music writer Chris Welch, it was precisely because 'the nation's dullards' were so inferior that they sought to cut the pop elite down to size. Welch blamed drug busts on the 'persecution of one section of society' by those envious of 'beauty, wealth, success and popularity'.[286] *IT* imagined the Harrisons and the authorities acting out these ascribed roles in the 'Free Theatre' of their drugs trial.[287]

Prudery accounted for some of the opposition to the Beatles' lifestyles. Their most implacable critics expressed a profound fear of sexuality as a disruptive force. John Sparrow confessed to a 'horror ... of the sheer, unadulterated physical side of sex'.[288] His denunciation of the 'animal appetites' on display in Lennon's portraits of Ono echoed the sentiments of colleague at All Souls Bryan Wilson, who feared the 'unsocialised primitive appetites' exhibited in and excited by youth culture.[289] At the same time, only someone as closeted as Sparrow could think that 'ALL sensuality is bad'.[290] Other Beatlephobes distinguished between a mature, monogamous and loving form of sexuality and the stunted, promiscuous and perverted variety. Christopher Booker saw the Beatles as epitomising an era which fetishised its amorality and abnormality through 'violations of order such as adultery, prostitution, transvestism, homosexuality, or incest'.[291]

Yet anti-permissiveness was based on much more than puritanism. The libertarian argument that people had a right to live as they pleased struck many commentators as selfish and anti-social. Hogg predicted the end of democracy if society permitted everyone to 'do what we like in the privacy of our own homes'.[292] He shared Anne Scott-James' fear that the Epicurean pursuit of 'individual happiness' threatened social cohesion and responsibility.[293] The Beatles' liberties accordingly had to be weighed against their family obligations. The ordinarily liberal agony aunt Marjorie Proops pointed to the 'abysmal sorrow' caused to loyal wives deserted by caddish husbands such as John Lennon.[294] Lennon's fitness as a husband and father was questioned further in 1971 custody proceedings brought by Ono's former husband Tony Cox. Cox accused Lennon of having 'seduced my wife and got her on drugs' and of having shared a bath with Kyoko, his daughter with Ono. 'I think it is immoral for a daughter to see her father in the nude, at any age', he argued.[295]

Accusations of irresponsibility and escapism undercut claims that drugs elevated the Beatles to a higher moral plane. The Catholic Auxiliary Bishop of Westminster spoke out against 'indulging an appetite for "thrills"' through psychedelics, much as the Anglican Bishop of Southwark saw no virtue in 'seek[ing] a way to escape in transitory pleasures and drugs'.[296] The *Express* attributed Epstein's death to his seeking an 'easy way out' through drugs, and the rabbi officiating at his funeral service sanctimoniously pronounced him to be 'a symbol of the malaise of our generation', not its redemption.[297]

In addition to shirking their responsibilities by taking drugs and indulging their sexual appetites, the Beatles stood accused of encouraging others to do likewise as public figures. The Beatles' privileges carried with them the responsibility to act as role models to impressionable young fans. Promiscuity, infidelity, obscenity and illegality set the worst possible example. Exposure of the Beatles' drug use in 1967 generated concerns about their influence over the young. In May, the BBC banned 'A Day in the Life' lest it might 'encourage a permissive attitude to drug-taking'.[298] The *Mirror* editorialised against 'B[loody]F[ool]' Paul McCartney the following month, arguing that teenagers would not follow his example in taking LSD only because they had 'more sense' than him.[299] In July columnist Robert Pitman denounced *Sgt. Pepper* as 'propaganda' for drugs and Home Office minister Alice Bacon accused McCartney of 'trying to influence the minds of young people and ... encourage them to take drugs'.[300]

The most histrionic anti-permissives viewed sex, drugs and rock 'n' roll as threatening the social fabric. Music lecturer Edward Lee blamed pop for the breakdown of the nuclear family. The unrealistic expectations produced by romantic lyrics were 'perhaps the biggest single contributory fact to our rising divorce rate', while unmarried mothers owed their plight to pop's detrimental effect on their powers of reasoning and verbal communication.[301] David Holbrook expanded Lee's sexual critique to include drugs when claiming that an untold number of young people had 'died and suffered' from addiction, venereal disease and unwanted pregnancy thanks to pop's 'dehumanisation'.[302] In *The Pseudo-Revolution* (1972), he used *The Beatles Illustrated Lyrics* (1969, 1971) to demonstrate the interconnection between drug use and sexual abandon. The indecent images in the volume had to have been produced under the influence of narcotics.[303] They in turn incited viewers to take drugs in order to experience for themselves the 'intense larger-than-life sexuality' on display, creating a vicious cycle of exploitation and perversion.[304]

Critics did not accept that the band formed part of a persecuted minority or could plead exemption from the law on account of their art and fame. 'Why should there be a special law for the Beatles and a different one for everyone else?' asked journalist Geoffrey Winn in response to a lawyer's call for a 'close season' after the drug convictions of Lennon and the Harrisons.[305] Claims of a generational shift towards acceptance of drugs were rudely contradicted by polls and surveys. McCartney's confession that he had taken LSD prompted *Melody Maker* to conduct a straw poll of young people in June 1967. Of the 100 people surveyed, 2 were willing to take LSD, 7 knew someone who had tried it, 18 favoured decriminalising it and 37 thought McCartney right to own up.[306]

A more robust opinion poll conducted by ORC in June 1969 testified to the Beatles' simultaneous prominence and marginality at the close of the decade. Alongside the questions discussed in Chapter 2 about positive and negative sixties developments was one asking respondents 'Which one of these events was the most important to you personally?' The national sample of over 1000 adults selected the following options (see Table 3.1):

The Beatles' prominence accounted for their appearance in the poll. The designers of the survey included them as one of seven options instead of events of global significance such as the Chinese Cultural Revolution, the Vietnam War, the ousting of Nikita Khrushchev, the Prague Spring, the Sharpeville Massacre, Vatican II, the trial and execution of Adolf Eichmann, the Six-Day War, Martin Luther King's Lincoln Memorial

Table 3.1 The sixties event of greatest personal importance to respondents in 1969

Man going to outer space	39
The death of President Kennedy	29
The death of Churchill	14
The marriage of Princess Margaret	2
The success of the Beatles	1
The Profumo scandal	1
The *Lady Chatterley* trial	-
None of these	10
Don't know	4

Source: Opinion Research Centre for *New Society*, November 1969 (N=1071)[307]

speech and assassination, the first heart transplant, Woodstock and the death of Marilyn Monroe. Even allowing for the poll's British focus, the Beatles appeared at the expense of England's World Cup triumph, Harold Wilson's election victories, the end of conscription, the abolition of capital punishment, the liberalisation of the laws on abortion and male homosexuality, the Moors Murders, the re-emergence of sectarian conflict in Northern Ireland, the maiden flight of Concorde, Charles de Gaulle's veto of Britain's application to join the Common Market and the end of British rule over vast tracts of Africa, Asia and the Caribbean.

The band's marginality resulted in just 1 per cent of respondents feeling more personally invested in 'the success of the Beatles' than in the other available options. It is possible that the figure would have been slightly higher had the question been phrased slightly differently ('success' being undefined and open to dispute) or asked at a time other than June 1969. The Beatles had generated headlines in the first half of 1969 for an unreleased album, a makeweight soundtrack album, two unpopular weddings, two Bed-Ins, two experimental solo albums, two poorly reviewed film projects, a drugs bust, a shady new manager, a failed takeover bid, the announcement of no more tours and rumours of band schisms and impending bankruptcy. These events were unlikely to make respondents identify strongly with the Beatles, even when allowing for two chart-topping singles and a rare public performance earlier that year. Furthermore, the Beatles were one of four options shunned by respondents, together with Princess Margaret's marriage, the Profumo affair and the *Chatterley* trial. The only domestic event to make it into double figures was Churchill's death, largely thanks to those aged 65 and above. It was not just the Beatles who seemed marginal to British people at the end of the sixties; it was Britain itself.[308]

The poll is nevertheless a sobering reminder of the context in which the Beatles lived and worked. It indicated that ordinary people did not identify with contemporary discourses about Britain's cultural pre-eminence in the 'swinging sixties', or at least identified more with an American president and a space race which placed a human on the moon a few weeks later. Being successful and iconic did not make the Beatles generally liked or appreciated. They became more inextricably linked with the sixties after their break-up in 1970 as memories changed, controversies raged and myths formed about the decade. While they were together, they faced being belittled, misrepresented and dismissed. The next chapters explore the cultural and political impact of the Beatles in the febrile climate of Britain in the 1960s.

4 | Culture: The Beatles as Artists

Figure 4.1 Intellectuals – Lionel Bart, Osbert Lancaster and Yehudi Menuhin with guest of honour John Lennon at a Foyle's luncheon, April 1964. Photo by *Evening Standard*/Getty Images

Were the Beatles artists? The question first received sustained attention in an article by the *Times'* music critic William Mann in December 1963. It stated that Lennon and McCartney were 'composers' who exhibited similarities to Gustav Mahler and Peter Maxwell Davies, and referred to 'the Beatle quartet' as if it bore comparison with the Amadeus or Végh.[1] The question acquired new meaning with the release of *Sgt. Pepper*, which was pronounced by theatre critic Kenneth Tynan to be a work of genius and 'Britain's most important contribution to the arts in 1967'.[2] And it implied something different still when Lennon and Ono were widely ridiculed in the late sixties for their experiments in conceptual art, performance, cinema, installations and lithography.[3]

From this one question regarding the artistry of the Beatles flowed scores more concerning the medium, genre, performance, composition, creation, reception, dissemination, evaluation and social context of popular music. Could art emerge from the hit parade? Was pop in competition with jazz and folk or did artistic recognition accorded to one benefit the rest? Was classical music inherently more artistic than other kinds? Were the Beatles' musical abilities a match for their songwriting? Were song lyrics poetry? Was the complexity of their later lyrics a sign of sophistication, pretension or drug-induced hallucination? Were their literary allusions homage, montage, pastiche or theft?

Who was primarily responsible for any artistry in the Beatles' recordings: the songwriters, the performers, the arranger or the producer? Did artistic intention matter? Would artists appear in pantomime or incite the passions of teenagers? Had they succeeded in translating their musical artistry to the fields of writing, acting, film-making and visual art? What did Yoko Ono mean by describing herself as a con artist?[4] Were the Beatles modernist, anti-modernist, postmodernist, primitivist or something else entirely?

Were artists born or made? What was the value of training, originality and authenticity? Assuming the Beatles were artists, were they great artists, even geniuses? What was the likelihood of two geniuses meeting as teenagers at a provincial church fete? Could you bop to art or scream at artists? Were 11-year-old girls better judges of quality than middle-aged men of letters? Had the Beatles replaced an unsophisticated audience with a discerning one in the late 1960s? Should the Beatles feature in newspapers' cultural coverage, television art programmes and radio stations devoted to serious music? Should the state counteract the Beatles' influence through teaching and subsidising unpopular culture?

Who decided who was and was not an artist? Was there still an agreed definition of art or was art simply in the eye of the beholder? Were formal musicology and literary criticism suited to the analysis of pop songs? Could high culture be popular? Could the insights of Matthew Arnold, F. R. Leavis and Theodor Adorno explain the relationship between culture, society and the economy exemplified by the Beatles? Did capitalism, democracy and mass communications help or hinder artistic creation and appreciation? Did the Beatles' ascendancy spell doom for Christendom and Western civilisation?

All of these questions were raised by the Beatles' cultural impact in 1960s Britain, which is the subject of this chapter. As Paul Gleed has noted, most analysis has considered the matter from the Beatles' perspective by seeking to discover 'when did the Beatles get all artsy?'[5] Mark Lewisohn's full answer will come in later volumes of his magisterial biography, but he has already identified 'their compelling urge to move on fast, to innovate and progress' as one of their defining characteristics from the Liverpool days onwards.[6] Matthew Schneider regards Lennon and McCartney's early compositions as evidence of their interest in exploring 'the personally expressive potential of the pop song' from the outset.[7] Kenneth Womack sees the artistic themes of authorship, nostalgia and irony which appear in their first recordings continuing throughout their recording career.[8] However, his narrative takes account of their 'self-conscious redefinition of themselves and their art' in the second half of the 1960s.[9] His characterisation of 'Penny Lane'/'Strawberry Fields Forever' (1967) as a 'pure work of art' chimes with Mark Hertsgaard's observation that the Beatles came to produce 'high art for the mass public'.[10] The question of whether the Beatles of the late 1960s can be classified as pioneering postmodernist artists has been explored by Gleed, Fredric Jameson, Kenneth Gloag and Ed Whitley.[11]

This chapter is not concerned with the extent to which the Beatles were artists or considered themselves to be so, but with whether they were regarded as such by their contemporaries in sixties Britain. Three existing explanations make the case for early acceptance, accreditation and rejection. They correspond to the three events mentioned above: Mann's 1963 article, the impact of *Sgt. Pepper* and the critical reception accorded to Lennon and Ono. Mann was not the first critic to rank the Beatles alongside classical composers; art critic David Sylvester had likened them to Monteverdi on the BBC the previous month.[12] But Mann's formal musicological analysis of their compositions, when combined with the *Times*' reputation as the paper of record, made his article a story in itself and seemed part of a trend when ballet critic Richard Buckle declared Lennon, McCartney and Harrison to be 'the greatest composers since Beethoven' in that week's *Sunday Times*.[13]

The early-acceptance model found favour in early writing on the Beatles. It appears in some of the first rock criticism, with Nik Cohn contending that Lennon 'trapped the intellectuals' by publishing volumes of comic prose and verse in 1964 and 1965.[14] In 1970, Lennon credited 'bullshitter' Mann for having 'got people talking about us in that intellectual way ... going, "Ooh, aren't they clever?"'.[15] The following year historian Arthur Marwick cited Mann's and Buckle's articles as evidence that the Beatles had conquered 'all sections of British society' by 1963, in an early rendering of Marwick's 'cultural revolution' thesis.[16] Ulf Lindberg provides a variation on the argument by suggesting that the 'intellectual appreciation' of popular music evident in Mann's piece and reviews of Lennon's work 'prevailed only during a rather short period, whereupon it more or less disappeared'.[17] The model has latterly been given a pejorative slant by Oded Heilbronner who, following in the tradition of New Left cultural criticism, argues that English popular musicians including the Beatles won acceptance from elites as 'consensual, anti-revolutionary phenomena mixing musical experimentation with conservatism, which modelled themselves on the cultural codes of the English middle class'.[18]

The second model sees the Beatles as achieving cultural accreditation in the second half of the 1960s. This is partly due to their increasing musical sophistication,[19] but in Bernard Gendron's influential account their accreditation is secured by key interventions from 'literary critics and musicologists ... and pundits from mass magazines' which focused on *Sgt. Pepper*.[20] Gendron sees the Beatles' 'acquisition of the status of "artist" as opposed to "entertainer"' as furthering the broader ambitions of young music writers to identify an elevated category of white male 'rock' music and assert their authority over its evaluation. The negative consequences of the Beatles' accreditation are explored by Elijah Wald in *How the Beatles Destroyed Rock 'n' Roll* (2009). He blames their 'complex artistic experimentation' for helping to resegregate American music between black dance music and cerebral white 'rock'.[21] Exhibit A is the creation and reception of *Sgt. Pepper*, described by George Martin as 'classical/rock crossover music that tore down the snobbery-sodden barriers that exist between the two types'.[22] Arthur Calder-Marshall's claim in 1968 that 'the Beatles have grown to command the respect of intellectuals' gained credence from their increasing visibility in polite company.[23] McCartney fondly recalled conversations at Ken Tynan's parties between 'a Beatle, a playwright, a novelist, an actress, an opera singer, a ballet dancer' as being integral to what 'made London *Swinging London*'.[24]

The third model, that of outright rejection, was advanced by the Beatles' publicist Derek Taylor in 1969 when berating 'all the fat and weary intellectuals' who condescended to the Beatles.[25] Taylor was writing in reaction to a televised spat between Lennon, Ono and the violinist Yehudi Menuhin over pacifism. Lennon was indeed the Beatle most criticised by his contemporaries and, in turn, the most critical of them. 'They don't take it seriously in England', he complained in 1969, referring to his recordings with the Beatles and collaborations with Ono.[26] He justified his decision to emigrate in 1971 on the grounds that he and Ono were 'treated like artists' in America but as mere celebrities at home.[27] Oblique support for this thesis comes from David Fowler's work on attacks on the Beatles by intellectuals in the *New Statesman* in 1963–4 and *Black Dwarf* in 1968–9.[28]

This chapter argues that each of these models offers a partial explanation of the Beatles' critical reception in 1960s Britain. The first section, which focuses on the Beatlemania era, suggests that the unparalleled attention paid to the band and its fans did not signal widespread early acceptance. On the contrary, novelist Anthony Burgess argued that it was precisely because 'Beatle drivel' was 'low [and] corrupting' that it deserved to be exposed.[29] Besides needing to produce copy, public intellectuals such as Burgess felt duty-bound to provide perspective and judgement on a matter of widespread concern. If the early-acceptance model does not account for the hostility initially facing the Beatles, nor does it explain the equivocation of their first supporters. Mann qualified his praise for the Beatles' music with patronising comments about their fans and pop music as a whole, while Buckle's comparison to Beethoven was facetious in intent.

Neither accreditation nor rejection fully captures the wide-ranging discussions about the cultural value of the Beatles in the later 1960s. The second half of the chapter highlights the divided reception of the Beatles' experiments in words, music and side projects, with *Sgt. Pepper* being a case in point. Producing an album 'to be listened to, rather than danced to' represented a breakthrough to musicologist Wilfrid

Mellers.[30] Yet some primitivist music critics denounced *Sgt. Pepper* for the same reason – that it appealed to the head rather than the feet and heart – while the music press more generally assessed the album in terms of its entertainment value.[31] Mann's recollection that his fulsome review of *Sgt. Pepper* 'made a lot of people very angry' indicates that the band's usual critics remained unmoved by the album.[32]

Further evidence against wholesale accreditation comes from the lumin-aries in other cultural fields who socialised with McCartney in the second half of the 1960s. While he recalled 'cross-fertilising' with enthusiasm, more than half of those he mentioned meeting by name were on occasion scathing about the Beatles.[33] They included novelist and barrister John Mortimer, who mocked the band for imbibing the Maharishi's 'Spirit of Universal Truth', and Kenneth Tynan, who doubted whether Harrison 'should think himself a poet' when unversed in English literary tradition.[34] Comedian Kenneth Williams surpassed himself in waspishness when dis-paraging Lennon and Ono's 'great foolishness' in 1969. He described Ono as 'Asiatic' and Lennon (whom he misidentified as 'Ringo Star' [sic]) as a singer in name only whose appearance was utterly 'grotesque'.[35] Playwright Arnold Wesker was the most complicated case. He took hand-outs from the Beatles for his Centre 42 arts project, then publicly criticised them for not doing more. In the same month that he described their cultural standing as symptomatic of the 'intellectual and emotional med-iocrity' in 1960s Britain, he chose 'Eleanor Rigby' (1966) as one of his *Desert Island Discs*.[36]

Whereas the first two models of early acceptance and accreditation underestimate opposition to the Beatles' cultural contribution, the third model of rejection overestimates it. Lennon's was a defensive reaction towards the unflattering reviews he and Ono had received for their various artistic collaborations. The couple's collaborative work displeased not only diehard opponents of popular culture, but also otherwise sympathetic critics who championed the Beatles' artistry in populist and anti-modernist terms. Characteristically, Lennon contra-dicted himself when claiming in 1970 that 'all the middle classes and intellectuals' followed Mann's lead in acclaiming the Beatles back in 1963.[37]

This chapter's findings diverge in part from these three models due to its different methodology. While Fowler views the Beatles almost exclusively from the perspective of their detractors, here the statements of such figures are contextualised within the full spectrum of contem-porary opinions on the band. For his part, Heilbronner cites almost no contemporaries who embraced the Beatles; in the single instance in which he lists primary sources in corroboration, two of the three references are untraceable.[38] Much of what makes Cohn's work so readable renders it unreliable. It is unabashedly subjective, his passion for 'genuine rock 'n' roll' leading him to dismiss all more complex fare from the late sixties.[39] More 'cynical' by his own account are his tactics of 'slagging the Beatles' as a sure-fire way to cause a 'mild sensation', and of fabricating quotations on the grounds that musicians are 'so dumb they need to be misquoted'.[40]

Bernard Gendron is a much more careful researcher, which paradoxically sits at odds with his highly schematised account of accreditation. His main claim that 'all had changed' in American cultural attitudes towards the Beatles between 1964 and 1967 is undermined by the mixed reception accorded to *Sgt. Pepper*.[41] Against the 'torrent of accolades' for the album must be weighed the misgivings he notes among several prominent critics.[42] His focus on the accreditation of *Sgt. Pepper* also leads him to simplify developments after 1967. Jon Landau and Robert Christgau did not speak for 'the rock critics' as a whole and they pursued a line on the Beatles disputed by other major rock critics such as Jann Wenner, Ralph Gleason and Greil Marcus.[43] It was not the case that 'highbrow' interest in popular music 'last[ed] little more than one year and was directed almost exclusively at the Beatles'.[44] On the contrary, the late sixties saw the publication of the first scholarly American works on pop. They included Carl Belz's *The Story of Rock* (1969), which compared the Beatles' development of 'Rock as Fine Art' with that of Bob Dylan and Frank Zappa.[45] The appearance from 1968 to 1970 of at least a dozen American academic theses and journal articles on the Beatles does not square with Gendron's claim that the 'brash new academic field of cultural studies' arrived along with punk in 1976.[46]

Gendron's American model also maps poorly onto Britain. There is little evidence to support his suggestion that there was 'greater toleration of British high culture toward mass culture' than was the case in the United States.[47] The Beatles entered a British intellectual world so elitist and circumscribed within a 'London-Oxford-Cambridge Axis' that embracing popular culture, the provinces and lower classes was an act of dissidence exhibited by 'Angry Young Men'.[48] Wald's thesis is a vital intervention in the cultural politics of race in twentieth-century America, but has little applicability to Britain, where 0.7 per cent of the population was non-white in 1961 and where the Beatles were prominent advocates of multiculturalism.[49] Moreover, the British critical reception of the Beatles was affected by a particular configuration of cultural institutions. No American equivalent existed to the British monopoly in licensed radio, duopoly in television, arts subsidies and competition between Fleet Street titles, and the capacity of established music newspapers in Britain to develop rock criticism.

This chapter pairs sources produced by all these institutions with contemporary satire, academic writings and fan magazines to explore the cultural impact of the Beatles on sixties Britain. As with the previous chapters on society, it is divided chronologically into two sections: the first section dealing with the period of Beatlemania up to 1965, and the second section with the Beatles' later career until their dissolution in 1970. Materials published from 1971 to 1975 which consider the Beatles primarily as a band rather than as solo performers are also included in this later section.

Early Debates

There was little interest in pop music among the intelligentsia in the decade prior to Beatlemania. '[T]he abysmal ignorance of educated persons about the popular music of the millions' was so profound, according to Colin MacInnes in 1958, that he felt compelled to define 'pop' and 'disc' for his readers.[50] The occasional mentions of the subject appeared in wider discussions of youth culture by left-wing critics, who were as troubled by mass culture as had been Matthew Arnold in the 1860s and F. R. Leavis in the 1930s.[51] Richard Hoggart's unsparing depiction of the aimless Juke Box Boys found echo in subsequent critiques by Eric Hobsbawm and T. R. Fyvel, who proposed extending education into late adolescence in order to combat 'the commercial mass attack directed against youthful minds'.[52]

The principal charge against the music industry was that it was just that: an industry which manufactured and marketed culture no differently from baked beans.[53] Critics emphasised the mechanical nature of the whole record-making process: from the recording of electrical instruments and amplified vocals by 'engineers', through the manipulation of these sounds by a 'producer' at a mixing desk, to the publicity campaigns which channelled 'spontaneous teenage enthusiasms' into profits.[54] Callow stars managed by cynical Svengalis produced ersatz music enriching greedy executives using manipulative marketing to con gullible children out of pocket money.

Early claims for the Beatles' cultural worth did not challenge this analysis head-on. Instead, they followed Brian Epstein's line that the band transcended the 'specious values of the [entertainment] industry' by dint of their authenticity and talent.[55] He conceded in October 1963 that 90 per cent of pop was devoid of 'artistic merit', while claiming the Beatles' music to be 'definitely ... an art form'.[56] Music journalist William Mann concurred that the generality of pop deserved no critical attention in his seminal 1963 *Times* article. It was in his opinion 'a genre of music in danger of ceasing to be music at all', which made the 'distinctive and exhilarating flavour' of the Beatles' music all the more noteworthy.[57] The 'trademark ... submediant switches' of Lennon–McCartney compositions did not appear in their cover versions and were almost unknown in 'other pop repertoires'.[58] He accordingly rejected any comparison between the Beatles and the Dave Clark Five when 'Glad All Over' replaced 'I Want to Hold Your Hand' at number one in January 1964. The Dave Clark Five were 'just pops', he insisted: 'You can't talk about *their* pandiatonic clusters.'[59]

Another influential early analysis of the Beatles, Stuart Hall and Paddy Whannel's *The Popular Arts* (1964), likewise disqualified the lion's share of pop music from consideration as 'genuine popular art'.[60] Hall and Whannel readily acknowledged that 'assembly line' production techniques led to a dismaying lack of 'variety', 'integrity' and 'inner musical life' in pop when compared with jazz.[61] Such arguments were only to be expected given that Whannel co-authored a 1960 *New Left Review* article that vilified the hit parade for seeking to 'narrow our sympathies, blunt our sensibilities and trivialise our feelings'.[62]

As well as contrasting the Beatles with other pop musicians, sympathetic critics also distinguished between ordinary fandom and their own appreciation of the band. Mann disclaimed any interest in a craze 'which finds expression in handbags, balloons and other articles bearing the likenesses of the loved ones'.[63] Moreover, while teenagers preferred the Beatles' 'noisy items', Mann heaped particular praise on their slower numbers: 'This Boy' with its 'chains of pandiatonic clusters' and the 'Aeolian cadence' of 'Not a Second Time' (both 1963).[64] Hall and Whannel were no more enamoured than Mann with 'the disturbing elements of mass hysteria' on display in Beatlemania, although they allowed that Beatles concerts engendered a more direct relationship between singers and their audience.[65]

The Beatles' adulthood and maleness made them less alien to commentators ill-equipped to fathom the motives of bobby-soxers. So did their apparent wit and education, which Terry Eagleton considered to be their defining characteristic. He detected 'a quality of sceptical self-aware detachment' in their performances, compositions, punning name and even their hairstyles: all of which signalled in his view pop's ascendancy 'from secondary modern to grammar school'.[66] Education helped to explain their unusual compositional abilities, which elevated them from entertainers to creators according to their supporters. 'I've never met rock stars who were so concerned with their writing', noted Adrian Mitchell in February 1963, after Lennon and McCartney boasted to him that they had completed 100 songs and 'a couple of plays' before hitting the big time.[67] Tony Barrow's liner notes for their first LP argued that the Beatles' songwriting betokened a broader creative self-sufficiency. 'They write their own lyrics, design and eventually build their own instrumental backdrops and work out their own vocal arrangements', he stated: 'The do-it-yourself angle ensures complete originality at all stages of the process.'[68]

The Beatles' artistry received further attention with the publication of Lennon's *In His Own Write* in March 1964 and the cinematic release of *A Hard Day's Night* in July 1964. Both received more attention than Beatles records in highbrow periodicals, which had yet to conceive of a 'rock critic', still less to employ one. *A Hard Day's Night* took reviewers by surprise with its wit and invention. Once again sympathisers reconciled an admiration for the Beatles with their denigration of youth culture. '[W]hat seems [like] a century of claptrap from teenagers, disc jockeys, journalists, publicity men, sociologists, trendsetters, and trend-followers' did not detract from the quality of the film.[69]

The audacity of a pop star trying his hand at literature ensured that *In His Own Write* caught the attention of intellectuals.[70] The book's credentials were burnished by being issued by a copper-bottomed publishing house, Jonathan Cape, and certified as 'marvellous stuff' by a 'stalwart body of critics and publishers' in advance of its publication.[71] The launch party was a star-studded occasion, as was the luncheon staged in Lennon's honour by Foyle's bookshop on the quatercentenary of Shakespeare's birth (see Fig. 4.1). Heavyweight reviewers were assigned to assess the book's merits, including Kenneth Allsop, John Willett, Adrian Mitchell, Hilary Corke and Jonathan Miller.

The early attention accorded to the Beatles did not, however, translate into ready acceptance of their cultural stature. There was no shortage of traditionalists, sceptics and assorted naysayers in the early sixties for whom the Beatles simply reinforced existing prejudices about popular culture in general and pop music in particular. Leavisites, Marxists and diehard Arnoldians united in their excoriation of the manufacturing and marketing of the Beatles. Music lecturer Donald Hughes saw the Beatles as corroborating his thesis that 'mass-produced pop' was an escapist and exploitative medium, and Roy Nash hypothesised that the music industry had perfected in the Beatles its 'hypnotic campaigns' to sell its wares.[72] 'Liverpool may have produced the Beatles, but Denmark Street is responsible for Beatlemania', concluded the jazz musician Humphrey Lyttleton.[73]

The Beatles' noise-making was so unrefined, according to Eric Hobsbawm, that it was best characterised not as 'music' but as a 'sound' which '[a]nyone can produce'.[74] The worthlessness of their music formed the basis of a legal challenge by the Cinematograph Exhibitors' Association against the Performing Rights Society. The cinema owners and concert promoters maintained that pop shows were 'entertainments' rather than musical performances because the music was of secondary importance to the act. According to their barrister Duncan Ranking, pop

consists of a rhythmic and monotonous beat, and while it is being played, the performers sing or hum into the microphone. In some instances they play the fool on the stage, grimacing and dancing, and they are often dressed in an unusual and outlandish way.[75]

That the Beatles were uppermost in Ranking's mind became clear when he described the audience's reaction. 'Instead of sitting quietly and attentively as they would if they were listening to a symphony by Beethoven', he said, 'they keep up a loud and almost hysterical screaming.'[76]

Though the Beatles' supporters drew attention to the age gap between the Beatles and their fans, critics pointed instead to the chasm between both and the adult population. Al Alvarez portrayed the Beatles as juveniles engaged in an 'adolescent revolt' which explained but did not excuse their mediocrity.[77] '[N]o one expects teenage art, however sincere, to be any good', he acknowledged, but their juvenilia showed no evidence of the band containing an 'embryo-Waugh or proto-Auden or baby-Amis'.[78]

The Beatles' early detractors were unimpressed by their intelligence. The band were 'moronic' in Malcolm Muggeridge's estimation.[79] Their inability to read music was held against them and their education, while a cut above that expected of pop stars, was hardly likely to impress university types. The publicity given to Harrison, Lennon and McCartney's selective secondary education invited otherwise well-disposed commentators to view them as having failed to progress beyond that level. Literary critic Michael Wood traced the 'intelligent, informed and infantile humour' of Lennon's writings back to grammar school: 'the "B" stream' in the precise estimation of Terry Eagleton.[80]

Lennon's education, or lack of it, affected evaluations of his writing. Favourable and unfavourable reviews of his fiction agreed on its resemblance to the nonsense verse of Edward Lear and Lewis Carroll and the wordplay of James Joyce.[81] What was in dispute was whether he had anything to add to these literary traditions or was indeed conversant with them. John Wain, Hilary Corke and Jonathan Miller concluded that Lennon was no more than a populariser, intro-ducing 'the young non-reader' to techniques commonplace in twen-tieth-century literature.[82]

The South African film critic M. M. Carlin noted a similarly patronising tone in reviews of *A Hard Day's Night*, however positive.[83] He had in mind comments like Gerald Kaufman's that 'The film falters only when it makes the mistake of taking itself seriously.'[84] In any case, many of the plaudits went to director Richard Lester and screenwriter Alun Owen. This was fair enough, but it meant that a film which lampooned the notion that the Beatles were ciphers of the entertainment industry appeared, from another perspective, to confirm it. *Help!* didn't help the following year, receiv-ing mixed reviews. Kenneth Tynan found virtue in its 'ferociously ephemeral' quality and declared it 'brilliant'.[85] The *Times* and *Telegraph* did not, drawing attention to its 'feeble' script and the 'absolute desperation' of its madcap pacing.[86] The *Mirror* pithily awarded it 'Half Marx'.[87]

Musical originality was another measure against which these four 'striplings' fell short.[88] Columnist Peter Fleming's 'square ear' heard nothing which differentiated their tunes from others in the hit parade and Donald Soper defied their defenders to point to 'one memorable chord, one inventive piece of counterpoint, one creative melodic line'.[89] Lennon and McCartney were held to lack the 'technical sophis-tication' of accomplished songwriters such as Gershwin, Porter, Kern and Rodgers and Hart.[90] The interwar standards performed by dance bands were just that: evergreen tunes setting a standard against which recent pop appeared 'trite and ephemeral'.[91] Folk music critic Karl Dallas claimed that the formulaic nature of early Beatles' compositions was the secret to their success, their 'genius for pastiche' putting them on a par with Lionel Bart, not Bach.[92] The 'bad words' of their early numbers made easy targets.[93] Musician and writer Fritz Spiegl doubted whether Lennon and McCartney deserved to be considered 'lyricists' or 'songwriters' after producing doggerel like 'I Wanna Be Your Man' (1963).[94] Humphrey Lyttleton used 'I Saw Her Standing There' (1963) as an example of how Beatles' songs lacked '[a]ny really close contact with everyday life'.[95]

It was no coincidence that Dallas, Spiegl and Lyttleton worked in three musical genres overshadowed by the Beatles' success: folk, classical and jazz. Most musicians and music critics in the early 1960s took it for granted that the music of the Beatles was inferior to that of their own chosen fields. Sir John Barbirolli flatly pronounced that 'Beat music isn't music at all.'[96] Less cutting if no less categorical was journalist Peter Laurie's assessment that in 1965 that 'we have in England two incomplete, polarised, but essentially complementary cultures ... the classical and pop cultures'. Drawing loosely upon C. P. Snow's contrast between the arts and the sciences, Laurie identified divergent 'attitudes and aspirations' in classical and pop artists. The classical musician entered his or her chosen field as a means of self-expression, whereas the pop star did so for money, fame or the sheer thrill of success.[97]

Although in a different league artistically, jazz, classical and folk music felt threatened by the Beatles' commercial success. Cassandra of the *Mirror* somehow held the band responsible for the financial troubles of the Philharmonia Orchestra.[98] The cancellation of a Stan Kenton gig in Liverpool and the axing of Victor Silvester's *Dance Club* after a sixteen-year run were likewise presented as confirmation that jazz and 'sweet' music had lost their audiences to the Beatles.[99] As jazz clubs closed their doors or opened them to pop acts, some jazz musicians expressed resentment bordering on contempt. Lyttleton blamed the media for providing publicity for 'four silly mop heads' and Ronnie Scott declared the 'overwhelming majority' of people to be too 'musically immature' to prefer jazz over beat music.[100] He urged fellow jazz musicians to resist making 'any concessions whatsoever' to public tastes.[101] Other jazz buffs bestowed faint praise on the Beatles. Singer George Melly allowed that the band had 'more to offer' than other pop combos, even though he blamed beat music for the death of trad.[102] Jazz critic Bob Dawburn likened their music to the best of music hall. It did not presume to match the manner in which jazz or classical music 'uplifted' its listeners. Bach and the Modern Jazz Quartet were 'culturally [and] aesthetically important' but the Beatles simply were not.[103]

Aficionados of classical music displayed their cultural capital by contrasting 'good-music lovers' to Beatlemaniacs.[104] Violinist Yehudi Menuhin and the conductor Otto Klemperer were likewise placed 'at the other extreme of the scale to the Beatles'.[105] The gulf between popular and 'serious' music was paradoxically confirmed by classical performances of Beatles' melodies. Fritz Spiegl's arrangement of *Eine Kleine Beatlemusik* (1965) for string quartet was as sardonic in intent as the Royal Liverpool Philharmonic Orchestra's rendition of 'I Want to Hold Your Hand' on April Fool's Day in 1964.[106]

Traditional folk and blues appealed to those in search of meaning and rawness.[107] A spokesperson for the English Folk Dance and Song Society drew much the same contrast between folk and the Beatles as *Guardian* columnist Sid Chaplin, who elevated the 'honest song' provided by the Elliotts of Birtley above the 'trivial noise' served up by the Beatles, with its 'amplified impersonations of alien words and tunes'.[108] An up-and-coming blues guitarist named Eric Clapton thought the band's deification 'despicable' when his heroes 'died unheard of, sometimes penniless and alone'. The popularity of Merseybeat threatened to make his blues evangelism seem like a 'lost cause'. It reduced bookings and 'forced musicians like me to almost go underground … plotting to overthrow the music establishment'.[109] Some commentators found authenticity in folk revival and folk rock acts, despite their lack of roots. The *Daily Telegraph*'s review of Bob Dylan's legendary 1965 Royal Albert Hall concert saw nothing in the Beatles' repertoire to compare with Dylan's 'sophisticated, socially conscious and biting' songs, which at their best married 'the earthiness of the blues' to 'the awareness of the intellectual'.[110]

The apparently crude arrangements, vapid lyrics and primitive musicianship of the Beatles' early recordings led detractors to conclude that Beatlemania had little to do with the band itself. It was fruitless to seek meaning in the words, tunes and actions of four fairly ordinary young men, and efforts to do so were disconcertingly redolent of the obsessive behaviour of their fans. Some critics therefore observed journalist Allen Brien's maxim that 'We don't study a shoe to understand a shoe fetishist' and directed their attention away from the Beatles and towards Beatlemaniacs.[111]

The composite portrait critics painted of Beatlemaniacs was as the opposite of themselves. The Beatlemaniac was young, female, hysterical, incoherent, ignorant, naïve, undiscriminating and conformist; the arche-typal critic was mature, male, composed, articulate, erudite, wise, discern-ing and independent.[112] The fans' youth accounted for their pathetic devotion to the Beatles, prompting Chaplin to express pity for the 'child-slaves' of the music industry.[113] Stupidity and ignorance further predis-posed youngsters towards Beatlemania. Anthony Burgess diagnosed a 'cutting-off of the higher centres' of Beatlemaniacs' brains and Douglas Gillies hypothesised that the appeal of the Beatles diminished 'as the IQ rises'.[114] The femaleness of most fans was an incurable condition, as was mental incapacity. Beatlephobes therefore pinned their hopes on fans simply growing out of Beatlemania. 'Let teenagers scream at the Beatles', counselled Auberon Waugh, until they came to their senses.[115]

Having cut the Beatles and Beatlemaniacs down to size, critics set about doing the same to their educated apologists. The *Daily Telegraph* invoked class loyalty when enjoining '[p]rofessors, writers, intellectuals [and] bishops' to spurn plebeian culture.[116] Donald Soper made a comparable appeal to generational solidarity. He upbraided his peer group for 'trying to cram itself into jeans' and engaging in a 'palsied twitching of bald heads' in time with the Beatles, before inexplicably confessing that 'I rather like Cilla Black.'[117] John Gross advanced a more considered argument against ced-ing cultural legitimacy to the Beatles. He reasoned that 'pop culture' was simply a new name for the same mass culture that had been exerting a corrupting influence for decades past. The 'myth of pop culture' was being propagated by publicists who invested the Beatles with a bogus significance and by critics who attempted to extract 'something that feels more authentic' from commercial dross.[118]

Variants of these class, generational and aesthetic arguments were used to roast every prominent early apologist for the Beatles. David Sylvester's comparison of the Beatles to Monteverdi prompted his fellow art critic Keith Roberts to accuse him of succumbing to 'the democratic pull of modern life'.[119] David Holbrook laid the graver charge that Hall and Whannel were guilty of 'blind *trahison*' for 'discriminating ... between pop and pop'.[120] Burgess twitted Kenneth Allsop for taking Lennon's writings seriously, and William Mann for believing that 'pop contains the same elements of emotional satisfaction and intellectual complexity as Beethoven, Brahms or Wagner'.[121] His criticism extended to the broad-casters and publishers who publicised them. Broadcasting pop could be justified if it served the didactic function of 'encourag[ing] an aesthetic', but as it was he suspected the BBC of being 'rather proud of its Philistinism'.[122]

Art and Criticism

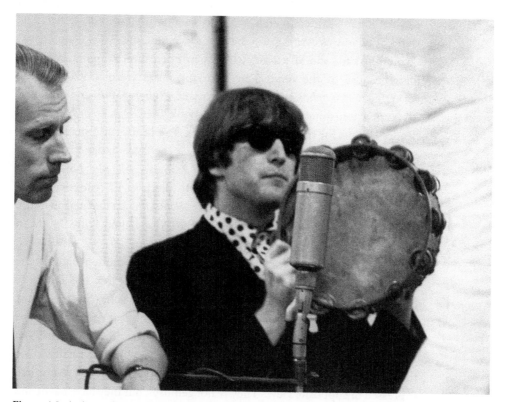

Figure 4.2 Artists – George Martin and John Lennon at Abbey Road Studios, 1965.
Photo by SSPL/Getty Images

The rapid evolution of the Beatles' music, lyrics and image meant that they represented a different cultural proposition in the second half of the 1960s (see Fig. 4.2). Their side projects made further incursions into fields hitherto associated with high art. They directed films, composed electronic music, exhibited art, wrote for the stage, sponsored artists, subsidised a theatre troupe and established a record label which promised to do for spoken-word recordings 'what the paperback revolution did to book publishing'.[123]

As the Beatles changed in the second half of the 1960s, so did the cultural environment in which they worked. The decision by Karl Miller in 1967 to revamp the *Listener*'s cultural coverage without regard for 'the categories of "high" and "low", "serious" and "vulgar"' had parallels in other publications of high repute.[124] Steve Race, who had wished rock 'n' roll 'Good riddance' in 1958, started reviewing pop LPs for the *Sunday Times* in 1965.[125] The *Observer* employed Nik Cohn and George Melly as rock critics, while the *Guardian* featured Geoffrey Cannon, until he agreed to edit the *Radio Times* and endow it with 'literary pretensions'.[126] By 1970, Derek Taylor was writing for the *Sunday Times* and Tony Palmer was a columnist for the *Spectator*, which permitted him to quote Lennon's infamous use of the F-word in 'Working Class Hero' (1970).[127] The venerable *Gramophone* magazine reviewed *Rubber Soul* and declared *Revolver* 'astonishing', and the reference book *The Great Records* included Beatles albums for the first time in 1967.[128] The Beatles also made regular appearances in BBC arts programmes in the late sixties.[129] In 1968 McCartney was interviewed for Tony Palmer's *All My Loving*, and Lennon and Ono played word games with the poet Christopher Logue on John Peel's *Night Ride*.[130] In 1969, *Late Night Line-Up* devoted an entire episode to *Abbey Road* and shortly afterwards dispatched Tony Bilbow to interview Starr in a rowing boat.[131]

The conversion of prominent music critics was another sign of the Beatles' rising cultural stock in the late sixties. In 1963, the *Listener*'s Deryck Cooke faintly praised the Beatles' songs as 'cheerful, engaging, unintellectual'; five years later, he heralded Lennon and McCartney as 'genuine creators of a "new music"' which displayed all the hallmarks of 'creative genius'.[132] Musician and writer George Melly likewise described the Beatles as 'totally convincing geniuses' in 1970, whereas in 1964 he had expressed the opposite view: 'They're not geniuses, but they have talent and charm.'[133] The most eminent convert to the Beatles' cause was the academic musicologist Wilfrid Mellers. During Beatlemania, he was willing to countenance teenagers 'accept[ing] Beatles and Bach', but saw the first as a stepping stone towards a mature appreciation of the second, and distanced himself from any 'inverted intellectual snobbery' suggesting otherwise.[134] He rated the Beatles' music as 'OK' and their lyrics as 'fatuous', grumbled about their earnings, viewed Beatlemania as a 'regrettable fashion' and condemned the electric guitar as a 'perversion' of the 'authentic Spanish variety'.[135] '[B]anality is sometimes inspired' was the backhanded compliment he gave them in 1966.[136] His remark that *Revolver*'s (1966) lyrics were 'decidedly worth listening to' also smacked of faint praise.[137] Mellers then experienced something of an epiphany with the release of *Sgt. Pepper* the following year. He had hitherto conceived of music in hierarchical terms between and within genres, so that the Beatles represented the best of the least kind of music. *Sgt. Pepper* convinced him that the once 'vast gap between the serious and the popular arts' was narrowing in terms of outlook and artistry.[138] '[T]hough it starts from the conventions of pop it becomes "art"', he argued, 'and art of an increasingly subtle kind.'[139] He was at this point unsure whether this signified the Beatles' evolution from entertainers to artists or a broader merger between pop and serious music. His curiosity impelled him to write the first scholarly monograph on the Beatles, published in 1973.[140]

These and other advocates of popular music in the late 1960s were more prepared to challenge the critics' indiscriminate attacks on the music industry than they had been just a few years earlier. Cannon disputed the notion that popular music was uniquely debased by commerce, arguing that 'vital music has no more (and no less) to do with the "pop music industry" than vital books, or movies, say, have to do with their industries'.[141] Richard Mabey took on the 'prejudice' that the 'laboratory manufacture' of music in the recording studio nullified its artistic value.[142] He claimed that electronic instruments were instruments like any other. In fact, synthesisers were arguably superior to pianos or violins because their ability to produce any sound allowed fuller artistic expression.[143] Nor could pop musicians be considered mere cogs in a moneymaking machine. Mabey argued that the idol as a 'creature of the public' had evolved into an artist who was 'very much his own man [sic]', uninclined to sing for their supper.[144]

The Beatles' champions turned the tables on those who saw popular culture as being debased by commercialism by advancing their own economic critique of elite culture. The poet Christopher Logue baldly stated that 'The word art stands for nothing except those morsels from the past upon which today's bourgeois place a high cash value.'[145] Critics charged that bourgeois patronage diminished the quality of art as well as distorting its definition. The *Guardian*'s art critic M. G. McNay thus preferred Stuart Sutcliffe's paintings over those of John Everett Millais because of Millais' decision to 'prostitute his remarkable talent to the middle class'.[146] Tony Palmer attacked latter-day patronage in the form of state subsidies for culture. He found common cause with Lennon in deriding 'the galleries, the museums, symphony concerts, opera' as constituting little more than 'a pretentious rat-race for the trendy'.[147]

The Beatles' fans, who had been something of an embarrassment to the band's defenders in the early 1960s, were now presented as a more discerning lot. The notion that, as Harrison observed in 1967, 'all the people who thought they were beyond the Beatles are fans' had two principal consequences.[148] The first was that fandom could be reimagined as being akin to connoisseurship. Mabey envisaged a new relationship between artist and fan now that 'more of the audience is listening', with music becoming a more mature form of communication.[149] The second was that the Beatles could no longer be accused of pandering to young, dumb Beatlemaniacs. The *Express* credited *Revolver* for making 'no attempt to hold the simpler souls in their following' and greeted *Sgt. Pepper* as the creation of 'a group now withdrawn from the screaming hysteria of pop world audiences and dedicated to originality and perfection'.[150]

The more sophisticated the Beatles and their ilk became, the more these critics questioned the value of pop as an analytical category. '"Pop" is now as indefinite a label as "jazz" or "classical music"', stated music critic Derek Jewell in 1968.[151] That same year, composer Tim Souster declared it 'worthless' to generalise about a genre encompassing everything from the Beatles to Leicester balladeer Engelbert Humperdinck.[152] One response was for critics to subdivide pop into categories, principally distinguishing between the Beatles and 'a small elite of other pop singers' on the one hand, and the cruder form represented by 'the raucous, long-haired rock 'n' roller, and the romantic crooner' on the other.[153] This distinction between supposedly serious and lightweight popular music eventually became codified as one between 'rock' and 'pop'. 'Rock', in its sense of a superior form of popular music, was an American coinage which had not fully established itself in Britain by the end of the 1960s: hence Nik Cohn's 1969 study was entitled *Rock from the Beginning* in the United States but *Pop from the Beginning* in the United Kingdom. Yet, as Table 4.1 shows, the perception of what *Melody Maker* described as a 'two-tier pop system' took root in Britain in the absence of an agreed terminology.[154] Those, like Bernard Levin, who refused to make any distinction between Procol Harum and the 1910 Fruitgum Company were those who dismissed all popular music as irredeemably crass and ephemeral.[155]

The origins of this hierarchical division have been heavily debated in popular music studies and its validity has been widely disputed.[156] For the purposes of this study, what matters is not whether 'rock' was objectively distinguishable from 'pop', but that contemporaries subjectively considered it to be so and credited the Beatles in part for rock's emergence.[157]

Evidence from musicians and fans shows that they largely concurred with critics in regarding the Beatles as 'the most influential mentors, catalysts and inspirers of ... pop adulthood' in the late 1960s.[158] It was true that fellow musicians found it less easy to pigeonhole them as 'rock' artists than, say, the Pink Floyd. The Beatles' career predated the concept of 'rock' and had initially conformed to much of the 'pop' archetype in its unabashed courting of a large, young and mostly female fan base.[159] For

Table 4.1 Divisions within popular music perceived by writers and musicians, 1965–1975

Writers		
William Mann, 1967	forward-looking pop	the sticky, sweaty, vacuous ballad[a]
Bob Dawburn, 1968	progressives	traditional-styled pop entertainers[b]
Nik Cohn, 1969	fashionable	square[c]
Charlie Gillett, 1969	art rock	bubble-gum[d]
Richard Mabey, 1969	musician	idol[e]
George Melly, 1970	hard pop	pop in the kiddy-mum-and-dad-Eurovision-song-contest sense[f]
Tony Palmer, 1970	technical virtuosity	musical illiteracy[g]
Tony Jasper, 1972	rock, progressive, head, acid, psychedelic, heavy	soul, tamla, bubble-gum[h]

Musicians		
Pete Townshend, 1965	pop-art	'showbiz' stuff[i]
Barry Gibb, 1967	blues groups	pop groups[j]
Manfred Mann, 1968	the semi-underground market	the pop market[k]
Dave Dee, 1969	the blues and the underground stuff	the Tom Joneses and the Engelberts[l]
John Lennon, 1970	students	working-class audience[m]

a   William Mann, *Times*, 29 May 1967, 9.
b   Dawburn, *Melody Maker*, 12 October 1968, 16.
c   Cohn, *Awopbopaloobop*, 168.
d   Charlie Gillett, *Record Mirror*, 14 June 1969, www.rocksbackpages.com/Library/SearchLinkRedirect?folder=born-to-sing-the-blues.
e   Mabey, *Pop*, 17.
f   Melly, *Revolt into Style*, 116.
g   Palmer, *Born under a Bad Sign*, 12.
h   Tony Jasper, *Understanding Pop* (London: S. C. M. Press, 1972), 16.
i   Cited in Nick Jones, *Melody Maker*, 3 July 1965, thewho.net/node/3848.
j   Cited in *Rolling Stone*, 23 November 1967, n.p.
k   Cited in Ian Stocks, *Oz*, no. 17 (1968), ro.uow.edu.au/ozlondon/17/.
l   Cited in *Melody Maker*, 29 March 1969, web.archive.org/web/20161111133826/http://davedeedozybeakymickandtich.nl/march-1969/.
m   Cited in Tariq Ali and Robin Blackburn, *Red Mole* 2, no. 5 (1971), 8.

these reasons, 'pop' acts such as Herman's Hermits, Love Affair, the Tremeloes and their friend Cilla Black remained loyal to the band in the late 1960s.[160] But musicians did not view the Beatles as invalidating the distinction between pop and rock so much as epitomising its evolution from one to the other. Eric Clapton in 1968 saw the Beatles as having created a new role for musicians since 1966, involving the (somewhat irksome) requirement to be 'intelligent' and display 'moral responsibility'.[161] Mick Jagger in 1967 pinpointed the release of *Revolver* in 1966 as 'the beginning of an appeal to the intellect' subsequently pursued by the Stones and 'most of the new groups'.[162] Members of Led Zeppelin, the most famous of these new groups, drew a distinction between the 'maturity' of the Beatles' psychedelic period and the era of Beatlemania, when '[y]ou didn't really bother what you were listening to' and their recordings were 'nothing to really write home about'.[163] It took an exceptionally cocky progressive musician such as Robert Wyatt to dismiss the Beatles as 'shallow' musicians who had not committed themselves to '[t]he discipline of the musical life'.[164] 'Pop' acts had to decide whether to follow the Beatles' path. Graham Nash chose to do so, even though it eventually meant leaving the Hollies. 'It's a question of "now follow that" after a Beatles' album ... and it's great to feel a part of this kind of progress', he commented after the release of *Revolver*.[165] Others decided against. *Revolver* was 'terrible' according to Tich of Dave Dee, Dozy, Beaky, Mick and Tich, principally because it featured jazz musicians, and Barry Gibb of the Bee Gees gave up listening to *The Beatles* double LP four tracks in.[166]

The pop–rock debate played out among consumers as well as producers of music. In 1967, the *Beatles Book* polled its readership on whether *Sgt. Pepper* was 'too advanced for the average pop fan to appreciate'.[167] A rump of Beatlemaniacs (estimated by the editor to be 5 per cent of readers) preferred the catchy tunes created by the band 'before they went stark raving mad and started to write rubbish'.[168] Jan and Chris from Luton pined for the 'head shaking, screaming and ooohing' records of yore and Ann Craig from Edinburgh found their later lyrics to be impenetrable, even though she considered herself no 'denser than most Beatle people'.[169] But Nancy Ryan of Cheshunt was pleased that 'the Beatles' music has grown up with me', and other correspondents had no hesitation in proclaiming the Beatles as 'true musicians' and future poet laureates.[170]

The male subcultures studied by Paul Willis in 1969 also drew sharp distinctions between the Beatles of the early and late sixties. The working-class 'motor-bike boys' were confirmed rockers who 'ranked the early Beatles very highly' as an extension of fifties rock 'n' roll. However, they 'despised some of their late "really stupid stuff"',[171] with exceptions made for the retro stylings of 'Lady Madonna' (1968), 'Get Back' (1969) and some Plastic Ono Band sides.[172] The very 'melodic asymmetry and complexity of rhythm' of the later Beatles' work which alienated bikers appealed to the hippies Willis encountered. Surveying the music scene from 'the post-Beatles high point of "progressive" music', hippies perceived the Beatles as having pioneered the crucial elements of prog rock – the concept album, artistry, integrity, uncommerciality – before being 'left behind' by still more adventurous acts.[173]

Among critics, the establishment of hierarchies within pop music criticism went hand in hand with the erosion of hierarchies between pop and other musical genres. It has been widely noted that the emerging field of rock criticism demanded the acceptance of 'rock' on terms equal or superior to those granted to folk, jazz, blues and sweet music owing to its newfound sophistication and 'social core'.[174] What is less acknowledged is that critics from within these fields increasingly agreed. *Telegraph* folk critic Maurice Rosenbaum argued that the Beatles' experiments, though largely originating in the folk revival, had repaid the favour by 1968 through 'encourag[ing], with almost every new song they produce, a more understanding and more penetrating approach to the whole world of demotic music'.[175] The Composers' Guild resolved in 1966 to admit to its ranks Lennon, McCartney and 'other "pop" composers with a serious, dedicated approach to music'.[176] The *Guardian*'s jazz critic Ian Breach declared the Beatles the equals of Billie Holiday, Hans Keller considered them 'truly creative' like Gershwin and the *Sunday Times*' Derek Jewell conceded that he saw little purpose in continuing to distinguish between pop and jazz, such was the overlap between the two.[177] He set about the task of 'establishing standards of discrimination in popular music', conscious that 'the barriers between categories are down' and that jazz was no longer 'the undisputed pacesetter' it had once been.[178]

Still more radical were the claims made in the late sixties for the best of pop to be accorded parity with classical music. Whereas early sixties debates on the Beatles' relationship to classical music had focused on Mann's comparisons with Mahler, those of the late sixties concentrated on Tony Palmer's assertion that 'Lennon and McCartney are the greatest song writers since Schubert' in his review of *The Beatles* (1968).[179] On the face of it, Schubert's *Lieder* offered a more natural comparison to the Beatles' songs. Other writers drew similar parallels between Schubert and the Beatles, who were by this point intermittently operating within the art song tradition.[180] But several factors combined to make Palmer's assertion so inflammatory. One was that Palmer was no 'middle-aged and very pleasant' classical music critic like Mann, but an up-and-coming rock critic who personified youth culture as much as he commented upon it.[181]

Furthermore, he made no secret of his ambition to destroy 'the rigid, authoritarian categorisation of music into "classical" and "popular"', and considered classical music to have 'little new to say to the now generation'.[182] Palmer's characterisation of Schubert as 'the inventor of Muzak' served to lower him to the Beatles' level rather than elevating them to his.[183] He doubled down on his claim that both Schubert and the Beatles wrote 'at great speed, for entertainment and with no regard for any high "artistic" content' by likening Liszt's female admirers to Beatlemaniacs and entitling an interview 'Paul McCartney – Composer'.[184]

William Mann, who had portrayed the Beatles as an exception to the general insignificance of pop music in 1963, claimed in 1971 that their work and other 'progressive stuff' had turned the best rock into an 'art form'.[185] The American expatriate Henry Pleasants went further in claiming that the terms 'classical' and 'popular' obscured the 'essentially indivisible' nature of music.[186] Both critics proposed that the pop–rock division could be applied within and across genres by distinguishing between music intended to entertain and that with higher aspirations.[187] Pleasants detected a generation gap among classical musicians, with a younger generation displaying more eclectic and ecumenical tastes.[188] There were certainly exceptions to this rule, but it was telling that Sir Malcolm Sargent and Sir John Barbirolli, both of whom boasted that they had never listened to the Beatles, had been born during Victoria's reign.[189] Classical musicians and composers born in the 1930s and 1940s had more time for the Beatles. Peter Maxwell Davies arranged 'Yesterday' (1965) for classical guitar and declared Beethoven and the Beatles to be 'both marvellous, but different': a sentiment echoed by fellow composers Gordon Crosse and John Tavener and the pianists John Ogdon and John Lill.[190]

Now that the best popular music had apparently achieved parity with classical music, some critics envisaged a fusion between the two. The ambitions of progressive rock in this regard were taken seriously by Jewell and Mann. They consequently applauded the song cycle on *Abbey Road* and the album's 'skilful but sparing use of symphonic resources'.[191] Henry Pleasants perceived in this and other 'mature' Beatles albums a shift in popular music from borrowing classical and jazz motifs to entering into an 'even exchange'.[192] However, the Beatles were not always seen as the best exponents of the 'exciting and creative confluence' between rock and classical music envisaged by Jewell.[193] He saw them as being overtaken by other progressive musicians in 1968 and welcomed their 'dethroning' in 1970 by more progressive acts such as Chicago, Pink Floyd, the Moody Blues, Fairport Convention and Crosby, Stills, Nash and Young.[194] Leading critic and musicologist Arthur Jacobs expected 'creative musical inter-course' to be realised by bolder musicians than the Beatles.[195]

Other critics warned against the mulish beast produced by the cross-breeding of pop and classical music. Tim Souster credited the Beatles with upholding the tonal musical tradition in popular music, but considered atonality better suited to composers of 'extended and complex musical expression' such as himself.[196] This argument gained credence from Lennon's musical collaborations with Ono, and Harrison's first two solo recordings. Jewell declared Ono responsible for the 'worst' and most 'ludicrous' music of 1968 and awarded *Unfinished Music No. 1: Two Virgins* (1968) booby prizes for the 'ugliest sleeve [and] most boring sound' of the year.[197] And while the promoter of avant-garde music, Victor Schonfield, urged Lennon and Ono in 1969 to 'think hard about giving up everything and getting serious about new music' on the strength of *Unfinished Music No. 2*, he dismissed Harrison's equally unlistenable *Electronic Sound* (1969) as 'absolutely empty . . . lifeless academicism'.[198]

An alternative objection to the marriage of pop and the classics was that classical music could not be saved from itself. Deryck Cooke used the Beatles as a stick with which to beat serialist and aleatoric composers who had eschewed the 'common musical language evolved by humanity at large' in favour of wilfully abstruse and atonal experimentation.[199] Cooke's preference for 'good pop songs' over other contemporary genres was echoed in pieces on the Beatles by Mann in 1968 and Pleasants in 1969.[200] It was therefore ironic that Cooke announced that he had 'finished with post-Schoenberg music' just as the Beatles began to dabble in it.[201] Cooke had confidently placed the Beatles and Karlheinz Stockhausen at 'extreme poles' of the musical spectrum in 1963, only to find the German composer appearing on the cover of *Sgt. Pepper* in 1967 and inspiring 'Revolution 9' the following year.[202] Another of McCartney's 'new idols' was John Cage, whose influence on Lennon and Ono's collaborations was readily apparent.[203]

Critics such as Mellers and Mann who shared the Beatles' catholic tastes took these developments in their stride.[204] But they posed difficulties for Cooke, who championed the romanticism of Schubert and Wagner, and for Pleasants, who criticised 'idolatry' of Cage and had made a splash in 1955 by declaring contemporary music 'A Dead Art'.[205] Pleasants pro-claimed the superiority of the Beatles over a pianist who 'bounced small white balls on the body [of the instrument] and rolled them down the fingerboard'.[206] Yet his ridicule might equally have been directed at McCartney, who had contributed to a concert by the improvisatory music ensemble AMM by 'running a penny along the coils of the old-fashioned steam radiator'.[207]

The Beatles' later lyrics also found their champions, although some otherwise well-disposed writers demurred. Literary critic Michael Wood and journalist Peter Cole did not rank them among the best songwriters, let alone poets, and Philip Larkin's fondness for their early music did not extend to him rating them as 'surrealists, mystics or political thinkers'.[208] As with music, their admirers were divided on whether the Beatles were contributing to high culture as well as popular culture and whether they offered an alternative to modernism. At a minimum, they accepted that the Beatles improved upon the 'formal and unrealistic' songs of the fifties and early sixties.[209] Most sympathetic writers agreed with John Willett that the decisive break with the 'old pop drivel' came in the second half of the 1960s.[210] Some went further. Adrian Mitchell was one of several poets who claimed kinship with the later Beatles. He traced their development from composing 'likeable' but inconsequential ditties in 1963 to bona fide poetry in 1966 and 'adventurous poetry' by 1967.[211] Christopher Logue declared Lennon and McCartney to have 'done as much' as anyone for verse in the 1960s, offering as proof extracts from 'For No One', 'Rain' (both 1966) and 'Sexy Sadie' (1968).[212] Thom Gunn pronounced McCartney's 'For No One' and 'Eleanor Rigby' to be 'excellent poems' and James Kirkup rated Lennon as 'one of the most gifted of younger English poets'.[213]

Poets who embraced the Beatles saw them as reviving 'popular poetry', separate from the 'academic or modernist' traditions.[214] Some went so far as to envisage them as rescuing poetry from the obscurantism and formalism of a prevailing modernist idiom. For example, Thom Gunn favoured 'Eleanor Rigby' (1966) over W. H. Auden's 'Miss Gee' (1937) for its greater empathy and economy of language.[215] Like the Beatles' defenders in the classical music field, admiring poets thought that their medium had become precious and aloof. '[A]uthorship and judgment are kept in the hands of white middle-class western men', claimed Logue.[216] Their 'harmless pastoral burburlings [sic]' had no connection to the lives of ordinary people, who seldom read books anyway.[217] The Beatles had succeeded where established poets failed. Their poetry was oral, popular, urban and relevant, full of the 'disobedience, sexuality, revolution, new values' to be found in almost all 'good new verse'.[218]

The theatre critics D. A. N. Jones and Harold Hobson similarly praised the Beatles' performance style as an alternative to the modernist techniques of agitprop or alienation. Jones advised theatre directors to take heed of the Beatles' 'courteous approach to audience participation' in the 'Hey Jude' promo (1968).[219] Hobson contrasted their crowd-pleasing manner with a contemporary drama scene which seldom 'cares about audiences' and applauded the 'good sense' of ordinary people who 'prefer (as I myself do) the Beatles to Brecht'.[220] The company manager of Apple Theatre, Wes Waring, also distanced himself from Brecht as well as the 'shock methods' of Peter Brook. Instead of confrontation, he sought to establish the same kind of 'connection between audience and performer' achieved by the Beatles and other empathetic artists.[221]

However, many of the Beatles' supporters did not pit them against modernists. Instead, they saw them as bridging the gap between the mainstream and the avant-garde and lowbrow and highbrow culture, especially in relation to visual art. The Beatles' commissioning of album covers by the pop artists Peter Blake, Jann Howarth and Richard Hamilton underlined the connection, and the *Sgt. Pepper* cover hammered home the point by sandwiching George Bernard Shaw between Stan Laurel and Oliver Hardy.[222]

The concept of Blake and Howarth's magnificent cover was not a novel one. In 1964, Mersey poet Adrian Henri imagined the Beatles in the company of jazz musicians (Charlie Parker and Thelonious Monk), modern and contemporary artists (James Ensor, Marcel Duchamp, Kurt Schwitters, Robert Rauschenberg and Jasper Johns) and the writers Alfred Jarry, Dylan Thomas and William Burroughs (two of whom appeared on the *Sgt. Pepper* cover).[223] And earlier in 1967, Edward Lucie-Smith's *The Liverpool Scene* pictured two of Henri's 'masters' (Jarry and Ensor) 'walk[ing] hand in hand with [jazz bassist] Charlie Mingus and Paul McCartney down Hope Street'.[224] Lucie-Smith saw something quintessentially Liverpudlian in the Beatles' transgression of cultural boundaries:

Liverpool 'fun' is often deliberately anarchic. It involves the rejection of many of the standards which those who officially promote and encourage the arts feel bound to uphold. The fragmentation of our culture doesn't bother them – they enjoy it.[225]

Artists and designers represented this state of cultural flux by juxtaposing the Beatles with canonical visual art. The *Yellow Submarine* film (1968) pastiched genres including expressionism, surrealism, pop art, op art and art nouveau with wit and gusto. The painter John McDonnell superimposed the Beatles' heads onto Caravaggio's figures in his updating of *The Musicians* (c. 1595). A *Vogue* feature by Elizabeth Bowen placed Richard Avedon's photographs of the band alongside medieval carvings, Japanese prints, paintings by Piero della Francesca, Fernand Léger and John D. Graham, and an image of Catherine Deneuve.[226] The 'elevation of pop music and allied pop culture by the Beatles' inspired Alan Aldridge not simply to devise *The Beatles Illustrated Lyrics* (1969, 1971), but to celebrate the collapse of cultural boundaries by inviting submissions from artists working in diverse fields.[227] Joining graphic artists like himself in the enterprise were the pop artists David Hockney, Allen Jones and Eduardo Paolozzi, the cartoonists Mel Calman, Ronald Searle and Ralph Steadman, the photographers David Bailey and John Deakin, the puppet-maker Roger Law, fan artists and many more.

Proponents of the 'New Poetry', 'new music' and related artistic endeavours had to decide whether the Beatles could be evaluated using the same criteria as high culture, or whether different yardsticks were required to map a transfigured cultural landscape.[228] For Palmer, the only valid distinction was one of quality. 'Ultimately, there can be only three kinds of music – whether it is composed by the Beatles or Brahms', he stated: 'good music, bad music and non-music'.[229] His absolutist approach chimed with that of critics who declared the Beatles to be geniuses. The word genius was applied to the Beatles in the 1960s in relation to a somewhat miscellaneous collection of works. William Mann dubbed McCartney a genius in a review of his first solo album and James Kirkup declared Lennon to be 'the only genius in modern English poetry' as early as 1965.[230] *Disc and Music Echo* saw 'musical genius' in *Sgt. Pepper*; New Age philosopher Alan Watts upped the ante by attributing 'serious musical genius' to the band as a whole.[231] Cooke and Melly invoked the traditional test of immortality in support of the Beatles' claims to genius, 'ultimate durability' being in Cooke's view 'the only realistic standard' to ascertain greatness.[232] Such claims would have appeared outlandish in the early sixties, when publicist Tony Barrow dared purchasers of a 1963 compilation to countenance the 'Lennon & McCartney Songbook' being discussed in ten years' time.[233]

Other critics preferred to devise new criteria befitting the new cultural forms emerging in the 1960s, starting with terminology. Jazz critic Peter Clayton found himself without a critical vocabulary to describe the invention he heard on *Revolver* (1966):

It isn't easy to describe what's here, since much of it involves things which are either new to pop music or which are being properly applied for the first time, and which can't be helpfully compared with anything.[234]

Music critic Geoffrey Cannon argued that rock was a 'culture' rather than an 'art form' and that its greatest creations could not be assessed according to 'any existing cultural frame'.[235] Whereas champions of the Beatles' genius compared them to past giants (as when Palmer likened the sentiments of 'Yellow Submarine' (1966) to the philosophy of Plato, Aristotle, Locke, Hume and John Stuart Mill), those emphasising the novelty of sixties culture were less interested in locating the Beatles within an existing canon.[236] They argued that the apparent 'formlessness' of the Beatles and their followers represented a 'form of freedom' of writers unbeholden to 'the literary achievements of the past', and even innocent of them: Tynan was disconcerted that Harrison had not heard of William Blake.[237] According to Clive James, such ignorance did not invalidate their artistry so much as require critics to reconsider their assumption that 'the ability to create in the arts is directly dependent on scholarly knowledge'.[238] New tools of criticism were needed to assess the Beatles and other 'talented yob[s]'.[239]

Culture and Anarchy

The eclecticism and experimentation of the Beatles in the second half of the 1960s did nothing to change the minds of their detractors. They continued to question the band members' abilities as musicians, composers and lyricists and found them wanting against a battery of standard tests of cultural value. Claims for the Beatles' canonical status were either rejected or left to posterity. In the early sixties, critics had confidently predicted that the Beatles would soon disappear and take their 'trivial and evanescent' music with them.[240] However, the Beatles lasted longer than anyone had expected (themselves included). Naysayers accordingly shifted to arguing that the Beatles' music needed to endure for several decades before it could be considered canonical. '[Arthur] Sullivan has attained immortality. The Beatles have not yet attained maturity', quipped Lord Goodman in 1966.[241] The poet Stephen Spender expressed relief when Starr did not recognise him when they met, since it reminded him of the difference between the fleeting celebrity of pop and the posthumous renown to which he aspired.[242] Since future generations could not yet pass judgement, critics spoke on their behalf. Muggeridge maintained that 'the eyes of posterity' would look unfavourably upon the Beatles, if at all, and Brian Magee found it inconceivable that the Beatles would be 'an unthinkingly accepted part of daily life all over the world in the 2000s'.[243]

Sceptics credited the greater artistry of the Beatles' later work to produ-cers and session musicians. Musicologist Sir Jack Westrup insisted that the 'harmonic ingenuities' attributed to pop performers were actually the work of 'the expert musicians who write the "backing"'.[244] Fritz Spiegl claimed that Lennon 'employed paid helpers to do some of his work for him' and disputed whether he or McCartney could be said to 'write' their music in any meaningful sense.[245] It was George Martin, after all, who had to 'transfer [their] hummings or strummings to paper, harmonise and, if necessary, orchestrate them'.[246] Composer Michael Nyman advanced 'the pathetic arrangement' of 'Yellow Submarine' for the Black Dyke Mills Band (1967) as evidence of McCartney's shoddy 'musical craftsmanship' when deprived of Martin's expertise, overlooking the fact that the arrangement was by Martin himself.[247]

Their 'modestly accomplished' musicianship came under scrutiny by the *Sunday Times* Insight team in 1966.[248] It pronounced Starr to be one of the 'most moderate' (that is, worst) professional drummers.[249] Harrison was deemed the best instrumentalist of the four, but that made him merely 'passable', one of the top thousand or so guitarists in the country.[250] Not that virtuosity could be put to any good effect in such a primitive musical form. Amplification removed nuance from pop and constituted a 'rape of the musical sense' according to the Leavisite Ian Robinson, a charge made more eloquently by George Steiner in his critique of 'decibel-culture'.[251]

Unchanged too was critics' relegation of the Beatles below their own preferred forms of popular music. The claims for jazz were made by Sandy Brown, who thought the Beatles were feted for 'ninth-hand' versions of techniques pioneered in New Orleans, and Edward Lee, who followed Hobsbawm in attributing pop's inferiority to its commerciality.[252] Traditional folk found its champion in Anthony Burgess, who perceived a 'genius' in broadside ballads of yore wholly absent from their modern equivalents.[253] Standards were praised by the poet Roy Fuller, whose paean to George Gershwin's setting of a single line from 'How Long Has This Been Going On?' (1927) sat oddly beside his ridiculing of comparable Beatles' tunes.[254] *Spectator* columnist Murray Kempton pitted the authenticity of blues singer Joe Turner against the superficiality of the Beatles, whose celebrity insulated them from everything 'raw and crude in life'.[255]

The superiority of classical music was stoutly defended by the Beatles' late-sixties critics, albeit in terms that made it appear demanding, difficult, abstruse and as such beyond the ken of ordinary people. A pair of *Times* editorials in 1967 and 1968 saw the Beatles' music and other 'ephemera' as evidence that popular music 'never ask[s] us to make exhausting efforts of mind or spirit'.[256] That the Beatles 'express what is going on in the popular mind' testified to their lack of artistry.[257] Further proof that they 'lag[ged] behind the conscious art' was found in their songs' 'emotional inflations', since such histrionics had been excised from high culture since the

1920s.[258] It was not clear from this depiction of classical music as draining, out of touch and buttoned-up why Beatles' fans should wish to cross the 'wide ... gulf' between low and high art, even if they were capable of doing so.[259]

The Beatles' excursions into poetry and philosophy also did nothing to improve their reputation among their detractors, who variously described their later lyrics as 'wretched', 'mostly rubbish' and 'so simple as to require no more chewing over than bubble-gum'.[260] Burgess saw the 'vapid sentiments' contained in 'Eleanor Rigby' (1966) and 'She's Leaving Home' (1967) as evidence that the Beatles concerned themselves with 'suburban little emotions' rather than the great themes tackled by great lyrical verse.[261] Hunter Davies ran up against the same prejudices when he sought to print the lyrics of 'Eleanor Rigby' alongside his *Sunday Times* interview with McCartney. His editors refused to countenance 'so much space wasted on humdrum pop songs'.[262] Such put-downs were directed less towards the Beatles than to what Burgess termed the 'pretentiousness and stupidity and cupidity' exhibited by their defenders among the literati.[263] *Punch* derided 'unembarrassed paeans' to pop poetry and proved their point by mock-auditioning Lennon for the vacant post of Poet Laureate.[264] Michael Smith ridiculed fellow rock critic Tony Palmer's over-interpretation of the pastiche and neo-primitivism of 'Birthday' and 'Goodnight' (both 1968).[265] Jillian Becker answered Christopher Logue's panegyric by comparing the Beatles' verse to that of Patience Strong and Hallmark cards.[266]

Critics' eyebrows arched ever higher when the Beatles branched out into other genres. They tore into the *Magical Mystery Tour* TV special (1967) for being 'witless, narcissistic, conceited' (*Daily Telegraph*), 'blatant rubbish' (*Daily Express*), 'a colossal conceit' (*Daily Mail*) and 'ill-constructed trash' (in a second *Daily Mail* panning).[267] Critics were divided over *Yellow Submarine* (1968), but united in their disdain for *Let It Be* (1970), the *Times* arguing that it failed to meet the 'minimum technical requirements' of *cinema verité*.[268] Still worse received were the Beatles' individual film ventures. *Candy* (1968) and *The Magic Christian* (1969) disillusioned critics who had seen comedic potential in Starr's performances in *A Hard Day's Night* and *Help!*. The 1969 ICA screening of Lennon's collaborations with Ono, which included slow-motion footage of Lennon's semi-tumescent penis, left Ian Christie unmoved. 'John Lennon's money has given him a licence to talk rubbish and be photographed doing it', was his withering judgement.[269]

Lennon's cultural stock fell with every other one of his side projects in the late 1960s and early 1970s. The mixed notices given to the stage adaptation of *In His Own Write* in 1968 indicated that the novelty of his literary works had worn off very quickly indeed. The skit he contributed to Kenneth Tynan's *Oh! Calcutta!* revue (1969, transferring to London in 1970) was considered 'marvellous' only by Ono.[270] Obscenity charges collapsed against his exhibition of explicit lithographs in 1970; harder to dismiss was the *Sunday Times*' accusation that the works failed to 'do anything for art'.[271] Even the owner of the gallery mounting the show accepted that it contained 'some ... bad art, some mediocre art and some ... good draughtsmanship'.[272]

Lennon's critics jumped on any sign of philistinism. Burgess dismissed him as having 'no great education and no great knowledge of our literary past' and his unfortunate combination of ignorance and pretension became a running joke in *Private Eye*.[273] It invented Spiggy Topes as a generic Lennon/Beatles/rock-star character given to dispensing the true wisdom granted to a 'mentally retarded idiot'.[274] Topes explained how he and his fellow Turds had reached the heights of Mozart, Beethoven and Elgar.[275] Brilliance was accomplished not by book learning ('Reading's a hang-up') or ability ('Talent's just a word like God'), but by spirituality and intuition.[276] 'You don't have to be educated to talk like I do', revealed Topes. 'You don't have to read nothing to know what I'm talking about. It's there.'[277] The arrival in Topes' life of 'Japanese pop sculptress and plastic flower arranger' Yoko Hama in 1968 provided boundless opportunities for parody, from staging a bedroom farce at Coventry Cathedral to screening art films of Topes belching and picking his nose.[278]

Such criticism went beyond mere disdain. In attacking the Beatles, traditionalists were defending culture as they understood it. They saw themselves as performing their public duty as a clerisy in apostolic succession to Britain's greatest public moralists.[279] The Oxford professor of poetry Roy Fuller pledged himself to Matthew Arnold's mission to ensure that 'the raw and unkindled masses of humanity are touched with sweetness and light'.[280] Arnold was explicitly invoked by journalist Maurice Wiggin in his jaundiced review of the 1967 *Our World* broadcast, and implicitly so by Malcolm Muggeridge in 1969 in his tendentious claim that 'all the works of the imagination are concerned with light'.[281] As Paul Long details in his *Only in the Common People: The Aesthetics of Class in Post-War Britain* (2008), F. R. Leavis was the touchstone for the educationalists and literary critics clustered around *The Use of English* and *Critical Quarterly*.[282] Brian Cox, the co-editor of *Critical Quarterly* and the associated *Black Papers on Education*, envisaged himself as engaged in a Leavisite 'battle' between upholders of 'the traditional justifications of high culture' and those pushing a '"value-free" concept of culture'.[283]

These critics founded their opposition to the Beatles on the conviction that, as Fuller put it, 'criticism's primary task [is] that of telling us whether the work of art under consideration is any good or not'. The 'chief cultural evil' which he confronted was that this truism was being ignored.[284] The 'cultural fog' permeating sixties culture made it possible for people to mistake John Lennon for James Joyce and 'A Day in the Life' (1967) for a work of art.[285] Fuller's indignation at 'Philistines' who failed to distinguish between 'highbrow' classical music and the Beatles' 'kitsch' indicated how closely he associated genre with worth.[286]

'Hierarchies exist', affirmed the *Daily Telegraph*'s music critic Colin Mason.[287] Music lecturer Edward Lee explained how 'serious art' was more valuable owing to its 'greater technical command, and technical subtlety, and ... greater moral insight and moral worth'.[288] But Lee's contention that these qualities were 'pretty well universally' acknowledged, much like Mason's categorical tone, belied the challenges facing champions of high culture in sixties Britain.[289] The novelist and critic John Wain saw Lennon's Joycean writings and the Beatles' MBEs as disconcerting evidence that 'no one cares to say any longer where one category ends and another begins':

The 1960s are witnessing a gigantic scrambling of cultural levels. Whereas even twenty years ago there was a culture for the few that was recognisably apart from the culture of the many, we have now reached a point where popular and non-popular forms have flowed together in a huge morass, whether fertile or poisonous remains to be seen.[290]

The Beatles' critics assumed the mantle of cultural authority, yet feared that those listening to the Beatles were no longer listening to them. Strident proclamations of the insignificance of the Beatles signalled the very opposite. Every time a bastion of culture fell to the Beatles, their detractors experienced a diminution in their power to police the production, dissemination and appreciation of art. Changes in broadcasting, the press and education drew ire and indignation. Malcolm Muggeridge's suggestion that Lord Reith would have given no airtime to the 'Beatles bleat' was corroborated by John Scupham, who had recently retired from his post as Controller of BBC Educational Broadcasting.[291] Scupham urged the BBC to 'renew with missionary zeal the attempt to create and maintain a common culture' of an unapologetically highbrow kind by elevating

Bach and Boulez above the Beatles.[292] Radio producer Charles Parker developed a conspiracy theory to explain why the BBC had abdicated its responsibility to educate and inform.[293] He claimed that his 1967 series *Vox Pop* (1967) had been suppressed because it contravened the BBC's plan to make pop music 'a master tool of social control by a ruling class'.[294]

The concurrent serialisation of Beatles biographies by the *Sunday Times* and the *Observer* led Michael Nyman to deploy scare quotes when discussing 'the "intellectual" Sundays' and served to 'cheapen' broadsheet journalism in the opinion of Bill Grundy, who later famously traded insults with the Sex Pistols.[295] *Punch* produced a mock-up of a *Sunday Times'* front page devoted entirely to the Beatles, including articles by the Bishop of Southwark, Beverley Nichols and Malcolm Muggeridge, and Lord Snowden's portraits of the Beatles' dogs.[296]

The Beatles were associated in the minds of conservative critics with the pernicious effects of progressive schooling.[297] Brian Cox blamed progressive educators for indoctrinating the young to accept the Beatles as 'major poets'.[298] The historian Max Beloff paired comparisons between Beethoven and the Beatles with the same misplaced egalitarianism that resisted 'excellence in education' and promoted comprehensivisation. He warned that clever children in comprehensives would become 'frustrated by being kept at the pace of slower brains or diverted from cultural pursuits by the ubiquity of "pop-culture" so-called in his environment'.[299] Anthony Burgess likewise fretted that comprehensives placed dull children in the same classrooms as 'the educable'.[300] These brighter pupils would be less likely as a consequence to grasp the 'true vision of reality' contained in the great literature, art and science and to distinguish it from 'the travesty-art of the Beatles'.[301]

The selectivity of higher education did not insulate it from the same levelling tendencies, causing Lee to express 'horror' at the prospect of 'university beat groups'.[302] Academic interest in the Beatles became a byword for lower educational standards. *Punch* accordingly imagined courses on the band being offered by the Open University and derided the 'people with degrees in socio-musicology or musico-sociology' who pontificated about pop while turning a blind eye to its 'sordid commercial and economic realities'.[303] Holbrook savaged a pair of further education lecturers who had the temerity to place the Beatles within a 'lesser tradition' of culture.[304] To him, the Beatles were fit only to condemn; to do otherwise was to be a 'traitor to humanity and to civilised values'.[305]

Besides speaking their minds, it was unclear what critics could do to right the situation. Suggested remedies ranged from the paternalistic to the coercive. Hoggart recommended that broadcasters steer listeners from the Beatles to Beethoven to give 'more of us ... more chance to hear these good – these better – things'.[306] Marghanita Laski made the case for the state to subsidise a 'high art' which 'consoled, renewed, strengthened [and] purified' its audience as opposed to a 'pop art' which made people 'happy, or excited, or relaxed'.[307] Her observation that 'many people want Beatles and only a few want art' was expressed in more confrontational terms by Arts Council chair Arnold Goodman, who spoke of a 'battle' between pop groups and high culture.[308] The marketplace did not merely sustain the lesser order of culture exemplified by the Beatles; it distracted people from what Goodman termed 'the worthwhile things in life'.[309] Goodman's call for more arts funding was as self-interested as that of educationalist Roy Shaw for educational projects to counteract 'the cultural immaturity of the majority'.[310] Shaw warned that '[m]ass democracy will mean cultural decay' in the absence of public largesse. But his proposal for government measures 'restrain[ing] the commercial providers of pop culture' was tellingly vague and indicated the weakness of cultural paternalism against the forces of mass culture.[311] Fellow educationalist Bryan Wilson was more concrete in his suggestion that the 'the entertainment industry ought to be placed under public examination' through a licensing system.[312] This was censorship by another name, and no more realistic than Wilson's plans to sequester students in 'the ivory tower' in order to protect them from 'dubious jazz-musicians, the popular press, pop singers, TV commentators, women of easy virtue and the contemporary satirists'.[313]

Conservative critics were acutely aware of their own marginality and weakness in the face of mass culture and what they perceived to be the treason of intellectuals who were supportive of the Beatles. In 'The Challenge of Barbarism' (1965), Max Beloff accused those 'fashionable pundits' who placed the Beatles on a par with Beethoven of participating in 'the treason of the intellectuals that is at the root of every society's decay'.[314] The poet and folklorist James Reeves similarly implicated Thom Gunn in a 'contemporary *trahison des clercs*' for celebrating the Beatles' creation of 'The New Music'.[315] Others charged educated Beatle-lovers of 'abdication', 'capitulation' and 'apostasy', but the meaning was the same. To portray the Beatles as great artists was to 'deceive oneself and damage the very standards that one should be trying to affirm'.[316]

The perceived strength of the forces ranged against them and the inadequacy of the remedies at their disposal induced despair among opponents of the Beatles. The tables had been turned, lamented the playwright Arnold Wesker in 1966. The traitors had become the establishment and now levelled charges of treachery against defenders of cultural standards. Critics of popular culture such as himself were not simply ignored. They were afraid to speak out. To state that Prokofiev was self-evidently superior to the Beatles was no longer socially acceptable. It violated the democratic principle that everyone was entitled to their own viewpoint, and the permissive consensus against 'priggishness or censoriousness'.[317] Like some recusant priest, he could only 'secretly value' the truly 'ennobling or stimulating qualities of art' altogether lacking in the Beatles' repertoire.[318]

The result was a cultural declinism verging on apocalypticism. A minority of Jeremiads came from left-wing figures such as Wesker. The veneration of the Beatles betokened 'decadence' to socialist poet Alan Bold and confirmation that 'the Enlightenment has turned into its opposite' to historian George Lichtheim.[319] But they were outdone in their doom-mongering by those on the right. The crowd at a 1965 Beatles concert so disturbed Noël Coward that he wondered whether 'we are whirling more swiftly into extinction than we know'.[320] Max Beloff associated the Beatles with 'Barbarism', Peter Simple invoked Spenglerian fears of the 'Suicide of the West' and Brian Cox warned of a 'revulsion from the achievements of Western civilisation' among the young.[321]

A defence of high culture spilled over into claims for the superiority of Western civilisation. George Steiner worried that the young no longer saw Western culture as 'self-evidently superior', while Quintin Hogg accused Lennon of renouncing 'the whole of Western culture and dynamism from Athens and Rome and Jerusalem down to the present day' by associating with the Maharishi.[322] The argument that 'western civilisation today was being challenged from within' was most fully developed by John Sparrow, the gadfly Warden of All Souls.[323] He pounced on the Beatles' 'muddied animism' and Lennon's comment that 'The Mona Lisa is a load of crap' as evidence of the young's 'desire to repudiate the traditional culture of the West and to reject in its totality the concept of Fine Art'.[324] Drawing inspiration from the profoundly Eurocentric vision of Kenneth Clark's *Civilisation* series (1969), Sparrow explained how 'a civilised society is superior to an uncivilised one'.[325] A cathedral organist was a 'superior specimen of humanity' to an 'African savage' and the rule of law was preferable to being 'scalped by savages or eaten by cannibals'.[326]

Sparrow presented an unappealing choice between order and liberty. His atavistic model of development envisaged the 'primitive' child growing into a 'civilised man' by sacrificing 'freshness of vision, the innocent eye, spontaneity and creative impulse, innocence of heart, directness in his personal relations' in favour of inhibition, hypocrisy and the subordination of the individual to the collective.[327] The individualism and experimental-ism espoused by the Beatles threatened the body politic. Following their lead, hippies sought to 'escape from the inhibitions imposed on them by western society' and 'live the life of the noble savage' through taking drugs and indulging in the 'hysterical worship of pop groups'.[328]

The most apocalyptic models of cultural decline came from religious writers. The Catholic convert Christopher Booker slotted the Beatles into his grand theories about the nature of art and its role in the rise and fall of civilisations. He identified 'two very different kinds of art' across time.[329] One was moral, truthful, profound, harmonious and in tune with 'true organic order'.[330] Its opposite was perverted, sensationalist, superficial, dissonant: a 'vitality fantasy' which fomented disorder in the name of 'freedom and excitement'.[331] He followed Plato in regarding music as instrumental in 'reflecting and shaping the moral character, mind and temper of the Greek citizens, and therefore ultimately the harmony of their society'.[332] Great music achieved 'the perfect marriage of life and order'; its corrupted form was as debased, discordant and neurotic as the society which spawned it.[333]

According to Booker, decolonisation, affluence and the erosion of class distinctions since 1956 had made Britain 'uniquely vulnerable' to vitality fantasies.[334] The impact of rock 'n' roll in 1955–6 was symptomatic of the nation's deteriorating 'psychic health', which was then dealt a body blow by Beatlemania.[335] The Beatles' 'Ooohs' constituted a 'disturbance of ordered normality' in the androgyny of their 'girlish falsetto' and the frenzy it created in their audience.[336] William Mann's 1963 *Times* article signalled 'the surrender of more traditional forms of culture to this new mass hysteria'.[337] Apostates like Mann saw '"self-expression"' in both Bach and the Beatles and analysed Lennon and McCartney compositions in the same way as Beethoven's.[338] To Booker, cultural relativism and moral relativism went hand in hand. A society which could not distinguish between the canon and the Beatles was equally incapable of drawing 'a clear distinction between good and evil'.[339]

The only 'Road Back from Fantasy' identified by Booker was the one he had chosen for himself: acceptance of 'that complete and unchanging world-view provided by Christianity throughout the past 2,000 years'.[340] His views chimed with those of Malcolm Muggeridge, who viewed Western civilisation as having experienced a 'Gadarene descent' from its Christian heyday into a 'Sargasso Sea of fantasy and fraud'.[341] Like Booker, Muggeridge pitted religious and artistic truth against the sordid fantasies of popular culture. The mass media conspired to 'draw people away from reality, which means away from Christ'.[342] The Beatles, the Maharishi and an assortment of modernist writers and artists also conveyed 'the bad dreams of a materialistic society'.[343] Their cultural contribution, such as it was, consisted of amassing wealth without talent or scruple, inciting lust among prepubescent girls and falling for the guff of Transcendental Meditation.[344]

Conclusion

'It is difficult for a civilised, literary man to understand pop', stated the journalist Ray Gosling in 1970.[345] So it proved, but the Beatles made many of them try. Their critical reception in sixties and early-seventies Britain reconfigured debates over the relationship between high and low culture in several crucial respects. The Beatles brought pop music from the margins of cultural discourse to its centre. They joined like-minded musicians in composing, recording, performing and discussing music which aspired to artistic recognition. Yet their background, youth, education, commerciality, popular audience and stylistic promiscuity challenged critics to rethink the very definition of art and its function in society.

However, this chapter has shown that the rethinking process was contested and protracted. It did not conform to the models of early acceptance, eventual accreditation or outright rejection which were advanced at the time and in subsequent scholarship. Instead, the Beatles provoked a fully fledged debate about the meaning of culture which showed no sign of resolution at the start of the 1970s. The debate was as much about its participants and their role as cultural critics as it was about the Beatles. The Beatles' detractors tended to be older and more right-wing, but there were many significant exceptions. Moreover, differing and often conflicting views of the Beatles could be found within every conceivable cultural group: poets, playwrights, composers and pop artists; literary critics, art critics and film critics; jazz, folk, rock and classical-music writers and musicians.

From one perspective, contemporary debates over the Beatles' artistry created more heat than light and exposed the educated at their most ignorant. They misspelt names ('Macartney'),[346] misdated albums ('*Sergeant Pepper's Lonely Hearts Club Band* (1966)'),[347] misnamed songs ('That Boy', 'Hullo Goodbye', 'Back Home in the USSR'),[348] misquoted lyrics ('I saw a film the other day', 'Couldn't be worse', 'I'm very stoned'),[349] misattributed compositions (Buckle crediting 'This Boy' to Harrison)[350] and misidentified instrumentalists (Mellers imagining that Starr played the sitar).[351] Richard Williams notoriously reviewed the blank sides of a test pressing of Lennon and Ono's *Wedding Album* (1969) as though they were experimental recordings.[352] Howard Barker wrote an entire play around the conceit that 'Lennon had actually known this girl Eleanor Rigby ... and served her up as song material', which would have made more sense if Lennon was the principal author of the song.[353] Laurie likewise contrasted Beatles' compositions to the sentimentality of Peter and Gordon's 'A World Without Love' (1964), unaware that it was a Lennon/McCartney cast-off.[354]

Champions and opponents of the Beatles sought to summarily dismiss each other's arguments. Tony Palmer maintained that 'only the ignorant will not hear and only the deaf will not acknowledge' the greatness of *The Beatles* double album.[355] Conversely, Fritz Spiegl refused to take seriously anyone who took pop seriously, lambasting the likes of Palmer as charlatans 'apply[ing] musical terms they do not understand to music which is beyond the music-critical pale'.[356] Spiegl's distinction as the composer of the *Z-Cars* theme tune established his superiority over the 'musically unlettered journalists' he criticised.[357] Similarly, Fuller's comment that any claim for the Beatles' artistic merits represented 'the abdication of the critic from the act of evaluation' served to bolster his own standing as a literary pundit.[358]

Yet the cultural authority of the Beatles' critics rested upon slenderer foundations than they cared to admit. Anthony Burgess was the only 'serious' composer whose criticism displayed more than a passing acquaintance with the Beatles' music.[359] Spiegl had once been an orchestral musician, but as a conductor he specialised in light music and composed theme tunes, one of which was released on Andrew Loog Oldham's Immediate Records. Non-musicians who based their preference for classical music on 'common sense' or their 'depths [being] stirred' faced similar criticisms to those levelled at untrained rock critics.[360] John Carey discerned no 'technical knowledge' in Paul Johnson's broadside and Clive James asked Roy Fuller to explain his criteria for elevating Rachmaninov above the Beatles.[361] James astutely observed that '"High culture" is being defended as a category, rather than as a set of qualities ... by people who are not qualified to defend it.'[362]

The very vehemence of the debate spoke to its significance. However poorly their arguments have aged, contemporaries who questioned the Beatles' cultural value were not simply tin-eared. To accept the Beatles as artists meant revising many of their most ingrained assumptions not simply about art, but their own status as artists, critics and intellectuals. The stakes for the Beatles' foremost defenders were almost as high. They found themselves accused of philistinism and culpability for 'the contemporary cultural crisis'.[363] That they persevered is testament to the originality and impact of the Beatles and to the border wars breaking out in postwar cultural criticism.

5 | Politics: The Beatles, Parliament and Revolution

Figure 5.1 Politicians – With Labour Party leader Harold Wilson, March 1964. Photo by © Hulton-Deutsch Collection/CORBIS/Corbis via Getty Images

In the general election of 1964, the Beatles propelled the Communist Party of Great Britain (CPGB) out of obscurity and into power. It all began when the main party leaders mishandled Beatlemania. The Liberals' coup of unveiling Ringo Starr at a campaign rally backfired when their leader Jo Grimond was revealed to be a Beatlephobe. The Tory leader Alec Douglas-Home agreed with his Labour counterpart Harold Wilson not to exploit the Beatles for electoral purposes, only to be accused of treachery when George Harrison, John Lennon and Paul McCartney unexpectedly joined him at a hustings. Wilson ignominiously failed to secure any 'platform Beatles' of his own. With Labour, Liberals and the Conservatives in disarray, the Beatles' decision to decamp to the Soviet Union resulted in a Communist landslide.[1]

These events did not happen. They were instead the premise of a *Punch* column written by Basil Boothroyd in March 1964, which neatly captures several themes of this chapter. The first is the sheer incongruity of pop stars having anything to do with politicians in the 1960s. The political leader most closely associated with the Beatles, Harold Wilson, might have confessed himself 'very fond of their [the Beatles'] programmes', but his biographer notes that 'fashion in music, dress and art was beyond his understanding' and he made the curtest of references to the band in his memoirs.[2] For their part, the Beatles cared less about Harold Wilson than they did about Brian Wilson of the Beach Boys or Mary Wilson of the Supremes. The two Beatles songs which mentioned him (1966's 'Taxman' and the unreleased 'Commonwealth Song' from 1969) skewered his immigration and taxation policies, prompting the author of one of them, George Harrison, to cite him alongside Edward Heath as exemplifying 'that silly cartoon world' from which he sought to escape.[3]

The second theme is the Beatles' unprecedented impact on political discourse. The *Punch* article was satirical rather than surreal because of the sporadic attempts by party leaders to align themselves with the band. Home had already made a number of positive references to the Beatles when the article appeared and Wilson was to meet them a few weeks afterwards (see Fig. 5.1).[4] Although Grimond did not join in, the General Secretary of the CPGB John Gollan felt it necessary to announce that his party had 'no line on the Beatles'.[5]

The third theme is that of politicians seeking to divine the Beatles' political leanings. The unseemly scramble for their favour envisaged in the article played on the idea that they had no confirmed party affiliation. This was indeed the case in the early sixties, allowing for claims and counterclaims to be projected onto them.[6] Whereas Boothroyd whimsically imagined them succumbing to communism, commentators from the left and right were more prone to detect an incipient fascism in Beatlemania.[7] The Beatles' political outspokenness in the second half of the 1960s did not resolve the matter so much as generate new areas of controversy.

The manner in which Boothroyd's piece has been misinterpreted in later accounts introduces the fourth theme: that existing scholarship on the Beatles' political impact resembles an echo chamber in which writers amplify each other's assertions and mistakes. Three recent examples illustrate the point. Chapters by Jeremy Tranmer use Bertrand Lemonnier as their source for several statements about the Beatles' significance in the 1964 general election. These include the claim that Alec Douglas-Home 'ask[ed] them jokingly to stand as candidates for the Conservative Party' and that 'Labour and the Conservatives came to a tacit agreement during the 1964 election campaign, according to which neither party would ... try to make excessive use of the group'.[8] Both events are wholly fictitious, and in fact appear in contemporary satires (one a cartoon, the other Boothroyd's column), the humour of which was lost on Lemonnier. David Fowler is similarly misinformed when stating that the Conservative Party 'instructed all Conservative candidates to mention the Beatles in their [general] election campaigns'.[9] There was no such instruction and accordingly no recorded mention of the band by politicians on the stump in the autumn of 1964 save by Screaming Lord Sutch and Major Arthur Braybrooke of the Patriotic Party, who proposed displacing the Beatles with a Gay Gordons revival.[10] Fowler proceeds to attribute half a dozen quotations to the Marxist scholar Eric Hobsbawm, all of which appeared in a riposte to Hobsbawm and other 'Beatles' detractors'.[11] This game of academic telephone is epitomised by an article by Oded Heilbronner, who writes of 'David Flower [*sic*] ... quoting the words of the conservative [*sic*] cabinet member William Deeds's [*sic*] in 1963 [*sic*]: "the Beatles were an example of youthful free enterprise that should be welcomed and nurtured by business leaders"'.[12] Both names are misspelt, the date is wrong and the quotation attributed to Deedes is actually Fowler's interpretation of the speech in question.

This chapter begins by examining why the Beatles provoked Parliament to discuss pop music for the first time in a concerted fashion.[13] It considers which politicians spoke about the Beatles, when they did so and how their comments fed into existing and emerging political debates. The main source for this section is every mention of the Beatles in parliamentary debates. In an attempt to introduce a modicum of precision to such textual analysis, each reference was classified by date, by debate, by the age, gender and party of the speaker, by theme, and by whether its tone was positive, negative, neutral or mixed. This material was supplemented by politicians' diaries and newspaper and periodical reports of statements made by parliamentarians outside Westminster.

It then turns to the Beatles' reception by Marxists and anarchists in the extra-parliamentary left. The left had more dealings than MPs with the band and was engaged in a similar quest to broaden the scope and constituency of politics beyond the concerns of Westminster. The left mattered to the Beatles to the extent that they became major funders of the radical press and supporters of certain campaigns, from CND to Troops Out. The Beatles mattered to the left because of their class origins, modernity, anti-authoritarianism, talent for creating controversy and appeal to the young. More broadly, left-wing writers and publications were instrumental in establishing pop music as a legitimate subject of analysis. Serious debates on pop appeared in *Marxism Today* and the *New Left Review* and the academic study of popular culture was pioneered by cultural Marxists based at the University of Birmingham. Simon Frith wrote for *Marxism Today*, Dave Laing and Pete Fowler wrote for *7 Days*, Richard Mabey and George Melly contributed to *Anarchy*, John Hoyland reviewed *Abbey Road* (1969) for *Black Dwarf* and articles by Karl Dallas appeared in the CPGB organ *Music and Life*. These authors and publications are among the main sources for the later portions of the chapter.

Previous chapters have examined conservative moralist critiques of the Beatles and their contribution to cultural and religious decline. The extra-parliamentary right nonetheless displayed little interest in the Beatles when compared to their left-wing adversaries. The newly formed National Front set off stink bombs at a screening of the 'Communist propaganda' film featuring Lennon, *How I Won the War* (1967), while members of Pokesdown Youth Club in Bournemouth burnt copies of 'I Am the Walrus' (1967) in protest against its 'lavatory poetry'.[14] But there was nothing in Britain to compare to the nationalist protests against their appearance at the Budokan Hall in Tokyo or the anti-communist, anti-atheist and anti-civil-rights activism against them in the southern United States.[15]

Parliament

The Beatles dominated parliamentary discussions of pop music every bit as much as they dominated the pop scene. The group and its members appeared in 57 debates and 5 written questions in the House of Commons and House of Lords up to the announcement of their break-up in April 1970: a total of 62 separate occasions. There appears to have been only 45 debates and questions mentioning any other pop musicians by name in the period between 1956, when Britain first encountered rock 'n' roll, and April 1970. The Rolling Stones and its members came second to the Beatles in Parliament as elsewhere, receiving mention in 15 debates or questions. The next most cited pop star in Parliament up to April 1970 was the since-forgotten Terry Dene, who featured in seven debates or questions concerning his discharge from national service on psychiatric grounds and swift return to his singing career. Of the rest, Elvis Presley appeared in 6 debates or questions, Tommy Steele and Adam Faith in 5 apiece and Marty Wilde in 4 (once again discussing his exemption from national service). An equal number of references was made to other pop musicians in the eight years prior to the Beatles' emergence and the eight years of their recording career (22 and 23 respectively), suggesting that parliamentarians' interest in the Beatles did not result in their paying greater attention to pop music more generally.

To determine when the Beatles appeared in parliamentary discussions, it is necessary to switch from looking at the number of debates or written questions to the total number of contributions made by Members of Parliament. This is because the Beatles were often mentioned by multiple speakers in the same debate. In all, 84 contributions were made by 76 different members (plus the unspecified number of Opposition MPs who added 'The Beatles!' to Quintin Hogg's list of 'top talent' lured to the United States), indicating that there were not just one or two eccentrics obsessing about the band.[16]

Table 5.1, which details the number of parliamentary references to the Beatles by year, shows that interest fluctuated during the band's short career. The bulk of references – 51 out of 84 – comes from the year and a half between November 1963, when the name of the Beatles was first uttered in Parliament, and June 1965, when it was announced that they were to receive official recognition as Members of the British Empire. The turning point came with the Beatles' conquest of America in

Table 5.1 Parliamentary comments on the Beatles by year, 1962 to April 1970

1962	0
1963	5
1964	30
1965	17
1966	2
1967	17
1968	5
1969	5
Jan.–Apr. 1970	3
Total	84

February 1964, which prompted no fewer than six parliamentary mentions of them in a single week. Beatlemania struck a good number of politicians as something remarkable in every sense of the word.

Parliamentary comments about the Beatles tailed off following the award of their MBEs in 1965, notwithstanding the Beatles' growing politicisation in the second half of the sixties. There were only mentioned twice in 1966: the year when they released their first overtly political song, 'Taxman', and when Lennon created a furore for remarking that the Beatles were 'more popular than Jesus'.[17] The Beatles attracted little parliamentary interest in that 'year of revolutions', 1968, when popular music provided the sound-track for radical protest. The same went for 1969, despite the publicity surrounding Lennon and Ono's Bed-Ins for peace and Lennon's return of his MBE.

One explanation for the decline in references to the Beatles after 1965 is that 'the end of the Beatle boom' perceived by Ian Gilmour in 1967 excused parliamentarians from attending to a subject which frankly baffled them.[18] It also indicates that any efforts by popular musicians to engage politicians could not expect to be reciprocated. Politicians were not particularly interested in what the Beatles or any other musicians had to say about them. Their interest derived from the way the Beatles encapsulated new social problems inviting political solutions. The year 1967 accordingly saw a rise in parliamentary comments on the Beatles because the band served as a handy reference point in debates on drugs, pirate radio and the youth question.

Parliamentary references to the Beatles did not fall neatly along party lines. Table 5.2 shows that Labour and Conservative Members of Parliament made almost the same number of contributions: 34 and 37

Table 5.2 Parliamentary comments on the Beatles by party, 1962 to April 1970

	Labour	Conservative	Other*	Total
Positive	11	10	3	24
Negative	9	6	5	20
Mixed	1	4	1	6
Neutral	13	17	4	34
Total	34	37	13	84

*   Includes Liberals, Ulster Unionists, cross-benchers and bishops. One National Liberal and Conservative MP is counted as a Conservative.

respectively. Labour parliamentarians were more likely to be negative than their Conservative counterparts, though were less hostile than members of minor parties and cross-benchers. But the two principal parties accounted for roughly the same proportion of positive and neutral comments, indicating that divisions about the Beatles emerged as much within parties as between them.

This is not to say that Labour and Tory attitudes to the Beatles were much of a muchness, for each party found different things to like and dislike about the band. Complimentary Conservative references to the Beatles portrayed them as exemplifying the work ethic, entrepreneurialism and the benefits of a free-market, low-taxation society. Labour had no truck with such economic liberalism and largely relied on the trademark opportunism of its leader, Harold Wilson, to stake its own claim to the Beatles. But when Labour and Conservative leaders fought over the band during the heyday of Beatlemania, they did so without any clear direction from their party colleagues.

The clearest division over the Beatles in Parliament occurred between the generations. Whereas MPs aged 50 or above made an equal number of positive and negative comments about the band, those under 50 were twice as likely to be positive as negative. The first MP to declare himself 'proud' to be both a fan and to belong to the same generation as the Beatles was, appropriately enough, the youngest member of the Commons, 25-year-old Leslie Huckfield. The 1967 debate on the age of majority provided him with the ideal occasion for defending the Beatles and other 'colourful facets of my generation' against parliamentary adversaries who 'seem to have lost touch completely with the way in which young people today are thinking and feeling and going about their lives'.[19] Younger MPs were not simply cheerleaders for the band. In fact, half of their contributions were neutral in tone, in comparison to a third of those by older MPs. It was rather that the Beatles featured on the mental map of the younger cohort, who felt obliged to acknowledge the band even when possessing no decided opinions about them.

So how did politicians interpret the Beatles? Table 5.3 indicates that humour was the most common theme. Mention of the band might serve as light relief from grave matters of governance, but it also involved politicians defining the Beatles as their binary opposites. They counterpoised the Beatles to such serious matters as military alliances ('from NATO to the Beatles'), the clergy ('from Beatles to bishops'), crop cultivation ('not the Liverpool "Beatle", but the betel nut, of course') and classical music ('for me to be non-controversial in a maiden speech is almost like asking

Table 5.3 Parliamentary comments on the Beatles by theme, 1962 to April 1970

Humour	24
Generation/youth	18
Art	14
Treatment by authorities	13
Crime	11
Merseyside, John Lennon	10 each
Economics, influence, wealth	8 each
Appearance	7
Drugs, education, modernity, music, state subsidy/intervention	6 each
Free market, Paul McCartney	5 each
Behaviour, Beatlemania, ephemerality, military, Ringo Starr, taxation	4 each
BBC, fame, personal enthusiasm, pirate radio	3 each
Yoko Ono, politics, public service, quotation of lyrics, religion	2 each
Britain, Brian Epstein, George Harrison, intellectual property	1 each

a Beatle to sing in grand opera').[20] Parliamentarians ordinarily had nothing in common with the Beatles, being modestly paid ('I only wish I had the salary of the Beatles') and sensibly coiffed ('would it be possible to get a Beatle wig in this house?').[21] Politics was represented as a serious business, in contrast to something as 'trivial or superficial' as a '"Beatle" hair-do'.[22] As such, it was best conducted by serious politicians, not pop stars, prompting one bemused MP to wonder why a constituent voted for 'someone called "Ringo"' instead of a parliamentary colleague.[23]

Direct comparisons between politicians and the Beatles appeared in the form of parliamentary insults in which one politician accused another of falling short of parliamentary ideals. The Speaker likened boisterous MPs to hysterical Beatlemaniacs when chiding them for 'treat[ing] the Prime Minister's question time as though it were a reception at London airport'.[24] The same analogy was used when dismissing the views of members of Her Majesty's Opposition as being 'of no more importance than whether the teen-agers are these days screaming for John or Paul or Ringo'.[25] An underperforming Leader of the Opposition drew comparisons to the hapless Pete Best, in severe need of replacement ('Get another drummer').[26]

A valuable article by Paul R. Kohl suggests one way of understanding why the Beatles signified a realm outside parliamentary concerns. He depicts the Beatles as 'agents of carnival' who challenged existing hierarchies through humour and role reversal.[27] This accurately describes how the Beatles and their admirers used humour, but politicians' jokes served the opposite purpose. By belittling the band, parliamentarians' witticisms reinscribed the political hierarchy on their own terms and in their own favour.

From this perspective, the Beatles' carnival was a sideshow that occasionally reminded politicians of the goings-on beyond the weighty matters occupying them at Westminster. Yet the Beatlemania sweeping Britain in late 1963 and the United States in early 1964 could not be ignored, however alien it seemed to the grown men (and occasional woman) in Parliament. The first prominent politicians to pronounce upon the Beatles betrayed their confusion. Edward Heath, having found himself labelled '[t]he most unpopular politician in Britain' by the *New York Times* for making snobbish remarks about their accents, sought to redeem himself by proclaiming the Beatles to be 'the salvation of the corduroy industry'.[28] Field-Marshal Viscount Montgomery similarly reversed himself, his initial fantasies about 'the Beatles having to get their hair cut' replaced by an equally unrealised ambition of inviting them 'down for the weekend'.[29]

While the earliest remarks by politicians merely acknowledged the Beatles' prominence, the manner in which Heath and Montgomery shifted from condescension to ingratiation testified to the band's power. They and their parliamentary colleagues suddenly found themselves having to compete for public attention with young men radically different from themselves in background, appearance, outlook and talents. Both politicians and musicians had constituencies of a sort. They vied for space in the newspapers and the broadcast schedules: an unfair competition given that Lennon was 'almost the most celebrated living Englishman'.[30] 'For anything to be acceptable just now, it has to be said by Marx or Marcuse, or by Lenin or Lennon", grumbled the aptly named Tom Iremonger in 1969.[31]

Politicians were by definition interested in power, and some speculated that the Beatles possessed a form of it that they lacked. They were omnipresent – 'the Mersey beat reaches even into Blaenau Ffestiniog' – and apparently omnipotent, leading Tony Benn to wonder whether the Soviet Union 'could be undermined by a single open air concert by the Beatles in Moscow'.[32] Tory MP Henry Price marvelled at the 'hypnotic' influence they exercised over their fans and Harold Wilson was one of several politicians expressing variations on the theme that 'the Beatles did more to keep kids off the streets than all the forces of law and order put together'.[33]

So, when not simply making jokes at the band's expense, politicians' responses to the Beatles revolved around issues of power. The most practical question was how the state should exercise its power over the Beatles: the subject of 13 parliamentary comments. The principle that citizens should be equal before the law led certain MPs to complain that the Beatles as celebrities received favourable treatment from the authorities. Sir Charles Taylor maintained in 1963 that 'the Beatles should no longer receive police protection in the London area from their admirers' and Sir Knox Cunningham objected in 1965 that 'people were refused admission to London Airport when the Beatles were flying to Europe'.[34] A related complaint was that the state should not bestow unwarranted praise on the Beatles as mere popular entertainers. Lord Willis deplored the sight of 'many grave, reverend and learned *seigneurs* climbing on the Beatles' bandwagon', and such indignation reached a crescendo when the Beatles were awarded MBEs in 1965.[35]

But arguments for equal treatment were made on behalf of the Beatles as well as against them on the grounds that, if they did not deserve to be mollycoddled, neither should they be mistreated or undervalued. Joan Quennell asked Rab Butler to explain why the Beatles had been 'manhandled by Foreign Office officials' during a Washington embassy reception in 1964 and the following year Ronald Lewis expressed himself dumbfounded that the Beatles were only awarded MBEs for 'making people happy' while Dr Beeching was ennobled for doing the precise opposite.[36] Arthur Lewis tabled two questions in 1968 suggesting that the arrest on drugs charges of John Lennon and Yoko Ono had been heavy-handed and publicity-seeking. The historian and peer John Julius Norwich thought the police had insufficient reason to impound Lennon's nude portraits of Ono two years later.[37]

The so-called 'Beatle clause' of the 1969 budget, which targeted the foreign earnings of entertainers, saw rival conceptions of equality being advanced by the two main political parties. Whereas Labour believed that taxing the rich would create a more equal society, the Conservatives held that all citizens had an equal right to earn money, and that singling out the Beatles for punitive taxation was a product of sheer envy. Shadow Chancellor Iain Macleod stated that Labour had 'set out to shoot the Beatles, probably not a particularly estimable thing to do since the Beatles make a lot of money for this country, much of it in foreign exchange'.[38]

The Conservatives' relatively liberal taxation policy was not the only instance of politicians advocating the relaxation of government control over the Beatles and their kind. Traditionalists and modernisers clashed over whether male prisoners and soldiers should be permitted Beatle-length hair. Montgomery welcomed the prospect of conscription forcing the Beatles to get short backs and sides, but such antediluvian views irked those keen for institutions to keep pace with the times.[39] 'I do not know why [the Beatles] should get their hair cut', said Emrys Hughes: 'Why should a soldier need to have his hair cut in a certain way?'[40] Hair length likewise presented Victor Yates with an issue on which to advocate penal reform. He condemned as 'repressive' and arbitrary prison regulations that would, for example, force the Beatles to be shorn.[41] Though the Beatles had split up by the time that they featured in a debate specifically about the permissive society, such exchanges weighed up the balance of power between state and the individual over matters of personal conduct.[42]

The extent to which the state should impose cultural standards appeared in debates over public sponsorship of the arts.[43] Even the most ardent *dirigistes* conceded that the state should not instruct people what to listen to in their free time. The Chairman of the Arts Council Lord Goodman despised the Beatles and despaired that 'The pop groups are winning the battle against those who would promote the arts'.[44] Yet he told Parliament that it was not the Arts Council's job to parachute classical musicians into areas where children were deserting Bartók for the Beatles.[45] '[W]e cannot legislate for leisure. That would be wrong. Leisure in itself is freedom', conceded his Labour colleague Lord Willis in his philippic against the Beatles, adding that 'we can only provide the conditions … the facilities' to foster cultural appreciation.[46] The provision of such 'facilities', however, allowed Willis to advocate a state-sponsored 'cultural offensive' against the 'cultural revolution' spearheaded by the Beatles. His suggestion that the state might subsidise high art with a 'culture tax' levied against pop music was a non-starter, unlike his opposition to profit-making radio stations '"chugged up" with "pop" music'.[47] As with the 'Beatle clause', Labour's antipathy to commercial broadcasting allowed the Conservatives to present themselves as champions of liberty (possibly buoyed by one pirate station transmitting from the good ship *Laissez-Faire*).

Disagreement over how the state should treat the Beatles was mirrored by that over how the Beatles should treat the state. Contributing to the national finances was the main way in which politicians saw the Beatles as being of service. It was widely assumed that they had been awarded MBEs for services to the export industry, though a supportive early-day motion tabled by Liverpudlian MPs credited them with producing 'great good and happiness' as well as 'great commercial advantage' to Britain.[48] Others wished that the Beatles would serve the nation by entertaining the troops in West Berlin or establishing a philanthropic institution in the mould of the Wolfson and Rayne Foundations or the Nuffield Trust.[49]

Politicians also hoped that the Beatles would serve as role models for the young, though what virtues they were meant to embody was a matter of dispute. Tory Vice-Chairman Dame Barbara Brooke and Bill Deedes encouraged youngsters to follow the Beatles' example of '[n]ot sitting waiting for other people to do for them, but getting about and doing on their own', the moral being that '[t]o be tops in the beat business demands work, skill, sweat'.[50] William Clark wondered if the Beatles could 'instil into our teen-agers the importance of saving' rather than earning money by lending their name to 'Beatle Bonds'.[51] Yet such materialistic concerns were secondary to Lord Aberdare, who considered the Beatles' involvement with the Maharishi to be 'one of the most significant things that has happened recently' inasmuch as it demonstrated 'worldly achievement' to be no substitute for 'spiritual satisfaction'.[52]

From a politician's point of view, however, the greatest public service that the Beatles could perform was to bestow electoral advantage on his or her party. The national press recorded only one occasion when a mainstream politician mentioned the Beatles on the hustings. This was during the Kinross by-election in November 1963, when Alec Douglas-Home 'gave the right answer at an election meeting to the wag who asked him "Would you let your daughter marry a Beatle?"'.[53] The Beatles went almost unmentioned during the general election campaign of autumn 1964. Yet there was an unmistakably electioneering tone to the way (as Brian Epstein put it) 'the Prime Minister and the Leader of the Opposition ... [made] voluble, rival claims to the ownership of the Beatles' earlier that year.[54]

Home and his Minister of Information Deedes displayed populist instincts in speeches which saluted the Beatles as representative of the export-driven, upwardly mobile and go-ahead country created by the Conservatives. Unfortunately for them, Wilson could not ignore so direct a challenge to his strategy of contrasting Labour's youthful and classless 'New Britain' with its Tory opposite. He retaliated using all the rhetorical skills at his disposal. Not only did he consider it preposterous for 'these apostles of a bygone age ... to pretend that they are with it by claiming the Beatles'. It was also opportunistic, with Wilson charging that Home 'would not hesitate' to appoint the Beatles to ambassadorial positions 'if he thought there were votes in it'.[55] While upbraiding the Conservatives for exploiting the Beatles for political gain, Wilson saluted them as young, classless achievers from Merseyside in the hope that voters would consider himself in a similar light. He was on hand to reopen the Cavern Club in 1966 and used his one face-to-face meeting with the band in March 1964 to secure a famous photo op and to denigrate 'attempts recently by a certain leader of a certain party . . . to involve our friends, the Beatles, in politics'.[56]

Wilson's decision to award MBEs to the Beatles testified as much to their symbolic power as to his tactical nous. The notion of the Beatles receiving honours first emerged during the 1964 general election campaign, but only as part of the platform of 'national teenage candidate' Screaming Lord Sutch.[57] *Melody Maker*'s call to 'Honour the Beatles: Do It Now!' in March 1965 met with widespread incredulity in Fleet Street.[58] Yet Wilson obliged within a matter of weeks, putting a Labour spin on the well-worn theme of the Beatles as incomparably iconic iconoclasts. Labour MP Eric Heffer accordingly dismissed protests against the MBEs as 'plain silly and rather snobbish' for their refusal to accept that 'nowadays honours are being given on a much wider and more democratic scale than before'.[59] The following year *Time* magazine portrayed 'good old 'arold' Wilson and the Beatles as part of the same 'swinging meritocracy'.[60]

As well as pondering how to respond to the Beatles as a band, politicians used the Beatles as test cases for the latest social theories: Michael Young's 'rise of the meritocracy', Richard Hoggart's 'candyfloss culture', John Kenneth Galbraith's 'affluent society', the Newsom Report's analysis of educational low achievement, and various models of juvenile delinquency. It was in this capacity as harbingers of modernity that the Beatles featured in three key political controversies concerning culture, social mobility and the generation gap.

The Beatles were inevitably invoked in parliamentary debates on the relationship between high and low culture at a time when the 'cultural capital' accorded to each was a matter of intense concern (see Chapter 4).[61] Most politicians agreed with Viscount Samuel in his sharp distinction between the Beatles and 'serious' art.[62] The Bishop of Southwark and Lawrie Pavitt accordingly contrasted them to the Royal Shakespeare Company and the soprano Joan Cross.[63] But while the likes of Lord Auckland and Sir Herbert Butcher were careful not to criticise the Beatles when distinguishing 'their form of culture' from the more august variety, others did not hesitate to do so.[64] The Duke of Atholl referred to the Beatles as mere 'noise', while Lord Willis saw the Beatles as personifying all that was wrong with contemporary culture and society.[65] Drawing upon Matthew Arnold's *Culture and Anarchy* (1869), Richard Hoggart's *The Uses of Literacy* (1957) and most especially Paul Johnson's *New Statesman* article 'The Menace of Beatlism' (1964), Willis declared that 'This is not culture. This is a cult – a cheap, plastic, candyfloss substitute for culture.' He charged that popular culture was not simply distinct from and inferior to high culture. It was destructive of it, supplanting its rightful place in the nation's hearts and minds. He used the metaphor of a 'tidal wave … under which we are in danger of becoming submerged' and lamented that firms had switched from making busts of Shakespeare to those of the Fab Four. Thus the twentieth century was becoming 'the century of Beatles and Bingo' in contrast to the eighteenth century ('the century of Bach and Beethoven') and the nineteenth century ('the century of Brahms').[66]

Willis was not the ideal champion of high culture since, although chairman of the Writers' Guild, he was by his own admission a 'first-class second-rate author'.[67] He had made his name as a screenwriter: most famously as the creator of *Dixon of Dock Green*, but was also responsible for melodramas, children's films, Norman Wisdom vehicles, the occasional musical and, somewhat later, the schlocky *Man-Eaters*, about tigers on the prowl in American suburbia. His dubious cultural credentials prompted Lady Gaitskell to state that she would choose the Beatles over his best known literary creation.[68] The other problem for Willis' argument was that the sixties were a time when the boundaries between high and low culture were coming under challenge. The Yardbirds duly sought to convince Willis of the merits of popular music by staging a concert in his back garden. Wilson showed himself better attuned to this development in a calculatedly light-hearted reference when he met the Beatles:

I'm sure the *Times* music correspondent spoke for all of us when he said of our friends, the Beatles, that harmonically, it is one of their most intriguing with its chains of pandiatonic clusters.[69]

Politicians were generally more comfortable when discussing music in less highfalutin terms, as a matter of personal preference. Lord Taylor confessed that he while he 'ought to have liked' all the canonical figures mentioned by Willis, he had not heard of some of them, disliked others and supplemented his enjoyment of the rest with music-hall and easy-listening artistes.[70] Lord Shackleton similarly admitted to being sufficiently 'lowbrow' to approve of the Beatles.[71] Lord Denham went still further by conceding that 'to the devotee, "pop" is an art form' and urging his fellow peers not to be 'intellectual snobs', although the remainder of his speech damned pop music with faint praise.[72] Less equivocal was the young Liverpudlian Labour MP Bill Rodgers. He expressed pride over having attended the same grammar school as two of the Beatles and declared that

It is important to realise that culture is indivisible and not to regard popular culture, which some people may not like, as something totally separate from the provision for music and the arts in the way that they are normally understood.[73]

Here was the germ of a more pluralistic view of culture, at odds with Willis' rigid if hypocritical hierarchical model.

The debate over meritocracy demonstrated that the Beatles were sufficiently ambiguous – and politicians sufficiently confused – that different conclusions could be reached by politicians applying similar models. Charles Curran used the concept of meritocracy along the same lines as its creator, Michael Young, when bemoaning the fate of those without 'a minimum standard of ability and education' in a society run by and for a skilled elite.[74] The one problem with his argument was his choice of John Lennon as a 'pathetic' example of how secondary-modern schools were leaving the residuum without the requisite academic skills to communicate, still less to succeed.[75] He was challenged by his Conservative colleagues Sir Harrison Harwood, who prized 'character' above book learning, and Norman Miscampbell, who more helpfully pointed out that Lennon and two other band members had attended grammar schools.[76]

While willing to credit the Beatles with being 'highly intelligent', Miscampbell shared Curran's assumption that their fans lacked 'deeper education'.[77] The same went for Richard Buchanan, who speculated that those who 'follow the Mersey beat' rather than 'the scholastic beat' ended up in jobs 'well below their intellectual capacity'.[78] Moreover, Miscampbell made the common error of portraying Young's dystopian vision in positive terms. He saw no problem in the Beatles being rewarded handsomely for their 'great skill', much as Bill Deedes commended them for showing that '[t]here is no place for the lazy, the incompetent, the slipshod' in a successful entertainment industry.[79]

Harold Wilson succeeded in devising a Labour version of meritocracy in which the Beatles were to be rewarded with medals instead of money, only for the Conservatives to regain the initiative in 1969 when opposing the 'Beatle clause'. John Nott received applause from his fellow Tories when he declared himself to be 'not envious' of pop stars and hoped that they would earn three times their current salary in recognition of their efforts.[80] Pop stars subsequently became one of the Conservatives' favourite examples when advocating low rates of personal taxation for the rich and enterprising in the 1970s and 1980s.

Notwithstanding Wilson's efforts, some Labour politicians used the example of the Beatles to question the very existence of a meritocracy. Tony Benn reasoned that 'the Beatles have done more for the royal family by accepting MBEs' than vice versa. A scourge of the status quo, Benn saw the Beatles' honours as 'strengthen[ing] all the forces of conservatism in society' by providing a democratic gloss to the archaic privileges of the monarch.[81] A more common concern was voiced by Lord Campbell of Eskan, who referred to the Beatles when ridiculing the idea of any 'recognisable relationship between productivity and reward'.[82] It once again fell to Ted Willis to launch the most uncompromising attack on the Beatles and, with it, the notion that the Beatles exemplified meritocratic accomplishment. It made no difference to him that they were 'technically very good' when their music lacked any cultural value. Nor could they take credit for satisfying a demand 'artificially created' by malign 'commercial interests'.[83] Their fans were not the 'highly discriminating critics' extolled by Deedes, but 'not-so-clever' educational failures engaged in the 'worship of "phoney" idols' like some 'savage and backward people'.[84] For the young to believe that 'They [the Beatles] did it; and I can do it' was not so much inspirational as delusional, the 'doctrine of cheap success' being but a temporary diversion from the 'drudgery and greyness' of their lives.[85] Meritocracy was meretricious.

The question of juvenile delinquency also exercised politicians a great deal in the 1960s.[86] They did not implicate the Beatles in the confrontations between mods and rockers in southern seaside resorts in 1964.[87] Better still, three parliamentarians that spring held Merseybeat responsible for the improved conduct of teenagers in the north-west. William Teeling credited 'the Beatles and similar groups of musicians' for the rapid decline of 'unruly behaviour' by young Northerners, a theory extended by the Bishop of Norwich to include skiffle groups and Birmingham in addition to the Beatles and Liverpool.[88] Norman Miscampbell likewise claimed that gang-related crime had 'largely disappeared' from Liverpool thanks to 'The Beatles, and groups like them' offering an alternative form of group membership. Miscampbell saw beat groups as a solution to the problem of youth alienation and atomisation inasmuch as they 'provided an outlet for many people who find it difficult to integrate themselves into society when they move into adolescence'.[89] Less idealistic was W. R. Rees-Davies, who called in 1965 for dance clubs to open on Sunday evenings on the grounds that teenagers who were prevented from 'listen[ing] to the

"Beatles", or whoever it may be … would be on the streets, getting into trouble'.[90] Willis condemned the 'attitude of complete defeat' of those content with 'keep[ing] them [adolescents] off the streets', but conceded that the Beatles served this basic if base purpose.[91]

In the late sixties and early seventies, however, politicians generally considered the Beatles to be inciting delinquency instead of quelling it. The 1967 Tory party conference showcased Quintin Hogg fulminating against the 'weakness, sophistry and ignorance' on display in the Beatles-sponsored advertisement in *The Times* questioning the laws on marijuana.[92] He proposed that 'addicts [*sic*] of hashish … however distinguished their position in the Top Ten … they will be treated as criminals deserve to be treated'.[93] That same year, Lord Stonham had denounced the 'contamination' represented by Lennon's apparent reference to LSD in 'Lucy in the Sky with Diamonds'.[94] Another Home Office minister, Alice Bacon, declared herself to be 'horrified' by the manner in which 'pop singers and managers of pop groups' were 'questioning traditional values and social judgments of all kinds'. She scolded McCartney and Epstein for justifying their use of LSD because 'young people take quite seriously what pop stars say'.[95] Indeed, such was the Beatles' presumed sway over youth that Paul Channon chastised Bacon for so much as mentioning their views on acid on the grounds that 'It is terribly dangerous to quote people like that when we are against drug taking.'[96] Richard Crossman reflected upon 'how useful' and 'respectable' the Beatles had seemed when granted MBEs when contrasted to the hippies they had become by 1970, much as Wilson conceded that Lennon went 'wrong, later' when promoting drugs.[97]

Given the scale of public anxiety and antipathy towards drugs and the counterculture, it is surprising that the Beatles did not receive more flak from politicians in the late 1960s. They presented sitting targets for conservative moralists such as Finchley MP Margaret Thatcher, who in 1969 expressed nostalgia for the 1950s when 'we had not heard of the Beatles or David Frost, there was no permissive society and no hippies'.[98] A more comprehensive attack came from the Labour peer Lord Sorensen. A Unitarian-cum-agnostic, Sorensen mocked the band's mysticism and devotion to the Maharishi.[99] As President of the Josephine Butler Society (formerly the Association for Moral and Social Hygiene), he took exception to 'the denunciation of conventional morality by such people as Yoko and her Hairy Spouse, Lennon the Beatle'.[100] And as someone born in the nineteenth century, he was no more affronted by their use of hallucinogens than the manner in which 'their appalling noises intoxicate the human young'.[101]

Yet the proportion of positive and negative comments about the band made by parliamentarians barely changed before and after 1967. From 1963 to 1966, 28 per cent of parliamentary comments were entirely positive and 22 per cent were entirely negative in tone. From 1967 to the dissolution of the band in April 1970, there were 30 per cent uniformly positive comments and 27 per cent uniformly negative ones. The big change – and irony – of the late sixties was that as the Beatles became more politicised and confrontational, they proved harder to incorporate into parliamentary discourse. They ridiculed Parliament, representative democracy and the party system and gravitated towards causes too utopian and internationalist to fall within Westminster's realm. Politicians and the Beatles regarded each other as largely irrelevant by the turn of the decade.

Marxists

In February 1964 – the month that Douglas-Home traded Beatles jokes with President Johnson and Paul Johnson sparred with Bill Deedes over their influence on the young – the Kremlin weighed in on the subject of the Beatles. Its youth paper *Moskovskij Komsomolets* opined that

The British authorities do not interfere [but] ... encourage the Beatles. Why? Because this diverts the attention of the young people of Britain from politics, from bitter reflections about their desecrated ideals and shattered hopes.[102]

Only the most doctrinaire Marxist organisations in Britain upheld such an unwaveringly hostile line.[103] One was the Maoist outfit the CPGB (Marxist-Leninist). Its Sussex University branch ingeniously combined attacks on the Beatles' wealth, reactionary politics and spirituality when imagining how 'from inside their Rolls Royces they sing "Revolution you can count me out", [*sic*] as they drive through India'.[104]

It was telling that the CPGB, which was formally affiliated to (and secretly funded by) the Soviet Union, felt no compunction to follow Moscow's line. In the same month as the *Moskovskij Komsomolets* article, the leader of the CPGB declared the party's neutrality towards the band.[105] The following month, the party journal *Music and Life* ran an article by John Evans which dismissed Soviet Bloc portrayals of the Beatles as 'an insidious class weapon to distract young people from political and social realities'.[106]

Marxists' uncertain reception of the Beatles was a product of their long and troubled interactions with popular music. The CPGB's approach belied its reputation for being mired in socialist realism.[107] As Andy Croft has noted, dogmatic statements about culture as a weapon of class struggle did a disservice to the party's genuine interest in creating 'an enriched and democratic human culture'.[108] Music was also integral to party members' self-contained world. David Aaronovitch recalls of his communist childhood that

The greatest carrier of the political message was not speeches or pamphlets or books. It was music. Emotion and ideology took fastest wing in song. The Party, knowing this well, always had good musicians and great tunes.[109]

The CPGB was wary of pop music owing to its all-consuming commerciality and propagandising for mainstream American values. The party-run Workers' Music Association cautioned in 1945 that '[t]he dance-band musician as a rule has not Ideals' to the same degree as the 'cultured musician'.[110] It did not consider popular music to be beyond redemption, but saw the solution in musicians recognising their 'social function' instead of indulging their individualism and employing their skills to 'educat[e] . . . people's emotions'.[111]

Jazz and folk were the popular genres deemed most appropriate for communist ends because they were held to operate outside and in opposition to capitalist mass culture. The two leading lights of the British folk revival, A. L. Lloyd and Ewan MacColl, were committed communists. The CPGB had strong links to the folk label Topic Records and the magazine *Sing* (1954–66), and contained within its ranks the eminent historian and jazz critic Eric Hobsbawm. Hobsbawm maintained that jazz and pop reflected their divergent modes of production. Whereas pop was 'standardised or mass-produced music', jazz was a 'folk music' which survived at the fringes of modern industrial capitalism.[112] The music industry controlled the pop musician and rendered his music 'insipid' through 'commercial processing'.[113] Jazz remained 'authentic' by resisting commercialisation and placing 'the individualities of the players' before all other concerns.[114]

If the Old Left was not as stodgy in its attitude to popular culture as might be thought, the New Left was not quite as open-minded as it has been given credit for.[115] To be sure, the *New Left Review* published notably sympathetic articles about youth culture, including one in which the historian and peace campaigner E. P. Thompson gamely presented Tommy Steele as a herald of the 'Aldermaston Generation'.[116] But on the whole New Left writers treated pop music as the least favoured of the popular arts. The non-Marxist Richard Hoggart equated rock 'n' roll with cultural deracination, the 'almost limitless freedom' of Juke Box Boys being dissipated in 'hedonistic but passive' diversions.[117] Raymond Williams echoed both Hoggart in his despair over 'cultural and educational colonisation' and Hobsbawm when contrasting jazz to 'the latest Tin-Pan drool'.[118] The most substantial *New Left Review* piece on popular music published before Beatlemania was by Paddy Whannel and Brian Groombridge. It made two bald propositions:

(1) that most of [pop] music is bad music – judged by its own standards, not by those of art music or folk song; (2) that the promotion of pops involves a fundamental but typical abuse of the means of communication in contemporary society.[119]

The Beatles and the bands which followed in their slipstream led Marxists to take another look at popular music. When Whannel returned to the topic in his collaboration with Stuart Hall, *The Popular Arts* (1964), he included a postscript on the Beatles which acknowledged their 'distinctive break' from pop's 'assembly line' pap. The Beatles' music was less 'tooled', their lyrics less 'moony' and their image less Americanised than standard pop.[120] Their authenticity was part cause, part consequence of a bond with their local fans that was not entirely mediated by marketing. Hall and Whannel's arguments overlapped with those made by the CPGB's John Evans in *Music and Life* earlier that year. To Evans, 'the exploitation of Beatlemania' did not nullify 'the intrinsic merits' of the Beatles' music.[121] These merits originated in the compositional talent of Lennon and McCartney, which made them 'largely independent of the mass-produced pop-song industries' and able to create 'something English and craftsmanlike' in an otherwise Fordist industry. He considered it churlish for British communists to decry the homegrown Beatles after having so long denounced 'the swamping of our native culture by American pop art, often of little musical worth and dubious morality'.[122]

Hall and Whannel did not mention the Beatles' politics and Evans disapproved of the political advantage sought by both East and West from these 'rather unpolitical but basically decent boys'.[123] But Marxists were impelled to consider the Beatles as political actors in their own right in the second half of the 1960s. Young Communist League (YCL) leader and one-time rock 'n' roll singer Pete Carter interpreted Lennon's 1966 call for 'a bloody revolution' as symptomatic of his generation's untapped militancy.[124] '[O]ur ideas are in accord with the direction of thought of young people', he argued: 'It is on this ground that communist ideas can make the biggest impact.'[125]

So could pop help the Marxist cause? The first issue to address was whether popular culture could become an arena of revolutionary activity. Marxists agreed that the entertainment industry represented capitalism at its most exploitative. Differences emerged about whether performers and fans exercised any agency in the production and consumption of music. Hall and Whannel's characterisation of youth culture as a 'contradictory mixture of the authentic and the manufactured' laid the foundations for subsequent Gramscian analyses.[126] Another unaligned intellectual, Alan Beckett, took on Theodor Adorno's reductionist model of the 'culture industry' in an influential *NLR* article published in 1966.[127]

Similar arguments appeared in party publications. Ian Birchall of the International Socialists (IS) conceived of pop music as being shaped by the 'two conflicting pressures' of capitalism and working-class youth.[128] The CPGB's *Marxism Today* ran heated debates about such matters in 1966 and again in 1973–5 in which the Beatles featured prominently.[129] Member of the CPGB and folk critic Karl Dallas broke ranks with 'folkier than thou' revivalists in 1968 by arguing that the 'showbiz power structure' was unable to control inventive acts like the Beatles.[130] His contention that 'the new pop people are virtually in control of the mass media' was echoed by the *soi-disant* Marxist Kenneth Tynan, who characterised Lennon and McCartney as 'working-class artists' who had 'take[n] over the means of artistic production'.[131] Perry Anderson imagined pop musicians who were 'clos[ing] the gap between those who produce and those who appropriate art' as modelling the role of artists in a future communist society.[132]

Marxist discussions of the music industry intertwined with those about youth. The CPGB had lost much of its membership following the suppression of the Hungarian Revolution of 1956 and saw the young as a potential source of renewal. Prominent members of the YCL were attuned to youth culture and achieved record sales for its newspaper *Challenge* when featuring the band on its cover in December 1963.[133] Evans warned older communists against 'playing the heavy father' by denouncing the Beatles. He pointed out that 'the Beatle generation are also ... the Aldermaston generation', unwilling to take instruction from their elders.[134] 'The potential idealism of youth is very strong. The harvest is there to be reaped', agreed his colleague Barney Davis: 'Unfortunately at the moment many of the harvesters are in the wrong field, using the wrong tools.'[135] Fellow YCL leader Pete Carter implied that the seeds of revolution were to be found among the young rather than the proletariat and urged the party to ditch 'the tactics, language and attitudes of yesterday' to rally them to the cause.[136]

The CPGB's youth drive faced strong competition from Trotskyist groups, whose dual critique of Western capitalism and Eastern socialism appealed to many graduates of the anti-nuclear, anti-Vietnam War and student-protest movements. By declaring students to be 'The New Revolutionary Vanguard', *Black Dwarf* went further than the YCL in questioning the doctrine of class struggle.[137] Its arts critic Roland Muldoon saw the potential of pop music to form part of 'a rival culture which reflects the aspirations of our movement' and which connected socialist doctrine to the everyday 'human predicament'.[138]

The Beatles were therefore integral in fuelling a debate among British Marxists about popular music, the young and the relationship between the two, yet fell short of effecting a decisive ideological shift during the 1960s and early 1970s. The balance of opinion in Marxist publications of the time rejected the notion that the music industry fostered revolutionary consciousness. The characterisation of pop culture as capitalist propaganda by the CPGB's Geoff Bowles differed little from that of Trotskyist Mick Launchbury, who deemed it 'the most advanced form of planned obsolescence in our sick society' and advocated a total boycott of its products.[139] From this perspective, the novelty of sixties youth culture was only superficial, its shifting styles a function of the industry's need 'to create and invent new demands' in order to shift new product.[140]

Marxist attacks on the entertainment industry acquired a conspiratorial flavour when applied to the Beatles. To radio producer and CPGB stalwart Charles Parker, the 'Beatles syndrome' provided incontrovertible evidence that pop was a form of social control 'sanctioned and utilised by the power elite to safeguard their position'.[141] Bowles portrayed 'the ruling class and their henchmen' as attempting to co-opt the Beatles by awarding them MBEs, while the Centre for Contemporary Cultural Studies (CCCS) presented the 'Beatles era' as a case study of how 'a subcultural style became transformed, through increasingly commercial organisation and fashionable expropriation, into a pure "market" or "consumer" style'.[142]

The idea of the young as a revolutionary vanguard seemed at best fanciful and at worst heretical to Marxists wedded to class struggle. Beatlemaniacs reminded classical composer Alan Bush of 'Voodoo in British Guiana'.[143] Bush's concern about the corrupting effects of pop lyrics on young minds was surprisingly echoed by John Evans in the same forum. He saw a link between 'sexy lyrics' and the rise in premarital

sex, and accepted that pop was somewhat to blame for delinquent behaviour such as amphetamine use and violence between mods and rockers.[144]

The appearance of hippies later in the decade dismayed some prominent
Marxist intellectuals. Peter Fryer thought them wilfully 'mindless', Stuart
Hall disparaged them as a 'pure American species' and George Lichtheim
diagnosed 'mental sickness' among their militant contingent.[145] For orthodox Marxists, the generation gap was an illusion 'deliberately fostered and
exploited' by the bourgeoisie to make profits and maintain power over
a fractured proletariat.[146] Cultural Marxists based in the CCCS developed
more sophisticated analyses of youth subcultures in the 1970s. Yet they
continued to view most pop culture as 'basically conformist in character',
with any subversive elements soon neutralised and commodified in
a process of 'renewal without revolution'.[147]

Many Marxists continued to denigrate pop on aesthetic grounds. At
a public discussion on 'The Good and Bad of Pop' organised by the CPGB's
Music Group in November 1964, a Musicians' Union official criticised the
technique of '"so-called" drummers' in beat groups, a retired musician
lamented pop's 'low artistic value' and Bush declared fan mania to be 'a
new low in mass culture'.[148] A jazz critic took issue with holding
a discussion in the first place. '[W]e should take the musical non-value of
present-day pop for granted', he maintained: 'There is nothing to discuss; it
is rubbish.'[149]

Champions of each genre of music approved by the CPGB came forward
to criticise the Beatles. Bush queried whether pop had 'any artistic value'
and *Music and Life* complained in January 1964 that EMI had stopped
pressing classical albums in order to meet the demand for Beatles' records.
It commended the practice of socialist economies of making classical
recordings cheaper than pop in order to elevate public taste.[150] When
Music and Life published Evans' article on the Beatles the next month, it
counterbalanced his positive assessment with a piece by the Hungarian
composer and folklorist Pál Járdányi. Járdányi's diatribe against dance
music, loudspeakers and transistor radios was included to provide
a 'wider perspective' on popular music, the editors explained.[151]

Hobsbawm considered 'products like the Beatles' to be musically insig-
nificant from his perspective as a jazz and blues connoisseur. 'Much of their
appeal has nothing to do with music at all', which was little different from
common-or-garden rock 'n' roll. It was the 'clothes, haircuts and stance'
which in his view accounted for their popularity, or rather provided 'an
excuse for (mainly feminine) teenage hysteria'.[152] Bert Lloyd accused the
Daily Worker of having become the '*Beatles' Daily*' for covering the band,

and fellow folklorist Parker saw the Beatles' visions of a 'false community' as a 'masterly confidence trick' detracting and distracting from the real thing.[153]

Parker's lyrical analysis followed an established method of sifting out 'positive' popular songs from the 'cynical' and 'decadent' ones.[154] Escapist lyrics served to 'distract the attention of young people away from the real problems of the world', while cynical ones inculcated a nihilism among the young.[155] Whether saccharine or acidic, pop in Ewan MacColl's view engendered a 'negative attitude' which absolved its producers and con-sumers of 'the responsibility of being committed to any idea [or] course of action'.[156] Marxists accordingly sought to identify 'what [were] the pro-gressive and reactionary elements in, say, T. S. Eliot's poetry or the songs of the Beatles'.[157] The simplicity of the early lyrics provided them with little to work with, although this did not stop Bush from declaring 'From Me to You' (1963) 'thoroughly obnoxious' for its advocacy of promiscuity.[158] Jim Cornelius was more generous in his interpretation of 'Can't Buy Me Love' (1964) in anti-capitalist terms as 'a condemnation of the values of society'.[159] The IS's Ian Birchall agreed, but pointed out that such senti-ments simply recapitulated 'the conservative convention of folk-song and fairy-story' that the poor were happy with their lot. As such, it was an object lesson in 'the individualism and quietism of all pop music'.[160]

The Beatles' psychedelic period divided opinion between those inspired by its transformative visions and others who objected that 'You need more than love to win the class war'.[161] Peter Fryer considered 'Within You Without You' (1967) 'puerile' for jettisoning 'collective efforts to solve humanity's problems' in favour of personal solutions.[162] Parker objected that *Sgt. Pepper*'s soundscapes bore no relation to 'the actual human communities in which people work, struggle and live together' and Jim Boyd argued that the line 'things are getting better all the time [*sic*]' was intended to deflect attention from the crisis of capitalism.[163] Yet CPGB critics of *Sgt. Pepper* were themselves criticised by other party members. Nick Kettle upbraided Boyd for his 'ludicrous analysis' of 'Getting Better' (1967) and the 'lachrymose banalities' detected by Parker in 'She's Leaving Home' (1967) were commended by veteran party official Betty Reid for their 'human and evocative' depiction of changes in family life.[164]

Marxists could at least unite against 'Revolution' (1968). Roland Muldoon's initial attack in *Black Dwarf* was swiftly followed by John Hoyland's two famous broadsides in the same paper.[165] Although Richard Neville described Hoyland's contretemps with Lennon as 'a classic New Left/psychedelic left dialogue', Lennon received little public support from the counterculture or any other quarter.[166] Neville himself cited the song as evidence that the Beatles 'sought to be excluded from the revolutionary vanguard', and the Old Left joined forces with the New Left in denouncing this 'piece of blatant anti-communism'.[167] Sheila Rowbotham privately dissented. Her desire for 'the "revolution" to combine the Johns [Hoyland and Lennon]' pointed the way towards an identity politics concerned with 'changing the outer world and building a new one within'.[168] Like Hoyland, she was a young revolutionary who had been inspired by the radical subjectivity of Beatles songs.[169] As a woman, however, she found the Beatles' masculinity at once arousing and disturbing. While watching the Beatles in *Magical Mystery Tour* (1967), her masturbatory fantasies were rudely interrupted by the striptease scene in Raymond's Revue Bar. She found herself simultaneously complicit in and distanced by the film's male gaze.[170]

Rowbotham recalled being unable at the time to resolve her quandaries about *Magical Mystery Tour* and the Lennon–Hoyland debate. For her and many other women involved in London's countercultural and left-wing circles, the answer to reconciling the personal and the political came in the form of the women's liberation movement.[171] British second-wave feminists were slow to develop critiques of popular music when compared to their American counterparts. Alan Beckett and Perry Anderson's quixotic defence of the Rolling Stones as exposing misogyny by trumpeting it went unchallenged in the feminist press until 1973, when *Spare Rib* published an article by the Australian Margaret Geddes.[172] In the meantime, the Stones made the playlists of women-only discos and Germaine Greer endorsed them for contributing to 'the revolution of sensibility which is the prerequisite of political revolution'.[173] Lennon and Ono's quirky brand of women's liberation made almost no impression on British feminists.[174] The sexual politics of the Beatles only began to be debated in earnest in the second half of the 1970s, when Terri Goddard and Liz Waugh's claim that their lyrics were 'notably free from sexism' was challenged by Elizabeth Wilson.[175] She maintained that they did not differ from the Stones in promoting the 'conscious and aggressive domination over women'.[176]

Class affiliation formed another test of the Beatles' bona fides. The first Marxist to write about the band, journalist Tom Spence, approved of the fact that the Beatles 'all live on the Merseyside [*sic*] and their relations work for a living'. He contrasted their class backgrounds with those of Alec Douglas-Home, and their earthy Scouse accents with the 'pseudo-Americanisms' of other British pop stars.[177] At the same time, Spence feared that 'spivs' would capitalise on their success and use it to distract workers from class conflict.[178] Spence reminded *Daily Worker* readers that Liverpool contained 'eighty thousand crumbling houses and thirty thousand people on the dole': a city in which the 'thud-thud-thud' of beat clubs helped the young to forget 'a worried outside, where Me Dad may be out of work and the telly is the only comfort in an unsanitary house'.[179]

As the Beatles' fame burgeoned and their horizons widened, Marxists accused them of embourgeoisement. Perry Anderson and Martin Jacques accepted that the band had spearheaded an 'implicitly class rebellion' in league with their proletarian fan base.[180] Anderson's complaint was that, having quickly achieved this 'certain sexual-cultural emancipation of working-class youth', the Beatles did not proceed to tackle the more intractable issue of economic inequality.[181] The resultant 'impasse' left the Beatles from 1967 onwards holed up in Abbey Road ('a null zone even of bourgeois London') conducting a 'musical radicalism' without political purpose.[182] Jacques likewise concluded the Beatles had become 'separated from their social and cultural backgrounds', but Marxist literary critic Terry Eagleton contended that the Beatles were not truly proletarian in the first place.[183] The grammar-school educations of Harrison, Lennon and McCartney has made them 'affluent, genial [and] uncommitted' in comparison to secondary-modern products such as Cliff Richard, whose rebellious streak was compounded by the racism he faced at school for being born in India.[184]

Marxists often wrote off the Beatles as class traitors at the turn of the decade. Harrison attracted criticism for his 'patronising sneer' at workers in 'Piggies' (1968), the anti-collectivist ethos of 'Within You Without You' (1967) and his belief in the 'miraculous powers of meditation'.[185] 'This might be a comforting creed to someone with Harrison's wealth, but unemployed workers in Birmingham or hungry peasants in Bengal are likely to be slightly less impressed', commented John Crump of the Socialist Party of Great Britain (SPGB).[186] The Socialist Labour League (SLL) lectured Starr on how the 'petty bourgeois vulgarity' of *The Magic Christian* (1969) paved the way for '[f]ascism's path', but it was Lennon's 'lamentable petty bourgeois cry of fear' in 'Revolution' (1968) that drew the greatest ire.[187] Hoyland's censure was a waste of time, according to one correspondent to *Black Dwarf*: 'Mr Hoyland should be told that bourgeoise [sic] like Lennon are cured not converted. There is not anything in Lennon's thinking that hunger and a few weeks in Fidel's canefields would not correct.'[188]

The Beatles' extramural activities in the late sixties did little to enhance their standing among Marxists. Few revolutionary socialists recognised McCartney's description of Apple as 'Western communism'.[189] Muldoon attributed the reactionary sentiments of 'Revolution' (1968) to the Beatles' interest in 'safeguarding their capitalist investment'.[190] The following year, the IS's David Widgery condemned Lennon as a 'quietist' for spending his time 'opening Oxfam bazaars and repelling takeover bids'.[191] As Widgery's quip about Oxfam indicated, philanthropy was too reformist for many on the left. Even Lennon and Ono's support for industrial action by the Upper Clyde Shipbuilders was criticised by Jack Bruce, musician and scion of a Glaswegian Communist family, on the grounds that the roses accompanying the donation were an insult to the workers' machismo.[192] Desmond Morris noted that the couple's pacifism also placed them at odds with the 'violent extremes in left-wing intellectualism'.[193] Lennon's Bed-Ins, his anthem 'Give Peace a Chance' (1969) and the return of his MBE in protest against Britain's involvement in Biafra went on to achieve legendary status, but received little attention in the Marxist press until Denver Walker pronounced them 'confused and idealistic' five years after they had taken place.[194] They also went unreported in the *Bulletin* of the Vietnam Solidarity Campaign (VSC), probably because the VSC was less anti-war than pro-Vietcong. Lennon's refusal to participate in VSC demonstrations on the grounds that he 'didn't like the violence' further blotted his copybook.[195]

Public confessions of drug use and infidelity appalled socialists of a puritanical bent. A correspondent to *Black Dwarf* contrasted the impeccable private lives of '[t]he great revolutionaries of history' with the 'amoral bums' of the pop world, including 'poor confused drug experimenter' Lennon.[196] A greater acceptance of drug use was 'among the things that defined a new Left, as against a traditional, rather stuffy old Left' according to Robin Blackburn of the International Marxist Group (IMG).[197] His IMG colleague Tariq Ali signed the 1967 Soma petition for the decriminalisation of cannabis alongside the Beatles, Brian Epstein and various left-wing luminaries including Peter Fryer, Tony Garnett, Clive Goodwin, Michael X and Adrian Mitchell. But the Beatles' funding of a full-page advertisement in *The Times* seemed decidedly tame in comparison to the conviction and brief incarceration of Mick Jagger and Keith Richards that same year.[198]

The ideological soundness of the Beatles was ultimately hard for Marxists to judge. Their politics changed from year to year and they were not card-carrying members of anything.[199] Lennon in particular spread his favours widely. He was in contact with unaligned leftists including Peter Watkins and Bertrand Russell, supported and corresponded with an array of underground publications and blithely informed IMGers Tariq Ali and Robin Blackburn that 'the first thing we did when we got back [to England] was contact you and Richard Neville and [Black Power leader] Michael [X], because in your individual ways you represent the movement in different spheres, all the different aspects of it'.[200]

Lennon's militant turn in the early seventies offered him the chance of redemption. Widgery applauded 'his remarkable musical self-analysis of the working-class hero, the serene socialist vision of *Imagine* and the deliberately unsubtle agit-prop of *Some Time In New York City*.'[201] For those schooled in the protest tradition, if for few others, the highlights of Lennon's songwriting career were his post-Beatles' revolutionary anthems 'Luck of the Irish', 'Sunday Bloody Sunday', 'Woman is the N****r of the World' (all 1972) and 'Power to the People' (1971). His four-figure donations in 1972 to Irish republicans and Scottish shipyard workers were tangible signs of commitment to the cause and Tariq Ali believed him to be on the verge of joining the IMG. His abrupt departure to the United States was therefore all the more disillusioning to his Marxist supporters. Ali disapproved of his new Yippie friends for their 'remoteness from the working class'.[202] Widgery bluntly called them 'middle-class bullshitters' and came to conclude that 'corporate America had killed Lennon long before Mark Chapman got to him'.[203]

Ali was not alone in hoping to attract a pop star to his cause. The YCL's Barney Davis had urged 'Marxists and progressives to help guide the work of these [pop and protest] singers' in 1966.[204] Pete Townshend had been a YCL member, the Kinks performed at the 1967 YCL annual conference and in 1968 John Hoyland 'fraternally' urged Lennon to commit himself to revolutionary socialism.[205] Had he or any of the other Beatles done so, it is difficult to imagine them lasting more than a few months before resigning or being expelled. Since they remained unattached, Marxists had to decide if they passed muster as fellow travellers. Imti Chounara conceded that 'none of the Beatles is a revolutionary Marxist-Leninist member of the Communist Party', but suggested that they should be treated no differently from radical trade unionists and politicians outside of the party.[206] Yet even Chounara admitted that Lennon was not a Marxist in all but name. Although he did not regard being 'idealistic in a Utopian sense' as a reason to dismiss Lennon out of hand, utopian socialism had highly pejorative connotations among communists since Marx and Engels coined the term in

1848.[207] Even Eurocommunists such as Martin Jacques believed that the counterculture's 'utopian-anarchism' had to be 'combat[ted] ... with the theory and practice of Marxism'.[208] Hardliners were less forgiving. Hippies' muddled anarchism, mysticism and reformism constituted 'An Abortion of Socialist Understanding' according to the SPGB publication *Socialist Standard*, while the CPGB (Marxist-Leninist) condemned the Beatles' 'utopian' misinterpretation of class war as spiritual quest.[209]

Anarchists

Many of the very same qualities which rendered the Beatles unpalatable to Marxists were what made them appealing to anarchists, who had their own reasons to consider the sixties a revolutionary era. In the late nineteenth and early twentieth centuries, there had been only a 'minuscule' number of self-declared anarchists in Britain.[210] The expressive politics of the anti-nuclear campaigns of the late 1950s and early 1960s, when combined with the waning appeal of the Soviet Union, generated an interest in anarchism which burgeoned during the 'permissive' 1960s. Britain's customary 'neglect of anarchism' abated as libertarianism grew, noted the New Left writer and historian Raphael Samuel.[211]

A major intervention in anarchist discussions of popular music in the 1960s came from Charles Radcliffe in his 'wild, experimental libertarian-socialist journal' *Heatwave* and related publications.[212] Radcliffe sought to 'alter the face of the earth' through 'the total extinction of all forms of exploitation or authority'.[213] The ideal society described in the first issue of *Heatwave* was standard anarchistic fare: a collectivised, decentralised, demilitarised 'federation of autonomous communes'.[214] By issue two, this had evolved into a more imaginative vision of '[a]n endless passion, an endless adventure, an endless banquet' founded on 'almost-total leisure'.[215]

For Radcliffe, 'total revolution' began with the destruction of all existing revolutionary doctrines and methods.[216] His ambitions far exceeded 'the rectification of economic and political structures' envisaged in the 'old revolutionary sacred texts'.[217] Eastern communism was as authoritarian and materialist as Western capitalism, and existing revolutionary organi-sations replicated the 'bureaucratic machine' they claimed to oppose.[218] Radcliffe also dismissed the insurrectionary potential of the proletariat, who were indistinguishable from the bourgeoisie in their consumerism and inertia.[219] The true new revolutionaries were the 'Provotariat', an assortment of subcultures which displayed 'the groping of youth towards explosive self-expression'.[220] The class base of these sundry 'groupings of disaffected youth' was beside the point. Whether cross-class mods, work-ing-class Teds, rockers and 'ton-up kids' or middle-class Beats, ravers and CNDers, they all refused to acquiesce to the status quo.[221] New methods of revolution were to be found not in strikes, party-building or 'disparate and fragmentary protests', but in the 'PROVOcation' of the ruling elite through youth culture, especially popular music.[222] The 'disquiet-factor' created by subcultures and their confrontational behaviour would provoke the autho-rities into overreacting, thereby creating a spiral of resistance and repres-sion until 'THE CRISIS WILL COME.'[223]

The centrality of popular music in Radcliffe's theory of revolution was partly a matter of personal enthusiasm:

I didn't really care much about the political coherence or otherwise of 'rock revolt'. It might be largely or entirely 'spectacular', but frankly I didn't give a shit. I simply liked listening passively or otherwise to some rock, most real blues and largely postwar jazz, and I wasn't about to stop![224]

He was friends with Eric Clapton, John Mayall, John McVie, Jimmy Page, Jeff Beck and Steve Winwood and wrote laudatory pieces about the Rolling Stones and The Who.[225] What made Radcliffe's own 'fusion of personal life-style and politics' timely and significant was that it fed into wider debates among anarchists about youth culture in the early 1960s.[226] Ian Vine's 1963 article 'Beatnik as Anarchist?' challenged 'armchair revolu-tionaries' to acknowledge that the nomadic and hedonistic existence of drop-outs allowed them to 'remain almost entirely free'.[227] While most such Beats-cum-tramps had no interest in wholesale social change, Radcliffe's American collaborators Penelope and Franklin Rosemont had transitioned from Beatniks to Wobblies convinced of the insurrectionary power of pop.[228]

The Beatles were the subject of Radcliffe's first and 'somewhat confused' article on popular music.[229] In 'Pop Goes the Beatle', published in November 1963, he found much to criticise. Their tunes lacked melody and harmony and their marketing was based on 'deception and manipula-tion of young people'. Beatlemania was a media-induced 'teenage orgasm-substitute' and the Beatlemaniacs themselves were 'not challenging anything'.[230] Even so, the Beatles were still an improvement on what he described elsewhere as 'the sickly gutlessness of orthodox pop'.[231] Merseybeat had begun as a form of self-expression and the music, however crude, was 'new and young and vigorous'.[232] The Beatles and their contemporaries were more independent of the music industry. So were the fans, who were increasingly able to select stars of their own choosing. The fulminations of Paul Johnson indicated that the Beatles and their fans constituted a 'PROVOcation' to the adults in power.[233] 'If anarchism has nothing to say' to the fans, he concluded, 'it has nothing to say at all.'[234]

A more full-throated anarchist defence of the Beatles appeared in *Peace News* the month after 'Pop Goes the Beatle'. It was written by Richard Mabey, sometime member of the Oxford anarchist group and future Penguin editor and nature writer. Mabey argued that the Beatles forced a wholesale reassessment of the music industry.[235] Their music and demeanour were refreshing and their stardom gave the lie to the idea that 'all financial success, hit parades, "latest sales gimmicks", heroes, agents, managers and promoters are all, a priori, wicked, reactionary and corrupting'.[236] The Beatles' pursuit of music as a 'way of life' was mirrored by their fans.[237] They were able to escape from the 'drab world of adult responsibility and obscure political squabblings' and experience unbridled joy in a 'blatantly subversive' fashion.[238]

Mabey's contention that the Beatles 'challenge[d] the assumptions of our society' did not convince correspondents to *Peace News*.[239] A teacher at a girls' comprehensive school saw little non-conformity in the Beatles fans in her classes, and an undergraduate accused Mabey of 'wish-fulfilment' for reading social progress into royal approval of the Beatles.[240] Mabey responded with the intriguing suggestion that orthodox models of revolution had things backwards. Instead of 'eliminating the baddies (Royalty, employers, etc.)' first and expecting the end of 'boredom, drabness, monotony' to follow, Beatlemania provided a 'revolutionary alternative to this world' in advance of structural transformation.[241]

The left-libertarian group Solidarity reprinted Radcliffe and Mabey's articles in a 1966 pamphlet, alongside a piece by the Chicago Wobbly Franklin Rosemont which answered the question 'Are the Beatles Subversive?' in the affirmative.[242] Yet scepticism towards youth culture was more common in anarchist publications of the early and mid-1960s. There was much suspicion of the protest movements favoured by the young, and anarchist critiques of the music industry overlapped with those of Marxists. A special youth issue of *Anarchy* in May 1963 denounced escapist fan worship and saw something suspicious in 'everyone [being] sympathetic' to teenagers after years of mistrust.[243] Older anarchist intellectuals differed little from their non-anarchist counterparts in their distaste for Beatlemania. The educationalist A. S. Neill viewed the Beatles' popularity as a symptom of defective schooling. Pupils engaged in 'making and doing' would not think of listening to their records and Beatlemania could be prevented if schools 'dealt with emotional things'.[244] The sexologist Alex Comfort was equally disconcerted by Beatlemania, likening its effect of 'The Beatles working up a teenage audience' to Adolf Hitler and 'the smoking of a marajuana [*sic*] cigarette'.[245]

The counterculture forced anarchists to reassess the Beatles in the late 1960s. It resembled anarchism in what Julie Stephens has termed its 'anti-disciplinary politics', and Elizabeth Nelson has identified an 'essentially anarchist critique of society' in the alternative press.[246] *International Times* (*IT*) encouraged readers to exercise autonomy over themselves: 'to be your own government' as well as 'taking on governments'.[247] *IT*'s great rival *Oz* noted how the underground sought to 'live peacefully but disparately' by creating its own autonomous institutions: 'It produces and reads its own newspaper, the *International Times*, runs its own boutiques and book-shops, organises its own finances and legal aid for members who get picked up by the police, goes about its own pop arts business.'[248]

Countercultural figures with anarchist leanings portrayed the hippie lifestyle in utopian terms. As a leading Western proponent of Zen Buddhism and an early enthusiast for LSD, Alan Watts naturally welcomed the counterculture's spiritual and chemical experimentation. In his 1969 essay 'Wealth versus Money', Watts portrayed hippies as pioneers of a new way of life in which people would value experiences over property and self-made items over mass-produced ones.[249] *Oz* editor Richard Neville's *Play Power* (1970) foresaw a future post-materialist society in which work was performed solely for fun as a 'pastime, obsession, hobby or art-form'.[250] As important as any ideological affinities between hippies and anarchists were the overlapping networks and personal friendships forged in London's embryonic alternative scene. One meeting place was London's Anti-University, whose roster of 'writers, poets, psychiatrists, sociologists, Marxists, anarchists, artists, musicians and filmmakers' included everyone from Jeff Nuttall and C. L. R. James to Yoko Ono and Barry Miles.[251] Another was Notting Hill Gate, with its stew of militancy, creativity, multiculturalism, communal living and drugs.

Anarchist intellectuals were conflicted over the meaning of the counter-culture. Their misgivings were captured in a round-table discussion broad-cast by BBC Radio 3 in 1968. Colin Ward characterised hippies as escapist, individualistic and juvenile.[252] Nicholas Walter adjudged the countercul-ture as 'relevant to' but not 'part of' the anarchist movement on account of its materialism.[253] For George Melly, the underground's obsession with drugs detracted from its laudable quest for love and freedom.[254] Timothy

Leary's drug-induced mysticism was also portrayed as 'sinister' by a 1967 Situationist manifesto co-authored by Radcliffe, Christopher Gray, Timothy Clark and Donald Nicholson-Smith, which went on to denounce *IT* as 'sanctimonious' for its pseudery and ambition to become part of a 'New Establishment'.[255] Yet Radcliffe and Gray 'hung out with hippies' regardless, and Radcliffe recognised that the Provotariat's 'countless and varied strands of autonomous post-war youth rebellion' had been brought together in the underground scene.[256] His belief in its revolutionary potential was shared by Alex Comfort, who was as sympathetic to hippies as he had been antipathetic to Beatlemaniacs. Comfort reasoned that the underground could be 'the most important … feature of our time' if it foreshadowed a coming generation 'which will no longer take orders, no longer respond to the conventional economic incentives, no longer value technology or discovery for their own unrelated selves'.[257]

Anarchists including George Melly, Richard Mabey, Jeff Nuttall and Mick Farren were responsible for a remarkable portion of the key texts on pop culture issued in the late sixties and early seventies.[258] These writers all saw popular music as a potentially subversive force. Melly argued that pop's commitment to 'total freedom' made its politics 'almost totally anarchist'.[259] Mabey saw fifties teenagers as erecting 'the scaffolding of an alternative society', Nuttall envisaged the counterculture as the beginnings of 'the erosion of the square society' and Farren saw postwar youth culture as 'revolution in its purest form':

Hundreds of thousands of white kids prepared to become social outcasts rather than join their parents' death culture, even in the role of oppressors, is surely the most positive, if disorganised, revolutionary statement in history.[260]

Farren, Melly, Mabey and Nuttall's assessments of the Beatles' contribution to youth culture corresponded to diverse strands of anarchist thought. Mick Farren hero-worshipped Lennon but nonetheless considered the Beatles 'part of a compromise of a revolution'.[261] They were too mainstream and insufficiently confrontational for his tastes. 'The Beatles have been trying to turn people on, gently', he remarked in 1968, whereas his band the Deviants were pursuing a 'harder line'.[262]

Melly thought the Beatles no different from other pop acts in lacking the social critique to develop their anti-authoritarian instincts into something more than libertarianism. He believed that Lennon's 'Revolution' deserved credit for exposing how 'Pop acts out revolt'.[263] The arguments for and against the Beatles' quest for 'total freedom' had been rehearsed in *Peace News*. In 1964, the radical educationalist Albert Hunt had ridiculed

Mabey's early pieces on the Beatles for parroting 'publicity handouts' about their cross-class appeal and had queried what '[w]etting your seat and putting your fingers in your mouth' at a concert did for the cause of revolution.[264] Four years later, he maintained that the Beatles' claim to self-sovereignty constituted a 'revolutionary demand' in a society which expected everyone to perform their allotted role.[265] However, fellow pacifist Roger Barnard attacked Hunt for endorsing a 'kind of anarchy' unattainable to all but the very rich.[266] Another contributor to *Peace News*, Laura Birch, argued that the band were not simply selfish, but parasitic. 'The Beatles could not be free if they had to produce all their needs for living', she stated: 'while it [their wealth] means that they themselves are free, [it] makes thousands of other people unfree', condemned to be the Beatles' 'lackeys and servants'.[267]

Richard Mabey and Jeff Nuttall shared Melly's concern that commodification had turned 'Revolt into Style', but were even more condemnatory of the Beatles' hippie phase. In *The Pop Process* (1969), Mabey described their abandonment of the 'toughness and common sense' characterising their earlier music as nothing short of 'infanticidal'.[268] To have 'surrendered meekly to the Maharishi' was as much of a political folly as a religious one, since their stay in the 'Maharishi's palace' removed them from the realities of poverty in India.[269] The charge of escapism also appeared in Nuttall's *Bomb Culture* (1970), which depicted the Beatles as 'absorbed in their navels, the novelty of the first trips wearing off'.[270] This 'pursuit of inner spaces', whether through drugs or religion, had diverted them and other countercultural artists from political and social involvement:

it behoves the artists . . . to turn away from the Nothingness. . . . It's time to apply their supremely informed sensibilities to action, decisive, constructive action that leaves behind it a concrete achievement as testimony to its worth. It's time to come away from the mobile arts, poetry, jazz, theatre, dance, clothes.[271]

These criticisms were stated forcefully by one 'Reg O'Lucian' in an *Anarchy* article published the month that the Beatles left for Rishikesh. To him, Transcendental Meditation epitomised 'the hippies' basic treason to their fellow men' in its quietism, individualism and passive acceptance of existing power structures. A '[r]evolution in your own soul' which left the state and economic inequality intact was in his view no revolution whatsoever.[272]

Music aside, anarchist discussions of the Beatles in the late 1960s and early 1970s centred on their activism, wealth, pacifism and art. Some of the Beatles' countercultural activities could be presented in anarchist terms.

Apple was (at least in theory) a non-state, not-for-profit organisation which placed the collective good above individual self-interest.[273] Epstein and the band briefly planned to establish a commune for themselves on a Greek island and, when that came to nothing, Lennon donated a less balmy island in the Irish Sea to communards in the Digger Action Movement.[274] Lennon's politics in 1968 and 1969 were more anarchistic than anything else, although he repeatedly dissociated himself from the term and neither he nor the Beatles received much credit from anarchists for their ventures.[275]

Anarchists' habitual mistrust of the rich and famous gained intellectual heft from the Situationist International (SI), which displayed an impeccably Gallic condescension towards Anglo-Saxon popular culture.[276] Before the Beatles appeared on the scene, *Internationale Situationniste* had mocked the Beats as 'mystical cretins' and Angry Young Men as 'tepidly literary' throwbacks to a pre-Dada era.[277] The journal shoehorned the Beatles' early fame into its model of a leisure industry based on 'forced consumption [and] pseudo-culture', noting their appeal to the bourgeoisie and their contribution to Britain's exports.[278] The Beatles featured alongside Minis and miniskirts in a list of 'prefabricated trifles' used to distract people from their oppression in Raoul Vaneigem's classic *The Revolution of Everyday Life* (1967).[279]

Formal links were established between the SI and British anarchists following visits to Vaneigem and Guy Debord by Charles Radcliffe, Christopher Gray and Diana Shelley late in 1966.[280] Although Radcliffe did not share their disdain for 'anything consumable that was in the slightest bit popular', he found little to admire in the later Beatles. He condemned their risible if quintessentially English ambition to become shopkeepers, mocked their 'foppishly absurd' attire and slated *Sgt. Pepper* for its 'grandiose superficiality'.[281] The Situationist manifesto he co-authored in 1967 replicated the SI's critique of culture as a spectacle designed to distract the populace from the reality of their own oppression and alienation.[282] The Beatles became a byword for conformity in British Situationist publications. They appeared as one of the 'most gratuitous, decadent and self-destructive products' of consumer society, while the filmmaker Jean-Luc Godard was denounced as 'just another bloody Beatle' on account of his celebrity.[283] A pamphlet distributed at a free concert in 1969 challenged concertgoers to recognise that the counterculture was just another form of popular entertainment:

WHAT THE FUCK ARE YOU DOING HERE? . . .

CAN'T YOU UNDERSTAND THAT THESE SCENES ARE NO DIFFERENT FROM THOSE THAT YOU ARE KICKING AGAINST?

TAKE YOUR PICK, SUNDAY NIGHT AT THE LONDON PALLADIUM, BEATLES, PINK FLOYD ITS [*sic*] ALL THE SAME SHIT.[284]

Out of this rage against pop culture's complicity with the spectacle came the ambition to create an anti-Beatles. Gray's original idea of 'a totally unpleasant pop group' was picked up by Malcolm McLaren and Jamie Reid and realised in the form of the Sex Pistols.[285]

Although there was considerable overlap between the anarchist and pacifist movements, Situationist ambitions to destroy the spectacle of capitalism often countenanced physical force, culminating in bombings by the Angry Brigade.[286] The Beatles' pacifism was mocked by King Mob, the militant offshoot of Situationism and the self-styled 'gangsters of the new freedom'.[287] King Mob's response to 'All You Need Is Love' was to daub 'All you need is dynamite' on a Tavistock Road wall.[288] More ominous was their hit list, inspired by Valerie Solanas' attempt on the life of Andy Warhol in 1968. Its call for the 'Murder of Artists' did not target the Beatles directly, but listed many of their friends and associates including Yoko Ono, Barry Miles, Richard Hamilton, Marianne Faithfull, Mick Jagger and Bob Dylan.[289] Lennon's murder in 1980 prompted one contributor to the anarchist newspaper *Freedom* to sympathise with the perpetrator, criticise the victim and ponder the 'fun' to be had writing satirical songs about the event.[290] Harry Harris' verdict was that Lennon's campaigns for love and peace had been credulous and futile. '[H]ow is it possible to respect a guy naive enough to think World Peace could simply be wished into existence?' he asked.[291]

Lennon's pacifism elicited more interest and support from John Papworth in the environmentalist journal he founded and edited, *Resurgence*. Papworth was an intriguing figure. An Anglican clergyman later defrocked for justifying shoplifting from supermarkets, he had the distinction of being jailed for civil rights protests in the United States and for anti-war protests in Britain. He helped to develop the small-is-beautiful philosophy with his friend E. F. Schumacher, and, less creditably, assisted the double agent George Blake to flee to Moscow after breaking out of prison.[292] Papworth approached Lennon and Ono as kindred spirits in an 'Open Letter' quite different in tone from Hoyland's more famous broadside. Responding to Lennon and Ono's promise to donate all future royalties to world peace, he pointed to the futility of all previous such ventures. Demonstrations and publications – his own included – did nothing to address the uncontrollable nature of large-scale economic and technological processes. It was these which caused wars, argued Papworth, so that only their complete replacement by thousands of largely self-sufficient 'village republics' would ensure peace. 'We can do nothing with their [leaders'] power except dissolve it at the base and create alternative structures on a small scale', he told Lennon and Ono, who uncharacteristically did not respond.[293]

British Situationists were unimpressed by the Beatles' artistic experimentalism. Theoretically, they were anti-art. They affirmed Antonin Artaud's assessment of culture as shit and fantasised about blowing up William Wordsworth's cottage in the Lake District.[294] Actually, they were in a direct line of descent from Dada, surrealism and other early twentieth-century modernists in their determination to remake culture into a subversive force. The Beatles were drawing upon many of the same artistic currents and knew some of the same artists and performers. Chris Gray was good friends with Lennon and Ono's assistant Dan Richter and later worked for McCartney, while Radcliffe knew Josje Leeger of The Fool, who designed clothes for the Apple Boutique. But Situationists critiqued the derivative and mercenary qualities displayed in the film *Help!* (1965), the *White Album* cover (1968) and Ono's art. *Help!* was a Happening devoid of any radical charge, according to David Wise. He objected to the film's jibes at abstract art and argued that the use of montage and rapid edits put a hip gloss on an artefact embedded 'firmly within the on-going capitalist order'.[295] Dick Lester's films and Lennon's side projects confirmed to him that 'English absurdity always ends up supporting the status quo'.[296] Richard Hamilton's blank cover for *The Beatles* was in Wise's view a copy of his own copy of Malevich's white-on-white coffin. Hamilton 'institutionalised' and 'emasculated' the motif by turning an avant-garde statement into yet another commodity ripe for exploitation.[297] Other anarchists charged that Yoko Ono's performance art represented a 'spectacle of revolt' designed to titillate and distract. The mourning for the murdered Lennon in 1980 was condemned as the ultimate spectacle in which 'sheep'-like consumers projected their dreams of community upon a commodified icon.[298]

Conclusion

Mutual disregard is the default state between politicians and pop musicians. The pioneering work of the CCCS (in common with 'serious' rock criticism of the 1960s and 1970s) operated on the reverse assumption that

Rock was good because it was authentic to subcultural and countercultural values. These values were in opposition to the dynamics of capitalism and their expression through the actions of the music industry was to be welcomed. Rock was political.[299]

Much subsequent research has undermined the premises of this model by questioning the existence of autonomous and oppositional subcultures and portraying political radicalism as either absent, spasmodic or ineffective among musicians and their audiences. 'It is becoming difficult to see where and how rock is, or could be, articulated to progressive political commitments', wrote Lawrence Grossberg in 1993: 'The once generally shared assumption that the two intersected at some point ... seems to have disappeared.'[300] If pop musicians were customarily detached from politics, it followed that politicians could afford to ignore pop music. '[A]lmost total indifference' is how the most prolific scholar on the subject, John Street, characterises British politicians' customary attitude to pop.[301] Simon Frith agrees, noting that 'British governments have never shown much interest in pop music' beyond the occasional photo opportunity.[302]

At the same time, popular music has evolved in such a way that occasional encounters with politics are inevitable. For the Beatles to become the first pop group to attract significant parliamentary attention was just one of many ways in which they were pioneers. To be sure, they received much less interest than, say, motorways, and made appearances on the edges of parliamentary discourse: in written questions, early-day motions, adjournment debates, Private Members' Bills, the free-for-all discussion of the Queen's Speech and in scattered references regarding everything from agriculture in Zanzibar to the siting of a district general hospital in Ilford. This testified in part to the Beatles' perceived marginality, for even admirers like Bill Deedes placed beat groups at the 'outer fringe' of his world view.[303] But it also pointed to their ubiquity in what Lord Balfour termed 'this Beatle-ridden age'.[304] The Beatles were a – possibly *the* – symbol of sixties Britain, who could be related to virtually any topic on virtually any occasion.

Quite what the Beatles symbolised provoked a bewildering number of questions in Parliament. Were they a force for good or ill? Was their power actual or symbolic? Were they deserving or undeserving of wealth, police protection and political honours? Were they cosseted or mistreated by the authorities? Should they be treasured as an economic asset or resented as a cost to the exchequer? Did they demonstrate the existence of a meritocracy and, if so, were they its beneficiaries or victims? Did they exemplify the failure of secondary-modern education or the success of a grammar school one? Were they the pride of the North or a symptom of its backwardness? Was John Lennon 'highly articulate'[305] or in a state of 'pathetic near-literacy'?[306] Was Paul McCartney 'a very good man' or leading youth astray?[307] Was their music 'art'[308] or 'noise'?[309] Was it the successor to or the antithesis of the classical tradition? Was its commercial success the product of a free market or a rigged one? Were the band members materialistic or spiritual? Did they promote 'the doctrine of cheap success' or point out its hollowness? Were their fans suckers or connoisseurs? Was their behaviour 'of very little consequence' or worthy of academic investigation?[310] Did they incite or prevent juvenile delinquency? Were they 'thumb[ing] their noses at the adult world and its conventions' or rightly 'rejecting some of the sloppy standards of their elders'?[311] If the Beatles joined the army or went to jail, should their hair be cropped? Assuming they needed it, would they merit state subsidy?

Westminster manufactured disputes, but these went beyond the usual parliamentary badinage in that they stemmed as much from confusion as dogmatism. No party line could be upheld towards characters as unpredictable and unprecedented as the Beatles. Nor could politicians draw upon their mental hinterland for clear guidance. Some broke the habit of a lifetime by declaring their ignorance on a matter of public interest, while others awkwardly admitted to gaining their knowledge through perusing glossy magazines.[312] To the four roles performed by politicians in relation to popular music identified by Martin Cloonan and John Street (legislators, policymakers, regulators and moral crusaders), perhaps we should add a fifth: that of perplexed bystanders.[313]

The closest parliamentarians came to agreement over the Beatles was to view them as funny peculiar. Wisecracks demonstrated a familiarity with the Beatles by the joker and his or her audience, who typically responded with 'self-conscious laughter'.[314] Yet they simultaneously served as a distancing mechanism, their humour stemming from the sheer improbability of a beat combo having anything to do with parliamentarians and their concerns.

Solemn consideration was given to how the state should treat these plenipotentiaries from the land of Youth. But the most serious issue raised by the Beatles concerned not the power of the state but its powerlessness. Harold Wilson was right that Alec Douglas-Home should have refrained from 'claiming credit for the Beatles'.[315] They had emerged unexpectedly, acted independently and represented forces outwith the comprehension of Westminster, still less its control. This explains why they appeared in debates about the most nebulous of topics and those most impervious to legislative action: 'The Problem of Leisure', 'Automation', 'Youth and Social Responsibilities', 'Drugs (Prevention of Misuse)'.

The most hyperbolic statements made by politicians about the Beatles were in retrospect the most realistic ones. Indeed, the very term used by Lord Willis – 'cultural revolution' – was that chosen by historian Arthur Marwick for his more positive characterisation of the sixties, which placed the Beatles at its centre.[316] Deedes applauded the same 'cultural movement among the young which may become part of the history of our times' so lamented by Willis.[317] But neither they nor any other politician could do very much about it. The Beatles represented changes in what Willis termed 'the human condition' that went beyond the limits of the knowable and actionable in Westminster.[318] From this perspective, it was not the Beatles but parliamentarians who were peripheral to the upheaval of the 1960s.

MPs and the revolutionary left held some attitudes in common towards the Beatles. Both perceived the band as rivals for public attention and affection. They envied the Beatles' sway over the young and enjoined them to use it to good effect, from the pacifist John Papworth's idea for a world of communes to the far-right MP John Biggs-Davison's suggestion that the state should leave anti-cigarette campaigns to celebrities like them. Politicians of all stripes liked to steal a little of the Beatles' limelight. Michael X's 1970 photo op with Ono and Lennon differed little from Harold Wilson's appearance with the band six years previously. Point-scoring over the Beatles between parties was a common occurrence inside and outside Westminster. The SLL's Bill Hunter pilloried Labour MP and one-time communist Eric Heffer for revealing his 'deep respect for the ruling class' in defence of the Beatles' MBEs.[319] The SPGB laid into the 'trendy imbecility' of the YCL for embracing pop culture in 1967, and an anonymous anarchist writing for *Freedom* in 1980 got in a dig at 'all the lefty rags' for being so conformist as to mourn Lennon's death.[320] Like their mainstream counterparts, Marxist parties and their publications were internally divided about the Beatles. Members of the CPGB exchanged insults in *Marxism Today* much like Trotskyists in *Black Dwarf*, and attitudes in the YCL ranged from praising Lennon's agitprop and Harrison's charity concerns to denouncing the false consciousness created by 'Sergeant Pep-up's Phoney Thoughts Club Band'.[321]

Extra-parliamentary and parliamentary attitudes nonetheless diverged in important respects. Parliamentary interest in the Beatles dipped in 1966 and declined precipitously from 1968 onwards. They attracted only ten mentions in Westminster from their break-up in April 1970 to 1979, when

Iain Sproat felt obliged to remind fellow MPs that the Beatles 'were big news 10 years ago'.[322] The revolutionary left conversely detected in 1966 the first overt signs of political consciousness in the Beatles, who went on to support some of their causes and publications in the late sixties and seventies. While (astonishingly) no one saw fit to comment in Parliament on Lennon's murder in December 1980, the CPGB's Political Committee had a minuted discussion on the subject.[323] Lengthy eulogies to Lennon were published by Simon Frith in *Marxism Today*, Mick Farren in *SoHo Weekly News* and Tariq Ali in *Socialist Challenge*, which was offering subscribers an 'Exclusive John Lennon poster' within days of his death.[324]

The revolutionary left's greater affinity with the Beatles existed for generational as well as ideological reasons. The Beatles were near-contemporaries of the young activists who joined far-left organisations during the 1960s. Furthermore, they moved in some of the same circles. The Beatles met Wilson once, but Lennon saw Michael X a number of times and gave him large sums of money over several years. Tariq Ali recalled that Lennon 'would ring me once or twice a month and talk about the state of the world' and Richard Neville was summoned to meet Lennon to discuss his libertarian manifesto *Play Power*.[325]

But the left's interest in the Beatles did not necessarily translate into affection or understanding. *Play Power* gave an equivocal answer to the question 'is rock music revolutionary?'[326] To Neville, 'The Paradox' was that the music was insurrectionary but 'the performers and promoters are not': an impression possibly reinforced when he was whisked away in a Rolls with tinted windows to Lennon's country pile.[327] Other left-wing analyses used the language of paradox and contradiction. Dave Laing's *The Sound of Our Time* (1969) suggested that the Beatles and Bob Dylan were turning on its head Lenin's maxim that 'Ethics are the Aesthetics of the future'. Instead, their music contained the germ of a better society which eliminated 'the notions of work, leisure and money as we know them'.[328] Martin Jacques and other embryonic Eurocommunists weighed up the 'positive and negative elements ... of the cultural rebellions of the sixties' and the Beatles' relationship to them.[329] Analyses of the band by the CCCS were a study in paradox, with the Beatles complicit in 'transcending class while preserving capitalism' and Beatlemania considered just another moral panic when compared to real threat posed by punk.[330]

More conventional Marxists saw little reason to be conflicted. To them, the Beatles were engaged in the wrong revolution: a cultural revolution which privileged generation over class, mistook bohemianism for rebellion and individualism for freedom.[331] 'Since property and work relations remained unaffected, nothing fundamental had been changed' by pop music in sixties Britain, argued Perry Anderson.[332] When Hoyland commented in *Black Dwarf* that the Beatles' psychedelic output formed 'part of what has made me into the kind of socialist I am', a correspondent snidely observed that the same could not be said for Che Guevara.[333] Such dogmatism threatened to make small groupings smaller in an age when 'a pop singer influences one thousand times more' young people than any left-wing outfit.[334] Hoyland instead entreated Lennon and his kind to 'come and join us', unsure of the outcome.[335]

Conclusion

Figure 6.1 Headliners – The Beatles' break-up goes public, April 1970. Photo by Mirrorpix/Getty Images

On 11 April 1970, the day after the news broke that Paul McCartney was leaving the Beatles (see Fig. 6.1), *Daily Mail* journalist Pearson Phillips reflected on 'How they changed and how they changed us'.[1] He presented a stark before–after picture. Before the Beatles, Britain had been a peaceable kingdom characterised by conformity, order, deference and innocence. Then 'when they arrived things changed' in every conceivable respect. Class hierarchies and sexual reticence collapsed. New looks and sounds announced themselves, as the North and the young led the way. Phillips hedged his bets on whether the Beatles were the agents or symptoms of change. 'Future historians will explain that in a footnote', he remarked, somewhat underestimating the complexity of the task. But that 'society changed' was undeniable from his perspective, as was the fact that without the Beatles it 'would not, could not, have happened with the same style'.[2]

John Lennon delivered a much bleaker assessment of the Beatles' societal impact when interviewed in December 1970 by the editor of *Rolling Stone*, Jann Wenner.[3] Wenner shared Phillips' belief in the catalytic effect of the Beatles, whom he had described earlier that year as 'the single dominant force in the new social thought and style for which the Sixties will forever be remembered'.[4] But, when asked by Wenner 'What do you think the effect of the Beatles was on the history of Britain?', Lennon was having none of it:

The people who are in control and in power and the class system and the whole bullshit bourgeois scene is exactly the same except that there is a lot of middle-class kids with long hair walking around London in trendy clothes and Kenneth Tynan's making a fortune out of the word 'fuck'. But apart from that, nothing happened except that we all dressed up. The same bastards are in control, the same people are runnin' everything, it's exactly the same.[5]

Lennon's pessimism had several causes. He had just emerged from purgative Primal Scream Therapy, which had offered him the possibility of being born again once he sloughed off the accrued pain of his past. To Lennon, the sixties and the Beatles were hang-ups to be overcome in order to forge a new career and face a new decade (he named 1970 'Year One').[6] He was also entering his most politically militant phase: hence his jibes at rich hippies offering no real challenge to the ruling class. Meeting the Trotskyists Tariq Ali and Robin Blackburn the next month, Lennon used the same line about 'trendy middle-class kids in pretty clothes' to underscore his position that 'the class system didn't change one little bit' in the 1960s.[7] He now accepted the Marxist orthodoxy that the cultural superstructure could not transform the economic base. When Ono ventured that 'the new music showed things could be transformed by new channels of communication' in the 1960s, he countered that 'nothing really changed' and sided with Ali and Blackburn against Ono by arguing that power could only be taken by force.[8] Lennon's demolition of 'the Beatles myth' in the Wenner interview served the personal aims of reinventing himself and reclaiming his artistic powers and the political aim of warning the likes of Wenner and Phillips not to project their hopes onto a pop group.[9] His declaration that 'the dream is over' was an attack on the broader folly of mistaking superficial and epiphenomenal events of the sixties for actual structural transformation.[10]

Phillips and Lennon stood at opposite poles when explaining the effect of the Beatles on sixties Britain. Phillips was at the tail-end of a tradition of sixties boosterism found in the journalism of Piri Halasz and John Crosby, the memoirs of Brian Epstein, Mary Quant and Vidal Sassoon, the films of Richard Lester and Peter Whitehead and the photographs of David Bailey.[11] Lennon's dourness was more in keeping with other commentators at the turn of the decade, which had been commemorated by a slew of instant histories-cum-obituaries of the sixties. Christopher Booker announced the implosion of the 'libertarian dream' epitomised by the Beatles, and Heather Cremonesi claimed that London's 'Permissive Paradise' had turned into 'a vision of hell'.[12] Even Peter Evans, who summed up the sixties as 'great fun', accepted that its cultural achievements were 'inevitably evaporative' when saying his farewells to the decade in 1969.[13]

The two most influential accounts of the Beatles to emerge in subsequent decades rejected both Lennon's contention that the Beatles made no significant impact on sixties Britain, and Phillips' view that they had changed it for the better. The titles of Philip Norman's *Shout! The Beatles in Their Generation* (1981; rev. 1993, 2003) and Ian MacDonald's *Revolution in the Head: The Beatles' Records and the Sixties* (1994; rev. 1997, 2005) testify to these works' ambition to relate the Beatles to their times. Each accepts Phillips' monochrome vision of Britain before the Beatles. According to Norman, 'respect' was the governing principle for 'the generation born [before] 1941' (a dividing line which oddly bisects the Beatles). The enduring power of 'Victorianism' dictated that

They had respect for their elders and their betters. They had respect for their country with its Empire, now Commonwealth, its God-given right to be called 'Great' Britain. Having just survived a world war, they had respect for politicians and soldiers. They had respect also for clergymen, policemen, schoolteachers and the Queen.[14]

The 'drab uniformity of postwar Britain' criticised by Norman also appears in MacDonald's account.[15] He depicts it as a 'slow-thinking world' in which 'conformism was universal', its 'stiff and pompous' façade hiding a 'festering mess of sexual ignorance'.[16]

MacDonald sees the Beatles as part of a 'flood of youthful energy' which breached this 'psychic dam' in the 1960s and ushered in a glorious if fleeting 'golden age' experienced by 'anyone' below the age of thirty.[17] Norman dates the turning point to 1956, when teenagers came into being in response to rock 'n' roll, and the Suez Crisis meant that 'England had become overnight a second-class power'.[18] These upheavals prepared the ground for the Beatles' ascendancy in the 1960s, when they symbolised the decade's 'vigour and optimism . . . idealism . . . abounding creativity . . . its childlike sense of discovering the whole world anew'.[19]

In Lennon's terms, MacDonald and Norman appear to embrace the Beatles myth and the sixties dream. They nonetheless share little of Phillips' enthusiasm for the social changes wrought by the 1960s. The only victims in Phillips' account are the collar-stud industry and the 'wrinkled balloons' of snobbery and pomposity, punctured by the Beatles' barbs.[20] For MacDonald and Norman, the price of sixties liberation was nothing less than the 'total fragmentation of Western society'.[21] MacDonald was a product of the counterculture who, as Richard Mills observes, remained faithful to its ideals in opposition to what he perceived to be the death of spirituality, debasement of culture and demise of community in the aftermath of the sixties.[22] In MacDonald's telling, the 'revolution in the head' experienced by ordinary people in the 1960s replaced 'consensus, hierarchy, and fixed values' with consumerism and the fetishisation of technology.[23] Stripped of their Christian beliefs and communal bonds, atomised individuals succumbed to a soulless materialism in the late twentieth century in which money alone was left 'holding Western civilisation together'.[24]

Norman came to share MacDonald's view that the Beatles opened a Pandora's box in the 1960s, which he characterises as the decade when 'civilisation ceased moving steadily forward and began taking quantum leaps backward'.[25] Lennon's irreverence at the 1963 Royal Variety Performance sparked the 'modern contempt for convention and self-restraint' manifested in IRA bombings, child abuse, the erosion of public services and 9/11.[26] *Sgt. Pepper*'s glorification of drug use led to the addictions plaguing contemporary society. The Pill (somewhat nebulously) allowed future generations of children 'to thieve and vandalise without the slightest fear of parental retribution'.[27] 'If we are honest we must accept the extent to which the heady new freedoms of youth in the sixties paved the way for the frightening, ungovernable world we see about us today', he maintains, and the Beatles' capacity to 'get away with anything' bore much of the blame.[28]

Much insight can be gained from the writings of MacDonald and Norman without subscribing to the metaphysics of one or the doom-mongering of the other. Their assessments of the Beatles' impact none-theless lack substantiation and verge on speculation. This book has set itself the more limited but achievable aim of understanding what the Beatles meant to sixties Britain through examining the thoughts of their contem-poraries recorded at the time. The available evidence indicates that the Beatles did what cultural figures seek to do above and beyond entertain-ment. As artists and celebrities, they advanced ways of living, loving, thinking, looking, talking, joking, worshipping and campaigning which surprised and occasionally provoked their contemporaries. Sometimes explicitly and sometimes unwittingly, they created a distinctive vision which critiqued society as it was and imagined society as it could be.

The chapters on society in this book show their impact to have been broad, rapid and multifaceted. By the end of 1963, the band and their fans had been used as a yardstick against which to measure virtually every facet of society: class and age, gender and sexuality, Church and Crown, region and nation, economics and politics. They did not create these debates. Late fifties and early sixties Britain was already awash with state-of-the-nation rumination.[29] Potboiling articles, books and pamphlets posed awkward questions: *Is Chastity Outmoded?*, *Suicide of a Nation?*, *Must Labour Lose?*, 'Does England Really Need a Queen?' Others delivered no less unsettling verdicts: *The Stagnant Society*, *The Glittering Coffin*, *The Angry Decade*, *The Rise of the Meritocracy*, *The Two Cultures*, *The American Invasion*. Writers blamed in-groups within 'The Establishment' for Britain's failures and identified out-groups giving cause for concern. These included the 'dark strangers' from the New Commonwealth, families leaving East End poverty and community for suburban affluence and isolation, wives jug-gling the 'two roles' of mother and worker, homosexuals who 'stand apart' and 'the unattached' and unclubbable young. A storied collection of young novelists, playwrights, satirists and New Wave directors dramatised hot-button issues: social mobility in *Room at the Top* and *Steptoe and Son*; manual labour in *Saturday Night and Sunday Morning* and *I'm All Right*

Jack; decolonisation in *The Entertainer*; individualism in *Look Back in Anger*, decency in *Lucky Jim*; marriage in *A Kind of Loving*; deference in *TW3*; heroism in *The Goon Show*; masculinity in *This Sporting Life*; alternative lifestyles in *A Taste of Honey*; delinquency in *The Loneliness of the Long-Distance Runner*; youth culture in *Absolute Beginners*; and race relations in *The Emigrants*, *The Lonely Londoners* and *City of Spades*.

It was testament to the Beatles' relevance and multivalence that they featured in discussions about all these issues and more. Still more striking was the way in which they – or rather, interpretations of them – changed the terms of the debates in several cases. Mass culture, Americanisation, the 'youth question', the 'generation gap' and the North–South divide looked different in light of the Beatles' stardom. Expectations that the bubble would burst and the craze collapse were confounded by their charm, ability and boundless creativity. But their continued salience did not rest entirely upon their capacity for reinvention. From the outset, reactions to the Beatles provoked reactions of their own. Contemporaries considered the social significance of Beatlemania, the political significance of parties identifying themselves with the band and the cultural significance of the *Times*' music critic naming Lennon and McCartney '[t]he outstanding English composers of 1963'.[30] These discussions about discussions about the Beatles created a snowball effect. The more fame the band acquired, the more publicity and sales they generated, the more fans they amassed and the more criticism they received, the more significant they seemed, making them still more famous. It was debatable who appeared oddest in the context of early sixties Britain: the Beatles; their indecorous young female fans; their incongruously male, middle-aged and middle-class admirers in journalism, politics and the arts; or the serried reactionaries ranged against them.

The condescension and outrage directed at them in the Beatlemania era was largely self-defeating. Critics drew attention to a band they believed to be beneath notice with a churlishness which undercut their claims to superiority. Epstein managed to provide the Beatles with substantial cover so long as they disclaimed artistic pretensions and social meaning and remained on the puckish side of offensive. But, as Chapter 3 argued, the Beatles essentially burst their own bubble in the second half of the 1960s. During Beatlemania, the band had debunked talk of their social, cultural and political import. Subsequently, this ingrained self-deprecation sat uncomfortably with their attempts to transmute their talent, fame and wealth into various unlikely ventures. They abjured the winning formula of tours, films, press conferences, publicity stunts and three-minute hits of their early years and cultivated a reputation for perversity.

Their popularity as a band survived the musical experimentation and eclecticism of the late 1960s, but they were paradoxically at their most marginal when at their most socially engaged. Post-materialism was a tough sell when most Britain households lacked telephones and central heating, especially if it was preached by monied pop stars.[31] The same went for 'Western communism' when its Eastern version sent tanks into Prague and persecuted its citizens in the name of Cultural Revolution. Eastern spirituality had little purchase in a Christian country of waning religiosity in which under 1 per cent of the population was of Asian descent.[32] Lennon and Ono unwisely expressed their support for Black Power by bankrolling a thug and espoused a version of second-wave feminism which did not appeal to second-wave feminists. The benefits of drugs were dubious and their risks obvious, while it was hard to disentangle unobjectionable calls for love, peace and understanding from crackpottery concerning chance, time travel and the power of positive thinking. Anyone hostile to drugs, hippies, obscenity, infidelity, permissiveness, law-breaking, social protest, the rich, the far left, avant-garde art, miscegenation, Americans, Indians or the Japanese had a reason to dislike the Beatles in the late 1960s. Under these circumstances, what is surprising is not the public criticism; it is the tolerance shown towards them.

The chapter on culture, like those on society, highlights the rapidity of the Beatles' impact. By the summer of 1964, they had produced songs, a film and a work of fiction which attracted highbrow scrutiny. Cultural critics, like social commentators, sought to divine the Beatles' representativeness, importance and desirability and were just as divided in their conclusions. Once again, the Beatles were initially unwitting agents of this discourse. There is no reason to think that Gustav Mahler inspired 'Not a Second Time' (1963) or that James Joyce directly influenced *In His Own Write* (1964). The Beatles subsequently became more self-conscious in their artistry. Though increasingly estranged from mainstream British society in the second half of the 1960s, they became more culturally connected. McCartney's exploration of the London scene, Ono's tutelage of Lennon, and album covers designed by famous artists testified to their burgeoning sophistication. As artists, they posed a more direct challenge to cultural norms than social ones: hence the ferocity of the arguments for and against their cultural worth. No agreement had emerged by the turn of the decade. For the Beatles to be admitted to the pantheon of great artists required art to be redefined and the boundaries between high and low culture to be redrawn.

The chapter on politics explores the Beatles' impact at the farthest reaches of their influence. In retrospect, their celebrated encounter with Harold Wilson appears more of a culture clash than a confluence between two modernising forces in sixties Britain, as representative as a lunar eclipse. Parliamentary interest in them was sporadic, and parasitic on discussions in the press. At best, MPs served their representative function in expressing the bewilderment shared by many of their age and background. More problematic was that their struggle to come to terms with the Beatles betrayed a wider incomprehension of new social and cultural currents. The same politicians who enacted permissive legislation displayed little understanding of the changing dynamics of sixties Britain that occasioned these reforms. They likewise expanded state sponsorship of the arts at the very time that culture was being democratised in a manner independent of subsidy and at variance with conventional notions of how art was created, consumed and conceived. The revolutionary left displayed more interest in and understanding of the Beatles than did Westminster politicians. Irrespective of their affiliations, most Marxists and anarchists adjudged the Beatles to be politically unsound. This was a correct analysis within its own terms, but testified to the difficulties encountered by revolutionary left organisations in accommodating countercultural values, and helps to explain why '68 in Britain was relatively small in scale.[33]

This book has shown how the Beatles acted as the sand in the oyster of sixties Britain: a disruptive presence inciting purposeful activity. Reactions to the Beatles dealt with the weightiest of subjects, however glibly: the condition of modernity, the meaning of art, the relationship between state and society. The volume, range and fractiousness of disagreement about them from their rise to their demise caution against generalising about the sixties. Phillips' model of change and Lennon's model of continuity, which respectively anticipated the historical work of Arthur Marwick and Dominic Sandbrook, do not account for the sheer lack of consensus about the Beatles. The band served as a common reference point around which people could argue about the present state and future direction of society.

By the end of the century, these disputes had faded in popular memory. This much was apparent in the interviews recorded by the BBC and archived by the British Library in the Millennium Memory Bank (MMB). This was a massive project, its 5,762 interviews making it the second-largest oral history archive in the world. Equally extensive was its range of interviewees, who came from every conceivable background, age group and region.[34] The summaries produced by the interviewers allow rough counts of the frequency of terms across the archive and allow us to identify especially pertinent interviews to be heard in full.[35]

Of the sixteen themes covered in the MMB's semi-structured interviews, those of Playtime and Growing Up were most likely to incite people to talk about the Beatles. And talk they did. In popular memory, as in contemporary discourse, the Beatles eclipsed all other popular musicians. They were mentioned a total of 237 times in the rough measure provided by the summaries. This was three times the number of references to Elvis and four times those to the Rolling Stones. There were approximately an eighth as many mentions of Cliff Richard, a ninth as many to Bob Dylan or Bill Haley and a tenth as many to Frank Sinatra or the Spice Girls. Wham!, Bing Crosby, Joe Loss, David Bowie, Duran Duran, Tommy Steele, Jimi Hendrix and Pink Floyd were the other popular musicians name-checked over ten times: that is, around a twentieth of the mentions of the Beatles. Those with mentions in single figures included The Who, the Kinks, the Shadows, the Bee Gees, the Sex Pistols, the Smiths, Abba, Oasis, Boy George and Culture Club, Bob Geldof, Band Aid and Live Aid, Madonna, Lulu, Eric Clapton, Cilla Black, Dusty Springfield, George Formby, Gracie Fields, Bob Marley, Vera Lynn, Harry Roy, Henry Hall, Johnny Ray, Adam Faith, Buddy Holly, Stevie Wonder, Diana Ross, Elton John and Kylie Minogue. There were more mentions of the Beatles than of whole genres and subcultures such as mods and rockers, hippies, punk and rock 'n' roll. References to films and television programmes seem paltry when placed alongside those to the Beatles. For every mention of *Coronation Street* or *EastEnders*, there were five or six to the Beatles. References to the band respectively outnumbered those to *Star Trek*, James Bond, *Star Wars* and *The Sound of Music* by factors of ten, twenty, thirty and a hundred to one.

The 135 people recorded as commenting on the Beatles in the MMB interviews were almost all drawn from the same age cohort. Five sixths of them were born between 1932 and 1960. This meant they had been between 10 and 30 years old at some point during the Beatles' recording career, compared to just a third of all interviewees. Those mentioning the Beatles did not differ substantially from their age cohort in terms of gender, ethnicity, occupation or education, but were over twice as likely to come from the north-west and (less predictably) the south-east.

The Beatles featured in people's life stories in three principal ways. One was to situate themselves in relation to famous historical events. At the turn of the millennium, the Beatles had joined wars and royal weddings as reference points in a shared narrative. An encounter with the Beatles related a personal story to a common history. Recollections of being shat on by pigeons while queuing for tickets, attending a concert, serving a Beatle or (as in many a Liverpudlian account) getting to know the band before they achieved fame, fed and fed off a repository of twentieth-century British identity.[36] Memories of the Beatles served a second, unsurprising purpose of evoking youthful passion. Interviewees wistfully recalled occasions when they were temporarily deafened by Beatlemaniacs[37] or heartbroken by McCartney's marriage.[38] Fans remembered wearing tights festooned with beetles[39] and eating packet after packet of Findus fish fingers to collect pictures of the band.[40] These anecdotes simultaneously distanced interviewees from their younger selves and allowed them to 'bathe in nostalgia' about the sixties, which was the third main reason for Beatles' references.[41] The band in this context served as a 'harbinger of some wonderful change' who appeared to bring 'everything else in [their] wake'.[42] In such accounts, 'the Beatles and the Pill' were unstoppable forces which ushered in 'total freedom' without serious problems or resistance:

the mid-sixties . . . was when you stopped dressing like your dad . . . the Beatles were obviously about then . . . the chains started to come off and people started to sort of really get free. And it really was like that, you know, sort of, everything started happening . . . everything just got turned on its head.[43]

The nostalgia at once conceals and reveals. Reading these accounts in isolation provides little inkling of the atypicality of the Beatles and their unsettling effect upon contemporaries. Hindsight smoothed out the conflicts, resolved the contradictions, marginalised the opposition. As this book has shown, the Beatles' meaning and worth were far from settled in the sixties. The same went for the social and cultural changes with which they were identified. What interviewees later remembered as a 'great feeling of freedom coming in' generated at the time anxiety as well as excitement, including among the young.[44] Only occasional glimpses of the 'other sixties' were available from the vantage point of the 1990s. The polarising effect of Beatlemania surfaced in one man's memory of spending his days fending off demands from home and school to cut his hair, and his nights sampling 'the city . . . full of bands, all combing their hair forward and wearing jackets without lapels on'.[45] A retired Liverpool policeman recalled having clocked Lennon after the 'foul-mouthed gutter snipe' told him to eff off and a clergyman related how the Eisteddfod disqualified his duo for contravening 'tradition' after girls screamed at its Beatles- and Everlys-influenced harmonies.[46] When Donna Bird reminisced about seeing 'all the top groups' at the Tower Ball Room in Great Yarmouth, her mother-in-law interjected that 'everybody didn't want the Beatles and rock stars. Things like that, I hated them, people of my age wanted Max Bygraves'.[47] Evidence of the opprobrium heaped upon the Beatles for their late sixties transgressions is confined to an ex-teacher recalling how their drug-taking made her 'go off them a bit' and an interior designer 'having to defend them because they did strange *Sgt. Pepper*-type things' and experimented with drugs. 'They . . . all went a bit weird, but so did the whole generation really', she recalled.[48]

These interviews offer a highly partial perspective on the sixties, but they speak volumes about its legacy. The Beatles are used not simply to define their era but to expose what was lacking beforehand: musically,[49] sexually,[50] sartorially,[51] emotionally.[52] The aftermath was disillusioning. While interviewees understood the loss of their youthful innocence in terms of personal maturation, the loss of sixties idealism was often perceived as societal degeneration. In these narratives, the Beatles symbolise a halcyon age poised between Victorian repression and 'the unpleasantness . . . associated later with some aspects of modern life'.[53] In 1963 16-year-old Cheryl Vines won a competition to meet the Beatles by writing that 'they personified the time'. In 1999 she cherished her memories of both band and decade:

I'm *so* glad I lived in the 60s . . . I mean the freedom was phenomenal. We really did think we could change the world. . . . It was a lovely time. It was gentle, it was peaceful, people were kind . . . there wasn't this terrible sort of grasping attitude.[54]

To people like her, the Beatles evoked a time of affluence before Thatcherism,[55] sex before AIDS,[56] drug experimentation before chronic addiction[57] and music before technology displaced 'real people or performers'.[58] Even those like Peter Allen, who conceded that the sixties 'didn't really swing' in his native Hull as they did in the metropolis, still remembered the decade as a 'tremendous time'. He declared himself 'very, very, very honoured to have been in my teens when the Beatles were at their height and been able to queue outside the ABC all night to get tickets to go and see them and to have felt that feel . . . of the *Sgt. Pepper's* era'.[59] The Beatles' ambivalent status in sixties Britain had been all but forgotten.

Notes

Preface: Imagining the Beatles

1. Unsigned, *Mail*, 26 February 1964, 1.
2. Vicky, *Mail*, 21 February 1963, www.cartoons.ac.uk/record/VY2145.
3. Joseph Lee, *Evening News*, 3 December 1963, www.cartoons.ac.uk/record/04760; Keith Waite, *Sun*, 21 February 1968, www.cartoons.ac.uk/record/12940; Stanley Franklin, *Mirror*, 29 May 1967, www.cartoons.ac.uk/record/11310; David Myers, *Standard*, 24 February 1969, www.cartoons.ac.uk/record/14886.
4. Keith Waite, *Sketch*, 6 May 1964, www.cartoons.ac.uk/record/05567; Osbert Lancaster, *Express*, 28 November 1963, www.cartoons.ac.uk/record/04718; Bernier, *Herald*, 1 February 1964, 8.
5. Joseph Lee, *Evening News*, 14 September 1964, www.cartoons.ac.uk/record/05985.
6. Emmwood, *Mail*, 25 February 1964, www.cartoons.ac.uk/record/05054; Emmwood, *Mail*, 27 February 1964, www.cartoons.ac.uk/record/05065; Keith Waite, *Sun*, 19 November 1965, www.cartoons.ac.uk/record/07987.
7. Keith Waite, *Sketch*, 5 November 1963, www.cartoons.ac.uk/record/04612; Emmwood, *Mail*, 24 December 1963, www.cartoons.ac.uk/record/MW2009.
8. Margaret Belsky, *Sun*, 21 November 1964, www.cartoons.ac.uk/record/06227.
9. *Honey*, August 1964, 63.
10. Keith Waite, *Mirror*, 1 January 1970, www.cartoons.ac.uk/record/16984; Jon, *Mail*, 28 December 1967, www.cartoons.ac.uk/record/12553.
11. Jak, *Standard*, 3 December 1964, www.cartoons.ac.uk/record/06413; Emmwood, *Mail*, 22 February 1964, www.cartoons.ac.uk/record/MW2023.
12. Jak, *Standard*, 17 August 1965, www.cartoons.ac.uk/record/07541.
13. Keith Waite, *Sun*, 9 March 1965, www.cartoons.ac.uk/record/07603.
14. Leslie Gilbert Illingworth, *Mail*, 10 February 1964, 6; cited in Richard Harrington, *Washington Post*, 9 February 1982, www.washingtonpost.com/archive/lifestyle/1982/02/09/remembering-the-beatles-debut-in-dc/789b6d0b-b89e-4298-8eac-2a65113303a6/.
15. Joseph Lee, *Evening News*, 26 October 1965, www.cartoons.ac.uk/record/07752.
16. Ralph Steadman, *THES*, 13 December 1968, www.cartoons.ac.uk/record/RSN0684; Jon, *Mail*, 14 January 1970, www.cartoons.ac.uk/record/17072; Mac, *Sketch*, 22 March 1969, www.cartoons.ac.uk/record/15077; Stanley

Franklin, *Mirror*, 16 December 1969, www.cartoons.ac.uk/record/16895; Paul Rigby, *Sun*, 17 January 1970, www.cartoons.ac.uk/record/17090.

17. Derek Taylor cited in Keith Badman, *The Beatles: Off the Record: Outrageous Opinions and Unreleased Interviews* (London: Omnibus, 2007), 495.
18. David Langdon, *Punch*, 3 June 1964, 828; Vicky, *Standard*, 1963, www .cartoons.ac.uk/record/VY2208; Trog, *Mail*, 7 November 1963, 22; Langdon, *Mail*, 9 November 1963, 12.
19. Marj Proops, *Mirror*, 9 September 1963, 7; Unsigned, *New Statesman*, 28 February 1964, 326.
20. Norman Mansbridge, *Sketch*, 2 March 1966, www.cartoons.ac.uk/record/ 08556.
21. Michael Heath, *Punch*, 14 October 1964, 25.
22. Osbert Lancaster, *Express*, 2 January 1971, www.cartoons.ac.uk/record/19339.
23. Norman Thelwell, *Punch*, 27 May 1964, 772; Lee, *Evening News*, 3 December 1963; Jon, *Mail*, 4 November 1963, www.cartoons.ac.uk/record/ 04607; Emmwood, *Mail*, 7 July 1964, www.cartoons.ac.uk/record/05868.
24. Stanley Franklin, *Mirror*, 3 January 1964, www.cartoons.ac.uk/record/04997; Joseph Lee, *Evening News*, 20 January 1966, www.cartoons.ac.uk/record/ 08332; Jon, *Mail*, 20 February 1965, www.cartoons.ac.uk/record/06732.
25. Stanley Franklin, *Mirror*, 18 October 1963, www.cartoons.ac.uk/record/04575. The same idea of bearskins cut down to moptops appeared when Prince Charles was rumoured to be a Beatles fan and when the Beatles visited Buckingham Palace to receive their MBEs (Emmwood, *Mail*, 23 April 1964, www.cartoons.ac.uk/record/05313;   Norman   Mansbridge,   *Sketch*, 27 October 1965, www.cartoons.ac.uk/record/07749).
26. Stanley Franklin, *Mirror*, 9 October 1964, www.cartoons.ac.uk/record/06178.
27. Giles, *Express*, 29 October 1963, www.cartoons.ac.uk/record/GA2047; Giles, *Express*, 27 November 1963, www.cartoons.ac.uk/record/GA2057.
28. Cyril Alfred Jacob, *Punch*, 11 March 1964, 387; Norman Mansbridge, *Sketch*, 16 September 1965, www.cartoons.ac.uk/record/07656.
29. Keith Waite, *Sketch*, 27 May 1964, www.cartoons.ac.uk/record/05467; Keith Waite, *Sun*, 28 October 1965, www.cartoons.ac.uk/record/07748.
30. Jak, *Standard*, 8 February 1964, www.cartoons.ac.uk/record/05097.
31. Giles, *Express*, 18 February 1964, www.cartoons.ac.uk/record/05024; Tony Holland, *Punch*, 17 March 1965, 14.
32. Norman Mansbridge, *Sketch*, 28 October 1965, www.cartoons.ac.uk/record/ 07744; Emmwood, *Mail*, 28 October 1965, www.cartoons.ac.uk/record/07745.
33. Lee, *Evening News*, 26 October 1965.
34. Emmwood, *Mail*, 12 November 1963, www.cartoons.ac.uk/record/MW1198A; Waite, *Mirror*, 1 January 1970.
35. Jak, *Standard*, 14 December 1963, www.cartoons.ac.uk/record/04809; Joseph Lee, *Evening News*, 22 November 1963, www.cartoons.ac.uk/record/04709; Thelwell, *Punch*, 27 May 1964, 772.

36. Emmwood, *Mail*, 22 November 1963, www.cartoons.ac.uk/record/MW1190; Lancaster, *Express*, 28 November 1963; Giles, *Express*, 7 July 1966, www.cartoons.ac.uk/record/GA2354; Norman Mansbridge, *Sketch*, 19 June 1967, www.cartoons.ac.uk/record/11452.

37. Michael Cummings, *Express*, 23 September 1964, www.cartoons.ac.uk/record/06079.

38. Jon, *Mail*, 6 February 1964, www.cartoons.ac.uk/record/05120; Leslie Gilbert Illingworth, *Mail*, 15 January 1964, www.cartoons.ac.uk/record/04949.

39. Cited in *New York Times*, 7 December 1962, 1; Emmwood, *Mail*, 12 August 1964, www.cartoons.ac.uk/record/MW2070.

40. Jak, *Standard*, 20 December 1968, www.cartoons.ac.uk/record/14483.

41. Jon, *Mail*, 12 March 1964, 1.

42. Jon, *Mail*, 16 June 1965, www.cartoons.ac.uk/record/07241; Emmwood, *Mail*, 17 June 1965, www.cartoons.ac.uk/record/MW2151.

43. Jak, *Standard*, 27 November 1969, www.cartoons.ac.uk/record/16764.

44. Unsigned, *Punch*, 23 November 1966, 8.

45. Emmwood, *Mail*, 20 December 1963, www.cartoons.ac.uk/record/MW2008; Eric Burgin, *Punch*, 20 November 1963, 744; unsigned, *Sketch*, 27 February 1964, www.cartoons.ac.uk/record/05144; Stanley Franklin, *Mirror*, 17 June 1965, www.cartoons.ac.uk/record/07247.

46. Jak, *Standard*, 5 November 1963, www.cartoons.ac.uk/record/04622; Jak, *Standard*, 12 November 1963, www.cartoons.ac.uk/record/04655.

47. David Langdon, *Sunday Mirror*, 25 February 1971, www.cartoons.ac.uk/record/LA0128B; Osbert Lancaster, *Express*, 3 December 1964, www.cartoons.ac.uk/record/06418.

48. Giles, *Express*, 9 December 1963, www.cartoons.ac.uk/record/04366; Giles, *Express*, 11 February 1964, www.cartoons.ac.uk/record/CG%2f1%2f4%2f1%2f3%2f18%2f53; Emmwood, *Mail*, 14 November 1963, www.cartoons.ac.uk/record/MW1185; Giles, *Express*, 3 December 1964, www.cartoons.ac.uk/record/06422.

49. Bernard Hollowood, *Punch*, 6 November 1963, 680; Hollowood, *Punch*, 19 January 1966, 6.

50. Clive Hudson, *Herald*, 25 February 1964, www.cartoons.ac.uk/record/05055.

51. Emmwood, *Mail*, 8 February 1964, www.cartoons.ac.uk/record/05109; Joseph Lee, *Evening News*, 14 April 1966, www.cartoons.ac.uk/record/08763; Stanley Franklin, *Mirror*, 6 July 1966, www.cartoons.ac.uk/record/09319; Emmwood, *Mail*, 12 November 1963; Stanley Franklin, *Mirror*, 30 April 1965, www.cartoons.ac.uk/record/07027; Waite, *Sketch*, 6 May 1964; Stanley Franklin, *Mirror*, 12 February 1965, www.cartoons.ac.uk/record/06769.

52. Jak, *Standard*, 13 February 1968, www.cartoons.ac.uk/record/12891; Trog, *Observer*, 25 June 1967, www.cartoons.ac.uk/record/11497; Bernard Cookson, *Evening News*, 24 March 1970, www.cartoons.ac.uk/record/17530;

Giles, *Sunday Express*, 18 January 1970, www.cartoons.ac.uk/record/GA2767; Jak, *Standard*, 27 November 1969, www.cartoons.ac.uk/record/16764.

53. Stanley Franklin, *Mirror*, 19 February 1968, www.cartoons.ac.uk/record/12927; Jak, *Standard*, 21 February 1968, www.cartoons.ac.uk/record/12941; Jak, *Standard*, 27 February 1968, www.cartoons.ac.uk/record/12982.

54. Norman Mansbridge, *Sketch*, 21 August 1967, www.cartoons.ac.uk/record/11840; Norman Mansbridge, *Sketch*, 22 August 1967, www.cartoons.ac.uk/record/11848.

55. Stanley Franklin, *Mirror*, 1 August 1968, www.cartoons.ac.uk/record/13807; Jak, *Standard*, 20 December 1968; Richard Willson, *Observer*, 23 March 1969, www.cartoons.ac.uk/record/15062.

56. Paul Rigby, *Sun*, 21 January 1971, www.cartoons.ac.uk/record/19485; Lancaster, *Express*, 2 January 1971.

57. Margaret Belsky, *Sun*, 3 July 1968, www.cartoons.ac.uk/record/13678; Jon, *Mail*, 25 February 1971.

58. Jon, *Mail*, 7 July 1970, www.cartoons.ac.uk/record/11575; Michael Cummings, *Express*, 3 May 1968, www.cartoons.ac.uk/record/13359.

59. Franklin, *Mirror*, 19 February 1968; Rigby, *Sun*, 17 January 1970; Mac, *Sketch*, 24 March 1970, www.cartoons.ac.uk/record/17529.

60. Stanley Franklin, *Mirror*, 15 September 1964, www.cartoons.ac.uk/record/06051; Stanley Franklin, *Mirror*, 31 December 1963, www.cartoons.ac.uk/record/067033.

61. Vicky, *Standard*, 12 September 1963, www.cartoons.ac.uk/record/04375; Stanley Franklin, *Mirror*, 26 September 1963, www.cartoons.ac.uk/record/15511.

62. Jak, *Standard*, 14 October 1963, www.cartoons.ac.uk/record/04442; Trog, *New Statesman*, 18 October 1963, www.cartoons.ac.uk/record/04470.

63. Lee, *Evening News*, 22 November 1963; Emmwood, *Mail*, 31 October 1963, www.cartoons.ac.uk/record/MW1180; Vicky, *Standard*, 31 October 1963, www.cartoons.ac.uk/record/VY2342.

64. Stanley Franklin, *Mirror*, 17 February 1964, www.cartoons.ac.uk/record/05020.

65. Michael Cummings, *Express*, 11 November 1963, www.cartoons.ac.uk/record/04648.

66. Glan Williams, *Sunday Citizen*, 17 November 1963, www.cartoons.ac.uk/record/04684; Stanley Franklin, *Mirror*, 12 December 1963, www.cartoons.ac.uk/record/04743.

67. Vicky, *Standard*, 7 February 1964, www.cartoons.ac.uk/record/VY2411; William Papas, *Guardian*, 14 February 1964, www.cartoons.ac.uk/record/05011.

68. Jon, *Mail*, 11 April 1964, www.cartoons.ac.uk/record/05391.

69. Cummings, *Express*, 4 December 1964.

70. Jon, *Mail*, 28 December 1967.

71. Vicky, *Standard*, 14 June 1965, www.cartoons.ac.uk/record/VY2759; Michael Cummings, *Express*, 16 June 1965, www.cartoons.ac.uk/record/07240.

72. Emmwood, *Mail*, 2 September 1967, www.cartoons.ac.uk/record/MW2361; Norman Mansbridge, *Sketch*, 6 March 1968, www.cartoons.ac.uk/record/ NM0026; Michael Cummings, *Express*, 1 January 1968, www.cartoons.ac.uk /record/12765.

73. Mac, *Sketch*, 22 March 1969; Emmwood, *Mail*, 27 March 1969, www .cartoons.ac.uk/record/15083; Mac, *Sketch*, 27 November 1969, www .cartoons.ac.uk/record/16759.

74. Cummings, *Express*, 3 May 1968; Cummings, *Express*, 2 February 1966, www .cartoons.ac.uk/record/08414.

75. Ernst Gombrich, *Meditations on a Hobby Horse and Other Essays on the Theory of Art* (London: Phaidon, 1963), 133.

76. Unsigned, *Mail*, 26 February 1964, 1. See also Keith Waite, *Sun*, 16 September 1965, www.cartoons.ac.uk/record/07654; and Norman Mansbridge, *Sketch*, 24 January 1966, www.cartoons.ac.uk/record/08367.

77. Stanley Franklin, *Mirror*, 23 May 1968, www.cartoons.ac.uk/record/13459; Mansbridge, *Sketch*, 22 August 1967; Jon, *Mail*, 24 January 1966, www .cartoons.ac.uk/record/08361.

78. Rigby, *Sun*, 21 January 1971; Leslie Gilbert Illingworth, *Mail*, 1 January 1964, www.cartoons.ac.uk/record/ILW3732; Giles, *Express*, 18 February 1964; Giles, *Sunday Express*, 11 October 1963, www.cartoons.ac.uk/record/GA2051; Emmwood, *Mail*, 24 December 1963; Emmwood, *Mail*, 25 April 1964, www .cartoons.ac.uk/record/05279; Emmwood, *Mail*, 7 July 1964; Emmwood, *Mail*, 12 August 1964; Lee, *Evening News*, 22 November 1963; Illingworth, *Mail*, 1 January 1964; Illingworth, *Mail*, 15 January 1964; Lancaster, *Express*, 28 November 1963; Vicky, *Standard*, 7 February 1964; Franklin, *Mirror*, 17 February 1964; Jon, *Mail*, 11 April 1964.

79. Emmwood, *Mail*, 18 December 1963, www.cartoons.ac.uk/record/ MW2006.

80. Margaret Belsky, *Herald*, 9 January 1964, www.cartoons.ac.uk/record/04969; Emmwood, *Mail*, 9 January 1964, www.cartoons.ac.uk/record/MW3284; Keith Waite, *Sketch*, 9 January 1964, www.cartoons.ac.uk/record/04968.

81. Emmwood, *Mail*, 8 February 1964; Giles, *Express*, 25 August 1964, www .cartoons.ac.uk/record/GA2143; Jak, *Standard*, 17 August 1965; Stanley Franklin, *Mirror*, 8 August 1966, www.cartoons.ac.uk/record/09520; Jak, *Standard*, 17 August 1966, www.cartoons.ac.uk/record/09555.

82. Franklin, *Mirror*, 6 July 1966; Giles, *Express*, 14 August 1966, www .cartoons.ac.uk/record/GA2366.

83. Jak, *Standard*, 13 February 1968; Jak, *Standard*, 21 February 1968; Jak, *Standard*, 27 February 1968; Waite, *Sun*, 21 February 1968.

84. Mansbridge, *Sketch*, 2 March 1966.

85. Nicholas Garland, *Telegraph*, 9 November 1966, www.cartoons.ac.uk/record/ 09995; David Langdon, *Sunday Mirror*, 20 November 1966, www .cartoons.ac.uk/record/10068.

86. Norman Mansbridge, *Sketch*, 7 December 1967, 12, www.cartoons.ac.uk /record/12455; Keith Waite, *Sun*, 2 August 1968, www.cartoons.ac.uk /record/13815; Emmwood, *Mail*, 3 August 1968, 6.

87. Emmwood, *Mail*, 28 December 1967, www.cartoons.ac.uk/record/ MW2396.

88. Giles, *Express*, 3 December 1964; Franklin, *Mirror*, 15 September 1964; Giles, *Express*, 12 March 1964, www.cartoons.ac.uk/record/GA2180; Cummings, *Express*, 4 December 1964; Lancaster, *Express*, 3 December 1964.

89. David Langdon, *Sunday Mirror*, 29 October 1967, www.cartoons.ac.uk /record/12227; Norman Mansbridge, *Sketch*, 24 November 1966, www .cartoons.ac.uk/record/10115; Keith Waite, *Sun*, 21 September 1967, https:// www.cartoons.ac.uk/record/12005.

90. Jak, *Standard*, 9 August 1966, https://www.cartoons.ac.uk/record/09526; Trog, *Observer*, 21 August 1966, www.cartoons.ac.uk/record/09562; David Myers, *Standard*, 9 August 1966, www.cartoons.ac.uk/record/09524; Giles, *Express*, 7 July 1966; Cummings, *Express*, 2 February 1966.

91. Cookson, *Evening News*, 24 March 1970; Giles, *Express*, 24 March 1970, www .cartoons.ac.uk/record/GA5537; Mac, *Sketch*, 24 March 1970; Paul Rigby, *Sun*, 24 March 1970, www.cartoons.ac.uk/record/17525.

92. Belsky, *Sun*, 3 July 1968; Jak, *Standard*, 20 December 1968; Willson, *Observer*, 23 March 1969; Giles, *Express*, 27 March 1969, www.cartoons.ac.uk/record/ GA5534; Stanley Franklin, *Mirror*, 1 April 1969, www.cartoons.ac.uk/record/ 15111; Paul Rigby, *Sun*, 27 November 1969, www.cartoons.ac.uk/record/ 16758; Mac, *Sketch*, 27 November 1969; Franklin, *Mirror*, 16 December 1969; Rigby, *Sun*, 17 January 1970.

93. Jak, *Standard*, 29 February 1964, www.cartoons.ac.uk/record/05075; Mansbridge, *Sketch*, 24 January 1966; Jon, *Mail*, 24 January 1966; Mac, *Sketch*, 13 March 1969, www.cartoons.ac.uk/record/14998; Keith Waite, *Sun*, 13 March 1969, www.cartoons.ac.uk/record/14997; Willson, *Observer*, 23 March 1969.

94. Waite, *Sun*, 16 September 1965; Osbert Lancaster, *Express*, 24 September 1965, www.cartoons.ac.uk/record/07689; Mansbridge, *Sketch*, 22 August 1967.

95. Lancaster, *Express*, 2 January 1971.

96. Gombrich, *Meditations*, 127.

97. Irene Morra, *Britishness, Popular Music, and National Identity: The Making of Modern Britain* (London: Routledge, 2013), 17–18.

98. Gombrich, *Meditations*, 132.

99. Waite, *Sun*, 16 September 1965; Lancaster, *Express*, 24 September 1965.

Introduction

1. For overviews of writing about the Beatles, see Marcus Collins, 'Introduction: Nothing You Can Know That Isn't Known?', *Popular Music History* 9, no. 1 (2014), 5–10; Marcus Collins, 'We Can Work It Out: Popular and Academic Writing on The Beatles', *Popular Music History* 9, no. 1 (2014), 79–101; Marcus Collins, 'Interpreting the Beatles', *Teaching History*, no. 136 (2009), 42; Erin Torkelson Weber, *The Beatles and the Historians: An Analysis of Writings about the Fab Four* (Jefferson, NC: McFarland, 2016); Olivier Julien, '50 ans des Beatles Studies', *Volume!* 12, no. 2 (2016), 15–42; Yrjö Heinonen, 'Introduction: (Being a Short Diversion to) Current Perspectives in Beatles' Research', in *Beatlestudies 1: Songwriting, Recording and Style Change*, ed. Yrjö Heinonen (Jyväskylä: University of Jyväskylä, 1998); Janne Mäkelä, '"The Greatest Story of Pop Music? Challenges of Writing the Beatles' History"' and Walter Everett, 'The Future of Beatles' Research', in *Beatlestudies 3*, ed. Yrjö Heinonen (Jyväskylä: University of Jyväskylä, 2000); James McGrath, 'Cutting up a Glass Onion: Reading the Beatles' History and Legacy', in *Fifty Years with the Beatles: The Impact of the Beatles on Contemporary Culture*, ed. Jerzy Jarniewicz and Alina Kwiatkowska (Łódź: Łódź University Press, 2010); Michael Brocken and Melissa Davis, 'Introduction', in *The Beatles Bibliography: A New Guide to the Literature* (Manitou Springs, CO: Beatle Works Limited, 2012). For introductions to the Beatles, see Ian Inglis, *The Beatles* (Sheffield: Equinox Publishing, 2017); Kenneth Womack, ed., *The Beatles Encyclopedia: Everything Fab Four* (Santa Barbara, CA: ABC-CLIO, 2016); Kenneth Womack, ed., *The Cambridge Companion to the Beatles* (Cambridge: Cambridge University Press, 2009).

2. Samuel H. Beer, *Britain against Itself: The Political Contradictions of Collectivism* (New York, NY: Norton, 1982), 139.

3. For revisionist accounts, see Trevor Harris and Monia O'Brien Castro, eds., *Preserving the Sixties: Britain and the 'Decade of Protest'* (Basingstoke: Palgrave Macmillan, 2014); Brian Harrison, 'Historiographical Hazards of Sixties Britain', in *Penultimate Adventures with Britannia: Personalities, Politics and Culture in Britain*, ed. William Roger Louis (London: I. B. Tauris, 2008); Brian Harrison, *Seeking a Role: The United Kingdom, 1951–1970* (Oxford: Clarendon Press, 2009), ch. 9; Dominic Sandbrook, *Never Had It So Good: A History of Britain from Suez to the Beatles* (London: Little, Brown, 2005); Dominic Sandbrook, *White Heat: A History of Britain in the Swinging Sixties* (London: Little, Brown, 2006). For Britain in the sixties, see also George L. Bernstein, *The Myth of Decline: The Rise of Britain since 1945* (London: Pimlico, 2004) ch. 8; Mark Donnelly, *Sixties Britain: Culture, Society, and Politics* (Harlow: Pearson Longman, 2005);

Marcus Collins, ed., *The Permissive Society and Its Enemies: Sixties British Culture* (London: Rivers Oram, 2007).

4. For the periodisation of the sixties, see Fredric Jameson, 'Periodizing the 60s', *Social Text*, no. 9/10 (1984), 178–209; Arthur Marwick, *The Sixties: Cultural Revolution in Britain, France, Italy, and the United States, c. 1958–c. 1974* (Oxford: Oxford University Press, 1998), ch. 1; Simon Hall, 'Protest Movements in the 1970s: The Long 1960s', *Journal of Contemporary History* 43, no. 4 (2008), 655–72; Andrew Hunt, '"When Did the Sixties Happen?" Searching for New Directions', *Journal of Social History* 33, no. 1 (1999), 147–61; Tor Egil Førland, 'Cutting the Sixties Down to Size: Conceptualizing, Historicizing, Explaining', *Journal for the Study of Radicalism* 9, no. 2 (2015), 125–48; Jeremy Varon, Michael S. Foley and John McMillian, 'Time Is an Ocean: The Past and Future of the Sixties', *The Sixties* 1, no. 1 (2008), 1–7.

5. Arthur Marwick, *Culture in Britain since 1945* (Oxford: Basil Blackwell, 1991), 96.

6. Oded Heilbronner, 'The Peculiarities of the Beatles: A Cultural-Historical Interpretation', *Cultural and Social History* 5, no. 1 (2008), 99–115.

7. Sandbrook, *White Heat*, 794.

8. David Fowler, *Youth Culture in Modern Britain, c. 1920–c. 1970: From Ivory Tower to Global Movement – a New History* (Basingstoke: Palgrave Macmillan, 2008), 174, 168. Musicologists working on the Beatles have their own methods and concerns and therefore have developed their own periodisations. That said, sociomusicological studies can be related to the tripartite model described above. For example, Wilfrid Mellers' claim that the Beatles had 'reinstated magic' within Western consciousness is a prime example of the 'Beatles as trailblazers' approach. Allan F. Moore's depiction of *Sgt. Pepper* as 'manag[ing] to capture, more vividly than almost anything contemporaneous, its own time and place' is closer to the 'Beatles as exemplars' approach. The same can be said of the quantitative song analysis undertaken by Matthias Mauch and his colleagues, which suggests that the Beatles should be considered more representative than innovative in terms of their musical style (Wilfrid Mellers, *Twilight of the Gods: The Music of the Beatles* (New York, NY: Viking Press, 1973), 184; Allen F. Moore, 'The Act You've Known for All These Years: A Re-Encounter with *Sgt. Pepper*', in *Sgt. Pepper and the Beatles: It Was Forty Years Ago Today*, ed. Olivier Julien (Aldershot: Ashgate, 2007), 140; Matthias Mauch, Robert M. MacCallum, Mark Levy and Armand M. Leroi, 'The Evolution of Popular Music: USA 1960–2010', *Royal Society Open Science* 2, no. 5 (2015), 7–9).

9. *Sgt. Pepper's Musical Revolution* (BBC Two, 3 June 2017).

10. *20th Century Greats: Lennon/McCartney* (C4, 27 November 2004).

11. Ibid. See also Howard Goodall, *The Story of Music: From Babylon to the Beatles – How Music Has Shaped Civilization* (London: Pegasus, 2013), ch. 8.

12. Norrie Drummond in *NME Annual* (London: IPC, 1967), 20.

13. Lennon cited in Cleave, *Standard*, 4 March 1966, 10.

14. Henry Pleasants, *Serious Music, and All That Jazz! An Adventure in Music Criticism* (London: Gollancz, 1969), 190–1.

15. Ray Coleman, *Melody Maker*, 16 November 1963, 8.

16. 'Iconic', *Cambridge Dictionary*, 2019, https://dictionary.cambridge.org /dictionary/english/iconic. For the Beatles' celebrity, see Ian Inglis, 'Ideology, Trajectory and Stardom: Elvis Presley and the Beatles', *International Review of the Aesthetics and Sociology of Music* 27, no. 1 (1996), 53–78; Janne Mäkelä, *John Lennon Imagined: Cultural History of a Rock Star* (New York, NY: Peter Lang, 2004); Anthony Elliott, 'Celebrity and Political Psychology: Remembering Lennon', *Political Psychology* 19, no. 4 (1998), 833–52; P. David Marshall, 'The Celebrity Legacy of the Beatles', in *The Beatles, Popular Music and Society*, ed. Ian Inglis (Basingstoke: Springer, 2000), 163–75.

17. 'Iconic'. For general works on celebrity, see P. David Marshall, *Celebrity and Power: Fame in Contemporary Culture* (Minneapolis, MN: University of Minnesota Press, 1997); Richard Schickel, *Intimate Strangers: The Culture of Celebrity in America* (Chicago, IL: Ivan R. Dee, 2000).

18. David R. Shumway, *Rock Star: The Making of Musical Icons from Elvis to Springsteen* (Baltimore, MD: Johns Hopkins University Press, 2014). For pop stardom, see Nick Stevenson, *David Bowie: Fame, Sound and Vision* (Cambridge: Polity Press, 2006), ch. 2; David Hepworth, *Uncommon People: The Rise and Fall of the Rock Stars 1955–1994* (London: Random House, 2017); David Buxton, 'Rock Music, the Star-System and the Rise of Consumerism', *Telos* 1983, no. 57 (1983), 93–106; Martin Cloonan, 'The Production of English Rock and Roll Stardom in the 1950s', *Popular Music History* 4, no. 3 (2009).

19. For example, see Geoff Wonfor and Bob Smeaton (dir.), *The Beatles Anthology* (ABC, 1995).

20. For example, see Jenny Diski, *The Sixties* (London: Profile, 2010); Jonathon Green, ed., *Days in the Life: Voices from the English Underground 1961–1971* (London: Minerva, 1989).

21. Alina Kwiatkowska, 'Roll Over, Shakespeare: References to Beatles' Songs in Contemporary English Texts', in Jarniewicz and Kwiatkowska, eds., *Fifty*, 269.

22. Gordon Heald and Robert J. Wybrow, *The Gallup Survey of Britain* (London: Croom Helm, 1986), 252.

23. YouGov, 'Survey Results 9–10 May 2016', https://d25d2506sfb94s .cloudfront.net/cumulus_uploads/document/7r92ujavz0/ InternalResults_160510_BestYear.pdf.

24. Jeffrey Weeks, *The World We Have Won: The Remaking of Erotic and Intimate Life* (London: Routledge, 2007).

25. When the BSA survey asked multiple iterations of the same question, the answers considered here are those asked closest in time to the year 2000.

26. British Social Attitudes, 'Survey Question Data (1993)', question 94B, www .britsocat.com/BodyTwoCol.aspx?control=CCESDSeriesMenu&SurveyID=9; British Social Attitudes, 'Survey Question Data (1998)', question 327, www .britsocat.com/BodyTwoCol.aspx?control=CCESDSeriesMenu&SurveyID=14.

27. British Social Attitudes, 'Survey Question Data (2008)', question 19f, www .britsocat.com/BodyTwoCol.aspx?control=CCESDSeriesMenu&SurveyID=24.

28. British Social Attitudes, 'Survey Question Data (1994)', question C2.44A, www .britsocat.com/BodyTwoCol.aspx?control=CCESDSeriesMenu&SurveyID=10.

29. British Social Attitudes, 'Survey Question Data (2006)', question 37c, www .britsocat.com/BodyTwoCol.aspx?control=CCESDSeriesMenu&SurveyID=22; British Social Attitudes, 'Survey Question Data (2000)', question 10b, www .britsocat.com/BodyTwoCol.aspx?control=CCESDSeriesMenu&SurveyID=16.

30. British Social Attitudes, 'Survey Question Data (1996)', question 502, www .britsocat.com/BodyTwoCol.aspx?control=CCESDSeriesMenu&SurveyID=12.

31. British Social Attitudes, 'Survey Question Data (2001)', question B.25, britsocat.com/BodyTwoCol.aspx?control=CCESDSeriesMenu&SurveyID=17.

32. For the Beatles and Liverpool, see Joe Flannery and Mike Brocken, *Standing in the Wings: The Beatles, Brian Epstein and Me* (Stroud: History Press, 2013); Spencer Leigh, *The Beatles in Liverpool: From Merseybeat to Stardom* (London: Omnibus, 2012); Marion Leonard, 'The "Lord Mayor of Beatle-Land": Popular Music, Local Government, and the Promotion of Place in 1960s Liverpool', *Popular Music and Society* 36, no. 5 (2013), 597–614; James McGrath, '"Where You Once Belonged": Class, Race and the Liverpool Roots of Lennon and McCartney's Songs', *Popular Music History* 9, no. 1 (2014): 11–31. For Hamburg, see Mark Lewisohn, *Tune In: The Beatles – All These Years* (New York, NY: Crown Archetype, 2013); Ian Inglis, *The Beatles in Hamburg* (London: Reaktion, 2012).

33. For the impact of Lennon's death, see Richard Aquila, 'Why We Cried: John Lennon and American Culture', *Popular Music and Society* 10, no. 1 (1985), 33–42; Fred Fogo, *'I Read the News Today': The Social Drama of John Lennon's Death* (Lanham, MD: Rowman & Littlefield, 1994); Anthony Elliott, *The Mourning of John Lennon* (Berkeley, CA: University of California Press, 1999).

34. Timothy Scott Brown, *West Germany and the Global Sixties: The Anti-Authoritarian Revolt, 1962–1978* (Cambridge: Cambridge University Press, 2013), 5. See also Uta G. Poiger, *Jazz, Rock, and Rebels: Cold War Politics and American Culture in a Divided Germany* (Berkeley, CA: University of California Press, 2000); and Julia Sneeringer, 'Meeting the Beatles: What Beatlemania Can Tell Us about West Germany in the 1960s', *The Sixties* 6, no. 2 (2013), 172–98.

35. For the history of the British press, see Adrian Bingham, 'Ignoring the First Draft of History? Searching for the Popular Press in Studies of Twentieth-Century Britain', *Media History* 18, no. 3–4 (2012), 311–26; Adrian Bingham, *Family Newspapers? Sex, Private Life, and the British Popular Press 1918–1978* (Oxford: Oxford University Press, 2009); Laurel Brake, Chandrika Kaul, and Mark W. Turner, eds., *The News of the World and the British Press, 1843–2011* (Basingstoke: Springer, 2016); Martin Conboy, *Tabloid Britain: Constructing a Community through Language* (London: Routledge, 2006), ch. 8; Adrian Bingham and Martin Conboy, *Tabloid Century: The Popular Press in Britain, 1896 to the Present* (New York, NY: Peter Lang, 2015); Kevin Williams, *Read All about It! A History of the British Newspaper* (London: Routledge, 2010).

36. For the study of periodicals, see David Finkelstein, 'The Role of the Literary and Cultural Periodical', in *The Routledge Companion to British Media History*, ed. Martin Conboy and John Steel (London: Routledge, 2015).

37. For girls' magazines, see Angela McRobbie, *Feminism and Youth Culture*, Rev. edn (Basingstoke: Macmillan, 2000), ch. 5; Chris Tinker, 'Shaping 1960s Youth in Britain and France: *Fabulous* and *Salut Les Copains*', *International Journal of Cultural Studies* 14, no. 6 (2011), 641–57; Chris Tinker, 'Mixed Masculinities in 1960s British and French Youth Magazines', *Journal of Popular Culture* 47, no. 1 (2014), 84–108; Melanie Tebbutt, 'From "Marriage Bureau" to "Points of View": Changing Patterns of Advice in Teenage Magazines', in *People, Places and Identities: Themes in British Social and Cultural History, 1700s–1980s*, ed. Alan Kidd and Melanie Tebbutt (Manchester: Manchester University Press, 2017).

38. For the British music press, see Ulf Lindberg, *Rock Criticism from the Beginning: Amusers, Bruisers, and Cool-Headed Cruisers* (New York, NY: Peter Lang, 2005), chs. 3 and 4; Pat Long, *The History of the NME: High Times and Low Lives at the World's Most Famous Music Magazine* (London: Portico, 2012); Steve Jones, ed., *Pop Music and the Press* (Philadelphia, PA: Temple University Press, 2002); Jon Savage, 'The Magazine Explosion: UK Pop Publications in the '60s', *Observer*, 6 September 2009, www .rocksbackpages.com/Library/Article/the-magazine-explosion-uk-pop-publications-in-the-60s; Patrick Glen, 'Sometimes Good Guys Don't Wear White: Morality in the Music Press, 1967–1983' (PhD Thesis, University of Sheffield, 2013); Paul Gorman, *In Their Own Write: Adventures in the Music Press* (London: Sanctuary Publishing, 2001).

39. For a preview, see Marcus Collins, 'I Feel Free: The Worldview of British Rock and Pop Musicians, c. 1965–1975', in *Popular Culture in Britain and America, 1950–1975* (Cheltenham: Adam Matthew Digital, 2013), www.rockandroll.amdigital.co.uk; Marcus Collins, 'The Beatles' Politics',

British Journal of Politics & International Relations 16, no. 2 (2014), 291–309.

40. Gerd-Rainer Horn, *The Spirit of '68: Rebellion in Western Europe and North America, 1956–1976* (Oxford: Oxford University Press, 2007), 243.

41. Keith Gildart, *Images of England through Popular Music: Class, Youth and Rock 'n' Roll, 1955–1976* (Basingstoke: Palgrave Macmillan, 2013), 2.

42. Ibid., 62.

43. David Simonelli, *Working Class Heroes: Rock Music and British Society in the 1960s and 1970s* (Lanham, MD: Lexington Books, 2013), ch. 2.

44. The seventies have received less attention. For overviews, see Alwyn W. Turner, *Crisis? What Crisis? Britain in the 1970s* (London: Aurum, 2013); Lawrence Black, Hugh Pemberton, and Pat Thane, eds., *Reassessing 1970s Britain* (Manchester: Manchester University Press, 2015); Dominic Sandbrook, *State of Emergency: The Way We Were – Britain, 1970–1974* (Harmondsworth: Penguin, 2011); Dominic Sandbrook, *Seasons in the Sun: The Battle for Britain, 1974–1979* (Harmondsworth: Penguin, 2012).

45. Marwick, *Sixties*; Arthur Marwick, *Britain in the Century of Total War* (London: Bodley Head, 1968).

46. Marwick, *Sixties*, 479.

47. Ibid., 3.

48. Kenneth Womack, *Long and Winding Roads: The Evolving Artistry of the Beatles* (New York, NY: Continuum, 2007); Matthew Schneider, *The Long and Winding Road from Blake to the Beatles* (Basingstoke: Palgrave Macmillan, 2008); John McMillian, *Beatles vs. Stones* (New York, NY: Simon & Schuster, 2013); Inglis, *Beatles.*

49. Dale C. Allison, *The Love There That's Sleeping: The Art and Spirituality of George Harrison* (London: Continuum, 2006); Joshua M. Greene, *Here Comes the Sun: The Spiritual and Musical Journey of George Harrison* (London: Random House, 2006); Ian Inglis, *The Words and Music of George Harrison* (New York, NY: Praeger, 2010).

50. Elliott, *Mourning*; Jon Wiener, *Come Together: John Lennon in His Time*, 2nd edn (London: Faber, 2000); Jon Wiener, *Gimme Some Truth: The John Lennon FBI Files* (Berkeley, CA: University of California Press, 2000); Mäkelä, *John Lennon Imagined*; Tim Kasser, *Lucy in the Mind of Lennon* (New York, NY: Oxford University Press, 2013).

51. Kenneth Womack, *Maximum Volume: The Life of Beatles Producer George Martin – the Early Years 1926–1966* (Chicago, IL: Chicago Review Press, 2017); Kenneth Womack, *Sound Pictures: The Life of Beatles Producer George Martin – the Later Years 1966–2016* (Chicago, IL: Chicago Review Press, 2018).

52. Mark Lewisohn, *The Beatles Live!* (London: Pavilion, 1986); Mark Lewisohn, *The Beatles Recording Sessions: The Official Abbey Road Session Notes,*

1962–1970 (New York, NY: Harmony Books, 1988); Mark Lewisohn, *The Complete Beatles Chronicles* (New York, NY: Harmony Books, 1992); Mark Lewisohn, *Tune In*; Ian MacDonald, *Revolution in the Head: The Beatles' Records and the Sixties*, 3rd edn (London: Pimlico, 2005); Kevin Courrier, *Artificial Paradise: The Dark Side of the Beatles' Utopian Dream* (New York, NY: Praeger, 2009); Philip Norman, *Shout! The True Story of the Beatles*, 3rd edn (New York, NY: Fireside/Simon and Schuster, 2005); Philip Norman, *John Lennon: The Life* (London: HarperCollins, 2009); Philip Norman, *Paul McCartney: The Biography* (London: Hachette UK, 2016); Peter Doggett, *You Never Give Me Your Money: The Battle for the Soul of the Beatles* (London: CCV, 2010); Tom Doyle, *Man on the Run: Paul McCartney in the 1970s* (Edinburgh: Birlinn, 2013); Howard Sounes, *Fab: An Intimate Life of Paul McCartney* (London: Harper, 2011); Paul Du Noyer, *Conversations with McCartney* (New York, NY: Overlook Press, 2016); Graeme Thomson, *George Harrison: Behind the Locked Door* (London: Omnibus Press, 2013); Jonathan Gould, *Can't Buy Me Love: The Beatles, Britain, and America* (New York, NY: Three Rivers Press, 2008); Albert Goldman, *The Lives of John Lennon* (New York, NY: Bantam, 1989); Michael Seth Starr, *Ringo: With a Little Help* (Mikwaukee, WI: Backbeat Books, 2016); Steve Turner, *Beatles '66: The Revolutionary Year* (London: HarperCollins, 2016).

53. For example, see Mike Marqusee, *Wicked Messenger: Bob Dylan and the 1960s* (New York, NY: Seven Stories Press, 2011); Philip Lambert, *Inside the Music of Brian Wilson: The Songs, Sounds, and Influences of the Beach Boys' Founding Genius* (London: Continuum, 2007); Alice Echols, *Scars of Sweet Paradise: The Life and Times of Janis Joplin* (Basingstoke: Macmillan, 1999); Greil Marcus, *The Doors* (London: Faber, 2012); Ulf Olsson, *Listening for the Secret: The Grateful Dead and the Politics of Improvisation* (Berkeley, CA: University of California Press, 2017).

54. Andrew August, 'Gender and 1960s Youth Culture: The Rolling Stones and the New Woman', *Contemporary British History* 23, no. 1 (2009), 79–100; Luke Dick and George Reisch, eds., *The Rolling Stones and Philosophy: It's Just a Thought Away* (Chicago, IL: Open Court, 2011); Marcus Collins, 'Sucking in the Seventies? The Rolling Stones and the Aftermath of the Permissive Society', *Popular Music History* 7, no. 1 (2012), 5–23; Marcus Collins, 'Permissiveness on Trial: Sex, Drugs, Rock, the Rolling Stones, and the Sixties Counterculture', *Popular Music and Society* 42, no. 2 (2019), 188–209; McMillian, *Beatles vs. Stones*.

55. Thomas M. Kitts, *Ray Davies: Not Like Everybody Else* (London: Routledge, 2008); Carey Fleiner, *The Kinks: A Thoroughly English Phenomenon* (Lanham, MD: Rowman & Littlefield, 2017); Keith Gildart, 'From "Dead End Streets" to "Shangri Las": Negotiating Social Class and Post-War

Politics with Ray Davies and the Kinks', *Contemporary British History* 26, no. 3 (2012), 273–98.

56. Mark Blake, *Pretend You're in a War: The Who and the Sixties* (London: Aurum, 2014); Casey Harison, *Feedback: The Who and Their Generation* (Lanham, MD: Rowman & Littlefield, 2014); Pamela Thurschwell, ed., *Quadrophenia and Mod(Ern) Culture* (Basingstoke: Springer, 2017).

57. Stevenson, *David Bowie*; Eoin Devereux, Aileen Dillane and Martin Power, eds., *David Bowie: Critical Perspectives* (London: Routledge, 2015).

58. Annie J. Randall, *Dusty! Queen of the Postmods* (New York, NY: Oxford University Press, 2008).

59. Susan Fast, *In the Houses of the Holy: Led Zeppelin and the Power of Rock Music* (Oxford: Oxford University Press, 2001).

60. Julian Palacios, *Syd Barrett and Pink Floyd: Dark Globe* (London: Plexus Publishing, 2015).

61. James J. Nott, *Music for the People: Popular Music and Dance in Interwar Britain* (Oxford: Oxford University Press, 2002).

62. George McKay, *Circular Breathing: The Cultural Politics of Jazz in Britain* (Durham, NC: Duke University Press, 2005).

63. Britta Sweers, *Electric Folk: The Changing Face of English Traditional Music* (New York, NY: Oxford University Press, 2005); Robert G. Burns, *Transforming Folk: Innovation and Tradition in English Folk-Rock Music* (Manchester: Manchester University Press, 2012); Michael Brocken, *The British Folk Revival: 1944–2002* (Aldershot: Ashgate, 2013).

64. Roberta Freund Schwartz, *How Britain Got the Blues: The Transmission and Reception of American Blues Style in the United Kingdom* (London: Routledge, 2016).

65. Cloonan, 'Production'; Gillian A. M. Mitchell, 'Reassessing "the Generation Gap": Bill Haley's 1957 Tour of Britain, Inter-Generational Relations and Attitudes to Rock 'n' Roll in the Late 1950s', *Twentieth Century British History* 24, no. 4 (2013), 573–605; Gillian A. M. Mitchell, 'From "Rock" to "Beat": Towards a Reappraisal of British Popular Music, 1958–1962', *Popular Music and Society* 36, no. 2 (2013), 194–215; Gildart, *Images*; Iain Chambers, *Urban Rhythms: Pop Music and Popular Culture* (Basingstoke: Macmillan, 1985), ch. 2; Dick Bradley, *Understanding Rock 'n' Roll: Popular Music in Britain 1955–1964* (Buckingham: Open University Press, 1992); Spencer Leigh, *Halfway to Paradise: Britpop, 1955–1962* (Folkestone: Finbarr International, 1996); Pete Frame, *The Restless Generation: How Rock Music Changed the Face of 1950s Britain* (London: Omnibus Press, 2011); Ian Inglis, 'Absolute Beginners: The Evolution of a British Popular Music Scene', in *The Ashgate Research Companion to Popular Musicology*, ed. Derek B. Scott (London: Routledge, 2016).

66. Richard Weight, *Mod: A Very British Style* (London: Bodley Head, 2013).

67. Brian Ward, *Just My Soul Responding: Rhythm and Blues, Black Consciousness, and Race Relations* (Berkeley, CA: University of California Press, 1998); Craig Hansen Werner, *A Change Is Gonna Come: Music, Race and the Soul of America* (Ann Arbor, MI: University of Michigan Press, 2006).

68. Sheila Whiteley, *The Space between the Notes: Rock and the Counter-Culture* (London: Routledge, 1992).

69. Edward Macan, *Rocking the Classics: English Progressive Rock and the Counterculture* (Oxford: Oxford University Press, 1997); Paul Hegarty and Martin Halliwell, *Beyond and Before: Progressive Rock since the 1960s* (London: Continuum, 2011); Bill Martin, *Listening to the Future: The Time of Progressive Rock, 1968–1978* (Chicago, IL: Open Court, 2015).

70. Philip Auslander, *Performing Glam Rock: Gender and Theatricality in Popular Music* (Ann Arbor, MI: University of Michigan Press, 2006).

71. Alice Echols, *Hot Stuff* (New York, NY: W.W. Norton, 2010); Tim Lawrence, *Love Saves the Day: A History of American Dance Music Culture, 1970–1979* (Durham, NC: Duke University Press, 2004).

72. Matthew Worley, *No Future: Punk, Politics and British Youth Culture, 1976–1984* (Cambridge: Cambridge University Press, 2017); Dave Laing, *One Chord Wonders: Power and Meaning in Punk Rock* (Oakland, CA: PM Press, 2015); Jon Savage, *England's Dreaming: Sex Pistols and Punk Rock* (London: Faber and Faber, 1991); Subcultures Network, *Fight Back: Punk, Politics and Resistance* (Oxford: Oxford University Press, 2017).

73. David Wilkinson, *Post-Punk, Politics and Pleasure in Britain* (Basingstoke: Springer, 2016); Simon Reynolds, *Rip It Up and Start Again: Postpunk 1978–1984* (London: Faber and Faber, 2009).

74. Matthew Bannister, *White Boys, White Noise: Masculinities and 1980s Indie Guitar Rock* (Aldershot: Ashgate, 2006); Wendy Fonarow, *Empire of Dirt: The Aesthetics and Rituals of British Indie Music* (Middletown, CT: Wesleyan University Press, 2006).

75. Robert Walser, *Running with the Devil: Power, Gender, and Madness in Heavy Metal Music* (Middletown, CT: Wesleyan University Press, 2014); Deena Weinstein, *Heavy Metal: The Music and Its Culture* (London: Hachette UK, 2009).

76. George McKay, *The Pop Festival: History, Music, Media, Culture* (New York, NY: Bloomsbury Publishing USA, 2015); Auslander, *Performing Glam Rock*.

77. Ian Goodyer, *Crisis Music: The Cultural Politics of Rock against Racism* (Oxford: Oxford University Press, 2009); Irene Morra, *Britishness, Popular Music, and National Identity: The Making of Modern Britain* (London: Routledge, 2013); Andy Bennett and Jon Stratton, eds., *Britpop and the English Music Tradition* (London: Routledge, 2016); Jon Stratton and Nabeel Zuberi, eds., *Black Popular Music in Britain since 1945* (London: Routledge, 2016).

78. Nathan Wiseman-Trowse, *Performing Class in British Popular Music* (Basingstoke: Palgrave Macmillan, 2008); Simonelli, *Working Class Heroes*.

79. Simon Reynolds and Joy Press, *The Sex Revolts: Gender, Rebellion, and Rock 'n' Roll* (Cambridge, MA: Harvard University Press, 1996); Sheila Whiteley, ed., *Sexing the Groove: Popular Music and Gender* (London: Routledge, 1997); Marion Leonard, *Gender in the Music Industry: Rock, Discourse and Girl Power* (Aldershot: Ashgate, 2007).

80. Mavis Bayton, *Frock Rock: Women Performing Popular Music* (Oxford: Oxford University Press, 1998); Jacqueline Warwick, *Girl Groups, Girl Culture: Popular Music and Identity in the 1960s* (London: Routledge, 2007); Sheila Whiteley, *Women and Popular Music: Sexuality, Identity and Subjectivity* (London: Routledge, 2013); Gayle Wald, 'Just a Girl? Rock Music, Feminism, and the Cultural Construction of Female Youth', *Signs: Journal of Women in Culture and Society* 23, no. 3 (1998), 585–610; Laurie Stras, ed., *She's So Fine: Reflections on Whiteness, Femininity, Adolescence and Class in 1960s Music* (Aldershot: Ashgate, 2010); Alexandra Marie Apolloni, 'Wishin' and Hopin': Femininity, Whiteness, and Voice in 1960s British Pop' (PhD Thesis, UCLA, 2013).

81. Bannister, *White Boys*; Stan Hawkins, *The British Pop Dandy: Masculinity, Popular Music and Culture* (Aldershot: Ashgate, 2009).

82. Morris Dickstein, *Gates of Eden: American Culture in the Sixties* (New York, NY: Basic Books, 1978); Sara Margaret Evans, *Personal Politics: The Roots of Women's Liberation in the Civil Rights Movement and the New Left* (New York, NY: Vintage Books, 1979).

83. See David Farber, 'The Sixties Legacy: "The Destructive Generation" or "Years of Hope"?', in *The Columbia Guide to America in the 1960s*, ed. David Farber and Beth Bailey (New York, NY: Columbia University Press, 2010); Alexander Bloom, *Long Time Gone: Sixties America Then and Now* (Oxford: Oxford University Press, 2001).

84. Alan Petigny, *The Permissive Society: America, 1941–1965* (Cambridge: Cambridge University Press, 2009).

85. Philip Jenkins, *Decade of Nightmares: The End of the Sixties and the Making of Eighties America* (Oxford: Oxford University Press, 2006); Van Gosse and Richard Moser, *The World the Sixties Made: Politics and Culture in Recent America* (Philadelphia, PA: Temple University Press, 2008).

86. Daniel Horowitz, *Consuming Pleasures: Intellectuals and Popular Culture in the Postwar World* (Philadelphia, PA: University of Pennsylvania Press, 2012); Andrew Ross, *No Respect: Intellectuals and Popular Culture* (London: Routledge, 2016).

87. Daniel Cavicchi, *Tramps Like Us: Music and Meaning among Springsteen Fans* (New York, NY: Oxford University Press, 1998); Fast, *In the Houses*;

Chris McDonald, *Rush, Rock Music and the Middle Class: Dreaming in Middletown* (Indianapolis, IN: Indiana University Press, 2009).

88. Elijah Wald, *How the Beatles Destroyed Rock 'n' Roll: An Alternative History of American Popular Music* (Oxford: Oxford University Press, 2009).

89. Shumway, *Rock Star*.

90. Devon Powers, *Writing the Record: The Village Voice and the Birth of Rock Criticism* (Amherst, MA: University of Massachusetts Press, 2013); Matt Brennan, *When Genres Collide: Down Beat, Rolling Stone, and the Struggle between Jazz and Rock* (New York, NY: Bloomsbury Publishing USA, 2017).

91. Julie Stephens, *Anti-Disciplinary Protest: Sixties Radicalism and Postmodernism* (Cambridge: Cambridge University Press, 1998); Christopher Gair, *American Counterculture* (Edinburgh: Edinburgh University Press, 2007); Peter Braunstein and Michael William Doyle, eds., *Imagine Nation: The American Counterculture of the 1960s and '70s* (London: Routledge, 2013); Anthony Ashbolt, *A Cultural History of the Radical Sixties in the San Francisco Bay Area* (London: Routledge, 2013); Mark Abraham, '"You Are Your Own Alternative": Performance, Pleasure, and the American Counterculture, 1965–1975' (PhD Thesis, York University, OT, 2014); W. J. Rorabaugh, *American Hippies* (Cambridge: Cambridge University Press, 2015).

92. Nadya Zimmerman, *Counterculture Kaleidoscope: Musical and Cultural Perspectives on Late Sixties San Francisco* (Ann Arbor, MI: University of Michigan Press, 2008); Sarah Hill, *San Francisco and the Long 60s* (New York, NY: Bloomsbury Publishing USA, 2016); Nicholas Bromell, *Tomorrow Never Knows: Rock and Psychedelics in the 1960s* (Chicago, IL: University of Chicago Press, 2000); Jim Derogatis, *Kaleidoscope Eyes: Psychedelic Music from the 1960s to the 1990s* (London: Fourth Estate, 1996).

93. Horn, *Spirit of '68*; Martin Klimke and Joachim Scharloth, eds., *1968 in Europe: A History of Protest and Activism, 1956–1977* (Basingstoke: Springer, 2008); Ingrid Gilcher-Holtey, ed., *A Revolution of Perception? Consequences and Echoes of 1968* (New York, NY: Berghahn Books, 2014); Robert Gildea, James Mark and Anette Warring, *Europe's 1968: Voices of Revolt* (Oxford: Oxford University Press, 2017); Phillip Gassert and Martin Klimke, eds., *1968: Memories and Legacies of a Global Revolt* (London: German Historical Institute, 2009).

94. Robert Adlington, ed., *Sound Commitments: Avant-Garde Music and the Sixties* (Oxford: Oxford University Press, 2009); Jeremi Suri, 'The Rise and Fall of an International Counterculture, 1960–1975', *The American Historical Review* 114, no. 1 (2009), 45–68; Grzegorz Kosc et al., eds., *The Transatlantic Sixties: Europe and the United States in the Counterculture Decade* (Bielefeld: transcript Verlag, 2013); Beate Kutschke and

Barley Norton, eds., *Music and Protest in 1968* (Cambridge: Cambridge University Press, 2013); Sheila Whiteley and Jedediah Sklower, eds., *Countercultures and Popular Music* (London: Routledge, 2014); Timothy Scott Brown and Andrew E. Lison, eds., *The Global Sixties in Sound and Vision: Media, Counterculture, Revolt* (Basingstoke: Palgrave Macmillan, 2014).

95. Christopher Leigh Connery, 'The World Sixties', in *The Worlding Project: Doing Cultural Studies in the Era of Globalization*, ed. Rob Wilson and Christopher Leigh Connery (Berkeley, CA: North Atlantic Books, 2007), 77–108; Marwick, *Sixties*; Gerard J. De Groot, *The 60s Unplugged: A Kaleidoscopic History of a Disorderly Decade* (London: Pan, 2009).

96. Kenneth Womack, 'Authorship and the Beatles', *College Literature* 34, no. 3 (2007), 161–82; Womack, *Long*; Kenneth Womack and Todd Davis, eds., *Reading the Beatles: Cultural Studies, Literary Criticism, and the Fab Four* (Binghamton, NY: SUNY Press, 2006); Schneider, *Long*; Jarniewicz and Kwiatkowska, eds., *Fifty Years*.

97. Stephanie Fremaux, *The Beatles on Screen* (New York, NY: Bloomsbury, 2018); Martin King, *Men, Masculinity and the Beatles* (Aldershot: Ashgate, 2013); James McGrath, 'Ideas of Belonging in the Work of John Lennon and Paul McCartney' (PhD Thesis, Leeds Metropolitan University, 2009); Holly Tessler, 'Beatles for Sale: The Role and Significance of Storytelling in the Commercialisation and Cultural Branding of the Beatles since 1970' (PhD Thesis, University of Liverpool, 2009); Peter Atkinson, 'The Beatles on BBC Radio in 1963: The "Scouse" Inflection and a Politics of Sound in the Rise of the Mersey Beat', *Popular Music and Society* 34, no. 2 (2011), 163–75; Peter Atkinson, 'The Beatles and the Broadcasting of British Cultural Revolution, 1958–63', in Jarniewicz and Kwiatkowska, eds., *Fifty Years*.

98. Stephen Daniels, 'Suburban Pastoral: "Strawberry Fields Forever" and Sixties Memory', *Cultural Geographies* 13, no. 1 (2006), 28–54; Robert J. Kruse, *A Cultural Geography of the Beatles: Representing Landscapes as Musical Texts (Strawberry Fields, Abbey Road, and Penny Lane)* (New York, NY: E. Mellen Press, 2005).

99. Michael Baur and Steven Baur, eds., *The Beatles and Philosophy: Nothing You Can Think That Can't Be Thunk* (Chicago, IL: Open Court, 2006).

100. Inglis, *Beatles*; idem, *Beatles in Hamburg*; Colin Campbell, *The Continuing Story of Eleanor Rigby: Analysing the Lyric of a Popular Beatles' Song* (Kibworth Beauchamp: Troubador, 2018); Colin Campbell and Allan R. Murphy, *Things We Said Today: The Complete Lyrics and a Concordance to the Beatles' Songs, 1962–1970* (Ann Arbor, MI: Pierian Press, 1980); John Astley, *Why Don't We Do It in the Road? The Beatles Phenomenon* (New Haven, CT: Company of Writers, 2006).

101. Michael R. Frontani, *The Beatles: Image and Media* (Oxford, MS: University Press of Mississippi, 2007); Thomas MacFarlane, *The Beatles and McLuhan: Understanding the Electric Age* (Lanham, MD: Rowman & Littlefield, 2013).

102. Kasser, *Lucy*. For an excellent overview of writing about the Beatles, see Brocken and Davis, *Beatles Bibliography*.

103. Richard Middleton, *Pop Music and the Blues: A Study of the Relationship and Its Significance* (London: Victor Gollancz, 1972); Yrjö Heinonen and Tuomas Eerola, 'Songwriting, Recording and Style Change: Problems in the Chronology and Periodization of the Musical Style of the Beatles', *Soundscapes: Journal on Media Culture* 3 (2000); Yrjö Heinonen, 'The Creative Process of the Beatles Revisited: A Multi-Level Analysis of the Interaction between Individual and Collaborative Creativity', *Popular Music History* 9, no. 1 (2014), 32–47; Walter Everett, *The Beatles as Musicians: The Quarry Men through Rubber Soul* (New York, NY: Oxford University Press, 1999); Walter Everett, *The Beatles as Musicians: Revolver through the Anthology* (Oxford: Oxford University Press, 1999). For the relationship between history and musicology, see Richard Middleton, 'Popular Music Analysis and Musicology: Bridging the Gap', *Popular Music* 12, no. 2 (1993), 177–90; Jeffrey H. Jackson and Stanley C. Pelkey, 'Introduction', in *Music and History: Bridging the Disciplines*, ed. Jeffrey H. Jackson and Stanley C. Pelkey (Oxford, MS: University Press of Mississippi, 2005).

104. Doggett, *You*; Holly Tessler, 'Let It Be? Exploring The Beatles Grey Market, 1970–1995', *Popular Music History* 9, no. 1 (2014), 48–63; Holly Tessler, 'The Role and Significance of Storytelling in the Creation of the "Post-Sixties" Beatles, 1970–1980', *Popular Music History* 5, no. 2 (2010), 169–89; Weber, *Beatles*; Fogo, *'I Read'*; John Kimsey, '"An Abstraction, Like Christmas": The Beatles For Sale and For Keeps', in Womack, ed., *Cambridge Companion*; Kenneth Womack and Todd F. Davis, 'Mythology, Remythology, and Demythology: The Beatles on Film', in *Reading The Beatles. Cultural Studies, Literary Criticism, and the Fab Four*, ed. Kenneth Womack and Todd F. Davis, 2006, 97–109.

105. Wald, *How*, 8.

106. Frontani, *Beatles*.

107. Womack, *Long*.

108. King, *Men*.

109. Steve Turner, *The Gospel According to the Beatles* (London: Westminster John Knox, 2006); Allison, *The Love There That's Sleeping*; Greene, *Here Comes the Sun*.

110. Schneider, *Long*.

111. MacFarlane, *Beatles and McLuhan*.

112. André Millard, *Beatlemania: Technology, Business, and Teen Culture in Cold War America* (Baltimore, MD: Johns Hopkins University Press, 2012).

113. McMillian, *Beatles vs. Stones*.

114. Inglis, *Beatles in Hamburg*; Kasser, *Lucy*; Turner, *Beatles '66*.

115. Allan F. Moore, *The Beatles: Sgt. Pepper's Lonely Hearts Club Band* (Cambridge: Cambridge University Press, 1997); Russell Reising, ed., *Every Sound There Is: The Beatles' Revolver and the Transformation of Rock and Roll* (Aldershot: Ashgate, 2002); Olivier Julien, ed., *Sgt. Pepper and the Beatles: It Was Forty Years Ago Today* (Aldershot: Ashgate, 2007); Kenneth Womack and Kathryn B. Cox, eds., *The Beatles, Sgt. Pepper, and the Summer of Love* (Lanham, MD: Lexington, 2017), 161–73; David Quantick, *Revolution: The Making of the Beatles' White Album* (New York, NY: A Capella Books, 2002); Mark Osteen, ed., *The Beatles through a Glass Onion: Reconsidering the White Album* (Ann Arbor, MI: University of Michigan Press, 2019); Thomas MacFarlane, *The Beatles' Abbey Road Medley: Extended Forms in Popular Music* (Lanham, MD: Scarecrow Press, 2007); Kenneth Womack, *Solid State: The Story of Abbey Road and the End of the Beatles* (Ithaca, NY: Cornell University Press, 2019).

116. Stephen Glynn, *A Hard Day's Night* (London: I. B. Tauris, 2005); Roland Reiter, *The Beatles on Film: Analysis of Movies, Documentaries, Spoofs and Cartoons* (Bielefeld: Transcript Verlag, 2008); Stephen Glynn, *The British Pop Music Film: The Beatles and Beyond* (Basingstoke: Springer, 2013), 82–104, 131–41; King, *Men*; David E. James, *Rock 'N' Film: Cinema's Dance with Popular Music* (New York, NY: Oxford University Press, 2017), chs. 8–9; Bob Neaverson, *The Beatles Movies* (London: Cassell, 1997).

117. Shumway, *Rock Star*, 22.

118. Cited in Richard M. Berrong, *Rabelais and Bakhtin: Popular Culture in Gargantua and Pantagruel* (Lincoln, NB: University of Nebraska Press, 2006), 111.

119. For an excellent overview, see Stephen Davies, *Empiricism and History* (Basingstoke: Palgrave, 2003).

120. Devin McKinney, *Magic Circles: The Beatles in Dream and History* (Cambridge, MA: Harvard University Press, 2003); Charles Hamm, 'Popular Music and Historiography', *Popular Music History* 1, no. 1 (2004): 13. For overviews of popular music studies, see Bradley, *Understanding*, introduction and ch. 1; Brian Longhurst, *Popular Music and Society*, 2nd edn (Cambridge: Polity, 2007); Tim Wall, *Studying Popular Music Culture* (Los Angeles, CA: Sage, 2013); Charles Hamm, *Putting Popular Music in Its Place* (Cambridge: Cambridge University Press, 1995).

121. Kasser, *Lucy*; Henry W. Sullivan, *The Beatles with Lacan: Rock 'n' Roll as Requiem for the Modern Age* (New York, NY: Peter Lang, 1995); Steven Baur, 'You Say You Want a Revolution: The Beatles and Karl Marx', in Baur and Baur, eds., *Beatles and Philosophy*; Gould, *Can't*; Jeffrey Roessner, 'We All Want to Change the World: Postmodern Politics and the Beatles' White

Album', in Womack and Davis, eds., *Reading the Beatles*, 147–58; MacFarlane, *Beatles and McLuhan*.

122. Dominic Sandbrook, *The Great British Dream Factory: The Strange History of Our National Imagination* (London: Allen Lane, 2015), xxx.

123. For pop memoirs, see Thomas Swiss, 'That's Me in the Spotlight: Rock Autobiographies', *Popular Music* 24, no. 2 (2005), 287–94; Oliver Lovesey, '"A Cellarful of Boys": The Swinging Sixties, Autobiography, and the Other Beatle', *Popular Music and Society* 38, no. 2 (2015), 160–75.

124. Paul Addison, *No Turning Back: The Peacetime Revolutions of Post-War Britain* (Oxford: Oxford University Press, 2010), 217, 216.

125. Harrison, *Seeking a Role*, 348; Kenneth O. Morgan, *Britain since 1945: The People's Peace* (Oxford: Oxford University Press, 2001), 582.

126. 'Editorial', *Beatles Book*, December 1969, 2.

127. Mike Kirkup, '"Some Kind of Innocence": The *Beatles Monthly* and the Fan Community', *Popular Music History* 9, no. 1 (2014), 64–78.

128. Greil Marcus, 'The Beatles (1979)', http://greilmarcus.net/2014/07/11/the-beatles-1979; Dave Marsh (1969) cited in Turner, *Gospel*, 2.

129. MacDonald, *Revolution*, xxiii.

130. Phil Sutcliffe, *Q*, April 2001, www.rocksbackpages.com/Library/Article/ian-macdonald-irevolution-in-the-head—the-beatles-records-and-the-sixtiesi-1994-revised-1995-pimlico.

131. McKinney, *Magic Circles*, 360; Rob Sheffield, *Dreaming the Beatles: The Love Story of One Band and the Whole World* (ebook: HarperCollins, 2017), n.p.

132. McKinney, *Magic Circles*, 360.

133. Ibid., 360.

134. Ibid., 342; Fowler, *Youth*, 166; Sandbrook, *Never*, 456, 461, 462, 466, 479, 762. For an extended version of the following critique of Fowler and Sandbrook's writing, see Collins, 'We Can', 86–93.

135. Fowler, *Youth*, 166–7.

136. Ibid., 189; Marwick, *Sixties*, 60.

137. Fowler, *Youth*, 173–4.

138. Ibid., 3.

139. Ibid., 168.

140. Ibid., 3.

141. Barbara Ehrenreich, Elizabeth Hess, and Gloria Jacobs, 'Beatlemania: Girls Just Want to Have Fun', in *The Adoring Audience: Fan Culture and Popular Media*, ed. Lisa A. Lewis (London: Routledge, 1992), 84–106. For a feminist critique of subcultural studies, see Angela McRobbie and Jenny Garber, 'Girls and Subcultures: An Exploration', in *Resistance through Rituals: Youth Subcultures in Post-War Britain*, ed. Stuart Hall and Tony Jefferson (London: Routledge, 2006).

142. Fowler, *Youth*, 167; John Hoyland, *Guardian*, 15 March 2008, www.theguardian.com/music/2008/mar/15/popandrock.pressandpublishing.

143. Fowler, *Youth*, 174.

144. Sandbrook, *White*, 748.

145. Ibid., 389–90.

146. Sandbrook, *Never*, 476.

147. Sandbrook, *White*, 389.

148. Sandbrook, *Never*, 462.

149. Sandbrook, *White*, 258; Sandbrook, *Great*, 413–17.

150. Sandbrook, *White*, 258.

151. *The Top 60 Best-Selling Records of the 60s* (BBC Radio 2, 31 May 2010).

152. Sandbrook, *White*, 389.

153. Sharon Mawer, '1969', www.sharonmawer1.wordpress.com/2017/06/17/1969/.

154. Collins, 'Beatles' Politics'. For the Beatles and radical politics in the late sixties, see Wiener, *Come Together*; Mäkelä, *John Lennon Imagined*, ch. 6; Kenneth L. Campbell, 'You Say You Want a Revolution', in Womack and Cox, eds., *Beatles*, 161–73; Roessner, 'We All Want'; Dorian Lynskey, *33 Revolutions Per Minute* (London: Faber and Faber, 2011), ch. 8; Peter Doggett, *There's a Riot Going On: Revolutionaries, Rock Stars and the Rise and Fall of '60s Counter-Culture* (Edinburgh: Canongate, 2007).

155. Sandbrook, *Great*, 419.

156. Martha Ann Bari, 'Mass Media Is the Message: Yoko Ono and John Lennon's 1969 Year of Peace' (PhD Thesis, University of Maryland, 2007). See also Kieran Curran, *Cynicism in British Post-War Culture* (Basingstoke: Palgrave Macmillan, 2015), ch. 6; Jonathan Harris, *The Utopian Globalists: Artists of Worldwide Revolution, 1919–2009* (Boston, MA: John Wiley & Sons, 2013), ch. 5.

157. Sandbrook, *Great*, 418.

158. Lewisohn, *Tune In*. See also Jonathan Paul Watson, '"Beats Apart": A Comparative History of Youth Culture and Popular Music in Liverpool and Newcastle upon Tyne, 1956–1965' (PhD Thesis, Northumbria University, 2010), ch. 5; Michael Brocken, *Other Voices: Hidden Histories of Liverpool's Popular Music Scenes, 1930s–1970s* (London: Routledge, 2016); Paul Du Noyer, *Liverpool: Wondrous Place: Music from the Cavern to the Coral* (London: Virgin, 2004).

159. Sandbrook, *Never*, 681.

160. Sandbrook, *White*, 210.

161. Sandbrook, *Never*, 457, 258.

162. Ibid., 258.

163. Sandbrook, *Great*, 414.

164. Ibid., 413–14.

165. For culture wars over the 1960s, see Francis Beckett, *What Did The Baby Boomers Ever Do For Us?* (London: Routledge, 2016); Gertrude Himmelfarb, *The De-Moralization Of Society: From Victorian Virtues to Modern Values*

(New York, NY: Vintage, 1996); Clive Bloom, *Literature, Politics, and Intellectual Crisis in Britain Today* (Basingstoke: Palgrave, 2001), ch. 6.

166. Dominic Sandbrook, '50 Years Ago a New Elite Came to Power in Britain', *Mail*, 1 January 2014, www.dailymail.co.uk/debate/article-2532051/Dominic-Sandbrook-50-years-ago-new-elite-came-power-Britain-Were-paying-price-contempt-ordinary-people.html.

167. Ibid.

168. A. N. Wilson, *Our Times* (London: Hutchinson, 2008), 192, 197.

169. Peter Hitchens, *The War We Never Fought: The British Establishment's Surrender to Drugs* (London: Bloomsbury, 2012), 270, 123.

170. Wilson, *Our Times*, 194; Peter Hitchens, *The Abolition of Britain: The British Cultural Revolution from Lady Chatterley to Tony Blair* (London: Quartet Books, 2000), 369.

171. Hitchens, *War*, chs. 15–16; Hitchens, *Abolition*, 133, xxxiii.

172. Blair cited in Hitchens, *Abolition*, xix; Hitchens, *Abolition*, xx, xxii.

173. Morgan, *Britain since 1945*, 261–2.

174. Ibid., 261, 259.

175. Ibid., 262.

176. Heilbronner, 'Peculiarities', 101.

177. Oded Heilbronner, '"Helter-Skelter"? The Beatles, the British New Left, and the Question of Hegemony', *Interdisciplinary Literary Studies* 13, no. 1/2 (2011), 88, 102.

178. Ibid., 102, 92, 101.

179. Dave Harker, 'Still Crazy After All These Years: What Was Popular Music in the 1960s?', in *Cultural Revolution? The Challenge of the Arts in the 1960s*, ed. Bart Moore-Gilbert and John Seed (London: Routledge, 1992).

180. Dave Harker, *One for the Money: Politics and Popular Song* (London: Hutchinson, 1980), 212–16.

181. Sandbrook, *Mail*, 1 January 2014.

182. Sandbrook, 'Why Britain Was Wrecked in 1965', *Mail*, 3 January 2015, www.dailymail.co.uk/news/article-2894963/Why-Britain-wrecked-1965–Fifty-years-ago-UK-socially-morally-culturally-different-country-ways-better-people-far-worse.html.

The Other Sixties: An Anti-Permissive Permissive Society?

1. Social Science Research Council (SSRC) Survey Unit, Future in Britain Survey (July 1970), data set at UK Data Archive (UKDA), SN 60.

2. For permissiveness, see Marcus Collins, 'Introduction: The Permissive Society and Its Enemies', in *The Permissive Society and Its Enemies: Sixties British Culture*, ed. Marcus Collins (London: Rivers Oram, 2007); Marcus Collins, *Modern Love: An Intimate History of Men and Women in Twentieth-Century*

Britain (London: Atlantic, 2003), ch. 5; Tim Newburn, *Permission and Regulation: Law and Morals in Post-War Britain* (London: Routledge, 1992); Christie Davies, *The Strange Death of Moral Britain* (Piscataway, NJ: Transaction Publishers, 2004); Mark Jarvis, *Conservative Governments, Morality and Social Change in Affluent Britain, 1957–64* (Manchester: Manchester University Press, 2005); Kate Gleeson, 'Consenting Adults in Private: In Search of the Sexual Subject' (PhD Thesis, University of New South Wales, 2006), ch. 1; Roger Davidson and Gayle Davis, *The Sexual State: Sexuality and Scottish Governance, 1950–80* (Edinburgh: Edinburgh University Press, 2012); Andrew Holden, *Makers and Manners: Politics and Morality in Postwar Britain* (London: Politico's, 2004).

3. Codebook for SSRC, Future in Britain Survey, 19.

4. SSRC, Future in Britain Survey.

5. Adrian Mitchell, 'Priests and Prophets of Permissiveness', in *The Permissive Society: The Guardian Inquiry*, ed. Harford Thomas (London: Panther, 1969); Christopher Booker, *Spectator*, 11 June 1970, 27.

6. David Stubbs, *Uncut*, November 2000, www.rocksbackpages.com/Library/SearchLinkRedirect?folder=the-death-of-the-beatles.

7. Cited in The Beatles, *The Beatles Anthology* (San Francisco, CA: Chronicle Books, 2000), 356.

8. Dominic Sandbrook, *White Heat: A History of Britain in the Swinging Sixties* (London: Little, Brown, 2006), 748.

9. NOP, *Report on Attitudes towards Crime, Violence and Permissiveness in Society* (London: NOP, 1970), 53, 44.

10. Arthur Marwick, *The Sixties: Cultural Revolution in Britain, France, Italy, and the United States, c. 1958–c. 1974* (Oxford: Oxford University Press, 1998); Jeffrey Weeks, *The World We Have Won: The Remaking of Erotic and Intimate Life* (London: Routledge, 2007), x.

11. Ibid., x.

12. For anti-permissiveness, see Amy C. Whipple, 'Speaking for Whom? The 1971 Festival of Light and the Search for the "Silent Majority"', *Contemporary British History* 24, no. 3 (2010), 319–39; Newburn, *Permission*, ch. 2; Lawrence Black, *Redefining British Politics: Culture, Consumerism and Participation, 1954–70* (Basingstoke: Springer, 2010), ch. 5; Dominic Sandbrook, 'Against the Permissive Society: The Backlash of the Late 1960s', in *Ultimate Adventures with Britannia: Personalities, Politics and Culture in Britain*, ed. William Roger Louis (London: I. B. Tauris, 2010); Ben Thompson, *Ban This Filth! Letters from the Mary Whitehouse Archive* (London: Faber and Faber, 2012); Matthew Grimley, 'Anglican Evangelicals and Anti-Permissiveness: The Nationwide Festival of Light, 1971–1982', in *Evangelicalism and the Church of England in the Twentieth Century: Reform, Resistance and Renewal*, ed. Andrew Atherstone and John G. Maiden (London: Boydell & Brewer, 2014).

13. Jarvis, *Conservative Governments*, 9.

14. Robert M. Worcester, *British Public Opinion: A Guide to the History and Methodology of Political Opinion Polling* (Oxford: Blackwell, 1991); Nick Moon, *Opinion Polls: History, Theory and Practice* (Manchester: Manchester University Press, 1999); Wolfgang Donsbach and Michael W. Traugott, eds., *The SAGE Handbook of Public Opinion Research* (Los Angeles, CA: Sage, 2008).

15. See especially the work of Ronald Inglehart, including *The Silent Revolution: Changing Values and Political Styles among Western Publics* (Princeton, NJ: Princeton University Press, 1977).

16. Jeffrey Richards and Dorothy Sheridan, *Mass-Observation at the Movies* (London: Routledge & Kegan Paul, 1987); Liz Stanley, *Sex Surveyed, 1949–1994: From Mass-Observation's 'Little Kinsey' to the National Survey and the Hite Reports* (London: Routledge, 1995); J. Michael Hogan, 'The Road Not Taken in Opinion Research: Mass-Observation in Great Britain, 1937–1940', *Rhetoric & Public Affairs* 18, no. 3 (2015), 409–39; Nick Hubble, *Mass Observation and Everyday Life: Culture, History, Theory* (Basingstoke: Springer, 2005); Gary Cross, *Worktowners at Blackpool: Mass-Observation and Popular Leisure in the 1930s* (London: Routledge, 2005); James Hinton, *Nine Wartime Lives: Mass-Observation and the Making of the Modern Self* (Oxford: Oxford University Press, 2010).

17. Brian Harrison, 'Historiographical Hazards of Sixties Britain', in *Penultimate Adventures with Britannia: Personalities, Politics and Culture in Britain*, ed. William Roger Louis (London: I. B. Tauris, 2008), 38. He quotes Larkin's comment that 'I don't think I have ever read a copy of *Private Eye*, seen a performance of *Beyond the Fringe*, *That Was The Week That Was*, or whatever David Frost does.' However, Harrison does not explain why Larkin is a representative figure of the provincial and middle-aged, how he was deterred from watching television or reading magazines by living in Hull or why his poems nonetheless contained some of the period's most famous reflections on the sexual revolution.

18. Michael Schofield, *The Sexual Behaviour of Young People* (London: Longmans, Green, 1965); Michael Schofield, *The Sexual Behaviour of Young Adults* (London: Allen Lane, 1973). For an insightful analysis of Schofield's findings, see Callum G. Brown, 'Sex, Religion, and the Single Woman c.1950–75: The Importance of a "Short" Sexual Revolution to the English Religious Crisis of the Sixties', *Twentieth Century British History* 22, no. 2 (2011), 189–215.

19. Geoffrey Gorer, *Exploring English Character* (New York, NY: Criterion, 1955); Geoffrey Gorer, *Sex and Marriage in England Today: A Study of the Views and Experience of the Under-45s* (London: Thomas Nelson, 1971). Gorer's findings are fascinating but unreliable. He admitted that 'there was no guarantee that the [1950] sample was representative' because the questionnaires had been completed by volunteers recruited by

a newspaper. He was determined not to repeat the mistake in 1969, stating that 'the validity of this study depends to a great extent on the validity of the sample'. Despite employing the reputable polling organisation ORC to conduct the second survey, there are several unexplained peculiarities in the sampling and analysis. It is unclear why there were over twice as many single males as females in the weighted sample or why 61 per cent of the AB class sample was female. Gorer further muddied the waters on class by misconstruing the meaning of the AB and DE classifications and then relying largely on self-classifications in his tables. The unrepresentative nature of the 1950 sample did not deter him from using it to make direct comparisons with the 1969 sample. He proceeded to misread the survey's findings by claiming that 'The belief that different standards should be applied to the sexual conduct of unmarried young men and unmarried young women is predominantly a feminine response among the English-born, though there are a few Englishmen who advance similar views.' In fact the double standard (as measured by subtracting the percentage who agreed that young women 'should have some sexual experience before marriage' from those who said the same about young men) was almost identical across gender: 17 per cent among men and 16 per cent among women. Gorer's well-known claims about the double standard are further weakened by a survey error which meant that a large minority of those who disapproved of premarital sex were not asked follow-up questions (*Sex and Marriage*, 2, 4, 6, 30, 13, 43, 276–7).

20. Andrew J. Taylor, '"The Record of the 1950s Is Irrelevant": The Conservative Party, Electoral Strategy and Opinion Research, 1945–64', *Contemporary British History* 17, no. 1 (2003), 81–110; Laura DuMond Beers, 'Whose Opinion?: Changing Attitudes towards Opinion Polling in British Politics, 1937–1964', *Twentieth Century British History* 17, no. 2 (2006), 177–205; Joe Moran, 'Mass-Observation, Market Research, and the Birth of the Focus Group, 1937–1997', *Journal of British Studies* 47, no. 4 (2008), 827–51; Mike Savage, *Identities and Social Change in Britain since 1940* (Oxford: Oxford University Press, 2010); Mark Roodhouse, '"Fish-and-Chip Intelligence": Henry Durant and the British Institute of Public Opinion, 1936–63', *Twentieth Century British History* 24, no. 2 (2013), 224–48; Claire Langhamer, '"The Live Dynamic Whole of Feeling and Behavior": Capital Punishment and the Politics of Emotion, 1945–1957', *Journal of British Studies* 51, no. 2 (2012), 416–41; Hogan, 'Road Not Taken'.

21. Brown, 'Sex'; Clive D. Field, *Britain's Last Religious Revival? Quantifying Belonging, Behaving, and Believing in the Long 1950s* (Basingstoke: Palgrave Pivot, 2015); Clive D. Field, *Secularization in the Long 1960s: Numerating Religion in Britain* (Oxford: Oxford University Press, 2017); Ben Clements, *Religion and Public Opinion in Britain: Continuity and Change* (Basingstoke: Palgrave Macmillan, 2015); Ben Clements, *Surveying Christian Beliefs and*

Religious Debates in Post-War Britain (Basingstoke: Palgrave Macmillan, 2016).

22. See Ben Clements and Clive D. Field, 'Public Opinion toward Homosexuality and Gay Rights in Great Britain', *Public Opinion Quarterly* 78, no. 2 (2014), 523–47; Ben Clements and Clive D. Field, 'Abortion and Public Opinion in Great Britain: A 50–Year Retrospective', *Journal of Beliefs & Values* 39, no. 4 (2018), 429–44; Marcus Collins, 'Immigration and Opinion Polls in Postwar Britain', *Modern History Review* 18, no. 4 (2016), 8–13.

23. Miriam Akhtar and Stephen Humphries, *The Fifties and Sixties: A Lifestyle Revolution* (London: Boxtree, 2001); Marwick, *Sixties*; Anthony Aldgate, James Chapman, and Arthur Marwick, eds., *Windows on the Sixties: Exploring Key Texts of Media and Culture* (London: I. B. Tauris, 2000).

24. Harrison, 'Historiographical'; Dominic Sandbrook, *Never Had It So Good: A History of Britain from Suez to the Beatles* (London: Little, Brown, 2005); Dominic Sandbrook, *White Heat*.

25. For a good introduction to methodological issues, see Christof Wolf et al., eds., *The SAGE Handbook of Survey Methodology* (Los Angeles, CA: Sage, 2016).

26. Gallup (November 1961) in George Gallup Jr (ed.), *The Gallup International Public Opinion Polls, Great Britain 1937–1975: Vol. 1 – 1937–1964* (New York, NY: Random House, 1976), 571. For homosexuality, see Rebecca Jennings, *Tomboys and Bachelor Girls: A Lesbian History of Post-War Britain 1945–71* (Manchester: Manchester University Press, 2007); Chris Waters, 'The Homosexual as a Social Being in Britain, 1945–1968', in *British Queer History: New Approaches and Perspectives*, ed. Brian Lewis (Manchester: Manchester University Press, 2013); Holden, *Makers and Manners*, ch. 3; Brian Lewis, *Wolfenden's Witnesses: Homosexuality in Postwar Britain* (Basingstoke: Springer, 2016); Sebastian Buckle, *The Way Out* (London: I. B. Tauris, 2015); Roger Davidson and Gayle Davis, 'Sexuality and the State: The Campaign for Scottish Homosexual Law Reform, 1967–80', *Contemporary British History* 20, no. 4 (2006), 533–58; Patrick Higgins, *Heterosexual Dictatorship: Male Homosexuality in Postwar Britain* (London: Trafalgar Square, 1996); Matt Houlbrook, *Queer London: Perils and Pleasures in the Sexual Metropolis, 1918–1957* (Chicago, IL: University of Chicago Press, 2006); Matt Cook, *Queer Domesticities: Homosexuality and Home Life in Twentieth-Century London* (Basingstoke: Springer, 2014); Charles Smith, 'The Evolution of the Gay Male Public Sphere in England and Wales 1967–c.1983' (PhD thesis, Loughborough University, 2015); Helen Smith, *Masculinity, Class and Same-Sex Desire in Industrial England, 1895–1957* (Basingstoke: Springer, 2015).

27. Gallup (November 1961) in Gallup, vol. 1, 571. For the *Chatterley* trial, see Mark Roodhouse, 'Lady Chatterley and the Monk: Anglican Radicals and the *Lady Chatterley* Trial of 1960', *Journal of Ecclesiastical History* 59, no. 3 (2008), 475–500; Nick Thomas, '"To-Night's Big Talking Point Is Still That

Book": Popular Responses to the *Lady Chatterley* Trial', *Cultural and Social History* 10, no. 4 (2013), 619–34.

28. Gallup (December 1962) in Gallup, vol. 1, 664.
29. *NOP Bulletin, Special Supplement II: Divorce*, October 1965, 1.
30. Gallup (July 1966) in George Gallup Jr (ed.), *The Gallup International Public Opinion Polls, Great Britain 1937–1975: Vol. 2 – 1965–1975* (New York, NY: Random House, 1976), 874.
31. Gallup (February 1967) in Gallup, vol. 2, 911.
32. Gallup (June 1968) in Gallup, vol. 2, 988.
33. *NOP Bulletin*, May 1965, 11; NOP, *Report on Attitudes*, 60. For abortion reform, see Newburn, *Permission*, ch. 6; Sylvie Pomies-Marechal and Matthew Leggett, 'The Abortion Act 1967: A Fundamental Change?', in *Preserving the Sixties: Britain and the 'Decade of Protest'*, ed. Trevor Harris and Monia O'Brien Castro (Basingstoke: Palgrave Macmillan, 2014); Stephen Brooke, *Sexual Politics: Sexuality, Family Planning, and the British Left from the 1880s to the Present Day* (Oxford: Oxford University Press, 2011), chs. 6 and 7; Barbara Brookes, *Abortion in England 1900–1967* (London: Routledge, 1988); Emma L. Jones, 'Attitudes to Abortion in the Era of Reform: Evidence from the Abortion Law Reform Association Correspondence', *Women's History Review* 20, no. 2 (2011), 283–98.
34. Gallup (June 1967) in Gallup, vol. 2, 930. For censorship, see John Sutherland, *Offensive Literature: Decensorship in Britain, 1960–1982* (London: Junction Books, 1982); Anthony Aldgate and James C. Robertson, *Censorship in Theatre and Cinema* (Edinburgh: Edinburgh University Press, 2005); Anthony Aldgate, *Censorship and the Permissive Society: British Cinema and Theatre, 1955–1965* (Oxford: Oxford University Press, 1995); Helen Freshwater, *Theatre Censorship in Britain: Silencing, Censure and Suppression* (Basingstoke: Springer, 2009).
35. NOP, *Report on Attitudes*, 68.
36. For moral panics, see Stanley Cohen, *Folk Devils and Moral Panics: The Creation of the Mods and Rockers*, 3rd edn (London: Routledge, 2002); Charles Krinsky, ed., *The Ashgate Research Companion to Moral Panics* (Aldershot: Ashgate, 2013); Kenneth Thompson, *Moral Panics* (London: Routledge, 2005).
37. Gallup (September 1958) in Gallup, vol. 1, 478.
38. Gallup (August 1964) in Gallup, vol. 1, 742.
39. Gallup (May 1968) in Gallup, vol. 2, 985.
40. Gallup (November 1959) in *World Political Opinion and Social Surveys: Series One – British Opinion Polls* (Reading: Research Publications, 1990), vol. 31, 55; Gallup (March 1969) in Gallup, vol. 2, 1042.
41. For attitudes to non-white migration in postwar Britain, see Camilla Schofield, *Enoch Powell and the Making of Postcolonial Britain* (Cambridge: Cambridge University Press, 2015); Amanda Bidnall, *West Indian Generation: Remaking British Culture in London, 1945–1965* (Oxford: Oxford University Press, 2017);

Amy Whipple, 'Revisiting the "Rivers of Blood" Controversy: Letters to Enoch Powell', *Journal of British Studies* 48, no. 3 (2009), 717–35; Wendy Webster, 'The Empire Comes Home: Commonwealth Migration to Britain', in *Britain's Experience of Empire in the Twentieth Century*, ed. Andrew Thompson (Oxford: Oxford University Press, 2012); Gavin Schaffer, *The Vision of a Nation: Making Multiculturalism on British Television, 1960–80* (Basingstoke: Palgrave Macmillan, 2014); John Davis, 'Containing Racism? The London Experience, 1957–1968', in *The Other Special Relationship: Race, Rights, and Riots in Britain and the United States*, ed. Robin D. G. Kelley and Stephen Tuck (Basingstoke: Palgrave Macmillan, 2015), 125–46; Elizabeth Buettner, '"Would You Let Your Daughter Marry a Negro?" Race and Sex in 1950s Britain', in *Gender, Labour, War and Empire*, ed. Philippa Levine and Susan R. Grayzel (Basingstoke: Springer, 2009), 219–37.

42. Field, *Britain's Last Religious Revival?*; Field, *Secularization*; Clements, *Religion and Public Opinion*; Clements, *Surveying Christian Beliefs*. For religion in postwar Britain, see Callum G. Brown, *Religion and Society in Twentieth-Century Britain* (Harlow: Longman, 2006); Grace Davie, *Religion in Britain: A Persistent Paradox* (Boston, MA: Wiley Blackwell, 2015); Steve Bruce, *Scottish Gods: Religion in Modern Scotland, 1900–2012* (Edinburgh: Edinburgh University Press, 2014); Nigel Yates, *Love Now, Pay Later? Sex and Religion in the Fifties and Sixties* (London: SPCK, 2011).

43. Callum G. Brown, *The Death of Christian Britain*, rev. edn (London: Routledge, 2013), 1; Social Surveys (Gallup Poll) Ltd, *Television and Religion* (London: University of London Press, 1964), 9.

44. Ibid., 35.

45. Ibid., 40, 48–9.

46. Ibid., 42. For secularisation, see Sam Brewitt-Taylor, 'The Invention of a "Secular Society"? Christianity and the Sudden Appearance of Secularization Discourses in the British National Media, 1961–4', *Twentieth Century British History* 24, no. 3 (2013), 327–50; Hugh McLeod, *The Religious Crisis of the 1960s* (Oxford: Oxford University Press, 2010); Field, *Secularization in the Long 1960s*; Brown, *Death*, ch. 8; Brown, 'Sex'; Brown, 'What Was the Religious Crisis of the 1960s?', *Journal of Religious History* 34, no. 4 (2010), 468–79; Jeremy Morris, 'The Strange Death of Christian Britain: Another Look at the Secularization Debate', *Historical Journal* 46, no. 4 (2003), 963–76; Morris, 'Secularization and Religious Experience: Arguments in the Historiography of Modern British Religion', *Historical Journal* 55, no. 1 (2012), 195–219; Steve Bruce and Tony Glendinning, 'When Was Secularization? Dating the Decline of the British Churches and Locating Its Cause', *British Journal of Sociology* 61, no. 1 (2010), 107–26.

47. Gallup (November 1959) in *World Political Opinion*, vol. 31, 55; Gallup (June 1968) in Gallup, vol. 2, 990; Gallup (March 1969) in Gallup, vol. 2, 1042.

48. Paul Barker and John Hanvey, *New Society*, 27 November 1969, 847.

49. Ibid., 849.

50. Paul Barker and John Hanvey, *New Society*, 27 November 1969, 847.

51. Reader's Digest, *Images of the World in the Year 2000: Great Britain International* (1967), data set at UKDA, SN 67025.

52. For fear of crime, see Stuart Hall, *Policing the Crisis: Mugging, the State, and Law and Order* (Basingstoke: Pan Macmillan, 1978); Pamela Hansford Johnson, *On Iniquity: Some Personal Reflections Arising Out of the Moors Murder Trial* (New York, NY: Scribner, 1967).

53. Gallup (September 1973) in Gallup, vol. 2, 1268–9.

54. For immigration policy, see Kathleen Paul, *Whitewashing Britain: Race and Citizenship in the Postwar Era* (Ithaca, NY: Cornell University Press, 1997).

55. Gallup (March 1938) in Gallup, vol. 1, 9.

56. Gallup (October 1949) in Gallup, vol. 1, 209. For gambling, see Jarvis, *Conservative Governments*, ch. 3; Mark Clapson, *A Bit of a Flutter: Popular Gambling and English Society, c. 1823–1961* (Manchester: Manchester University Press, 1992).

57. Gallup (March 1958) in Gallup, vol. 1, 459.

58. For the 'permissive moment', see Jeffrey Weeks, *Sex, Politics and Society: The Regulation of Sexuality since 1800*, rev. edn (Longman, 1989), ch. 13.

59. For the politics of divorce, see B. H. Lee, *Divorce Law Reform in England* (London: Peter Owen, 1974).

60. NOP, *Report on Attitudes*, 54.

61. NOP for *Gay News*, Attitudes to Social Issues (April 1975), data set at UKDA, SN 1105.

62. For capital punishment, see Langhamer, "'Live Dynamic Whole'"; Neville Twitchell, *The Politics of the Rope: The Campaign to Abolish Capital Punishment in Britain 1955–1969* (Bury St. Edmunds: Arena, 2012).

63. Gallup (January 1954) in Gallup, vol. 1, 314; Gallup (February 1969) in Gallup, vol. 2, 1041.

64. Appendix to *NOP Political Bulletin* (December 1969), 3.

65. Gallup (August 1963) in Gallup, vol. 1, 700; Social Surveys, *Television and Religion*, 122.

66. For birth control, see Simon Szreter and Kate Fisher, *Sex Before the Sexual Revolution: Intimate Life in England 1918–1963* (Cambridge: Cambridge University Press, 2010); Brooke, *Sexual Politics*; Hera Cook, *The Long Sexual Revolution: English Women, Sex, and Contraception 1800–1975* (Oxford: Oxford University Press, 2005); Kate Fisher, *Birth Control, Sex and Marriage in Britain 1918–1960* (Oxford: Oxford University Press, 2006); Lara Marks, *Sexual Chemistry: A History of the Contraceptive Pill* (New Haven, CT: Yale University Press, 2001).

67. Gallup (September 1973) in Gallup, vol. 2, 1005.

68. NOP, *Report on Attitudes*, 56.

69. Appendix to *NOP Political Bulletin* (December 1969), 3. For debates over corporal punishment, see Jarvis, *Conservative Governments*, ch. 2.

70. Gallup (October 1961) in Gallup, vol. 1, 602; Gallup (July 1962) in Gallup, vol. 1, 638.

71. NOP (February 1964), dataset at UKDA SN 64004.

72. Gallup (December 1965) in Gallup, vol. 2, 844; Gallup (June 1967) in Gallup, vol. 2, 934.

73. Gallup (September 1971) in Gallup, vol. 2, 1145.

74. *NOP Bulletin*, May 1968, 12–13.

75. *NOP Bulletin*, April 1976, 9.

76. Gallup (November 1959) in Gallup, vol. 1, 545; Gallup (September 1965) in Gallup, vol. 1, 829.

77. Gallup (October 1954) in Gallup, vol. 1, 336. For the moral panic over comics, see Martin Barker, *A Haunt of Fears: The Strange History of the British Horror Comics Campaign* (Oxford, MS: University Press of Mississippi, 1984).

78. Gallup (September 1957) in Gallup, vol. 1, 427. For prostitution, see Julia Laite, 'A Global History of Prostitution: London', in *Selling Sex in the City: A Global History of Prostitution, 1600s–2000s*, ed. Magaly Rodriguez Garcia, Lex Heerma van Voss and Elise van Nederveen Meerkerk (Amsterdam: Brill, 2017), 111–37; Frank Mort, *Capital Affairs: London and the Making of the Permissive Society* (New Haven, CT: Yale University Press, 2010), ch. 4.

79. Gallup (August 1967) in Gallup, vol. 2, 941.

80. Gallup (November 1961) in Gallup, vol. 1, 610–11.

81. Gallup (April 1968) in Gallup, vol. 2, 979.

82. Gallup (March 1971) in Gallup, vol. 2, 1128.

83. Gallup (July 1966) in Gallup, vol. 1, 874; Gallup (September 1967) in Gallup, vol. 1, 945. For pirate radio, see Robert Chapman, *Selling the Sixties: The Pirates and Pop Music Radio* (London: Routledge, 2012).

84. For the history of drugs in postwar Britain, see Alex Mold, *Heroin: The Treatment of Addiction in Twentieth-Century Britain* (DeKalb, IL: Northern Illinois University Press, 2008); Alex Mold, 'The Changing Role of NGOs in Britain: Voluntary Action and Illegal Drugs', in *NGOs in Contemporary Britain: Non-State Actors in Society and Politics since 1945*, edited by N. J. Crowson, Matthew Hilton and James McKay, 164–81 (Basingstoke: Palgrave Macmillan, 2009); Steve Abrams, 'The Wooton Retort: The Decriminalisation of Cannabis in Britain', 1997, www.nedprod.com /cannabis/essays/wraltnet.txt; Martin Booth, *Cannabis: A History* (London: Bantam, 2004); R. P. T. Davenport-Hines, *The Pursuit of Oblivion: A Social History of Drugs* (London: Orion, 2004); Chris Hallam, 'Script Doctors and Vicious Addicts: Subcultures, Drugs, and Regulation under the "British System", *c*.1917 to *c*.1960' (PhD Thesis, London School of Hygiene & Tropical Medicine, 2016); Peter Hitchens, *The War We Never Fought: The British Establishment's Surrender to Drugs* (London: Bloomsbury, 2012).

85. Gallup (June 1967) in Gallup, vol. 2, 934.

86. Gallup (August 1967) in Gallup, vol. 2, 941; Gallup (May 1973) in Gallup, vol. 2, 1247.

87. *NOP Bulletin*, April 1972, 11–12.

88. *NOP Bulletin*, May 1971, xv, 10.

89. Ibid.

90. For women's rights in postwar Britain, see Elizabeth Wilson, *Only Halfway to Paradise: Women in Postwar Britain 1945–1968* (London: Tavistock, 1980); Ina Zweiniger-Bargielowska, ed., *Women in Twentieth-Century Britain* (Harlow: Longman, 2001); Jane E. Lewis, *Women in Britain since 1945: Women, Family, Work and the State in the Post-War Years* (Oxford: Blackwell, 1994).

91. Steven Marcus, *The Other Victorians: A Study of Sexuality and Pornography in Mid-Nineteenth-Century England* (London: Weidenfeld and Nicholson, 1966), xix, 283.

92. Ibid., xx, 285.

93. Marcus Collins, 'Introduction', in Collins, ed., *Permissive Society*, 34, 36–7. For Foucault's critique of permissiveness and *The Other Victorians*, see Michel Foucault, *The History of Sexuality, vol. 1: An Introduction* (New York, NY: Pantheon, 1978).

94. 'Abolition of Obscenity Law Opposed', *Telegraph*, 21 July 1969, 15.

95. NOP, *Report on Attitudes*, 43.

96. Julian Holland, *Mail*, 29 November 1967, 6.

97. Louis Harris Research, *Express*, 28 June 1971, 4.

98. Ibid., 4.

99. Peter Chambers, *Express*, 5 February 1964, 8.

Society, 1963–1965: The Beatles and Modernity

1. *Mirror*, 6 November 1963, 6.

2. *Express*, 22 January 1964, 1.

3. Michael Walsh, *Express*, 5 November 1963, 5.

4. John Sandiford, *Mirror*, 23 November 1963, 4; 'Beatle Uniform for Girls', *Mirror*, 22 November 1963, 13.

5. Benedict Nightingale, *Guardian*, 2 April 1964, 7; John Sandilands, *Mail*, 20 April 1965, 10; Clive Barnes, *Spectator*, 27 December 1963, 16.

6. *Express*, 20 February 1965, 13; *Express*, 10 December 1963, 4; Kenneth Allsop, *Mail*, 5 November 1963, 8; *Guardian*, 4 November 1963, 4; *Express*, 31 March 1964, 7; Marcus Collins, '"The Age of the Beatles": Parliament and Popular Music in the 1960s', *Contemporary British History* 27, no. 1 (2013), 85–107.

7. Patrick Gibbs, *Telegraph*, 30 July 1965, 19; *Express*, 18 November 1963, 11; Nancy Banks-Smith, *Express*, 18 October 1963, 10; David Ash, *Express*, 31 October 1963, 10.

8. 'No Time to Scream', *Sunday Telegraph*, 17 November 1963, 6.

9. 'No Beatles, No Work', *Telegraph*, 19 November 1963, 1.

10. *Mail*, 18 December 1964, 1.

11. Derek Taylor, sleeve notes for *Beatles For Sale* (Parlophone, 1964); Frederick James, *Beatles Book*, March 1964, 27.

12. Hilton Tims, *Mail*, 9 January 1964, 6.

13. For overviews of postwar British society, see Pat Thane, *Unequal Britain: Equalities in Britain since 1945* (London: A&C Black, 2010); Peter Hennessy, *Having It So Good: Britain in the Fifties* (Harmondsworth: Penguin, 2007); David Kynaston, *Austerity Britain, 1945–51* (London: Bloomsbury, 2008); Kynaston, *Family Britain, 1951–1957* (London: A&C Black, 2009); Kynaston, *Modernity Britain: Opening the Box, 1957–59* (London: Bloomsbury, 2013); Kynaston, *Modernity Britain: A Shake of the Dice, 1959–62* (London: Bloomsbury, 2014); Paul Addison, *No Turning Back: The Peacetime Revolutions of Post-War Britain* (Oxford: Oxford University Press, 2010); George L. Bernstein, *The Myth of Decline: The Rise of Britain since 1945* (London: Pimlico, 2004); Paul Addison and Harriet Jones, eds., *A Companion to Contemporary Britain, 1939–2000* (Oxford: Blackwell, 2007); Kathleen Burk, ed., *The British Isles since 1945* (Oxford: Oxford University Press, 2003); Andrew Rosen, *The Transformation of British Life, 1950–2000: A Social History* (Manchester: Manchester University Press, 2003).

14. Dick Hebdige, *Hiding in the Light: On Images and Things* (Philadelphia, PA: Psychology Press, 1988), 19.

15. For youth in postwar Britain, see Selina Todd and Hilary Young, 'From Baby-Boomers to "Beanstalkers": Making the Modern Teenager in Postwar Britain', *Cultural and Social History* 9, no. 3 (2012), 451–67; Melanie Tebbutt, *Making Youth: A History of Youth in Modern Britain* (Basingstoke: Palgrave Macmillan, 2016); Mike Brake, *The Sociology of Youth Culture and Youth Subcultures: Sex and Drugs and Rock 'n' Roll* (London: Routledge & Kegan Paul, 1980); Bill Osgerby, '"Seized By Change, Liberated By Affluence": Youth Consumption and Cultural Change in Postwar Britain', in *Twentieth-Century Mass Society in Britain and the Netherlands*, ed. Bob Moore and Henk van Nierop (Oxford: Berg, 2006); Mathew Thomson, *Lost Freedom: The Landscape of the Child and the British Post-War Settlement* (Oxford: Oxford University Press, 2013). For the significance of music in youth culture, see Keith Gildart, *Images of England through Popular Music: Class, Youth and Rock 'n' Roll, 1955–1976* (Basingstoke: Palgrave Macmillan, 2013); Daniel Laughey, *Music and Youth Culture* (Edinburgh: Edinburgh University Press, 2006); Simon Frith, *Sound Effects: Youth, Leisure and the Politics of Rock*, rev. edn (London: Constable, 1983), chs. 8 and 9; James Nott, *Going to the Palais: A Social and Cultural History of Dancing and Dance Halls in Britain, 1918–1960* (Oxford: Oxford University Press, 2015) ch. 10; Andy Bennett, *Popular Music and Youth*

Culture: Music, Identity and Place (Basingstoke: Macmillan, 2000), chs. 1 and 2; Lucy Robinson et al., 'Introduction: Making a Difference by Making a Noise', in *Youth Culture and Social Change: Making a Difference by Making a Noise* (Basingstoke: Springer, 2017); Dick Hebdige, *Subculture: The Meaning of Style* (London: Methuen, 1979); Charles Mueller, 'Were British Subcultures the Beginnings of Multitude?', in *Countercultures and Popular Music*, ed. Sheila Whiteley and Jedediah Sklower (London: Routledge, 2014); Sarah Thornton, *Club Cultures: Music, Media and Subcultural Capital* (Boston, MA: John Wiley & Sons, 2013); John Davis, *Youth and the Condition of Britain: Images of Adolescent Conflict* (London: Athlone Press, 1990), ch. 8.

16. *New Society*, 2 January 1964, 4.
17. For Beatlemania, see Barbara Ehrenreich, Elizabeth Hess, and Gloria Jacobs, 'Beatlemania: Girls Just Want to Have Fun', in *The Adoring Audience: Fan Culture and Popular Media*, ed. Lisa A. Lewis (London: Routledge, 1992), 84–106; John Muncie, 'The Beatles and the Spectacle of Youth', in *The Beatles, Popular Music and Society*, ed. Ian Inglis (Basingstoke: Springer, 2000), 35–52; John Blaney, *Beatles for Sale: How Everything They Touched Turned to Gold* (London: Jawbone Press, 2008), ch. 5; Nicolette Rohr, 'Yeah Yeah Yeah: The Sixties Screamscape of Beatlemania', *Journal of Popular Music Studies* 29, no. 2 (2017); Mike Kirkup, '"Some Kind of Innocence": The *Beatles Monthly* and the Fan Community', *Popular Music History* 9, no. 1 (2014), 64–78; Millard, *Beatlemania*. For music fandom more generally, see Lawrence Grossberg, 'Another Boring Day in Paradise: Rock and Roll and the Empowerment of Everyday Life', *Popular Music* 4 (1984), 225–58; Linda Duits, Koos Zwaan and Stijn Reijners, eds., *The Ashgate Research Companion to Fan Cultures* (Aldershot: Ashgate, 2014); Matthew Hills, *Fan Cultures* (London: Routledge, 2003).
18. Joanne Hallifax cited in *Church Times*, 6 March 1964, 16; cited in Michael Braun, *Love Me Do: The Beatles' Progress* (Harmondsworth: Penguin, 1964), 65.
19. Vincent Mulchrone, *Mail*, 21 October 1963, 8.
20. Mulchrone, *Mail*, 22 October 1963, 6.
21. Winifred Carr, *Telegraph*, 1 November 1963, 12.
22. Cited in *Times*, 28 May 1964, 7.
23. *Mirror*, 22 November 1963, 13.
24. Sandiford, 4.
25. Frederick Dalby Flower, *Language and Education* (London: Longmans, 1966), 41.
26. Cited in Merrick Winn, *Express*, 9 October 1963, 6.
27. Cited in Charles Hamblett and Jane Deverson, *Generation X* (New York, NY: Tandem Books, 1964), 16.

28. D. W. Winnicott, *New Society*, 28 May 1964, 6; Clive Borrell, *Mail*, 22 April 1965, 6.

29. *Mirror*, 20 April 1967, 15.

30. Robert Pitman, *Express*, 6 November 1963, 10.

31. Cited in *Express*, 4 January 1964, 4. The England team valiantly overcame the handicap of Beatlemania to win the World Cup two years later.

32. *Telegraph*, 2 November 1963, 8.

33. David Holbrook cited in Charles Greville, *Mail*, 6 August 1964, 4.

34. Cited in *Times*, 28 May 1964, 7.

35. Roy Nash, *Mail*, 6 February 1964, 8.

36. Sid Chaplin, *Guardian*, 16 November 1963, 14.

37. A. P. Garland, *Telegraph*, 6 November 1963, 14.

38. Nash, 8.

39. Pitman, 10.

40. Marshall Pugh, *Mail*, 20 May 1964, 8.

41. Cited in David Lewin, *Mail*, 5 June 1964, 10.

42. For the symbolism of hair in the sixties, see Annie J. Randall, *Dusty! Queen of the Postmods* (New York, NY: Oxford University Press, 2008), ch. 1.

43. Mirror Reporter, *Mirror*, 5 June 1964, 3; *Mail*, 5 June 1964, 1.

44. 'Tipping the Scales', *Telegraph*, 10 December 1964, 15; *Mirror*, 6 December 1963, 15; 'Beatle Cuts Ban', *Telegraph*, 10 June 1966, 22.

45. *Express*, 8 November 1963, 1; *Express*, 29 February 1964, 4.

46. 'Haircut Protest', *Telegraph*, 3 March 1965, 16.

47. 'GCE Boy Quits School over Beatle Cut', *Telegraph*, 22 November 1963, 17.

48. Ann Steele, *Telegraph*, 2 September 1964, 13; 'Head Ties Boys' Hair in Ribbon', *Telegraph*, 18 July 1964, 9; *Herald*, 11 January 1964, 5.

49. O. W. Walston, *New Statesman*, 20 March 1964, 448.

50. McCartney (1965) cited in Mark Swearingen and Don Christian, eds., *The Beatles 'Speaking Words of Wisdom': Beatles Interviews 1962–1970* (Scotts Valley, CA: Createspace, 2014), 252. Liberace's successful libel suit against the *Daily Mirror* in 1956 might have deterred the British media from making any mention of homosexuality. For the Liberace trial, see Darden Asbury Pyron, 'The Days of the Understated Suit', 2000, University of Chicago Press, www.press.uchicago.edu/Misc/Chicago/686671.html.

51. Bernice Ryan cited in *Mirror*, 24 October 1963, 15; *Telegraph*, 18 July 1964, 9; Gallup (October 1965) in George Gallup Jr, *The Gallup International Public Opinion Polls, Great Britain 1937–1975: Vol. 2 – 1965–1975* (New York, NY: Random House, 1976), 833.

52. *Mirror*, 17 August 1963, 3.

53. *Mirror*, 11 January 1964, 18; cited in *Mail*, 28 February 1964, 9.

54. 'An executive of the youth employment bureau' cited in *Times*, 29 December 1964, 4.

55. WPC Carol and anonymous Cavern employee cited in Merrick Winn, *Express*, 7 October 1963, 8.

56. Colin Fletcher, *New Society*, 20 February 1964, 11–14.

57. Ibid., 14. Fletcher's account was strongly disputed by an erstwhile member of a rival gang, Roger Corlett, but it found favour with several influential writers on youth culture; see Roger P. Corlett, *New Society*, 12 March 1964, 32; Geoffrey Moorhouse, *Britain in the Sixties: The Other England* (Harmondsworth: Penguin, 1964), 138.

58. Cited in *Mirror*, 21 February 1964, 10; George Green cited in *Mirror*, 21 February 1964, 2; cited in *Express*, 20 February 1964, 14; cited in *Times*, 26 February 1964, 7.

59. Brian Epstein, *A Cellarful of Noise* (New York, NY: Doubleday, 1964), 73. Proceeds from the Washington embassy reception for the Beatles in February 1964 were diplomatically donated to anti-delinquency initiatives; see Jeffrey Blyth, *Mail*, 11 February 1964, 10. For Mods, see Stanley Cohen, *Folk Devils and Moral Panics: The Creation of the Mods and Rockers*, 3rd edn (London: Routledge, 2002); Richard Weight, *Mod: A Very British Style* (London: Bodley Head, 2013); Pamela Thurschwell, ed., *Quadrophenia and Mod(Ern) Culture* (Basingstoke: Springer, 2017).

60. Hubert F. Allen, *Mail*, 11 May 1964, 8.

61. Cited in Douglas Marlborough, *Mail*, 7 April 1964, 7.

62. Epstein, *A Cellarful of Noise*, 72. For girls and young women in postwar Britain, see Carol Dyhouse, *Girl Trouble: Panic and Progress in the History of Young Women* (London: Zed Books, 2013).

63. Epstein, *A Cellarful of Noise*, 75.

64. Daniel McGeachie, *Express*, 10 December 1963, 7.

65. Ibid., 7. For the Beatles' tours, see Mark Lewisohn, *The Beatles Live!* (London: Pavilion, 1986); Martin Creasy, *Beatlemania! The Real Story of the Beatles UK Tours 1963–1965* (London: Omnibus, 2011).

66. Keith Graves, *Express*, 31 October 1964, 1; *Mail*, 24 September 1964, 2.

67. Cited in *Mail*, 15 June 1966, 9.

68. Cassandra, *Mirror*, 28 October 1963, 6.

69. *Mirror*, 5 March 1964, 1.

70. *Express*, 3 March 1964, 12.

71. *Mirror*, 20 December 1963, 3.

72. Rosina Rutherford cited in *Mirror*, 20 December 1963, 3.

73. Music therapist cited in Carr, 12.

74. *Telegraph*, 2 November 1963, 8.

75. Anthony Burgess, *Listener*, 25 July 1963, 142; Anthony Burgess, *Listener*, 19 December 1963, 1042; Anthony Burgess, *Listener*, 7 September 1967, 315; Paul Johnson, *New Statesman*, 28 February 1964, 326–7.

76. Cassandra, *Mirror*, 28 October 1963, 6; Bishop Brunner of Middlesbrough cited in *Catholic Herald*, 14 April 1964, 2.

77. Charles Hamblett, *Here Are the Beatles* (London: New English Library, 1964), n.p.
78. Cited in Kenneth Harris, *Observer*, 17 May 1964, 28. For similar accounts, see Peter Laurie, *Mail*, 5 November 1963, 8; and Braun, *Love Me Do*, 20.
79. Gerry Marsden cited in Winn, *Express*, 9 October 1963, 6.
80. Winn, *Express*, 9 October 1963, 6.
81. Peter Laurie, *The Teenage Revolution* (London: A. Blond, 1965), 151.
82. Ibid., 154.
83. Ibid., 156.
84. Richard Lester (dir.), *A Hard Day's Night* (Walter Shenson Films, 1964). For the Beatles and masculinity, see Martin King, *Men, Masculinity and The Beatles* (Aldershot: Ashgate, 2013); Martin King, 'The Beatles in *Help!* Re-Imagining the English Man in Mid-1960s Britain', *Global Journal of Human-Social Science Research* 14, no. 4 (2014), https://socialscienceresearch.org/index.php/GJHSS/article/view/1066; Martin King, '"Roll up for the Mystery Tour": Reading the Beatles' *Magical Mystery Tour* as a Countercultural Anti-Masculinist Text', *Global Journal of Interdisciplinary Social Sciences* 4, no. 3 (2015), 102–10.
85. Hamblett, *Here Are the Beatles*, n.p.; Henry Fairlie, *Spectator*, 3 June 1964, 4.
86. Consultant psychiatrist cited in Winn, *Express*, 9 October 1963, 6; Mike Hennessey, *Melody Maker*, 25 September 1965, 10–11.
87. Edith Summerskill cited in *Mail*, 10 January 1964, 1.
88. For contemporary attitudes to the sexuality of girls and young women, see Rosalind Watkiss Singleton, '"(Today I Met) The Boy I'm Gonna Marry": Romantic Expectations of Teenage Girls in the 1960s West Midlands', in *Youth Culture and Social Change*, ed. Keith Gildart, Anna Gough-Yates and Sian Lincoln (Basingstoke: Palgrave Macmillan, 2017), 119–46; Louise A. Jackson, '"The Coffee Club Menace": Policing Youth, Leisure and Sexuality in Post-War Manchester', *Cultural and Social History* 5, no. 3 (2008), 289–308; Janet Fink and Penny Tinkler, 'Teetering on the Edge: Portraits of Innocence, Risk and Young Female Sexualities in 1950s and 1960s British Cinema', *Women's History Review* 26, no. 1 (2017), 9–25.
89. *Jackie*, 29 February 1964, 1.
90. Maurice Woodruff, *Girl*, 13 July 1963, 12.
91. Helena Harding, *Beatles Book*, November 1963, 20.
92. Monica Furlong, *Mail*, 8 November 1963, 18.
93. Cited in *Times*, 28 May 1964, 7.
94. Julian Huxley, 'Introduction', *Philosophical Transactions of the Royal Society of London. Series B, Biological Sciences* 251, no. 772 (1966), 265; Alex Comfort, 'The Technological Age and Human Needs: An Emotional "Technology"', in *Technology and Society: The First Bath Conference, 1965*, ed. Gerald Walters and Kenneth Hudson (Bath: Bath University Press, 1966), 173.

95. Malcolm Muggeridge, 'Down with Sex (1965)', in *Tread Softly, for You Tread on My Jokes* (London: Collins, 1966), 46.

96. David Griffiths, *Listener*, 30 July 1964, 935. For pop on television, see Ian Inglis, ed., *Popular Music and Television in Britain* (Aldershot: Ashgate, 2010).

97. Entry for 4 July 1965 in Graham Payn and Sheridan Morley, eds., *Noël Coward Diaries* (New York, NY: Da Capo Press, 2000), 602.

98. David Holbrook, *New Statesman*, 13 March 1964, 397.

99. Ibid., 398.

100. Walston, 448.

101. David Holbrook, *Creativity and Popular Culture* (Rutherford, NJ: Fairleigh Dickinson University Press, 1994), 169.

102. Ibid., 172.

103. Ibid., 170.

104. Ibid., 169.

105. Ibid., 168.

106. Ibid., 171.

107. Ibid., 173, 171, 172.

108. Deryck Cooke, *New Statesman*, 20 March 1964, 448.

109. Cited in Philip Norman, *Shout! The True Story of the Beatles*, 3rd edn (New York, NY: Fireside/Simon and Schuster, 2005), 223.

110. Ibid., 223; Vincent Mulchrone, *Mail*, 22 October 1963, 6.

111. Alan Brien, *Sunday Telegraph*, 2 August 1964, 5; Peter Leslie, *Fab: The Anatomy of a Phenomenon* (London: MacGibbon & Kee, 1965), 132.

112. Richard Mabey, *The Pop Process* (London: Hutchinson Educational, 1969), 33.

113. For social histories of class in postwar Britain, see Selina Todd, *The People: The Rise and Fall of the Working Class, 1910–2010* (London: John Murray, 2015); Mike Savage, *Identities and Social Change in Britain since 1940* (Oxford: Oxford University Press, 2010); Ben Jones, *The Working Class in Mid-Twentieth-Century England: Community, Identity and Social Memory* (Manchester: Manchester University Press, 2012); Jon Lawrence, 'Class, "Affluence" and the Study of Everyday Life in Britain, c. 1930–64', *Cultural and Social History* 10, no. 2 (2013), 273–99; Jon Lawrence, 'The British Sense of Class', *Journal of Contemporary History* 35, no. 2 (2000), 307–18. For representations of class, see Stephen Brooke, '"Slumming" in Swinging London? Class, Gender and the Post-War City in Nell Dunn's *Up the Junction* (1963)', *Cultural and Social History* 9, no. 3 (2012), 429–49; Dominic Head, *The Cambridge Introduction to Modern British Fiction, 1950–2000* (Cambridge: Cambridge University Press, 2002), ch. 2; Stuart Laing, *Representations of Working-Class Life, 1957–1964* (Basingstoke: Macmillan, 1986).

114. Cited in Harris, 28.

115. Hamblett, *Here Are the Beatles*, n.p.

116. Mulchrone, *Mail*, 21 October 1963, 8.
117. Cited in Shawn Levy, *Ready, Steady, Go! Swinging London and the Invention of Cool* (London: Fourth Estate, 2002), 137.
118. Cited in *Express*, 20 February 1964, 14.
119. Jonathan Aitken, *The Young Meteors* (London: Secker & Warburg, 1967), 272.
120. Robin Douglas-Home, *Express*, 3 February 1966, 8.
121. Ibid., 8.
122. Cited in Harris, 28; Tony Barrow, sleeve notes for *All My Loving* EP (Parlophone, 1964).
123. Richard Mabey, *Peace News*, 20 December 1963; *Mirror*, 6 November 1963, 6; Cyril Dunn and Peter Dunn, *Observer*, 10 November 1963, 29; Ash, 10; Maureen Cleave, *Standard*, 24 December 1963, 1; *Express*, 1 November 1963, 6.
124. Marjorie Proops, *Mirror*, 16 June 1964, 5.
125. Derwent J. May, *TLS*, 5 December 1963, 1011.
126. Brien, 5.
127. For attitudes to affluence, see Lawrence Black and Hugh Pemberton, eds., *An Affluent Society? Britain's Post-War 'Golden Age' Revisited* (Aldershot: Ashgate, 2004); Avner Offer, 'British Manual Workers: From Producers to Consumers, c. 1950–2000', *Contemporary British History* 22, no. 4 (2008), 537–71; John Rule, 'Time, Affluence and Private Leisure: The British Working Class in the 1950s and 1960s', *Labour History Review* 66, no. 2 (2001), 223–42.
128. *Sun*, 4 December 1964, 3.
129. Robert Bickford, *Mail*, 1 April 1964, 3.
130. *Express*, 11 February 1963, 1.
131. Cited in *Express*, 2 January 1967, 1.
132. Lord Russell of Liverpool and Charles Hodgson cited in Charles Greville, *Mail*, 25 February 1964, 4.
133. David English, *Express*, 13 February 1964, 2.
134. Epstein, *A Cellarful of Noise*, 15. For gentlemanliness, see Marcus Collins, 'The Fall of the English Gentleman: The National Character in Decline, c. 1918–1970', *Historical Research* 75, no. 187 (2002), 90–111.
135. *Express*, 27 June 1963, 17; Douglas Marlborough, *Mail*, 17 August 1964, 3.
136. Ibid., 3.
137. *Express*, 13 February 1965, 13.
138. Robert Head, *Mirror*, 16 February 1965, 17.
139. *Express*, 20 February 1965, 13; Jon, *Mail*, 20 February 1965, www .cartoons.ac.uk/record/06732.
140. For the monarchy, see Andrzej Olechnowicz, ed., *The Monarchy and the British Nation, 1780 to the Present* (Cambridge: Cambridge University Press, 2007).
141. Don Short, *Mirror*, 5 November 1963, 16.

142. Derek Taylor (1964) cited in Al Aronowitz, *The Blacklisted Journalist*, no. 17 (1997), www.blacklistedjournalist.com/column17.htm. For the reinvention of tradition, see Richard Cawston, *The Royal Family* (BBC One, 21 June 1969).
143. *Express*, 24 March 1964, 15.
144. Walsh, 5; cited in Mike Evans, *The Beatles Literary Anthology* (London: Plexus, 2004), 131. Different accounts attribute the comment to Lennon or McCartney.
145. *Mail*, 3 April 1964, 1; 'Princess Anne Wearing a Beatle Style Cap as She Left', *Telegraph*, 19 September 1966, 14.
146. The Beatles refused to play at further Royal Variety Performances; see Derek Johnson, *NME*, 29 October 1965, 2.
147. David Lewin, *Mail*, 6 March 1964, 1.
148. *Express*, 24 March 1964, 15; cited in Charles Greville, *Mail*, 30 July 1965, 4.
149. *Telegraph*, 2 November 1963, 8; Johnson, 327.
150. Peregrine Worsthorne, *The Socialist Myth* (New York, NY: Weybright and Talley, 1971).
151. Max Beloff, 'The Challenge of Barbarism (1965)', in *The Intellectual in Politics and Other Essays* (New York, NY: Library Press, 1971), 47; Bryan Wilson, 'The Social Context of the Youth Problem (1965)', in *The Youth Culture and the Universities* (London: Faber and Faber, 1970), 165.
152. Bryan Wilson, 'The Needs of Students (1965)', in *Youth Culture*, 127.
153. Bryan Wilson, 'Social Context', 165.
154. George Melly, *New Statesman*, 6 March 1964, 364; Fairlie, 4; Alexander Cockburn, *Oz*, no. 1 (1967), 7; John Carey, *Listener*, November 1971, 624.
155. Hunter Davies, *Sunday Times*, 16 November 1969, 50; *Melody Maker*, 3 July 1965, 2.
156. For national identity, see Raphael Samuel, *Theatres of Memory, Volume II. Island Stories: Unravelling Britain* (London: Verso, 1998); Richard Weight, *Patriots: National Identity in Britain, 1940–2000* (London: Macmillan, 2002); Robert Colls, *Identity of England* (Oxford: Oxford University Press, 2002); Paul Ward, *Britishness since 1870* (London: Routledge, 2004); Wendy Webster, *Imagining Home: Gender, Race and National Identity, 1945–1964* (London: Routledge, 2005).
157. Judith Simons, *Express*, 24 May 1963, 16. For metropolitan coverage of the 'Mersey Sound', see Ian Inglis, '"I Read the News Today, Oh Boy": The British Press and the Beatles', *Popular Music and Society* 33, no. 4 (2010), 558–9. For representations of Northernness, see Dave Russell, *Looking North: Northern England and the National Imagination* (Manchester: Manchester University Press, 2004).
158. Judith Simons, *Express*, 24 May 1963, 16; Judith Simons, *Express*, 25 September 1963, 6; Peter Black, *Mail*, 7 May 1964, 3. For the tangled relationship between race and popular music, see Jack Hamilton, *Just Around*

Midnight: Rock and Roll and the Racial Imagination (Cambridge, MA: Harvard University Press, 2016); Jon Stratton, *When Music Migrates: Crossing British and European Racial Faultlines, 1945–2010* (Aldershot: Ashgate, 2014).

159. Cited in Dunn and Dunn, 29.

160. For the Beatles and Britishness, see Andy Bennett, '"Sitting in an English Garden": Comparing Representations of "Britishness" in the Songs of the Beatles and 1990s Britpop Groups', in *The Beatles, Popular Music and Society*, ed. Ian Inglis (Basingstoke: Springer, 2000), 189–206; Edward Macan, 'The Beatles and the Origins of "Britishness" in Rock Music', in *Fifty Years with the Beatles: The Impact of the Beatles on Contemporary Culture*, ed. Jerzy Jarniewicz and Alina Kwiatkowska (Łódź: Łódź University Press, 2010); Kathryn B. Cox, 'Mystery Trips, English Gardens, and Songs Your Mother Should Know: The Beatles and British Nostalgia in 1967', in *New Critical Perspectives on the Beatles: Things We Said Today*, ed. Kenneth Womack and Katie Kapurch (Basingstoke: Springer, 2016), 31–50.

161. Hamblett, *Here Are the Beatles*, n.p.

162. Ibid., n.p.

163. Hamblett and Deverson, *Generation X*, 138.

164. Peter Laurie, *Mail*, 5 November 1963, 8; cited in Desmond Zwar, *Mail*, 4 December 1964, 10. The first Bond film, *Dr. No* premiered on the same day that Love Me Do was released, 5 October 1962.

165. Colin MacInnes, *Encounter*, December 1957, 3. For American influences on British popular music, see Laura E. Cooper and B. Lee Cooper, 'The Pendulum of Cultural Imperialism: Popular Music Interchanges between the United States and Britain, 1943–1967', *The Journal of Popular Culture* 27, no. 3 (1993), 61–78; Randall, *Dusty!*, ch. 2; Simon Philo, *British Invasion: The Crosscurrents of Musical Influence* (Lanham, MD: Rowman & Littlefield, 2014); Allison Abra, *Dancing in the English Style: Americanisation and National Identity in Britain 1918–50* (Oxford: Oxford University Press, 2017). For broader studies of Americanisation, see Adrian Horn, *Juke Box Britain: Americanisation and Youth Culture, 1945–60* (Manchester: Manchester University Press, 2009); Howard Malchow, *Special Relations: The Americanization of Britain?* (Stanford, CA: Stanford University Press, 2011); John F. Lyons, *America in the British Imagination: 1945 to the Present* (Basingstoke: Springer, 2013), chs. 1 and 2.

166. MacInnes, 6.

167. Mordecai Richler, *Commentary* 39, no. 5 (1965), 67.

168. Tony Barrow, sleeve notes for *Please Please Me* (Parlophone, 1963).

169. William Mann, *Times*, 23 December 1963, 4; Dunn and Dunn, 29.

170. Derek Malcolm, *Guardian*, 20 February 1964, 9.

171. Barnes, 16.

172. Cited in 'Beatle Haircut For The Lion', *Times*, 15 April 1966, 7.

173. Cited in ibid., 7.

174. Charles De Hoghton, *Times*, 19 June 1965, 9.

175. *New York Times*, 10 November 1996, SM27; *Times*, 9 August 1966, 6.

176. Israel State Archives, 'Israel Bans the Beatles', *Israel's Documented Story*, 11 December 2013, http://israelsdocuments.blogspot.com/2013/12/israel-bans-beatles.html.

177. Geoffrey Thursby, *Express*, 2 February 1965, 2.

178. Robin Smyth, *Mail*, 5 April 1966, 1; Ian Brodie, *Express*, 16 February 1967, 8; *Express*, 20 January 1967, 1.

179. *Guardian*, 5 December 1968, 11; *Mirror*, 4 March 1964, 7. For the Beatles' infiltration of the Eastern Bloc, see Leslie Woodhead, *How the Beatles Rocked the Kremlin* (London: Bloomsbury, 2013).

180. Peter Knight, *Telegraph*, 22 May 1964, 17; Head, 17.

181. *Vogue*, 1 August 1965, 87.

182. Piri Halasz, *Time*, 15 April 1966, 30–34. For the London scene, see Becky E. Conekin, 'Fashioning Mod: Twiggy and the Moped in "Swinging" London', *History and Technology* 28, no. 2 (2012), 209–15; Levy, *Ready, Steady, Go!* ; Frank Mort, *Capital Affairs: London and the Making of the Permissive Society* (New Haven, CT: Yale University Press, 2010), ch. 5; David Mellor, *The Sixties Art Scene in London* (London: Phaidon, 1993); Simon Rycroft, *Swinging City: A Cultural Geography of London 1950–1974* (London: Routledge, 2016).

183. For the Beatles as a transatlantic phenomenon, see Jonathan Gould, *Can't Buy Me Love: The Beatles, Britain, and America* (New York, NY: Three Rivers Press, 2008); Steven D. Stark, *Meet the Beatles: A Cultural History of the Band That Shook Youth, Gender, and the World* (London: HarperCollins, 2005).

184. Patrick Doncaster, *Mirror*, 24 January 1963, 15.

185. David Lewin, *Mail*, 14 September 1964, 8.

186. *Mirror*, 29 June 1966, 11. See also Patrick Doncaster, *Mirror*, 15 August 1963, 11.

187. Cited in *Express*, 24 March 1964, 15.

188. *Guardian*, 4 January 1964, 3.

189. Simons, *Express*, 25 September 1963, 6.

190. Wilson, 'Social Context', 165.

191. Cited in *Times*, 28 May 1964, 7; Erwin Stengel, 'Review of *Transcultural Psychiatry* by A. V. S. de Reuck', *British Medical Journal* 2, no. 5505 (1966), 100; cited in *Times*, 30 December 1964, 4.

192. Cassandra, *Mirror*, 7 July 1964, 6.

193. Rev E. L. Hebden Taylor cited in *Times*, 2 May 1966, 6.

194. A. Culverhouse, *Express*, 17 January 1964, 8.

195. *Express*, 17 January 1964, 8.

196. Clifford Hanley, *Spectator*, 19 July 1963, 76.

197. Cassandra, *Mirror*, 10 August 1966, 8.

198. Cited in Cassandra, *Mirror*, 10 January 1966, 8.
199. Jeremy Hornsby, *Express*, 13 February 1965, 8.
200. Black, 3; *Express*, 20 February 1964, 14; Cassandra, *Mirror*, 3 December 1964, 8.
201. Chaplin, 14; *Times*, 27 December 1963, 4; Hamblett, *Here Are the Beatles*, n.p.
202. Sheila Duncan, *Mirror*, 13 April 1964, 10; *Mail*, 28 May 1964, 10; William Sargant, 'Psychiatric Treatment in General Teaching Hospitals: A Plea for a Mechanistic Approach', *British Medical Journal* 2, no. 5508 (1966), 257–62.
203. Cited in *Mail*, 5 March 1964, 16.
204. Callum G. Brown, *The Death of Christian Britain*, rev. edn (London: Routledge, 2013). For the liberalisation of Christianity in sixties Britain, see Laura Monica Ramsay, 'The Church of England, Homosexual Law Reform, and the Shaping of the Permissive Society, 1957–1979', *Journal of British Studies* 57, no. 1 (2018), 108–37; Sam Brewitt-Taylor, 'Christianity and the Invention of the Sexual Revolution in Britain, 1963–1967', *Historical Journal* 60, no. 2 (2017), 519–46; Keith Robbins, 'Contextualizing a "New Reformation": John A. T. Robinson and the Church of England in the Early Sixties', *Kirchliche Zeitgeschichte* 23, no. 2 (2010), 428–46; Matthew Grimley, 'Law, Morality and Secularisation: The Church of England and the Wolfenden Report, 1954–1967', *Journal of Ecclesiastical History* 60, no. 4 (2009), 725–41; G. I. T. Machin, *Churches and Social Issues in Twentieth-Century Britain* (Oxford: Clarendon Press, 1998), ch. 6.
205. Rev. Michael Brierley cited in *Express*, 5 December 1963, 2.
206. Cited in *Express*, 13 March 1965, 2.
207. Ian Ramsey, *Guardian*, 10 September 1964, 7.
208. Ian T. Ramsey, 'Talking about God: Models, Ancient and Modern', in *Myth and Symbol*, vol. 7, ed. Frederick William Dillistone (London: SPCK, 1966), 93.
209. Ibid., 93.
210. *Mail*, 20 April 1965, 12.
211. *Guardian*, 31 January 1964, 23. For popular music in church, see Peter Webster and Ian Jones, 'Anglican "Establishment" Reactions to "Pop" Church Music in England c. 1956–1991', in *Elite and Popular Religion: Papers Read at the 2004 Summer Meeting and the 2005 Winter Meeting of the Ecclesiastical History Society*, ed. Kate Cooper and Jeremy Gregory (Woodbridge: Boydell Press, 2006).
212. *Guardian*, 13 February 1964, 4.
213. *Church Times*, 19 June 1964.
214. Cited in *Express*, 18 November 1963, 11.
215. Cited in ibid., 11.
216. Cited in ibid., 11.
217. Anne Scott-James, *Mail*, 21 November 1963, 10.

218. *Times*, 8 August 1964, 7; *Telegraph*, 7 August 1964, 22; *Church Times*, 14 August 1964, 3.

219. Henry Fairlie, *Spectator*, 13 August 1964, 4.

220. Cited in Edward Vale, *Mirror*, 12 June 1965, 1.

221. Cited in ibid., 1; cited in Simon Frith, *Marxism Today*, January 1981, 24.

222. *Melody Maker*, 6 March 1965, 13; cited in Weight, *Patriots*, 359.

223. Cited in 'The Beatles: MBEs Awarded by The Queen', *The Beatles*, www .thebeatles.com/feature/beatles-mbes-awarded-queen.

224. Cited in Evans, *Beatles Literary Anthology*, 131. Different accounts attribute the phrase to Lennon or McCartney.

225. Joseph Lee, *Evening News*, 26 October 1965, www.cartoons.ac.uk/record/ 07752.

226. 'MBE', *Mirror*, 17 June 1965, 7; Harry Rabinowitz et al., *Mail*, 18 June 1965, 10; 'Two to One against Beatles', *Times*, 17 June 1965, 6.

227. Patrick Sergeant, *Mail*, 22 February 1964, 8.

228. Donald Zec, *Mirror*, 12 June 1965, 9.

229. Cited in David Pritchard and Alan Lysaght, *The Beatles: An Oral History* (Hyperion, 1998), 191.

230. Bernard Levin, *Mail*, 14 June 1965, 8.

231. Peregrine Worsthorne cited in *Tribune*, 15 October 1965.

232. Entry for 4 July 1965 in Payn and Morley, eds., *Noël Coward Diaries*, 602.

233. George Melly, *Observer*, 27 June 1965, 23.

234. *Catholic Herald*, 10 June 1966, 2.

235. Quoodle, *Spectator*, 18 June 1965.

236. Richard Pape cited in *Telegraph*, 15 June 1965, 1.

237. Cited in *Times*, 22 June 1965, 10.

238. Cited in 'Protest at Honour for Beatles', *Times*, 15 June 1965, 12.

239. Cited in 'Beatles MBE Protests Mount', *Telegraph*, 16 June 1965, 17.

240. *Mirror*, 17 June 1965, 3.

241. Pete Shotton and Nicholas Schaffner, *John Lennon: In My Life* (New York, NY: Stein & Day, 1983), 96–7.

242. Cited in Anthony Fawcett, *John Lennon: One Day at a Time* (New York, NY: Grove Press, 1981), 58.

243. Paul McCartney, *Scene and Heard*, interview by David Wigg, 19 September 1969, www.beatlesinterviews.org/db1969.0919.beatles.html.

244. Mark Lewisohn, *The Complete Beatles Chronicles* (New York, NY: Harmony Books, 1992), 180.

245. For Epstein, see Debbie Geller, *In My Life: The Brian Epstein Story* (Basingstoke: Macmillan, 2014); Ray Coleman, *Brian Epstein: The Man Who Made the Beatles* (Harmondsworth: Penguin, 1989).

246. Lennon cited in G. Barry Golson, ed., *The Playboy Interviews with John Lennon and Yōko Ono* (New York, NY: Putnam Publishing Group, 1981), 149. For the evolution of the Beatles' lyrics, see Colin Campbell, *The*

Continuing Story of Eleanor Rigby: Analysing the Lyric of a Popular Beatles' Song (Kibworth Beauchamp: Troubador, 2018); James McGrath, 'Reading Post-War Britain in Lennon and McCartney's Imagined Communities', in *New Perspectives in British Cultural History*, ed. Ros Crone, David Gange and Katie Jones (Newcastle: Cambridge Scholars, 2007); Hunter Davies, *The Beatles Lyrics: The Stories Behind the Music, Including the Handwritten Drafts of More than 100 Classic Beatles Songs* (London: Hachette UK, 2014).

247. See James M. Decker, '"Try Thinking More": *Rubber Soul* and the Beatles' Transformation of Pop', in *The Cambridge Companion to the Beatles*, ed. Kenneth Womack (Cambridge: Cambridge University Press, 2009).

248. Diana Vreeland cited in John Crosby, *Weekend Telegraph*, 16 April 1965, n.p. For sixties British culture, see Bart Moore-Gilbert and John Seed, eds., *Cultural Revolution? The Challenge of the Arts in the 1960s* (London: Routledge, 1992); Eleanor Bell and Linda Gunn, eds., *The Scottish Sixties: Reading, Rebellion, Revolution?* (Amsterdam: Rodopi, 2013); Robert Hewison, *Too Much: Art and Society in the Sixties 1960–75* (London: Methuen, 1986); David Mellor and Laurent Gervereau, eds., *The Sixties: Britain and France, 1962–1973: The Utopian Years* (London: Philip Wilson, 1997); Angela Bartie, *The Edinburgh Festivals: Culture and Society in Postwar Britain* (Edinburgh: Edinburgh University Press, 2013).

249. Interdepartmental Committee on Drug Addiction, *Drug Addiction: The Second Report* (London: HMSO, 1965), n.p. https://web .archive.org/web/20141017120149/, www.drugtext.org/Second-Brain-Report/drug-addiction-2.html

250. Ibid., n.p.

Society, 1966–1970: The Beatles Go Too Far

1. Cited in Kurt Loder, *Rolling Stone*, 11 September 1986, www .rollingstone.com/music/music-news/paul-mccartney-the-rolling-stone-interview-41087/.

2. Bernard Levin, *Mail*, 29 December 1967, 4.

3. Bernard Levin, *The Pendulum Years: Britain and the Sixties* (London: Jonathan Cape, 1970), 318.

4. Cited in *Sunday Times*, 25 August 1968, 1.

5. *Jackie*, 11 November 1967, 12.

6. John King, *Petticoat*, December 1966, 17.

7. *Jackie*, 29 March 1969, 1; Jackie, 2 May 1970, 11.

8. Maureen Cleave, *Standard*, 24 December 1963, 1; Robert McKenzie, *Observer*, 8 December 1963, 10; Robert Bickford, *Mail*, 1 January 1964, 3.

9. Don Short, *Mirror*, 27 December 1969, 9; Mike Hennessey, *Record Mirror*, 3 January 1970 cited in William Fraser Sandercombe, *The Beatles: The Press Reports, 1961–1970* (Burlington, ON: Collectors Guide Pub., 2007), 291.

10. Hunter Davies cited in *Sunday Times*, 28 December 1969, 41.

11. *Man of the Decade* (ATV, 12 December 1969); Robert Speaight, *Times*, 31 December 1969, 7.

12. George Melly, *Revolt into Style: The Pop Arts in Britain* (Harmondsworth: Penguin, 1970); David Bailey and Peter Evans, *Goodbye Baby & Amen: A Saraband for the Sixties* (London: Condé Nast, 1969); Christopher Booker, *The Neophiliacs: A Study of the Revolution in English Life in the Fifties and Sixties* (London: Collins, 1969); Levin, *Pendulum Years*.

13. Kenneth Allsop, 'Pop Goes Young Woodley', in *Class: A Symposium*, ed. Richard Mabey (London: Antony Blond, 1967), 127–43.

14. T. R. Fyvel, *Intellectuals Today: Problems in a Changing Society* (London: Chatto and Windus, 1968), 54; Janet Daley, *Guardian*, 29 January 1968, x; *Man of the Decade*.

15. Karl Miller, *Listener*, 1 May 1969, 602; Tony Palmer, *Observer*, 17 November 1968, 24.

16. Tony Barrow, *Melody Maker*, 10 February 1968, 7.

17. Frederick James, *Beatles Book*, March 1964, 27; Barrow, *Melody Maker*, 10 February 1968, 7.

18. G. M. Carstairs, *Listener*, 14 September 1972, 329.

19. Ibid., 329.

20. Edmund Leach, *A Runaway World? The Reith Lectures 1967* (London: British Broadcasting Corporation, 1967), 39, 40.

21. For the evolution of the Beatles' image, see Paolo Hewitt, *Fab Gear* (London: Prestel, 2011), chs. 3 and 4; Charlotte Wilkins and Ian Inglis, 'Fashioning the Fab Four: The Visual Identities of the Beatles', *Fashion, Style & Popular Culture* 2, no. 2 (2015), 207–21.

22. Aubrey Walter, 'Introduction', in Aubrey Walter, ed., *Come Together: The Years of Gay Liberation, 1970–73* (London: Gay Men's Press, 1980), 14.

23. Jann Wenner, *Rolling Stone*, 21 January 1971, 36–43.

24. Michael Wood, *New Society*, 4 January 1968, 287.

25. Julian Critchley, *Times*, 21 November 1969, 11.

26. *Times*, 3 October 1968, 2.

27. Cited in *Mail*, 1 September 1967, 1.

28. F. Norman Lewis, *Church Times*, 22 September 1967, 9; Andrew Ritchie, *Church Times*, 30 July 1971, 4; Hilary Wakeman, *Church Times*, 26 January 1973, 12. For New Age religion, see Colin Campbell, *The Easternization of the West: A Thematic Account of Cultural Change in the Modern Era* (London: Routledge, 2008); Paul Heelas, *The New Age Movement* (Oxford: Blackwell, 1996).

29. *Church Times*, 2 January 1970, 1; *Church Times*, 31 October 1969, 1. The same issues belatedly brought the Beatles to the attention of Catholic intellectuals. Except for the local pride displayed by the Archbishop of Liverpool, Catholic clergymen had little to say about the Beatles during Beatlemania. Instead, the *Catholic Herald* faithfully reported the *Osservatore Romano*'s fulminations against their 'ridiculous and repugnant' music and Pope Paul VI's denunciation of 'frenzied agitation over some foolish entertainment' at a gathering of 10,000 Catholic girls a week after a Beatles' concert in Rome. But in 1968, the prominent Brazilian liberation theologian Archbishop Helder Câmara told his British audience that the Beatles were 'in the vanguard of youth's protest in every continent' against what he termed the seven deadly sins of the modern world: racism, colonialism, war, paternalism, Pharisaism, estrangement, and fear. The opposite case was made by the Catholic novelist John Braine, for whom Lennon and Ono represented perfect examples of why '[s]ocial justice is the modern heresy'. 'Christianity ... isn't about material equality, it isn't about housing or education or racialism or hospitals or wages or working conditions, it is about individual salvation', he stated: a roundabout way of saying that he had divine sanction to pay less tax (cited in *Times*, 1 October 1965, 8; cited in *Catholic Herald*, 19 June 1964, 5; cited in *Mail*, 5 July 1965, 3; cited in *Times*, 11 April 1969, 4; John Braine, *Catholic Herald*, 29 September 1972, 5).

30. Ringo Starr, *Scene and Heard*, interview by David Wigg (BBC Radio 1, 25 January 1970).

31. Ibid.; John Lennon and Yoko Ono, interview by Maurice Hindle, December 1968, http://imaginepeace.com/archives/9171.

32. Paul McCartney cited in Jonathan Cott, *Rolling Stone*, 10 February 1968, 6; Lennon and Ono, Hindle interview, December 1968.

33. Starr, *Scene and Heard* interview; McCartney cited in Ray Coleman, *Disc and Music Echo*, 11 June 1966, 9.

34. Cited in *Vancouver Sun*, 19 August 1966, 66.

35. Cited in Coleman, *Disc and Music Echo*, 11 June 1966, 9.

36. For the value placed upon authenticity in rock, see Yuval Barker and Hugh Taylor, *Faking It: The Quest for Authenticity in Popular Music* (London: Faber and Faber, 2007); Robert Pattison, *The Triumph of Vulgarity: Rock Music in the Mirror of Romanticism* (New York, NY: Oxford University Press, 1987); Theodore A. Gracyk, 'Romanticizing Rock Music', *Journal of Aesthetic Education* 27, no. 2 (1993), 43–58; Hans Weisethaunet and Ulf Lindberg, 'Authenticity Revisited: The Rock Critic and the Changing Real', *Popular Music and Society* 33, no. 4 (2010), 465–85.

37. James T. Coffman, '"Everybody Knows This Is Nowhere": Role Conflict and the Rock Musician', *Popular Music and Society* 1, no. 1 (1971), 20–32.

38. Cited in *Top of the Pops*, interview by Brian Matthew (BBC One, 20 March 1967), www.beatlelinks.net/forums/showthread.php?t=17253.

39. Cited in B. P. Fallon, *Melody Maker*, 12 April 1969, 4.

40. Starr, *Scene and Heard* interview.

41. Brian Epstein, *A Cellarful of Noise* (New York, NY: Doubleday, 1964), 82.

42. *Beatles Book,* December 1963, 2; James, *Beatles Book*, March 1964, 27; James, *Beatles Book*, January 1964, 25.

43. *Beatles Book*, March 1964, 29; George Harrison cited in Billy Shepherd and Johnny Dean, *Beatles Book*, September 1964, 23.

44. Ibid., 23.

45. Peter Laurie, *The Teenage Revolution* (London: A. Blond, 1965), 82; Alan Smith, *NME*, 16 May 1963, 10.

46. Alan Whittaker in *News of the World* (1964) cited in Mark Paytress, *Rolling Stones: Off The Record* (London: Omnibus, 2009), 63; *Mirror*, 6 November 1963, 2.

47. *Telegraph*, 2 November 1963, 8.

48. Dominic Sandbrook, *Never Had It So Good: A History of Britain from Suez to the Beatles* (London: Little, Brown, 2005), 475. For press coverage of the Beatles, see David Simonelli, *Working Class Heroes: Rock Music and British Society in the 1960s and 1970s* (Lanham, MD: Lexington Books, 2013), ch. 2; John Blaney, *Beatles for Sale: How Everything They Touched Turned to Gold* (London: Jawbone Press, 2008), ch. 4; Ian Inglis, "'I Read the News Today, Oh Boy": The British Press and the Beatles', *Popular Music and Society* 33, no. 4 (2010), 549–562; Michael R. Frontani, *The Beatles: Image and Media* (Oxford, MS: University Press of Mississippi, 2007).

49. Don Short, *Mirror*, 21 June 1963, 28.

50. Peter Evans, *Express*, 1 March 1965, 8.

51. Lennon cited in Ray Coleman, *Disc and Music Echo*, 18 January 1969, in Sandercombe, *Beatles*, 254.

52. Maureen Cleave, *Standard*, 1 April 1966, 8; Maureen Cleave, *Standard*, 11 March 1966, 10.

53. Cited in Maureen Cleave, *Standard*, 25 March 1966, 8.

54. Cited in Maureen Cleave, *Standard*, 4 March 1966, 10.

55. Cited in Maureen Cleave, *Standard*, 18 March 1966, 8. For excellent accounts of the Cleave interviews, see Steve Turner, *Beatles '66: The Revolutionary Year* (London: HarperCollins, 2016), 73–132; and Jon Savage, *1966: The Year the Decade Exploded* (London: Faber & Faber, 2015); ch. 4.

56. Tony Palmer, *Born under a Bad Sign* (London: William Kimber, 1970), 51.

57. Cited in Richie Yorke, *Detroit Free Press*, 29 November 1968, 52.

58. Cited in Alan Smith, *NME*, 17 August 1968, 3.

59. 'Help the Mail Help Oxfam Help the Beatles . . . to Save the Children', *Mail*, 12 December 1963, 1. Lennon also drew a Christmas charity card for Oxfam in 1965.

60. For memoirs by Apple Scruffs, see Carolyn Lee Mitchell and Michael Munn, *All Our Loving: A Beatles Fan's Memoirs* (London: Robson Books, 1988);

Carol Bedford, *Waiting for the Beatles: An Apple Scruff's Story* (London: Blandford Press, 1984).

61. Sean O'Mahony, *Beatles Book*, December 1969, 15.

62. Ibid., 14; 'Editorial', *Beatles Book*, January 1969, 2; Mal Evans, *Beatles Book*, July 1969, 22–9; 'Editorial', *Beatles Book*, August 1969, 2.

63. Cited in Stephen Daniels, 'Suburban Pastoral: "Strawberry Fields Forever" and Sixties Memory', *Cultural Geographies*. 13, no. 1 (2006), 44.

64. 'Monkees Versus Beatles', *Melody Maker*, 25 March 1967, 10–11; For the Monkees' significance, see Rosanne Welch, *Why the Monkees Matter: Teenagers, Television and American Pop Culture* (Jefferson, NC: McFarland, 2016).

65. Cited in Ray Coleman, *Disc and Music Echo*, 27 May 1967, in Sandercombe, *Beatles*, 191.

66. Ibid., 191.

67. Ibid., 191. For *Sgt. Pepper*, see Simon Warner, *Text and Drugs and Rock 'n' Roll: The Beats and Rock Culture* (London: A&C Black, 2013) ch. 6; Ben Winsworth, 'Psychic Liberation in *Sgt. Pepper's Lonely Hearts Club Band*', in *Preserving the Sixties: Britain and the 'Decade of Protest'*, ed. Trevor Harris and Monia O'Brien Castro (Basingstoke: Palgrave Macmillan, 2014); Jörg Helbig, ed., *Summer of Love: The Beatles, Art and Culture in the Sixties* (Trier: Wissenschaftlicher Verlag Trier, 2008); Clinton Heylin, *The Act You've Known for All These Years: The Life, and Afterlife, of Sgt. Pepper* (Edinburgh: Canongate, 2007); Olivier Julien, ed., *Sgt. Pepper and the Beatles: It Was Forty Years Ago Today* (Aldershot: Ashgate, 2007); Allan F. Moore, *The Beatles: Sgt Pepper's Lonely Hearts Club Band* (Cambridge: Cambridge University Press, 1997); Kenneth Womack and Kathryn B. Cox, eds., *The Beatles, Sgt. Pepper, and the Summer of Love* (Lanham, MD: Lexington Books, 2017).

68. Alan Walsh, *Melody Maker*, 20 May 1967, 3.

69. Ibid., 3.

70. 'Australians Greet Beatles', *Express*, 13 June 1964, 5.

71. Lord Denning cited in *Mail*, 21 August 1964, 2; cited in *Express*, 8 January 1964, 1.

72. 'A nurse' cited in *Mail*, 6 October 1964, 11.

73. Tom Read, *Mirror*, 1 May 1964, 13.

74. General Frederick Coutts cited in Robert Bickford, *Mail*, 26 November 1963, 3; A. E. Dillon, *Mail*, 1 April 1964, 6.

75. Cited in Douglas Marlborough, *Mail*, 4 September 1964, 3.

76. *Mirror*, 2 May 1964, 2.

77. Dr Maurice Williams cited in *Mail*, 29 April 1964, 9.

78. Cited in *Newsfront*, interview by Mitchell Krause, 14 May 1968, www .beatlesinterviews.org/db1968.0514.beatles.html.

79. Lennon (1980) cited in G. Barry Golson, ed., *The Playboy Interviews with John Lennon and Yōko Ono* (New York, NY: Putnam Publishing Group, 1981), 176.

80. For the counterculture in Britain, see Theodore Roszak, *The Making of a Counter Culture: Reflections on the Technocratic Society and Its Youthful Opposition* (Garden City, NY: Doubleday, 1969); Harriet Vyner, *Groovy Bob: The Life and Times of Robert Fraser* (London: Heni Publishing, 2016); Jonathon Green, ed., *Days in the Life: Voices from the English Underground 1961–1971* (London: Minerva, 1989); Sharif Gemie and Brian Ireland, *The Hippie Trail: A History* (Oxford: Oxford University Press, 2017); Chad Martin, 'Paradise Now: Youth Politics and the British Counterculture, 1958–74' (PhD Thesis, Stanford University, 2003); Elizabeth Nelson, *British Counter-Culture 1966–73: A Study of the Underground Press* (Basingstoke: Springer, 1989); Christopher John McGowan, 'Harmony and Discord within the English "Counter-Culture", 1965–1975, with Particular Reference to the "Rock Operas" *Hair*, *Godspell*, *Tommy* and *Jesus Christ Superstar*' (PhD Thesis, Queen Mary, London, 2012); Barry Miles, *London Calling: A Countercultural History of London since 1945* (London: Atlantic, 2011); Christoph Grunenberg and Jonathan Harris, eds., *Summer of Love: Psychedelic Art, Social Crisis and Counterculture in the 1960s* (Liverpool: Liverpool University Press, 2005).

81. Cited in Green, ed., *Days*, 115.

82. Ibid., 225.

83. Su Small, Graham Keen and Barry Miles cited in Green, ed., *Days*, 279, 230, 212.

84. Barry Miles, John Dunbar and Joe Boyd cited in Green, ed., *Days*, 79, 80, 202.

85. For Apple, see Peter McCabe and Robert D. Schonfeld, *Apple to the Core: The Unmaking of the Beatles* (London: Martin Brian and O'Keeffe, 1972); Richard DiLello, *The Longest Cocktail Party: An Insider's Diary of the Beatles, Their Million-Dollar Apple Empire, and Its Wild Rise and Fall* (Edinburgh: Canongate, 2005); Fred Goodman, *Allen Klein: The Man Who Bailed Out the Beatles, Made the Stones, and Transformed Rock & Roll* (Boston, MA: Houghton Mifflin Harcourt, 2015), prologue, chs. 9–11.

86. Barry Miles, *Oz*, no. 14 (1968), 25.

87. Cited in Green, ed., *Days*, 225; Wes Waring, *IT*, no. 52 (1969), 9.

88. Lennon cited in Pete Shotton and Nicholas Schaffner, *John Lennon: In My Life* (New York, NY: Stein & Day, 1983), 139.

89. McCartney cited in Hunter Davies, *Sunday Times*, 24 December 1967.

90. John Lennon and Yoko Ono, Vienna press conference, 31 March 1969, www
.beatlesinterviews.org/db1969.0331.beatles.html; John Lennon, Queen Elizabeth Hotel, interview by Howard Smith, 26 July 1969, www
.pastemagazine.com/articles/2012/01/john-lennon-yoko-ono-at-the-queen-
elizabeth-hotel.html; John Lennon and Yoko Ono, interview by David Frost,

24 August 1968, www.beatlesbible.com/1968/08/24/television-john-lennon-yoko-ono-frost-on-saturday/2/.

91. Cited in Ray Connolly, *Stardust Memories: Talking About My Generation* (London: Pavilion, 1983), 33.

92. *Beatles Book*, April 1968, 31.

93. Blackburn cited in Tariq Ali and Robin Blackburn, *Red Mole* 2, no. 5 (1971), 8; *Times*, 4 October 1966, 1; James Davies, *Express*, 14 September 1970, 1.

94. For the rooftop concert, see Tony Barrell, *The Beatles on the Roof* (London: Omnibus, 2017).

95. Alan Walsh, *Melody Maker*, 1 June 1968, 9.

96. Cited in Alan Walsh, *Melody Maker*, 7 December 1968, 18.

97. Cited in *Melody Maker*, 27 July 1968, 13.

98. Cited in Jeff Burger, ed., *Lennon on Lennon: Conversations with John Lennon* (London: Omnibus ebook, 2017), 50.

99. Germaine [Greer], *Oz*, no. 22 (1969), 4.

100. Richard Neville, *Oz*, no. 9 (1968), 27.

101. Miles, *Oz*, no. 14 (1968), 25.

102. Cited in Tony Barrow, *John, Paul, George, Ringo and Me* (London: Andre Deutsch, 2006), 232.

103. Cited in Kevin Howlett, *The Beatles: The BBC Archives 1962–1970* (London: Ebury Press, 2013), 232. See also Barry J. Faulk, *British Rock Modernism, 1967–1977: The Story of Music Hall in Rock* (London: Routledge, 2016), ch. 2.

104. Cited in Julius Fast, *The Beatles: The Real Story* (New York, NY: G.P. Putnam's Sons, 1968), 197.

105. Maurice Wiggin, *Sunday Times*, 31 December 1967, 20.

106. See Doug Sulpy and Ray Schweighardt, *Get Back: The Beatles' Let It Be Disaster* (London: Helter Skelter, 2003).

107. Cited in Jonathan Cott and David Dalton, *The Beatles Get Back* (London: Apple, 1970) n.p.

108. Cited in Ibid., n.p.

109. D. Dicks, *Beatles Book*, July 1969, 19.

110. Elaine Danson, *Beatles Book*, January 1969, 19.

111. 'London girl' cited in Frederick James, *Beatles Book*, October 1968, 31.

112. Cited in Jonathan Cott, *Rolling Stone*, 23 November 1968, www.rollingstone.com/music/music-news/john-lennon-the-rolling-stone-interview-186264/.

113. Cited in Spencer Leigh, ed., *Speaking Words of Wisdom: Reflections on the 'Beatles'* (Liverpool: Cavern City Tours, 1991), 72.

114. Tony Palmer, *Spectator*, 23 July 1971, 27.

115. Evan Anthony, *Spectator*, 2 December 1972, 23; George Barker, *Listener*, 11 June 1970, 792. Wilfrid Mellers was equally unsure whether to read irony into Ono's 'Sisters, O Sisters' (1972). Treated as a 'joke against utopianism', it was nihilistic; taken seriously, it envisaged a world he had

no wish to see (Wilfrid Mellers, *Twilight of the Gods: The Music of the Beatles* (New York, NY: Viking Press, 1973), 195).

116. Cited in Philip Oakes, *Sunday Times*, 14 July 1968, 15. For the sixties art college scene, see Simon Frith and Howard Horne, *Art into Pop* (London: Methuen, 1987); Alex Seago, *Burning the Box of Beautiful Things: The Development of a Postmodern Sensibility* (Oxford: Oxford University Press, 1995); Lisa Tickner, *Hornsey 1968: The Art School Revolution* (London: Frances Lincoln, 2008).

117. Cited in Michael Watts, *Melody Maker*, 2 October 1971, 24; cited in Burger, *Lennon on Lennon*, 91.

118. Ono (1983) cited in Nick Johnstone, *Yoko Ono 'Talking'* (London: Omnibus Press, 2010), 48.

119. Cited in David Skan, *Record Mirror*, 11 October 1969, in Sandercombe, *Beatles*, 278.

120. Alan Walsh, *Melody Maker*, 14 June 1969, 7.

121. Donald Zec, *Mirror*, 18 December 1969, 13.

122. For an overview of social activism in this period, see Adam Lent, *British Social Movements since 1945: Sex, Colour, Peace and Power* (Basingstoke: Palgrave Macmillan, 2001).

123. Cited in Palmer, *Born*, 47.

124. For the 'more popular than Jesus' controversy, see Steve Turner, *The Gospel According to the Beatles* (London: Westminster John Knox, 2006), ch. 2; Eyal Regev, 'Lennon and Jesus: Secularization and the Transformation of Religion', *Studies in Religion* 41, no. 4 (2012), 534–63; Brian Ward, '"The 'C' Is for Christ": Arthur Unger, *Datebook* Magazine and the Beatles', *Popular Music and Society* 35.4 (2012), 541–60.

125. Bryan Forbes, 'No Bone Showing', *Transition*, no. 31 (1967), 46–50.

126. David Frost, *Spectator*, 8 December 1966, 10.

127. Stanley Franklin, *Mirror*, 8 August 1966, www.cartoons.ac.uk/record/09520; Jak, *Standard*, 17 August 1966, www.cartoons.ac.uk/record/09555; Keith Waite, *Sun*, 17 August 1966, www.cartoons.ac.uk/record/09553.

128. *Melody Maker*, 13 August 1966, 1.

129. Maurice Wiggin, *Sunday Times*, 28 August 1966, 8.

130. *Catholic Herald*, 2 September 1966, 3.

131. Rev John Grover cited in *Express*, 9 September 1966, 16.

132. Rev J. M. Mather cited in *Mirror*, 17 August 1966, 4; Eric, Bishop of Reading, *Telegraph*, 19 August 1966, 14.

133. A. Dinsdale Young, *Sunday Telegraph*, 21 August 1966, 9.

134. For the Maharishi Mahesh Yogi, see Paul Saltzman, *The Beatles in Rishikesh* (New York, NY: Viking Studio, 2000); Paul Oliver, *Hinduism and the 1960s: The Rise of a Counter-Culture* (London: Bloomsbury, 2014), ch. 5; Jane Iwamura, *Virtual Orientalism: Asian Religions and American Popular Culture* (New York, NY: Oxford University Press, 2011), ch. 3.

135. Jeremy Hornsby, *Express*, 20 September 1967, 6.

136. Alix Palmer, *Express*, 2 October 1967, 8.
137. Donald Zec, *Mirror*, 6 October 1967, 17; Don Short, *Melody Maker*, 9 March 1968, 13.
138. See Turner, *Gospel*.
139. *The Frost Programme* (Rediffusion, 4 October 1967).
140. Cited in Jonathan Gould, *Can't Buy Me Love* (New York, NY: Three Rivers Press, 2008), 447; Barry Miles, *IT* 1, no. 23 (1968), 2.
141. Peregrine Worsthorne, *Sunday Telegraph*, 3 September 1967, 12.
142. Christopher Booker, *The Seventies: The Decade That Changed the Future* (New York, NY: Stein and Day, 1981), 328.
143. Monica Furlong, *Mail*, 30 July 1964, 3.
144. Monica Furlong, *The End of Our Exploring* (New York, NY: Coward, McCann & Geoghegan, 1973), 116, 113, 114.
145. Ibid., 114–18.
146. For the Beatles and India, see Peter Lavezzoli, *The Dawn of Indian Music in the West* (London: A&C Black, 2006), ch. 9; David Reck, 'The Inner Light: George Harrison's Indian Songs' and Monika Kocot, 'The Indian Beatle(s), From "Norwegian Wood" to "The Hare Krishna Mantra": Indian Influences on the Lyrics and Music of the Beatles', in *Fifty Years with the Beatles: The Impact of the Beatles on Contemporary Culture*, ed. Jerzy Jarniewicz and Alina Kwiatkowska (Łódź: Łódź University Press, 2010).
147. Nigel Gosling, *Observer*, 18 January 1970, 31.
148. Desmond Shawe-Taylor, *Sunday Times*, 16 June 1968, 51.
149. John Grigg, *Guardian*, 6 October 1966, 16; Mellers, *Twilight*, 183.
150. Wilfrid Mellers, *Harper's Bazaar* 100, no. 3068 (1967), 44–5, 113.
151. Cited in Burger, *Lennon On Lennon*, 64. See also Ali and Blackburn, 9. For attitudes to mixed marriages, see Clive Webb, 'Special Relationships: Mixed-Race Couples in Post-War Britain and the United States', *Women's History Review* 26, no. 1 (2017), 110–29; Marcus Collins, 'Pride and Prejudice: West Indian Men in Mid-Twentieth-Century Britain', *Journal of British Studies* 40, no. 3 (2001), 405–410.
152. *Private Eye*, 24 May 1968, 12; Malcolm Muggeridge, 'Looking through the Eye (1976)', in *Seeing Through the Eye: Malcolm Muggeridge on Faith*, ed. Cecil C. Kuhne III (San Francisco, CA: Ignatius Press, 2005), 94; Malcolm Muggeridge, *Listener*, 21 September 1967, 367.
153. Cited in Tom Scott, *Gandalf's Garden*, no. 2 (1968), 5.
154. Neville Maxwell, *Times*, 14 October 1967, 9; Richard Mabey, *The Pop Process* (London: Hutchinson Educational, 1969), 23; Henry Fairlie, *Encounter*, August 1971, 3–13.
155. George Melly, *Observer*, 4 June 1967, 21; Nik Cohn, *Awopbopaloobop Alopbamboom: Pop from the Beginning* (London: Minerva, 1969), 126; Charles Shaar Murray, *NME*, 25 May 1974, www.rocksbackpages.com

/Library/SearchLinkRedirect?folder=the-beatles-silly-charlie-and-the-not-so
-red-hot-pepper.

156. Melly, *Revolt into Style*, 115; Tony Palmer, *All You Need Is Love: The Story of Popular Music* (Harmondsworth: Penguin, 1977), 177.

157. Jeremy Hornsby, *Express*, 18 July 1967, 6; Donald Walker, *Mirror*, 26 September 1969, 9. Frank Zappa and Timothy Leary were the other archetypal hippies mentioned in the article.

158. For student radicalism, see David Fowler, *Youth Culture in Modern Britain, c. 1920–c. 1970: From Ivory Tower to Global Movement – a New History* (Basingstoke: Palgrave Macmillan, 2008), ch. 8; Caroline Hoefferle, *British Student Activism in the Long Sixties* (London: Routledge, 2012).

159. John Prince, *Telegraph*, 7 September 1967, 26; Anne Crichton, *New Society*, 15 April 1965, 20; Bryan Wilson, 'The Needs of Students (1965)', in *The Youth Culture and the Universities* (London: Faber and Faber, 1970), 126; L. Neville Brown, 'Student Protest in England', *American Journal of Comparative Law* 17, no. 3 (1969), 395.

160. Paul Barker and John Hanvey, *New Society*, 27 November 1969, 847; NOP, *Report on Attitudes Towards Crime, Violence and Permissiveness in Society* (London: NOP, 1970), 43.

161. Anne Scott-James, *Mail*, 5 October 1967, 6.

162. *Mirror*, 19 June 1967, 2.

163. Michael Wood, *New Society*, 27 June 1968, 949.

164. Alix Palmer, *Express*, 31 August 1967, 4.

165. Godfrey Winn, *Mail*, 2 September 1967, 6. See also Arnold Lunn and Garth Lean, *Christian Counter-Attack* (London: Blandford, 1969), 36.

166. John Sparrow, *Sunday Times*, 6 September 1970, 25.

167. Rudolf Klein, *Observer*, 20 October 1968, 10. Klein was referring to Lennon's statement that 'Beethoven is a con, just like we are now. He was just knocking out a bit of work, that was all' (cited in Hunter Davies, *The Beatles: The Authorised Biography* (New York, NY: McGraw-Hill, 1968), 321).

168. Peter Simple, *Telegraph*, 16 November 1967, 18.

169. For the peace movement, see Holger Nehring, *Politics of Security: British and West German Protest Movements and the Early Cold War, 1945–1970* (Oxford: Oxford University Press, 2013).

170. Glyndwr Chambers, *Beatles Book*, July 1969, 19.

171. For McCartney's views on just wars, see Gavin Martin, *Independent*, 15 November 2001, www.rocksbackpages.com/article.html?ArticleID=5564.

172. Cited in Cleave, *Standard*, 18 March 1966, 8.

173. Dilys Powell, *Sunday Times*, 22 October 1967, 51; Gillian Ingham, *Mail*, 25 July 1967, 6.

174. John Lennon and Yoko Ono, 'Amsterdam', *Wedding Album* (Apple, 1969); Lennon cited in Philip Evans, *Telegraph*, 26 November 1969, 1.

175. John Lennon, interview by Marshall McLuhan, 19 December 1969, www
.beatlesinterviews.org/db1969.1219.beatles.html.

176. *Frendz*, 29 May 1970, 6; Frendz, 16 September 1971, 4.

177. John Hoyland, *Black Dwarf* 13, no. 7 (1968), 6.

178. John Lennon, *Black Dwarf* 13, no. 9 (1969), 4; John Hoyland, *Black Dwarf* 14,
no. 24 (1969), 7.

179. Ibid., 7.

180. *Melody Maker*, 13 August 1966, 1; Frost, 10.

181. See Peter Mandler, *The English National Character: The History of an Idea
from Edmund Burke to Tony Blair* (New Haven, CT: Yale University Press,
2006), ch. 6.

182. Virginia Ironside, *Mail*, 1 August 1968, 6; Robert Pitman, *Express*, 7 August
1968, 6.

183. Don Short, *Mirror*, 26 October 1968, 9.

184. Desmond Morris in *Man of the Decade*.

185. Palmer, *Born*, 192.

186. Cited in Derek Taylor, *Fifty Years Adrift* (Guildford: Genesis Publications,
1984), 382.

187. Michael Steemson, *Express*, 1 September 1967, 4; A. C. Bhaktivedanta Swami
Prabhupāda, *Search for Liberation: Featuring a Conversation between John
Lennon and Swami Bhaktivedanta* (Los Angeles, CA: Bhaktivedanta Book
Trust, 1981), 4.

188. Peter Finch, *Gandalf's Garden*, no. 2 (1968), 15.

189. Ibid., 15; Audrey Slaughter cited in Taylor, *Fifty Years Adrift*, 382;
B. P. Fallon, *Melody Maker*, 19 April 1969, 16; Derek Taylor, *Disc and
Music Echo*, 30 November 1968, www.rocksbackpages.com/Library/
SearchLinkRedirect?folder=john-lennon-fighting-the-good-fight-with-all-of
-his-might.

190. Taylor, *Fifty Years Adrift*, 340.

191. Derek Taylor, *Disc and Music Echo*, 30 November 1968.

192. Derek Taylor, sleeve notes for *Yellow Submarine* (Apple, 1969).

193. Cited in Brenda Giuliano and Geoffrey Giuliano, eds., *Things We Said Today:
Conversations with the Beatles* (Holbrook, MA: Adams Media Corporation,
1998), 237; Derek Taylor, *As Time Goes By: Living in the Sixties with John
Lennon, Paul McCartney* . . . (London: Straight Arrow Books, 1973), 178, 116;
cited in Walsh, *Melody Maker*, 7 December 1968, 18; cited in Martin Lewis,
Variety, 26 November 2007, 11.

194. O'Mahony, 14.

195. Frederick James, *Beatles Book*, May 1967, 7, 31; Mal Evans and Neil Aspinall,
Beatles Book, April 1967, 10–12; Frederick James, *Beatles Book*, August 1967,
24–7.

196. Frederick James, *Beatles Book*, May 1967, 31.

197. *Beatles Book*, June 1967, 2.

198. Steve Turner, *Beatles Book*, October 1969, 13.

199. *Beatles Book*, November 1968, 2.

200. Billy Shepherd, *Beatles Book*, December 1969, 28.

201. Ibid., 28.

202. Joyce Nobbs, *Beatles Book*, March 1969, 19.

203. Harrison cited in Ray Coleman, *Disc and Music Echo*, 10 August 1968, in Sandercombe, *Beatles*, 242.

204. John Lennon, *Skywriting by Word of Mouth* (New York, NY: HarperCollins, 1987), 15.

205. Anne Scott-James, *Mail*, 14 November 1963, 10; Anne Scott-James, *Mail*, 5 October 1967, 6. McCartney's comment originally appeared in Norrie Drummond, *NME*, 9 September 1967, 3.

206. Vincent Mulchrone, *Mail*, 27 November 1969, 10; Mulchrone, *Mail*, 21 October 1963, 8.

207. Mulchrone, *Mail*, 4 January 1965, 6; Mulchrone, *Mail*, 27 November 1969, 10.

208. Winn, *Mail*, 2 September 1967, 6.

209. Winn, *Mail*, 2 April 1969, 10.

210. Virginia Ironside, *Mail*, 19 May 1967, 8.

211. Idem, *Mail*, 1 August 1968, 6.

212. Idem, *Mail*, 1 October 1969, 3.

213. Cited in Scott, 5.

214. Cited in Andy Davis, *The Beatles Files* (London: MetroBooks, 2000), 116.

215. *Sunday Times*, 8 September 1968, 2.

216. Gould, *Can't Buy Me Love*, 497.

217. Ned Sherrin, *Spectator*, 10 November 1968, 16; Bill Grundy, *Spectator*, 12 September 1968, 9.

218. Francis Williams, *Punch*, 11 September 1968, 265.

219. Alan Walsh, *Melody Maker*, 17 August 1968, 14; Gordon Brook-Shepherd, *Sunday Telegraph*, 11 August 1968, 14; Ironside, *Mail*, 1 August 1968, 6; *Private Eye*, 30 August 1968, 7.

220. Don Short, *Mirror*, 26 August 1968, 9; 'The Beatles' Top 50 Biggest Selling Songs Revealed', Official Charts, 27 August 2015, www.officialcharts.com/chart-news/the-official-top-50-biggest-selling-beatles-singles-revealed__10575/. The sales figures for the single include those for the 1986 and 1988 reissues, when it respectively reached number 12 and number 52 in the charts.

221. Shepherd, 28.

222. Walsh, *Melody Maker*, 17 August 1968, 14; cited in Taylor, *Fifty Years Adrift*, 382.

223. Winn, *Mail*, 2 April 1969, 10.

224. Joanna Thomson, *Beatles Book*, October 1968, 19.

225. Diana Cavaghan, *Beatles Book*, August 1967, 18; Lucy Weir, *Beatles Book*, August 1967, 18.

226. Alison Moss, *Beatles Book*, August 1967, 19; American College Student, *Beatles Book*, July 1969, 18; Derrick Harrison, *Beatles Book*, June 1969, 18.

227. Wendy Sandiford, *Beatles Book*, November 1968, 19; Ken Kingborn, *Beatles Book*, May 1969, 19; Nobbs, 19; Chambers, 19.

228. Derrick Harrison, 18.

229. McCartney cited in *Melody Maker*, 14 September 1968, 5.

230. Cited in Jack Hutton, *Melody Maker*, 2 December 1967, in Sandercombe, *Beatles*, 222.

231. Cited in Judith Simons and Arnold Latcham, *Express*, 1 April 1968, 9; John Lennon and Yoko Ono, interview by David Wigg, 8 May 1969, www .beatlesinterviews.org/db1969.0331.beatles.html.

232. Andru J. Reeve, *Turn Me On, Dead Man: The Beatles and the Paul Is Dead Hoax* (Bloomington, IN: AuthorHouse, 2004).

233. Anthony Fawcett, *John Lennon: One Day at a Time* (New York, NY: Grove Press, 1981), 77.

234. Lennon cited in Maureen Cleave, *Standard*, 2 February 1963, 9.

235. Victor Unit, *Frendz*, 15 May 1970, 39.

236. Felicity Green, *Mirror*, 8 August 1968, 7; Zec, *Mirror*, 18 December 1969, 13; James Wilson, *Mirror*, 28 March 1969, 3.

237. 'Should a Pop Singer Discuss Teenage Sex Problems in Public?', *Melody Maker*, 3 February 1963, 2.

238. 'Sex in Songs', *Melody Maker*, 22 June 1963, 6.

239. *Music and Life*, no. 26 (1965), 4; David Griffiths, *Listener*, 30 July 1964, 935.

240. Tony Barrow cited in Peter Doggett, *There's a Riot Going On: Revolutionaries, Rock Stars and the Rise and Fall of '60s Counter-Culture* (Edinburgh: Canongate, 2007), 16.

241. Ray Coleman, *Lennon* (New York, NY: McGraw-Hill, 1986), 330.

242. Cynthia Lennon, *A Twist of Lennon* (London: Star Books, 1978), 163.

243. Joan Peyser, *New York Times*, 29 September 1968, BR7; Jann Wenner, *Rolling Stone*, 26 October 1968, 16. As late as 1973, Tony Palmer expressed uncertainty over whether 'Brian Epstein may or may not have been a repressed homosexual' (Tony Palmer, *New Society*, 15 November 1973, 416).

244. Harold Fielding cited in *Express*, 12 December 1963, 4. See also Cassandra, *Mirror*, 4 June 1964, 6.

245. Anonymous psychiatrist cited in Scott-James, *Mail*, 14 November 1963, 10; Monica Furlong, *Mail*, 8 November 1963, 18.

246. *Mirror*, 6 November 1963, 2; *Express*, 13 February 1964, 8.

247. Cyril Dunn and Peter Dunn, *Observer*, 10 November 1963, 29.

248. Chris Welch, *Melody Maker*, 21 August 1965, 14.

249. Mike Hennessey, *Melody Maker*, 25 September 1965, 10.

250. Ibid., 11.

251. *Melody Maker*, 10 September 1966, 3. For the role of groupies in sixties pop, see Lisa Rhodes, *Electric Ladyland: Women and Rock Culture* (Philadelphia, PA: University of Pennsylvania Press, 2005), chs. 4–6.

252. For censorship of pop, see Martin Cloonan, 'You Can't Do That: The Beatles, Artistic Freedom and Censorship', in *The Beatles, Popular Music and Society*, ed. Ian Inglis (Basingstoke: Springer, 2000), 126–49; Martin Cloonan, *Banned! Censorship of Popular Music in Britain, 1967–92* (London: Arena, 1996).

253. David Mairowitz, *IT*, no. 47 (1969), 14.

254. See Claire Langhamer, 'Adultery in Post-War England', *History Workshop Journal*, no. 62 (2006), 86–115.

255. Cited in Carol Clerk, *Uncut*, 2003, www.rocksbackpages.com/Library/Article/the-ballad-of-john–yoko.

256. Public attitudes to illegitimacy during the period drew a distinction between culpable parents and their blameless offspring. The media were held to be at least partly responsible, with celebrities having children out of wedlock thought to exert a particularly baleful influence upon impressionable young females (NOP, *Report on Attitudes*, 56). For a history of the topic, see Pat Thane and Tanya Evans, *Sinners? Scroungers? Saints? Unmarried Motherhood in Twentieth-Century England* (Oxford: Oxford University Press, 2012).

257. Epstein, *A Cellarful of Noise*, 109.

258. Hennessey, *Melody Maker*, 25 September 1965, 10.

259. Cited in Dawn James, *Rave*, March 1966, 6.

260. *Melody Maker*, 13 August 1966, 8.

261. *People* (1966) cited in Michael Hollingshead, *The Man Who Turned on the World* (London: Blond and Briggs, 1973), www.psychedelic-library.org/holl6.htm.

262. Marcus Collins, 'Permissiveness on Trial: Sex, Drugs, Rock, the Rolling Stones and the Sixties Counterculture', *Popular Music and Society* 42, no. 2 (2019), 188–209. For drugs and the British counterculture, see Andy Roberts, *Albion Dreaming: A Popular History of LSD in Britain* (London: Marshall Cavendish, 2008); Antonio Melechi, ed., *Psychedelia Britannica: Hallucinogenic Drugs in Britain* (London: Turnaround, 1997); Alex Mold, '"The Welfare Branch of the Alternative Society?" The Work of Drug Voluntary Organization Release, 1967–1978', *Twentieth Century British History* 17, no. 1 (2005), 50–73; John Davis, 'The London Drug Scene and the Making of Drug Policy, 1965–73', *Twentieth Century British History* 17, no. 1 (2006), 26–49; Jock Young, *The Drugtakers: The Social Meaning of Drug Use* (London: MacGibbon and Kee, 1971).

263. McCartney praised Leary in a *Punch* interview later in 1966 (cited in Patrick Skene Catling, *Punch*, 23 November 1966, 770).

264. Cited in ibid., 770; Robert Pitman, *Express*, 24 May 1967, 10.

265. Cited in *Mirror*, 3 December 1966, 21. For the circumstances of the ban, see Gordon Thompson, '"A Day in the Life": The Beatles and the BBC,

May 1967', in *The Oxford Handbook of Music Censorship*, ed. Patricia Hall (Oxford: Oxford University Press, 2017).

266. In his excellent study of the Beatles' drug use, Joe Goodden notes that the Beatles had first referred to LSD in an interview for the American *Datebook* magazine in 1965. However, McCartney was the first Beatle to admit to using drugs almost two years later (Joe Goodden, *Riding So High: The Beatles and Drugs* (London: Pepper & Pearl, 2017, n.p.)).

267. Walsh, *Melody Maker*, 17 August 1968, 14. See also Don Short, *Mirror*, 29 April 1969, 23.

268. *Beatles Book*, February 1969, 2; *Beatles Book*, January 1967, 10–12; *Beatles Book*, February 1967, 9–11; *Beatles Book*, March 1967, 8–11; *Beatles Book*, October 1967, 9–11; *Beatles Book*, November 1967, 13–14.

269. *Beatles Book*, August 1968, 2. See also Freda Kelly, *Beatles Book*, September 1968, 4.

270. Sandiford, 19. See also Ryk Lussenburg, *Beatles Book*, September 1968, 19.

271. Lilian Hunter, Janet Brown and Dorothy Wilson, *Beatles Book*, March 1969, 18.

272. O'Mahony, 15.

273. *Melody Maker*, 19 August 1967, 11; Adrian Mitchell, *Listener*, 3 October 1968, 447.

274. Don Short, *Mirror*, 23 November 1967, 25.

275. Thompson, *Ban This Filth!*, 87–88.

276. *Sunday Times*, 9 March 1969, 49.

277. Cited in Donald Zec, *Mirror*, 16 October 1968, 7; cited in *Express*, 4 February 1970, 1. For Lennon's art, see Jon Wiener, 'Pop and the Avant-Garde: The Case of John and Yoko', *Popular Music and Society* 22, no. 1 (1998), 1–16; Wulf Herzogenrath and Dorothee Hansen, eds., *John Lennon: Drawings, Performances, Films* (Berlin: Cantz, 1995).

278. Bernard Levin, *Mail*, 29 April 1970, 6; Barbara Griggs, *Express*, 17 January 1970, 6.

279. Ibid., 6.

280. Gosling, *Observer*, 18 January 1970, 31.

281. Irving Wardle, *Times*, 28 July 1970, 7.

282. Cited in *Express*, 29 July 1967, 5.

283. Cited in Tim Hewat, *Rolling Stones File* (London: Panther, 1967), 114.

284. Palmer, *Observer*, 17 November 1968, 24.

285. Taylor, *Disc and Music Echo*, 30 November 1968.

286. Chris Welch, *Melody Maker*, 21 October 1967, 15.

287. *IT*, no. 53 (1969), 14.

288. Cited in John Lowe, *The Warden: A Portrait of John Sparrow* (London: HarperCollins, 1998), 171.

289. Bryan Wilson, 'The Social Context of the Youth Problem (1965)', in *Youth Culture*, 165.

290. Cited in Lowe, *Warden*, 171.

291. Booker, *Neophiliacs*, 65. For a Marxist version of the same argument, see Charles Parker, 'Pop Song, the Manipulated Ritual', in *The Black Rainbow: Essays on the Present Breakdown of Culture*, ed. Peter Abbs (London: Heinemann Educational, 1975), 146.

292. Cited in *Times*, 21 October 1967, 1.

293. Scott-James, *Mail*, 5 October 1967, 6.

294. Marjorie Proops, *Mirror*, 9 November 1968, 7.

295. Cited in *Express*, 29 September 1971, 7.

296. Cited in *Catholic Herald*, 4 August 1967, 2; cited in *Express*, 31 July 1967, 6. Mervyn Stockwood's 'South Bank theology' was not permissive to the point of espousing atomised individualism.

297. *Express*, 9 September 1967, 5; Norman Solomon cited in Tony Bramwell and Rosemary Kingsland, *Magical Mystery Tours: My Life with the Beatles* (Basingstoke: Macmillan, 2006), 220.

298. Unnamed BBC official cited in *Mail*, 20 May 1967, 1.

299. *Mirror*, 19 June 1967, 2.

300. Robert Pitman, *Express*, 18 July 1967, 6; Alice Bacon, 28 July 1967, *Debates (Commons)*, vol. 751, col. 1163.

301. Edward Lee, *Music of the People: A Study of Popular Music in Great Britain* (London: Barrie & Jenkins, 1970), 250.

302. David Holbrook, 'Predatory Beatles', *The Use of English* 20 (1969), 212.

303. David Holbrook, *The Pseudo-Revolution: A Critical Study of Extremist 'Liberation' in Sex* (London: Tom Stacey, 1972), 128.

304. Ibid., 165.

305. Winn, *Mail*, 2 April 1969, 10.

306. *Melody Maker*, 1 July 1967, 9.

307. Barker and Hanvey, 848.

308. Ibid., 348.

Culture: The Beatles as Artists

1. William Mann, *Times*, 23 December 1963, 4.

2. Kenneth Tynan, *Observer*, 21 January 1968, 27.

3. For Ono's art, see Kevin Concannon, 'Yoko Ono's "Cut Piece": From Text to Performance and Back Again', *PAJ: A Journal of Performance and Art* 30.3 (2008), 81–93; Julia Bryan-Wilson, 'Remembering Yoko Ono's "Cut Piece"', *Oxford Art Journal* 26, no. 1 (2003), 101–23; Thomas Kellein, *Yoko Ono: Between the Sky and My Head* (Cologne: Walther Konig, 2008); Alexandra Munroe, ed., *YES Yoko Ono* (New York, NY: Japan Society, 2003).

4. Cited in Peter McCabe and Robert D. Schonfeld, *Apple to the Core: The Unmaking of the Beatles* (London: Martin Brian and O'Keeffe, 1972), 55.

5. Paul Gleed, 'The Rest of You, If You'll Just Rattle Your Jewelry: The Beatles and Questions of Mass and High Culture', in *Reading the Beatles: Cultural Studies, Literary Criticism, and the Fab Four*, ed. Kenneth Womack and Todd Davis (Binghamton, NY: SUNY Press, 2006), 164.

6. Mark Lewisohn, *Tune In: The Beatles – All These Years* (New York, NY: Crown Archetype, 2013), xi.

7. Matthew Schneider, *The Long and Winding Road from Blake to the Beatles* (Basingstoke: Palgrave Macmillan, 2008), viii.

8. Kenneth Womack, *Long and Winding Roads: The Evolving Artistry of the Beatles* (New York, NY: Continuum, 2007), 54.

9. Ibid., 129.

10. Ibid., 167; Mark Hertsgaard, *A Day in the Life: The Music and Artistry of the Beatles* (New York, NY: Delacorte Press, 1995), 317.

11. Fredric Jameson, 'Periodizing the 60s', *Social Text*, no. 9/10 (1984), 178–209; Kenneth Gloag, 'Situating the 1960s: Popular Music – Postmodernism – History', *Rethinking History* 5, no. 3 (2001), 397–410; Kenneth Gloag, 'The Beatles: High Modernism and/or Postmodernism?', in *Beatlestudies 3*, ed. Yrjö Heinonen (Jyväskylä: University of Jyväskylä, 2000), 79–84; Ed Whitley, 'The Postmodern White Album', in *The Beatles, Popular Music and Society: A Thousand Voices*, ed. Ian Inglis (New York, NY: St. Martin's Press, 2000); Gleed, 'The Rest of You, If You'll Just Rattle Your Jewelry'.

12. Cited in Alan Medanock, 'These Musical Times', *Musical Times* 105, no. 1451 (1964), 24.

13. Charles Greville, *Mail*, 28 December 1963, 4; Richard Buckle, *Buckle at the Ballet* (New York, NY: Atheneum, 1980), 362.

14. Nik Cohn, *Awopbopaloobop Alopbamboom: Pop from the Beginning* (London: Minerva, 1969), 128.

15. Cited in Jann Wenner, *Lennon Remembers*, rev. edn (London: Verso, 2000), 48.

16. Arthur Marwick, *The Explosion of British Society, 1914–1970* (Basingstoke: Macmillan, 1971), 175.

17. Ulf Lindberg, *Rock Criticism from the Beginning: Amusers, Bruisers, and Cool-Headed Cruisers* (New York, NY: Peter Lang, 2005), 72.

18. Oded Heilbronner, 'The Peculiarities of the Beatles: A Cultural-Historical Interpretation', *Cultural and Social History* 5, no. 1 (2008), 110.

19. See Womack, *Long*; Walter Everett, *The Beatles as Musicians: The Quarry Men through Rubber Soul* (New York, NY: Oxford University Press, 1999); Walter Everett, *The Beatles as Musicians: Revolver through the Anthology* (Oxford: Oxford University Press, 1999); Allan F. Moore, *The Beatles: Sgt. Pepper's Lonely Hearts Club Band* (Cambridge: Cambridge University Press, 1997).

20. Bernard Gendron, *Between Montmartre and the Mudd Club: Popular Music and the Avant-Garde* (Chicago, IL: University of Chicago Press, 2002), 162.

21. Ibid., 161, 203–24; Elijah Wald, *How the Beatles Destroyed Rock 'n' Roll: An Alternative History of American Popular Music* (Oxford: Oxford University Press, 2009), 246.
22. George Martin and William Pearson, *Summer of Love: The Making of Sgt. Pepper* (Basingstoke: Macmillan, 1994), 137.
23. Arthur Calder-Marshall, *TLS*, 4 July 1968, 708.
24. Cited in Barry Miles, *Paul McCartney: Many Years from Now* (London: Secker & Warburg, 1996), 124.
25. Derek Taylor, *As Time Goes By: Living in the Sixties with John Lennon, Paul McCartney . . .* (London: Straight Arrow Books, 1973), 177.
26. John Lennon and Yoko Ono, Ontario, interview by Marshall McLuhan, 19 December 1969, www.beatlesinterviews.org/db1969.1219.beatles.html.
27. Cited in Michael Watts, *Melody Maker*, 10 February 1971, www.rocksbackpages.com/Library/SearchLinkRedirect?folder=john-and-yoko-a-press-conference-at-apple.
28. David Fowler, *Youth Culture in Modern Britain, c. 1920–c. 1970: From Ivory Tower to Global Movement – a New History* (Basingstoke: Palgrave Macmillan, 2008), ch. 9.
29. Anthony Burgess, *Listener*, 17 October 1963, 626. For Burgess' attitudes to popular culture, see John J. Stinson, 'Anthony Burgess: Novelist on the Margin', *Journal of Popular Culture* 7, no. 1 (1973), 136–51.
30. Wilfrid Mellers, *Twilight of the Gods: The Music of the Beatles* (New York, NY: Viking Press, 1974), 86.
31. Olivier Julien, '"Their Production Will Be Second to None": An Introduction to *Sgt. Pepper*', in *Sgt. Pepper and the Beatles: It Was Forty Years Ago Today*, ed. Olivier Julien (Aldershot: Ashgate, 2008), 8.
32. Cited in Roy Hollingworth, *Melody Maker*, 9 October 1971, 21.
33. Cited in Miles, *Paul McCartney*, 124.
34. Entry for 25 February 1971 in John Lahr, ed., *The Diaries of Kenneth Tynan* (London: A&C Black, 2002), 29.
35. Entry for 15 June 1969 cited in Russell Davies, ed., *The Kenneth Williams Diaries* (London: HarperCollins, 1993), 352.
36. Arnold Wesker, *Six Sundays in January* (London: Jonathan Cape, 1971), 158; Arnold Wesker, cited in Michael Gill, *Three Swings on a Pendulum* (BBC One, 8 June 1967), www.bbc.co.uk/programmes/p00rzw31; Arnold Wesker, *Encounter*, November 1966, 7; *Desert Island Discs* (BBC Home Service, 7 November 1966), www.bbc.co.uk/programmes/p009y36x/segments.
37. Cited in Wenner, *Lennon Remembers*, 48.
38. Heilbronner, 'Peculiarities', 114.
39. Cited in Steve Turner, *Beat Instrumental*, May 1972, www.rocksbackpages.com/Library/SearchLinkRedirect?folder=nik-cohn-my-book-is-rubbish-but-its-the-best.
40. Cited in ibid. For Nik Cohn, see also Lindberg, *Rock Criticism*, ch. 4.5.

41. Gendron, *Between Montmartre*, 163.

42. Ibid., 163.

43. Ibid., 217–18. For the emergence of rock criticism, see Simon Frith, *Performing Rites: On the Value of Popular Music* (Cambridge, MA: Harvard University Press, 1998), pt. I; Steve Jones, 'Re-Viewing Rock Writing: The Origins of Popular Music Criticism', *American Journalism* 9, no. 1–2 (1992), 87–107; Barney Hoskyns, 'Music Journalism at 50', *Rock's Backpages*, 2013, www.rocksbackpages.com/Library/Article/music-journalism-at-50; Lindberg, *Rock Criticism*.

44. Ibid., 203.

45. Carl Belz, *The Story of Rock* (New York, NY: Oxford University Press, 1969), ch. 5.

46. Gendron, *Between Montmartre*, 224.

47. Ibid., 164. For distinctions between high and low culture in the modern era, see Lawrence W. Levine, *Highbrow/Lowbrow: The Emergence of Cultural Hierarchy in America* (Cambridge, MA: Harvard University Press, 1990).

48. Edward Shils, *Encounter*, April 1955, 11. For postwar British intellectual life, see Stefan Collini, *Absent Minds: Intellectuals in Britain* (Oxford: Oxford University Press, 2006); Peter Mandler and Susan Pedersen, eds., *After the Victorians: Private Conscience and Public Duty in Modern Britain* (London: Routledge, 2005); Paul T. Phillips, *Contesting the Moral High Ground: Popular Moralists in Mid-Twentieth-Century Britain* (Toronto: McGill-Queen's University Press, 2013); Neil Nehring, *Flowers in the Dustbin: Culture, Anarchy and Postwar England* (Ann Arbor, MI: University of Michigan Press, 1993); Jonathan Rose, *The Intellectual Life of the British Working Classes* (New Haven, CT: Yale University Press, 2010); Noel Annan, *Our Age: Portrait of a Generation* (London: Weidenfeld and Nicolson, 1990); Alastair Davies and Alan Sinfield, *British Culture of the Post-War: An Introduction to Literature and Society 1945–1999* (London: Routledge, 2013); Peter Mandler, 'Two Cultures – One – Or Many?', in *The British Isles since 1945*, ed. Kathleen Burk (Oxford: Oxford University Press, 2003).

49. Roger Ballard, 'Britain's Visible Minorities: A Demographic Overview' (1999), CrossAsia-Repository, 5, http://crossasia-repository.ub.uni-heidelberg.de/286/1/demography.pdf.

50. Colin MacInnes, 'Pop Songs and Teenagers (1958)', in *England, Half English* (London: MacGibbon & Kee, 1961), 46, 45.

51. For British intellectuals and twentieth-century popular culture, see Dennis L. Dworkin, *Cultural Marxism in Postwar Britain: History, the New Left, and the Origins of Cultural Studies* (Durham, NC: Duke University Press, 1997), ch. 3; Simon Frith and Jon Savage, 'Pearls and Swine: Intellectuals and the Media', *NLR* 198 (1993), https://newleftreview.org/issues/I198/articles/jon-savage-simon-frith-pearls-and-swine-intellectuals-and-the-media; D. L. LeMahieu, *A Culture for Democracy: Mass Communication and the*

Cultivated Mind in Britain between the Wars (Oxford: Clarendon, 1988); Adrian Bingham, 'Cultural Hierarchies and the Interwar British Press', in *Middlebrow Literary Cultures: The Battle of the Brows, 1920–1960*, ed. Erica Brown and Mary Grover (Basingstoke: Springer, 2011).

52. Richard Hoggart, *The Uses of Literacy: Aspects of Working-Class Life with Special Reference to Publications and Entertainments* (Harmondsworth: Pelican, 1958), 202–5; Francis Newton, *The Jazz Scene* (London: MacGibbon & Kee, 1959); T. R. Fyvel, *The Insecure Offenders: Rebellious Youth in the Welfare State* (Harmondsworth: Penguin, 1966), 328.

53. This critique was most famously (but by no means exclusively) developed by Theodor Adorno; see *The Culture Industry: Selected Essays on Mass Culture* (London: Routledge, 2005), ch. 1. For the British music industry in the twentieth century, see Gordon Thompson, *Please Please Me: Sixties British Pop, Inside Out* (New York, NY: Oxford University Press, 2008); Simon Frith, 'The Popular Music Industry' and Will Straw, 'Consumption', in *The Cambridge Companion to Pop and Rock*, ed. Simon Frith, Will Straw and John Street (Cambridge: Cambridge University Press, 2010); James Nott, *Music for the People: Popular Music and Dance in Interwar Britain* (Oxford: Oxford University Press, 2002), pt. I; David Harker, *One for the Money: Politics and Popular Song* (London: Hutchinson, 1980); Mary Harron, 'McRock: Pop as a Commodity', in *Facing the Music*, ed. Simon Frith (New York, NY: Pantheon, 1988), 173–220.

54. Humphrey Lyttleton, *Spectator*, 30 July 1964, 10.

55. Brian Epstein, *A Cellarful of Noise* (New York, NY: Doubleday, 1964), 82.

56. Cited in Noel Whitcomb, *Mirror*, 22 October 1963, 16.

57. Mann, *Times*, 23 December 1963, 4.

58. Ibid., 4.

59. Cited in Charles Greville, *Mail*, 9 January 1964, 4.

60. Stuart Hall and Paddy Whannel, *The Popular Arts* (London: Hutchinson Educational, 1964), 310.

61. Ibid., 307, 310.

62. Brian Groombridge and Paddy Whannel, *NLR* I, no. 1 (1960), 54.

63. Mann, *Times*, 23 December 1963, 4.

64. Ibid., 4.

65. Hall and Whannel, *Popular Arts*, 312.

66. Terry Eagleton, 'New Bearings: The Beatles', *Blackfriars* 65, no. 4 (1964), 176.

67. Adrian Mitchell, *Mail*, 1 February 1963, 10; McCartney cited in ibid., 10.

68. Tony Barrow, sleeve notes for *Please Please Me* (Parlophone, 1963).

69. *Guardian*, 27 July 1964, 4. For the reception of *A Hard Day's Night*, see Andrew Caine, *Interpreting Rock Movies: The Pop Film and Its Critics in Britain* (Manchester: Manchester University Press, 2004), ch. 6; Stephen Glynn, *A Hard Day's Night* (London: I. B. Tauris, 2005).

70. For Lennon's writings, see James Sauceda, *The Literary Lennon* (Ann Arbor, MI: Pierian Press, 1984); Jörg Helbig, 'John Lennon as a Writer: Shun the Punman!', in *John Lennon: Drawings, Performances, Films*, ed. Wulf Herzogenrath and Dorothee Hansen (Berlin: Cantz, 1995).

71. Cited in Michael Braun, *Love Me Do: The Beatles' Progress* (Harmondsworth: Penguin, 1964), 68.

72. Donald Hughes, 'Recorded Music', in *Discrimination and Popular Culture*, ed. Denys Thompson (Harmondsworth: Penguin, 1964), 154, 173; Roy Nash, *Mail*, 6 February 1964, 8.

73. Lyttleton, *Spectator*, 30 July 1964, 10.

74. Francis Newton, *New Statesman*, 8 November 1963, 673.

75. Duncan Ranking cited in *Express*, 10 December 1963, 4.

76. Ibid., 4.

77. A. Alvarez, *Spectator*, 12 November 1964, 300.

78. Ibid., 300.

79. Malcolm Muggeridge, *TV Guide*, 3 June 1965, 22.

80. Michael Wood, *New Society*, 27 June 1968, 949; Eagleton, 176.

81. For Carroll's influence on Lennon, see Michael E. Roos, 'The Walrus and the Deacon: John Lennon's Debt to Lewis Carroll', *Journal of Popular Culture* 18, no. 1 (1984), 19–29.

82. John Wain, *New Republic*, 7 August 1965, 20; Jonathan Miller, *TLS*, 6 August 1964, 703; Hilary Corke, *Listener*, 24 June 1965, 959.

83. M. M. Carlin, 'Love on Film', *Transition*, no. 17 (1964), 37.

84. Gerald Kaufman, *Listener*, 23 July 1964, 131.

85. Kenneth Tynan, 'Review of *Help!* (1965)', in *The Beatles Literary Anthology*, ed. Mike Evans (London: Plexus, 2004), 144.

86. *Times*, 29 July 1965, 14; Patrick Gibbs, *Telegraph*, 30 July 1965, 19.

87. Donald Zec, *Mirror*, 28 July 1965, 7. For *Help!*, see Stephen Glynn, 'The Beatles' *Help!* Pop Art and the Perils of Parody', *Journal of British Cinema and Television* 8, no. 1 (2011), 23–43; King, 'Beatles in *Help!*'.

88. Cassandra, *Mirror*, 7 July 1964, 6.

89. Strix, *Spectator*, 15 November 1963, 621; cited in *Mail*, 5 March 1964, 16.

90. *Sunday Times*, 13 November 1966, 8.

91. Eric David Mackerness, *A Social History of English Music* (London: Routledge and Kegan Paul, 1964), 279.

92. Karl Dallas, *Singers of an Empty Day: Last Sacraments for the Superstars* (London: Kahn & Averill, 1971), 62.

93. *New Statesman*, 17 January 1964, 82.

94. Fritz Spiegl, *Listener*, 8 March 1979, 341.

95. Lyttleton, *Spectator*, 30 July 1964, 10.

96. Cited in Malcolm Keogh, *Mirror*, 7 October 1963, 25.

97. Peter Laurie, *The Teenage Revolution* (London: A. Blond, 1965), 76, 84. For the impact of Snow, see Guy Ortolano, *The Two Cultures Controversy:*

Science, Literature and Cultural Politics in Postwar Britain (Cambridge: Cambridge University Press, 2011).

98. Cassandra, *Mirror*, 13 March 1964, 6.

99. Martin Jackson, *Express*, 27 February 1964, 7; *Express*, 20 September 1963, 16.

100. Humphrey Lyttleton, *Melody Maker*, 4 April 1964, 7; cited in Bob Houston, *Melody Maker*, 18 April 1964, 12.

101. Cited in ibid., 12.

102. George Melly, *New Statesman*, 6 March 1964, 364; George Melly, *Owning Up: The Trilogy* (Harmondsworth: Penguin, 2006), 590–91.

103. Bob Dawburn, *Melody Maker*, 23 November 1963, 5. Ever the contrarian, Leicester's answer to Albert Camus, Colin Wilson, put the Beatles on a par with jazz music in 1964 in order to demonstrate that jazz was 'still a very long way from what is absurdly called "serious music"' (Colin Wilson, *Colin Wilson on Music* (London: Pan, 1967), 126–7).

104. Peter Chambers, *Express*, 20 April 1964, 8.

105. Marshall Pugh, *Mail*, 24 October 1963, 6; Neville Cardus, *Express*, 31 October 1963, 10.

106. Benedict Nightingale, *Guardian*, 2 April 1964, 7.

107. For folk music, see Michael Brocken, *The British Folk Revival: 1944–2002* (Aldershot: Ashgate, 2013).

108. Cited in *Express*, 19 December 1963, 6; Sid Chaplin, *Guardian*, 16 November 1963, 14.

109. Eric Clapton and Christopher Sykes, *Eric Clapton: The Autobiography* (London: Century, 2007), 42.

110. 'R.F.D.G.', *Telegraph*, 10 May 1965, 18.

111. Cited in Julius Fast, *The Beatles: The Real Story* (New York, NY: G. P. Putnam's Sons, 1968), 124.

112. For the denigration of mass culture as feminised, see Andreas Huyssen, *After the Great Divide: Modernism, Mass Culture, Postmodernism* (Bloomington, IN: Indiana University Press, 1988), ch. 3. For critics' animosity towards fans, see Joly Jenson, 'Fandom as Pathology: The Consequences of Characterization', in *The Adoring Audience: Fan Culture and Popular Media*, ed. Lisa A. Lewis (London: Routledge, 1992), 9–26.

113. Chaplin, 14.

114. Burgess, *Listener*, 17 October 1963, 626; Douglas Gillies, 'Teachers and Teenagers', *Musical Times* 105, no. 1459 (1965), 656.

115. Auberon Waugh, *Catholic Herald*, 8 November 1963, 5.

116. *Telegraph*, 2 November 1963, 8.

117. Cited in *Mail*, 5 March 1964, 16.

118. John Gross, *Observer*, 15 December 1963, 21.

119. Keith Roberts, 'London', *Burlington Magazine* 105, no. 729 (1963), 577.

120. David Holbrook, 'Quite Useful Neutrals', *The Use of English* 17, no. 3 (1966), 196.

121. Anthony Burgess, *Listener*, 2 April 1964, 566; cited in Tony Palmer, *Born under a Bad Sign* (London: William Kimber, 1970), 117.

122. Burgess, *Listener*, 17 October 1963, 626.

123. Zapple advertisement cited in Barry Miles, *In the Sixties* (London: Jonathan Cape, 2002), 258. For Zapple, see Barry Miles, *The Zapple Diaries: The Rise and Fall of the Last Beatles Label* (New York, NY: Abrams, 2016).

124. Karl Miller, *Listener*, 1 May 1969, 602.

125. Cited in Steve Turner, *Cliff Richard: The Biography* (Oxford: Lion Books, 2008), 103.

126. Geoffey Cannon and David Driver, *Guardian*, 23 July 2009, www .guardian.co.uk/global/2009/jul/23/gordon-burns-obituary-letters.

127. Tony Palmer, *Spectator*, 26 December 1970, 857. For contemporary controversies over swearing, see David Hendy, 'Bad Language and BBC Radio Four in the 1960s and 1970s', *Twentieth Century British History* 17, no. 1 (2006), 74–102.

128. Peter Clayton, *Gramophone*, October 1966, 233; Ivan March, ed., *The Great Records* (Blackpool: Long Playing Record Library, 1967).

129. For late sixties coverage of popular music on the BBC, see David Simonelli, 'BBC Rock Music Programming on Radio and Television and the Progressive Rock Audience, 1967–1973', *Popular Music History* 2, no. 1 (2007), 95–112.

130. Tony Palmer, 'All My Loving', *Omnibus* (BBC One, 3 November 1968); *Night Ride* (BBC Radio 1, 11 December 1968).

131. *Late Night Line-Up* (BBC Two, 19 September 1969); *Late Night Line-Up* (BBC Two, 10 December 1969).

132. Deryck Cooke, *Listener*, 26 December 1963, 1083; Deryck Cooke, *Listener*, 1 February 1968, 157.

133. George Melly, *Revolt into Style: The Pop Arts in Britain* (Harmondsworth: Penguin, 1970), 123; George Melly, *New Statesman*, 6 March 1964, 364.

134. Wilfrid Mellers, 'Music for 20th-Century Children. 3: The Teenager's World', *Musical Times* 105, no. 1457 (1964), 502, 501.

135. Ibid., 501; cited in Charles Greville, *Mail*, 6 August 1964, 4. Wilfrid Mellers, 'The Avant-Garde in America', *Proceedings of the Royal Musical Association* 90 (1963), 9; Wilfrid Mellers, 'Music for 20th-century Children. 3', 502.

136. Wilfrid Mellers, 'Review of Debussy, Preludes (Books I & II). Leonard Pennario', *Musical Times* 107, no. 1483 (1966), 784.

137. Wilfrid Mellers, *Harper's Bazaar* 100, no. 3068 (1967), 44.

138. Wilfrid Mellers, *New Statesman*, 2 June 1967, 770.

139. Ibid., 770.

140. Wilfrid Mellers, *Twilight of the Gods*.

141. Geoffrey Cannon, *Socialist Commentary*, January 1969, 43.

142. Richard Mabey, *The Pop Process* (London: Hutchinson Educational, 1969), 18.

143. Ibid., 18.

144. Ibid., 17.

145. Logue, *Times*, 26 July 1969, 17.

146. M. G. McNay, *Guardian*, 15 March 1967, 7. For Stuart Sutcliffe, see Pauline Sutcliffe, *The Beatles' Shadow: Stuart Sutcliffe & His Lonely Hearts Club* (London: Pan Macmillan, 2016); Lewisohn, *Tune In*.

147. Palmer, *Spectator*, 26 December 1970, 857.

148. Cited in Christopher Porterfield, *Time*, 22 September 1967, http://content .time.com/time/magazine/article/0,9171,837319,00.html.

149. Mabey, *Pop*, 15.

150. *Express*, 8 August 1966, 7; Judith Simons, *Express*, 19 May 1967, 6.

151. Derek Jewell, *Sunday Times*, 11 August 1968, 39.

152. Tim Souster, 'Notes on Pop Music', *Tempo*, no. 87 (1968–9), 2–6.

153. Jonathan Aitken, *The Young Meteors* (London: Secker & Warburg, 1967), 259.

154. Bob Dawburn, *Melody Maker*, 12 October 1968, 16–17.

155. Bernard Levin, *Pendulum Years: Britain and the Sixties* (London: Jonathan Cape, 1970), 318.

156. For the construction of the dichotomy between rock and pop, see Motti Regev, 'Producing Artistic Value: The Case of Rock Music', *Sociological Quarterly* 35, no. 1 (1994), 85–102; Simon Frith, *Sound Effects: Youth, Leisure and the Politics of Rock*, rev. edn (London: Constable, 1983), ch. 3; David Pattie, *Rock Music in Performance* (Basingstoke: Springer, 2007), ch. 4; Peter Wicke, *Rock Music: Culture, Aesthetics and Sociology* (Cambridge: Cambridge University Press, 1990), ch. 1; Matt Brennan, 'Down Beats and Rolling Stones: The American Jazz Press Decides to Cover Rock in 1967', *Popular Music History* 1, no. 3 (2004), 263–84; Wald, *How*; Marcus Collins, 'I Feel Free: The Worldview of British Rock and Pop Musicians, c. 1965–1975', in *Popular Culture in Britain and America, 1950–1975* (Cheltenham: Adam Matthew Digital, 2013), www .rockandroll.amdigital.co.uk; Stan Hawkins, *Pop Music and Easy Listening* (London: Routledge, 2017); Keir Keightley, 'The Historical Consciousness of Sunshine Pop', *Journal of Popular Music Studies* 23, no. 3 (2011), 343–61; Keir Keightley, 'Reconsidering Rock', in Frith, Straw and Street, eds., *Cambridge Companion*, 109–42.

157. For the Beatles and the origins of 'rock', see Sheila Whiteley, 'No Fixed Agenda: The Position of the Beatles within Popular/Rock Music', in *Beatlestudies 3*; John Covach, 'From "Craft" to "Art": Formal Structure in the Music of the Beatles', in *Reading the Beatles*; Stephen Valdez, 'It's All Too Much: The Beatles' Formal, Sonic, and Lyrical Contributions to the Change from Rock 'n' Roll to Rock' and Colin Campbell, 'From Romance to Romanticism: The Beatles 1964/5–1970', in *Fifty Years with the Beatles: The Impact of the Beatles on Contemporary Culture*, ed. Jerzy Jarniewicz and Alina Kwiatkowska (Łódź: Łódź University Press, 2010).

158. Jewell, *Sunday Times*, 11 August 1968, 39.

159. For musicians' attitudes to 'pop' and 'rock' in Britain, see Collins, 'I Feel Free'; Alan Clayson, *Beat Merchants: The Origins, History, Impact, and Rock Legacy of the 1960s British Pop Groups* (London: Blandford, 1995); Thompson, *Please Please Me*; Simonelli, *Working Class Heroes*.

160. Peter Noone cited in *Super Sound* (New York, NY: Benjamin Company, n.d.), 2; Alan Howard cited in Chris Welch, 'The Tremeloes: War of the Groups', *Melody Maker*, 3 February 1968, www.rocksbackpages.com/Library/SearchLinkRedirect?folder=the-tremeloes-war-of-the-groups; Mick Jackson cited in Chris Welch, 'Love Affair: A Love Affair to Remember', *Melody Maker*, 20 January 1968, www.rocksbackpages.com/Library/SearchLinkRedirect?folder=love-affair-a-love-affair-to-remember; Cilla Black, *What's It All About?* (London: Random House, 2009).

161. Cited in *Rolling Stone*, 11 May 1968, www.rollingstone.com/music/features/the-rolling-stone-interview-eric-clapton-19680511.

162. Cited in *The History of Rock 1967*, ed. John Mulvey (London: Time Inc., 2015), 110.

163. Jimmy Page (1976) and Jon Bonham (1970) cited in Hank Bordowitz, ed., *Led Zeppelin on Led Zeppelin: Interviews and Encounters* (Chicago, IL: Chicago Review Press, 2014), 198, 20.

164. Cited in 'Inside the Soft Machine', *Gandalf's Garden*, no. 5 (1969), 21.

165. Cited in Keith Altham, *NME*, 28 October 1966, www.rocksbackpages.com/Library/SearchLinkRedirect?folder=hollie-graham-nash-finds-his-face.

166. Cited in Richard Green, *Record Mirror*, 25 June 1966, https://web.archive.org/web/20141220163722/, http://davedeedozybeakymickandtich.nl/june-1966/; cited in Jan Nesbit, *NME*, 7 December 1968, www.beegees-world.com/archives113.html.

167. Frederick James, *Beatles Book*, August 1967, 24–27.

168. 'Editorial', *Beatles Book*, July 1967, 2; Jan Williams cited in James, *Beatles Book*, August 1967, 27.

169. Jan and Chris, *Beatles Book*, May 1967, 19; Ann Craig, *Beatles Book*, July 1967, 19.

170. Cited in Frederick James, *Beatles Book*, August 1967, 27; Janet and Susan, *Beatles Book*, August 1967, 19; Kristin Santose, *Beatles Book*, October 1967, 19.

171. Paul E. Willis, *Profane Culture* (Princeton, NJ: Princeton University Press, 2014), 89.

172. Ibid., 86.

173. Ibid., 86, 10, 204, 140.

174. Alan Walsh, *Melody Maker*, 14 September 1968, 10.

175. Maurice Rosenbaum, *Telegraph*, 29 November 1968, 16.

176. Cited in Benedict Nightingale, *Guardian*, 12 May 1966, 3.

177. Ian Breach, *Guardian*, 26 April 1967, 7; Hans Keller, *Listener*, 20 April 1967, 536; Jewell, *Sunday Times*, 11 August 1968, 39.

178. Ibid., 39.

179. Tony Palmer, *Observer*, 17 November 1968, 24.

180. Cooke, *New Statesman*, 20 March 1964, 448; Richard Middleton, *Pop Music and the Blues: A Study of the Relationship and Its Significance* (London: Victor Gollancz, 1972), 172; *Times*, 16 July 1966, 11; George Martin and Jeremy Hornsby, *All You Need Is Ears* (Basingstoke: Macmillan, 1979), 167.

181. Hollingworth, 21.

182. Palmer, *Born*, 22; Peter Heyworth and Tony Palmer, *Observer*, 1 February 1970, 758.

183. Palmer, *Born*, 19.

184. Ibid., 45, 125.

185. Cited in Hollingworth, 21.

186. Henry Pleasants, *Serious Music, and All That Jazz! An Adventure in Music Criticism* (London: Gollancz, 1969), 29.

187. Ibid., 29; cited in Hollingworth, 21.

188. Pleasants, *Serious Music*, 234.

189. Charles Reid, *Malcolm Sargent: A Biography* (New York, NY: Taplinger, 1970), 339; cited in Arnold Field, *Sunday Times*, 23 November 1969, 54.

190. Peter Maxwell Davies, *Yesterday (Lennon and McCartney)*, WoO 124, 1974; Peter Maxwell Davies cited in Kenneth Eastaugh, *Mirror*, 14 April 1969, 11; Kenneth Eastaugh, *Mirror*, 8 August 1970, 16; cited in Eastaugh, *Mirror*, 14 April 1969, 11; cited in *Express*, 7 August 1967, 6; cited in Wilfred De'Ath, *Listener*, 14 September 1967, 348.

191. Derek Jewell, *Sunday Times*, 28 September 1969, 59; William Mann, *Times*, 5 December 1969, 7.

192. Pleasants, *Serious Music*, 197.

193. Jewell, *Sunday Times*, 11 August 1968, 39.

194. Jewel, *Sunday Times*, 20 September 1970, 30.

195. Arthur Jacobs, *A Short History of Western Music* (Harmondsworth: Penguin, 1972), 347. Jacobs had in mind the Velvet Underground and the Grateful Dead, whereas Michael Wood touted Brian Wilson as the most innovative of popular musicians (Michael Wood, *New Society*, 2 January 1969, 374).

196. Tim Souster, *Listener*, 3 October 1968, 430.

197. *Sunday Times*, 29 December 1968, 5. For more positive assessments of Ono's music, see Shelina Brown, 'Scream from the Heart: Yoko Ono's Rock and Roll Revolution', in *Countercultures and Popular Music*, ed. Sheila Whiteley and Jedediah Sklower (London: Routledge, 2014); Barry Shank, 'Abstraction and Embodiment: Yoko Ono and the Weaving of Global Musical Networks', *Journal of Popular Music Studies* 18, no. 3 (2006), 282–300.

198. Victor Schonfield, *IT*, no. 58 (1969), 19. For avant-garde music in Britain, see Virginia Anderson, '"1968" and the Experimental Revolution in Britain', in *Music and Protest in 1968*, ed. Beate Kutschke and Barley Norton (Cambridge: Cambridge University Press, 2013); Robert Adlington, ed., *Sound*

Commitments: Avant-Garde Music and the Sixties (Oxford: Oxford University Press, 2009); David Addison, 'Politics, Patronage, and the State in British Avant-Garde Music, c.1959–c.1974', *Twentieth Century British History* 27, no. 2 (2016), 242–65.

199. Cooke, *Listener*, 1 February 1968, 157.
200. Cooke, *Listener*, 20 July 1968, 808; William Mann, *Times*, 22 November 1968, 9; Henry Pleasants, *Encounter*, April 1969, 94–5. See also Christopher Ballantine, *New Society*, 3 July 1969, 779, 781.
201. Cooke, *Listener*, 1 February 1968, 157.
202. Cooke, *Listener*, 26 December 1963, 1083.
203. Cited in Barry Miles, 'Miles Interviews Paul McCartney', *IT*, no. 6 (1967), http://oobujoobu.tumblr.com/post/6073808597/miles-interviews-paul-mccartney.
204. Wilfrid Mellers, *TLS*, 19 November 1971, 1454; William Mann, *Times*, 28 August 1967, 8; William Mann cited in Hollingworth, 21.
205. Deryck Cooke, *The Language of Music* (Oxford: Oxford University Press, 1959); Deryck Cooke, *I Saw the World End: A Study of Wagner's Ring* (Oxford: Oxford University Press, 1979); Pleasants, *Serious Music*, 77; Pleasants, *New York Times Magazine*, 13 March 1955, 14.
206. Pleasants, *Serious Music*, 95.
207. Miles, *Paul McCartney*, 237. For McCartney's experimental music, see Ian Peel, *The Unknown Paul McCartney: McCartney and the Avant-Garde* (London: Reynolds and Hearn, 2002).
208. Wood, *New Society*, 27 June 1968, 949; Peter Cole, 'Lyrics in Pop', in *Anatomy of Pop*, ed. Anthony Cash (London: British Broadcasting Corporation, 1970), 18; Philip Larkin, *Observer*, 9 October 1983, 32. The primitivist rock critic Nik Cohn considered the 'limp-wristed, pompous and fake' lyrics of *Abbey Road* (1969) as decidedly inferior to the 'real', 'personal' and 'evocative' language of their first recordings. Their lyrics came out poorly from Perry Anderson's comparison to the Stones', and resembled 'cave paintings' according to Michael Gray when judged against Bob Dylan's masterpieces (Nik Cohn, *New York Times*, 5 October 1969, sec. hi fi and recordings; Richard Merton, *NLR* I, no. 47 (1968), 29–31; Michael Gray, *Oz*, no. 7 (1967), 5).
209. Thom Gunn, *Listener*, 3 August 1967, 129.
210. John Willett, *TLS*, 25 August 1966, 763.
211. Mitchell, *Listener*, 3 October 1968, 447.
212. Christopher Logue, *Times*, 26 July 1969, 17.
213. Gunn, 129; cited in *TLS*, 4 December 1969, 1391.
214. Introduction to Paul McCartney, *Blackbird Singing: Poems and Lyrics 1965–1999* (London: Faber, 2001), xviii.
215. Gunn, 129. Strangely enough, W. H. Auden mused about using the Beatles as a cultural influence to 'bounce off' towards the end of his life (cited in Grevel Lindop, *TLS*, 3 July 1981, 759).

216. Logue, *Times*, 26 July 1969, 17.
217. Ibid., 17.
218. Ibid., 17.
219. D. A. N. Jones, *Listener*, November 1969, 648.
220. Harold Hobson, *Sunday Times*, 28 December 1969, 47.
221. Waring, *IT*, no. 52 (1969), 9. For Apple Theatre, see G. D. White, 'Digging for Apples: Reappraising the Influence of Situationist Theory on Theatre Practice in the English Counterculture', *Theatre Survey* 42, no. 2 (2001), 177–90.
222. For the Beatles' album covers, see Ian Inglis, '"Nothing You Can See That Isn't Shown": The Album Covers of the Beatles', *Popular Music* 20, no. 1 (2001), 83–97; and Ian Inglis, 'Cover Story: Magic, Myth and Music', in *Sgt. Pepper and the Beatles: It Was Forty Years Ago Today*, edited by Olivier Julien, 91–102 (Aldershot: Ashgate, 2007).
223. Adrian Henri, *TLS*, 6 August 1964, 707.
224. Edward Lucie-Smith, *Sunday Times*, 21 May 1967, 50. Lucie-Smith's mention of Mingus is an allusion to Adrian Henri's painting, *The Entry of Christ into Liverpool*, 1962–4. Adrian Henri's poems and art were major influences on the *Sgt. Pepper* cover, as I explain further in a forthcoming article.
225. Ibid., 50. See also John Willett, *Art in a City* (Liverpool: Bluecoat Society of Arts/Methuen, 1967), 167. For Liverpool's sixties art scene, see Simon Warner, *Text and Drugs and Rock'n'Roll: The Beats and Rock Culture* (London: A&C Black, 2013), ch. 4; Robert Knifton, 'Centre of the Creative Universe: Liverpool and the Avant-Garde' (PhD Thesis, Manchester Metropolitan University, 2007).
226. Elizabeth Bowen, *Vogue*, December 1968, 188–203.
227. Alan Aldridge, *The Beatles Illustrated Lyrics* (Boston, MA: Houghton Mifflin Harcourt, 1969), 9.
228. Logue, *Times*, 26 July 1969, 17; Gunn, 129.
229. Palmer, *Born*, 22.
230. William Mann, *Times*, 17 April 1970, 17; James Kirkup, 'Review of *Unwrinkling Plays* by Paul Reps', *Japan Quarterly* 12, no. 2 (1965), 261.
231. Cited in Steve Turner, 'The Beatles: *Sergeant Pepper*, the Inside Story Part II', Q, July 1987, www.rocksbackpages.com/Library/SearchLinkRedirect?folder=the-beatles-isgt-pepper-ithe-inside-story-part-ii; Alan W. Watts, 'Wealth versus Money (1969)', in *Does It Matter? Essays on Man's Relation to Materiality* (Novato, CA: New World Library, 2010), 12.
232. Melly, *Revolt into Style*, 123; Cooke, *Listener*, 1 February 1968, 157.
233. Tony Barrow, sleeve notes for *The Beatles' Hits* EP (Parlophone, 1963).
234. Clayton, 233.
235. Geoffrey Cannon, *Listener*, 4 July 1968, 17.
236. Palmer, *Born*, 66.
237. Wes Magee, *Tribune*, 5 September 1969, 10; entry for 25 February 1971 in Lahr, *Diaries of Kenneth Tynan*, 29.

238. Clive James, *Listener*, 30 April 1970, 574.

239. Ibid., 574.

240. *Telegraph*, 5 March 1964, 17.

241. Cited in Hunter Davies, *Sunday Times*, 15 June 1966, 9.

242. Stephen Spender, *Listener*, 23 March 1972, 366.

243. Malcolm Muggeridge, *TLS*, 17 August 1967, 743; Bryan Magee, *Listener*, 23 February 1967, 264.

244. Jack Westrup, 'Editorial', *Music & Letters* 49, no. 1 (1968), 1.

245. Fritz Spiegl, *Listener*, 8 January 1981, 60; Fritz Spiegl, *Listener*, 8 March 1979, 341.

246. Ibid., 341.

247. Michael Nyman, *Spectator*, 12 September 1968, 19.

248. *Sunday Times*, 13 November 1966, 8.

249. Ibid., 8.

250. Ibid., 8.

251. Ian Robinson, 'Paper Tygers, or the Circus Animals' Desertion in the New Pop Poetry', in *The Black Rainbow: Essays on the Present Breakdown of Culture*, ed. Peter Abbs (London: Heinemann Educational, 1975), 30; George Steiner, *In Bluebeard's Castle: Some Notes towards the Redefinition of Culture* (New Haven, CT: Yale University Press, 1974), 90.

252. Sandy Brown, *Listener*, 1 February 1973, 759.

253. Anthony Burgess, *Sunday Times*, 29 May 1966, 32.

254. Roy Fuller, *Professors and Gods: Last Oxford Lectures on Poetry* (London: André Deutsch, 1973), 86.

255. Murray Kempton, *Spectator*, 9 February 1966, 279.

256. *Times*, 20 July 1968, 9.

257. *Times*, 1 April 1967, 11.

258. Ibid., 11.

259. *Times*, 20 July 1968, 9.

260. Cited in *Sunday Times*, 29 September 1968, 15; Ruari Maclean, *TLS*, 7 December 1973, 1522; Alan Bold, *Marxism Today*, July 1971, 214.

261. Cited in Palmer, *Born*, 118. The same two songs later featured in Ruth Finnegan's *The Penguin Book of Oral Poetry* (London: Allen Lane, 1978).

262. Hunter Davies, *The Beatles: The Authorised Biography*, rev. edn (New York, NY: McGraw-Hill, 1985), xiv; Hunter Davies, *Sunday Times*, 18 September 1966, 11.

263. Anthony Burgess, *Punch*, 20 September 1967, 431.

264. Peter Dickinson, *Punch*, 9 August 1967, 205; 'Laureates Galore', *Punch*, 31 May 1967, 778.

265. Michael Smith, *Melody Maker*, 30 November 1968, 5.

266. Jillian Becker, *Times*, 2 August 1969, 17.

267. *Telegraph*, 15 November 1967, 16; James Thomas, *Express*, 27 December 1967, 4; Peter Black, *Mail*, 27 December 1967, 3; Bernard Levin, *Mail*, 29 December 1967, 4.

268. John Russell Taylor, *Times*, 22 May 1970, 7.

269. Ian Christie, *Express*, 11 September 1969, 15. For Lennon and Ono's experimental films, see Dorothee Hansen, 'The Films', in *John Lennon: Drawings, Performances, Films*, ed. Wulf Herzogenrath and Dorothee Hansen (Berlin: Cantz, 1995).

270. Cited in Philip Norman, 'Yoko Ono: Life Without John', *Sunday Times*, June 1981, www.rocksbackpages.com/Library/SearchLinkRedirect?folder=yoko-ono -life-without-john.

271. John Russell, *Sunday Times*, 3 May 1970, 32.

272. Eugene Schuster cited in Rodney Tyler, *Mail*, 28 April 1970, 7.

273. Cited in Palmer, *Born*, 117–18.

274. *Private Eye*, 7 June 1968, 5.

275. *Private Eye*, 13 September 1968, 5; *Private Eye*, 5 January 1968, 5; *Private Eye*, 16 April 1968, 1.

276. *Private Eye*, 1 March 1969, 13.

277. *Private Eye*, 1 October 1968, 8.

278. *Private Eye*, 5 July 1968, 7; *Private Eye*, 2 August 1968, 8.

279. The term was coined by Stefan Collini; see *Public Moralists: Political Thought and Intellectual Life in Britain 1850–1930* (Oxford: Clarendon Press, 1991).

280. Cited in Roy Fuller, *Owls and Artificers: Oxford Lectures on Poetry* (London: André Deutsch, 1971), 17.

281. Maurice Wiggin, *Sunday Times*, 31 December 1967, 20; Malcolm Muggeridge, *Catholic Herald*, 29 August 1969, 4.

282. Paul Long, *Only in the Common People: The Aesthetics of Class in Post-War Britain* (Newcastle: Cambridge Scholars, 2008), 221–53. See also Dave Laing, 'Scrutiny to Subcultures: Notes on Literary Criticism and Popular Music', *Popular Music* 13, no. 2 (1994), 179–90.

283. C. B. Cox, 'Editorial', *Critical Quarterly* 13, no. 3 (1971), 196.

284. Fuller, *Owls and Artificers*, 15.

285. Fuller, *TLS*, 13 April 1967, 305.

286. Fuller, *Owls and Artificers*, 12, 14. Fuller claimed in one of his poems that his reactionary opinions were primarily intended 'to raise a laugh', but Neil Powell notes their centrality to his world view (Neil Powell, 'An Aquarian Talent', in *Roy Fuller: A Tribute*, ed. A. Trevor Tolley (Toronto, ON: McGill-Queen's Press, 1993), 55).

287. Colin Mason, *Encounter*, April 1969, 93.

288. Edward Lee, *Music of the People: A Study of Popular Music in Great Britain* (London: Barrie & Jenkins, 1970), 258.

289. Ibid., 258.

290. Wain, 20.

291. Malcolm Muggeridge, *Listener*, 30 November 1967, 685.

292. Cited in Maurice Wiggin, *Sunday Times*, 9 April 1967, 52.

293. Charles Parker, 'Pop Song, the Manipulated Ritual', in Abbs, *Black Rainbow*, 139.

294. Ibid., 139. For Parker's acrimonious departure from the BBC, see Long, *Only*, 156–7.

295. Nyman, 19; Bill Grundy, *Spectator*, 12 September 1968, 9.

296. 'On Other Pages', *Punch*, 18 September 1968, 388–9.

297. For the politics of education, see Brian Simon, *Education and the Social Order: 1940–1990* (London: Lawrence & Wishart, 2000).

298. C. B. Cox, *Encounter*, April 1973, 209.

299. Max Beloff, 'The Challenge of Barbarism (1965)', in *The Intellectual in Politics and Other Essays* (New York, NY: Library Press, 1971), 47.

300. Anthony Burgess, *Spectator*, 3 March 1967, 11.

301. Ibid., 11.

302. Lee, *Music*, 207.

303. *Punch*, 25 September 1963, 452; *Punch*, 1 November 1967, 650.

304. D. F. Chorley and A. C. Nicholls, 'Letter', *The Use of English* 20, no. 1 (1968), 48.

305. David Holbrook, 'Predatory Beatles', *The Use of English* 20 (1969), 212.

306. Richard Hoggart, *Listener*, 16 December 1971, 837. For Hoggart and the Beatles, see James McGrath, 'John, Paul, George and Richard: The Beatles' Uses of Literacy', in *Richard Hoggart: Culture and Critique*, ed. Michael Bailey and Mary Eagleton (London: Critical, Cultural and Communications Press, 2011).

307. Marghanita Laski, *Listener*, 8 April 1965, 508.

308. Ibid., 508; cited in Andrew Loog Oldham, *2Stoned* (New York, NY: Random House, 2012), 304.

309. Cited in *The Stage and Television Today*, 17 March 1966, 1.

310. Roy Shaw, *Culture and Equality: The Role of Adult Education* (Keele: University of Keele, 1969), 5.

311. Ibid., 5.

312. Bryan Wilson, 'The War of the Generations (1964)', in *The Youth Culture and the Universities* (London: Faber and Faber, 1970), 100.

313. Bryan Wilson, 'The Social Context of the Youth Problem (1965)', in *Youth Culture*, 132.

314. Beloff, 'The Challenge of Barbarism', 47. The previous year, Paul Johnson had labelled those who took jazz seriously as 'treasonable clerks', but stopped short of blaming jazz critics for 'The Menace of Beatlism' (*New Statesman*, 28 February 1964, 326).

315. James Reeves, 'The World of Sergeant Pepper', *The Use of English* 19, no. 3 (1968), 235–40; Gunn, 129.

316. Wiggin, *Sunday Times*, 9 April 1967, 52; Roy Fuller, *Encounter*, December 1971, 44; Wesker, *Encounter*, November 1966, 4; Fuller, *Owls and Artificers*, 43; Donald Mitchell, *Socialist Commentary*, May 1967, 36.

317. Wesker, *Encounter*, November 1966, 4.

318. Ibid., 6, 4.

319. Bold, 214; George Lichtheim, *TLS*, 12 March 1970, 272.

320. Entry for 4 July 1965 in Graham Payn and Sheridan Morley, eds., *Noël Coward Diaries* (New York, NY: Da Capo Press, 2000), 603.

321. Beloff 'The Challenge of Barbarism'; Peter Simple, *Telegraph*, 16 November 1967, 18; Cox, *Encounter*, April 1973, 9.

322. Steiner, *In Bluebeard's Castle*, 63; cited in Tom Scott, *Gandalf's Garden*, no. 2 (1968), 5.

323. John Sparrow, *Listener*, 8 May 1969, 629.

324. Ibid., 629; John Sparrow, *Times*, 23 January 1971, 15. Sparrow was probably referring to Lennon's 1963 remark that 'I took a look at the original mouldy Mona Lisa in Paris – eccch, crap!' (cited in Braun, *Love Me Do*, 34).

325. *Civilisation: A Personal View* (BBC2, 23 February to 18 May 1969); Sparrow, *Listener*, 8 May 1969, 629.

326. Ibid., 629.

327. Ibid., 629.

328. Ibid., 629.

329. Christopher Booker, *The Neophiliacs: A Study of the Revolution in English Life in the Fifties and Sixties* (London: Collins, 1969), 355.

330. Ibid., 348.

331. Ibid., 66.

332. Ibid., 358.

333. Ibid., 357.

334. Ibid., 81.

335. Ibid., 358.

336. Ibid., 65.

337. Ibid., 232.

338. Ibid., 354, 359.

339. Ibid., 353–4.

340. Booker, *Sunday Telegraph*, 5 October 1969, 10.

341. Malcolm Muggeridge, *Chronicles of Wasted Time* (New York, NY: W. W. Morrow, 1973), 19.

342. Malcolm Muggeridge, 'Looking through the Eye (1976)', in *Seeing Through the Eye: Malcolm Muggeridge on Faith*, ed. Cecil C. Kuhne III (San Francisco, CA: Ignatius Press, 2005), 75.

343. Malcolm Muggeridge, *Another King: A Sermon* (Edinburgh: Saint Andrew Press, 1968), 12.

344. Malcolm Muggeridge, *Observer*, 12 December 1965, 27; Muggeridge, 'Down with Sex (1965)', in *Tread Softly, for You Tread on My Jokes* (London: Collins, 1966), 46; M *Another King*, 12.

345. Ray Gosling, *Times*, 23 November 1970, 11.

346. Laurie, *Teenage Revolution*, 22; Ned Sherrin, *Spectator*, 11 October 1968, 16; John Willett, *TLS*, 26 March 1964, 250.

347. Raymond Durgnat, 'Rock, Rhythm and Dance', *British Journal of Aesthetics* 11, no. 1 (1971), 45.
348. Mann, *Times*, 23 December 1963, 4; Cannon, *Listener*, 4 July 1968, 17; Cannon, *Guardian*, 7 January 1969, 6.
349. D. A. N. Jones, *Listener*, August 1967, 163; Jones, *Listener,* November 1969, 648; Peter Fryer, *Encounter*, October 1967, 13.
350. Buckle, *Buckle*, 361.
351. Wilfrid Mellers, *Caliban Reborn: Renewal in Twentieth-Century Music* (London: Gollancz, 1967), 144.
352. Richard Williams, 'The History of Rock', *Melody Maker*, 15 November 1969, https://ia801208.us.archive.org/35/items/TheHistoryOfRock1969/TheHistoryOfRock1969.pdf.
353. Cited in David I. Rabey and Henk Huijser, *Howard Barker: Politics and Desire – An Expository Study of His Drama and Poetry, 1969–87* (Basingstoke: Springer, 1989), 20.
354. Laurie, *Teenage Revolution*, 85–6.
355. Palmer, *Observer*, 17 November 1968, 24.
356. Spiegl, *Listener*, 8 March 1979, 341.
357. Ibid., 341.
358. Fuller, *Encounter*, December 1971, 44.
359. Burgess, *Punch*, 20 September 1967, 431.
360. John Crosby, *Observer*, 5 January 1969, 8; Wesker, *Encounter*, November 1966, 4.
361. John Carey, *Listener*, 3 June 1971, 734; Clive James, *TLS*, 25 June 1971, 723.
362. Ibid., 723.
363. Martin Dodsworth, *Listener*, 11 December 1969, 829.

Politics: The Beatles, Parliament and Revolution

1. Basil Boothroyd, *Punch*, 4 March 1964, 332.
2. Cited in *Mail*, 31 January 1964, 9; Ben Pimlott, *Harold Wilson* (London: HarperCollins, 1992), 268; Harold Wilson, *A Personal Record: The Labour Government, 1964–1970* (Boston, MA: Little, Brown, 1971), 261.
3. George Harrison, *I, Me, Mine* (New York, NY: Simon and Schuster, 1981), 67.
4. Alec Douglas-Home, 'Empire Club of Canada Diamond Jubilee Dinner', 11 February 1964, http://speeches.empireclub.org/59924/data.
5. Cited in Boothroyd, 332.
6. See Marcus Collins, 'The Beatles' Politics', *British Journal of Politics and International Relations* 16, no. 2 (2014), 291–309.
7. *Telegraph*, 2 November 1963, 8; William Sargent cited in *Times*, 30 December 1964, 4; Alex Comfort, 'The Technological Age and Human

Needs: An Emotional "Technology"', in *Technology and Society: The First Bath Conference, 1965*, ed. Gerald Walters and Kenneth Hudson (Bath: Bath University Press, 1966), 173; Peter Watkins (dir.), *Privilege* (Universal, 1967).

8. Jeremy Tranmer, 'The Radical Left and Popular Music in the 1960s', in *Preserving the Sixties: Britain and the 'Decade of Protest'*, ed. Trevor Harris and Monia O'Brien Castro (Basingstoke: Palgrave Macmillan, 2014), 91; Jeremy Tranmer, '"Within You Without You": les Beatles et la gauche britannique', *Volume!* 12, no. 2 (2016), 75–85; Bertrand Lemonnier, *La révolution pop dans l'Angleterre des années soixante* (Paris: Le table ronde, 1986); Bertrand Lemonnier, *L'Angleterre des Beatles: une histoire culturelle des années soixante* (Paris: Editions Kimé, 1998).

9. David Fowler, *Youth Culture in Modern Britain, c. 1920–c. 1970: From Ivory Tower to Global Movement – a New History* (Basingstoke: Palgrave Macmillan, 2008), 170.

10. Nicholas Tomalin, *Sunday Times*, 11 October 1964, 11.

11. David Fowler, *Youth*, 169; 'Beats and Beatles', *New Statesman*, 17 January 1964, 82.

12. Oded Heilbronner, '"Helter-Skelter"? The Beatles, the British New Left, and the Question of Hegemony', *Interdisciplinary Literary Studies* 13, no. 1/2 (2011), 87–8.

13. For a fuller account, see Marcus Collins, '"The Age of the Beatles": Parliament and Popular Music in the 1960s', *Contemporary British History* 27, no. 1 (2013), 85–107.

14. Daniel McEachie, *Express*, 24 October 1967, 1; *Mail*, 5 January 1968, 7.

15. See Carolyn S. Stevens, *The Beatles in Japan* (London: Routledge, 2017), chs. 2 and 3; Mark Sullivan, '"More Popular than Jesus": The Beatles and the Religious Far Right', *Popular Music* 6, no. 3 (1987), 313–26.

16. Cited in *Times*, 25 February 1964, 4. In several cases, more than one of the Beatles are mentioned in the same debate or question, which explains why the total number of references to musicians does not equal the total number of debates or questions in which they appear.

17. Cited in Maureen Cleave, *Standard*, 4 March 1966, 10.

18. Ian Gilmour, 15 February 1967, *Debates (Commons)*, vol. 741, col. 730.

19. Leslie Huckfield, 20 November 1967, *Debates (Commons)*, vol. 754, col. 1005.

20. Earl of Bessborough, 11 March 1964, *Debates (Lords)*, vol. 256, col. 520; John Biggs-Davison, 8 May 1964, *Debates (Commons)*, vol. 694, col. 1691; Lord Ogmore, 28 November 1963, *Debates (Lords)*, vol. 253, col. 818; Raymond Fletcher, 23 November 1964, *Debates (Commons)*, vol. 702, col. 960.

21. Ernest Marples, 12 February 1964, *Debates (Commons)*, vol. 659, col. 357; Knox Cunningham, 17 May 1965, *Debates (Commons)*, vol. 752, col. 987.

22. Baroness Wootton, 3 November 1964, *Debates (Lords)*, vol. 261, col. 15.

23. Walter H. Loveys, 12 February 1965, *Debates (Commons)*, vol. 706, col. 738.

24. Harry Hylton-Foster, Mr Speaker, 25 February 1964, *Debates (Commons)*, vol. 690, col. 235.
25. Russell Kerr, 24 July 1967, *Debates (Commons)*, vol. 751, cols 145–6.
26. Geoffrey Hirst, 25 February 1964, *Debates (Commons)*, vol. 690, col. 235.
27. Paul R. Kohl, 'A Splendid Time Is Guaranteed for All: The Beatles as Agents of Carnival', *Popular Music and Society* 20, no. 4 (1996), 81–8.
28. Frederick Lewis, *New York Times Magazine*, 1 December 1963, 125; Edward Heath, 'Institute of Directors' (ITN, 6 November 1963).
29. Viscount Montgomery of Alamein, 19 November 1963, *Debates (Lords)*, vol. 253, col. 275; cited in Michael Braun, *Love Me Do: The Beatles' Progress* (Harmondsworth: Penguin, 1964), 69.
30. Charles Curran, 19 June 1964, *Debates (Commons)*, vol. 696, col. 1745.
31. T. L. Iremonger, 23 May 1969, *Debates (Commons)*, vol. 784, col. 886.
32. David Price, 7 February 1964, *Debates (Commons)*, vol. 688, col. 1576; entry for 15 April 1970 in Tony Benn, *Office without Power: Diaries 1968–72* (London: Random House, 2012), 267. Unfortunately Benn's theory was never put to the test, the Beatles having split up earlier that week.
33. Cited in Charles Hamblett, *Here Are the Beatles* (London: New English Library, 1964), n.p.; cited in Bill Harry, *The John Lennon Encyclopaedia* (London: Virgin, 2000), 922.
34. Charles Taylor, 21 November 1963, *Debates (Commons)*, vol. 684, col. 120W; Knox Cunningham, 30 June 1965, *Debates (Commons)*, vol. 715, col. 101W.
35. Lord Willis, 13 May 1964, *Debates (Lords)*, vol. 258, col. 265.
36. Joan Quennell, 21 February 1964, *Debates (Commons)*, vol. 689, col. 250W; Ronald Lewis, 16 November 1965, *Debates (Commons)*, vol. 720, col. 1042.
37. Arthur Lewis, 24 October 1968, *Debates (Commons)*, vol. 770, col. 341W; Arthur Lewis, 7 November 1968, *Debates (Commons)*, vol. 772, col. 145W; Viscount Norwich, 18 February 1970, *Debates (Lords)*, vol. 307, cols 1168–9.
38. Iain Macleod, 18 July 1969, *Debates (Commons)*, vol. 787, col. 1161. See also Kenneth Baker, 17 July 1969, *Debates (Commons)* vol. 787, no. 921.
39. Viscount Montgomery of Alamein, 19 November 1963, *Debates (Lords)*, vol. 253, col. 275.
40. Emrys Hughes, 9 December 1963, *Debates (Commons)*, vol. 686, col. 70.
41. Victor Yates, 23 January 1964, *Debates (Commons)*, vol. 687, col. 1361.
42. Lord Goodman, 19 April 1967, *Debates (Lords)*, vol. 282, col. 236.
43. For cultural policy, see Lawrence Black, '"Making Britain a Gayer and More Cultivated Country": Wilson, Lee and the Creative Industries in the 1960s', *Contemporary British History* 20, no. 3 (2006), 323–42.
44. Arnold Goodman, *Tell Them I'm On My Way: Memoirs* (London: Chapmans, 1993), 135; Cited in Andrew Loog Oldham, *2Stoned* (New York, NY: Random House, 2012), 304.
45. Lord Goodman, 19 April 1967, *Debates (Lords)*, vol. 282, col. 236.
46. Lord Willis, 13 May 1964, *Debates (Lords)*, vol. 258, col. 266.

47. Ibid., vol. 258, cols 266, 270, 269.

48. Cited in *Times*, 16 June 1965, 12.

49. Clive Bossom, 5 March 1964, *Debates (Commons)*, vol. 690, col. 1598; Graham Page, 17 March 1967, *Debates (Commons)*, vol. 743, col. 921.

50. Cited in David Simonelli, *Working Class Heroes: Rock Music and British Society in the 1960s and 1970s* (Lanham, MD: Lexington Books, 2013), 30. For the background to Deedes' speech, see Stephen Robinson, *The Remarkable Lives of Bill Deedes* (London: Little, Brown, 2008), 254.

51. William Clark, 20 April 1964, *Debates (Commons)*, vol. 693, col. 946.

52. Lord Aberdare, 15 November 1967, *Debates (Lords)*, vol. 307, col. 975.

53. Frederick Lewis, 125.

54. Brian Epstein, *A Cellarful of Noise* (New York, NY: Doubleday, 1964), 110.

55. Cited in *Times*, 9 March 1964, 10.

56. Harold Wilson, 'Variety Club Awards Ceremony', 19 March 1964, http://members.aol.com/dinsdalep/640319.txt, http://members.aol.com/dinsdalep/640319.txt.

57. *Times*, 23 September 1964, 8.

58. *Melody Maker*, 6 March 1965, 13; *Melody Maker*, 13 March 1965, 1.

59. Cited in *Times*, 16 June 1965, 12.

60. Piri Halasz, *Time*, 15 April 1966, 30.

61. For a classic analysis of 'cultural capital', see Pierre Bourdieu, *Distinction: A Social Critique of the Judgement of Taste* (Cambridge, MA: Harvard University Press, 1987).

62. Viscount Samuel, 23 June 1965, *Debates (Lords)*, vol. 267, col. 583.

63. Bishop of Southwark, 3 March 1965, *Debates (Lords)*, vol. 263, col. 1183; Laurence Pavitt, 12 June 1964, *Debates (Commons)*, vol. 696, col. 896.

64. Lord Auckland, 3 June 1964, *Debates (Lords)*, vol. 258, cols 494–5; Herbert Butcher, 18 March 1964, *Debates (Commons)*, vol. 691, cols 1468–9.

65. Iain Murray, Duke of Atholl, 5 April 1967, *Debates (Lords)*, vol. 281, col. 973.

66. Paul Johnson, *New Statesman*, 28 February 1964, 326–7; Lord Willis, 13 May 1964, *Debates (Lords)*, vol. 258, cols 264–6.

67. Cited in John Grant, *Independent*, 9 January 1993, www.independent.co.uk/news/people/obituary-lord-willis-1477520.html.

68. Cited in *Times*, 15 May 1964, 8.

69. Wilson, 'Variety Club Awards Ceremony'.

70. Lord Taylor, 13 May 1964, *Debates (Lords)*, vol. 258, col. 322.

71. Lord Shackleton, 13 May 1964, *Debates (Lords)*, vol. 258, cols 348–9.

72. Lord Denham, 18 April 1967, *Debates (Lords)*, vol. 282, col. 125.

73. W. T. Rodgers, 22 June 1964, *Debates (Commons)*, vol. 697, col. 55.

74. Charles Curran, 19 June 1964, *Debates (Commons)*, vol. 696, col. 1738.

75. Ibid., vol. 696, col. 1745.

76. Harrison Harwood, 19 June 1964, *Debates (Commons)*, vol. 696, cols 1757–8; Norman Miscampbell, 19 June 1964, *Debates (Commons)*, vol. 696, col. 1751.

77. Ibid., vol. 696, col. 1751.

78. Richard Buchanan, 2 April 1965, *Debates (Commons)*, vol. 709, cols 2009–10.

79. Norman Miscampbell, 19 June 1964, *Debates (Commons)*, vol. 696, col. 1751; cited in Reuters, *Ottawa Journal*, 21 February 1964, 7.

80. Cited in *Times*, 24 June 1969, 4.

81. Entry for 13 June 1965 in Tony Benn, *Out of the Wilderness: Diaries 1963–67* (London: Hutchinson, 1987), 273.

82. Lord Campbell of Eskan, 1 August 1966, *Debates (Lords)*, vol. 276, col. 1131.

83. Lord Willis, 13 May 1964, *Debates (Lords)*, vol. 258, col. 264.

84. Cited in Reuters, 7; Lord Willis, 13 May 1964, *Debates (Lords)*, vol. 258, cols 261, 265.

85. Ibid., cols 263–265.

86. For Labour attitudes to the 'youth question', see Lawrence Black, *The Political Culture of the Left in Affluent Britain, 1951–64: Old Labour, New Britain?* (Basingstoke: Palgrave Macmillan, 2003), ch. 4; and Steven Fielding, *The Labour Governments 1964–70, Volume 1: Labour and Cultural Change* (Manchester: Manchester University Press, 2003), ch. 7.

87. For politicians' attitudes to mods and rockers, see Richard S. Grayson, 'Mods, Rockers and Juvenile Delinquency in 1964: The Government Response', *Contemporary British History* 12, no. 1 (1998), 19–47; Catherine Ellis, 'No Hammock for the Idle: The Conservative Party, "Youth" and the Welfare State in the 1960s', *Twentieth Century British History* 16, no. 4 (2005), 441–70.

88. William Teeling, 23 June 1964, *Debates (Commons)*, vol. 697, col. 261; Lord Bishop of Norwich, 13 May 1964, *Debates (Lords)*, vol. 258, col. 285.

89. Norman Miscampbell, 19 June 1964, *Debates (Commons)*, vol. 696, col. 1751.

90. W. R. Rees-Davies, 15 February 1965, *Debates (Commons)*, vol. 706, col. 931.

91. Lord Willis, 13 May 1964, *Debates (Lords)*, vol. 258, col. 265.

92. Cited in *Times*, 21 October 1967, 1.

93. Cited in David Stafford-Clark, *Times*, 12 April 1967, 11.

94. Lord Stonham, 21 July 1967, *Debates (Lords)*, vol. 285, col. 561.

95. Alice Bacon, 28 July 1967, *Debates (Commons)*, vol. 751, cols 1163–4.

96. Paul Channon, 28 July 1967, *Debates (Commons)*, vol. 751, col. 1164.

97. Entry for 1 January 1970 in Richard Howard Stafford Crossman, *The Diaries of a Cabinet Minister, vol. 3: Secretary of State for Social Services, 1968–1970* (New York, NY: Holt, Rinehart and Winston, 1978), 773; cited in Simon Frith, *Marxism Today*, January 1981, 24.

98. Margaret Thatcher, 'Speech to Finchley Conservative Association Ball', Margaret Thatcher Foundation, 1969, www.margaretthatcher.org /document/101689.

99. Reginald Sorensen, *Ethical Record*, May 1968, 13, http://conwayhall.org.uk /wp-content/uploads/2015/01/ETHICAL-RECORD-MAY-1968.pdf.

100. Reginald Sorensen, *Ethical Record*, May 1970, 6, http://conwayhall.org.uk/wp-content/uploads/2015/01/ETHICAL-RECORD-MAY-1970.pdf.

101. Reginald Sorensen, *Ethical Record*, May 1968, 13.

102. Cited in Victor Zorza, *Guardian*, 14 February 1964, 13. The Soviet Minister of Culture later maligned the Beatles as the 'idols of a society which had no ideals' in response to British criticism of the invasion of Czechoslovakia (cited in Squire Barraclough, *Express*, 4 December 1968, 1).

103. For the revolutionary left in Britain, see Jodi Burkett, *Constructing Post-Imperial Britain: Britishness, 'Race' and the Radical Left in the 1960s* (Basingstoke: Springer, 2013); Celia Hughes, *Young Lives on the Left: Sixties Activism and the Liberation of the Self* (Oxford: Oxford University Press, 2015); Evan Smith and Matthew Worley, eds., *Against the Grain: The British Far Left from 1956* (Oxford: Oxford University Press, 2014).

104. Sussex Communist Caucus (M-L), *The Marxist* 1, no. 9 (1969), 2.

105. Cited in Boothroyd, 332.

106. John Evans, *Music and Life*, no. 23 (1964), 5.

107. For the Communist Party of Great Britain, see Geoff Andrews, *Endgames and New Times: The Final Years of British Communism, 1964–1991* (London: Lawrence & Wishart, 2004); Andy Croft, ed., *A Weapon in the Struggle: The Cultural History of the Communist Party in Britain* (London: Pluto Press, 1998); Kevin Morgan, Gidon Cohen and Andrew Flinn, *Communists and British Society, 1920–1991* (London: Rivers Oram, 2007).

108. Andy Croft, 'Introduction', in *idem*, ed., *Weapon*, 2.

109. David Aaronovitch, *Party Animals: My Family and Other Communists* (London: Random House, 2016), 98.

110. Workers' Music Association, *A Policy for Music in Post-War Britain* (London: Workers' Music Association, 1945), 3–4.

111. Ibid., 7.

112. Francis Newton, *The Jazz Scene* (London: MacGibbon & Kee, 1959), 15. Hobsbawm wrote music criticism under a pseudonym; see Philip Bounds, 'From Folk to Jazz: Eric Hobsbawm, British Communism and Cultural Studies', *Critique* 40, no. 4 (2012), 575–93.

113. Newton, *Jazz Scene*, 20.

114. Ibid., 29.

115. For the New Left in Britain, see Geoff Andrews et al., eds., *New Left, New Right and Beyond: Taking the Sixties Seriously* (Basingstoke: Springer, 1999); Dennis L. Dworkin, *Cultural Marxism in Postwar Britain: History, the New Left, and the Origins of Cultural Studies* (Durham, NC: Duke University Press, 1997).

116. E. P. Thompson, *New Reasoner*, no. 9 (1959), 1.

117. Richard Hoggart, *The Uses of Literacy: Aspects of Working-Class Life with Special Reference to Publications and Entertainments* (Harmondsworth: Pelican, 1958), 205.

118. Raymond Williams, ed., *May Day Manifesto: 1968* (Harmondsworth: Penguin, 1968), 140; Raymond Williams, *NLR* I, no. 5 (1960), 53.

119. Brian Groombridge and Paddy Whannel, *NLR* I, no. 1 (1960), 52. For New Left analyses of youth, see Nick Bentley, 'The Young Ones: A Reassessment of the British New Left's Representation of 1950s Youth Subcultures', *European Journal of Cultural Studies* 8, no. 1 (2005), 65–83; Dworkin, *Cultural Marxism*, ch. 3.

120. Stuart Hall and Paddy Whannel, *The Popular Arts* (London: Hutchinson Educational, 1964), 312.

121. Evans, 5.

122. Ibid., 5.

123. Ibid., 5.

124. Pete Carter, *Marxism Today*, June 1966, 190. For Carter, see Morgan, Cohen and Flinn, *Communists and British Society*, 97.

125. Carter, 190.

126. Hall and Whannel, *Popular Arts*, 276.

127. Alan Beckett, *NLR* 1, no. 39 (1966), 87–90.

128. Ian Birchall, *International Socialism*, no. 23 (1965), 16–17.

129. For the later debates, see Matthew Worley, 'Marx-Lenin-Rotten-Strummer: British Marxism and Youth Culture in the 1970s', *Contemporary British History* 30, no. 4 (2016), 505–21.

130. Karl Dallas, *Music and Life*, no. 40 (1968), 7.

131. Ibid., 7; Kenneth Tynan, *Observer*, 21 January 1968, 27.

132. Richard Merton, *NLR* I, no. 59 (1970), 88–96.

133. Tom Spence, *Challenge*, 10 December 1963, 2.

134. Evans, 5.

135. Barney Davis, *Marxism Today*, March 1966, 82.

136. Carter, 190.

137. Cover of *Black Dwarf* 13, no. 2 (1968).

138. Roland Muldoon, *Black Dwarf* 13, no. 8 (1968), 3.

139. Geoff Bowles, *Marxism Today*, April 1972, 110–15; Mick Launchbury, *Black Dwarf* 13, no. 8 (1968), 3.

140. Don Milligan, *Marxism Today*, May 1966, 155.

141. Charles Parker, 'Pop Song, the Manipulated Ritual', in *The Black Rainbow: Essays on the Present Breakdown of Culture*, ed. Peter Abbs (London: Heinemann Educational, 1975), 165.

142. Bowles, 115; John Clarke, 'Style', in *Resistance Through Rituals: Youth Subcultures in Post-War Britain*, ed. Tony Jefferson and Stuart Hall (London: Routledge and Kegan Paul, 1975), 187.

143. Cited in *Music and Life*, no. 26 (1965), 4. The record of this meeting does not name the speaker but identifies him as a professor at the Royal Academy of

Music. Richard Hanlon and Mike Waite state that the speaker was 'almost certainly Bush' (Richard Hanlon and Mike Waite, 'Notes from the Left: Communism and British Classical Music', in Croft, ed., *Weapon*, 84). For Bush, see Joanna Bullivant, *Alan Bush, Modern Music, and the Cold War: The Cultural Left in Britain and the Communist Bloc* (Cambridge: Cambridge University Press, 2017).

144. Cited in *Music and Life*, no. 26 (1965), 4.

145. Peter Fryer, *Encounter*, October 1967, 20; cited in Julie Stephens, *Anti-Disciplinary Protest: Sixties Radicalism and Postmodernism* (Cambridge: Cambridge University Press, 1998), 7; George Lichtheim, *From Marx to Hegel* (London: Orbach and Chambers, 1971), 116.

146. John Boyd, *Marxism Today*, December 1973, 375.

147. Graham Murdock and Robin McCron, 'Consciousness of Class and Consciousness of Generation', in Jefferson and Hall (ed.), *Resistance through Rituals*, 197.

148. Cited in *Music and Life*, no. 26 (1965), 4.

149. Cited in ibid., 4.

150. Cited in ibid., 4; *Music and Life*, no. 23 (1964), 2.

151. Pál Járdányi, *Music and Life*, no. 23 (1964), n.p.

152. Francis Newton, *New Statesman*, 8 November 1963, 673.

153. Cited in Evans, 3; Parker, 'Pop Song', 159.

154. Carter, 190.

155. Dave Ashby, *Keep Left*, June 1965, 5; Milligan, 155.

156. MacColl (1967) cited in David Holbrook, *Creativity and Popular Culture* (Rutherford, NJ: Fairleigh Dickinson University Press, 1994), 191.

157. Jeremy Hawthorn, *Marxism Today*, December 1973, 365.

158. *Music and Life*, no. 26 (1965), 4.

159. Jim Cornelius, *Marxism Today*, September 1974, 281.

160. Birchall, 17.

161. Challenge cited in *Lansing State Journal*, 3 December 1967, 37.

162. Fryer, 20.

163. Parker, 'Pop Song', 165; Boyd, 376.

164. Nick Kettle, *Marxism Today*, July 1974, 214; Parker, 'Pop Song', 165; Betty Reid, 'Some Thoughts on the Women's Liberation Movement: A Contribution to Discussion', January 1971, CPGB archives. Women's Department: Miscellaneous Women's Department Files – Papers on the Women's Liberation Movement.

165. Roland Muldoon, *Black Dwarf* 13, no. 6 (1968), 16; John Hoyland, *Black Dwarf* 13, no. 7 (1968), 6; John Hoyland, *Black Dwarf* 13, no. 9 (1969), 4. For the American reception of 'Revolution', see John Platoff, 'John Lennon, "Revolution", and the Politics of Musical Reception', *Journal of Musicology* 22, no. 2 (2005), 241–67.

166. Richard Neville, *Play Power* (London: Jonathan Cape, 1970), 84.

167. Ibid., 84; Walker, 216.

168. Sheila Rowbotham, *Promise of a Dream: Remembering the Sixties* (London: Verso, 2001), 199.

169. Ibid., 209.

170. Sheila Rowbotham, *Woman's Consciousness, Man's World* (Harmondsworth: Penguin, 1973), 40–1.

171. For second-wave feminism, see Elizabeth Homans, 'Visions of Equality: Women's Rights and Political Change in 1970s Britain' (PhD Thesis, Bangor University, 2015); Natalie Thomlinson, *Race, Ethnicity and the Women's Movement in England, 1968–1993* (Basingstoke: Springer, 2016); Sarah F. Browne, *The Women's Liberation Movement in Scotland* (Manchester: Manchester University Press, 2014); Marcus Collins, *Modern Love: An Intimate History of Men and Women in Twentieth Century Britain* (London: Atlantic, 2003), ch. 6.

172. Alan Beckett, *NLR* I, 1, no. 47 (1968), 28; Richard Merton, *NLR* I, no. 47 (1968), 31; *idem*, *NLR* I, no. 59 (1970), 94; Margaret Geddes, 'Roll Over and Rock Me Baby', *Spare Rib* no. 11 (1973), 8.

173. Mavis Bayton (2000) cited in Helen Reddington, *The Lost Women of Rock Music: Female Musicians of the Punk Era* (Aldershot: Ashgate, 2007), 104; Germaine [Greer], *Oz*, no. 24 (1969), 28.

174. One exception was Joy Farren's review of Ono's *Approximately Infinite Universe* (*Oz* 47 (1973), 56).

175. Terri Goddard and Liz Waugh, *Spare Rib* no. 38 (1975), 39.

176. Elizabeth Wilson, *Women and the Welfare State* (London: Tavistock, 1977), 71.

177. Spence, 2.

178. Ibid., 2.

179. Idem, *Daily Worker*, 7 September 1963. Thanks lots to Mark Lewisohn for sharing this reference.

180. Martin Jacques, *Marxism Today*, September 1973, 272.

181. Merton, *NLR* I, no. 59 (1970), 90.

182. Ibid., 90, 93.

183. Jacques, *Marxism Today*, September 1973, 272.

184. Terry Eagleton, 'New Bearings: The Beatles', *Blackfriars* 65, no. 4 (1964), 176, 175.

185. Pete Fowler, *7 Days*, 24 November 1971, 19; Fryer, 20; John Crump, *Socialist Standard*, February 1968, n.p., www.worldsocialism.org/spgb/socialist-standard/1960s/1968/no-762-february-1968/politics-pop.

186. Ibid., n.p.

187. Tom Kemp, *Keep Left*, 17 December 1969; Merton, *NLR* I, no. 59 (1970), 93.

188. R. Sentes, *Black Dwarf* 13, no. 10 (1969), 4.

189. Cited in Ray Connolly, *Stardust Memories: Talking About My Generation* (London: Pavilion, 1983), 33.

190. Muldoon, *Black Dwarf* 13, no. 6 (1968), 16.

191. David Widgery, *Oz*, no. 20 (1969), 25.
192. Cited in *Frendz*, no. 37 (1971), 3.
193. *Man of the Decade* (ATV, 12 December 1969).
194. Denver Walker, *Marxism Today*, July 1974, 217.
195. Cited in Tariq Ali, *Street Fighting Years: An Autobiography of the Sixties* (London: Verso, 2005), 331.
196. Pat McVeigh, *Black Dwarf* 8, no. 3 (1968), 3.
197. Cited in Jonathon Green, ed., *Days in the Life: Voices from the English Underground 1961–1971* (London: Minerva, 1989), 55.
198. See Marcus Collins, 'Permissiveness on Trial: Sex, Drugs, Rock, the Rolling Stones and the Sixties Counterculture', *Popular Music and Society* 42, no. 2 (2019), 188–209. Suspicions lingered that the Beatles were too big to bust until the arrests of Lennon and Ono in October 1968 and Harrison in March 1969.
199. See Collins, 'Beatles' Politics'.
200. Cited in Jeff Burger, ed., *Lennon on Lennon: Conversations with John Lennon* (London: Omnibus eBook, 2017), n.p.
201. David Widgery, *International Socialism*, June 1973, 25.
202. Ali, *Street Fighting Years*, 335.
203. Widgery, *International Socialism*, June 1973, 25; Widgery, *Preserving Disorder: Selected Essays 1968–1988* (London: Pluto Press, 1989), 75.
204. Davis, 78.
205. Hoyland, *Black Dwarf* 13, no. 7 (1968), 6.
206. Imtiaz Chounara, *Marxism Today*, October 1974, 318.
207. Ibid., 318.
208. Jacques, *Marxism Today*, September 1973, 280; Jacques, *Marxism Today*, April 1975, 115. See also Paul Fauvet, *Marxism Today*, March 1974, 93; and John Green, *Marxism Today*, November 1974, 350.
209. *Socialist Standard*, December 1969, n.p., www.worldsocialism.org/spgb/socialist-standard/1960s/1969/no-784-december-1969/hippies-abortion-socialist-understanding; Sussex Communist Caucus (M-L), 2.
210. David Goodway, *Anarchist Seeds Beneath the Snow: Left-Libertarian Thought and British Writers from William Morris to Colin Ward* (Oakland, CA: PM Press, 2011), 326.
211. Raphael Samuel, *New Society*, 2 October 1987, xxxix. For anarchism in Britain, see Goodway, *Anarchist Seeds*; Matthew S. Adams, *Kropotkin, Read and the Intellectual History of British Anarchism* (Basingstoke: Palgrave, 2015); and Carissa Honeywell, *A British Anarchist Tradition: Herbert Read, Alex Comfort and Colin Ward* (London: A&C Black, 2011).
212. 'HEATWAVE: First Statement', *Heatwave*, no. 1 (July 1966), 2. For Heatwave, see Franklin Rosemont and Charles Radcliffe, eds., *Dancin' in the Streets! Anarchists, IWWs, Surrealists, Situationists & Provos in the 1960s as Recorded in the Pages of The Rebel Worker & Heatwave* (Chicago,

IL: Charles H. Kerr, 2005); Sam Cooper, 'Heatwave: Mod, Cultural Studies and the Counterculture', in *Quadrophenia and Mod(Ern) Culture*, ed. Pamela Thurschwell (Basingstoke: Springer, 2017).

213. 'HEATWAVE: First Statement', 2.
214. Ibid., 2.
215. Christopher Gray and Charles Radcliffe, 'All Or Not At All', *Heatwave*, no. 2 (October 1966), 2–4.
216. Ibid., 4.
217. Ibid., 4; Charles Radcliffe, 'The Seeds of Social Destruction', *Heatwave*, no. 1 (July 1966), 15.
218. Gray and Radcliffe, 'All Or Not At All', 2.
219. 'Provo: What Is the Provotariat', *Heatwave*, no. 1 (July 1966), 3.
220. Ibid., 3–5; Radcliffe, 'The Seeds of Social Destruction', 23.
221. Ibid., 15.
222. Gray and Radcliffe, 'All Or Not At All', 3; 'Provo: What Is the Provotariat', 4.
223. Radcliffe, 'The Seeds of Social Destruction', 24; 'Provo: What Is the Provotariat', 4.
224. Charles Radcliffe, 'Two Fiery Flying Rolls: The *Heatwave* Story, 1966–1970', in Rosemont and Radcliffe, eds., *Dancin' in the Streets!*, 369.
225. Ben Covington (aka Charles Radcliffe), 'Only Lovers Left Alive', *Heatwave*, no. 1 (1966), 13; Ben Covington (aka Charles Radcliffe), *Anarchy*, May 1965, 129–33; Charles Radcliffe, 'The Who: Crime Against The Bourgeoisie', in Rosemont and Radcliffe, eds., *Dancin' in the Streets!*, 199–202.
226. Radcliffe, 'Two Fiery Flying Rolls', *348*.
227. Ian Vine, *Anarchy*, September 1963, 287, 284.
228. Franklin Rosemont, 'To Be Revolutionary in Everything: The *Rebel Worker* Story, 1964–1968', in Rosemont and Radcliffe, eds., *Dancin' in the Streets!*, 1–82.
229. Radcliffe, 'Two Fiery Flying Rolls', 336.
230. Radcliffe, 'Pop Goes The Beatle', in Rosemont and Radcliffe, eds., *Dancin' in the Streets!*, 252–3.
231. Covington, *Anarchy*, May 1965, 130.
232. Radcliffe, 'Pop', 252.
233. Radcliffe, 'Seeds', *24*.
234. Radcliffe, 'Pop', 253.
235. Mabey, 'Twist and Shout', *Peace News*, 20 December 1963.
236. Mabey, 'Subversion by Grinning', *Peace News*, 24 January 1964.
237. Mabey, 'Twist and Shout'.
238. Ibid.
239. Mabey, 'Subversion by Grinning'.
240. June Freeman, *Peace News*, 17 January 1964; Patrick Parrinder, *Peace News*, 3 January 1964.
241. Mabey, 'Subversion by Grinning'.

242. Franklin Rosemont, Charles Radcliffe, and Richard Mabey, *Mods, Rockers and the Revolution* (London: Solidarity Bookshop, 1966).

243. Joe Benjamin, *Anarchy*, May 1963, 129.

244. A. S. Neill, *Freedom – Not License!* (New York, NY: Hart Publishing Company, 1966), 149; A. S. Neill, *Anarchy*, January 1966, 23.

245. Comfort, 'Technological Age', 173.

246. Stephens, *Anti-Disciplinary Protest*; Elizabeth Nelson, *British Counter-Culture 1966–73: A Study of the Underground Press* (Basingstoke: Springer, 1989), 102. For the underground press, see also Alessandro Bratus, 'Scene through the Press: Rock Music and Underground Papers in London, 1966–73', *Twentieth-Century Music* 8, no. 2 (2011), 227–52; Chris Atton, 'A Reassessment of the Alternative Press', *Media, Culture and Society* 21, no. 1 (1999), 51–76; Nigel Fountain, *Underground: The London Alternative Press, 1966–74* (London: Routledge, 1988).

247. Barry Miles, *IT*, no. 1 (1966), 8.

248. *Oz*, no. 16 (1968), 3.

249. Alan W. Watts, 'Wealth versus Money (1969)', in *Does It Matter? Essays on Man's Relation to Materiality* (Novato, CA: New World Library, 2010), 12.

250. Neville, *Play Power*, 263.

251. *IT*, no. 24 (1968), 3.

252. Cited in Richard Boston, *Anarchy*, no. 85 (1968), 73.

253. Cited in ibid., 74.

254. Cited in ibid., 73.

255. Timothy Clark et al., 'The Revolution of Modern Art and the Modern Art of Revolution' (unpublished, 1967), www.cddc.vt.edu/sionline/si/modernart.html.

256. Radcliffe, 'Two Fiery Flying Rolls', 351.

257. Alex Comfort, *Guardian*, 6 December 1968, 11.

258. For Farren's politics, see Mick Farren, *Give the Anarchist a Cigarette* (London: Random House, 2010). For Mabey, see *Anarchy*, February 1969, 33–7. For Melly, see George Melly, *Owning Up: The Trilogy* (Harmondsworth: Penguin, 2006). For Nuttall, see Jeff Nuttall, *Bomb Culture* (London: Paladin, 1970); Gillian Whiteley, 'Sewing the "Subversive Thread of Imagination": Jeff Nuttall, *Bomb Culture* and the Radical Potential of Affect', *The Sixties* 4, no. 2 (2011), 109–33.

259. George Melly, *Revolt into Style: The Pop Arts in Britain* (Harmondsworth: Penguin, 1970), 120.

260. Richard Mabey, *The Pop Process* (London: Hutchinson Educational, 1969), 55; Nuttall, *Bomb Culture*, 241; Mick Farren and Edward Barker, *Watch Out Kids* (London: Open Gate Books, 1972), n.p.

261. Mick Farren, *SoHo Weekly News*, 10 December 1980, https://www.rocksbackpages.com/Library/Article/the-snuff-of-dreams-the-death-of-john-lennon-; Farren and Barker, *Watch Out Kids*, n.p.

262. Cited in Bob Dawburn, *Melody Maker*, 26 October 1968, 13.

263. Melly, *Revolt into Style*, 120.
264. Albert Hunt, *Peace News*, 31 January 1964.
265. Albert Hunt, *Peace News*, 1 May 1968, 2.
266. Roger Barnard, *Peace News*, 19 January 1968, 3.
267. Laura Birch, *Peace News*, 26 January 1968, 2.
268. Mabey, *Pop*, 25.
269. Ibid., 24.
270. Nuttall, *Bomb Culture*, 203.
271. Ibid., 203, 243.
272. Reg O'Lucian (pseud.), *Anarchy*, February 1968, 60–4.
273. Miles, *Oz*, no. 14 (1968), 25.
274. *Oz*, no. 25 (1969), 53.
275. For Lennon's disavowal of anarchism, see Ray Coleman, *Disc Weekly*, 2 April 1966, 6.
276. For the Situationist International, see Sadie Plant, *The Most Radical Gesture: The Situationist International in a Postmodern Age* (London: Routledge, 2002); McKenzie Wark, *The Beach Beneath the Street: The Everyday Life and Glorious Times of the Situationist International* (London: Verso Books, 2015).
277. *Internationale Situationniste*, no. 1 (1958), www.cddc.vt.edu/sionline/si/soundfury.html.
278. *Internationale Situationniste*, no. 9 (1964), www.cddc.vt.edu/sionline/si/leisure.html.
279. Raoul Vaneigem, 'The Revolution of Everyday Life' (1967), The Anarchist Library, 30, https://theanarchistlibrary.org/library/raoul-vaneigem-the-revolution-of-everyday-life.pdf.
280. For Situationism in Britain, see Sam Cooper, *The Situationist International in Britain: Modernism, Surrealism and the Avant-Garde* (London: Taylor & Francis, 2016); Britt Eversole, 'Occupy the Fun Palace', *Thresholds* 41 (2013), 32–45.
281. Charles Radcliffe, *Don't Start Me Talking: Subculture, Situationism and the Sixties* (ebook: Bread and Circuses, 2018), n.p.
282. Charles Radcliffe, 'Two Fiery Flying Rolls', 369; Clark et al., 'Revolution'.
283. David Robins, *IT*, no. 47 (1969), 3; cited in David Wise, 'A Critical Hidden History of King Mob', Revolt Against Plenty, 2003, www.revoltagainstplenty.com/index.php/archive-local/93-a-hidden-history-of-king-mob.html.
284. Dave Walton, '1969: Revolution as Personal and as Theatre', Revolt Against Plenty, 2001, www.revoltagainstplenty.com/index.php/archive-local/26-1969-revolution-as-personal-and-as-theatre.html.
285. David Wise and Stuart Wise, 'The End of Music', in *What Is Situationism? A Reader*, ed. Stewart Home (London: AK Press, 1996), 67. For the Situationist roots of the Sex Pistols, see also Greil Marcus, *Lipstick Traces: A Secret History of the Twentieth Century* (Cambridge, MA: Harvard University Press, 1989).

286. For the Angry Brigade, see Tom Vague, *Anarchy in the UK: The Angry Brigade* (Edinburgh: AK Press, 1997); Gianfranco Sanguinetti et al., *Red Army Faction, Red Brigades, Angry Brigade: The Spectacle of Terror in Post War Europe* (ebook: Bread and Circuses, 2015); J. D. Taylor, 'The Party's Over? The Angry Brigade, the Counterculture, and the British New Left, 1967–1972', *Historical Journal* 58, no. 3 (2015), 877–900.

287. Cited in Timothy Scott Brown, 'The Sixties in the City: Avant-Gardes and Urban Rebels in New York, London, and West Berlin', *Journal of Social History* 46, no. 4 (2013), 832.

288. Cooper, *Situationist International*, 123. A photograph of the graffiti can be seen at Servando Rocha, 'La camiseta de los odios y las bendiciones', Agente Provocador, 2016, www.agenteprovocador.es/publicaciones/la-camiseta-de-los-odios-y-las-bendiciones.

289. King Mob, 'The Death of Art Spells the Murder of Artists. The Real Anti-Artist Appears (1968)', in *An Endless Adventure, an Endless Passion, an Endless Banquet: A Situationist Scrapbook*, ed. Iwona Blazwick (London: ICA, 1989), 70.

290. 'Chapman', *Freedom Anarchist Weekly* 41, no. 25 (1980), 4.

291. Harry Harris, 'Death of a Walrus', libcom.org, 1981, http://libcom.org/library/death-walrus.

292. 'Controversial Priest Is Reprimanded', *Chicago Tribune*, 30 March 1997, http://articles.chicagotribune.com/1997-03-30/news/9703300263_1_george-blake-shoplifting-british-double-agent.

293. John Papworth, *Resurgence* 2, no. 12 (1970), 3.

294. King Mob, *Smash the Plastic Death*, n.d., www.tate.org.uk/context-comment/articles/mob-who-shouldnt-really-be-here; Cooper, *Situationist International*, 126.

295. Wise, 'Critical'.

296. Diary jotting by David Wise (1972) cited in ibid.

297. Wise, 'Ferry Across the Tyne', *Revolt Against Plenty*, 2008, www.revoltagainstplenty.com/index.php/archive-local/54-on-bryan-ferry-qferry-across-the-tyneq.html.

298. Clark et al., 'Revolution'; Harris, 'Death of a Walrus'.

299. Tony Bennett et al., 'Introduction', in *Rock and Popular Music: Politics, Policies, Institutions*, ed. Tony Bennett (London: Routledge, 2005), 3. For the politics of popular music, see John Street, *Rebel Rock: The Politics of Popular Music* (Oxford: Blackwell, 1986).

300. Lawrence Grossberg, 'The Framing of Rock: Rock and the New Conservatism', in Bennett (ed.), *Rock and Popular Music*, 195.

301. Street, *Rebel Rock*, 16.

302. Simon Frith, 'Popular Music and the Local State', in Bennett (ed.), *Rock and Popular Music*, 14.

303. Cited in *Times*, 18 April 1964, 6.

304. Harold Harington Balfour, *Times*, 18 April 1964, 15.
305. Miscampbell, 19 June 1964, *Debates (Commons)*, vol. 696, col. 1751.
306. Charles Curran, 19 June 1964, *Debates (Commons)*, vol. 696, col. 1745.
307. Tom Driberg, 28 July 1967, *Debates (Commons)*, vol. 751, col. 1164.
308. Denham, 18 April 1967, *Debates (Lords)*, vol. 282, col. 125.
309. Murray, Duke of Atholl, 5 April 1967, *Debates (Lords)*, vol. 281, col. 973.
310. Russell Kerr, 24 July 1967, *Debates (Commons)*, vol. 751, cols 145–6.
311. Lord Willis, 13 May 1964, *Debates (Lords)*, vol. 258, col. 264; Deedes cited in Reuters, *Ottawa Journal*, 21 February 1964, 7.
312. Charles Curran, 19 June 1964, *Debates (Commons)*, vol. 696, col. 1745; Laurence Pavitt, 21 March 1969, *Debates (Commons)*, vol. 780, col. 963; Alice Bacon, 28 July 1967, *Debates (Commons)*, vol. 751, col. 1163.
313. John Street and Martin Cloonan, 'Politics and Popular Music: From Policing to Packaging', *Parliamentary Affairs* 50, no. 2 (1997), 223–35.
314. *Times*, 26 February 1964, 10.
315. Harold Wilson, 25 February 1964, *Debates (Commons)*, vol. 690, col. 235.
316. Lord Willis, 13 May 1964, *Debates (Lords)*, vol. 258, col. 270; Arthur Marwick, *The Sixties: Cultural Revolution in Britain, France, Italy, and the United States, c. 1958–c. 1974* (Oxford: Oxford University Press, 1998). Another Labour politician critical of the Beatles, Barry Jones, spoke in similar terms of the Beatles being part of a 'social revolution' in 1971 (Barry Jones, 1 March 1971, *Debates (Commons)* 812, no. 1313).
317. Cited in Reuters, 7.
318. Lord Willis, 13 May 1964, *Debates (Lords)*, vol. 258, col. 259.
319. Bill Hunter, *The Newsletter*, 26 June 1965, 4.
320. David Ramsay Steele, *Socialist Standard*, June 1967, n.p., www.worldsocialism.org/spgb/socialist-standard/1960s/1967/no-754-june-1967/ycls-land-hope-and-glory; 'Chapman', 4.
321. Cited in Pendennis, *Observer*, 5 November 1967, 40.
322. Iain Sproat, 24 January 1979, *Debates (Commons)*, vol. 961, col. 586.
323. Minutes of Political Committee meeting, 17 December 1980, CPGB archives, CP/CENT/PC.
324. Frith, 'John Lennon'; Mick Farren, *SoHo Weekly News*, 10 December 1980, www.rocksbackpages.com/Library/Article/the-snuff-of-dreams-the-death-of-john-lennon; Tariq Ali, *Socialist Challenge*, 26 February 1981, 1, 8–9; 'Advert', *Socialist Challenge*, 17 December 1980, 1.
325. Ali, *Street Fighting Years*, 330.
326. Neville, *Play Power*, 105.
327. Ibid., 105; Neville, *Hippie Hippie Shake* (London: Gerald Duckworth & Co, 2012).
328. Dave Laing, *The Sound of Our Time* (London: Sheed & Ward, 1969), 183. See also Dave Laing, *Marxism Today*, April 1978, 123–8.
329. Jacques, *Marxism Today*, April 1975, 112.

330. Murdock and McCrone, 197; Dick Hebdige, *Subculture: The Meaning of Style* (London: Methuen, 1979), 162.

331. See Willie Thompson and Marcus Collins, 'The Revolutionary Left and the Permissive Society', in Collins (ed.), *Permissive Society*, 155–68.

332. Merton, *NLR* I, no. 59 (1970), 90.

333. Hoyland, *Black Dwarf* 13, no. 9 (1969), 4; Sentes, 4.

334. Chounara, 318.

335. Hoyland, *Black Dwarf* 13, no. 7 (1968), 6.

Conclusion

1. Pearson Phillips, *Mail*, 11 April 1970, 5.

2. Ibid., 5.

3. For the background to the interview, see Joe Hagan, *Sticky Fingers: The Life and Times of Jann Wenner and Rolling Stone Magazine* (Edinburgh: Canongate, 2017), prologue and ch. 8.

4. Jann Wenner, *Rolling Stone*, 7 February 1970, 24.

5. Cited in Jann Wenner, *Lennon Remembers* (San Francisco, CA: Straight Arrow Books, 1971), 11–12.

6. Cited in Richie Yorke, *Rolling Stone*, 7 February 1970, 22.

7. Cited in Tariq Ali and Robin Blackburn, *Red Mole* 2, no. 5 (1971), 1.

8. Cited in ibid., 3.

9. Cited in Wenner, *Lennon Remembers*, 31, 45.

10. Cited in ibid., 12, 31.

11. Piri Halasz, *Time*, 15 April 1966, 30–4; John Crosby, *Weekend Telegraph*, 16 April 1965, n.p.; Brian Epstein, *A Cellarful of Noise* (New York, NY: Doubleday, 1964); Mary Quant, *Quant by Quant* (London: Cassell, 1966); Vidal Sassoon, *Sorry I Kept You Waiting, Madam* (London: Cassell, 1968); Richard Lester (dir.), *A Hard Day's Night* (Walter Shenson Films, 1964); Richard Lester (dir.), *Help!* (Walter Shenson Films, 1965); Peter Whitehead (dir.), *Wholly Communion* (Lorrimer Films, 1965); Peter Whitehead (dir.), *Tonite Let's All Make Love In London* (Lorrimer Films, 1967); David Bailey and Francis Wyndham, *David Bailey's Box of Pin-Ups* (London: Weidenfeld and Nicolson, 1965).

12. Christopher Booker, *The Neophiliacs: A Study of the Revolution in English Life in the Fifties and Sixties* (London: Collins, 1969), 298; Heather Cremonesi, 'Yeah, Yeah', in *Young London: Permissive Paradise*, ed. Frank Habicht (London: Harrap, 1969), xiv.

13. David Bailey and Peter Evans, *Goodbye Baby & Amen: A Saraband for the Sixties* (London: Condé Nast, 1969), 237, 5.

14. Philip Norman, *Shout! The Beatles in Their Generation* (New York, NY: Fireside/Simon and Schuster, 1981), 31.

15. Ibid., 32.

16. Ian MacDonald, *Revolution in the Head: The Beatles' Records and the Sixties*, 3rd edn (London: Pimlico, 2005), 8–9.

17. Ibid., 7, 37, 221.

18. Norman, *Shout!*, 1981 edn, 31.

19. Philip Norman, *Shout! The True Story of the Beatles*, 3rd edn (New York, NY: Fireside/Simon and Schuster, 2005), xxiv.

20. Phillips, 5.

21. MacDonald, *Revolution*, 32.

22. Richard Mills, 'Expert Textpert: Ian MacDonald's Revolution in the Head: The Beatles' Records and the Sixties (1994)', in *Fifty Years with the Beatles: The Impact of the Beatles on Contemporary Culture*, ed. Jerzy Jarniewicz and Alina Kwiatkowska (Łódź: Łódź University Press, 2010), 327–40.

23. MacDonald, *Revolution*, 28.

24. Ibid., 32.

25. Norman, *Shout!*, 2005 edn, xxiv.

26. Ibid., xxiii–xxiv.

27. Ibid., xxiii.

28. Ibid., xxiii.

29. For an overview, see Matthew Grant, 'Historians, the Penguin Specials and the "State-of-the-Nation" Literature, 1958–64', *Contemporary British History* 17, no. 3 (2003), 29–54. For the relationship between the Beatles and the 'Angry Young Men', see Matthew Schneider, 'Getting Better: The Beatles and the Angry Young Men', in *New Critical Perspectives on the Beatles: Things We Said Today*, ed. Kenneth Womack and Katie Kapurch (Basingstoke: Springer, 2016), 13–30; Ian Inglis, 'Men of Ideas? Popular Music, Anti-Intellectualism and the Beatles', in *The Beatles, Popular Music and Society*, ed. Ian Inglis (Basingstoke: Springer, 2000), 18–20; Jonathan Gould, *Can't Buy Me Love: The Beatles, Britain, and America* (New York, NY: Three Rivers Press, 2008), 22–4, 90–2.

30. William Mann, *Times*, 23 December 1963, 4.

31. Office for National Statistics, 'Percentage of households with landline telephones in the United Kingdom (UK) from 1970 to 2018', www .statista.com/statistics/289158/telephone-presence-in-households-in-the-uk /; *idem*, 'Percentage of households with central heating systems in the United Kingdom (UK) from 1970 to 2018', www.statista.com/statistics/289137/central-heating-in-households-in-the-uk/.

32. Roger Ballard, 'Britain's Visible Minorities: A Demographic Overview' (1999), CrossAsia-Repository, 5, http://crossasia-repository.ub.uni-heidelberg.de/286/1/demography.pdf.

33. For Britain's '68, see Steffen Bruendel, 'Global Dimensions of Conflict and Cooperation: Public Protest and the Quest for Transnational Solidarity in

Britain, 1968–1973', in *A Revolution of Perception? Consequences and Echoes of 1968*, ed. Ingrid Gilcher-Holtey (New York, NY: Berghahn Books, 2014), 35–68; Holger Nehring, 'Great Britain', in *1968 in Europe: A History of Protest and Activism, 1956–1977*, ed. Martin Klimke and Joachim Scharloth (Basingstoke: Springer, 2008); Hans Righart, 'Moderate Versions of the "Global Sixties": A Comparison of Great Britain and the Netherlands', *Journal of Area Studies* 6, no. 13 (1998), 82–96.

34. For the Millennium Memory Bank, see Rob Perks, 'The Century Speaks: A Millennium Oral History Project', in *Aural History: Essays on Recorded Sound*, ed. Andy Linehan (London: British Library, 2001), 27–40; April Gallwey, 'The Rewards of Using Archived Oral Histories in Research: The Case of the Millennium Memory Bank', *Oral History* 41, no. 1 (2013), 37–50.

35. For the first histories to draw on MMB interviews, see Mark Roodhouse, *Black Market Britain: 1939–1955* (Oxford: Oxford University Press, 2013); Lizzie Seal, *Capital Punishment in Twentieth-Century Britain: Audience, Justice, Memory* (London: Routledge, 2014), ch. 8; Alana Harris, *Faith in the Family: A Lived Religious History of English Catholicism, 1945–82* (Oxford: Oxford University Press, 2016); Florence Sutcliffe-Braithwaite, *Class, Politics, and the Decline of Deference in England, 1968–2000* (Oxford: Oxford University Press, 2018).

36. Janice Boswell, summary of interview by Julia Letts for BBC Hereford and Worcester, *Millennium Memory Bank* (*MMB*), 1998, http://explore.bl.uk /BLVU1:LSCOP-ALL:BLLSA5615697.

37. Alan Page, summary of interview by Simon Evans for BBC Radio Kent, *MMB*, 1999, http://explore.bl.uk/BLVU1:LSCOP-ALL:BLLSA5958929.

38. Miriam Forster, summary of interview by Virtue Jones for BBC Radio Newcastle, *MMB*, 1998, http://explore.bl.uk/BLVU1:LSCOP-ALL: BLLSA5959765.

39. Jenny Porter, summary of interview by Siobhan Logue for BBC Radio Gloucestershire, *MMB*, 1999, http://explore.bl.uk/BLVU1:LSCOP-ALL: BLLSA5897963.

40. Alison Andrews, summary of interview by Andy Vivian for BBC Radio Gloucestershire, *MMB*, 1999, http://explore.bl.uk/BLVU1:LSCOP-ALL: BLLSA5958837.

41. Milan Pavasovic, summary of interview by Mike Hally for BBC GMR, *MMB*, 1999, http://explore.bl.uk/BLVU1:LSCOP-ALL:BLLSA5651004.

42. Deborah Sutcliffe, recorded interview by Lucy Ashwell for BBC Radio Humberside, *MMB*, 1999, C900/07131.

43. Jennie Gower, summary of interview by Amanda Kennett for BBC Southern Counties Radio, *MMB*, 1999, http://explore.bl.uk/BLVU1:LSCOP-ALL: BLLSA5628263; Steve Graham, recorded interview by Simon Evans for BBC Radio Kent, *MMB*, 1999, C900/07594.

44. Phil Fryer, summary of interview by Eka Morgan for BBC Thames Valley, *MMB*, 1999, http://explore.bl.uk/BLVU1:LSCOP-ALL:BLLSA5651503.

45. Peter Allen, recorded interview by Lucy Ashwell for BBC Radio Humberside, *MMB*, 1998, C900/07016.

46. Arthur Schmul, recorded interview by Evelyn Draper for BBC Radio Merseyside, *MMB*, 1999, C900/10065; Ray Bevan cited in Herbert Williams, *Voices of Wales: The Century Speaks* (Stroud: History Press, 1999), 103.

47. Donna Bird and Miriam Bird, summary of interview for BBC Radio Norfolk, *MMB*, 1998, http://explore.bl.uk/BLVU1:LSCOP-ALL:BLLSA6014820.

48. Ann Simpson, recorded interview by Neil Gander for BBC Radio Cleveland, *MMB*, 1999, C900/01603; Cheryl Vines, recorded interview by Julia Letts for BBC Hereford and Worcester, *MMB*, 1999, C900/06638.

49. Bruce Findlay, summary of interview for BBC Radio Scotland, *MMB*, 1998, http://explore.bl.uk/BLVU1:LSCOP-ALL:BLLSA6477281.

50. Joanna Cole, summary of interview by Neil Gander for BBC Radio Cleveland, *MMB*, 1999, http://explore.bl.uk/BLVU1:LSCOP-ALL:BLLSA5592786.

51. Thomas Anthony Eccleston, summary of interview by Evelyn Draper for BBC Radio Merseyside, *MMB*, 1999, http://explore.bl.uk/BLVU1:LSCOP-ALL: BLLSA5959648.

52. Joan Wakeling, summary of interview by Cristina Parry for BBC Thames Valley, *MMB*, 1999, http://explore.bl.uk/BLVU1:LSCOP-ALL:BLLSA5651546.

53. Simpson, recorded interview, C900/01603. Here she is paraphrasing her mother's impression of the 1960s.

54. Vines, recorded interview, C900/06638.

55. Bent Larsen, summary of interview by Eva Simmons for BBC Radio Cambridgeshire, *MMB*, 1998, http://explore.bl.uk/BLVU1:LSCOP-ALL: BLLSA5627229.

56. Joan Wakeling, summary of interview by Cristina Parry for BBC Thames Valley, *MMB*, 1999, http://explore.bl.uk/BLVU1:LSCOP-ALL:BLLSA5651546; John Steele, summary of interview by Virtue Jones for BBC Radio Newcastle, *MMB*, 1998, http://explore.bl.uk/BLVU1:LSCOP-ALL:BLLSA5959778.

57. Ian Ayres, summary of interview by Chris Eldon Lee for BBC Radio Shropshire, *MMB*, 1998, http://explore.bl.uk/BLVU1:LSCOP-ALL:BLLSA5962965; Brian Hogg, summary of interview for BBC Radio Scotland, *MMB*, 1999, http://explore.bl.uk/BLVU1:LSCOP-ALL:BLLSA6477216.

58. Tony Allen, summary of interview by Evelyn Draper for BBC Radio Merseyside, *MMB*, 1998, http://explore.bl.uk/BLVU1:LSCOP-ALL:BLLSA6869337.

59. Peter Allen, recorded interview, C900/07016.

Bibliography

Primary Sources

Archives

BBC Genome Project, https://genome.ch.bbc.co.uk

BBC Written Archives Centre, Caversham

British Cartoon Archive: www.cartoons.ac.uk

British Library Sound Archive, London

British Social Attitudes Information System, www.britsocat.com

Communist Party of Great Britain Archive, www.communistpartyarchive
.org.uk

GESIS Data Archive for the Social Sciences, www.gesis.org/en/institute/
departments/data-archive-for-the-social-sciences

Hansard 1803–2005, https://api.parliament.uk/historic-hansard/index
.html

Inter-University Consortium for Political and Social Research, www
.icpsr.umich.edu

Popular Culture in Britain and America, 1950–1975, www
.rockandroll.amdigital.co.uk

Rock's Backpages, www.rocksbackpages.com/

Special Collections and Archives of Liverpool John Moores University,
Liverpool

Statista, www.statista.com

UK Data Archive, www.data-archive.ac.uk

Periodicals

To save space, articles in non-academic periodicals are not listed separately in the bibliography. Full references to these, as well as to websites and broadcasts, are provided in the endnotes using the abbreviated titles in parentheses.

7 Days

Anarchy

The Beatles Book (Beatles Book)
Black Dwarf
Blackfriars/New Blackfriars
The Catholic Herald
Challenge
The Church Times
The Daily Express (Express)
The Daily Herald (Herald)
The Daily Mail (Mail)
The Daily Mirror (Mirror)
The Daily Telegraph (Telegraph)
Disc and Music Echo
Disc Weekly
The Economist
Encounter
Ethical Record
Fabulous 208
Freedom Anarchist Weekly
Frendz
Gandalf's Garden
Girl
Gramophone
The Guardian (Guardian)
Harper's Bazaar
Heatwave
Honey
Ink
Internationale Situationniste
International Socialism
International Times (IT)
Jackie
Keep Left
The Listener (Listener)
The London Evening Standard (Standard)
Marxism Today
The Marxist
Melody Maker
Music and Life
The Musical Times
New Left Review (NLR)

New Musical Express (NME)
The New Reasoner
New Society
New Statesman
New York Times
NOP Political Bulletin
The Observer (Observer)
Oz
Partisan Review
Peace News
Petticoat
Private Eye
Punch
Rave
Record Mirror
Red Mole
Resurgence
Rolling Stone
Socialist Challenge
Socialist Commentary
Socialist Standard
The Spectator (Spectator)
The Sun (Sun)
The Sunday Express (Sunday Express)
The Sunday Mirror (Sunday Mirror)
The Sunday Telegraph (Sunday Telegraph)
The Sunday Times (Sunday Times)
The Times (Times)
The Times Higher Education Supplement (THES)
The Times Literary Supplement (TLS)
Transition
Tribune
Vogue
VSC Bulletin

Sound Recordings by the Beatles (in Chronological Order)

'Love Me Do'/'P. S. I Love You'. Parlophone R 4949, 5 October 1962.
'Please Please Me'/'Ask Me Why'. Parlophone R 4983, 11 January 1963.
Please Please Me. Parlophone PCS 3042, 22 March 1963.

'From Me to You'/'Thank You Girl'. Parlophone R 5015, 12 April 1963.

'Twist and Shout'/'A Taste of Honey'/'Do You Want to Know a Secret?'/ 'There's a Place'. Parlophone GEP 8882, 12 July 1963.

'She Loves You'/'I'll Get You'. Parlophone R 5055, 23 August 1963.

With the Beatles. Parlophone PCS 3045, 22 November 1963.

'I Want to Hold Your Hand'/'This Boy'. Parlophone R 5084, 29 November 1963.

'Can't Buy Me Love'/'You Can't Do That'. Parlophone R 5114, 20 March 1964.

'Long Tall Sally'/'I Call Your Name'/'Slow Down'/'Matchbox'. Parlophone GEP 8913, 19 June 1964.

'A Hard Day's Night'/'Things We Said Today'. Parlophone R 5160, 10 July 1964.

A Hard Day's Night. Parlophone PCS 3058, 10 July 1964.

'I Feel Fine'/'She's a Woman'. Parlophone R 5200, 27 November 1964.

Beatles for Sale. Parlophone PCS 3062, 4 December 1964.

'Ticket to Ride'/'Yes It Is'. Parlophone R 5265, 9 April 1965.

'Help!'/'I'm Down'. Parlophone R 5303, 23 July 1965.

Help! Parlophone PCS 3071, 6 August 1965.

Rubber Soul. Parlophone PCS 3075, 3 December 1965.

'Day Tripper'/'We Can Work It Out'. Parlophone R 5389, 3 December 1965.

'Paperback Writer'/'Rain'. Parlophone R 5452, 10 June 1966.

'Eleanor Rigby'/'Yellow Submarine'. Parlophone R 5493, 5 August 1966.

Revolver. Parlophone PCS 7009, 5 August 1966.

A Collection of Beatles Oldies (But Goldies). Parlophone PCS 7016, 10 December 1966.

'Penny Lane'/'Strawberry Fields Forever'. Parlophone R 5570, 17 February 1967.

Sgt. Pepper's Lonely Hearts Club Band. Parlophone PCS 7027, 1 June 1967.

'All You Need Is Love'/'Baby, You're a Rich Man'. Parlophone R 5620, 7 July 1967.

'Hello Goodbye'/'I Am the Walrus'. Parlophone R 5655, 24 November 1967.

Magical Mystery Tour. Parlophone SMMT 1/2, 8 December 1967.

'Lady Madonna'/'The Inner Light'. Parlophone R 5675, 15 March 1968.

'Hey Jude'/'Revolution'. Apple R 5722, 30 August 1968.

The Beatles. Apple PCS 7067/8, 22 November 1968.

Yellow Submarine. Apple PCS 7070, 17 January 1969.

'Get Back'/'Don't Let Me Down'. Apple R 5777, 11 April 1969.

'The Ballad of John and Yoko'/'Old Brown Shoe'. Apple R 5786, 30 May 1969.

Abbey Road, Apple PCS 7088, 26 September 1969.

'Something'/'Come Together', Apple R 5814, 31 October 1969.

'Let It Be'/'You Know My Name (Look Up the Number)'. Apple R 5833, 6 March 1970.

Let It Be. Apple PXS 1, 8 May 1970.

'How Do You Do It', *Anthology 1.* Apple 7243 8 34445 2 6, 21 November 1995.

Sound Recordings by Other Artists (in Alphabetical Order)

The Barock and Roll Ensemble, *Eine Kleine Beatlemusik.* HMV 7EG 8887, 1965.

The Barron Knights with Duke D'Mond, 'Call Up The Groups' (Medley). Columbia DB 7317, 1964.

Black Dyke Mills Band, 'Thingumybob'/'Yellow Submarine'. Apple APPLE 4, 1968.

The Dave Clark Five, 'Glad All Over'/'I Know You'. Columbia DB 7154, 1963.

Bill Elliott and the Elastic Oz Band, 'God Save Us'/'Do the Oz'. Apple APPLE 36, 1971.

George Harrison, *All Things Must Pass.* Apple, STCH 639, 1970.

Engelbert Humperdinck, 'Release Me'/'Ten Guitars'. Decca F.12541, 1967.

Frank Ifield with Norrie Paramor and His Orchestra, 'The Wayward Wind'/'I'm Smiling Now'. Columbia 45–DB 4960, 1963.

John Lennon, *Imagine.* Apple PAS 10004, 1971.

John Lennon/Plastic Ono Band, 'Imagine'/'It's So Hard'. Apple (US) 1840, 1971.

John Lennon and Yoko Ono, *Unfinished Music No. 1: Two Virgins.* Apple/Track, SAPCOR 2/61301, 1968.

John Lennon and Yoko Ono, *Wedding Album.* Apple, SAPCOR 11, 1969.

John Lennon and Yoko Ono/Plastic Ono Band, 'Power to the People'/'Open Your Box'. Apple R 5892, 1971.

John Lennon and Yoko Ono/Plastic Ono Band with Elephant's Memory, *Some Time in New York City.* Apple PCSP 716, 1972.

John Lennon and Yoko Ono/Plastic Ono Band with Elephant's Memory, 'Woman Is the Nigger of the World'/'Sisters O Sisters'. Apple (US) 1848, 1972.

The London Waits, 'Softly Softly'/'Serenadio (Italian Serenade)'. Immediate IM 030, 1966.

Paul McCartney, *McCartney*. Apple PCS 7102, 1970.

Yoko Ono, *Approximately Infinite Universe*. Apple SAPDO 1001, 1973.

Peter and Gordon, 'A World without Love'/'If I Were You'. Columbia DB 7225, 1964.

Peter Sellers, 'A Hard Day's Night'/'Help!' Parlophone R 5393, 1965.

Plastic Ono Band, 'Cold Turkey'/'Don't Worry Kyoko (Mummy's Only Looking for a Hand in the Snow)'. Apple APPLES 1001, 1969.

Plastic Ono Band, 'Give Peace a Chance'/'Remember Love'. Apple APPLE 13, 1969.

Films

Lester, Richard, dir. *A Hard Day's Night*. Walter Shenson Films, 1964.

Lester, Richard, dir. *Help!* Walter Shenson Films, 1965.

Lester, Richard, dir. *How I Won the War*. United Artists, 1967.

Marquand, Christian, dir. *Candy*. ABC Pictures, 1968.

McGrath, Joseph, dir. *The Magic Christian*. Commonwealth United Corporation, 1969.

Watkins, Peter, dir. *Privilege*. Universal, 1967.

Whitehead, Peter, dir. *Tonite Let's All Make Love in London*. Lorrimer Films, 1967.

Whitehead, Peter, dir. *Wholly Communion*. Lorrimer Films, 1965.

Wonfor, Geoff, and Bob Smeaton, dir. *The Beatles Anthology*. ABC, 1995.

Young, Terence, dir. *Dr. No*. Eon Productions, 1962.

Books, Book Chapters and Scholarly Articles

Aaronovitch, David. *Party Animals: My Family and Other Communists*. London: Random House, 2016.

Aitken, Jonathan. *The Young Meteors*. London: Secker & Warburg, 1967.

Aldridge, Alan. *The Beatles Illustrated Lyrics*. Boston, MA: Houghton Mifflin Harcourt, 1969.

Ali, Tariq. *Street Fighting Years: An Autobiography of the Sixties*. London: Verso, 2005.

Allsop, Kenneth. 'Pop Goes Young Woodley'. In *Class: A Symposium*, edited by Richard Mabey, 127–43. London: Antony Blond, 1967.

Badman, Keith. *The Beatles: Off the Record – Outrageous Opinions and Unreleased Interviews*. London: Omnibus, 2007.

Bailey, David, and Francis Wyndham. *David Bailey's Box of Pin-Ups*. London: Weidenfeld and Nicolson, 1965.

Bailey, David, and Peter Evans. *Goodbye Baby & Amen: A Saraband for the Sixties*. London: Condé Nast, 1969.

Barrow, Tony. *John, Paul, George, Ringo and Me*. London: André Deutsch, 2006.

Beatles, The. *The Beatles Anthology*. San Francisco, CA: Chronicle Books, 2000.

Bedford, Carol. *Waiting for the Beatles: An Apple Scruff's Story*. London: Blandford Press, 1984.

Beloff, Max. 'The Challenge of Barbarism (1965)'. In *The Intellectual in Politics and Other Essays*. New York, NY: Library Press, 1971.

Benn, Tony. *Office without Power: Diaries 1968–72*. London: Random House, 2012.

Benn, Tony. *Out of the Wilderness: Diaries 1963–67*. London: Hutchinson, 1987.

Berke, Joseph H., ed. *Counter Culture: The Creation of an Alternative Society*. London: Peter Owen, 1969.

Black, Cilla. *What's It All About?* London: Random House, 2009.

Booker, Christopher. *The Neophiliacs: A Study of the Revolution in English Life in the Fifties and Sixties*. London: Collins, 1969.

Booker, Christopher. *The Seventies: The Decade That Changed the Future*. New York, NY: Stein and Day, 1981.

Bordowitz, Hank, ed. *Led Zeppelin on Led Zeppelin: Interviews and Encounters*. Chicago, IL: Chicago Review Press, 2014.

Bramwell, Tony, and Rosemary Kingsland. *Magical Mystery Tours: My Life with the Beatles*. Basingstoke: Macmillan, 2006.

Braun, Michael. *Love Me Do: The Beatles' Progress*. Harmondsworth: Penguin, 1964.

Brown, L. Neville. 'Student Protest in England'. *The American Journal of Comparative Law* 17, no. 3 (1969): 395–402.

Buckle, Richard. *Buckle at the Ballet*. New York, NY: Atheneum, 1980.

Burger, Jeff, ed. *Lennon on Lennon: Conversations with John Lennon*. London: Omnibus ebook, 2017.

Carlin, M. M. 'Love on Film'. *Transition*, no. 17 (1964): 35–8.

Chorley, D. F., and A. C. Nicholls. 'Letter'. *The Use of English* 20, no. 1 (1968): 48.

Clapton, Eric, and Christopher Sykes. *Eric Clapton: The Autobiography*. London: Century, 2007.

Clark, Timothy, Christopher Gray, Donald Nicholson-Smith and Charles Radcliffe. 'The Revolution of Modern Art and the Modern Art of Revolution'. Unpublished, 1967. www.cddc.vt.edu/sionline/si/modernart.html.

Clarke, John. 'Style'. In *Resistance through Rituals: Youth Subcultures in Post-War Britain*, edited by Tony Jefferson and Stuart Hall, 175–91. London: Routledge and Kegan Paul, 1975.

Cohn, Nik. *Awopbopaloobop Alopbamboom: Pop from the Beginning*. London: Minerva, 1969.

Cole, Peter. 'Lyrics in Pop'. In *Anatomy of Pop*, edited by Anthony Cash, 9–30. London: British Broadcasting Corporation, 1970.

Comfort, Alex. 'The Technological Age and Human Needs: An Emotional "Technology"'. In *Technology and Society: The First Bath Conference, 1965*, edited by Gerald Walters and Kenneth Hudson, 170–3. Bath: Bath University Press, 1966.

Connolly, Ray. *Stardust Memories: Talking about My Generation*. London: Pavilion, 1983.

Cooke, Deryck. *I Saw the World End: A Study of Wagner's Ring*. Oxford: Oxford University Press, 1979.

Cooke, Deryck. *The Language of Music*. Oxford: Oxford University Press, 1959.

Cox, C. B. 'Editorial'. *Critical Quarterly* 13, no. 3 (1971): 195–200.

Cremonesi, Heather. 'Yeah, Yeah'. In *Young London: Permissive Paradise*, edited by Frank Habicht. London: Harrap, 1969.

Crossman, Richard Howard Stafford. *The Diaries of a Cabinet Minister. Vol. 3: Secretary of State for Social Services, 1968–1970*. New York, NY: Holt, Rinehart and Winston, 1978.

Dallas, Karl. *Singers of an Empty Day: Last Sacraments for the Superstars*. London: Kahn & Averill, 1971.

Davies, Hunter. *The Beatles: The Authorised Biography*. New York, NY: McGraw-Hill, 1968.

Davies, Hunter. *The Beatles: The Authorised Biography*. Rev. edn. New York, NY: McGraw-Hill, 1985.

Davies, Russell, ed. *The Kenneth Williams Diaries*. London: HarperCollins, 1993.

DiLello, Richard. *The Longest Cocktail Party: An Insider's Diary of the Beatles, Their Million-Dollar Apple Empire, and Its Wild Rise and Fall*. Edinburgh: Canongate, 2005.

Du Noyer, Paul. *Conversations with McCartney*. New York, NY: Overlook Press, 2016.

Durgnat, Raymond. 'Rock, Rhythm and Dance'. *British Journal of Aesthetics* 11, no. 1 (1971): 28.

Epstein, Brian. *A Cellarful of Noise*. New York, NY: Doubleday, 1964.

Evans, Mike, ed. *The Beatles Literary Anthology*. London: Plexus, 2004.

Farren, Mick. *Give the Anarchist a Cigarette*. London: Random House, 2010.

Farren, Mick, and Edward Barker. *Watch Out Kids*. London: Open Gate Books, 1972.

Fast, Julius. *The Beatles: The Real Story*. New York, NY: G. P. Putnam's Sons, 1968.

Fawcett, Anthony. *John Lennon: One Day at a Time*. New York, NY: Grove Press, 1981.

Finnegan, Ruth, ed. *The Penguin Book of Oral Poetry*. London: Allen Lane, 1978.

Flower, Frederick Dalby. *Language and Education*. London: Longmans, 1966.

Forbes, Bryan. 'No Bone Showing'. *Transition*, no. 31 (1967): 46–50.

Fuller, Roy. *Owls and Artificers: Oxford Lectures on Poetry*. London: André Deutsch, 1971.

Fuller, Roy. *Professors and Gods: Last Oxford Lectures on Poetry*. London: André Deutsch, 1973.

Furlong, Monica. *The End of Our Exploring*. New York, NY: Coward, McCann & Geoghegan, 1973.

Fyvel, T. R. *The Insecure Offenders: Rebellious Youth in the Welfare State*. Harmondsworth: Penguin, 1966.

Fyvel, T. R. *Intellectuals Today: Problems in a Changing Society*. London: Chatto and Windus, 1968.

Golson, G. Barry, ed. *The Playboy Interviews with John Lennon and Yoko Ono*. New York, NY: Putnam Publishing Group, 1981.

Gombrich, Ernst. *Meditations on a Hobby Horse and Other Essays on the Theory of Art*. London: Phaidon, 1963.

Goodman, Arnold. *Tell Them I'm on My Way: Memoirs*. London: Chapmans, 1993.

Gorer, Geoffrey. *Exploring English Character*. New York, NY: Criterion, 1955.

Gorer, Geoffrey. *Sex and Marriage in England Today: A Study of the Views and Experience of the Under-45s*. London: Thomas Nelson, 1971.

Green, Jonathon, ed. *Days in the Life: Voices from the English Underground 1961–1971*. London: Minerva, 1989.

Hall, Stuart, and Paddy Whannel. *The Popular Arts*. London: Hutchinson Educational, 1964.

Hamblett, Charles. *Here Are the Beatles*. London: New English Library, 1964.

Hamblett, Charles, and Jane Deverson. *Generation X*. New York, NY: Tandem Books, 1964.

Harrison, George. *I, Me, Mine*. New York, NY: Simon and Schuster, 1981.

Hewat, Tim. *Rolling Stones File*. London: Panther, 1967.

Hoggart, Richard. *The Uses of Literacy: Aspects of Working-Class Life with Special Reference to Publications and Entertainments*. Harmondsworth: Pelican, 1958.

Holbrook, David. *Creativity and Popular Culture*. Rutherford, NJ: Fairleigh Dickinson University Press, 1994.

Holbrook, David. 'Predatory Beatles'. *The Use of English* 20 (1969): 204–12.

Holbrook, David. *The Pseudo-Revolution: A Critical Study of Extremist 'Liberation' in Sex*. London: Tom Stacey, 1972.

Holbrook, David. 'Quite Useful Neutrals'. *The Use of English* 17, no. 3 (1966): 195–8.

Hollingshead, Michael. *The Man Who Turned on the World*. London: Blond and Briggs, 1973.

Hughes, Donald. 'Recorded Music'. In *Discrimination and Popular Culture*, edited by Denys Thompson, 152–75. Harmondsworth: Penguin, 1964.

Huxley, Julian. 'Introduction'. *Philosophical Transactions of the Royal Society of London. Series B, Biological Sciences* 251, no. 772 (1966): 249–71.

Interdepartmental Committee on Drug Addiction. *Drug Addiction: The Second Report*. London: HMSO, 1965. https://web.archive.org/web/20141017120149/http://www.drugtext.org/Second-Brain-Report/drug-addiction-2.html.

Jacobs, Arthur. *A Short History of Western Music*. Harmondsworth: Penguin, 1972.

Jasper, Tony. *Understanding Pop*. London: S. C. M. Press, 1972.

Johnson, Pamela Hansford. *On Iniquity: Some Personal Reflections Arising Out of the Moors Murder Trial*. New York, NY: Scribner, 1967.

King Mob. 'The Death of Art Spells the Murder of Artists. The Real Anti-Artist Appears (1968)'. In *An Endless Adventure, an Endless Passion, an Endless Banquet: A Situationist Scrapbook*, edited by Iwona Blazwick, 70. London: ICA, 1989.

Kirkup, James. 'Review of *Unwrinkling Plays* by Paul Reps'. *Japan Quarterly* 12, no. 2 (1965): 260-2.

Lahr, John, ed. *The Diaries of Kenneth Tynan*. London: A&C Black, 2002.

Laing, Dave. *The Sound of Our Time*. London: Sheed & Ward, 1969.

Laurie, Peter. *The Teenage Revolution*. London: A. Blond, 1965.

Leach, Edmund. *A Runaway World? The Reith Lectures 1967*. London: British Broadcasting Corporation, 1967.

Lee, Edward. *Music of the People: A Study of Popular Music in Great Britain*. London: Barrie & Jenkins, 1970.

Leigh, Spencer, ed. *Speaking Words of Wisdom: Reflections on the 'Beatles'*. Liverpool: Cavern City Tours, 1991.

Lennon, Cynthia. *A Twist of Lennon*. London: Star Books, 1978.

Lennon, John. *Skywriting by Word of Mouth*. New York, NY: HarperCollins, 1987.

Lennon, John. 'The Ballad of John and Yoko'. In *Skywriting by Word of Mouth*. New York, NY: HarperCollins, 1987.

Leslie, Peter. *Fab: The Anatomy of a Phenomenon*. London: MacGibbon & Kee, 1965.

Levin, Bernard. *The Pendulum Years: Britain and the Sixties*. London: Jonathan Cape, 1970.

Lichtheim, George. *From Marx to Hegel*. London: Orbach and Chambers, 1971.

Lunn, Arnold, and Garth Lean. *Christian Counter-Attack*. London: Blandford, 1969.

Mabey, Richard. *The Pop Process*. London: Hutchinson Educational, 1969.

MacInnes, Colin. *England, Half English*. London: MacGibbon & Kee, 1961.

Mackerness, Eric David. *A Social History of English Music*. London: Routledge and Kegan Paul, 1964.

March, Ivan. ed., *The Great Records*. Blackpool: Long Playing Record Library, 1967.

Martin, George, and Jeremy Hornsby. *All You Need Is Ears*. Basingstoke: Macmillan, 1979.

Martin, George, and William Pearson. *Summer of Love: The Making of Sgt. Pepper*. Basingstoke: Macmillan, 1994.

McCabe, Peter, and Robert D. Schonfeld. *Apple to the Core: The Unmaking of the Beatles*. London: Martin Brian and O'Keeffe, 1972.

McCartney, Paul. *Blackbird Singing: Poems and Lyrics 1965–1999*. London: Faber, 2001.

Medanock, Alan. 'These Musical Times'. *Musical Times* 105, no. 1451 (1964): 24.

Mellers, Wilfrid. *Caliban Reborn: Renewal in Twentieth-Century Music*. London: Gollancz, 1967.

Mellers, Wilfrid. 'Music for 20th-Century Children. 3: The Teenager's World'. *The Musical Times* 105, no. 1457 (1964): 500–5.

Mellers, Wilfrid. 'Review of Debussy, Preludes (Books I & II). Leonard Pennario'. *The Musical Times* 107, no. 1483 (1966): 784.

Mellers, Wilfrid. 'The Avant-Garde in America'. *Proceedings of the Royal Musical Association* 90 (1963): 1–13.

Mellers, Wilfrid. *Twilight of the Gods: The Music of the Beatles*. New York, NY: Viking Press, 1974.

Melly, George. *Owning Up: The Trilogy*. Harmondsworth: Penguin, 2006.

Melly, George. *Revolt into Style: The Pop Arts in Britain*. Harmondsworth: Penguin, 1970.

Middleton, Richard. *Pop Music and the Blues: A Study of the Relationship and Its Significance*. London: Victor Gollancz, 1972.

Miles, Barry. *In the Sixties*. London: Jonathan Cape, 2002.

Miles, Barry. *The Zapple Diaries: The Rise and Fall of the Last Beatles Label*. New York, NY: Abrams, 2016.

Mitchell, Adrian. 'Priests and Prophets of Permissiveness'. In *The Permissive Society: The Guardian Inquiry*, edited by Harford Thomas. London: Panther, 1969.

Mitchell, Carolyn Lee, and Michael Munn. *All Our Loving: A Beatles Fan's Memoirs*. London: Robson Books, 1988.

Moorhouse, Geoffrey. *Britain in the Sixties: The Other England*. Harmondsworth: Penguin, 1964.

Muggeridge, Malcolm. *Another King: A Sermon*. Edinburgh: Saint Andrew Press, 1968.

Muggeridge, Malcolm. *Chronicles of Wasted Time*. New York, NY: W. W. Morrow, 1973.

Muggeridge, Malcolm. 'Down With Sex (1965)'. In *Tread Softly, For You Tread on My Jokes*. London: Collins, 1966.

Muggeridge, Malcolm. 'Looking through the Eye (1976)'. In *Seeing through the Eye: Malcolm Muggeridge on Faith*, edited by Cecil C. Kuhne III, 75–88. San Francisco, CA: Ignatius Press, 2005.

Murdock, Graham, and Robin McCron. 'Consciousness of Class and Consciousness of Generation'. In *Resistance through Rituals: Youth Subcultures in Post-War Britain*, edited by Tony Jefferson and Stuart Hall, 192–207. London: Routledge and Kegan Paul, 1975.

Neill, A. S. *Freedom – Not License!* New York, NY: Hart Publishing Company, 1966.

Neville, Richard. *Hippie Shake*. London: Gerald Duckworth & Co., 2010.

Neville, Richard. *Play Power*. London: Jonathan Cape, 1970.

Newton, Francis. *The Jazz Scene*. London: MacGibbon & Kee, 1959.

NOP. *Report on Attitudes towards Crime, Violence and Permissiveness in Society* London: NOP, 1970.

Nuttall, Jeff. *Bomb Culture*. London: Paladin, 1970.

Oldham, Andrew Loog. *2Stoned*. New York, NY: Random House, 2012.

Palmer, Tony. *All You Need Is Love: The Story of Popular Music*. Harmondsworth: Penguin, 1977.

Palmer, Tony. *Born under a Bad Sign*. London: William Kimber, 1970.

Parker, Charles. 'Pop Song, the Manipulated Ritual'. In *The Black Rainbow: Essays on the Present Breakdown of Culture*, edited by Peter Abbs, 134–65. London: Heinemann Educational, 1975.

Payn, Graham, and Sheridan Morley, eds. *Noël Coward Diaries*. New York, NY: Da Capo Press, 2000.

Paytress, Mark. *Rolling Stones: Off the Record*. London: Omnibus, 2009.

Pleasants, Henry. *Serious Music, and All That Jazz! An Adventure in Music Criticism*. London: Gollancz, 1969.

Prabhupāda, A. C. Bhaktivedanta, Swami. *Search for Liberation: Featuring a Conversation between John Lennon and Swami Bhaktivedanta*. Los Angeles, CA: Bhaktivedanta Book Trust, 1981.

Quant, Mary. *Quant by Quant*. London: Cassell, 1966.

Radcliffe, Charles. *Don't Start Me Talking: Subculture, Situationism and the Sixties*. ebook: Bread and Circuses, 2018.

Radcliffe, Charles. 'Pop Goes the Beatle'. In *Dancin' in the Streets! Anarchists, IWWs, Surrealists, Situationists & Provos in the 1960s as Recorded in the Pages of The Rebel Worker & Heatwave*, edited by Franklin Rosemont and Charles Radcliffe. Chicago, IL: Charles H. Kerr, 2005.

Radcliffe, Charles. 'Two Fiery Flying Rolls: The *Heatwave* Story, 1966–1970'. In *Dancin' in the Streets! Anarchists, IWWs, Surrealists, Situationists & Provos in the 1960s as Recorded in the Pages of The Rebel Worker & Heatwave*, edited by Franklin Rosemont and Charles Radcliffe. Chicago, IL: Charles H. Kerr, 2005.

Ramsey, Ian T. 'Talking about God: Models, Ancient and Modern'. In *Myth and Symbol*, vol. 7, edited by Frederick William Dillistone, 76–96. London: SPCK, 1966.

Reeves, James. 'The World of Sergeant Pepper'. *The Use of English* 19, no. 3 (1968): 235–40.

Robinson, Ian. 'Paper Tygers, or the Circus Animals' Desertion in the New Pop Poetry'. In *The Black Rainbow: Essays on the Present Breakdown of Culture*, edited by Peter Abbs, 19–30. London: Heinemann Educational, 1975.

Rosemont, Franklin, Charles Radcliffe and Richard Mabey. *Mods, Rockers and the Revolution*. London: Solidarity Bookshop, 1966.

Rosemont, Franklin. 'To Be Revolutionary in Everything: The *Rebel Worker* Story, 1964–1968'. In *Dancin' in the Streets! Anarchists, IWWs, Surrealists, Situationists & Provos in the 1960s as Recorded in the Pages of The Rebel Worker & Heatwave*, edited by Franklin Rosemont and Charles Radcliffe. Chicago, IL: Charles H. Kerr, 2005.

Roszak, Theodore. *The Making of a Counter Culture: Reflections on the Technocratic Society and Its Youthful Opposition*. Garden City, NY: Doubleday, 1969.

Rowbotham, Sheila. *Promise of a Dream: Remembering the Sixties*. London: Verso, 2001.

Rowbotham, Sheila. *Woman's Consciousness, Man's World*. Harmondsworth: Penguin, 1973.

Saltzman, Paul. *The Beatles in Rishikesh*. London: Viking Studio, 2000.

Sargant, William. 'Psychiatric Treatment in General Teaching Hospitals: A Plea for A Mechanistic Approach'. *British Medical Journal* 2, no. 5508 (1966): 257–62.

Sassoon, Vidal. *Sorry I Kept You Waiting, Madam*. London: Cassell, 1968.

Schofield, Michael. *The Sexual Behaviour of Young Adults*. London: Allen Lane, 1973.

Schofield, Michael. *The Sexual Behaviour of Young People*. London: Longmans, Green, 1965.

Shaw, Roy. *Culture and Equality: The Role of Adult Education*. Keele: University of Keele, 1969.

Shotton, Pete, and Nicholas Schaffner. *John Lennon: In My Life*. New York, NY: Stein & Day, 1983.

Social Surveys (Gallup Poll) Ltd. *Television and Religion*. London: University of London Press, 1964.

Souster, Tim. 'Notes on Pop Music'. *Tempo*, no. 87 (1968–1969): 2–6.

Steiner, George. *In Bluebeard's Castle: Some Notes towards the Redefinition of Culture*. New Haven, CT: Yale University Press, 1974.

Stengel, Erwin. 'Review of *Transcultural Psychiatry* by A. V. S. de Reuck'. *British Medical Journal* 2, no. 5505 (9 July 1966): 100–1.

Swearingen, Mark, and Don Christian, eds. *The Beatles 'Speaking Words of Wisdom': Beatles Interviews 1962–1970*. Scotts Valley, CA: Createspace, 2014.

Taylor, Derek. *As Time Goes By: Living in the Sixties with John Lennon, Paul McCartney . . ..* London: Straight Arrow Books, 1973.

Taylor, Derek. *Fifty Years Adrift*. Guildford: Genesis Publications, 1984.

Tynan, Kenneth. 'Review of *Help!* (1965)'. In *The Beatles Literary Anthology*, edited by Mike Evans, 144–5. London: Plexus, 2004.

Vaneigem, Raoul. 'The Revolution of Everyday Life'. *The Anarchist Library*, 1967. https://theanarchistlibrary.org/library/raoul-vaneigem-the-revolution-of-everyday-life.pdf.

Walter, Aubrey, ed. *Come Together: The Years of Gay Liberation, 1970–73*. Gay Men's Press, 1980.

Watts, Alan W. 'Wealth versus Money (1969)'. In *Does It Matter? Essays on Man's Relation to Materiality*, 1–23. Novato, CA: New World Library, 2010.

Wenner, Jann. *Lennon Remembers*. San Francisco, CA: Straight Arrow Books, 1971.

Wenner, Jann. *Lennon Remembers*. Rev. edn. London: Verso, 2000.

Wesker, Arnold. *Six Sundays in January*. London: Jonathan Cape, 1971.

Westrup, Jack. 'Editorial'. *Music & Letters* 49, no. 1 (1968): 1–3.

Widgery, David. *Preserving Disorder: Selected Essays 1968–1988*. London: Pluto Press, 1989.

Willett, John. *Art in a City*. Liverpool: Bluecoat Society of Arts/Methuen, 1967.

Williams, Herbert. *Voices of Wales: The Century Speaks*. Stroud: History Press, 1999.

Williams, Raymond, ed. *May Day Manifesto: 1968*. Harmondsworth: Penguin, 1968.

Wilson, Bryan. *The Youth Culture and the Universities*. London: Faber and Faber, 1970.

Wilson, Colin. *Colin Wilson on Music*. London: Pan, 1967.

Wilson, Elizabeth. *Women and the Welfare State*. London: Tavistock, 1977.

Wilson, Harold. *A Personal Record: The Labour Government, 1964–1970*. Boston, MA: Little, Brown, 1971.

Wise, David, and Stuart Wise. 'The End of Music'. In *What Is Situationism? A Reader*, edited by Stewart Home, 63–102. London: AK Press, 1996.

Workers' Music Association. *A Policy for Music in Post-War Britain*. London: Workers' Music Association, 1945.

Worsthorne, Peregrine. *The Socialist Myth*. New York, NY: Weybright and Talley, 1971.

Secondary Sources

Abra, Allison. *Dancing in the English Style: Americanisation and National Identity in Britain 1918–50*. Oxford: Oxford University Press, 2017.

Abraham, Mark. '"You Are Your Own Alternative": Performance, Pleasure, and the American Counterculture, 1965–1975'. PhD Thesis, York University, OT, 2014.

Abrams, Steve. 'The Wooton Retort: The Decriminalisation of Cannabis in Britain', 1997. www.nedprod.com/cannabis/essays/wraltnet.txt.

Adams, Matthew S. *Kropotkin, Read and the Intellectual History of British Anarchism*. Basingstoke: Palgrave, 2015.

Addison, David. 'Politics, Patronage, and the State in British Avant-Garde Music, c. 1959–c. 1974'. *Twentieth Century British History* 27, no. 2 (2016): 242–65.

Addison, Paul. *No Turning Back: The Peacetime Revolutions of Post-War Britain*. Oxford: Oxford University Press, 2010.

Addison, Paul, and Harriet Jones, eds. *A Companion to Contemporary Britain, 1939–2000*. Oxford: Blackwell, 2007.

Adlington, Robert, ed. *Sound Commitments: Avant-Garde Music and the Sixties*. Oxford: Oxford University Press, 2009.

Adorno, Theodor W. *The Culture Industry: Selected Essays on Mass Culture.* London: Routledge, 2005.

Akhtar, Miriam, and Stephen Humphries. *The Fifties and Sixties: A Lifestyle Revolution.* London: Boxtree, 2001.

Aldgate, Anthony. *Censorship and the Permissive Society: British Cinema and Theatre, 1955–1965.* Oxford: Oxford University Press, 1995.

Aldgate, Anthony, James Chapman and Arthur Marwick, eds. *Windows on the Sixties: Exploring Key Texts of Media and Culture.* London: I. B. Tauris, 2000.

Aldgate, Anthony, and James C. Robertson. *Censorship in Theatre and Cinema.* Edinburgh: Edinburgh University Press, 2005.

Allison, Dale C. *The Love There That's Sleeping: The Art and Spirituality of George Harrison.* London: Continuum, 2006.

Anderson, Virginia. '"1968" and the Experimental Revolution in Britain'. In *Music and Protest in 1968*, edited by Beate Kutschke and Barley Norton, 171–87. Cambridge: Cambridge University Press, 2013.

Andrews, Geoff. *Endgames and New Times: The Final Years of British Communism, 1964–1991.* London: Lawrence & Wishart, 2004.

Andrews, Geoff, Richard Cockett, Alan Hooper and Michael Williams, eds. *New Left, New Right and Beyond: Taking the Sixties Seriously.* Basingstoke: Springer, 1999.

Annan, Noel. *Our Age: Portrait of a Generation.* London: Weidenfeld and Nicolson, 1990.

Apolloni, Alexandra Marie. 'Wishin' and Hopin': Femininity, Whiteness, and Voice in 1960s British Pop'. PhD Thesis, UCLA, 2013.

Aquila, Richard. 'Why We Cried: John Lennon and American Culture'. *Popular Music and Society* 10, no. 1 (1985): 33–42.

Ashbolt, Anthony. *A Cultural History of the Radical Sixties in the San Francisco Bay Area.* London: Routledge, 2013.

Astley, John. *Why Don't We Do It in the Road? The Beatles Phenomenon.* New Haven, CT: Company of Writers, 2006.

Atkinson, Peter. 'The Beatles and the Broadcasting of British Cultural Revolution, 1958–63'. In *Fifty Years with the Beatles: The Impact of the Beatles on Contemporary Culture*, edited by Jerzy Jarniewicz and Alina Kwiatkowska, 15–28. Łódź: Łódź University Press, 2010.

Atkinson, Peter. 'The Beatles on BBC Radio in 1963: The "Scouse" Inflection and a Politics of Sound in the Rise of the Mersey Beat'. *Popular Music and Society* 34, no. 2 (2011): 163–175.

Atton, Chris. 'A Reassessment of the Alternative Press'. *Media, Culture & Society* 21, no. 1 (1999): 51–76.

August, Andrew. 'Gender and 1960s Youth Culture: The Rolling Stones and the New Woman'. *Contemporary British History* 23, no. 1 (2009): 79–100.

Auslander, Philip. *Performing Glam Rock: Gender and Theatricality in Popular Music.* Ann Arbor, MI: University of Michigan Press, 2006.

Ballard, Roger. 'Britain's Visible Minorities: A Demographic Overview'. 1999. CrossAsia-Repository. http://crossasia-repository.ub.uni-heidelberg.de/286/1/demography.pdf.

Bannister, Matthew. *White Boys, White Noise: Masculinities and 1980s Indie Guitar Rock*. Aldershot: Ashgate, 2006.

Bari, Martha Ann. 'Mass Media Is the Message: Yoko Ono and John Lennon's 1969 Year of Peace'. PhD Thesis, University of Maryland, 2007.

Barker, Martin. *A Haunt of Fears: The Strange History of the British Horror Comics Campaign*. Oxford, MS: University Press of Mississippi, 1984.

Barker, Yuval, and Hugh Taylor. *Faking It: The Quest for Authenticity in Popular Music*. London: Faber and Faber, 2007.

Barrell, Tony. *The Beatles on the Roof*. London: Omnibus, 2017.

Bartie, Angela. *The Edinburgh Festivals: Culture and Society in Postwar Britain*. Edinburgh: Edinburgh University Press, 2013.

Baur, Steven. 'You Say You Want a Revolution: The Beatles and Karl Marx'. In *The Beatles and Philosophy: Nothing You Can Think That Can't Be Thunk*, edited by Michael Baur and Steven Baur. Chicago, IL: Open Court, 2006.

Baur, Michael, and Steven Baur, eds. *The Beatles and Philosophy: Nothing You Can Think That Can't Be Thunk*. Chicago, IL: Open Court, 2006.

Bayton, Mavis. *Frock Rock: Women Performing Popular Music*. Oxford: Oxford University Press, 1998.

Beckett, Francis. *What Did the Baby Boomers Ever Do for Us?* London: Routledge, 2016.

Beer, Samuel H. *Britain against Itself: The Political Contradictions of Collectivism*. New York, NY: Norton, 1982.

Beers, Laura DuMond. 'Whose Opinion? Changing Attitudes towards Opinion Polling in British Politics, 1937–1964'. *Twentieth Century British History* 17, no. 2 (2006): 177–205.

Bell, Eleanor, and Linda Gunn, eds. *The Scottish Sixties: Reading, Rebellion, Revolution?* Amsterdam: Rodopi, 2013.

Belz, Carl. *The Story of Rock*. New York, NY: Oxford University Press, 1969.

Bennett, Andy. *Popular Music and Youth Culture: Music, Identity and Place*. Basingstoke: Macmillan, 2000.

Bennett, Andy. '"Sitting in an English Garden": Comparing Representations of "Britishness" in the Songs of the Beatles and 1990s Britpop Groups'. In *The Beatles, Popular Music and Society*, edited by Ian Inglis, 189–206. Basingstoke: Springer, 2000.

Bennett, Andy, and Jon Stratton, eds. *Britpop and the English Music Tradition*. London: Routledge, 2016.

Bennett, Tony, Simon Frith, Larry Grossberg, John Shepherd and Graeme Turner. 'Introduction'. In *Rock and Popular Music: Politics, Policies, Institutions*, edited by Tony Bennett, 1–5. London: Routledge, 2005.

Bentley, Nick. 'The Young Ones: A Reassessment of the British New Left's Representation of 1950s Youth Subcultures'. *European Journal of Cultural Studies* 8, no. 1 (2005): 65–83.

Bernstein, George L. *The Myth of Decline: The Rise of Britain since 1945*. London: Pimlico, 2004.

Berrong, Richard M. *Rabelais and Bakhtin: Popular Culture in Gargantua and Pantagruel*. Lincoln, NB: University of Nebraska Press, 2006.

Bidnall, Amanda. *West Indian Generation: Remaking British Culture in London, 1945–1965*. Oxford: Oxford University Press, 2017.

Bingham, Adrian. 'Cultural Hierarchies and the Interwar British Press'. In *Middlebrow Literary Cultures: The Battle of the Brows, 1920–1960*, edited by Erica Brown and Mary Grover, 55–68. Basingstoke: Springer, 2011.

Bingham, Adrian. *Family Newspapers? Sex, Private Life, and the British Popular Press 1918–1978*. Oxford: Oxford University Press, 2009.

Bingham, Adrian. 'Ignoring the First Draft of History? Searching for the Popular Press in Studies of Twentieth-Century Britain'. *Media History* 18, no. 3–4 (2012): 311–26.

Bingham, Adrian, and Martin Conboy. *Tabloid Century: The Popular Press in Britain, 1896 to the Present*. New York, NY: Peter Lang, 2015.

Black, Lawrence. '"Making Britain a Gayer and More Cultivated Country": Wilson, Lee and the Creative Industries in the 1960s'. *Contemporary British History* 20, no. 3 (2006): 323–42.

Black, Lawrence. *The Political Culture of the Left in Affluent Britain, 1951–64: Old Labour, New Britain?* Basingstoke: Palgrave Macmillan, 2003.

Black, Lawrence. *Redefining British Politics: Culture, Consumerism and Participation, 1954–70*. Basingstoke: Springer, 2010.

Black, Lawrence, and Hugh Pemberton, eds. *An Affluent Society? Britain's Post-War 'Golden Age' Revisited*. Aldershot: Ashgate, 2004.

Black, Lawrence, Hugh Pemberton and Pat Thane, eds. *Reassessing 1970s Britain*. Manchester: Manchester University Press, 2015.

Blake, Mark. *Pretend You're in a War: The Who and the Sixties*. London: Aurum, 2014.

Blaney, John. *Beatles for Sale: How Everything They Touched Turned to Gold*. London: Jawbone Press, 2008.

Bloom, Alexander. *Long Time Gone: Sixties America Then and Now*. Oxford: Oxford University Press, 2001.

Bloom, Clive. *Literature, Politics, and Intellectual Crisis in Britain Today*. Basingstoke: Palgrave, 2001.

Booth, Martin. *Cannabis: A History*. London: Bantam, 2004.

Bounds, Philip. 'From Folk to Jazz: Eric Hobsbawm, British Communism and Cultural Studies'. *Critique* 40, no. 4 (2012): 575–93.

Bourdieu, Pierre. *Distinction: A Social Critique of the Judgement of Taste*. Cambridge, MA: Harvard University Press, 1987.

Bradley, Dick. *Understanding Rock 'n' Roll: Popular Music in Britain 1955–1964.* Buckingham: Open University Press, 1992.

Brake, Laurel, Chandrika Kaul and Mark W. Turner, eds. *The News of the World and the British Press, 1843–2011.* Basingstoke: Springer, 2016.

Brake, Mike. *The Sociology of Youth Culture and Youth Subcultures: Sex and Drugs and Rock 'n' Roll.* London: Routledge & Kegan Paul, 1980.

Bratus, Alessandro. 'Scene through the Press: Rock Music and Underground Papers in London, 1966–73'. *Twentieth-Century Music* 8, no. 2 (2011): 227–52.

Braunstein, Peter, and Michael William Doyle, eds. *Imagine Nation: The American Counterculture of the 1960s and '70s.* London: Routledge, 2013.

Brennan, Matt. 'Down Beats and Rolling Stones: The American Jazz Press Decides to Cover Rock in 1967'. *Popular Music History* 1, no. 3 (2004): 263–84.

Brennan, Matt. *When Genres Collide: Down Beat, Rolling Stone, and the Struggle between Jazz and Rock.* New York, NY: Bloomsbury Publishing USA, 2017.

Brewitt-Taylor, Sam. 'Christianity and the Invention of the Sexual Revolution in Britain, 1963–1967', *Historical Journal* 60, no. 2 (2017): 519–46.

Brewitt-Taylor, Sam. 'The Invention of a "Secular Society"? Christianity and the Sudden Appearance of Secularization Discourses in the British National Media, 1961–4'. *Twentieth Century British History* 24, no. 3 (2013): 327–50.

Brocken, Michael. *Other Voices: Hidden Histories of Liverpool's Popular Music Scenes, 1930s–1970s.* London: Routledge, 2016.

Brocken, Michael. *The British Folk Revival: 1944–2002.* Aldershot: Ashgate, 2013.

Brocken, Michael, and Melissa Davis. 'Introduction'. In *The Beatles Bibliography: A New Guide to the Literature* . Manitou Springs, CO: Beatle Works Limited, 2012.

Brocken, Michael, and Melissa Davis, eds. *The Beatles Bibliography: A New Guide to the Literature.* Manitou Springs, CO: Beatle Works Limited, 2012.

Bromell, Nicholas. *Tomorrow Never Knows: Rock and Psychedelics in the 1960s.* Chicago, IL: University of Chicago Press, 2000.

Brooke, Stephen. *Sexual Politics: Sexuality, Family Planning, and the British Left from the 1880s to the Present Day.* Oxford: Oxford University Press, 2011.

Brooke, Stephen. '"Slumming" in Swinging London? Class, Gender and the Post-War City in Nell Dunn's *Up the Junction* (1963)'. *Cultural and Social History* 9, no. 3 (2012): 429–49.

Brookes, Barbara. *Abortion in England 1900–1967.* London: Routledge, 1988.

Brown, Callum G. *Religion and Society in Twentieth-Century Britain.* Harlow: Longman, 2006.

Brown, Callum G. 'Sex, Religion, and the Single Woman c. 1950–75: The Importance of a "Short" Sexual Revolution to the English Religious Crisis of the Sixties'. *Twentieth Century British History* 22, no. 2 (2011): 189–215.

Brown, Callum G. *The Death of Christian Britain*. Rev. edn. London: Routledge, 2013.

Brown, Callum G. 'What Was the Religious Crisis of the 1960s?' *Journal of Religious History* 34, no. 4 (2010): 468–479.

Brown, Erica, and Mary Grover, eds. *Middlebrow Literary Cultures: The Battle of the Brows, 1920–1960*. Basingstoke: Springer, 2011.

Brown, Shelina. 'Scream from the Heart: Yoko Ono's Rock and Roll Revolution'. In *Countercultures and Popular Music*, edited by Sheila Whiteley and Jedediah Sklower, 171–90. London: Routledge, 2014.

Brown, Timothy Scott. 'The Sixties in the City: Avant-Gardes and Urban Rebels in New York, London, and West Berlin'. *Journal of Social History* 46, no. 4 (2013): 817–42.

Brown, Timothy Scott. *West Germany and the Global Sixties: The Anti-Authoritarian Revolt, 1962–1978*. Cambridge: Cambridge University Press, 2013.

Brown, Timothy Scott, and Andrew E. Lison, eds. *The Global Sixties in Sound and Vision: Media, Counterculture, Revolt*. Basingstoke: Palgrave Macmillan, 2014.

Browne, Sarah F. *The Women's Liberation Movement in Scotland*. Manchester: Manchester University Press, 2014.

Bruce, Steve. *Scottish Gods: Religion in Modern Scotland, 1900–2012*. Edinburgh: Edinburgh University Press, 2014.

Bruce, Steve, and Tony Glendinning. 'When Was Secularization? Dating the Decline of the British Churches and Locating Its Cause'. *The British Journal of Sociology* 61, no. 1 (2010): 107–26.

Bruendel, Steffen. 'Global Dimensions of Conflict and Cooperation: Public Protest and the Quest for Transnational Solidarity in Britain, 1968–1973'. In *A Revolution of Perception? Consequences and Echoes of 1968*, edited by Ingrid Gilcher-Holtey, 35–68. New York, NY: Berghahn Books, 2014.

Bryan-Wilson, Julia. 'Remembering Yoko Ono's "Cut Piece"'. *Oxford Art Journal* 26, no. 1 (2003): 101–23.

Buckle, Sebastian. *The Way Out*. London: I. B. Tauris, 2015.

Buettner, Elizabeth. '"Would You Let Your Daughter Marry a Negro?" Race and Sex in 1950s Britain'. In *Gender, Labour, War and Empire*, edited by Philippa Levine and Susan R. Grayzel, 219–37. Basingstoke: Springer, 2009.

Bullivant, Joanna. *Alan Bush, Modern Music, and the Cold War: The Cultural Left in Britain and the Communist Bloc*. Cambridge: Cambridge University Press, 2017.

Burk, Kathleen, ed. *The British Isles since 1945*. Oxford: Oxford University Press, 2003.

Burkett, Jodi. *Constructing Post-Imperial Britain: Britishness, 'Race' and the Radical Left in the 1960s*. Basingstoke: Springer, 2013.

Burns, Robert G. *Transforming Folk: Innovation and Tradition in English Folk-Rock Music*. Manchester: Manchester University Press, 2012.

Buxton, David. 'Rock Music, the Star-System and the Rise of Consumerism'. *Telos* 1983, no. 57 (1983): 93–106.

Caine, Andrew. *Interpreting Rock Movies: The Pop Film and Its Critics in Britain.* Manchester: Manchester University Press, 2004.

Campbell, Colin. *The Continuing Story of Eleanor Rigby: Analysing the Lyric of a Popular Beatles' Song.* Kibworth Beauchamp: Troubador, 2018.

Campbell, Colin. *The Easternization of the West: A Thematic Account of Cultural Change in the Modern Era.* London: Routledge, 2008.

Campbell, Colin, and Allan R. Murphy. *Things We Said Today: The Complete Lyrics and a Concordance to the Beatles' Songs, 1962–1970.* Ann Arbor, MI: Pierian Press, 1980.

Campbell, Kenneth L. 'You Say You Want a Revolution'. In *The Beatles, Sgt. Pepper, and the Summer of Love,* edited by Kenneth Womack and Kathryn B. Cox, 161–73. Lanham, MD: Lexington, 2017.

Cavicchi, Daniel. *Tramps Like Us: Music and Meaning among Springsteen Fans.* New York, NY: Oxford University Press, 1998.

Chambers, Iain. *Urban Rhythms: Pop Music and Popular Culture.* Basingstoke: Macmillan, 1985.

Chapman, Robert. *Selling the Sixties: The Pirates and Pop Music Radio.* London: Routledge, 2012.

Clapson, Mark. *A Bit of a Flutter: Popular Gambling and English Society, c. 1823–1961.* Manchester: Manchester University Press, 1992.

Clayson, Alan. *Beat Merchants: The Origins, History, Impact, and Rock Legacy of the 1960s British Pop Groups.* London: Blandford, 1995.

Clements, Ben. *Religion and Public Opinion in Britain: Continuity and Change.* Basingstoke: Palgrave Macmillan, 2015.

Clements, Ben. *Surveying Christian Beliefs and Religious Debates in Post-War Britain.* Basingstoke: Palgrave Macmillan, 2016.

Clements, Ben, and Clive D. Field. 'Abortion and Public Opinion in Great Britain: A 50-Year Retrospective'. *Journal of Beliefs & Values* 39, no. 4 (2018): 429–44.

Clements, Ben, and Clive D. Field. 'Public Opinion toward Homosexuality and Gay Rights in Great Britain'. *Public Opinion Quarterly* 78, no. 2 (2014): 523–47.

Cloonan, Martin. *Banned! Censorship of Popular Music in Britain, 1967–92.* London: Arena, 1996.

Cloonan, Martin. 'The Production of English Rock and Roll Stardom in the 1950s'. *Popular Music History* 4, no. 3 (2009).

Cloonan, Martin. 'You Can't Do That: The Beatles, Artistic Freedom and Censorship'. In *The Beatles, Popular Music and Society,* edited by Ian Inglis, 126–49. Basingstoke: Springer, 2000.

Coffman, James T. '"Everybody Knows This Is Nowhere": Role Conflict and the Rock Musician'. *Popular Music & Society* 1, no. 1 (1971): 20–32.

Cohen, Stanley. *Folk Devils and Moral Panics: The Creation of the Mods and Rockers.* 3rd edn. London: Routledge, 2002.

Coleman, Ray. *Brian Epstein: The Man Who Made the Beatles*. Harmondsworth: Penguin, 1989.

Coleman, Ray. *Lennon*. New York, NY: McGraw-Hill, 1986.

Collini, Stefan. *Absent Minds: Intellectuals in Britain*. Oxford: Oxford University Press, 2006.

Collini, Stefan. *Public Moralists: Political Thought and Intellectual Life in Britain 1850–1930*. Oxford: Clarendon Press, 1991.

Collins, Marcus. '"The Age of the Beatles": Parliament and Popular Music in the 1960s'. *Contemporary British History* 27, no. 1 (2013): 85–107.

Collins, Marcus. 'The Beatles' Politics'. *The British Journal of Politics & International Relations* 16, no. 2 (2014): 291–309.

Collins, Marcus. 'The Fall of the English Gentleman: The National Character in Decline, c. 1918–1970'. *Historical Research* 75, no. 187 (2002): 90–111.

Collins, Marcus. 'I Feel Free: The Worldview of British Rock and Pop Musicians, c. 1965–1975'. In *Popular Culture in Britain and America, 1950–1975*. Cheltenham: Adam Matthew Digital, 2013. www.rockandroll.amdigital.co.uk/.

Collins, Marcus. 'Immigration and Opinion Polls in Postwar Britain'. *Modern History Review* 18, no. 4 (2016): 8–13.

Collins, Marcus. 'Interpreting the Beatles'. *Teaching History*, no. 136 (2009): 42.

Collins, Marcus. 'Introduction: Nothing You Can Know That Isn't Known?' *Popular Music History* 9, no. 1 (2014): 5–10.

Collins, Marcus. 'Introduction: The Permissive Society and Its Enemies'. In *The Permissive Society and Its Enemies: Sixties British Culture*, edited by Marcus Collins, 1–40. London: Rivers Oram, 2007.

Collins, Marcus. *Modern Love: An Intimate History of Men and Women in Twentieth Century Britain*. London: Atlantic, 2003.

Collins, Marcus. 'Permissiveness on Trial: Sex, Drugs, Rock, the Rolling Stones, and the Sixties Counterculture'. *Popular Music and Society* 42, no. 2 (2019): 188–209.

Collins, Marcus. 'Pride and Prejudice: West Indian Men in Mid-Twentieth-Century Britain'. *Journal of British Studies* 40, no. 3 (2001): 391–418.

Collins, Marcus. 'Sucking in the Seventies? The Rolling Stones and the Aftermath of the Permissive Society'. *Popular Music History* 7, no. 1 (2012): 5–23.

Collins, Marcus. 'We Can Work It Out: Popular and Academic Writing on The Beatles'. *Popular Music History* 9, no. 1 (2014): 79–101.

Collins, Marcus, ed. *The Permissive Society and Its Enemies: Sixties British Culture*. London: Rivers Oram, 2007.

Colls, Robert. *Identity of England*. Oxford: Oxford University Press, 2002.

Conboy, Martin. *Tabloid Britain: Constructing a Community through Language*. London: Routledge, 2006.

Concannon, Kevin. 'Yoko Ono's "Cut Piece": From Text to Performance and Back Again'. *PAJ: A Journal of Performance and Art* 30, no. 3 (2008): 81–93.

Conekin, Becky E. 'Fashioning Mod: Twiggy and the Moped in "Swinging" London'. *History and Technology* 28, no. 2 (2012): 209–15.

Connery, Christopher Leigh. 'The World Sixties'. In *The Worlding Project: Doing Cultural Studies in the Era of Globalization*, edited by Rob Wilson and Christopher Leigh Connery, 77–108. Berkeley, CA: North Atlantic Books, 2007.

Cook, Hera. *The Long Sexual Revolution: English Women, Sex, and Contraception 1800–1975*. Oxford: Oxford University Press, 2005.

Cook, Matt. *Queer Domesticities: Homosexuality and Home Life in Twentieth-Century London*. Basingstoke: Springer, 2014.

Cooper, Laura E., and B. Lee Cooper. 'The Pendulum of Cultural Imperialism: Popular Music Interchanges between the United States and Britain, 1943–1967'. *The Journal of Popular Culture* 27, no. 3 (1993): 61–78.

Cooper, Sam. 'Heatwave: Mod, Cultural Studies, and the Counterculture'. In *Quadrophenia and Mod(ern) Culture*, edited by Pamela Thurschwell, 67–81. Basingstoke: Springer, 2017.

Cooper, Sam. *The Situationist International in Britain: Modernism, Surrealism, and the Avant-Garde*. London: Taylor & Francis, 2016.

Courrier, Kevin. *Artificial Paradise: The Dark Side of the Beatles' Utopian Dream*. New York, NY: Praeger, 2009.

Covach, John. 'From "Craft" to "Art": Formal Structure in the Music of the Beatles'. In *Reading the Beatles: Cultural Studies, Literary Criticism, and the Fab Four*, edited by Kenneth Womack and Todd Davis, 37–53. Binghamton, NY: SUNY Press, 2006.

Cox, Kathryn B. 'Mystery Trips, English Gardens, and Songs Your Mother Should Know: The Beatles and British Nostalgia in 1967'. In *New Critical Perspectives on the Beatles: Things We Said Today*, ed. Kenneth Womack and Katie Kapurch, 31–50. Basingstoke: Springer, 2016.

Creasy, Martin. *Beatlemania! The Real Story of the Beatles UK Tours 1963–1965*. London: Omnibus, 2011.

Croft, Andy. 'Introduction'. In *A Weapon in the Struggle: The Cultural History of the Communist Party in Britain*, edited by Andy Croft, 1–6. London: Pluto Press, 1998.

Croft, Andy, ed. *A Weapon in the Struggle: The Cultural History of the Communist Party in Britain*. London: Pluto Press, 1998.

Cross, Gary. *Worktowners at Blackpool: Mass-Observation and Popular Leisure in the 1930s*. London: Routledge, 2005.

Curran, Kieran. *Cynicism in British Post-War Culture*. Basingstoke: Palgrave Macmillan, 2015.

Daniels, Stephen. 'Suburban Pastoral: "Strawberry Fields Forever" and Sixties Memory'. *Cultural Geographies* 13, no. 1 (2006): 28–54.

Davenport-Hines, R. P. T. *The Pursuit of Oblivion: A Social History of Drugs*. London: Orion, 2004.

Davidson, Roger, and Gayle Davis. 'Sexuality and the State: The Campaign for Scottish Homosexual Law Reform, 1967–80'. *Contemporary British History* 20, no. 4 (2006): 533–58.

Davidson, Roger, and Gayle Davis. *The Sexual State: Sexuality and Scottish Governance, 1950–80*. Edinburgh: Edinburgh University Press, 2012.

Davie, Grace. *Religion in Britain: A Persistent Paradox*. Boston, MA: Wiley Blackwell, 2015.

Davies, Alastair, and Alan Sinfield. *British Culture of the Post-War: An Introduction to Literature and Society 1945–1999*. London: Routledge, 2013.

Davies, Christie. *The Strange Death of Moral Britain*. Piscataway, NJ: Transaction Publishers, 2004.

Davies, Hunter. *The Beatles Lyrics: The Stories behind the Music, Including the Handwritten Drafts of More than 100 Classic Beatles Songs*. London: Hachette UK, 2014.

Davies, Stephen. *Empiricism and History*. Basingstoke: Palgrave, 2003.

Davis, Andy. *The Beatles Files*. London: MetroBooks, 2000.

Davis, John. 'Containing Racism? The London Experience, 1957–1968'. In *The Other Special Relationship: Race, Rights, and Riots in Britain and the United States*, edited by Robin D. G. Kelley and Stephen Tuck, 125–46. Basingstoke: Palgrave Macmillan, 2015.

Davis, John. 'The London Drug Scene and the Making of Drug Policy, 1965–73'. *Twentieth Century British History* 17, no. 1 (2006): 26–49.

Davis, John. *Youth and the Condition of Britain: Images of Adolescent Conflict*. London: Athlone Press, 1990.

De Groot, Gerard J. *The 60s Unplugged: A Kaleidoscopic History of a Disorderly Decade*. London: Pan, 2009.

Decker, James M. '"Try Thinking More": *Rubber Soul* and the Beatles' Transformation of Pop'. In *The Cambridge Companion to the Beatles*, edited by Kenneth Womack, 75–89. Cambridge: Cambridge University Press, 2009.

Derogatis, Jim. *Kaleidoscope Eyes: Psychedelic Music from the 1960s to the 1990s*. London: Fourth Estate, 1996.

Devereux, Eoin, Aileen Dillane and Martin Power, eds. *David Bowie: Critical Perspectives*. London: Routledge, 2015.

Dick, Luke, and George Reisch, eds. *The Rolling Stones and Philosophy: It's Just a Thought Away*. Chicago, IL: Open Court, 2011.

Dickstein, Morris. *Gates of Eden: American Culture in the Sixties*. New York, NY: Basic Books, 1978.

Diski, Jenny. *The Sixties*. London: Profile, 2010.

Doggett, Peter. *There's a Riot Going on: Revolutionaries, Rock Stars, and the Rise and Fall of '60s Counter-Culture*. Edinburgh: Canongate, 2007.

Doggett, Peter. *You Never Give Me Your Money: The Battle for the Soul of the Beatles*. London: CCV, 2010.

Donnelly, Mark. *Sixties Britain: Culture, Society, and Politics.* Harlow: Pearson Longman, 2005.

Donsbach, Wolfgang, and Michael W. Traugott, eds. *The SAGE Handbook of Public Opinion Research.* Los Angeles, CA: Sage, 2008.

Doyle, Tom. *Man on the Run: Paul McCartney in the 1970s.* Edinburgh: Birlinn, 2013.

Du Noyer, Paul. *Liverpool: Wondrous Place: Music from the Cavern to the Coral.* London: Virgin, 2004.

Duits, Linda, Koos Zwaan and Stijn Reijners, eds. *The Ashgate Research Companion to Fan Cultures.* Aldershot: Ashgate, 2014.

Dworkin, Dennis L. *Cultural Marxism in Postwar Britain: History, the New Left, and the Origins of Cultural Studies.* Durham, NC: Duke University Press, 1997.

Dyhouse, Carol. *Girl Trouble: Panic and Progress in the History of Young Women.* London: Zed Books, 2013.

Echols, Alice. *Hot Stuff.* New York, NY: W. W. Norton, 2010.

Echols, Alice. *Scars of Sweet Paradise: The Life and Times of Janis Joplin.* Basingstoke: Macmillan, 1999.

Ehrenreich, Barbara, Elizabeth Hess and Gloria Jacobs. 'Beatlemania: Girls Just Want to Have Fun'. In *The Adoring Audience: Fan Culture and Popular Media*, edited by Lisa A. Lewis, 84–106. London: Routledge, 1992.

Elliott, Anthony. 'Celebrity and Political Psychology: Remembering Lennon'. *Political Psychology* 19, no. 4 (1998): 833–52.

Elliott, Anthony. *The Mourning of John Lennon.* Berkeley, CA: University of California Press, 1999.

Ellis, Catherine. 'No Hammock for the Idle: The Conservative Party, "Youth" and the Welfare State in the 1960s'. *Twentieth Century British History* 16, no. 4 (2005): 441–70.

Emsley, Clive. *Exporting British Policing During the Second World War: Policing Soldiers and Civilians.* London: Bloomsbury Publishing, 2017.

Evans, Sara Margaret. *Personal Politics: The Roots of Women's Liberation in the Civil Rights Movement and the New Left.* New York, NY: Vintage Books, 1979.

Everett, Walter. *The Beatles as Musicians: Revolver through the Anthology.* Oxford: Oxford University Press, 1999.

Everett, Walter. *The Beatles as Musicians: The Quarry Men through Rubber Soul.* New York, NY: Oxford University Press, 1999.

Everett, Walter. 'The Future of Beatles' Research'. In *Beatlestudies 3*, edited by Yrjö Heinonen, 25–44. Jyväskylä: University of Jyväskylä, 2000.

Eversole, Britt. 'Occupy the Fun Palace'. *Thresholds* 41 (2013): 32–45.

Farber, David. 'The Sixties Legacy: "The Destructive Generation" or "Years of Hope"?' In *The Columbia Guide to America in the 1960s*, edited by David Farber and Beth Bailey. New York, NY: Columbia University Press, 2010.

Fast, Susan. *In the Houses of the Holy: Led Zeppelin and the Power of Rock Music.* Oxford: Oxford University Press, 2001.

Faulk, Barry J. *British Rock Modernism, 1967–1977: The Story of Music Hall in Rock.* London: Routledge, 2016.

Field, Clive D. *Britain's Last Religious Revival? Quantifying Belonging, Behaving, and Believing in the Long 1950s.* Basingstoke: Palgrave Pivot, 2015.

Field, Clive D. *Secularization in the Long 1960s: Numerating Religion in Britain.* Oxford: Oxford University Press, 2017.

Fielding, Steven. *The Labour Governments 1964–70, Volume 1: Labour and Cultural Change.* Manchester: Manchester University Press, 2003.

Fink, Janet, and Penny Tinkler. 'Teetering on the Edge: Portraits of Innocence, Risk and Young Female Sexualities in 1950s and 1960s British Cinema'. *Women's History Review* 26, no. 1 (2017): 9–25.

Finkelstein, David. 'The Role of the Literary and Cultural Periodical'. In *The Routledge Companion to British Media History*, edited by Martin Conboy and John Steel, 263–72. London: Routledge, 2015.

Fisher, Kate. *Birth Control, Sex and Marriage in Britain 1918–1960.* Oxford: Oxford University Press, 2006.

Flannery, Joe, and Mike Brocken. *Standing in the Wings: The Beatles, Brian Epstein and Me.* Stroud: History Press, 2013.

Fleiner, Carey. *The Kinks: A Thoroughly English Phenomenon.* Lanham, MD: Rowman & Littlefield, 2017.

Fogo, Fred. *'I Read the News Today': The Social Drama of John Lennon's Death.* Lanham, MD: Rowman & Littlefield, 1994.

Fonarow, Wendy. *Empire of Dirt: The Aesthetics and Rituals of British Indie Music.* Middletown, CT: Wesleyan University Press, 2006.

Førland, Tor Egil. 'Cutting the Sixties Down to Size: Conceptualizing, Historicizing, Explaining'. *Journal for the Study of Radicalism* 9, no. 2 (2015): 125–48.

Foucault, Michel. *The History of Sexuality, vol. 1: An Introduction.* New York, NY: Pantheon, 1978.

Fountain, Nigel. *Underground: The London Alternative Press, 1966–74.* London: Routledge, 1988.

Fowler, David. *Youth Culture in Modern Britain, c. 1920–c. 1970: From Ivory Tower to Global Movement – a New History.* Basingstoke: Palgrave Macmillan, 2008.

Frame, Pete. *The Restless Generation: How Rock Music Changed the Face of 1950s Britain.* London: Omnibus Press, 2011.

Fremaux, Stephanie. *The Beatles on Screen.* New York, NY: Bloomsbury, 2018.

Freshwater, Helen. *Theatre Censorship in Britain: Silencing, Censure and Suppression.* Basingstoke: Springer, 2009.

Frith, Simon. *Performing Rites: On the Value of Popular Music.* Cambridge, MA: Harvard University Press, 1998.

Frith, Simon. 'Popular Music and the Local State'. In *Rock and Popular Music: Politics, Policies, Institutions*, edited by Tony Bennett, Simon Frith, Larry Grossberg, John Shepherd and Graeme Turner, 14–24. London: Routledge, 1993.

Frith, Simon. *Sound Effects: Youth, Leisure and the Politics of Rock*. Rev. edn. London: Constable, 1983.

Frith, Simon. 'The Popular Music Industry'. In *The Cambridge Companion to Pop and Rock*, edited by Simon Frith, Will Straw, and John Street, 26–52. Cambridge: Cambridge University Press, 2010.

Frith, Simon, and Angela McRobbie. 'Rock and Sexuality'. In *On Record: Rock, Pop and the Written Word*, edited by Simon Frith and Andrew Goodwin, 371–89. London: Routledge, 1990.

Frith, Simon, and Howard Horne. *Art into Pop*. London: Methuen, 1987.

Frith, Simon, and Jon Savage. 'Pearls and Swine: Intellectuals and the Media', *NLR* 198 (1993), https://newleftreview.org/issues/I198/articles/jon-savage-simon-frith-pearls-and-swine-intellectuals-and-the-media.

Frontani, Michael R. *The Beatles: Image and Media*. Oxford, MS: University Press of Mississippi, 2007.

Gair, Christopher. *American Counterculture*. Edinburgh: Edinburgh University Press, 2007.

Gallup, George, Jr. *The Gallup International Public Opinion Polls, Great Britain 1937–1975: Vol. 1 – 1937–1964*. New York, NY: Random House, 1976.

Gallup, George, Jr. *The Gallup International Public Opinion Polls, Great Britain 1937–1975: Vol. 2 – 1965–1975*. New York, NY: Random House, 1976.

Gallwey, April. 'Love Beyond the Frame: Stories of Maternal Love Outside Marriage in the 1950s and 1960s'. In *Love and Romance in Britain, 1918–1970*, edited by Alana Harris and Tim Harris, 100–23. Basingstoke: Springer, 2015.

Gallwey, April. 'The Rewards of Using Archived Oral Histories in Research: The Case of the Millennium Memory Bank'. *Oral History* 41, no. 1 (2013): 37–50.

Gassert, Phillip, and Martin Klimke, eds. *1968: Memories and Legacies of a Global Revolt*. London: German Historical Institute, 2009.

Gassert, Phillip, and Martin Klimke. 'Introduction: 1968 from Revolt to Research'. In *1968: Memories and Legacies of a Global Revolt*, edited by Philipp Gassert and Martin Klimke, 5–24. London: German Historical Institute, 2009.

Geller, Debbie. *In My Life: The Brian Epstein Story*. Basingstoke: Macmillan, 2014.

Gemie, Sharif, and Brian Ireland. *The Hippie Trail: A History*. Oxford: Oxford University Press, 2017.

Gendron, Bernard. *Between Montmartre and the Mudd Club: Popular Music and the Avant-Garde*. Chicago, IL: University of Chicago Press, 2002.

Gilcher-Holtey, Ingrid, ed. *A Revolution of Perception? Consequences and Echoes of 1968*. New York, NY: Berghahn Books, 2014.

Gildart, Keith. 'From "Dead End Streets" to "Shangri Las": Negotiating Social Class and Post-War Politics with Ray Davies and the Kinks'. *Contemporary British History* 26, no. 3 (2012): 273–98.

Gildart, Keith. *Images of England through Popular Music: Class, Youth and Rock 'n' Roll, 1955–1976*. Basingstoke: Palgrave Macmillan, 2013.

Gildea, Robert, James Mark and Anette Warring. *Europe's 1968: Voices of Revolt*. Oxford: Oxford University Press, 2017.

Giuliano, Brenda, and Geoffrey Giuliano, eds. *Things We Said Today: Conversations with the Beatles*. Holbrook, MA: Adams Media Corporation, 1998.

Gleed, Paul. 'The Rest of You, If You'll Just Rattle Your Jewelry: The Beatles and Questions of Mass and High Culture'. In *Reading the Beatles: Cultural Studies, Literary Criticism, and the Fab Four*, edited by Kenneth Womack and Todd Davis, 161–8. Binghamton, NY: SUNY Press, 2006.

Gleeson, Kate. 'Consenting Adults in Private: In Search of the Sexual Subject'. PhD Thesis, University of New South Wales, 2006.

Glen, Patrick. 'Sometimes Good Guys Don't Wear White: Morality in the Music Press, 1967–1983'. PhD Thesis, University of Sheffield, 2013.

Gloag, Kenneth. 'The Beatles: High Modernism and/or Postmodernism?' In *Beatlestudies 3*, edited by Yrjö Heinonen, 79–84. Jyväskylä: University of Jyväskylä, 2000.

Gloag, Kenneth. 'Situating the 1960s: Popular Music – Postmodernism – History'. *Rethinking History* 5, no. 3 (2001): 397–410.

Glynn, Stephen. 'The Beatles' *Help!* Pop Art and the Perils of Parody'. *Journal of British Cinema and Television* 8, no. 1 (2011): 23–43.

Glynn, Stephen. *The British Pop Music Film: The Beatles and Beyond*. Basingstoke: Springer, 2013.

Glynn, Stephen. *A Hard Day's Night*. London: I. B. Tauris, 2005.

Goldman, Albert. *The Lives of John Lennon*. New York, NY: Bantam, 1989.

Goodall, Howard. *The Story of Music: From Babylon to the Beatles – How Music Has Shaped Civilization*. London: Pegasus, 2013.

Goodden, Joe. *Riding So High: The Beatles and Drugs*. London: Pepper & Pearl, 2017.

Goodman, Fred. *Allen Klein: The Man Who Bailed Out the Beatles, Made the Stones, and Transformed Rock & Roll*. Boston, MA: Houghton Mifflin Harcourt, 2015.

Goodway, David. *Anarchist Seeds beneath the Snow: Left-Libertarian Thought and British Writers from William Morris to Colin Ward*. Oakland, CA: PM Press, 2011.

Goodyer, Ian. *Crisis Music: The Cultural Politics of Rock against Racism*. Oxford: Oxford University Press, 2009.

Gorman, Paul. *In Their Own Write: Adventures in the Music Press*. London: Sanctuary Publishing, 2001.

Gosse, Van, and Richard Moser. *The World the Sixties Made: Politics and Culture in Recent America*. Philadelphia, PA: Temple University Press, 2008.

Gould, Jonathan. *Can't Buy Me Love: The Beatles, Britain, and America*. New York, NY: Three Rivers Press, 2008.

Gracyk, Theodore A. 'Romanticizing Rock Music'. *Journal of Aesthetic Education* 27, no. 2 (1993): 43–58.

Granados, Stefan. *Those Were the Days: An Unofficial History of the Beatles Apple Organization, 1967–2001*. London: Cherry Red, 2002.

Grant, Matthew. 'Historians, the Penguin Specials and the "State-of-the-Nation" Literature, 1958–64'. *Contemporary British History* 17, no. 3 (2003): 29–54.

Grayson, Richard S. 'Mods, Rockers and Juvenile Delinquency in 1964: The Government Response'. *Contemporary British History* 12, no. 1 (1998): 19–47.

Greene, Joshua M. *Here Comes the Sun: The Spiritual and Musical Journey of George Harrison*. London: Random House, 2006.

Grimley, Matthew. 'Anglican Evangelicals and Anti-Permissiveness: The Nationwide Festival of Light, 1971–1982'. In *Evangelicalism and the Church of England in the Twentieth Century: Reform, Resistance and Renewal*, edited by Andrew Atherstone and John G. Maiden, 183–205. London: Boydell & Brewer, 2014.

Grimley, Matthew. 'Law, Morality and Secularisation: The Church of England and the Wolfenden Report, 1954–1967'. *The Journal of Ecclesiastical History* 60, no. 4 (2009): 725–41.

Grossberg, Lawrence. 'Another Boring Day in Paradise: Rock and Roll and the Empowerment of Everyday Life'. *Popular Music* 4 (1984): 225–58.

Grossberg, Lawrence. 'The Framing of Rock: Rock and the New Conservatism'. In *Rock and Popular Music: Politics, Policies, Institutions*, edited by Tony Bennett, Simon Frith, Larry Grossberg, John Shepherd and Graeme Turner. 193–209. London: Routledge, 1993.

Grunenberg, Christoph, and Jonathan Harris, eds. *Summer of Love: Psychedelic Art, Social Crisis and Counterculture in the 1960s*. Liverpool: Liverpool University Press, 2005.

Hagan, Joe. *Sticky Fingers: The Life and Times of Jann Wenner and Rolling Stone Magazine*. Edinburgh: Canongate, 2017.

Hall, Simon. 'Protest Movements in the 1970s: The Long 1960s'. *Journal of Contemporary History* 43, no. 4 (2008): 655–72.

Hall, Stuart. *Policing the Crisis: Mugging, the State, and Law and Order*. Basingstoke: Pan Macmillan, 1978.

Hallam, Chris. 'Script Doctors and Vicious Addicts: Subcultures, Drugs, and Regulation under the "British System", *c.* 1917 to *c.* 1960'. PhD Thesis, London School of Hygiene & Tropical Medicine, 2016.

Hamilton, Jack. *Just around Midnight: Rock and Roll and the Racial Imagination*. Cambridge, MA: Harvard University Press, 2016.

Hamm, Charles. 'Popular Music and Historiography'. *Popular Music History* 1, no. 1 (2004): 9–14.

Hamm, Charles. *Putting Popular Music in Its Place*. Cambridge: Cambridge University Press, 1995.

Hansen, Dorothee. 'The Films'. In *John Lennon: Drawings, Performances, Films*, edited by Wulf Herzogenrath and Dorothee Hansen, 182–7. Berlin: Cantz, 1995.

Harison, Casey. *Feedback: The Who and Their Generation*. Lanham, MD: Rowman & Littlefield, 2014.

Harker, David. *One for the Money: Politics and Popular Song*. London: Hutchinson, 1980.

Harker, Dave. 'Still Crazy after All These Years: What Was Popular Music in the 1960s?' In *Cultural Revolution? The Challenge of the Arts in the 1960s*, edited by Bart Moore-Gilbert and John Seed. London: Routledge, 1992.

Harris, Alana. *Faith in the Family: A Lived Religious History of English Catholicism, 1945–82*. Oxford: Oxford University Press, 2016.

Harris, Jonathan. *The Utopian Globalists: Artists of Worldwide Revolution, 1919–2009*. Boston, MA: John Wiley & Sons, 2013.

Harris, Trevor, and Monia O'Brien Castro, eds. *Preserving the Sixties: Britain and the 'Decade of Protest'*. Basingstoke: Palgrave Macmillan, 2014.

Harrison, Brian. 'Historiographical Hazards of Sixties Britain'. In *Penultimate Adventures with Britannia: Personalities, Politics and Culture in Britain*, edited by William Roger Louis, 33–53. London: I. B. Tauris, 2008.

Harrison, Brian. *Seeking a Role: The United Kingdom, 1951–1970*. Oxford: Clarendon Press, 2009.

Harron, Mary. 'McRock: Pop as a Commodity'. In *Facing the Music*, edited by Simon Frith, 173–220. New York, NY: Pantheon, 1988.

Harry, Bill. *The John Lennon Encyclopedia*. London: Virgin, 2000.

Hawkins, Stan. *The British Pop Dandy: Masculinity, Popular Music and Culture*. Aldershot: Ashgate, 2009.

Hawkins, Stan. *Pop Music and Easy Listening*. London: Routledge, 2017.

Head, Dominic. *The Cambridge Introduction to Modern British Fiction, 1950–2000*. Cambridge: Cambridge University Press, 2002.

Heald, Gordon, and Robert J. Wybrow. *The Gallup Survey of Britain*. London: Croom Helm, 1986.

Hebdige, Dick. *Hiding in the Light: On Images and Things*. Philadelphia, PA: Psychology Press, 1988.

Hebdige, Dick. *Subculture: The Meaning of Style*. London: Methuen, 1979.

Heelas, Paul. *The New Age Movement*. Oxford: Blackwell, 1996.

Hegarty, Paul, and Martin Halliwell. *Beyond and Before: Progressive Rock since the 1960s*. London: Continuum, 2011.

Heilbronner, Oded. '"Helter-Skelter"? The Beatles, the British New Left, and the Question of Hegemony'. *Interdisciplinary Literary Studies* 13, no. 1/2 (2011): 87–107.

Heilbronner, Oded. 'The Peculiarities of the Beatles: A Cultural-Historical Interpretation'. *Cultural and Social History* 5, no. 1 (2008): 99–115.

Heinonen, Yrjö. 'The Creative Process of the Beatles Revisited: A Multi-Level Analysis of the Interaction between Individual and Collaborative Creativity'. *Popular Music History* 9, no. 1 (2014): 32–47.

Heinonen, Yrjö. 'Introduction: (Being a Short Diversion to) Current Perspectives in Beatles' Research'. In *Beatlestudies 1: Songwriting, Recording and Style Change*, edited by Yrjö Heinonen, i–iv. Jyväskylä: University of Jyväskylä, 1998.

Heinonen, Yrjö, and Tuomas Eerola. 'Songwriting, Recording and Style Change: Problems in the Chronology and Periodization of the Musical Style of the Beatles'. *Soundscapes: Journal on Media Culture* 3 (2000). www.icce.rug.nl/~soundscapes/VOLUME03/Songwriting_recording.shtml.

Helbig, Jörg. 'John Lennon as a Writer: Shun the Punman!' In *John Lennon: Drawings, Performances, Films*, edited by Wulf Herzogenrath and Dorothee Hansen. Berlin: Cantz, 1995.

Helbig, Jörg, ed. *Summer of Love: The Beatles, Art and Culture in the Sixties*. Trier: Wissenschaftlicher Verlag Trier, 2008.

Hendy, David. 'Bad Language and BBC Radio Four in the 1960s and 1970s'. *Twentieth Century British History* 17, no.1 (2006): 74–102.

Hennessy, Peter. *Having It so Good: Britain in the Fifties*. Harmondsworth: Penguin, 2007.

Hepworth, David. *Uncommon People: The Rise and Fall of the Rock Stars 1955–1994*. London: Random House, 2017.

Hertsgaard, Mark. *A Day in the Life: The Music and Artistry of the Beatles*. New York, NY: Delacorte Press, 1995.

Herzogenrath, Wulf, and Dorothee Hansen, eds. *John Lennon: Drawings, Performances, Films*. Berlin: Cantz, 1995.

Hewison, Robert. *Too Much: Art and Society in the Sixties 1960–75*. London: Methuen, 1986.

Hewitt, Paolo. *Fab Gear*. London: Prestel, 2011.

Heylin, Clinton. *The Act You've Known for All These Years: The Life, and Afterlife, of Sgt. Pepper*. Edinburgh: Canongate, 2007.

Higgins, Patrick. *Heterosexual Dictatorship: Male Homosexuality in Postwar Britain*. London: Trafalgar Square, 1996.

Hill, Sarah. *San Francisco and the Long 60s*. New York, NY: Bloomsbury Publishing USA, 2016.

Hills, Matthew. *Fan Cultures*. London: Routledge, 2003.

Himmelfarb, Gertrude. *The De-Moralization of Society: From Victorian Virtues to Modern Values*. New York, NY: Vintage, 1996.

Hinton, James. *Nine Wartime Lives: Mass-Observation and the Making of the Modern Self.* Oxford: Oxford University Press, 2010.

Hitchens, Peter. *The Abolition of Britain: The British Cultural Revolution from Lady Chatterley to Tony Blair.* London: Quartet Books, 2000.

Hitchens, Peter. *The War We Never Fought: The British Establishment's Surrender to Drugs.* London: A&C Black, 2012.

Hoefferle, Caroline. *British Student Activism in the Long Sixties.* London: Routledge, 2012.

Hogan, J. Michael. 'The Road Not Taken in Opinion Research: Mass-Observation in Great Britain, 1937–1940'. *Rhetoric & Public Affairs* 18, no. 3 (2015): 409–39.

Holden, Andrew. *Makers and Manners: Politics and Morality in Postwar Britain.* London: Politico's, 2004.

Homans, Elizabeth. 'Visions of Equality: Women's Rights and Political Change in 1970s Britain'. PhD Thesis, Bangor University, 2015.

Honeywell, Carissa. *A British Anarchist Tradition: Herbert Read, Alex Comfort and Colin Ward.* London: A&C Black, 2011.

Horn, Adrian. *Juke Box Britain: Americanisation and Youth Culture, 1945–60.* Manchester: Manchester University Press, 2009.

Horn, Gerd-Rainer. *The Spirit of '68: Rebellion in Western Europe and North America, 1956–1976.* Oxford: Oxford University Press, 2007.

Horowitz, Daniel. *Consuming Pleasures: Intellectuals and Popular Culture in the Postwar World.* Philadelphia, PA: University of Pennsylvania Press, 2012.

Houlbrook, Matt. *Queer London: Perils and Pleasures in the Sexual Metropolis, 1918–1957.* Chicago, IL: University of Chicago Press, 2006.

Howlett, Kevin. *The Beatles: The BBC Archives 1962–1970.* London: Ebury Press, 2013.

Hubble, Nick. *Mass Observation and Everyday Life: Culture, History, Theory.* Basingstoke: Springer, 2005.

Hughes, Celia. *Young Lives on the Left: Sixties Activism and the Liberation of the Self.* Oxford: Oxford University Press, 2015.

Hunt, Andrew. '"When Did the Sixties Happen?" Searching for New Directions'. *Journal of Social History* 33, no. 1 (1999): 147–61.

Huyssen, Andreas. *After the Great Divide: Modernism, Mass Culture, Postmodernism.* Bloomington, IN: Indiana University Press, 1988.

Inglehart, Ronald. *The Silent Revolution: Changing Values and Political Styles among Western Publics.* Princeton, NJ: Princeton University Press, 1977.

Inglis, Ian. 'Absolute Beginners: The Evolution of a British Popular Music Scene'. In *The Ashgate Research Companion to Popular Musicology*, edited by Derek B. Scott, 379–95. London: Routledge, 2016.

Inglis, Ian. 'Cover Story: Magic, Myth and Music'. In *Sgt. Pepper and the Beatles: It Was Forty Years Ago Today*, edited by Olivier Julien, 91–102. Aldershot: Ashgate, 2007.

Inglis, Ian. 'Ideology, Trajectory and Stardom: Elvis Presley and the Beatles'. *International Review of the Aesthetics and Sociology of Music* 27, no.1 (1996): 53–78.

Inglis, Ian. '"I Read the News Today, Oh Boy": The British Press and the Beatles'. *Popular Music and Society* 33, no. 4 (2010): 549–62.

Inglis, Ian. 'Men of Ideas? Popular Music, Anti-Intellectualism and the Beatles'. In *The Beatles, Popular Music and Society*, edited by Ian Inglis. Basingstoke: Springer, 2000.

Inglis, Ian. '"Nothing You Can See That Isn't Shown": The Album Covers of the Beatles'. *Popular Music* 20, no. 1 (2001): 83–97.

Inglis, Ian. *The Beatles*. Sheffield: Equinox Publishing, 2017.

Inglis, Ian. *The Beatles in Hamburg*. London: Reaktion, 2012.

Inglis, Ian. *The Words and Music of George Harrison*. New York, NY: Praeger, 2010.

Inglis, Ian, ed. *Popular Music and Television in Britain*. Aldershot: Ashgate, 2010.

Iwamura, Jane. *Virtual Orientalism: Asian Religions and American Popular Culture*. New York, NY: Oxford University Press, 2011.

Jackson, Jeffrey H., and Stanley C. Pelkey. 'Introduction'. In *Music and History: Bridging the Disciplines*, ed. Jeffrey H. Jackson and Stanley C. Pelkey. Oxford, MS: University Press of Mississippi, 2005.

Jackson, Louise A. '"The Coffee Club Menace": Policing Youth, Leisure and Sexuality in Post-War Manchester'. *Cultural and Social History* 5, no. 3 (2008): 289–308.

James, David E. *Rock 'N' Film: Cinema's Dance with Popular Music*. New York, NY: Oxford University Press, 2017.

Jameson, Fredric. 'Periodizing the 60s'. *Social Text*, no. 9/10 (1984): 178–209.

Jamison, Andrew, and Ron Eyerman. *Seeds of the Sixties*. Berkeley, CA: University of California Press, 1994.

Jarniewicz, Jerzy, and Alina Kwiatkowska, eds. *Fifty Years with the Beatles*. Łódź: Łódź University Press, 2010.

Jarvis, Mark. *Conservative Governments, Morality and Social Change in Affluent Britain, 1957–64*. Manchester: Manchester University Press, 2005.

Jenkins, Philip. *Decade of Nightmares: The End of the Sixties and the Making of Eighties America*. Oxford: Oxford University Press, 2006.

Jennings, Rebecca. *Tomboys and Bachelor Girls: A Lesbian History of Post-War Britain 1945–71*. Manchester: Manchester University Press, 2007.

Jenson, Joly. 'Fandom as Pathology: The Consequences of Characterization'. In *The Adoring Audience: Fan Culture and Popular Media*, edited by Lisa A. Lewis, 9–26. London: Routledge, 1992.

Johnstone, Nick. *Yoko Ono 'Talking'*. London: Omnibus Press, 2010.

Jones, Ben. *The Working Class in Mid-Twentieth-Century England: Community, Identity and Social Memory*. Manchester: Manchester University Press, 2012.

Jones, Emma L. 'Attitudes to Abortion in the Era of Reform: Evidence from the Abortion Law Reform Association Correspondence'. *Women's History Review* 20, no. 2 (2011): 283–98.

Jones, Steve. 'Re-Viewing Rock Writing: The Origins of Popular Music Criticism'. *American Journalism* 9, no. 1–2 (1992): 87–107.

Jones, Steve, ed. *Pop Music and the Press*. Philadelphia, PA: Temple University Press, 2002.

Julien, Olivier. '50 ans des Beatles Studies'. *Volume!* 12, no. 2 (2016): 15–42.

Julien, Olivier, ed. *Sgt. Pepper and the Beatles: It Was Forty Years Ago Today*. Aldershot: Ashgate, 2007.

Julien, Olivier. '"Their Production Will Be Second to None": An Introduction to *Sgt. Pepper*'. In *Sgt. Pepper and the Beatles: It Was Forty Years Ago Today*, edited by Olivier Julien, 1–9. Aldershot: Ashgate, 2008.

Kane, Daniel. 'Wholly Communion, Literary Nationalism, and the Sorrows of the Counterculture'. *Framework: The Journal of Cinema and Media* 52, no. 1 (2011): 102–27.

Kasser, Tim. *Lucy in the Mind of Lennon*. New York, NY: Oxford University Press, 2013.

Keightley, Keir. 'Reconsidering Rock'. In *The Cambridge Companion to Pop and Rock*, edited by Simon Frith, Will Straw, and John Street, 109–42. Cambridge: Cambridge University Press, 2001.

Keightley, Keir. 'The Historical Consciousness of Sunshine Pop'. *Journal of Popular Music Studies* 23, no. 3 (2011): 343–61.

Kellein, Thomas. *Yoko Ono: Between the Sky and My Head*. Cologne: Walther Konig, 2008.

Kimsey, John. '"An Abstraction, Like Christmas": The Beatles For Sale and For Keeps'. In *The Cambridge Companion to the Beatles*, edited by Kenneth Womack, 230–54. Cambridge: Cambridge University Press, 2011.

King, Martin. *Men, Masculinity and the Beatles*. Aldershot: Ashgate, 2013.

King, Martin. '"Roll up for the Mystery Tour": Reading the Beatles' *Magical Mystery Tour* as a Countercultural Anti-Masculinist Text'. *Global Journal of Interdisciplinary Social Sciences* 4, no. 3 (2015): 102–10.

King, Martin. 'The Beatles in *Help!* Re-Imagining the English Man in Mid-1960s Britain'. *Global Journal of Human-Social Science Research* 14, no. 4 (2014). https://socialscienceresearch.org/index.php/GJHSS/article/view/1066.

Kirkup, Mike. '"Some Kind of Innocence": The *Beatles Monthly* and the Fan Community'. *Popular Music History* 9, no. 1 (2014): 64–78.

Kitts, Thomas M. *Ray Davies: Not Like Everybody Else*. London: Routledge, 2008.

Klimke, Martin, and Joachim Scharloth, eds. *1968 in Europe: A History of Protest and Activism, 1956–1977*. Basingstoke: Springer, 2008.

Knifton, Robert. 'Centre of the Creative Universe: Liverpool and the Avant-Garde'. PhD Thesis, Manchester Metropolitan University, 2007.

Kocot, Monika. 'The Indian Beatle(s): From "Norwegian Wood" to "The Hare Krishna Mantra". Indian Influences on the Lyrics and Music of the Beatles'. In *Fifty Years with the Beatles: The Impact of the Beatles on Contemporary Culture*, edited by Jerzy Jarniewicz and Alina Kwiatkowska, 183–97. Łódź: Łódź University Press, 2010.

Kohl, Paul R. 'A Splendid Time Is Guaranteed for All: The Beatles as Agents of Carnival'. *Popular Music & Society* 20, no. 4 (1996): 81–8.

Kosc, Grzegorz, Clara Juncker, Sharon Monteith and Britta Waldschmidt-Nelson, eds. *The Transatlantic Sixties: Europe and the United States in the Counterculture Decade*. Bielefeld: transcript Verlag, 2013.

Krinsky, Charles, ed. *The Ashgate Research Companion to Moral Panics*. Aldershot: Ashgate, 2013.

Kruse, Robert J. 'The Beatles as Place Makers: Narrated Landscapes in Liverpool, England'. *Journal of Cultural Geography* 22, no. 2 (2005): 87–114.

Kruse, Robert J. *A Cultural Geography of the Beatles: Representing Landscapes as Musical Texts (Strawberry Fields, Abbey Road, and Penny Lane)*. New York, NY: E. Mellen Press, 2005.

Kutschke, Beate, and Barley Norton, eds. *Music and Protest in 1968*. Cambridge: Cambridge University Press, 2013.

Kwiatkowska, Alina. 'Roll over, Shakespeare: References to Beatles' Songs in Contemporary English Texts'. In *Fifty Years with the Beatles: The Impact of the Beatles on Contemporary Culture*, edited by Jerzy Jarniewicz and Alina Kwiatkowska, 269–85. Łódź: Łódź University Press, 2010.

Kynaston, David. *Austerity Britain, 1945–51*. London: Bloomsbury, 2008.

Kynaston, David. *Family Britain, 1951–1957*. London: A&C Black, 2009.

Kynaston, David. *Modernity Britain: Opening the Box, 1957–59*. London: Bloomsbury, 2013.

Kynaston, David. *Modernity Britain: A Shake of the Dice, 1959–62*. London: Bloomsbury, 2014.

Laing, Dave. *One Chord Wonders: Power and Meaning in Punk Rock*. Oakland, CA: PM Press, 2015.

Laing, Dave. 'Scrutiny to Subcultures: Notes on Literary Criticism and Popular Music', *Popular Music* 13, no. 2 (1994): 179–90.

Laing, Stuart. *Representations of Working-Class Life, 1957–1964*. Basingstoke: Macmillan, 1986.

Laite, Julia. 'A Global History of Prostitution: London'. In *Selling Sex in the City: A Global History of Prostitution, 1600s–2000s*, edited by Magaly Rodriguez Garcia, Lex Heerma van Voss and Elise van Nederveen Meerkerk, 111–37. Amsterdam: Brill, 2017.

Lambert, Philip. *Good Vibrations: Brian Wilson and the Beach Boys in Critical Perspective*. Ann Arbor, MI: University of Michigan Press, 2016.

Lambert, Philip. *Inside the Music of Brian Wilson: The Songs, Sounds, and Influences of the Beach Boys' Founding Genius*. London: Continuum, 2007.

Langhamer, Claire. 'Adultery in Post-War England'. *History Workshop Journal*, no. 62 (2006): 86–115.

Langhamer, Claire. '"The Live Dynamic Whole of Feeling and Behavior": Capital Punishment and the Politics of Emotion, 1945–1957'. *Journal of British Studies* 51, no. 2 (2012): 416–41.

Laughey, Daniel. *Music and Youth Culture*. Edinburgh: Edinburgh University Press, 2006.

Lavezzoli, Peter. *The Dawn of Indian Music in the West*. London: A&C Black, 2006.

Lawrence, Jon. 'Class, "Affluence" and the Study of Everyday Life in Britain, c. 1930–64'. *Cultural and Social History* 10, no. 2 (2013): 273–99.

Lawrence, Jon. 'The British Sense of Class'. *Journal of Contemporary History* 35, no. 2 (2000): 307–18.

Lawrence, Tim. *Love Saves the Day: A History of American Dance Music Culture, 1970–1979*. Durham, NC: Duke University Press, 2004.

Lee, B. H. *Divorce Law Reform in England*. London: Peter Owen, 1974.

Leigh, Spencer. *Halfway to Paradise: Britpop, 1955–1962*. Folkestone: Finbarr International, 1996.

Leigh, Spencer. *The Beatles in Liverpool: From Merseybeat to Stardom*. London: Omnibus, 2012.

LeMahieu, D. L. *A Culture for Democracy: Mass Communication and the Cultivated Mind in Britain between the Wars*. Oxford: Clarendon, 1988.

Lemonnier, Bertrand. *L'Angleterre des Beatles: Une histoire culturelle des années soixante*. Paris: Editions Kimé, 1998.

Lemonnier, Bertrand. *La révolution pop dans l'Angleterre des années soixante*. Paris: Le table ronde, 1986.

Lent, Adam. *British Social Movements since 1945: Sex, Colour, Peace and Power*. Basingstoke: Palgrave Macmillan, 2001.

Leonard, Marion. *Gender in the Music Industry: Rock, Discourse and Girl Power*. Aldershot: Ashgate, 2007.

Leonard, Marion. 'The "Lord Mayor of Beatle-Land": Popular Music, Local Government, and the Promotion of Place in 1960s Liverpool'. *Popular Music and Society* 36, no. 5 (2013): 597–614.

Levine, Lawrence W. *Highbrow/Lowbrow: The Emergence of Cultural Hierarchy in America*. Cambridge, MA: Harvard University Press, 1990.

Levy, Shawn. *Ready, Steady, Go! Swinging London and the Invention of Cool*. London: Fourth Estate, 2002.

Lewis, Brian. *Wolfenden's Witnesses: Homosexuality in Postwar Britain*. Basingstoke: Springer, 2016.

Lewis, Jane E. *Women in Britain since 1945: Women, Family, Work and the State in the Post-War Years*. Oxford: Blackwell, 1994.

Lewisohn, Mark. *The Beatles Live!* London: Pavilion, 1986.

Lewisohn, Mark. *The Beatles Recording Sessions: The Official Abbey Road Session Notes, 1962–1970*. New York, NY: Harmony Books, 1988.

Lewisohn, Mark. *The Complete Beatles Chronicles*. New York, NY: Harmony Books, 1992.

Lewisohn, Mark. *Tune In: The Beatles – All These Years*. New York, NY: Crown Archetype, 2013.

Lindberg, Ulf. *Rock Criticism from the Beginning: Amusers, Bruisers, and Cool-Headed Cruisers*. New York, NY: Peter Lang, 2005.

Long, Pat. *The History of the NME: High Times and Low Lives at the World's Most Famous Music Magazine*. London: Portico, 2012.

Long, Paul. *Only in the Common People: The Aesthetics of Class in Post-War Britain*. Newcastle: Cambridge Scholars, 2008.

Longhurst, Brian. *Popular Music and Society*. 2nd edn. Cambridge: Polity, 2007.

Lovesey, Oliver. "'A Cellarful of Boys': The Swinging Sixties, Autobiography, and the Other Beatle'. *Popular Music and Society* 38, no. 2 (2015): 160–75.

Lowe, John. *The Warden: A Portrait of John Sparrow*. London: HarperCollins, 1998.

Lynskey, Dorian. *33 Revolutions Per Minute*. London: Faber and Faber, 2011.

Lyons, John F. *America in the British Imagination: 1945 to the Present*. Basingstoke: Springer, 2013.

Macan, Edward. 'The Beatles and the Origins of "Britishness" in Rock Music'. In *Fifty Years with the Beatles: The Impact of the Beatles on Contemporary Culture*, edited by Jerzy Jarniewicz and Alina Kwiatkowska, 107–29. Łódź: Łódź University Press, 2010.

Macan, Edward. *Rocking the Classics: English Progressive Rock and the Counterculture*. Oxford: Oxford University Press, 1997.

MacDonald, Ian. *Revolution in the Head: The Beatles' Records and the Sixties*. 3rd edn. London: Pimlico, 2005.

MacFarlane, Thomas. *The Beatles' Abbey Road Medley: Extended Forms in Popular Music*. Lanham, MD: Scarecrow Press, 2007.

MacFarlane, Thomas. *The Beatles and McLuhan: Understanding the Electric Age*. Lanham, MD: Rowman & Littlefield, 2013.

Machin, G. I. T. *Churches and Social Issues in Twentieth-Century Britain*. Oxford: Clarendon Press, 1998.

Mäkelä, Janne. "'The Greatest Story of Pop Music? Challenges of Writing the Beatles" History"'. In *Beatlestudies 3*, edited by Yrjö Heinonen, 47–55. Jyväskylä: University of Jyväskylä, 2000.

Mäkelä, Janne. *John Lennon Imagined: Cultural History of a Rock Star*. New York, NY: Peter Lang, 2004.

Malchow, Howard. *Special Relations: The Americanization of Britain?* Stanford, CA: Stanford University Press, 2011.

Mandler, Peter. *The English National Character: The History of an Idea from Edmund Burke to Tony Blair*. New Haven, CT: Yale University Press, 2006.

Mandler, Peter. 'Two Cultures – One – Or Many?' In *The British Isles since 1945*, edited by Kathleen Burk. Oxford: Oxford University Press, 2003.

Mandler, Peter, and Susan Pedersen, eds. *After the Victorians: Private Conscience and Public Duty in Modern Britain*. London: Routledge, 2005.

Marcus, Greil. *Lipstick Traces: A Secret History of the Twentieth Century*. Cambridge, MA: Harvard University Press, 1989.

Marcus, Greil. *The Doors*. London: Faber, 2012.

Marcus, Steven. *The Other Victorians: A Study of Sexuality and Pornography in Mid-Nineteenth-Century England*. London: Weidenfeld and Nicholson, 1966.

Marks, Lara. *Sexual Chemistry: A History of the Contraceptive Pill*. New Haven, CT: Yale University Press, 2001.

Marqusee, Mike. *Wicked Messenger: Bob Dylan and the 1960s*. New York, NY: Seven Stories Press, 2011.

Marshall, P. David. *Celebrity and Power: Fame in Contemporary Culture*. Minneapolis, MN: University of Minnesota Press, 1997.

Marshall, P. David. 'The Celebrity Legacy of the Beatles'. In *The Beatles, Popular Music and Society*, edited by Ian Inglis, 163–75. Basingstoke: Springer, 2000.

Martin, Bill. *Listening to the Future: The Time of Progressive Rock, 1968–1978*. Chicago, IL: Open Court, 2015.

Martin, Chad. 'Paradise Now: Youth Politics and the British Counterculture, 1958–74'. PhD Thesis, Stanford University, 2003.

Marwick, Arthur. *Britain in the Century of Total War*. London: Bodley Head, 1968.

Marwick, Arthur. *Culture in Britain since 1945*. Oxford: Basil Blackwell, 1991.

Marwick, Arthur. *The Explosion of British Society, 1914–1970*. Basingstoke: Macmillan, 1971.

Marwick, Arthur. *The Sixties: Cultural Revolution in Britain, France, Italy, and the United States, c. 1958–c. 1974*. Oxford: Oxford University Press, 1998.

Mauch, Matthias, Robert M. MacCallum, Mark Levy and Armand M. Leroi. 'The Evolution of Popular Music: USA 1960–2010'. *Royal Society Open Science* 2, no. 5 (2015): 7–9.

McDonald, Chris. *Rush, Rock Music and the Middle Class: Dreaming in Middletown*. Indianapolis, IN: Indiana University Press, 2009.

McGowan, Christopher John. 'Harmony and Discord within the English "Counter-Culture", 1965–1975, with Particular Reference to the "Rock Operas" *Hair, Godspell, Tommy* and *Jesus Christ Superstar*'. PhD Thesis, Queen Mary, London, 2012.

McGrath, James. 'Cutting up a Glass Onion: Reading the Beatles' History and Legacy'. In *Fifty Years with the Beatles: The Impact of the Beatles on Contemporary Culture*, edited by Jerzy Jarniewicz and Alina Kwiatkowska, 303–25. Łódź: Łódź University Press, 2010.

McGrath, James. 'Ideas of Belonging in the Work of John Lennon and Paul McCartney'. PhD Thesis, Leeds Metropolitan University, 2009.

McGrath, James. 'John, Paul, George and Richard: The Beatles' Uses of Literacy'. In *Richard Hoggart: Culture and Critique*, ed. Michael Bailey and Mary Eagleton. London: Critical, Cultural and Communications Press, 2011.

McGrath, James. 'Reading Post-War Britain in Lennon and McCartney's Imagined Communities'. In *New Perspectives in British Cultural History*, edited by Ros Crone, David Gange, and Katie Jones, 244–54. Newcastle: Cambridge Scholars, 2007.

McGrath, James. '"Where You Once Belonged": Class, Race and the Liverpool Roots of Lennon and McCartney's Songs'. *Popular Music History* 9, no. 1 (2014): 11–31.

McKay, George. *Circular Breathing: The Cultural Politics of Jazz in Britain*. Durham, NC: Duke University Press, 2005.

McKay, George. *The Pop Festival: History, Music, Media, Culture*. New York, NY: Bloomsbury Publishing USA, 2015.

McKinney, Devin. *Magic Circles: The Beatles in Dream and History*. Cambridge, MA: Harvard University Press, 2003.

McLeod, Hugh. *The Religious Crisis of the 1960s*. Oxford: Oxford University Press, 2010.

McMillian, John. *Beatles vs. Stones*. New York, NY: Simon & Schuster, 2013.

McRobbie, Angela. *Feminism and Youth Culture*. Rev. edn. Basingstoke: Macmillan, 2000.

McRobbie, Angela, and Jenny Garber. 'Girls and Subcultures: An Exploration'. In *Resistance through Rituals: Youth Subcultures in Post-War Britain*, edited by Stuart Hall and Tony Jefferson, 209–22. London: Routledge, 2006.

Melechi, Antonio, ed. *Psychedelia Britannica: Hallucinogenic Drugs in Britain*. London: Turnaround, 1997.

Mellor, David. *The Sixties Art Scene in London*. London: Phaidon, 1993.

Mellor, David, and Laurent Gervereau, eds. *The Sixties: Britain and France, 1962–1973: The Utopian Years*. London: Philip Wilson, 1997.

Miles, Barry. *London Calling: A Countercultural History of London since 1945*. London: Atlantic, 2011.

Miles, Barry. *Paul McCartney: Many Years from Now*. London: Secker & Warburg, 1996.

Millard, André. *Beatlemania: Technology, Business, and Teen Culture in Cold War America*. Baltimore, MD: Johns Hopkins University Press, 2012.

Mills, Richard. 'Expert Textpert: Ian MacDonald's *Revolution in the Head: The Beatles' Records and the Sixties* (1994)'. In *Fifty Years with the Beatles: The Impact of the Beatles on Contemporary Culture*, edited by Jerzy Jarniewicz and Alina Kwiatkowska, 327–39. Łódź: Łódź University Press, 2010.

Mitchell, Gillian A. M. 'From "Rock" to "Beat": Towards a Reappraisal of British Popular Music, 1958–1962'. *Popular Music and Society* 36, no. 2 (2013): 194–215.

Mitchell, Gillian A. M. 'Reassessing "the Generation Gap": Bill Haley's 1957 Tour of Britain, Inter-Generational Relations and Attitudes to Rock 'n' Roll in the Late 1950s'. *Twentieth Century British History* 24, no. 4 (2013): 573–605.

Mold, Alex. 'The Changing Role of NGOs in Britain: Voluntary Action and Illegal Drugs'. In *NGOs in Contemporary Britain: Non-State Actors in Society and Politics since 1945*, edited by N. J. Crowson, Matthew Hilton, and James McKay, 164–81. Basingstoke: Palgrave Macmillan, 2009.

Mold, Alex. *Heroin: The Treatment of Addiction in Twentieth-Century Britain*. DeKalb, IL: Northern Illinois University Press, 2008.

Mold, Alex. '"The Welfare Branch of the Alternative Society?" The Work of Drug Voluntary Organization Release, 1967–1978'. *Twentieth Century British History* 17, no. 1 (2005): 50–73.

Moon, Nick. *Opinion Polls: History, Theory and Practice*. Manchester: Manchester University Press, 1999.

Moore, Allan F. 'The Act You've Known for All These Years: A Re-Encounter with *Sgt. Pepper*'. In *Sgt. Pepper and the Beatles: It Was Forty Years Ago Today*, ed. Olivier Julien. Aldershot: Ashgate, 2007.

Moore, Allan F. *The Beatles: Sgt. Pepper's Lonely Hearts Club Band*. Cambridge: Cambridge University Press, 1997.

Moore-Gilbert, Bart, and John Seed, eds. *Cultural Revolution? The Challenge of the Arts in the 1960s*. London: Routledge, 1992.

Moran, Joe. 'Mass-Observation, Market Research, and the Birth of the Focus Group, 1937–1997'. *Journal of British Studies* 47, no. 4 (2008): 827–51.

Morgan, Kenneth O. *Britain since 1945: The People's Peace*. Oxford: Oxford University Press, 2001.

Morgan, Kevin, Gidon Cohen and Andrew Flinn. *Communists and British Society, 1920–1991*. London: Rivers Oram, 2007.

Morra, Irene. *Britishness, Popular Music, and National Identity: The Making of Modern Britain*. London: Routledge, 2013.

Morris, Jeremy. 'Secularization and Religious Experience: Arguments in the Historiography of Modern British Religion'. *The Historical Journal* 55, no. 1 (2012): 195–219.

Morris, Jeremy. 'The Strange Death of Christian Britain: Another Look at the Secularization Debate'. *The Historical Journal* 46, no. 4 (2003): 963–76.

Mort, Frank. *Capital Affairs: London and the Making of the Permissive Society*. New Haven, CT: Yale University Press, 2010.

Mueller, Charles. 'Were British Subcultures the Beginnings of Multitude?' In *Countercultures and Popular Music*, edited by Sheila Whiteley and Jedediah Sklower. London: Routledge, 2014.

Muncie, John. 'The Beatles and the Spectacle of Youth'. In *The Beatles, Popular Music and Society*, edited by Ian Inglis, 35–52. Basingstoke: Springer, 2000.

Munroe, Alexandra, ed. *YES Yoko Ono*. New York, NY: Japan Society, 2003.

Neaverson, Bob. *The Beatles Movies*. London: Cassell, 1997.

Nehring, Holger. 'Great Britain'. In *1968 in Europe: A History of Protest and Activism, 1956–1977*, edited by Martin Klimke and Joachim Scharloth, 125–36. Basingstoke: Springer, 2008.

Nehring, Holger. *Politics of Security: British and West German Protest Movements and the Early Cold War, 1945–1970*. Oxford: Oxford University Press, 2013.

Nehring, Neil. *Flowers in the Dustbin: Culture, Anarchy and Postwar England*. Ann Arbor, MI: University of Michigan Press, 1993.

Nelson, Elizabeth. *British Counter-Culture 1966–73: A Study of the Underground Press*. Basingstoke: Springer, 1989.

Newburn, Tim. *Permission and Regulation: Law and Morals in Post-War Britain*. London: Routledge, 1992.

Norman, Philip. *John Lennon: The Life*. London: HarperCollins, 2009.

Norman, Philip. *Paul McCartney: The Biography*. London: Hachette UK, 2016.

Norman, Philip. *Shout! The Beatles in Their Generation*. New York, NY: Fireside/Simon and Schuster, 1981.

Norman, Philip. *Shout! The True Story of the Beatles*. 3rd edn. New York, NY: Fireside/Simon and Schuster, 2005.

Nott, James. *Going to the Palais: A Social and Cultural History of Dancing and Dance Halls in Britain, 1918–1960*. Oxford: Oxford University Press, 2015.

Nott, James. *Music for the People: Popular Music and Dance in Interwar Britain*. Oxford: Oxford University Press, 2002.

Offer, Avner. 'British Manual Workers: From Producers to Consumers, c. 1950–2000'. *Contemporary British History* 22, no. 4 (2008): 537–71.

Olechnowicz, Andrzej, ed. *The Monarchy and the British Nation, 1780 to the Present*. Cambridge: Cambridge University Press, 2007.

Oliver, Paul. *Hinduism and the 1960s: The Rise of a Counter-Culture*. London: Bloomsbury, 2014.

Olsson, Ulf. *Listening for the Secret: The Grateful Dead and the Politics of Improvisation*. Berkeley, CA: University of California Press, 2017.

Ortolano, Guy. *The Two Cultures Controversy: Science, Literature and Cultural Politics in Postwar Britain*. Cambridge: Cambridge University Press, 2011.

Osgerby, Bill. '"Seized By Change, Liberated By Affluence": Youth Consumption and Cultural Change in Postwar Britain'. In *Twentieth-Century Mass Society in Britain and the Netherlands*, edited by Bob Moore and Henk van Nierop, 175–88. Oxford: Berg, 2006.

Osteen, Mark, ed. *The Beatles through a Glass Onion: Reconsidering the White Album*. Ann Arbor, MI: University of Michigan Press, 2019.

Palacios, Julian. *Syd Barrett and Pink Floyd: Dark Globe*. London: Plexus Publishing, 2015.

Pattie, David. *Rock Music in Performance*. Basingstoke: Springer, 2007.

Pattison, Robert. *The Triumph of Vulgarity: Rock Music in the Mirror of Romanticism*. New York, NY: Oxford University Press, 1987.

Paul, Kathleen. *Whitewashing Britain: Race and Citizenship in the Postwar Era*. Ithaca, NY: Cornell University Press, 1997.

Peel, Ian. *The Unknown Paul McCartney: McCartney and the Avant-Garde*. London: Reynolds and Hearn, 2002.

Perks, Rob. 'The Century Speaks: A Millennium Oral History Project'. In *Aural History: Essays on Recorded Sound*, edited by Andy Linehan, 27–40. London: British Library, 2001.

Petigny, Alan. *The Permissive Society: America, 1941–1965*. Cambridge: Cambridge University Press, 2009.

Phillips, Paul T. *Contesting the Moral High Ground: Popular Moralists in Mid-Twentieth-Century Britain*. Toronto: McGill-Queen's University Press, 2013.

Philo, Simon. *British Invasion: The Crosscurrents of Musical Influence*. Lanham, MD: Rowman & Littlefield, 2014.

Pimlott, Ben. *Harold Wilson*. London: HarperCollins, 1992.

Plant, Sadie. *The Most Radical Gesture: The Situationist International in a Postmodern Age*. London: Routledge, 2002.

Platoff, John. 'John Lennon, "Revolution", and the Politics of Musical Reception'. *The Journal of Musicology* 22, no. 2 (2005): 241–67.

Poiger, Uta G. *Jazz, Rock, and Rebels: Cold War Politics and American Culture in a Divided Germany*. Berkeley, CA: University of California Press, 2000.

Pomies-Marechal, Sylvie, and Matthew Leggett. 'The Abortion Act 1967: A Fundamental Change?' In *Preserving the Sixties: Britain and the 'Decade of Protest'*, edited by Trevor Harris and Monia O'Brien Castro, 51–72. Basingstoke: Palgrave Macmillan, 2014.

Powell, Neil. 'An Aquarian Talent'. In *Roy Fuller: A Tribute*, edited by A. Trevor Tolley, 53–8. Toronto, ON: McGill-Queen's Press, 1993.

Powers, Devon. *Writing the Record: The Village Voice and the Birth of Rock Criticism*. Amherst, MA: University of Massachusetts Press, 2013.

Pritchard, David, and Alan Lysaght, eds. *The Beatles: An Oral History*. London: Hyperion, 1998.

Pyron, Darden Asbury. 'The Days of the Understated Suit'. 2000. University of Chicago Press. www.press.uchicago.edu/Misc/Chicago/686671.html.

Quantick, David. *Revolution: The Making of the Beatles' White Album*. New York, NY: A Capella Books, 2002.

Rabey, David I., and Henk Huijser. *Howard Barker: Politics and Desire – An Expository Study of His Drama and Poetry, 1969–87*. Basingstoke: Springer, 1989.

Ramsay, Laura Monica. 'The Church of England, Homosexual Law Reform, and the Shaping of the Permissive Society, 1957–1979'. *Journal of British Studies* 57, no. 1 (2018): 108–37.

Randall, Annie J. *Dusty! Queen of the Postmods*. New York, NY: Oxford University Press, 2008.

Reck, David. 'Beatles Orientalis: Influences from Asia in a Popular Song Tradition'. *Asian Music* 16, no. 1 (1985): 83–149.

Reck, David. 'The Inner Light: George Harrison's Indian Songs'. In *Fifty Years with the Beatles: The Impact of the Beatles on Contemporary Culture*, edited by Jerzy Jarniewicz and Alina Kwiatkowska, 167–81. Łódź: Łódź University Press, 2010.

Reck, David. 'The Beatles and Indian Music'. In *Sgt. Pepper and The Beatles: It Was Forty Years Ago Today*, edited by Olivier Julien, 63–74. Aldershot: Ashgate, 2007.

Reddington, Helen. *The Lost Women of Rock Music: Female Musicians of the Punk Era*. Aldershot: Ashgate, 2007.

Reeve, Andru J. *Turn Me On, Dead Man: The Beatles and the Paul Is Dead Hoax*. Bloomington, IN: AuthorHouse, 2004.

Regev, Eyal. 'Lennon and Jesus: Secularization and the Transformation of Religion'. *Studies in Religion* 41, no. 4 (2012): 534–63.

Regev, Motti. 'Producing Artistic Value: The Case of Rock Music'. *The Sociological Quarterly* 35, no. 1 (1994): 85–102.

Reid, Charles. *Malcolm Sargent: A Biography*. New York, NY: Taplinger, 1970.

Reising, Russell, ed. *Every Sound There Is: The Beatles' Revolver and the Transformation of Rock and Roll*. Aldershot: Ashgate, 2002.

Reiter, Roland. *The Beatles on Film: Analysis of Movies, Documentaries, Spoofs and Cartoons*. Bielefeld: Transcript Verlag, 2008.

Reynolds, Simon. *Rip It Up and Start Again: Postpunk 1978–1984*. London: Faber and Faber, 2009.

Reynolds, Simon, and Joy Press. *The Sex Revolts: Gender, Rebellion, and Rock 'n' Roll*. Cambridge, MA: Harvard University Press, 1996.

Rhodes, Lisa. *Electric Ladyland: Women and Rock Culture*. Philadelphia, PA: University of Pennsylvania Press, 2005.

Richards, Jeffrey, and Dorothy Sheridan. *Mass-Observation at the Movies*. London: Routledge & Kegan Paul, 1987.

Righart, Hans. 'Moderate Versions of the "Global Sixties": A Comparison of Great Britain and the Netherlands'. *Journal of Area Studies* 6, no. 13 (1998): 82–96.

Robbins, Keith. 'Contextualizing a "New Reformation": John A. T. Robinson and the Church of England in the Early Sixties'. *Kirchliche Zeitgeschichte* 23, no. 2 (2010): 428–46.

Roberts, Andy. *Albion Dreaming: A Popular History of LSD in Britain*. London: Marshall Cavendish, 2008.

Robinson, Lucy, Anna Gough-Yates, Sian Lincoln, Bill Osgerby, John Street, Peter Webb and Matthew Worley. 'Introduction: Making a Difference by

Making a Noise'. In *Youth Culture and Social Change: Making a Difference by Making a Noise*, 1–13. Basingstoke: Springer, 2017.

Robinson, Stephen. *The Remarkable Lives of Bill Deedes*. London: Little, Brown, 2008.

Roessner, Jeffrey. 'We All Want to Change the World: Postmodern Politics and the Beatles' White Album'. In *Reading the Beatles: Cultural Studies, Literary Criticism, and the Fab Four*, edited by Kenneth Womack and Todd Davis, 147–58. Binghamton, NY: SUNY Press, 2006.

Rohr, Nicolette. 'Yeah Yeah Yeah: The Sixties Screamscape of Beatlemania'. *Journal of Popular Music Studies* 29, no. 2 (2017): 1–13.

Roodhouse, Mark. *Black Market Britain: 1939–1955*. Oxford: Oxford University Press, 2013.

Roodhouse, Mark. '"Fish-and-Chip Intelligence": Henry Durant and the British Institute of Public Opinion, 1936–63'. *Twentieth Century British History* 24, no. 2 (2013): 224–48.

Roodhouse, Mark. 'Lady Chatterley and the Monk: Anglican Radicals and the Lady Chatterley Trial of 1960'. *The Journal of Ecclesiastical History* 59, no. 3 (2008): 475–500.

Roos, Michael E. 'The Walrus and the Deacon: John Lennon's Debt to Lewis Carroll'. *Journal of Popular Culture* 18, no. 1 (1984): 19–29.

Rorabaugh, W. J. *American Hippies*. Cambridge: Cambridge University Press, 2015.

Rose, Jonathan. *The Intellectual Life of the British Working Classes*. New Haven, CT: Yale University Press, 2010.

Rosemont, Franklin, and Charles Radcliffe, eds. *Dancin' in the Streets! Anarchists, IWWs, Surrealists, Situationists & Provos in the 1960s as Recorded in the Pages of The Rebel Worker & Heatwave*. Chicago, IL: Charles H. Kerr, 2005.

Rosen, Andrew. *The Transformation of British Life, 1950–2000: A Social History*. Manchester: Manchester University Press, 2003.

Ross, Andrew. *No Respect: Intellectuals and Popular Culture*. London: Routledge, 2016.

Rule, John. 'Time, Affluence and Private Leisure: The British Working Class in the 1950s and 1960s'. *Labour History Review* 66, no. 2 (2001): 223–42.

Russell, Dave. *Looking North: Northern England and the National Imagination*. Manchester: Manchester University Press, 2004.

Rycroft, Simon. *Swinging City: A Cultural Geography of London 1950–1974*. London: Routledge, 2016.

Samuel, Raphael. *Theatres of Memory, Volume II. Island Stories: Unravelling Britain*. London: Verso, 1998.

Sandbrook, Dominic. 'Against the Permissive Society: The Backlash of the Late 1960s'. In *Ultimate Adventures with Britannia: Personalities, Politics and Culture in Britain*, edited by William Roger Louis, 55–71. London: I. B. Tauris, 2010.

Sandbrook, Dominic. *Never Had It So Good: A History of Britain from Suez to the Beatles*. London: Little, Brown, 2005.

Sandbrook, Dominic. *The Great British Dream Factory: The Strange History of Our National Imagination*. Harmondsworth: Penguin, 2015.

Sandbrook, Dominic. *Seasons in the Sun: The Battle for Britain, 1974–1979*. Harmondsworth: Penguin, 2012.

Sandbrook, Dominic. *State of Emergency: The Way We Were – Britain, 1970–1974*. Harmondsworth: Penguin, 2011.

Sandbrook, Dominic. *White Heat: A History of Britain in the Swinging Sixties*. London: Little, Brown, 2006.

Sandercombe, William Fraser. *The Beatles: The Press Reports, 1961–1970*. Burlington, ON: Collectors Guide Pub., 2007.

Sanguinetti, Gianfranco, John Barker, Charity Scribner and Tom Wise. *Red Army Faction, Red Brigades, Angry Brigade: The Spectacle of Terror in Post War Europe*. ebook: Bread and Circuses, 2015.

Sauceda, James. *The Literary Lennon*. Ann Arbor, MI: Pierian Press, 1984.

Savage, Jon. *1966: The Year the Decade Exploded*. London: Faber and Faber, 2015.

Savage, Jon. *England's Dreaming: Sex Pistols and Punk Rock*. London: Faber and Faber, 1991.

Savage, Mike. *Identities and Social Change in Britain since 1940*. Oxford: Oxford University Press, 2010.

Schaffer, Gavin. *The Vision of a Nation: Making Multiculturalism on British Television, 1960–80*. Basingstoke: Palgrave Macmillan, 2014.

Schickel, Richard. *Intimate Strangers: The Culture of Celebrity in America*. Chicago, IL: Ivan R. Dee, 2000.

Schneider, Matthew. 'Getting Better: The Beatles and the Angry Young Men'. In *New Critical Perspectives on the Beatles: Things We Said Today*, edited by Kenneth Womack and Katie Kapurch, 13–30. Basingstoke: Springer, 2016.

Schneider, Matthew. *The Long and Winding Road from Blake to the Beatles*. Basingstoke: Palgrave Macmillan, 2008.

Schofield, Camilla. *Enoch Powell and the Making of Postcolonial Britain*. Cambridge: Cambridge University Press, 2015.

Schwartz, Roberta Freund. *How Britain Got the Blues: The Transmission and Reception of American Blues Style in the United Kingdom*. London: Routledge, 2016.

Seago, Alex. *Burning the Box of Beautiful Things: The Development of a Postmodern Sensibility*. Oxford: Oxford University Press, 1995.

Seal, Lizzie. *Capital Punishment in Twentieth-Century Britain: Audience, Justice, Memory*. London: Routledge, 2014.

Shank, Barry. 'Abstraction and Embodiment: Yoko Ono and the Weaving of Global Musical Networks'. *Journal of Popular Music Studies* 18, no. 3 (2006): 282–300.

Sheffield, Rob. *Dreaming the Beatles: The Love Story of One Band and the Whole World*. London: HarperCollins, 2017.

Shumway, David R. *Rock Star: The Making of Musical Icons from Elvis to Springsteen*. Baltimore, MD: Johns Hopkins University Press, 2014.

Simon, Brian. *Education and the Social Order: 1940–1990*. London: Lawrence & Wishart, 2000.

Simonelli, David. 'BBC Rock Music Programming on Radio and Television and the Progressive Rock Audience, 1967–1973'. *Popular Music History* 2, no. 1 (2007): 95–112.

Simonelli, David. *Working Class Heroes: Rock Music and British Society in the 1960s and 1970s*. Lanham, MD: Lexington Books, 2013.

Singleton, Rosalind Watkiss. '"(Today I Met) The Boy I'm Gonna Marry": Romantic Expectations of Teenage Girls in the 1960s West Midlands'. In *Youth Culture and Social Change*, edited by Keith Gildart, Anna Gough-Yates and Sian Lincoln, 119–46. Basingstoke: Palgrave Macmillan, 2017.

Smith, Charles. 'The Evolution of the Gay Male Public Sphere in England and Wales 1967–c. 1983'. PhD thesis, Loughborough University, 2015.

Smith, Evan, and Matthew Worley, eds. *Against the Grain: The British Far Left from 1956*. Oxford: Oxford University Press, 2014.

Smith, Helen. *Masculinity, Class and Same-Sex Desire in Industrial England, 1895–1957*. Basingstoke: Springer, 2015.

Sneeringer, Julia. 'Meeting the Beatles: What Beatlemania Can Tell Us about West Germany in the 1960s'. *The Sixties* 6, no. 2 (2013): 172–98.

Sounes, Howard. *Fab: An Intimate Life of Paul McCartney*. London: Harper, 2011.

Stanley, Liz. *Sex Surveyed, 1949–1994: From Mass-Observation's 'Little Kinsey' to the National Survey and the Hite Reports*. London: Routledge, 1995.

Stark, Steven D. *Meet the Beatles: A Cultural History of the Band That Shook Youth, Gender, and the World*. London: HarperCollins, 2005.

Starr, Michael Seth. *Ringo: With a Little Help*. Milwaukee, WI: Backbeat Books, 2016.

Stephens, Julie. *Anti-Disciplinary Protest: Sixties Radicalism and Postmodernism*. Cambridge: Cambridge University Press, 1998.

Stevens, Carolyn S. *The Beatles in Japan*. London: Routledge, 2017.

Stevenson, Nick. *David Bowie: Fame, Sound and Vision*. Cambridge: Polity Press, 2006.

Stinson, John J. 'Anthony Burgess: Novelist on the Margin'. *Journal of Popular Culture* 7, no. 1 (1973): 136–51.

Stras, Laurie, ed. *She's so Fine: Reflections on Whiteness, Femininity, Adolescence and Class in 1960s Music*. Aldershot: Ashgate, 2010.

Stratton, Jon. *When Music Migrates: Crossing British and European Racial Faultlines, 1945–2010*. Aldershot: Ashgate, 2014.

Stratton, Jon, and Nabeel Zuberi, eds. *Black Popular Music in Britain since 1945*. London: Routledge, 2016.

Street, John. *Rebel Rock: The Politics of Popular Music*. Oxford: Blackwell, 1986.

Street, John, and Martin Cloonan. 'Politics and Popular Music: From Policing to Packaging'. *Parliamentary Affairs* 50, no. 2 (1997): 223–35.

Subcultures Network. *Fight Back: Punk, Politics and Resistance*. Oxford: Oxford University Press, 2017.

Sullivan, Henry W. *The Beatles with Lacan: Rock 'n' Roll as Requiem for the Modern Age*. New York, NY: Peter Lang, 1995.

Sullivan, Mark. '"More Popular than Jesus": The Beatles and the Religious Far Right'. *Popular Music* 6, no. 3 (1987): 313–26.

Sulpy, Doug, and Ray Schweighardt. *Get Back: The Beatles' Let It Be Disaster*. London: Helter Skelter, 2003.

Suri, Jeremi. 'The Rise and Fall of an International Counterculture, 1960–1975'. *The American Historical Review* 114, no. 1 (2009): 45–68.

Sutcliffe, Pauline. *The Beatles' Shadow: Stuart Sutcliffe & His Lonely Hearts Club*. London: Pan Macmillan, 2016.

Sutcliffe-Braithwaite, Florence. *Class, Politics, and the Decline of Deference in England, 1968–2000*. Oxford: Oxford University Press, 2018.

Sutherland, John. *Offensive Literature: Decensorship in Britain, 1960–1982*. London: Junction Books, 1982.

Sweers, Britta. *Electric Folk: The Changing Face of English Traditional Music*. New York, NY: Oxford University Press, 2005.

Swiss, Thomas. 'That's Me in the Spotlight: Rock Autobiographies'. *Popular Music* 24, no. 2 (2005): 287–94.

Szreter, Simon, and Kate Fisher. *Sex before the Sexual Revolution: Intimate Life in England 1918–1963*. Cambridge: Cambridge University Press, 2010.

Taylor, Andrew J. '"The Record of the 1950s Is Irrelevant": The Conservative Party, Electoral Strategy and Opinion Research, 1945–64'. *Contemporary British History* 17, no. 1 (2003): 81–110.

Taylor, J. D. 'The Party's Over? The Angry Brigade, the Counterculture, and the British New Left, 1967–1972'. *The Historical Journal* 58, no. 3 (2015): 877–900.

Tebbutt, Melanie. 'From "Marriage Bureau" to "Points of View": Changing Patterns of Advice in Teenage Magazines'. In *People, Places and Identities: Themes in British Social and Cultural History, 1700s–1980s*, edited by Alan Kidd and Melanie Tebbutt, 180–201. Manchester: Manchester University Press, 2017.

Tebbutt, Melanie. *Making Youth: A History of Youth in Modern Britain*. Basingstoke: Palgrave Macmillan, 2016.

Tessler, Holly. 'Beatles for Sale: The Role and Significance of Storytelling in the Commercialisation and Cultural Branding of the Beatles since 1970'. PhD Thesis, University of Liverpool, 2009.

Tessler, Holly. 'Let It Be? Exploring the Beatles Grey Market, 1970–1995'. *Popular Music History* 9, no. 1 (2014): 48–63.

Tessler, Holly. 'The Role and Significance of Storytelling in the Creation of the "Post-Sixties" Beatles, 1970–1980'. *Popular Music History* 5, no. 2 (2010): 169–89.

Thane, Pat. *Unequal Britain: Equalities in Britain since 1945*. London: A&C Black, 2010.

Thane, Pat, and Tanya Evans. *Sinners? Scroungers? Saints? Unmarried Motherhood in Twentieth-Century England*. Oxford: Oxford University Press, 2012.

Thomas, Nick. '"To-Night's Big Talking Point Is Still That Book": Popular Responses to the Lady Chatterley Trial'. *Cultural and Social History* 10, no. 4 (2013): 619–34.

Thomlinson, Natalie. *Race, Ethnicity and the Women's Movement in England, 1968–1993*. Basingstoke: Springer, 2016.

Thompson, Ben. *Ban This Filth! Letters from the Mary Whitehouse Archive*. London: Faber and Faber, 2012.

Thompson, Gordon. '"A Day in the Life": The Beatles and the BBC, May 1967'. In *The Oxford Handbook of Music Censorship*, edited by Patricia Hall, 535–55. Oxford: Oxford University Press, 2017.

Thompson, Gordon. *Please Please Me: Sixties British Pop, Inside Out*. New York, NY: Oxford University Press, 2008.

Thompson, Kenneth. *Moral Panics*. London: Routledge, 2005.

Thompson, Willie, and Marcus Collins. 'The Revolutionary Left and the Permissive Society'. In *The Permissive Society and Its Enemies: Sixties British Culture*, edited by Marcus Collins, 155–68. London: Rivers Oram, 2007.

Thomson, Graeme. *George Harrison: Behind the Locked Door*. London: Omnibus Press, 2013.

Thomson, Mathew. *Lost Freedom: The Landscape of the Child and the British Post-War Settlement*. Oxford: Oxford University Press, 2013.

Thornton, Sarah. *Club Cultures: Music, Media and Subcultural Capital*. Boston, MA: John Wiley & Sons, 2013.

Thurschwell, Pamela, ed. *Quadrophenia and Mod(ern) Culture*. Basingstoke: Springer, 2017.

Tickner, Lisa. *Hornsey 1968: The Art School Revolution*. London: Frances Lincoln, 2008.

Tinker, Chris. 'Mixed Masculinities in 1960s British and French Youth Magazines'. *The Journal of Popular Culture* 47, no. 1 (2014): 84–108.

Tinker, Chris. 'Shaping 1960s Youth in Britain and France: *Fabulous* and *Salut Les Copains*'. *International Journal of Cultural Studies* 14, no. 6 (2011): 641–57.

Todd, Selina. *The People: The Rise and Fall of the Working Class, 1910–2010*. London: John Murray, 2015.

Todd, Selina, and Hilary Young. 'From Baby-Boomers to "Beanstalkers": Making the Modern Teenager in Postwar Britain'. *Cultural and Social History* 9, no. 3 (2012): 451–67.

Tranmer, Jeremy. 'The Radical Left and Popular Music in the 1960s'. In *Preserving the Sixties: Britain and the 'Decade of Protest'*, edited by

346 *Bibliography*

Trevor Harris and Monia O'Brien Castro, 90–104. Basingstoke: Palgrave Macmillan, 2014.
Tranmer, Jeremy. "'Within You Without You": les Beatles et la gauche britannique'. *Volume!* 12, no. 2 (2016): 7585.
Turner, Alwyn W. *Crisis? What Crisis? Britain in the 1970s.* London: Aurum, 2013.
Turner, Steve. *Beatles '66: The Revolutionary Year.* London: HarperCollins, 2016.
Turner, Steve. *Cliff Richard: The Biography.* Oxford: Lion Books, 2008.
Turner, Steve. *The Gospel According to the Beatles.* London: Westminster John Knox, 2006.
Twitchell, Neville. *The Politics of the Rope: The Campaign to Abolish Capital Punishment in Britain 1955–1969.* Bury St. Edmunds: Arena, 2012.
Vague, Tom. *Anarchy in the UK: The Angry Brigade.* Edinburgh: AK Press, 1997.
Valdez, Stephen. 'It's All Too Much: The Beatles' Formal, Sonic, and Lyrical Contributions to the Change from Rock 'n' Roll to Rock'. In *Fifty Years with the Beatles: The Impact of the Beatles on Contemporary Culture*, edited by Jerzy Jarniewicz and Alina Kwiatkowska, 149–66. Łódź: Łódź University Press, 2010.
Varon, Jeremy, Michael S. Foley and John McMillian. 'Time Is an Ocean: The Past and Future of the Sixties'. *The Sixties* 1, no. 1 (2008): 1–7.
Vyner, Harriet. *Groovy Bob: The Life and Times of Robert Fraser.* London: Heni Publishing, 2016.
Wald, Elijah. *How the Beatles Destroyed Rock 'n' Roll: An Alternative History of American Popular Music.* Oxford: Oxford University Press, 2009.
Wald, Gayle. 'Just a Girl? Rock Music, Feminism, and the Cultural Construction of Female Youth'. *Signs: Journal of Women in Culture and Society* 23, no. 3 (1998): 585–610.
Wall, Tim. *Studying Popular Music Culture.* Los Angeles, CA: Sage, 2013.
Walser, Robert. *Running with the Devil: Power, Gender, and Madness in Heavy Metal Music.* Middletown, CT: Wesleyan University Press, 2014.
Ward, Brian. "'The 'C' Is for Christ": Arthur Unger, *Datebook* Magazine and the Beatles'. *Popular Music and Society* 35, no. 4 (2012): 541–60.
Ward, Brian. *Just My Soul Responding: Rhythm and Blues, Black Consciousness, and Race Relations.* Berkeley, CA: University of California Press, 1998.
Ward, Paul. *Britishness since 1870.* London: Routledge, 2004.
Wark, McKenzie. *The Beach beneath the Street: The Everyday Life and Glorious Times of the Situationist International.* London: Verso Books, 2015.
Warner, Simon. *Text and Drugs and Rock 'n' Roll: The Beats and Rock Culture.* London: A&C Black, 2013.
Warwick, Jacqueline. *Girl Groups, Girl Culture: Popular Music and Identity in the 1960s.* London: Routledge, 2007.
Waters, Chris. 'The Homosexual as a Social Being in Britain, 1945–1968'. In *British Queer History: New Approaches and Perspectives*, edited by Brian Lewis, 188–218. Manchester: Manchester University Press, 2013.

Watson, Jonathan Paul. '"Beats Apart": A Comparative History of Youth Culture and Popular Music in Liverpool and Newcastle upon Tyne, 1956–1965'. PhD Thesis, Northumbria University, 2010.

Webb, Clive. 'Special Relationships: Mixed-Race Couples in Post-War Britain and the United States'. *Women's History Review* 26, no. 1 (2017): 110–29.

Weber, Erin Torkelson. *The Beatles and the Historians: An Analysis of Writings about the Fab Four*. Jefferson, NC: McFarland, 2016.

Webster, Peter, and Ian Jones. 'Anglican "Establishment" Reactions to "Pop" Church Music in England c. 1956–1991'. In *Elite and Popular Religion: Papers Read at the 2004 Summer Meeting and the 2005 Winter Meeting of the Ecclesiastical History Society*, edited by Kate Cooper and Jeremy Gregory, 429–41. Woodbridge: Boydell Press, 2006.

Webster, Wendy. *Imagining Home: Gender, Race and National Identity, 1945–1964*. London: Routledge, 2005.

Webster, Wendy. 'The Empire Comes Home: Commonwealth Migration to Britain'. In *Britain's Experience of Empire in the Twentieth Century*, edited by Andrew Thompson, 122–60. Oxford: Oxford University Press, 2012.

Weeks, Jeffrey. *Sex, Politics and Society: The Regulation of Sexuality since 1800*. Rev. edn. Harlow: Longman, 1989.

Weeks, Jeffrey. *The World We Have Won: The Remaking of Erotic and Intimate Life*. London: Routledge, 2007.

Weight, Richard. *Mod: A Very British Style*. London: Bodley Head, 2013.

Weight, Richard. *Patriots: National Identity in Britain, 1940–2000*. London: Macmillan, 2002.

Weinstein, Deena. *Heavy Metal: The Music and Its Culture*. London: Hachette UK, 2009.

Weisethaunet, Hans, and Ulf Lindberg. 'Authenticity Revisited: The Rock Critic and the Changing Real'. *Popular Music and Society* 33, no. 4 (2010): 465–85.

Welch, Rosanne. *Why the Monkees Matter: Teenagers, Television and American Pop Culture*. Jefferson, NC: McFarland, 2016.

Werner, Craig Hansen. *A Change Is Gonna Come: Music, Race and the Soul of America*. Ann Arbor, MI: University of Michigan Press, 2006.

Whipple, Amy. 'Revisiting the "Rivers of Blood" Controversy: Letters to Enoch Powell'. *Journal of British Studies* 48, no. 3 (2009): 717–35.

Whipple, Amy C. 'Speaking for Whom? The 1971 Festival of Light and the Search for the "Silent Majority"'. *Contemporary British History* 24, no. 3 (2010): 319–39.

White, G. D. 'Digging for Apples: Reappraising the Influence of Situationist Theory on Theatre Practice in the English Counterculture'. *Theatre Survey* 42, no. 2 (2001): 177–90.

Whiteley, Gillian. 'Sewing the "Subversive Thread of Imagination": Jeff Nuttall, Bomb Culture and the Radical Potential of Affect'. *The Sixties* 4, no. 2 (2011): 109–33.

Whiteley, Sheila. 'No Fixed Agenda: The Position of the Beatles within Popular / Rock Music'. In *Beatlestudies 3*, edited by Yrjö Heinonen, 3–13. Jyväskylä: University of Jyväskylä, 2000.

Whiteley, Sheila, ed. *Sexing the Groove: Popular Music and Gender*. London: Routledge, 1997.

Whiteley, Sheila. *The Space between the Notes: Rock and the Counter-Culture*. London: Routledge, 1992.

Whiteley, Sheila. *Women and Popular Music: Sexuality, Identity and Subjectivity*. London: Routledge, 2013.

Whiteley, Sheila, and Jedediah Sklower, eds. *Countercultures and Popular Music*. London: Routledge, 2014.

Whitley, Ed. 'The Postmodern White Album'. In *The Beatles, Popular Music and Society: A Thousand Voices*, edited by Ian Inglis, 105–25. New York, NY: St. Martin's Press, 2000.

Wicke, Peter. *Rock Music: Culture, Aesthetics and Sociology*. Cambridge: Cambridge University Press, 1990.

Wiener, Jon. *Come Together: John Lennon in His Time*. 2nd edn. London: Faber, 2000.

Wiener, Jon. *Gimme Some Truth: The John Lennon FBI Files*. Berkeley, CA: University of California Press, 2000.

Wiener, Jon. 'Pop and the Avant-Garde: The Case of John and Yoko'. *Popular Music and Society* 22, no. 1 (1998): 1–16.

Wilkins, Charlotte, and Ian Inglis. 'Fashioning the Fab Four: The Visual Identities of the Beatles'. *Fashion, Style & Popular Culture* 2, no. 2 (2015): 207–21.

Wilkinson, David. *Post-Punk, Politics and Pleasure in Britain*. Basingstoke: Springer, 2016.

Williams, Kevin. *Read All about It! A History of the British Newspaper*. London: Routledge, 2010.

Willett, John. *Art in a City*. Liverpool: Bluecoat Society of Arts/Methuen, 1967.

Willis, Paul E. *Profane Culture*. Princeton, NJ: Princeton University Press, 2014.

Wilson, A. N. *Our Times*. London: Hutchinson, 2008.

Wilson, Elizabeth. *Only Halfway to Paradise: Women in Postwar Britain 1945–1968*. London: Tavistock, 1980.

Winsworth, Ben. 'Psychic Liberation in *Sgt. Pepper's Lonely Hearts Club Band*'. In *Preserving the Sixties: Britain and the 'Decade of Protest'*, edited by Trevor Harris and Monia O'Brien Castro, 160–72. Basingstoke: Palgrave Macmillan, 2014.

Wiseman-Trowse, Nathan. *Performing Class in British Popular Music*. Basingstoke: Palgrave Macmillan, 2008.

Wolf, Christof, Dominique Joye, Tom W. Smith and Yang-chih Fu, eds. *The SAGE Handbook of Survey Methodology*. Los Angeles, CA: Sage, 2016.

Womack, Kenneth. 'Authorship and the Beatles'. *College Literature* 34, no. 3 (2007): 161–82.

Womack, Kenneth. *Long and Winding Roads: The Evolving Artistry of the Beatles.* New York, NY: Continuum, 2007.

Womack, Kenneth. *Maximum Volume: The Life of Beatles Producer George Martin – the Early Years 1926–1966.* Chicago, IL: Chicago Review Press, 2017.

Womack, Kenneth. *Solid State: The Story of Abbey Road and the End of the Beatles.* Ithaca, NY: Cornell University Press, 2019.

Womack, Kenneth. *Sound Pictures: The Life of Beatles Producer George Martin – the Later Years 1966–2016.* Chicago, IL: Chicago Review Press, 2018.

Womack, Kenneth, ed. *The Beatles Encyclopedia: Everything Fab Four.* Santa Barbara, CA: ABC-CLIO, 2016.

Womack, Kenneth, ed. *The Cambridge Companion to the Beatles.* Cambridge: Cambridge University Press, 2009.

Womack, Kenneth, and Kathryn B. Cox, eds. *The Beatles, Sgt. Pepper, and the Summer of Love.* Lanham, MD: Lexington Books, 2017.

Womack, Kenneth, and Todd F. Davis. 'Mythology, Remythology, and Demythology: The Beatles on Film'. In *Reading the Beatles: Cultural Studies, Literary Criticism, and the Fab Four,* edited by Kenneth Womack and Todd F. Davis, 97–109. Binghamton, NY: SUNY Press, 2006.

Womack, Kenneth, and Todd Davis, eds. *Reading the Beatles: Cultural Studies, Literary Criticism, and the Fab Four.* Binghamton, NY: SUNY Press, 2006.

Woodhead, Leslie. *How the Beatles Rocked the Kremlin.* London: Bloomsbury, 2013.

Worcester, Robert M. *British Public Opinion: A Guide to the History and Methodology of Political Opinion Polling.* Oxford: Blackwell, 1991.

World Political Opinion and Social Surveys: Series One – British Opinion Polls. Reading: Research Publications, 1990.

Worley, Matthew. 'Marx–Lenin–Rotten–Strummer: British Marxism and Youth Culture in the 1970s'. *Contemporary British History* 30, no. 4 (2016): 505–21.

Worley, Matthew. *No Future: Punk, Politics and British Youth Culture, 1976–1984.* Cambridge: Cambridge University Press, 2017.

Yates, Nigel. *Love Now, Pay Later? Sex and Religion in the Fifties and Sixties.* London: SPCK, 2011.

Young, Jock. *The Drugtakers: The Social Meaning of Drug Use.* London: MacGibbon and Kee, 1971.

Zimmerman, Nadya. *Counterculture Kaleidoscope: Musical and Cultural Perspectives on Late Sixties San Francisco.* Ann Arbor, MI: University of Michigan Press, 2008.

Zweiniger-Bargielowska, Ina, ed. *Women in Twentieth-Century Britain.* Harlow: Longman, 2001.

Index